Seedtime of the Republic

Look back, therefore, with reverence look back to the times of ancient virtue and renown. Look back to the mighty purposes which your fathers had in view, when they traversed a vast ocean, and planted this land. Recal to your minds their labours, their toils, their perseverance, and let their divine spirit animate you in all your actions.

Look forward also to distant posterity. Figure to yourselves millions and millions to spring from your loins, who may be born *freemen* or *slaves*, as Heaven shall now approve or reject your councils. Think, that on you may depend, whether this great country, in ages hence, shall be filled and adorned with a virtuous and inlightened people; enjoying *Liberty* and all its concomitant blessings . . . or covered with a race of men more contemptible than the savages that roam the wilderness.

—REV. WILLIAM SMITH, 1775

I always consider the settlement of America with reverence and wonder, as the opening of a grand scheme and design in Providence for the illumination and emancipation of the slavish part of mankind all over the earth. —JOHN ADAMS, 1765

Clinton Rossiter

SEEDTIME OF THE REPUBLIC

THE ORIGIN OF THE AMERICAN TRADITION
OF POLITICAL LIBERTY

New York

HARCOURT, BRACE AND COMPANY

This book is for

WINTON GOODRICH ROSSITER

and

DOROTHY SHAW ROSSITER

*whose lives have been a witness to the dignity
and durability of the virtues of their ancestors*

INDUSTRY · FRUGALITY · PIETY

CHARITY · INTEGRITY

and

THE LOVE OF LIBERTY

Preface

THE research for this book led to many inspiring places and kind people. I am glad to acknowledge publicly the warm welcome and interest of the staffs of these institutions: in Salem, the Essex Institute; in Cambridge, the Houghton Library and Harvard University Archives; in Boston, the Boston University Library and Massachusetts Historical Society; in Worcester, the American Antiquarian Society; in Providence, the Brown University Library, Rhode Island Historical Society, and John Carter Brown Library; in Hartford, the Connecticut Historical Society and Connecticut State Library; in New Haven, the Yale University Library; in New York, the New York Public Library, New-York Historical Society, Columbia University Library, and New York Society Library; in Philadelphia, the Historical Society of Pennsylvania, American Philosophical Society, and Free Library of Philadelphia; in Baltimore, the Maryland Historical Society; in Annapolis, the Maryland State Library; in Washington, the Rare Book and Manuscript Divisions of the Library of Congress; in Williamsburg, Colonial Williamsburg and the William and Mary College Library; in Richmond, the Virginia State Library; in Raleigh, the North Carolina State Department of Archives; in Charleston, the Charleston Library Society; in San Marino, California, the Huntington Library. Yale University, Boston University, the Massachusetts Historical Society, and the American Philosophical Society have all granted permission to quote from manuscripts in their keeping.

Of all these places and people, I presumed most heavily on the staffs of the John Carter Brown Library and the Rare Book Room of the New York Public Library. The town clerks of Ipswich, Massachusetts; Little Compton, Rhode Island; and Simsbury, Connecticut kindly permitted me to read their original town records. A generous grant from the Social Science Research Council made it possible for me to visit most of these institutions. It should be recorded, however, that I was able to do a major part of my research

ix

right at home in the Cornell University Library. To the staff of this library—and to that great man, Andrew D. White, who purchased the private collection of Jared Sparks—I am profoundly grateful.

Although I have tried my best to follow an original line of thought through newspapers, documents, letters, sermons, broadsides, magazines, narratives, and diaries, I have profited greatly from the guidance of an array of brilliant historians. This is especially true of Part I. There are at least seventy names I would gladly list in this preface, but I shall let these ten most faithful guides represent the rest: Andrews, Bridenbaugh, Greene, Labaree, Perry Miller, Morison, Nettels, Savelle, Schlesinger, and Wertenbaker. I should also avow, some fourteen years after the event, that my simultaneous discoveries of Tyler and Parrington first set me on this road.

Parts of each of the biographies in Part II have appeared in the *New England Quarterly*, *William and Mary Quarterly*, *American Quarterly*, and *Pennsylvania Magazine of History and Biography*. The editors of these journals have kindly given me permission to use this material.

John Roche of Haverford College read Part III, and my wife, Mary Crane Rossiter, the whole of this book. Each of them, but particularly the latter, knows how much I value the help and criticism thus extended.

CLINTON ROSSITER

Ithaca, New York
October 1952

Contents

1

THE CIRCUMSTANCES

2

THE MEN

3

THE HERITAGE

Seedtime of the Republic

Introduction

THIS book is a study of the political ideas that sustained the rise of liberty in colonial and Revolutionary America. I have planned and written it in pursuit of four assumptions, two having to do with the making and two with the writing of history.

The assumptions of history were: First, the men who made the Revolution held a philosophy of ethical, ordered liberty that the American people still cherish as their most precious intellectual possession; and second, this philosophy was the product of long generations of colonial experience, not an exotic doctrine hastily imported to justify resistance to an overweening Parliament. The assumptions of historiography were: First, Whatever its defects as technique of social or economic history, biography recommends itself strongly to the historian of ideas; and second, this historian has no right to make use of the creators and carriers of significant ideas unless he describes the environment in which they lived and worked.

The organization of this book follows these assumptions in reverse order. Part I, "The Circumstances," is a selective account of the government, religion, economy, social structure, and intellectual life of the thirteen colonies. I hold no unusual ideas about the influence of environment on either the instruments or ethics of human freedom. Certainly I would not attempt to weigh each of the many physical and human-directed forces that shaped the destiny of the American colonies, or to establish a precise cause-and-effect relationship between any one force or set of forces and any one value or set of values. What I have tried to do is describe the total environment as one extremely favorable to the rise of liberty, and to single out those forces—"the factors of freedom," as I have called them—which seemed most influential in creating this environment. This, it seems to me, is the essential first step to a full understanding of the remainder of the book. In describing the colonial environment, I have concentrated

I

inevitably upon the eighteenth century, the years that Parrington described as the *saeculum politicum*—the age of politics—of our colonial history.

Part 2, "The Men," presents the lives and philosophies of six men I consider to have been the most notable political thinkers in the colonial period: Thomas Hooker, Roger Williams, John Wise, Jonathan Mayhew, Richard Bland, and Benjamin Franklin. Hooker and Williams were seventeenth-century thinkers, transplanted Englishmen who lived in a more primitive America than that described in Part 1. In their biographies I have therefore called attention to the peculiar political environment in which they acted and wrote. The prophetic nature of their ideas, especially those of Williams, made their exclusion from this book unthinkable. The credentials of all these men will be examined in Part 2, but I should say at this point that each of them, with the possible exception of Franklin, was more important as a representative than influential thinker, a fact that makes them especially useful to my purposes. Among them they expressed every article of faith in the American philosophy of liberty as it had developed to 1765.

Part 3, "The Heritage," is an extensive description of the political theory of the American Revolution, of the noble aggregate of "self-evident truths" that vindicated the campaign of resistance (1765-1775), the resolution for independence (1776), and the establishment of the new state governments (1776-1780). It is important to remember that most of these truths had been no less self-evident to the preachers, merchants, planters, and lawyers who were the mind of colonial America. In this third part, I have done my best to let the men of the Revolution, both great and small, speak for themselves. But I have also made a special effort to bring a reasonable amount of order to a political philosophy marked by charming disorder.

This book, then, is an interpretive account of the seedtime of the Republic, of the first great period of American liberty. It tells of an environment in which human liberty expanded as a fact of life, of men who preached a faith to match and justify this fact, and of the uses to which other men, themselves products of this environment, put this inherited faith in their hour of need and decision. I have thought it important to tell this story because of the devotion Americans continue to pay to the political values of the colonial and Revolutionary periods. If this devotion is to be intelligent and meaningful, they must know more exactly what these values were. Ignorance should be no part of a philosophy of liberty.

Part 1

THE CIRCUMSTANCES

In the year 1765 there lived along the American seaboard 1,450,000 white and 400,000 Negro subjects of King George III of England. The area of settlement stretched from the Penobscot to the Altamaha and extended inland, by no means solidly, to the Appalachian barrier. Within this area flourished thirteen separate political communities, subject immediately or ultimately to the authority of the Crown, but enjoying in fact large powers of self-government. Life was predominantly rural, the economy extractive and commercial, religion Protestant, descent English, and politics the concern of men of property.

To the best of the average man's knowledge, whether his point of observation were in the colonies or England, all but a handful of these Americans were contented subjects of George III. It was hard for them to be continually enthusiastic about a sovereign or mother country so far away, yet there were few signs that the imperial bonds were about to chafe so roughly. Occasionally statements appeared in print or official correspondence accusing the colonists of republicanism, democracy, and a hankering for independence, but these could be written off as the scoldings of overfastidious travelers or frustrated agents of the royal will.[1] Among the ruling classes sentiments of loyalty to the Crown were strongly held and eloquently expressed, while the attitude of the mass of men was not much different from that of the plain people of England: a curious combination of indifference and obeisance. Benjamin Franklin, who had more firsthand information about the colonies than any other man, could later write in all sincerity, "I never had heard in any Conversation from any Person drunk or sober, the least Expression of a wish for a Separation, or Hint that such a Thing would be advantageous to America." [2]

Yet in the summer and fall of this same year the colonists shook off their ancient habits of submission in the twinkling of an eye and stood revealed as almost an alien people. The passage of the Stamp Act was greeted by an overwhelming refusal to obey, especially among colonial leaders who saw ruin in its provisions—lawyers, merchants, planters, printers, and ministers. Although the flame of resistance was smothered by repeal of the obnoxious act, the next ten years were at best a smoldering truce. In 1775 the policies of Lord North forced a final appeal to arms, and enough Americans answered it to bring off a successful revolution.

Dozens of able historians have inquired into the events and forces that drove this colonial people to armed rebellion. Except among extreme patriots and equally extreme economic determinists, fundamental agreement now prevails on the immediate causes of the American Revolution. Less attention has been devoted to the question: What made this people ripe for rebellion, or, more exactly, what made the colonists so willing in 1765 to engage in open and unanimous defiance of a major imperial policy? One answer, perhaps the best and certainly the best-known, was volunteered in 1818 by John Adams, himself a cause of the American Revolution: "The Revolution was effected before the war commenced. The Revolution was in the minds and hearts of the people. . . . This radical change in the principles, opinions, sentiments, and affections of the people, was the real American Revolution." [3]

What Adams seems to have argued was that by 1765 there existed a collective outlook and understanding called the American (or at least English-American) mind, a mind whose chief characteristics, so we learn in other parts of his writings, were self-reliance, patriotism, practicality, and love of liberty, with liberty defined as freedom from alien dictation. Adams did not find it necessary to describe in detail the forces that had produced this mind, perhaps because that extraordinary student of political realities, Edmund Burke, had already given so perceptive a description. In his magnificent speech on conciliation with the colonies (March 22, 1775), Burke singled out "six capital sources" to account for the American "love of freedom," that "fierce spirit of liberty" which was "stronger in the English colonies probably than in any other people of the earth": their English descent; their popular forms of government; "religion in the northern provinces"; "manners in the southern"; education, especially in the law; and "the remoteness of the situation from the first mover of government." [4]

The first part of this book is an elaboration of Adams and Burke, an analysis of those forces which helped create a people dedicated to liberty and qualified for independence. Before we proceed to examine these forces in the convenient categories of government, religion, economics, society, and thought and culture, it would be helpful to point to four common, all-pervading features of the colonial experience—what we may properly call "forces-behind-the-forces"—that were hastening the day of liberty, independence, and democracy. Over only one of these primary factors did the colonists or English authorities have the slightest degree of control, and the political wisdom that was needed to keep it in tight rein simply did not exist in empires of that time. These were the four ingredients of colonial liberty: [5]

THE ENGLISH HERITAGE. Burke acknowledged this "capital source" in words that his countrymen could understand but apparently not act upon.

> The people of the colonies are descendants of Englishmen. England, Sir, is a nation which still I hope respects, and formerly adored, her freedom. The colonists emigrated from you when this part of your character was most predominant; and they took this bias and direction the moment they parted from your hands. They are therefore not only devoted to liberty, but to liberty according to English ideas, and on English principles.[6]

"Wee humbly pray," wrote the General Assembly of Rhode Island to the Board of Trade in 1723, "that their Lordships will believe wee have a Tincture of the ancient British Blood in our veines." [7] The colonists had considerably more than a tincture: At least seven in ten were English in blood, and virtually all their institutions, traditions, ideas, and laws were English in origin and inspiration. The first colonists had brought over both the good and evil of seventeenth-century England. The good had been toughened and in several instances improved; much of the bad had been jettisoned under frontier conditions. As a result of this interaction of heredity and environment, the eighteenth-century American was simply a special brand of Englishman. When it pleased him he could be more English than the English, and when it pleased him most was any occurrence in which questions of liberty and self-government were at issue. In a squabble over the question of a fixed salary between Governor Joseph Dudley and the Massachusetts Assembly, the latter could state without any sense of pretension:

> It hath been the Priviledge from Henry the third & confirmed by Edward the first, & in all Reigns unto this Day, granted, & is now allowed to be the just & unquestionable Right of the Subject, to raise when & dispose of how they see Cause, any Sums of money by Consent of Parliament, the which Priviledge We her Majesty's Loyal and Dutiful Subjects have lived in the Enjoym^t of, & do hope always to enjoy the same, under Our most gracious Queen Ann & Successors, & shall ever endeavour to discharge the Duty incumbent on us; But humbly conceive the Stating of perpetual Salaries not agreable to her Majesty's Interests in this Province, but prejudicial to her Majesty's good Subjects.[8]

Southerners were, if anything, even more insistent. In 1735 the South Carolina legislature resolved:

> That His Majesty's subjects in this province are entitled to all the liberties and privileges of Englishmen . . . [and] that the Commons House of Assembly in South Carolina, by the laws of England and South Carolina, and ancient usage and custom, have all the rights and privileges pertaining to Money bills that are enjoyed by the British House of Commons.[9]

And the men of the frontier, who were having the same trouble with assemblies that assemblies were having with governors, made the echo ring.

> 1st. We apprehend, as Free-Men and English Subjects, we have an indisputable Title to the same Privileges and Immunities with his Majesty's other Subjects, who reside in the interior Counties of Philadelphia, Chester and Bucks, and therefore ought not to be excluded from an equal Share with them in the very important Privilege of Legislation.[10]

These were the words of men who made much of the English tie, even when, as in the last of these instances, some of them were Scotch-Irish or German. Their great traditions—representative government, supremacy of law, constitutionalism, liberty of the subject—belonged to them as Englishmen. Their key institutions, especially the provincial assembly, were often looked upon as sound to the extent that they conformed to English models, or at least to colonial interpretations or recollections of those models. The rights for which they contended were not the natural rights of all men but the ancient rights of Englishmen.[11] "It is no Little Blessing of God," said Cotton Mather to the Massachusetts Assembly in 1700, "that we are a part of the *English Nation*." [12]

Throughout the colonial period the English descent and attitudes of the great majority of Americans gave direction and impetus to their struggles for liberty. It is a decisive fact of American history that until 1776 it was a chapter in English history as well. Just as England in 1765 was ahead of the Continent in the struggle for law and liberty, so America, this extraordinary part of England, was even further ahead, not least because most of its inhabitants could think of themselves as Englishmen.

> If we consider ourselves as *British* subjects, and entitled to the liberties and privileges of such, both civil and sacred; we must acknowledge that providence has, in this respect, favoured us above most *other* protestants: Very few of whom, I might perhaps say none, live under so happy and excellent a form of government as ourselves.[13]

Men who believed this proud assertion, as most articulate Americans certainly did, would not easily be cheated or argued out of their heritage—a truth that Burke did his best to advertise:

> The temper and character which prevail in our colonies are, I am afraid, unalterable by any human art. We cannot, I fear, falsify the pedigree of this fierce people, and persuade them that they are not sprung from a nation in whose veins the blood of freedom circulates. The language in which they would hear you tell them this tale would detect the imposition; your speech would betray you. An Englishman is the unfittest person on earth to argue another Englishman into slavery.[14]

THE CONFLICT OF ENGLISH AND AMERICAN INTERESTS. The clash of imperial policy and colonial desire for self-direction is almost always productive of the spirit of liberty. This is especially true if the policy of the parent state is conceived purely in its own interests, and if the colonists are men of high political aptitude and proud descent. Such was the pattern of Anglo-American relations in the colonial period. From the time of the earliest settlement, which like all the important settlements was the result of private initiative, English and American opinions on the political and economic status of the colonies were in sharp and ultimately fatal conflict.[15]

The conduct of colonial affairs by the English government rested on these assumptions: The colonies were perpetual dependents of the parent state. Since their interests were completely subordinate to those of England, the welfare of the latter was to be the one concern of all agencies charged with governing them. They were therefore to serve, apparently forever, as a source of wealth and support to the land out of which their inhabitants had departed.[16]

If the English government had acted on these assumptions consistently throughout the colonial period, the contrasting ideas of the colonists would have had less chance to strike deep root. But confusion at the beginning, domestic troubles in the middle, and "salutary neglect" throughout most of this period permitted the colonists to build not only a theory but a condition of self-government. And it was this condition, of course, as some perceptive Englishmen were aware, that helped the colonies develop into prizes worth retaining by force of arms. The interests of England were, in an important sense, self-contradictory.

The views of the colonists on their place in the imperial structure were somewhat mixed, ranging from the arrogant independence asserted by Massachusetts in the seventeenth century [17] to the abject dependence argued by a handful of Tory apologists in the eighteenth. In general, the colonial attitude was one looking to near-equality in the present and some sort of full partnership in the future, all within the confines of a benevolent and protecting empire.[18] The colonist acknowledged that for certain diplomatic and commercial purposes his destiny would rest for some time to come in the hands of men in London. But in all other matters, especially in that of political self-determination, he considered himself a "freeborn subject of the Crown of England." Theories of the origin and nature of the colonial assemblies are a good example of these divergent views. In English eyes the assemblies were founded by royal grant and existed at royal pleasure; in American eyes they existed as a matter of right. The Board of Trade looked upon them as inferior bodies enjoying certain rule-making powers under the terms of their charters; [19] the men of Virginia and Massachusetts looked upon them as miniature Houses of Commons with power to make all laws they could get away with in practice. The struggle between these assemblies and the royal governors sent to control them was the focus of conflict of colonial and imperial interests.

Had Parliament not decided to intrude its authority into colonial affairs, the old-fashioned imperial views of the English authorities and the prophetic self-governing claims of the American colonists might have coexisted for decades without producing a violent break. The tardy policies of stern control initiated by the Grenville ministry brought this long-standing conflict fully into the open. In the years before 1765 the push-and-pull of imperialism and home rule had been an important spur to the growth of liberty in the colonies. In the next decade it ignited a revolution.

ISOLATION. Let us hear again from the member for Bristol.

> The last cause of this disobedient spirit in the colonies is hardly less powerful than the rest, as it is not merely moral, but laid deep in the natural constitution of things. Three thousand miles of ocean lie between you and them. No contrivance can prevent the effect of this distance in weakening government. Seas roll, and months pass, between the order and the execution; and the want of a speedy explanation of a single point is enough to defeat a whole system. . . . In large bodies, the circulation of power must be less vigorous at the extremities. Nature has said it. The Turk cannot govern Egypt, and Arabia, and Curdistan, as he governs Thrace; nor has he the same dominion in Crimea and Algiers, which he has at Brusa and Smyrna. Despotism itself is obliged to truck and huckster. The Sultan gets such obedience as he can. He governs with a loose rein, that he may govern at all; and the whole of the force and vigour of his authority in his centre is derived from a prudent relaxation in all his borders. Spain, in her provinces, is, perhaps, not so well obeyed as you are in yours. She complies too; she submits; she watches times. This is the immutable condition, the eternal law, of extensive and detached empire.[20]

This cardinal fact of nature, the remoteness of the colonies, increased the difference between imperial purpose and colonial aspiration. The early colonists, thrown willy-nilly on their own devices, developed habits of self-government and passed them on to their descendants. The descendants, still just as far if not farther from London, fell naturally into an attitude of provincialism well suited to their condition but corrosive of empire. The lack of contact between one colony and another, the result of distance and unbelievably bad roads, allowed each to develop pretty much on its own. The diversity in character of the key colonies of Virginia, Massachusetts, New York, and Pennsylvania made a mockery of any notion of uniform imperial policy.

Worst of all from the imperial point of view, the ill effects of the inconsistency, inefficiency, corruption, stupidity, arrogance, and ignorance displayed to some degree at all times and to a perilous degree at some times by the English authorities were doubled and redoubled by the rolling seas and passing months. English laxity in enforcing the Navigation Acts and colonial evasion in obeying them were one instance of the extent to which three thousand miles of ocean could water down a policy of strict control. The technique of royal disallowance, which seemed so perfectly designed to keep the colonial assemblies in check, was likewise weakened by the mere fact of distance. For example, the disallowance in 1706 of two New Hampshire judiciary acts passed in 1699 and 1701 was never reported properly to the province, and the judiciary in that colony continued to function under these laws for a half century.[21] And the royal governor, the linchpin of empire, was a far more accommodating fellow in Boston or Charleston than he appeared in his commissions and instructions issued from London. A governor like Sir Matthew Johnson of North Carolina, whose correspondence to the Board of Trade went astray four years in a row (1742-1746),[22] could not have been much of a buffer against colonial urges to independence. When we realize that no regular mail-service of any kind existed until 1755, and that war disrupted communications more than one third of the time between 1689 and 1763, we can understand how the ocean was at once a highway to freedom and a barrier to imperialism. Rarely in history have the laws of geopolitics worked so powerfully for liberty.[23]

THE FRONTIER, AND FRONTIER CONDITIONS OF LIFE. Had Burke ever lived in the colonies, he might have listed a seventh "capital source" to explain the rise of liberty in America, and thus have anticipated Frederick Jackson Turner and his celebrated thesis. We need not go all the way with Turner—"American democracy is fundamentally the outcome of the experiences of the American people in dealing with the West" [24]—to acknowledge the significance of the frontier in early American history. Whatever the extent of that influence in the nineteenth century, in the seventeenth and eighteenth centuries—when America was one vast frontier and perhaps one in three Americans a frontiersman at some time in his life—it was clearly of the first importance. If we may take the word "frontier" to mean not only the line of farthest settlement to the west, but also the primitive conditions of life and thought which in the seventeenth century extended throughout the colonies and during most of the eighteenth continued to prevail in many areas east of the Appalachians, we may point to at least a half-dozen indications of the decisive influence of the American environment.

First, the frontier impeded the transfer to America of outworn attitudes and institutions. Although classes existed from the outset, and although an authentic aristocracy developed eventually in the colonies, both classes and aristocracy were shaped to American requirements. The wilderness frustrated completely such attempts to plant feudalism in America as the schemes of Sir Ferdinando Gorges and the stillborn Fundamental Constitutions of Carolina,[25] and everywhere archaic laws and customs were simplified, liberalized, or rudely abandoned. In the matter of church-state relations the frontier was especially influential as a decentralizing and democratizing force. The positive result of this process of sloughing off the old ways was an increase in mobility, experimentation, and self-reliance among the settlers.

The wilderness demanded of those who would conquer it that they spend their lives in unremitting toil. Unable to devote any sizable part of their energies to government, the settlers insisted that government let them alone and perform its severely limited tasks at the amateur level.[26] The early American definition of liberty as freedom *from* government was given added popularity and meaning by frontier conditions. It was a new and invigorating experience for tens of thousands of Englishmen, Germans, and Scotch-Irish to be able to build a home where they would at last be "let alone."

The frontier produced, in ways that Turner and his followers have made clear,[27] a new kind of individual and new doctrines of individualism. The wilderness did not of itself create democracy; indeed, it often encouraged the growth of ideas and institutions hostile to it. But it did help produce some of the raw materials of American democracy—self-reliance, social fluidity, simplicity, equality, dislike of privilege, optimism, and devotion to liberty. At the same time, it emphasized the importance of voluntary co-operation. The group, too, had its uses on the frontier, whether for defense or barn-raising or cornhusking. The phrases "free association," "mutual subjection," and "the consent of the governed" were given new content in the wilderness.

Next, the fact that wages were generally higher and working conditions better in the colonies than in England did much to convince Americans that they were better off if left to their own devices. The reason for this happy condition was a distinct shortage of labor, and a prime reason for the shortage was land for the asking. The frontier population was made up of thousands of men who had left the seaboard to toil for themselves in the great forest. The results of this constant migration were as important for the seaboard as they were for the wilderness.

Fifth, from the beginning the frontier was an area of protest and thus a nursery of republican notions. Under-represented in assemblies that made a habit of overtaxing them, scornful of the privileges and leadership assumed by the tidewater aristocracy, resentful of attempts to saddle them with unwanted ministers and officials, the men of the back country were in fact if not in print the most outspoken radicals of the colonial period. If their quaint and strangely deferential protests contributed very little to the literature of a rising democracy, they nevertheless made more popular the arguments for liberty and self-government. And no people could have talked so incessantly of their own rights without coming to acknowledge the rights of others.

Finally, all these factors conspired to give new force and content to the English heritage of law, liberty, and self-government. The over-refined and often archaic institutions that the settlers brought along as part of their intellectual baggage were thrust once again into the crucible of primitive conditions. If these institutions emerged in shapes that horrified royal governors, they were nevertheless more simple, workable, and popular than they had been for several centuries in England. The laws and institutions of early Rhode Island or North Carolina would not have worked in more civilized societies, but they had abandoned most of their outworn features and were ready to develop along American lines. The hardworking, long-suffering men and women of the frontier—"People a litle wilful Inclined to doe when and how they please or not at al"—[28] were themselves a primary force in the rise of colonial self-government.

The English descent and heritage of the colonists, the conflict of imperial and colonial interests, the rolling ocean, the all-pervading frontier—these were the forces-behind-the-forces that shaped the history of the colonies, just as the history shaped the developing American mind. Of these forces we shall speak or think on almost every page of this book.

CHAPTER ONE

Colonial Government
and the Rise of Liberty

THE bisection of early American history into periods separated by the events of the Glorious Revolution has special application to colonial government. The first period of political development, which lasted from the Jamestown settlement (1607) to the withdrawal, alteration, and restoration of the Massachusetts charter (1684-1691), was one of "alarum and excursion" in the mother country and resultant self-determination in the colonies. The second, which began with the creation of the Board of Trade (1696) and ended with the outburst of resistance to the Stamp Act (1765), was one of fast-growing imperial concern in England and even faster-growing political maturity and self-consciousness in America. The influence of the first period upon the second, of the century of neglect upon the century of oversight, was great if not indeed decisive. Habits of self-government were implanted in New England and Virginia that no new policy of empire, no matter how autocratic in conception and efficient in execution, could ever have rooted out.

Except for short terms, in isolated localities, and among small groups of pioneers, there was very little political democracy in the colonial period. Generations of well-meaning historians and patriots have done the colonists no service by insisting that they and their institutions were democratic.[1] There was a good deal of practical content injected into the ancient phrase "liberty of the subject"; there were unusual opportunities for self-government at all levels; and there was thinking and talking about political democracy that outran actual performance. Yet for the most part government in the colonies was simply a less corrupt and oppressive, more popular and easy-going version of government at home, and thus was characterized by limited suffrage, aristocratic leadership, and both deference and indifference among the mass of men. The governments of the continental colonies were a stage in the development of American democracy rather than democracy itself. The thoughts of good colonials were thoughts of liberty and self-government rather than of equality and mass participation. The course of political freedom was halting, full of starts and stops and some discouraging retreats, yet over the generations it went slowly and painfully upward to ultimate triumph.

THE PATTERN OF GOVERNMENT

The pattern of government in the thirteen American colonies was marked by unity of basic form and diversity of detail. It provides an arresting example of the adaptation of established institutions and procedures, in this case those of seventeenth-century England, to an unusual environment, in this case that of the agrarian frontier. A brief description of this pattern is necessary before we attempt to isolate the strictly political forces that were hastening the advent of free government.[2]

THE CONSTITUTIONS OF THE COLONIES. The shape of government in each colony was determined by what we may conveniently term its "constitution," leading elements of which were such instruments as the original charter, grant, or patent and its renewals, commissions and instructions to the governor, orders-in-council and other directions from the mother country, codes of laws, and local custom and practice. The charter, grant, or patent was the basic document, and according to it the colonies were divided into three distinct types:

Royal.[3] The royal colony was, from a constitutional point of view, a political entity in which the Crown was immediately supreme and sovereign. In theory, all officials and institutions existed at the pleasure of the King; in practice, the colonists shared heavily in determining their political destinies, especially through the assembly and institutions of local government. The royal colony was easily the most satisfactory type in terms of English interests. Had the early imperialists had their way, royal government would have been installed without delay throughout the empire. Even though it was not, the trend toward centralization of power in the Crown became increasingly insistent, and by the middle of the eighteenth century eight of thirteen colonies were royal in constitution: Virginia (the model of this type), New York, New Hampshire, Massachusetts, New Jersey, North Carolina, South Carolina, and Georgia.

Proprietary.[4] The proprietary was a type of colony in which political power and ownership of the land were placed in the hands of one or more private individuals. The model of such proprietaries as Maryland and the Carolinas was the county palatine of Durham, a feudal principality in which the Bishop of Durham, for reasons of state, had been permitted to exercise the powers of a virtually absolute king. Because of weaknesses inherent in its constitutional structure, weaknesses that took little time coming to the surface under wilderness conditions, the proprietary form was pretty much of a failure in colonial America. Some proprietorships were converted into royal colonies; others made such heavy concessions to imperial demands from above and popular urges from below as to be scarcely distinguishable from royal colonies. Although nine continental colonies were originally constituted as proprietorships under royal favor, only three—Pennsylvania, Delaware (under the same proprietorship as Pennsylvania), and Maryland—were in existence in 1765.

Corporate.[5] Connecticut and Rhode Island, both of which were founded without express authority from the Crown, were granted royal charters of incorporation at the time of the Restoration. Despite repeated threats of judicial or legislative revocation, these colonies clung to their corporate charters and unique status of independence throughout the eighteenth century. In these two colonies the pattern of self-government was most firmly established. Although the Crown retained considerable authority over their military, diplomatic, and commercial affairs, the actual extent of supervision was spotty and discontinuous.[6] An especially sour Tory, John Mein of Boston, was not too far from the truth when he wrote of Connecticut and Rhode Island: "The people in those Colonies chuse their Governors, Judges, Assemblymen, Counsellors, and all the rest of their Officers; and the King and Parliament have as much influence there as in the wilds of Tartary."[7] In the commonwealth period (1630-1684) Massachusetts was an extraordinary type of corporate colony[8]—extraordinary alike in origin, form, and pretensions to independence. Although the charter of 1691 established Massachusetts as a royal colony, the corporate features could never be entirely eradicated.

GOVERNORS. The governor—in the royal colonies a viceroy appointed by the King, in the proprietaries a special agent selected by the proprietors, in Connecticut and Rhode Island a local gentleman chosen by the assembly acting as court of election—was the key official in each of the colonies.[9] In the royal and proprietary colonies he was the focus of internal politics and external relations. As representative of the sponsoring agency in England, especially of the Crown, he exercised most of the ancient executive prerogatives: command of the forces; the summoning, proroguing, and dissolution of the assembly; an absolute veto over legislation; the power of appointment to subordinate offices; leadership of the church wherever established; the royal prerogative of mercy; large powers, at least by instruction, in financial affairs; and often, with the council, the responsibility of serving as the colony's court of last resort. In short, he was the symbol and fact of royal or proprietary authority—a dignified chief of state, a powerful political and military official, a direct participant in legislative and judicial affairs, and the linchpin of empire.

ASSEMBLIES.[10] Over against the governor, representative of England and monarchy, was set the assembly, representative of colony and people. The political and constitutional history of colonial America appears often to have been nothing so much as a huge, ill-tempered tug-of-war between governors and assemblies,[11] and it was the latter that grew steadily more robust in the struggle for power. Some assemblies were established under royal, proprietary, or trading-company favor; others were spontaneous creations of the men on the spot.[12] Grounded firmly in representative and electoral systems that were the direct ancestors of present American practice,[13] converted sooner or later by circumstance into a bicameral structure (everywhere except Pennsylvania),[14] persuaded through experience that they possessed and could wield all traditional legislative powers and privileges,[15] the assemblies were the most important instruments of popular government in colonial America. The growth of such techniques of representation as residence requirements, constituency payments, annual elections, instructions, voting by ballot, and bans on place-holding by assemblymen is evidence that the assemblies were far more advanced toward the idea of a popular legislature than was the House of Commons.[16]

COUNCILS. In each colony there was also a conciliar body, generally made up of twelve gentlemen of property and prestige, which exercised important functions of an executive, legislative, and judicial character.[17] The council acted for the governor as advisory cabinet, with the assembly as upper house of a bicameral legislature, and again with the governor as highest provincial court of appeals in civil cases (and in Virginia in criminal cases as well). It was often as powerful an agent of royal authority as the governor. The normal method of appointment of councilors was by the Crown, on recommendation of the governor.[18] The principal instance of deviation from this scheme was to be found in Massachusetts: The charter of 1691, which could not ignore the years of republican independence, provided for a council of twenty-eight to be chosen annually by the general court subject to the veto of the governor.

COURTS. In its origins and early development the judicial system of colonial America was less influenced by English precedents than almost any other set of institutions or procedures.[19] In the seventeenth century the differences between the courts of one colony and the next were so pronounced that it is impossible to make any general statement about them. What existed in most colonies was a profoundly practical and popular system of law and courts in which there was much emphasis on the colonists' own rude notions of equity and justice and little on uniform practice or a trained bench and bar. In Massachusetts lawyers were forbidden to practice, and in all colonies the prejudice against them was surprisingly strong. In part this could be traced to English antecedents; the Fundamental Constitutions of Carolina labeled it "a base and vile thing to plead for money or reward." [20] In part it was a natural frontier-reaction to a profession identified with the complexities of civilization.

In the eighteenth century, chiefly at the behest of the Crown and under the pressures of a more developed society, the trend was everywhere toward uniformity in organization and improvement in professional standards. By 1765 the judicial system in most of the colonies was regularized and independent, and the chief props of the system, the lawyers, were climbing into the political saddle. The trial of Captain John Preston and his men and the all-but-unanimous judicial resistance to general writs of assistance are proof of the vitality of the court system inherited by the Revolutionary generation.

LOCAL GOVERNMENT. The agencies through which the colonists governed themselves at the local level will be described in some detail at a later stage in this chapter. It should be enough to remark at this point that the preponderance of political power was exercised in towns, parishes, counties, and boroughs, and that these entities were even more independent of the colony than the colony was of the Crown. Self-government was doubly the rule in colonial America.

INSTRUMENTS OF IMPERIAL SUPERVISION. No account of government in colonial America would be complete without some reference to the complexity of officials active in England and the colonies as agents of the Crown's belated attempt to prosecute a consistent imperial policy.[21] The word "complexity" is used advisedly, for in the eighteenth century there were so many officials and committees engaged in overseeing the colonies that it is no easy matter to fix with exactness their powers, functions, and relations to one another. Several features of imperial administration, however, are beyond dispute. Control of the colonies was exercised in the name of the King and thus as an extraordinary assertion of the royal prerogative, which by this time had lost most of its meaning in the mother country. Parliament was preoccupied with what it considered weightier affairs and was quite unsure of its right to legislate in support or restraint of this last significant manifestation of the once-proud prerogative. Neither Crown nor Parliament created much in the way of special machinery for colonial affairs, and for the most part regular executive agencies expanded their activities to include the colonies. Final authority over the colonies resided in the Privy Council, but the actual task of supervision was carried on by committees of the Council, regular agencies, and one specially constituted board. The most important of these varied instruments were:

The Board of Trade,[22] or "Lords Commissioners of Trade and Plantations," a staff and advisory agency independent of the Privy Council. The Board was charged with drafting instructions for the governors,[23] hearing colonial complaints, suggesting appointments, collecting information for purposes of more effective oversight and direction, and reviewing colonial laws. Although the Board was inferior in legal status and had no sanctions at its command, it wielded much influence through its correspondence with governors and through reports and recommendations to the Crown. Rarely, for example, did the Privy Council disregard its advisory verdict on the wisdom or legality of colonial legislation.

The Committee of the Privy Council, often known as "the Lords of the Committee of Council for hearing appeals and complaints from the plantations," an agency whose functions are clear in its title. This committee provided, for those colonists able and willing to make use of its machinery, a reasonably impartial and efficient high court of appeals. Its chief purpose was not to do justice or develop an imperial common law, but to protect prerogative and mercantilism against colonial interference.

The Treasury Board, which dealt with the larger problems of colonial finance, especially in time of war, and exercised important discretion in settling American claims for money.

The Commissioners of the Customs, an agency of the Treasury, which took the lead in enforcing the Navigation Acts and collected the duties levied under them. The commissioners drafted special instructions to the governors in matters of trade and revenue and tendered advice to other branches of the government concerning commercial policy.

The Admiralty, which directed the navy's commercial and martial operations in American waters.

The War Office, which first came into prominence in the French and Indian War as the agency for organizing and equipping the British armies in America.

Last in order, but in many ways first in importance, the Secretary of State for the Southern Department, the chief official for colonial affairs in the developing cabinet system. The primary concern of the Secretary of State was war and diplomacy with France and Spain; it was therefore inevitable that his conduct of office should bear directly upon problems of security for the colonies.

The actual division of responsibility for colonial affairs among these many agencies is as difficult to state today as it must have been to understand in the eighteenth century. For the most part, the Secretary of State confined his attention to diplomatic and military affairs, the Board of Trade to the defense of mercantilism, the Privy Council to final action in appeals and disallowances, and the other agencies to their special provinces. A good deal of overlapping in certain areas and undersupervision in others developed and was tolerated. The makings of a unified system of colonial control were present in the office of Secretary of State, but for several reasons—the lack of interest in colonial affairs of most incumbents (especially the Duke of Newcastle, 1724-1748), the preoccupation of the Secretary with the over-all pattern of war and diplomacy, and the rapid turnover in personnel—these potentialities were never realized.

The result of this conjunction of too much organization for detail and too little concern for unity—especially when intensified by distance, slowness of communication, inferiority of personnel, corruption, bribery, and colonial obstinacy—was a large measure of self-government for the colonies. Each of the chief weapons of imperial control—the viceregal authority of the governor, the system of appeals to the Privy Council, and the practice of royal disallowance of colonial legislation—proved either defective or inadequate in action. The governor was one thing in the instructions of the Board of Trade and quite another in Williamsburg, Boston, or New York. The system of appeals to the Privy Council was workable enough, but was confined to cases in which a sizable sum was at stake. In the entire colonial period less than two hundred cases from the American colonies were prosecuted before the Privy Council.[24] Whatever it was to become in later years, it was not in the eighteenth century a supreme court of empire. The extent of imperial control exercised through the technique of royal disallowance may be judged from the figures: From 1691 to the end of the colonial period roughly 8,500 laws were submitted for approval.[25] Of these some 470, or 5.5 per cent, were disallowed. The practice of submission and examination was loose and was particularly hampered by the fact of distance. Considerable success was achieved by English authorities in blocking laws that encroached on the prerogative, affected England's commercial interests, interfered with the established church, tampered with the currency, and altered the laws of inheritance; yet for the most part the fact or threat of royal disallowance had surprisingly little effect on the course of colonial self-government.

All sorts of officials were active in the colonies as instruments of royal supervision and control. Of these the most important in each colony were the royal governor, his council, and such executive officials as the secretary and attorney-general. In addition, strewn through all the colonies, even in self-contained Rhode Island and Connecticut, was an ever-growing band of emissaries and executors for the agencies at home: naval officers, customs officials, military and naval commanders, deputy postmasters, and judges of vice-admiralty.[26] "He has erected a multitude of New Offices," complained Jefferson in the Declaration of Independence, "and sent hither swarms of Officers to harass our people, and eat out their substance."

COLONIAL AGENTS.[27] One of the interesting developments of the colonial period was the eventual establishment, by the colonies, of permanent representatives at the seat of empire—a development that was encouraged by the Board of Trade. The duties of the colonial agent, who was generally an American resident in England, were determined largely by circumstance: to represent the interests of the colony before the agencies of imperial control, and when necessary before Parliament; to gather and transmit information in both directions; to see to the colony's commercial, financial, and judicial interests; and generally to further its fortunes in all possible ways, even (as in the famous instances of Dummer and Franklin) to the extent of writing pamphlets to influence English opinion. As the eighteenth century progressed and the split between governor and assembly widened, it became common practice for each of these political branches to maintain its own agent. By the end of the colonial period eight assemblies had agents in London.

Such was the scheme of colonial government at the center and extremities of empire—at the center a hodgepodge of administration with standards of solicitude and performance that varied radically from one agency to another and from one period to the next, at the extremities a swarm of officials dedicated either to Crown or to colony, rarely to both. The push-and-pull of these two opposing forces is the substance of American political and constitutional history in the eighteenth century.[28]

POPULAR PARTICIPATION IN POLITICS

If the pattern of colonial politics was marked by an ever-increasing measure of self-government and home rule, then the question naturally arises: Who were the "selves" who did the governing? Who ruled at home? The answer must be sought in these three considerations: the nature of the suffrage in the various colonies; the extent to which the suffrage was actually exercised; the intensity of popular interest and participation in the political affairs of town and colony.

The history of the colonial suffrage, like the history of almost all early American institutions, was one of primitive diversity in the seventeenth century and maturing uniformity in the eighteenth.[29] A wide variety of practice prevailed before 1690, ranging from the narrow limitation of church membership in Hebraic Massachusetts to something quite close to white manhood suffrage during the first years in Virginia, Rhode Island, West Jersey, and several other localities. As the settlements developed into more stable and complicated societies, ever more insistent demands arose for a broader suffrage in the autocratic colonies and a narrower one in the popular. By the turn of the century, some sort of property qualification for voting had been established in every colony;[30] this feature of American politics was to continue in force until well after the winning of independence. In part the requirement of property-holding was fostered by the English authorities, who had begun to insist in charters and instructions that

> You shall take care that the members of the assembly be elected only by ffreeholders, as being more agreeable to the custome of England, to which you are as nigh as conveniently you can to conforme yourselfe.[31]

In part it could be traced to the fact that the colonists, too, were Englishmen, and therefore felt, consciously or unconsciously, the urge to conform to ancient ways. It was all but inevitable that men of their blood and understanding should have been impelled by the rise of a propertied class to restrict the suffrage to those who had achieved a visible measure of competence and stability.

The details of these property requirements furnish yet another instance of English practice adapted to American conditions. In most colonies the basic qualification was the famous "forty-shilling freehold." Seven of them—New Hampshire, Rhode Island, New York, New Jersey, Virginia, North Carolina, and Georgia—made the possession of land an absolute requirement, while the others held out alternatives to this real estate qualification: personal property or payment of taxes. Everywhere a "stake-in-society" was the key to political enfranchisement, and almost everywhere additional restrictions kept women, youths, Catholics, Jews, infidels, Negroes, Indians, mulattoes, indentured servants, and other "inferior" persons from the polls. A few, but only a very few, voices were lifted in protest against limited suffrage. Perhaps the clearest of these spoke through an advertisement in a Philadelphia newspaper in 1737:

A PECUNIARY Gratification is offered to any of the learned or unlearned, who shall *Mathematically* prove, that a Man's having a Property in a Tract of Land, more or less, is thereby entitled to any Advantage, *in point of understanding*, over another Fellow, who has no other Estate, than

"THE AIR . . . *to breathe in*, THE EARTH . . . *to walk upon*, and ALL THE RIVERS OF THE WORLD . . . *to drink of*." [32]

Accurate figures of the voting potential in each of the colonies are not easy to establish.[33] The best estimate—arrived at by a study of population statistics, land- and tax-records, and poll lists in representative localities—would be that something like one out of every two to eight white males was eligible to vote for representatives in the assembly, perhaps one out of two to five for elective officers in towns and in boroughs with open charters of incorporation. There were many deviations, both upward and downward, from these averages, depending, for example, upon the local price and availability of land, proximity to the frontier, and the origins and attitudes of the inhabitants. It must be emphasized that these figures are estimates only, for reliable statistics are just not to be found.

If these figures are discouraging to the modern democrat, even more discouraging are estimates of exercise of the suffrage. Again the pattern is one of extreme variation from one time and locality to the next, but in general there existed what appears at first glance to have been an attitude of astounding apathy toward campaigns and elections. Not only was but one in four white males eligible to vote; in many places but one in four of those eligible even bothered to vote. Nonvoting is no new thing in the American experience. Rather it would appear that the flight from the poll was far more general in colonial times than today. The records of the late eighteenth century show that in several supposedly hotly contested elections in Massachusetts an average of one qualified voter in five took the trouble to vote.[34] The figures are better, but not too much better, in Virginia and the middle colonies. Although no generalized percentages can be established, the generalized statement that nonvoting was a widespread feature of colonial politics seems to be true beyond any shadow of doubt.

The third point of inquiry, the intensity of popular interest and participation in the political affairs of town and colony, has already been largely answered. What was true of voting was doubly true of office-holding: Restrictions were many and aspirants few.[35] In an age when breadwinning consumed all a man's time and energy, when travel was difficult and organized political parties nonexistent, when government was severely limited in scope and touched many men not at all, and when the pace of life and the progress of institutions went slowly, political indifference—to elections, to office-holding, and to issues—was well-nigh inevitable. Despite eloquent references to "an aroused people" in certain memorable debates in the assemblies, politics in colonial America was the province of those with particular interests to defend or with a natural flair for public action.[36] The number of such persons was never and nowhere very large. The political apathy of the colonial press, punctured only occasionally before 1765 by a thorough airing of some local squabble, is proof of the slow pace of political life. "Publick Lethargy" was under constant attack by colonial penmen.[37]

This does not mean that the declarations and decisions of the attentive few or the experiences and instincts of the indifferent many were any the less important to the progress of American liberty. The few in their assemblies, town meetings, and polls held the democratic future in trust and acted out on a small stage the great drama of constitutional government that was in time to call millions into the supporting cast. The many, too, had their own notion of liberty and self-government: to be left alone to pursue their own destinies. When government became important or oppressive enough, they found ways other than politics to express their wishes and to influence action. Sullen resistance, riots, and "going out west" are not generally recommended as effective techniques of political freedom, but in colonial times they served a very real purpose.

These are the facts of political participation in the American colonies: Only a fraction could participate and even a lesser fraction did; the colonies were still well ahead of practice in almost all other countries; and many men never cared one way or the other about the exercise of political power. Nor should it be forgotten that in a society so amazingly fluid for the age, a society where men could "move on" and where land was cheap and plentiful, the privilege of the suffrage was something that any man could win. The records prove that everywhere, even in aristocratic New York and South Carolina, men of mean birth and menial occupation could aspire to political power and prominence.[38] And that a man in eighteenth-century Virginia or New England had neither opportunity nor desire to vote or hold office did not mean that he considered himself a slave. In an age when politics was one of the least of man's worries, the poll lists were one of the lesser criteria of the progress of liberty.

THE FACTORS OF FREEDOM: I

Upon this stage and within these limits at least four major political forces were at work for liberty in those times and democracy in these: the rise of the assembly and its contest for power with the governor; the development of institutions of local government; the winning of several of the key political freedoms, especially freedom of press; and the establishment of the institutions and spirit of constitutionalism.

ASSEMBLY AND GOVERNOR. Seeds of contention between governor and assembly were sown with profusion in the constitutions of the colonies.[39] The inherent contradictions between the interests and attitudes of the mother country and those of the distant, misunderstood colonies were especially apparent and decisive in this instance. On one hand stood the royal or proprietary governor—in four cases out of five an Englishman, in the fifth a loyal colonial, in any case an agent of the prerogative with a commission and instructions that made him an autocrat not beholden to colonial direction. On the other stood the provincial assembly—the articulate organ of a breed of men who were more English than the English in their obstinacy, pride, and hypersensitivity in matters of self-government. From the outset the system gaped at the middle, and the final triumph of the assembly was almost foreordained. Although the governor occupied a position of overwhelming constitutional and legitimate superiority, it was one repeatedly undercut by circumstances in colony and empire.

The governors got far more verbal than moral or practical support from the authorities at home. The remoteness of colonial capitals and the lack of either an imperial policy or the will to execute it created a situation in which the governor was left pretty much on his own. It was he, not the Board of Trade, who had to live with the colonists; it was his estimate of the expedient, not the Board's demand of the impossible, that controlled decisions taken on the spot. The governor was far too often left defenseless against what Governor Clinton of New York labeled the assembly's "continued Grasping at Power." [40]

The colonists fell naturally into the opinion of their governors best summed up in Franklin's reference to "men of vicious characters and broken fortunes, sent by a Minister to get them out of the way." [41] We know today that this was rarely the case, that the governors were "typical British officials, neither better nor worse than those who were carrying on the administration in England." [42] There were men as bad as Cornbury and Fletcher, but there were also men as good as Dinwiddie, the Wentworths, Spotswood, Hunter, Pownall, Burnet, Shirley, Glen, and Dobbs. [43] No matter who the governors were, however, most colonists agreed with the New York Assembly of 1749 that they were

> generally entire Strangers to the People they are sent to govern . . . their Interest is entirely distinct . . . they seldom regard the Welfare of the People, otherwise than as they can make it subservient to their own particular Interest. [44]

In this instance the myth was more telling than the fact, and the myth was one of "men of broken fortunes, dissolute and ignorant, too vile to be employed near home," [45] a calumny that the English press printed and the colonial press reprinted with glee. [46] Recognition of the alien purposes of the royal governors and misrepresentation of their personal traits did much to strengthen the pretensions of the colonial assemblies.

Colonial legislators were persistent, clever, and vigilant, and over the years advanced a surprisingly coherent policy in constitutional matters. The struggle for power was not always so bitter and decisive as the history books would have it, for several colonies enjoyed extended periods of political quiescence and good will. Yet always the trend was toward power in the assembly, which fought its way ever higher in the name of "the people" and "our ancient and undoubted rights and priviledges as Englishmen."

The lack of real toughness in the imperialists in England permitted the colonists to exploit to the limit the great and fatal defect of the colonial constitutions: the location of the power of the purse in colonial hands, a defect compounded by the failure of the Crown to provide a permanent civil list in any of the colonies. No one was more aware than the governor himself that "the Want of a certain and adequate civil List to each Colony" was "the Root of the American Disorders." [47] Far too many officials, institutions, and necessities of empire were left dependent upon the willingness of the assemblies to tax friends and neighbors and upon their natural desire to fix conditions upon any and all grants.

Occasionally in spectacular political warfare accompanied by newspaper attacks on the governors,[48] but more often through unpublicized day-to-day encroachments, the assemblies grasped for privileges and powers like those of the House of Commons. Several of Parliament's hard-earned privileges—control over procedure, freedom of debate, determination of disputed elections—were secured by the assemblies. Others—the "Speaker's Petition," control over sessions, regulation of elections, creation of new electoral districts—were not, and over these the struggle raged in almost every colony. The Crown defended with particular tenacity the governor's power to prorogue and dissolve the assembly and the final weapons of gubernatorial veto and royal disallowance. Yet the area of assembly freedom grew ever wider, especially as it came home to more and more colonials that the fight for parliamentary privilege was at bottom a fight for the liberty of the subject.[49]

The assemblies also used the purse to pry their way into executive affairs. For example, by designating a specific person to receive the salary of an office they usurped the power of appointment; by naming their own committees and even their own treasurer to verify expenditures they encroached substantially on the governor's command of the militia and control over military stores;[50] and by the famous expedient of tampering with the governor's salary they brought more than one recalcitrant to heel in such matters as the personnel and jurisdiction of colonial courts. The governors of Georgia and Virginia were the only viceroys whose salaries were not dependent on the pleasure of the assembly or, as in the case of the North Carolina quit-rents, on an unsatisfactory substitute arrangement. Especially acrimonious battles were fought in New York and Massachusetts over the assembly's calculated practice of annual grants to the governor—with the assembly emerging victorious.[51] The provision in the Constitution of 1787 forbidding the raising or lowering of the President's compensation attests the respect in which eighteenth-century Americans held this technique.

By 1760 the assemblies were dominant in almost every colony in continental America. The royal power of disallowance was potent enough to prevent a complete overriding of the governor and other imperial officials, but shrewd observers were beginning to realize that only the full power of Parliament was now equal to the centrifugal practices of the assemblies. Most discouraging to proponents of empire was the inability of English authorities to secure positive accomplishments. The record of colonial co-operation, or rather nonco-operation, in time of war must have been hard to swallow. The assemblies recorded their most spectacular gains, especially in their campaign to control the public purse, in the French and Indian War. Many a governor was thoroughly convinced that the lower house considered him rather than the French the enemy to be brought to terms.

The struggles of the colonial assemblies provide an instructive example of the way in which men distrustful of democracy in one century can, by fighting for their own privileges and opinions, open the way to democracy in the next.[52] Indeed, "distrustful of democracy" is the very best that can be said of cliques that controlled assemblies in New Hampshire, Pennsylvania, the Carolinas, and Virginia. The records show up many colonial parliamentarians as ill-tempered, petty, self-seeking, tiresome little men, more often than not committed to the intolerant side of questions of religious and economic freedom. Yet on the whole the assemblies included an unusual range of strong and able men, many of whom were genuinely liberal in their opinions. The Whigs in the colonial legislatures had a limited popularism as their goal, but in driving toward it they unloosed forces that would not be halted short of total political democracy. And their arguments proved in time to be fully convertible to democratic currency.

The colonial assemblies, like the dissenting churches, were influential schools of American political thought. The system under which delegates were chosen was one as representative of "the people" as could be erected in those days of concern for Whig ideals of liberty. The proceedings of the assemblies were open to public inspection and criticism,[53] their journals were printed and distributed, and their exchanges with the governors, especially those of a pungent nature, got an ever more thorough coverage in the colonial press. Just about all that the people of South Carolina knew of Massachusetts was that there, too, the assembly hacked away continually at the governor's position and powers.[54] There can be no argument with Charles M. Andrews's conclusion: "In the development of American political ideas and social practices, the influence of the popular assembly . . . is the most potent single factor underlying our American system of government." [55]

LOCAL GOVERNMENT.[56] Both the fact and tradition of local self-government bear the stamp of the colonial experience. Self-sustaining institutions of local government have always been a sure sign of political freedom. The flourishing condition of such institutions in colonial times was at once a factor in the evolution of a democratic faith and evidence of the progress of American liberty. It was evidence of other things as well: the English origins of the founders of the various colonies; the remarkable display of pragmatic ingenuity, or of plain horse-sense, that they devoted to fitting their inherited experience to new conditions of geography and economic structure; the pronounced influence in several areas of corporate forms and traditions; the intense political self-reliance of the first settlers and their descendants; and the widespread distrust of arbitrary or centralized or simply remote government. In general, the central governments of the colonies exercised even less control over local institutions than did the mother country over the colonies.

The over-all pattern of local government was typically colonial, exhibiting primitive diversity in the seventeenth century, maturing uniformity in the eighteenth, and sharp differences always between North and South, frontier and seaboard, city and village. In New England the influence of corporate forms and incidence of local self-direction were especially pronounced. The basic units were the county,[57] which in most of New England was a judicial-military district and in Massachusetts handled problems of land titles, probate administration, highway planning, licensing, and taxation as well, and the town,[58] which dealt pragmatically with "prudential affairs": care of highways, poor relief, preservation of the peace, elementary education, land disposal and registration, assessment and collection of taxes and tithes, and just about any other matter of local interest, including the enforcement of "blue laws." The county's affairs were directed by justices and other officers appointed by the governor, who rarely if ever ignored local opinion in making his selections. There was no representative body for county affairs, nor does there seem to have been any demand for one.

Although colonial assemblies passed many laws dealing with the organization and powers of the towns, these units were in fact quite independent of central control. More important, they were self-governing in the most obvious sense—through the famous town meeting, the selectmen, and a host of unpaid minor officials: constables, tithingmen, surveyors, fence-viewers, field-drivers, haywards, notice-givers, assessors, pound-keepers, corders of wood, leather-sealers, overseers of the poor, "hogg constables," cutters of fish, and "cometies" for almost every conceivable purpose, all chosen from and by the citizenry. In 1720 an average Massachusetts town, Ipswich, had ninety-seven regular officials.[59]

Town government in colonial New England has never deserved more than a fraction of the encomiums heaped indiscriminately upon it, for the records tell us that oligarchy and apathy were common in those days, too. The same names appear year after year in important offices; the same concern over nonattendance at town meeting is displayed in resolves ordering delinquents to show up or be fined. Yet the town was a species of artless democracy, however limited; it was far more popular a scheme of government than local institutions in the homeland; and it provided, for those who took part in elections, meetings, and public service, important schooling in the techniques of political freedom. The town governments of New England were, quite without hyperbole, the most memorable form of local self-government in colonial America.[60]

Local government in the Southern colonies was aristocratic, even oligarchical in character, and was thus quite different from the New England plan.[61] In neither of the two major units, county and parish, were officers elected, nor was there any sort of representative body. The county—the key unit for military, judicial, administrative, and electoral affairs—was governed by a court of eight or more justices appointed by the governor on the recommendation of the justices themselves. In practice, this converted the court into a closed, self-perpetuating organ of the local gentry. The parish, which was much less important than the county and dealt with such problems as government of the local church, ferries, land boundaries, and care of the poor, was equally closed and self-perpetuating. Yet in the vital tests of self-reliance and freedom from central supervision, the counties and parishes—and, of course, the plantations—of Virginia and South Carolina were as typically colonial as the towns of New England.[62] The select vestries of Bristol and Stratton Major were not too different in character from the selectmen of Little Compton and Simsbury. The records [63] give much substance to Jefferson's observations on the vestrymen:

> These are usually the most discreet farmers, so distributed through their parish, that every part of it may be under the immediate eye of some one of them. They are well acquainted with the details and economy of private life, and they find sufficient inducements to execute their charge well, in their philanthropy, in the approbation of their neighbors, and the distinction which that gives them.[64]

The "publicity of familiarity" was apparently almost as salutary a check on the parish clerk in Virginia as was the town meeting on the town clerk in Massachusetts.

Local government in the middle colonies was neither so popular as in the North nor select as in the South.[65] New York and Pennsylvania went through their own processes of evolution, which in each instance led to the natural selection of the county as the principal unit. County government in New York was in the hands of a board of supervisors; each town in the county elected one member of this board. In Pennsylvania a law of 1724 established a somewhat different system, under which three commissioners were elected from the whole county to manage fiscal, civil, and judicial affairs.[66] These two systems were destined to spread from New York and Pennsylvania throughout the Union. They, too, were marked by a considerable degree of self-determination in the colonial period. The town meeting was carried into several areas of the middle colonies, but failed to take fast root except in the settlements on Long Island. There—in Oyster Bay, Southampton, Brookhaven, Huntington, and other still pleasant towns—descendants of New Englanders governed themselves in the New England way.[67]

Two special types of local arrangement were relatively uniform in appearance and spirit through most of the colonies: government in the incorporated city,[68] and government on the frontier. Many of the more populous localities—Boston, Baltimore, New Haven, Newport, Charleston—were governed through most or all of the colonial period under much the same forms as were their small neighbors. Others—including such important centers as New York, Albany, Philadelphia, Annapolis, Norfolk, and Williamsburg, as well as a dozen or so lesser communities—were granted charters of incorporation.[69] Several of these were "close" corporations, in which mayor, councilors, aldermen, and other officials were empowered to choose their own successors. The majority, however, enjoyed charters of a more popular character. In New York, for example, councilors and aldermen were elected by the freemen and freeholders of the borough. Colonial incorporations exercised almost complete control over their own affairs, and in several of them political activity reached its peak in the colonial period. The independence of local units was dramatically demonstrated in 1734 by the refusal of officials of the city of New York to obey Governor Cosby's order to attend the burning of the offensive numbers of John Peter Zenger's *Weekly Journal*.[70]

The scheme of self-government on the advancing frontier was a tremendous spiritual if not institutional force in the development of American democracy. We know very little about the politics of the wilderness. The chief sources of information are the priceless records of the very first settlements, when the frontier was everywhere and every man a frontiersman.[71] These records tell us that a practical, primitive householders' democracy, grounded in the fact and theory of free consent, was the usual form of government in almost every English settlement except Massachusetts Bay. Later pioneers, especially the Scotch-Irish in Pennsylvania, Virginia, and the Carolinas, were not so literate and articulate as Roger Williams and John Pory, yet we learn something of their ways through occasional minutes, letters, and travelers' descriptions. The general picture is one of the barest bones of government.[72] Yet even in their state of near-anarchy there was active that peculiar combination of individualism and co-operation—"free association"—which was enforced by circumstances of the agrarian frontier. When organs of town, parish, or county government were finally set up in the settlements, they were cast in a rudely popular mold. The institutions were those of the tidewater, but the spirit and suffrage were often those of the democratic frontier.

By way of summation, these common features of local government in the colonies should be noted: the broader suffrage for local than for colony-wide elections;[73] the multiplicity of unpaid offices and duties, a system under which a much greater percentage of the citizens performed at least some sort of public duty than is the case today; the healthy publicity that went along with "government by friends and neighbors"; the absence of control, supervision, and tampering by governor or assembly; the limited scope of action and service as contrasted with modern local government; and the devotion of the average man's political attention to affairs of town rather than colony. All these are signs of a pragmatic sort of popularism, which was especially strong in the New England towns, frontier settlements, and open boroughs. Historians were later to rhapsodize about the "democracy" of these experiments, but the colonists themselves valued their local institutions for their simplicity and utility. Whatever their worth as techniques of public service, these institutions taught the colonists one more sturdy lesson in freedom from pomp and arbitrary power.

THE FACTORS OF FREEDOM: II

THE RISE OF POLITICAL LIBERTY; FREEDOM OF PRESS. By 1765 a healthy
portion of the American people had been conditioned to a lively concern
for political liberty. Unsophisticated and intuitive as colonial notions of
liberty might seem to us today, they were held in such esteem and expressed with such fervor as to work decisive influence on the course of
events. The early colonials—good Englishmen they were—had talked incessantly of their rights and privileges. As the settlements progressed toward
social maturity and political self-consciousness, developments in the assembly
and local governments gave new content to old phrases. From this experience flowed new ideas of liberty, and these ideas in turn gave rise to even
more liberty. By the middle of the eighteenth century freedom as both
fact and condition was flourishing in the colonies far more vigorously than
in England. "They augur misgovernment at a distance," cried Burke, "and
snuff the approach of tyranny in every tainted breeze." What Tories derided
and yet feared as "republican notions" had swept America from leveling
Vermont to aristocratic Charleston.

Most of the liberties essential to the growth of democracy and democratic thought are mentioned at other points in this book: suffrage, elections,
assembly privileges, and equality before the law; liberty of individual conscience and separation of church and state; freedom of opportunity and
social mobility; free inquiry and the right to dissent from political or
religious orthodoxy. All these liberties were developing at different speeds
in the different colonies, most vigorously on the frontier and in the cities
of the northern and middle colonies. There were people everywhere who
cherished and enjoyed them, and who were ready at the snuff of a tainted
breeze to defend them with philosophical and practical argument—and ultimately with their blood.

Let us concentrate here on one basic liberty. Freedom of press—the uncontrolled and uncensored exchange in print of ideas, information, arguments, and accusations—is in many ways the most essential political liberty.
The effective conduct of free government is dependent upon the existence
of a free press; the fortunes of each seem always to rise and fall together.
The establishment of a free press in eighteenth-century America was therefore a fact of great moment, not only for the popularization of libertarian
values, but also for the winning of independence. The struggle for a free
and unlicensed press was long and frustrating, but by the time of the Stamp
Act the victory had been sealed.[74]

In seventeenth-century America there was no such thing as freedom of
press. Indeed, in many colonies there was no press at all. The disrupting
power of the printed word was well understood by those who ruled in
Europe and America. Governor Berkeley of Virginia was only a trifle
tougher than his fellow autocrats when he wrote to the lords commissioners
in 1671:

But, I thank God, *there are no free schools* nor *printing;* and I hope we shall not have these hundred years; for *learning* has brought disobedience, and heresy, and sects into the world, and *printing* has divulged them, and libels against the best government. God keep us from both! [75]

One of the standard royal commands issued to governors between 1686 and 1732 was this:

Forasmuch as great inconveniences may arise by the liberty of printing in our said province, you are to provide by all necessary orders that no person keep any press for printing, nor that any book, pamphlet, or other matters whatsoever be printed without your especial leave and license first obtained.[76]

In the few places where printing presses were permitted in the seventeenth-century settlements, they were sponsored or watched closely by the ruling authorities. Massachusetts took the lead: A press was established at Cambridge in 1638 for orthodox purposes, and thirty-odd years later Marmaduke Johnson set up, under strict licensing, another press in Boston.[77] It was here on September 25, 1690, that *Publick Occurrences*, America's first newspaper, appeared—and was immediately suppressed.

The rise of a free press in colonial America was therefore a development of the eighteenth century. The bare facts of this development indicate its extent and character: In 1715 there was one newspaper in the colonies, John Campbell's weekly *Boston News-Letter*, which carried news of England a year old, had a circulation of 250, and was "published by authority." In 1765 there were twenty-three, at least one in each colony but New Jersey and Delaware,[78] carrying news and letters of every variety and political hue, reaching tens of thousands of subscribers and their friends, and being printed everywhere without censorship and almost everywhere without fear of governor or assembly. Several of these were already quite partisan in character, while others discharged their obligations to full and free discussion by publishing documents and letters on all sides of an issue, thus fulfilling the motto of Rind's *Virginia Gazette:* "Open to All Parties but influenced by None." Until 1765 the press engaged for the most part in straight reporting, with emphasis on "European Intelligence" (especially war news and speculation about such problems as the Queen of Denmark's rupture and the Queen of Spain's "inward Disorders"), ship arrivals and clearings, exchanges of pleasantries between King and Parliament, horror stories, moralizing, and essays on such subjects as "The Faithfulness of Dogs" and "Early Rising." [79]

The decision of Parliament to tax the colonies brought the press to life. The reaction of newspapers to the Stamp Act was clamorous and unanimous.[80] The transition from political apathy to political frenzy was especially noticeable in such newspapers as the *Georgia Gazette, Pennsylvania Journal, Connecticut Gazette, South-Carolina Gazette, New-York Gazette, New-York Mercury,* and above all the *Boston Gazette.* In 1763 some of these journals were devoting eleven in twelve columns to paid advertisements; in

1765 they were devoting eleven in twelve to letters from Britannicus Americanus, Á Friend to Both Peoples, Sydney, and Mucius Scaevola.

Of equal importance in this eighteenth-century development was the increasingly vigorous practice of political pamphleteering. The success of Thomas Paine's *Common Sense* was made possible by decades of other pamphlets that had helped transfer this habit from England to America. Much less significant politically, but no less interesting, were the fourteen magazines that were published for brief intervals during these years.[81]

We should pay tribute to the journalists who did most to defy authority in the struggle for an uncensored press: to James Franklin and his saucy *New-England Courant* (1721), the third paper in Boston and first to be published without authority; to Benjamin Edes and John Gill and their *Boston Gazette* (founded 1719, first published by them 1755), so outspoken a defender of colonial liberties as to win for itself from the Tories the title of "The Weekly Dung-Barge"; to Andrew Bradford of Philadelphia and the *American Weekly Mercury* (1719), the first paper outside Boston and one much concerned with political liberty; to his nephew William Bradford and the *Pennsylvania Journal* (1741), one of the bravest supporters of the cause of American freedom; to Benjamin Franklin and the *Pennsylvania Gazette* (1729), one of the liveliest and best-written colonial weeklies; to William Parks and the *Maryland Gazette* (1727) and *Virginia Gazette* (1736), the earliest journals in these pivotal colonies; and above all to John Peter Zenger and his *New-York Weekly Journal* (1733). Nor should we forget old Andrew Hamilton of Philadelphia, who appealed to the jury over the heads of a hostile court to win for Zenger a verdict of "not guilty" on the charge of seditious libel. The Zenger trial (1735) is rightly celebrated as an epic of American liberty.[82] Although the principles argued by Hamilton —the admissibility of evidence concerning the truth of an alleged libel and the right of the jury to decide whether a piece of writing is seditious or defamatory—were still many decades from final establishment in law, the release of Zenger was widely acclaimed and did much to put fiber in colonial editors and ginger in their political reporting. Pamphlets and newspapers everywhere printed accounts of the trial,[83] and colonists who had been hitherto indifferent to controversies over liberty and authority discussed it with interest.

The rise of a free press and of a philosophy to defend it is an outstanding example of the manner in which a variety of historical forces combined to bring liberty, independence, and finally democracy to America.[84] Among these may be singled out once again the English descent and interests of the colonists, who drew constantly upon the mother country for political ideas and literary manners; the increase in literacy, learning, and popular desire for news and knowledge, which made widespread printing financially possible; the struggle of factions in the assembly and local governments, which enticed colonial editors into ever more positive comment on political matters; the fluidity of society and economy, which made it possible for poor but ambitious men like Franklin and Louis Timothée to make a success of printing and publishing; and the increasing recognition among printers and readers that a free press was every man's interest. "THE PRESS," wrote the printer of the *Connecticut Gazette,* "is not so much considered, as the Property of the Men who carry on the Trade of Printing, as of the Publick." [85] And an anonymous correspondent told Zenger, as if he didn't already know:

> The *Liberty of the Press* is the *Foundation* of all our other *Liberties,* whether *Civil* or *Religious* and whenever the Liberty of the Press is taken away, either by *open Force,* or any *little, dirty infamous Arts,* we shall immediately become as *wretched,* as *ignorant,* and as *despicable* SLAVES, as any one Nation in all *Europe.* [86]

The muscular press of the Revolution was the gift of a score of independent journeymen, few of whom were aware of the collective importance of their modest ventures in publishing the news, yet all of whom made a rich contribution to American liberty.

WRITTEN CONSTITUTIONS AND STANDING LAW. One of the popular slogans of the Revolutionary generation was "a government of laws and not of men." Even the most politically sophisticated American found meaning and comfort in this admonition. The able men of Massachusetts who placed it in their constitution of 1780 knew very well that they, not some words on paper, would govern in the future as they had governed in the past; yet they flattered themselves that they had constructed a political system in which the laws of all generations rather than the discretion of one would be the decisive factor in the conduct of government. By 1765 most colonists believed implicitly that government should be run by men whose status, term of office, duties, powers, and limitations were outlined in organic laws and charters comprehensible to all citizens. Americans counted it a blessing that they were relatively free from the power of magistrates exercising uncontrolled discretion, that they lived under a government prohibited by law from acting out of whim or caprice. As a leader of the North Carolina Regulators wrote, even "if we are all rogues, there must be Law, and all we want is to be Governed by Law, and not by the *Will* of Officers, which to us is perfectly despotick and arbitrary." [87] The colonists not only held to this belief but had institutions to express it. When they thought the mother country had turned to ruling them with whim and caprice, they resisted with the aid of two institutions in particular: written constitutions and standing law.

The American doctrine of a written constitution owes much to England but even more to colonial experience. [88] The state constitutions of 1776-1780 and the federal constitutions of 1778 and 1787 attest the determination of eighteenth-century Americans to live under governments organized, enabled, and limited by written documents. The immediate cause of this flurry of constitution-making was the fact of revolution, which generally compels men who start with a clean slate to fill it up at once with careful directions to themselves and their descendants. Yet the virtual unanimity with which politically minded Americans turned to writing constitutions proves that they were acting on principle as well as out of necessity.

It is difficult to fix the origins of the American belief in a written constitution. It is possible, however, to point to a half-dozen varieties of fundamental law in colonial times and to suggest that they must have done a great deal to advertise this principle to the awakening American mind. Among these were:

Charters. Whether commercial, proprietary, corporate, or royal, the charter or other basic document of each colony was recognized, however vaguely or grudgingly, as a species of written and controlling law. Neither companies, proprietors, nor colonial assemblies had authority to alter the conditions of these documents; as a result, the colonists learned through experience that men could govern successfully within the confines of a written higher law. Important in this respect was the so-called "conformity clause," which appeared in one form or other in almost all colonial charters. Self-governing powers were granted the persons or entities named in the charter so long as their "Statutes, Ordinances and Proceedings as near as conveniently may be, be agreeable to the Laws, Statutes, Government, and Policy of this our Realm of England," [89] and colonial lawmakers were therefore constantly concerned to shape their statutes to a higher law. At the same time, the assemblies learned to appeal to the charter and to make capital out of the blessed word "unconstitutional." In some ways the charter was quite different from the modern constitution, but in certain essential features it was itself a constitution, for it was *written, higher, controlling,* and *law.* The direct line of descent from colonial charter to state constitution is shown in the fact that the Connecticut charter of 1662 was in force until 1818, the Rhode Island charter of 1663 until 1842.

English Documents. Such frustrated or short-lived experiments in English constitution-making as the Agreement of the People (1647) and the Instrument of Government (1653) had no more effect on the colonies than they did on the mother country. English practice and thought worked upon the American constitutional tradition in other ways, principally through the transmission of the great tradition of government under law and of the habits of devotion and appeal to Magna Charta and the Bill of Rights. In their insistence upon written constitutions the Revolutionists were children of the colonial experience; in their insistence upon constitutionalism they were children of England.

The Bible. In Puritan Massachusetts and New Haven, as well as in other scattered localities that tried consciously to live by Scripture, the Bible gave a healthy spur to the belief in a written constitution. The Mosaic Code, too, was a higher law that men could live by—and appeal to against the decrees and whims of ordinary men.

Compacts. A full accounting of the influence of the compact or contract upon colonial history will be rendered at a later stage, but it should be mentioned in passing that such written expressions of this ancient doctrine as the Mayflower Compact (1620) and the Fundamental Orders of Connecticut (1639) were primitive forms of constitution-making in which the colonists themselves engaged. We must be careful, however, not to regard these as constitutions in the currently accepted sense of the word.

Church Organization. The articles of association of many of the separatist or other dissenting churches were a special type of compact or agreement. In areas where church organization had a pronounced effect upon civil government, the covenant did much to encourage the tradition and practices of constitutionalism. Nor should it be forgotten that rules of conduct and mutual assistance adopted by groups of these churches—for example, the Platform of Church Discipline adopted at Cambridge in 1649—assumed with the passing of the years those characteristics of sanctity and untouchability which add so much to the influence of our modern constitutions.

Plans of Government. Finally, we ought not overlook the plans of government bestowed upon certain colonies by their well-meaning sponsors. Some of these were miserable failures, notably John Locke's grandiose Fundamental Constitutions of Carolina; some were reasonably successful experiments, notably William Penn's Frames of Government. All were ancestors of our modern constitutions.

One final point should be made about these numerous forerunners of the American constitutions: Not only were they written, higher, sacred, and in some sense controlling law; not only did they stimulate the principles and habits of constitutionalism; but most of them included some sort of grant or acknowledgment of individual liberties, immunities, or privileges. The American assumption that no constitution is complete unless it incorporates a special bill of rights may also be traced back through colonial experience to the English past.

The growth of standing law in the colonies did much to give practical content to the slogan "a government of laws and not of men." [90] By the middle of the eighteenth century the relations of man to man and of man to community were governed almost everywhere by codes, statutes, and established principles that were known, certain, comprehensible, and to a large extent equal in application. Just as the written constitution was designed primarily to limit the whim of executive and legislature, so the standing law served primarily to regularize the procedures and punishments of the judiciary and its agents in the executive branch. The history of law and courts in colonial times is largely one of the steady reduction of judicial discretion to limits consistent with the dictates of free government. In this instance in particular, the advance from primitive diversity to mature uniformity was marked by an increase in individual liberty.

Popular demand for standing law, and thus for legal control of executive and judicial discretion, was as old as the colonies. As early as 1618 in Virginia,[91] 1641 in Massachusetts,[92] 1647 in Rhode Island, 1650 in Connecticut, and 1656 in New Haven, codes of laws based on experience and English usage had been enacted in response to popular demand.[93] As other colonies were founded, the inhabitants of these, too, were quick to seek procedural guaranties in codes, statutes, and fundamental orders. And in all colonies, old and new, the standing law was sporadically revised and elaborated by assemblies and courts.

The law of seventeenth-century America was simple, practical, and often quite primitive.[94] The magistrates retained an unusual degree of discretion, but they exercised this discretion in keeping with the mores and needs of the homogeneous community. Justice was rough and ready, but so was society. The common law had very little influence either in detail or general principle,[95] except in such colonies as New York, where the homogeneity of other colonies was lacking, and Maryland, which seems to have made a special effort to import certain elements of the English system.[96] One reason for the lack of influence of the common law was the active colonial prejudice against lawyers and consequent untrained character of bench and bar. This primitive experience aided the growth of popular elements in American law. In his ground-breaking studies of "legal engineering" in the colonies,[97] Richard B. Morris has revealed the simplifying, equalizing, and ultimately humanizing influences of the frontier period of our legal history. Many legal historians would agree with Judge Samuel D. Bell of the Supreme Judicial Court of New Hampshire:

> We regard the ignorance of the first colonists of the technicalities of the common law as one of the most fortunate things in the history of the law; since, while the substance of the common law was preserved, we happily lost a great mass of antiquated and useless rubbish, and gained in its stead a course of practice of admirable simplicity.[98]

In the eighteenth century the common law was imported into American jurisprudence on a large scale.[99] Among the reasons for this turn of events were the growing maturity and complexity of the settled regions, the increase in imperial control, and the development of a trained bench and bar.[100] It was natural for lawyers and judges, many of whom had been educated at the Inns of Court in London,[101] to "turn to the great reservoir of legal experience in their own language for guidance and information." [102] By the middle of the century the standing law in America was a unique amalgam of elements drawn from colonial experience and English precedent. In one sense, the importation of the property-conscious common law was a triumph for conservatism or even reaction. In other ways, however, it furthered the cause of liberty and democracy. The common law helped reinvigorate that "sturdy sense of right" inherited from the mother country; [103] it became, through the appeal to several of its more libertarian features, a synonym for liberty and thus a weapon of the Revolutionists; and it trained a whole generation of patriots like Jefferson and John Adams. Burke was sure that the "untractable spirit" of the Americans could be traced to the fact that "In no country perhaps in the world is the law so general a study." [104] The rights of Englishmen were soon to become the rights of all men, and of these none was more precious than to live and do business under a standing law.

Several important details of organization and philosophy were missing in 1765 from the American doctrines of constitutionalism and the rule of law. The constitutional convention, popular ratification, judicial review, and "constitution-worship" were not yet incorporated into the belief in a written constitution. The writ of habeas corpus and other common-law liberties were secured in most colonies only by imported precedents and the willingness of judges and magistrates to follow them.[105] But the spirit of constitutionalism was fixed in the colonial mind. Americans were becoming ever more attached to the conviction that free government demands a high level of political morality, that political morality is best expressed through constitutional procedures, and that constitutionalism is therefore not only a product but a prerequisite of freedom and democracy. The American democracy, like all true democracies, has been pre-eminently a *constitutional* democracy. The transfer of the ancient tenets of English constitutionalism to the colonies, and their conversion to colonial requirements, was a memorable stage of American liberty.

For the most part, of course, the colonists had their political sights set a good deal lower than these lofty notions of law and constitutionalism. Most of them seem to have been far too concerned with problems of existence to give much thought or energy to problems of government. The mass of men went about their business quite indifferent to issues and election, cultivating in their own nonpolitical ways those attitudes of liberty, justice, and individualism which were to stand them in such good stead in the era of the Revolution. The minority that was enfranchised and attentive to public affairs pursued the politics of freedom on a limited stage. Whatever political democracy did exist was a democracy of white male property-owners.

Yet the important truth remains that these people, though they were chiefly concerned with their own short-range interests and had no intention of sharing political power with the disqualified majority, made use of institutions and arguments that were to prove readily convertible to democratic purposes. Their institutions were elective, representative, secular, constitutional, and limited by law; their arguments were framed in terms of "liberty" and "the people." When to these elements were finally added an expanded suffrage and a faith in the average man's political capacity, the triumph of political democracy was secure. The groundwork of this triumph was laid in the colonial period. Before there could be democracy there had to be liberty and self-government.

CHAPTER TWO

Colonial Religion
and the Rise of Liberty

THE influence of religion on government has always been profound. If it is dangerous to frame general laws about the political consequences of religious belief and practice, especially to insist that authoritarianism or democracy or anarchy in the church leads to authoritarianism or democracy or anarchy in the state, it is equally dangerous to refuse to acknowledge that at certain times in certain countries the effects of religion have been decisive.

One thing is certain about church and state in the Atlantic community, and history does not teach us a more emphatic lesson: The great struggles for religious liberty, whatever the motivations of each group or individual taking part in them, contributed directly to the rise of political liberty.

> The Western world . . . as we live in it and think it, was really forged in the clash of warring sects and opinions, in the secular feuds between the clergy and laity, Catholic and Protestant, Lutheran and Calvinist. . . . It is not too much to say that political liberty would not now-a-days exist anywhere but for the claim to ecclesiastical independence.[1]

If this claim of Father Figgis is a bit too sweeping for secular minds, we have Harold Laski's opinion that "the political liberty of the seventeenth and eighteenth centuries was the outcome of the protest against religious intolerance." [2] The student of history can hardly escape the conclusion that political democracy flourished first, and flourishes most vigorously today, in those countries where religion has been most liberal, tolerant, and humane.

The free state rests squarely, both logically and historically, on freedom of religion.[3]

The rise of political liberty in colonial America is an exciting testament to this great truth.[4] The unending struggles for toleration, disestablishment, and liberty of profession were one of the most powerful human-directed forces working for individual freedom, constitutional government, and ultimately democracy. The establishment of religious freedom was no less momentous an achievement than the clearing of the great forest or the winning of independence, for the twin doctrines of separation of church and state and liberty of individual conscience are the marrow of our democracy, if not indeed America's most magnificent contribution to the freeing of Western man. In this chapter we shall re-examine the political consequences of this achievement, first, by tracing the pattern of religion in the colonies; second, by calling attention to those details in this pattern most important for the growth of political liberty; third, by evaluating the contributions of the leading churches and religious movements; and finally, by reflecting on the meaning of this experience for the future republic.

THE PATTERN OF RELIGION

The pattern of religion in colonial America was diversified and shifting, varying significantly and often sharply from one colony to another and from one decade to the next.[5] From the welter of complexity and detail these salient features loom up:

An overwhelming proportion of the colonists were Protestant in persuasion or background.[6] Catholics, except for a few short seasons in scattered locations, were feared, despised, slandered, and "warned out," not least, as one colonial penman put it, because "Popery is a great Friend to *arbitrary Government*." [7] The wars with France and Spain and the Pretender's rebellion of 1746 strengthened the colonist's loathing of the "Papist." [8] Throughout most of the colonial period—"The Penal Period," as Catholic historians label it [9]—every colony carried anti-Catholic legislation on its books. The Protestants were, as we shall see, a special brand. Dissent rather than unity and Calvinism rather than Lutheranism were the marks of American colonial Protestantism.

It should never be forgotten, even or especially in an age of economic determinism, that religion was a leading motive in some of the most important explorations and settlements.[10] Several colonies were established as havens for the oppressed of one persuasion, several others as havens for the oppressed of all, still others as primarily economic undertakings in which toleration of dissenting consciences was encouraged as "good for business." [11] Equally important, throughout the colonial period the Protestant crusade against Roman Catholicism was a prime reason for settling and defending the American colonies. Any interpretation of early American history that ignores religious motivation is essentially unsound.

The English origin of the early colonists was the deciding factor in the relations of church and state in the various colonies. The men of Virginia, the Carolinas, and Massachusetts had come from a country where the union of church and state, with the latter generally the dominant partner, was part of the accepted way of life. It should therefore occasion no surprise to learn that in nine of the thirteen colonies a state church was established and maintained in the colonial period—the Anglican Church in Virginia, Maryland (after 1702), the Carolinas, Georgia, and the southern counties of New York;[12] the Congregational Church in Massachusetts[13] (as well as Plymouth), Connecticut (as well as New Haven), and the towns of New Hampshire. No church was ever established in Rhode Island, Pennsylvania, or Delaware, nor, after the coming of the English, in New Jersey. Despite the growth of dissent and toleration, despite the fact that in several colonies the established Anglican Church claimed only a fraction of the inhabitants, nine of the thirteen colonies went into the Revolution with religious privilege fixed in their laws and charters. The dissolving of the political bands that had connected them with a superior power brought an early end to establishment in most of the new states.

Eighteenth-century America was the world's warmest nursery of sects and sectarians. The most reliable census of early American churches and congregations lists these figures for 1775:[14] Congregational, 668; Presbyterian, 588; Anglican, 495; Baptist, 494; Quaker, 310; German Reformed, 159; Lutheran, 150; Dutch Reformed, 120; Methodist, 65; Catholic, 56; Moravian, 31; Congregational-Separatist, 27; Dunker, 24; Mennonite, 16; French Protestant, 7; Sandemanian, 6; Jewish, 5; Rogerene, 3—a catalogue that could be rendered even more motley by calling attention to severe doctrinal conflicts in several of these groupings, for example, between "New Lights" and "Old Lights" in Connecticut Congregationalism and between "New Sides" and "Old Sides" in Virginia Presbyterianism. A study of Pennsylvania in 1776 gives this count of churches in the dissenters' paradise: German Reformed, 106; Presbyterian, 68; Lutheran, 63; Quaker, 61; Anglican, 33; Baptist, 27; Moravian, 14; Mennonite, 13; Dunker, 13; Catholic, 9; Dutch Reformed, 1.[15] Even in seventeenth-century Massachusetts unity of doctrine was more apparent than real. As to the eighteenth century, when the splintering effects of Protestantism and the American environment had done their worst, one town in Massachusetts (Rehoboth) is reported to have harbored six different and mutually independent Baptist churches. Diversity of creed and organization was another mark of religion in colonial America.[16]

Despite this network of highways to heaven, or turnpikes to Tophet, an astounding number of colonists belonged to no church at all. One reason was the poverty of such colonies as North Carolina and of such colonists as the early Germans and Scotch-Irish in Pennsylvania. Another was the fact that church membership in all colonies was a matter of individual choice, and that religion was therefore personalized rather than institutionalized. A third reason was the largely indifferent attitude toward religion prevalent, for quite different reasons, in both the lowest and highest strata of colonial

society. By the middle of the eighteenth century there was a larger percentage of "non-professing Christians" in the American colonies than in
any state in Western Europe.

Throughout the colonial period—amid scenes of establishment and disestablishment, struggle and brotherhood, persecution and toleration, decline
and revival, consecration and indifference—the course of American religion
moved ever away from feudalism and onward toward modern times.[17] The
line from John Cotton to Jonathan Mayhew extends from one pole of
Puritanism to the other, yet it is astonishingly direct and easily followed.
Under the pressure of the American environment Christianity grew more
humanistic and temperate—more tolerant with the struggle of the sects, more
liberal with the growth of optimism and rationalism, more experimental
with the rise of science, more individualistic with the advent of democracy.
Equally important, increasing numbers of colonists, as a legion of preachers
loudly lamented,[18] were turning secular in curiosity and skeptical in attitude.
They might still believe, but their theology had softened, their sense of
sin had disappeared, and their thoughts were of performance in this world
rather than of the promise of the other. The violence of the Great Awakening was a lefthanded tribute to the sweep of this trend. "That old-time
religion" was a far less potent element in colonial life in 1765 than it had
been in 1630, 1675, or even 1700.

THE FACTORS OF FREEDOM

Out of all these forces, movements, and trends three conditions were working most powerfully for political liberty: the spirit and institutions of
Protestantism; the multiplicity of religions; and the increasing proportion of
the unchurched, worldly, and indifferent. These three factors in turn helped
create a fourth, the struggle for religious liberty, and this factor had as
much direct influence as did all the others combined on the rise of political
liberty in colonial America.

PROTESTANTISM. Burke caught the spirit of American religion in words
that could not conceivably be improved upon:

> The people are Protestants; and of that kind which is the most adverse
> to all implicit submission of mind and opinion. This is a persuasion not only
> favourable to liberty, but built upon it. I do not think, Sir, that the reason
> of this averseness in the dissenting churches, from all that looks like abso-
> lute government, is so much to be sought in their religious tenets, as in their
> history. Every one knows that the Roman Catholic religion is at least coeval
> with most of the governments where it prevails; that it has generally gone
> hand in hand with them, and received great favour and every kind of sup-
> port from authority. The Church of England too was formed from her
> cradle under the nursing care of regular government. But the dissenting
> interests have sprung up in direct opposition to all the ordinary powers of
> the world; and could justify that opposition only on a strong claim to nat-
> ural liberty. Their very existence depended on the powerful and unremitted
> assertion of that claim. All Protestantism, even the most cold and passive,

is a sort of dissent. But the religion most prevalent in our northern colonies is a refinement on the principle of resistance; it is the dissidence of dissent, and the Protestantism of the Protestant religion.[19]

Dissent and resistance were the effective impulses of American Protestantism in the seventeenth and eighteenth centuries, and dissent and resistance have always been first causes of religious freedom. Yet the Protestant strain spurned the growth of liberty in ways other than the ceaseless struggle for religious freedom. Church government in the colonies, which even in Anglican Virginia emphasized the self-directing competence of the congregation at the expense of hierarchy, helped democratize political organization. The belief in an infallible Bible advertised the glories of higher law; Locke rode into New England on the backs of Moses and the prophets. At the same time, the Old Testament was a channel through which some of the liberating doctrines of the Hebraic tradition were fed into the American stream.[20] And the concept of the chosen people, which was as strong in seventeenth-century Boston as it had been in ancient Israel, was to prove easily convertible—by such men as Mayhew, Edwards, John Adams, Washington, and Jefferson—into the noble democratic doctrine of the American Mission.

American democracy owes its greatest debt to colonial Protestantism for the momentum it gave to the growth of individualism. The Reformation, which was powered by the revolutionary notion that man could commune with God without the intercession of a priest, did as much as the rise of capitalism to spread the doctrine of individualism. As the Protestants of Protestantism, the dissidents of dissent, the American churches stressed the salvation of the individual rather than the maintenance of communal unity or doctrinal purity. Calvinist in inspiration and Puritan in essence, the great dissenting churches helped breed a new person, and this man, multiplied millions of times over, was to give American democracy its peculiar flavor. In its best aspects and moments Protestantism was a main source of these great political principles of American democracy: freedom of thought and expression, separation of church and state, local self-government, higher law, constitutionalism, the American Mission, and the free individual.[21]

Even in its worst aspects and moments Protestantism in America seemed intent on making certain a democratic future. The seasons of persecution and intolerance, in which the New England churches engaged most deplorably, only hastened the seasons of brotherhood and indifference. At least one reason for the strength of the American doctrine of religious liberty is the fact that men not only had to flee persecution in Europe but had to fight it in America. The Puritans did their part for religious liberty when they hanged Mary Dyer. It may be a case of having one's cake and eating it, too, to argue that oppression did as much as toleration to lead the colonies to more humane and liberal religion. Yet it is hard to suppress the feeling that the stern Puritans—and the superior Anglicans, too—were leading actors in the great drama of religious liberty.

MULTIPLICITY OF RELIGIONS. The pattern of religious diversity in colonial America has already been described in actual figures. This amazing variety, the delight or despair of dozens of articulate European visitors, aided the growth of liberty in several ways. First, it is a commonplace that diversity—sectional, economic, racial, religious—has been the sign, strength, and test of American democracy. The earliest of these diversities was in religious belief and practice. The great religious problem of colonial America was to create an environment in which men of differing faiths could live together in peace. The fact that such an environment was created seems all the more remarkable when we remember that dissent and treason were still synonymous in much of the Christian world. The pluralistic nature of American society may be traced in part to the multiple pattern of colonial faith.

Second, the early American tendency to splinter into sects over fine points of doctrine and worship carried the spirit of Protestantism to its logical conclusion.[22] If the right of private judgment was achieved at the expense of a sense of community, if the hopes of one great Christian edifice were smashed into the rubble of a hundred raucous creeds, the Protestant ethic had none the less been fulfilled. Nowhere in the eighteenth-century world, with one or two possible exceptions, did the Protestant urge to protest have freer play. Nowhere was the impact of Protestantism more destructive of medieval notions of man, society, church, and God.

The rapid multiplication of the sects made toleration, and in time religious liberty, a social necessity. The doctrine of political equality of faiths was not the result of sweet reasoning about the brotherhood of man, but of the plain necessity that each sect in order to live had also to let live. A child of necessity, too, was the doctrine of separation of church and state. Even the religions that insisted most vociferously on their exclusive claims to truth contributed to this liberalizing process. The Catholic in seventeenth-century Maryland and the Anglican in eighteenth-century Massachusetts plumped as hard as any Baptist for religious freedom, not out of conviction but in the interests of self-preservation.

Finally, the increasing variety of religious elements, especially in the middle colonies and certain areas in the South, accustomed colonials to live on mutually respectful if not loving terms with men whose creeds were different from their own. The fact of religious diversity taught individuals as well as governments the practical advantages of toleration and religious liberty. A man who does business, especially profitable business, with all sorts of heretics may come in time to suspect that they are not heretics at all.

THE UNCHURCHED, THE WORLDLY, THE INDIFFERENT. A factor of immense importance for the rise of liberty in America was the half-forgotten truth that large numbers of colonists took no part at all in the religious life of their communities. Some of these people were "unchurched" in the physical sense: They could not have gone to church or asked counsel of a minister even had they wanted to. An eyewitness account of religious life in the Carolinas in the early eighteenth century had this to say:

This is *South-Carolina*, extending in Length on the Sea-Coast, 300 Miles; and into the main Land near 200 Miles. It was granted by Patent from the Crown, in the Year 1663, and settled soon after, containing in the Year 1701, above 7000 Persons, besides *Negroes* and Indians, and was divided into several Parishes and Towns. Yet tho' peopled at its first Settlement with the Natives of these Kingdoms, there was, until the Year 1701, no Minister of the Church of *England* Resident in this Colony; tho' great Numbers of the Inhabitants were very desirous of having Ministers of the Church of *England;* and with very few Teachers of any other Kind; neither had they any Schools for the Education of their Children.

The next Colony, *North-Carolina*, extending on the Sea-Coast above 100 Miles, and into the Land about 100, was divided into several Townships, and peopled from *England*. It contained above 5000 Inhabitants, besides *Negroes* and *Indians*, in the Year 1701, all living without any Form of Divine Worship publickly performed, and without Schools for the Education of their Children in the Elements of Learning and Principles of Religion.[23]

And in 1729 Colonel Byrd wrote of the capital of North Carolina:

> I believe this is the only Metropolis in the Christian or Mahometan World, where there is neither Church, Chappel, Mosque, Synagogue, or any other place of Publick Worship of any Sect or Religion whatsoever.[24]

Throughout the colonial period people in many areas were simply too poor to support even the lowest grade of minister, especially if their doctrinal differences made it impossible to unite in one church. Many of the colonists had come from the lower economic classes in England and Germany. In the old countries their attachment to the church had been nominal; in the new they lost contact completely. The struggle for existence had much to do with the unchurching of the poor.

A second group that carried on quite oblivious of organized religion was composed of people more toward the middle or even the upper end of the social and economic scale. The attitudes of secularism, of concern with one world at a time and even disbelief in any other, appealed to thousands of colonists whose fathers had been stout believers in the finer shadings of doctrine. Governor Dongan of New York, himself a liberal Catholic, testified to the presence of such people in his province in 1687:

> New York has first a Chaplain belonging to the Fort of the Church of England; secondly a Dutch Calvinist, thirdly a French Calvinist; fourthly a Dutch Lutheran—Here bee not many of the Church of England; few Roman Catholicks; abundance of Quakers preachers men and women especially; Singing Quakers; Ranting Quakers; Sabbatarians; Antisabbatarians; some Anabaptists some Independants; some Jews; in short of all sorts of opinion there are some, and the most part, of none at all.[25]

Even then New York was a haven for those whose religion was "none at all," but in other colonies, too, the early fervor was on the wane. The rantings of the later Mathers and the explosiveness of the Great Awakening show how far the worldly attitude had penetrated even orthodox Massachusetts. Religion cooled off in eighteenth-century America, and a dozen awakenings would not have got the old fires going again.

A third group was made up of those who were outside any church not by compulsion or carelessness but by choice. Men of this description— Franklin, John Adams, and Jefferson were typical—were not so much indifferent to religion as they were to religions. Some were rationalists, some deists; some were completely unchurched, others nominal adherents but actual nonparticipants. Most of them proclaimed their allegiance to the person and teachings of Jesus, but for them he was not much more than a magnificent moralist. Most of them, being practical men, supported the churches as indispensable aids to ordered liberty. The deists and rationalists, and there were ministers among them, were two more sects for sectarian America. The Masons, too, must be included in this reckoning.

All these men—the frontier farmer in his harsh poverty, the tavernkeeper in his worldly apathy, the merchant in his rationalized indifference [26]—were foes of establishment, tithes, intolerance, and doctrinal dispute. To them as much as to any group we owe our state without a church. An entire nation of them would have been a calamity for stability and freedom, but as a third or fourth of a nation they were unwitting workers for liberty. Again we are having our cake and relishing it, too, but history teaches that irreligion, taken in moderate doses, has helped more than one body politic to win through to true religious and social liberty.

THE GROWTH OF RELIGIOUS LIBERTY

Had religious freedom existed from the outset in all colonies, it could hardly have been so vigorous an ingredient in the rise of American liberty. But the fact that nine of thirteen colonies sooner or later set up a state church, and that only in Rhode Island was pure religious liberty established at the beginning and maintained (with one questionable exception) through the years, makes clear that whatever freedom existed in 1765 was the harvest of a long season of growth. The winning of religious liberty can be understood partly in terms of tension and conflict, partly in terms of silent, almost unnoticed development. A mass of social and economic pressures was working for freedom of religion, a mass of memory and vested interests against it. One result was struggle,[27] and the result of struggle was liberty, not only in the religious, but also in the social, economic, and political phases of colonial life.

From the beginning it was plain to men in each colony that the fight against religious autocracy was likewise a fight against political autocracy. In Puritan Massachusetts, where until 1691 a man could not vote unless he had been admitted to the one church in town, any blow struck for religious liberty was struck just as hard for political liberty. In Anglican Virginia, where the royal governor headed the established church, the campaign for toleration was always regarded as a form of political subversion. Said Governor Gooch of certain Presbyterians who were trying his patience, "It is not liberty of conscience, but freedom of speech, they so earnestly prosecute." [28] Freedom of speech, representation, constitutionalism, official responsibility, the suffrage, and the prized colonial right to be left alone and not taxed for other men's interests (especially for the support of their clergy)—all these principles of political liberty were constantly invigorated by the arguments and techniques of the dissenting churches. At the same time, the men who would not be stilled, above all Quaker and Baptist, got more support than they realized from the ever-increasing multitude that dissented in silence.

It would hardly be profitable to trace the ups and downs of religious freedom in each of the colonies.[29] In those where nonconformity came hardest, and thus where the struggle had the most influence on politics, the area of religious freedom was increased by painful steps. Toleration rather than separation was the immediate goal of the Quaker in Massachusetts, Anglican in Connecticut, Presbyterian in Virginia, and Catholic everywhere. The actual achievements of colonial America were toleration in all colonies, disestablishment in four of them, and the philosophy of complete religious liberty that triumphed at last during and after the Revolution. Hardly less important was the spread of a general spirit of live-and-let-live, which meant, for example, that dozens of severe laws punishing all manner of alleged heresies were rarely enforced in the eighteenth century. If Pennsylvanians are reminded that the Charter of Privileges of 1701 limited residence to those who believed in God, and political activity to those who believed in "*Jesus Christ*, the Saviour of the World," they may answer that there is no instance on record of the application of these restrictions, not even in the case of Benjamin Franklin.

The circumstances that made possible the victory over religious oppression and privilege are an especially satisfying example of the interplay of ethics and environment. We have already noted three of these circumstances: Protestantism, multiplicity of religions, and the great unchurched. These were the fundamental reasons for the absence in almost every colony of a recognizable religious majority, and thus for the growth of a general awareness that any other course but toleration, and in time separation, would be inexpedient if not impossible to follow. Most colonials had a minority attitude on relations of church and state, and the core of this attitude could have been no other than the "permission of dissenting consciences."

A fourth influence for religious liberty in the colonies was English practice and persuasion. Although the main pressure from England was for Anglican uniformity, and although the mother country lagged behind many of her colonies in the progress of religious freedom, Englishmen helped the cause of dissent in several important ways. Proprietors and stockholders in many of the first settlements realized that some measure of toleration was necessary to induce colonists to hazard their fortunes in the new world. Even so orthodox a monarch as Charles II approved charters with liberty-of-conscience clauses, in the interest of imperial prosperity. The Board of

Trade warned Virginia in 1752 not to persecute dissenters, for "Toleration and a free Exercise of Religion" were "essential to the enriching and improving of a Trading Nation." [30] And in 1704 the King-in-Council disallowed two Maryland anti-Catholic laws as tending "to depopulate that profitable colony." [31]

Perhaps the most convincing testimony to English insistence on the policy of toleration as commercially advisable was the statement of Charles Calvert of Maryland in 1675:

> At the first planting of this Province by my father . . . He found very few who were inclyned to goe and seat themselves in those parts But such as for some Reason or other could not lyve with ease in other places And of these a great part were such as could not conforme in all particulars to the several Lawes of England relateing to Religion Many there were of this sort of People who declared their Wyllingness to goe and Plant themselves in this Province so as they might have a Generall Toleraccōn settled there by a Lawe by which all sorts who professed Christianity in Generall might be at Liberty to Worship God in such Manner as was most agreeable with their respective Judgmts and Consciences without being subject to any penaltyes whatsoever for their so doeing provyded the civill peace were preserved And that for the secureing the Civill peace and preventing all heats [and] Feuds which were generally observed to happen amongst such as differ in oppynions upon Occasion of Reproachfull Nicknames and Reflecting upon each Other's Oppynions It might by the same Lawe be made Penall to give any Offence in that kynde these were the condicōns proposed by such as were willing to goe and be the first planters of this Provynce and without the complying with these condicōns in all probability This Province had never been planted. [32]

"Without the complying with these condicōns" in all probability half of America "had never been planted." Other English influences for religious liberty were important—for example, the large measure of freedom granted out of principle rather than expediency by proprietors like William Penn and the Earl of Shaftesbury, the political pressure exerted by Quakers in England for royal intervention in behalf of persecuted colleagues in Massachusetts, [33] and the extension of the Act of Toleration of 1689 to several colonies that needed it badly. [34] The commercial motive, however, was the most influential. [35] Here was a clear case of economic determinism.

Many colonial leaders shared this experience-proved opinion that oppression and persecution were bad for business. Indeed, most of them were convinced that a policy of government noninterference in religious affairs was an essential not only of commercial prosperity but of survival itself. The arguments from expediency of the leaders of commerce were some of the heaviest guns in the campaign for religious liberty.

The example of such experiments as Rhode Island and the Quaker colonies was still another force for freedom. Biographers of Williams and Penn have claimed too much for Rhode Island and Pennsylvania, forgetting that the struggle for religious liberty had to go forward in what were essentially thirteen separate and often isolated salients. Yet the prosperity of the free colonies, advertised through the growing network of intercolonial contacts, did teach many openminded leaders in Massachusetts, Virginia, Maryland, and New York that religious freedom was a support rather than a subversion of political stability.

A seventh reason was the gospel of freedom preached and practiced by those individuals, such as Roger Williams and John Clarke, and those sects, notably Baptists and Quakers, who believed in religious liberty as a matter of principle. Most Protestant groups argued for toleration or liberty out of sheer expediency, because they were a hunted minority in an intolerant colony or were sensible enough to see the impossibility of achieving meaningful unity in a situation of hopeless diversity. A few brave men, however, made their contribution to the liberty of later generations directly rather than accidentally. American religious liberty has its share of prophets, philosophers, saints, and martyrs.

A final ingredient of religious liberty was the struggle for self-government. This chapter has stressed the historical and logical influence of religion on politics, but the reverse of this process might also have been argued. The reform elements in colonial America—levelers, popularists, radical Whigs, republicans, and just plain troublemakers—were all opponents of the powerful state. In their attacks on arbitrary power, even when their only purpose was to grasp a little power for themselves, they undercut the dominance of the state over the churches. Wherever political and religious oligarchy went hand in hand, an assault on the former, even for the most secular purposes, was sure to be an assault on the latter. Particularly in Massachusetts did the attempt to wrest power from the magistrates weaken the position of the ministers, while in all royal colonies from Maryland to South Carolina the political victories of the assemblies resulted sooner or later in weaker establishments. The fight of the frontier for equitable taxation, and for representation as well, did much to bring about separation of state and church in Virginia.

We need not exaggerate the progress of religious liberty in colonial America to establish its importance for the growth of free government.[36] It can be no hardship for modern patriots to acknowledge that the colonies went into the Revolution with a hodgepodge of religious legislation still on the books, for the swiftness with which the relics of privilege and discrimination were abandoned in state after state between 1776 and 1790 is evidence that the spirit of the people had far outrun the statutes. Pennsylvania demanded belief in God yet put no man to the test; Massachusetts taxed for support of the church yet permitted Anglicans to direct their payments to their own churches and all-out Quakers and Baptists to escape this tax completely; Rhode Island passed a law (probably in 1719) limiting political participation to Protestant Christians yet passed other laws admitting specific Jews and Catholics to citizenship;[37] New York had an establishment in the four southern counties, yet the establishment was nameless; and Virginia swung from the most complete establishment in 1765 to freedom of religion in 1776 and full separation in 1785. Of all the revolutions of '76, the colonists seemed most ready for that in church-state relations.

By the beginning of the new century religious liberty, even for the long-suffering "Papist," had been achieved in the American states. Although Connecticut, Massachusetts, and New Hampshire still retained the system of church rates, these were all abandoned by 1833; and although several state constitutions carried nonsensical clauses about the duty of the citizen to believe this or that, these admonitions went unenforced. Separation of church and state and entire liberty of conscience have been part of the American way for a century and a half. And lest there be any mistake about the terms of this heritage from colonial America, we might quote a leading authority's list of the essentials of religious liberty willed to the new nation by the old empire:

1. The civil power has no authority in, or over, the individual or the Church, touching matters of faith, worship, order, discipline, or polity.

2. The Church has no power in the state to direct its policy or action, otherwise than its influence may be felt in the persuasion of the public mind towards the principles it teaches.

3. The state cannot appropriate public moneys to the Church, or for the propagation of religion, or any particular form of religion.

4. The Church cannot look to the state for any support of its worship or institutions, otherwise than, like all other corporations, it may appeal, and must submit, to legislation and judicial decisions in matters of pecuniary trusts and foundations, the ground of which legislation and decisions is not at all religious, but strictly civil.

5. The civil power cannot exercise any preference among the various churches or sects, but must hold all as having equal rights under the law, and as equally entitled to whatever protection under the law circumstances may furnish need for.

6. The civil power may not make any distinction among citizens on account of religion, unless the following thereof is dangerous to society. Neither the right to vote nor to hold office is to be invalidated because of opinions on the matter of religion. Nor, again, is a citizen's right to bear witness, or to inherit property to be called in question for reasons of religion.[38]

CONTRIBUTIONS OF PARTICULAR CHURCHES TO RELIGIOUS AND POLITICAL LIBERTY

Of all the churches and sects that gained a hold in the American colonies, five or six proved popular and steadfast enough to work visible effects upon the spirit and institutions of the rising democracy. The contributions of each of the most prominent churches should be briefly noted.

QUAKERS AND LIBERTY. The Society of Friends was a force to be reckoned with in the social and political life of almost every colony. From the founding of their sect the Quakers of old England looked to the west for a refuge from persecution. Although the hopes of many leaders for a general triumph of Quaker principles in the colonies came to nothing,[39] the ideas and methods of this most persecuted of Christian faiths helped prepare the ground for liberty.

The doctrines of the Quakers were democratic to the core, emphasizing brotherly love, mutual aid and comfort, pacifism, justice for all on equal terms, rejection of priestly authority, and complete religious individualism. The good Quaker, who centered his worldly thoughts upon the problem of individual conduct, would have denied that he possessed any particular theories of state and government. Yet since democracy is simply the presence of a certain number of democrats, and since the good democrat believes in principles that the Quakers put first in their catalogue of virtues, it is plain that the teachings of this sect gave substance to the growing theory of political liberty.

In practice, colonial Quakers aided the cause of liberty in several ways: their meetings were a prime example of democracy in being; they gave the rising nation its only real martyrs to religious persecution in colonial America and fought out of principle for liberty of conscience and abolition of establishments; they provided in Pennsylvania, thanks to the rare nobility of William Penn, a "free colony for all mankind," [40] one of the few areas in the colonies unstained by actual persecution; they took the lead, thanks to the even rarer nobility of John Woolman,[41] in the movement against slavery; and they had easily the best colonial record in dealings with the Indians.[42] The colonies in which they shared or held the reins of political power—Rhode Island, Pennsylvania, early New Jersey,[43] early North Carolina—were some of the most democratic in the colonial period.[44]

As time went by, many Quakers, particularly in prosperous, nonpersecuting Newport and Philadelphia, lost much of the old fire, surrounded as they were by slaves, wealth, and worldly power. Yet the principles remained the same, principles of liberty, justice, peace, and love; and in Virginia, the Carolinas,[45] Massachusetts, and Maryland radical Quakerism held out strongly against oaths, tithes, military service, slavery, and social inequality. The widening social rift among "the People called Quakers" merely called attention to the democracy ingrained in their doctrine and practice.[46]

BAPTISTS AND LIBERTY. Baptists were in the colonies almost from the beginning.[47] Until well into the eighteenth century, however, they were few, scattered, and friendless, and were persecuted severely in Massachusetts. As late as 1740, long after toleration had been finally secured, only about twenty Baptist congregations could be found in New England, half of these in Rhode Island.

In the meantime, Baptists were flourishing in the middle colonies. Friendly Philadelphia became the center of American Baptism, and from here and the British Isles the church spread its gospel and influence into Virginia and the Carolinas.[48] The Great Awakening had more influence on the Baptists than on any other church, and the growth of this persuasion in the years just before the Revolution was nothing short of astounding. It was a long journey from Rhode Island in 1639 to Virginia in 1776, from the twelve friends of Roger Williams to the enthusiastic horde that outnumbered the Anglicans, and one of deep significance for religious and political liberty.

The Baptists were Calvinist in theology and independent in church polity, differing in doctrine from New England Puritanism only in their opposition to infant baptism and to union of church and state. Their doctrine was basically illiberal and their zeal often rudely excessive. This was especially true of the Separate Baptists, who poured into Virginia and the Carolinas in the third quarter of the eighteenth century. Yet their form of church government, which emphasized the compact, equality, and congregational autonomy, nourished the growth of republican notions, as more than one royal governor acknowledged with his policy of persecution. The organization of the Baptists was more important than their theology, and their organization was as democratic as any in colonial America. Said an early historian of the Baptists, "Our religious education agrees with, and perfectly corresponds with, a government by the people." [49]

American democracy will always be indebted to the colonial Baptists for their singleminded devotion to complete religious liberty. Their methods were not always sensible nor their zeal free from prejudice, but their peculiar hatred for the established church, especially in Virginia, earned them glory that more than made up for their temporary sufferings.[50] The Baptists of New England,[51] the middle colonies, and the South were the largest single group committed to an uncompromising campaign for complete separation of church and state. Where most other churches sought freedom within the law, the Baptists would not be satisfied until all laws on religion had been swept away completely.

PRESBYTERIANS AND LIBERTY. The history of the Presbyterian Church in colonial America is largely a history of that extraordinary multitude of eighteenth-century immigrants, the Scotch-Irish.[52] Although Presbyterian churches or tendencies existed in the northern colonies throughout the seventeenth century, not until 1706 was the first American presbytery established, at Philadelphia under the leadership of Francis Makemie. Of the seven ministers who formed it—acting, it should be noted, on their own responsibility—six were Scotch-Irish and one a New Englander.[53] Except for the lack of a delegate from the Dutch or German Reformed churches, which were always closely associated with Presbyterianism in doctrine and action, this proportion was representative of the relative strength of the elements making up the Presbyterian churches. The great wave of migration from Ulster to America, which began around 1710 and lasted through the Revolution, spread Scotch-Irish Presbyterianism through all the colonies, especially into the back country from Pennsylvania to the Carolinas. Puritans outside New England entered in strength into this great advancing front of Calvinism and individualism. The first synod was formed at Philadelphia in 1716.

The contributions of the Presbyterians to the rise of colonial liberty were not quite so forceful as those of the Baptists. In both theology and organization they were a good deal more autocratic than several other prominent churches. Yet these points are certainly worth considering: their traditional emphasis on covenant and compact; their efforts to maintain a learned ministry, which led to the establishment of several colleges; the receptivity of the clergy, which was widely devoted to the Scotch philosophy of common sense, to the ideas of the Enlightenment; their activities for toleration, however much in their own interest, especially in Virginia under the devoted leadership of Samuel Davies; and the severe social disruption, the struggle between New Sides and Old Sides, that resulted from the Great Awakening. Most important of all was the unusual fact that the Scotch-Irish were generally more democratic in politics and social attitudes than in religion. In colonial Presbyterianism the stream of democracy flowed in a reverse course. Many a staunch radical in politics was a staunch conservative in religion; many a Scotch-Irish frontiersman moved from an original faith in political man to a more liberal point of view on the possibilities of universal salvation.

PIETISM AND LIBERTY. The German Pietist sects—Mennonites, Moravians, Schwenkfelders, Dunkers, and other groups—formed a small but vital religious element in Pennsylvania and scattered localities to the south. The common feature of these groups was their literal devotion, with the usual sectarian shadings, to the tenets of primitive Christianity: dominance of the inner spirit, individual judgment, freedom of conscience, informal worship, sovereignty of the congregation (indeed of each individual who made it up), and often some form of pacifism.[54] All these essentially democratic principles have obvious counterparts in libertarian political theory. Although the Pietists stood aloof from the push-and-pull of colonial politics, the sincerity and simplicity of their methods were yet another support to the upbuilding of American liberty. Benjamin Franklin came in contact with most of these sects, and his tribute to one of them, the Dunkers at Ephrata, was as warm as it was charming:

> I was acquainted with one of the founders, Michael Welfare. . . . He complained to me that they were grievously calumniated by the zealots of other persuasions, and charged with abominable principles and practices to which they were utter strangers. I told him this had always been the case with new sects and that to put a stop to such abuse, I imagined it might be well to publish the articles of their belief and the rules of their discipline. He said that it had been proposed among them, but not agreed to for this reason: "When we were first drawn together as a society," says he, "it had pleased God to enlighten our minds so far as to see that some doctrines which we once esteemed truths were errors, and that others which we had esteemed errors were real truths. From time to time he has been pleased to afford us further light, and our principles have been improving and our errors diminishing. Now we are not sure that we are arrived at the end of this progression, and at the perfection of spiritual or theological knowledge; and we fear that if we should once print our confession of faith, we should feel ourselves as if bound and confined by it, and perhaps be unwilling to receive further improvement, and our successors still more so, as conceiving what their elders and founders had done to be something sacred, never

to be departed from." This modesty in a sect is perhaps a singular instance in the history of mankind.[55]

A little of this spirit goes a long way in a system that encourages the multiplication of groups and opinions.

ANGLICANISM AND LIBERTY. It is impossible to make a case for orthodox Anglicanism as a force for colonial liberty,[56] except for the lefthanded manner in which its intolerance of dissent forced dissenters to redouble their efforts for toleration. An intriguing example of Anglican action that ended up producing a libertarian reaction was the eighteenth-century move-ment—a weak movement at that—for an American bishop.[57] The cause of political independence prospered noticeably from the outcry of opposition to this "Popish plot," and at least some of the outcry burst from Anglican throats.[58]

Nevertheless, the development of the Anglican Church in the Southern colonies provides a convincing case-study of the liberalizing, or perhaps simply enfeebling, effects of the American environment on religious ortho-doxy. For a variety of reasons—for example, the fact that no Bishop of London (in whose see the colonies were included) ever visited America—colonial Anglicanism was a sorry example of a supposedly hierarchical church. In Virginia the ministry grew ever more worldly and uninstructed,[59] the parish ever more self-directing, the average adherent ever more skeptical, the discharge of devotions ever more formal, and the priestly support ac-corded political orthodoxy ever more strident and yet feckless.[60] Even the devoted efforts of men like Commissaries James Blair of Virginia and Thomas Bray of Maryland, and of missionaries of the Society for the Propagation of the Gospel in Foreign Parts, could do little to stem the tide of laxity that seeped through American Anglicanism. Although authorities in England were inclined to agree that the ministers they sent out were "most miserably handled by their Plebeian Juntos, the Vestries," [61] there was not much they were willing or able to do toward restoring the purity of the colonial establishment. The thoughts of able ministers in England were summarized by an Anglican missionary who complained to his superiors that he "would rather be vicar to the Bear Garden than Bishop of North Carolina." [62]

The pattern of evolution of colonial Anglicanism was that of an aristo-cratic, hierarchical religion growing ever more congregational in organiza-tion and rationalist in doctrine. Although for the most part the churches remained supporters of the conservative party, and although many ministers would have no truck with the patriot cause, Anglicanism passed through the Revolution into its Episcopalian phase without too much disruption or loss of continuity. This pillar of English orthodoxy was decisively Americanized in the colonial period. When Commissary Martyn of Charleston wrote his bishop in 1765, "The Principles of most of the Colonists in America are independent in Matters of Religion, as well as republican in those of Govern-ment," [63] he could just as easily have added that this was true of some of his own ministers and most of their parishioners. Fully half the signers of the Declaration of Independence were at least nominal Anglicans.

JEWS, CATHOLICS, AND LIBERTY. The influence of these two great and ancient religions, which were later to have such an impact on American life, was hardly noticeable in the colonial period. The small numbers of Jews and slightly larger numbers of Catholics who trickled into the colonies through all this time existed so precariously and anonymously as to leave precious few lasting traces.[64] Jews may take pride in the influence of the Hebraic tradition on the development of American democracy, but must acknowledge that this tradition was fed into the colonies by other hands than those of Israel. Catholics may take pride in the part played by their forefathers in the celebrated Maryland Act of Toleration (1649), but must acknowledge that this law is the most clear-cut instance in colonial history of toleration secured by religionists—Puritans and Catholics—who believed in toleration not at all. Indeed, "suffered" rather than "secured" would be the proper word in this instance, for the Act of 1649 was jammed through the Maryland Assembly on the insistence of the second Lord Baltimore, whose own motives were an undecipherable combination of principle and expediency. The honor would seem to belong to him rather than to his church. In any case, in Maryland alone in seventeenth-century America did Catholics and Protestants live side by side with any show of forbearance.[65]

As to the eighteenth century, perhaps the less said the better. Still, it is good and humbling for modern Americans, Catholics as well as Protestants, to recall the difficulties of Catholicism in the generations before the Revolution. Of physical suffering there was little if any, for the policy of almost every colony was much simpler than that: exclusion. In this policy the English authorities concurred thoroughly. After 1679 a standard instruction to the governor of each royal colony ran:

> You are to permit a liberty of conscience to all persons EXCEPT PAPISTS, so they be contented with a quiet and peaceable enjoyment of the same, not giving offense or scandal to the government.[66]

The Catholic occupied much the same position in colonial America that the Communist does today. Though few colonists had ever seen or could have recognized a real live Catholic, they knew everything about "the Papists" and shared a morbid interest in their doctrine and practice. They were also quick to brand people Papists who were not Papists at all. The press found Catholicism excellent copy, especially if the "facts" were bloody or erotic, and especially in times of war with Catholic countries.[67] Certainly the Catholic was feared and despised with the same unthinking passion as is the Communist today, and he was therefore the acid test of the good intentions of the new Republic. The speed with which disqualifications were erased from state laws and constitutions was, considering the heritage of hate and fear, a stunning triumph of reason and democracy. On the eve of the Revolution mass was celebrated publicly only in easy-going Pennsylvania. On the morrow it was celebrated in every state.

Puritans were confirmed believers in higher law, going most men
etter in being able to point to its existence in writing! The ancient
ian idea of a universal moral order appealed strongly to Calvin, and
nore strongly to those of his disciples called Puritans. It was their con-
n—and here they broke most sharply with the mother church in Eng-
that the Scriptures offered correct answers to all problems of individual
ict, church government, and social and political organization. Al-
h the Puritan determination to adhere rigidly to Hebraic mandates
ened and gave way under the stresses of human nature and the Ameri-
nvironment, the belief in higher law—law that could be appealed to
st the arbitrariness of rulers—carried over irresistibly into the develop-
American creed. The law of nature, like the social contract, got an
ially warm reception among descendants of Puritans. And the tra-
al American insistence on a written constitution owes something
e insistence of the Puritan that higher law could be written law.

third contribution of Puritanism to liberty was the substance it gave
e doctrine of individualism. It is strange to think of Puritanism, with
oncepts of human depravity, predestination, and political authoritarian-
as a wellspring of eighteenth-century and modern individualism. Yet
r this cruel exterior lurked notions of a liberating character, and these
to emerge in good season as a rich inheritance for American democracy.
the most rigidly orthodox Puritans betrayed suspicions that man was
:how responsible, competent, and potentially decent; that his own
pretation of Scripture, not a priest's thirdhand account of revealed
na, was to control his actions; that salvation was the result of an inner
rience, not of conformity to certain modes of worship; and that the
to eternity was open to all men without regard to political, economic,
ocial standing. Most important, as Roscoe Pound has written, "Puritan-
put individual judgment and individual conscience in the first place
re the traditional modes of thought had put authority and the reason
judgment of the prince." [73] In challenging the claims of hierarchy the
itans had to stress the competence of the individual, and in so doing
r opened the door to religious and political equality. The uncompromis-
insistence of eighteenth-century liberal preachers on the "right of
ate judgment" was the democratic fruit of these seeds of orthodox
itanism.[74]

conomic individualism—a conspicuous feature of the American model
oolitical democracy—also owes a healthy debt to Puritanism. The Puritans
e not, as we shall learn in Chapter 3, laissez-faire capitalists. Govern-
it regulation of the economy was an accepted part of their scheme of
igs. But by insisting that a sober and godly life was both a sign of salva-
n and a path to prosperity, by sanctifying the virtues of industry,
gality, and self-reliance, they helped create a collective state of mind
I morality that would make possible the rise of American capitalism.
ierican democracy has been, in the best and truest sense of the terms,
Idle-class, bourgeois, free-enterprise democracy, and Puritanism did as

PURITANISM, REVIVALISM, ANI

We turn now to the two most interesting contributi
to American liberty: one the legacy of an entire w
the other the result of the first great popular movem
the Great Awakening.

PURITANISM AND DEMOCRACY.[68] The starting-point
Puritanism and American democracy must be the unv
the two great men of Massachusetts Bay. Said John Wi
"A Democratie is, among most civill nations, accounte
of all formes of Governm^t . . . & Historyes doe reco
allwayes of least continuance & fullest of troubles." [69]
minister: "Democracy, I do not conceyve that ever
a fitt government eyther for church or commonwealth.
ernors, who shall be governed?" [70] Building their case
ward expressions of Puritan political theory and on t
oligarchy in Massachusetts, some historians have insiste
proud New England, that American democracy has o
Puritanism, rather that certain nasty elements of author
can culture may be traced directly to the Puritan stra

These arguments are hard to meet, especially since t
weight of partial validity. They lean too heavily, howe
logical interpretation of history and fail to make a valid
Puritans and Puritanism, between the magnificent autoc
Salem and their inherently revolutionary way of life and
of good or evil we owe Winthrop and Cotton, we owe
of the toughest elements of our constitutional democr
liberty and self-government in colonial America was no
Puritan principles.[71]

First, the Puritan concept of the covenant helped swe
the dominant notion of eighteenth-century popularism, tl
The first Puritans were, as Perry Miller and others hav
obsessed with the covenant or contract, relying on this
to explain almost every relation of man to man and man
seven or eight covenants recognized in orthodox Purita
covenant was the particular forerunner of the eighteenth-
The Puritan theory of the origin of the church in the conser
led directly to the popular theory of the origin of governi
sent of the governed. The doctrines of popular governme
a Massachusetts village were largely a secularized and expa
tionalism. It was hardly accidental that New England mi
first and most cordial reception to the arguments of John I
great English liberals, and broadcast from their pulpits the
government by consent.

much as any other "way of life" to give our democracy this special flavor. Puritanism was not free enterprise, but some of the best Puritans were conscious free-enterprisers.

Next, a key source of the American belief in the dependence of liberty on an educated citizenry was the Puritan emphasis on general education. Some early American radicals, most prominently Roger Williams, simply ignored the problem of education; others were actually hostile to the founding of schools and colleges. It was the much-maligned Puritan of Massachusetts and Connecticut—the man who insisted on a learned ministry, enlightened saints, and common men at least able to read the Bible and write their wills—who first showed faith in the efficacy of education. The instruments of education erected by the early New England Puritans in the face of overwhelming odds were not designed to further liberty as we understand it. Yet these instruments and the philosophy that sustained them were to prove readily convertible to the broader, more humane uses of later generations. Though few if any realized it at the time, the founding of Harvard College opened at least one door to American liberty, as John Wise and Jonathan Mayhew were to prove to the dismay of latter-day orthodox Puritans.

Finally, it must never be forgotten, especially in an age of upheaval and disillusionment, that American democracy rests squarely on the assumption of a pious, honest, self-disciplined, moral people. For all its faults and falterings, for all the distance it has yet to travel, American democracy has been and remains a highly *moral* adventure. Whatever doubts may exist about the sources of this democracy, there can be none about the chief source of the morality that gives it life and substance. From Puritanism, from the way of life that exalted individual responsibility, came those homely rules of everyday conduct—or, if we must, those rationalizations of worldly success—that have molded the American mind into its unique shape. Puritanism was the goad to the American conscience that insisted on communal responsibility before individual freedom, constitutionalism before democracy, order before liberty. If democracy has flourished in these states as strongly as anywhere in the world, it is because we are drawing still upon the moral vigor of Puritanism.

This was the legacy of Puritanism, especially of Congregational Puritanism, to American democracy: the contract and all its corollaries; the higher law as something more than a "brooding omnipresence in the sky"; the concept of the competent and responsible individual; certain key ingredients of economic individualism; the insistence on a citizenry educated to understand its rights and duties; and the middle-class virtues, that high plateau of moral stability on which, so Americans believe, successful democracy must always build. When we recall that the Presbyterian, Baptist, Reformed, and even early Anglican churches in the colonies were likewise Calvinistic, there can be no argument that here was the major religious element in the rise of an American brand of liberty. Early American Protestantism was largely Puritan Protestantism.[75]

REVIVALISM AND DEMOCRACY: THE GREAT AWAKENING. In the second quarter of the eighteenth century a surge of revivalistic emotion swept through the colonies.[76] The Great Awakening, the American phase of a widespread reaction against formalism and indifference, converted tens of thousands to personal religion, left telling marks on colonial society, and earned the reputation of "the first spontaneous outburst of popular feeling in American history." [77] The spontaneity of this movement is evident in the fact that no one place could claim to be its origin, no one man its originator, no one church its chief beneficiary. The revival was aimed at re-establishing piety in all religions rather than reforming doctrine in any one.

The leading lights of the revival were Theodore Frelinghuysen of New Jersey, a Dutch Reformed minister who hit his stride about 1725; William Tennent and his four sons, Presbyterians who awakened the middle colonies in the 1730's; Jonathan Edwards, whose severe but evangelical preaching began to take effect at Northampton, Massachusetts, in 1734; [78] and a swarm of Baptists and Presbyterians, most notably Samuel Davies, who spread the new fervor through the southern colonies in the 1740's and later. The man whose preaching bound these diverse movements together, whose American career shows how the awakening cut across denominational lines, was the English revivalist, George Whitefield. His glory-shouting tours through the colonies, the first beginning in Philadelphia in 1739, the last ending with his death in Newburyport in 1770, were marked by the most dramatic, effective, and well-attended preaching of the Great Awakening.[79] He was for a generation the best-known man in colonial America.[80]

The effects of the Great Awakening, especially the ways in which it hastened or delayed the day of democracy, are the chief concern of these few pages. As in all popular movements of this sweep, the results were mixed and the record controversial. Certainly such social by-products as the upsurge of intolerance in Connecticut and Massachusetts, the crude emotionalism of the extremist sects, and the bad feeling generated for purely personal reasons in dozens of communities did not benefit the fragile spirit of mutual respect upon which true liberty depends. Yet for all its excesses, which revolted such religious liberals as Jonathan Mayhew and Charles Chauncy,[81] the Great Awakening was a tremendous spur to the coming of American democracy, especially social democracy. Here in brief were its principal democratizing effects: [82]

The revival of piety accelerated the trend toward multiplication of religions. "If religion had been broken into segments by the Protestant revolt of the sixteenth century, it was atomized now by the Great Awakening of the eighteenth." [83] All those liberating social forces which derived from the splintering of the sects were given added impetus by the schisms created in Congregationalism and Presbyterianism, by the founding of new and short-lived churches on the frontier, and by the breaking of ground for the coming of Methodism.

The increase in number of dissenting churches and the upsurge of fervor in men and women of all denominations gave new strength to the campaign for separation of church and state. Certainly disestablishment and religious liberty would not have come so swiftly in Virginia had not the Great Awakening helped create a social situation in which any other course would have been impractical and disruptive. The Declaration of Rights of 1776 and the Act for Establishing Religious Freedom of 1785 were made possible by changes in the religious pattern of Virginia in the 1750's and 1760's.

Equality rather than liberty or fraternity was the chief beneficiary of the Great Awakening. The revival spirit placed emphasis on the importance of the regenerated individual, without regard to his social standing, national background, calling, or religion. The rise of personalized religion among the poor folk of the colonies gave a lift to those doctrines of individual worth and social equality which were to lead the new nation to Jacksonian democracy. By insisting that heaven, the greatest prize of all, was open to all men on equal terms, the preachers of the Awakening aroused leveling sentiments among tens of thousands of common men.

A natural result of these new feelings of individualism and equality was the further democratizing of organization and methods in the churches. More democracy in the church led in turn to more democracy in the community, and so the great historical interaction of religion and politics continued to work to liberate man from the tyranny of the past. Conservatives condemned the excesses of the Awakening as menaces not only to social stability but to the established political order.

If the Great Awakening led many people to distrust learning and intelligence and to insist that their ministers be no better men than they, it led other men, especially Presbyterians, to a more lively concern for education—an example of the mixed character of such broadly popular movements. William Tennent's "Log College" at Neshaminy, Pennsylvania, was the most important boost to education at the time of the Great Awakening; Princeton, Brown, Rutgers, Dartmouth, Washington and Lee, and Hampden-Sydney are modern reminders of the thorough shaking-up visited upon colonial society by the Great Awakening.

Still another product of eighteenth-century revivalism was an increase in social consciousness and humanitarianism. Some historians trace the beginnings of the antislavery movement in America to the egalitarian preaching of men like Samuel Hopkins of Great Barrington, and certainly several left-wing sects emerged from this period with new and radical attitudes on Negro slavery. The Great Awakening also revived interest in Indian missions, and everywhere there was renewed concern for abnormal and unfortunate members of society.

Finally, the revival aroused latent feelings of class antagonism. It appealed primarily to the poor and despised; it revolted the well-born, well-educated, and well-to-do. As a result, it spread like wildfire among Baptists, stirred up bitter opposition among Anglicans, and split the Presbyterian, Congregational, and Reformed churches into conservative and radical factions that conformed amazingly to class lines.[8] Especially in Virginia, where revivalism seems to have worked the most profound changes all along the line, did eager Baptists and New Side Presbyterians awaken socially and politically as well as religiously. The challenge of religious radicalism to the formalistic religion of the ruling class carried with it new doubts about the claims of this class to social and political superiority. The old habits of deference were weakened severely by the Great Awakening, not only in Virginia but all over America.

By 1765 religion in the colonies had taken on a new and unmistakable look and would henceforth be recognized as "characteristically American." The chief elements of American religion were varied and contradictory: Protestantism, especially the left-wing Puritan variety; diversity of doctrine and organization, with no one church claiming anything like a clear majority; skepticism, rationalism, and bored indifference among a large fraction of all classes; and a long-range trend toward the fact and principle of religious liberty. The result of their blending in the colonial environment was a pattern of faith more individualistic and liberating than that of any other Christian land.

Openminded colonists had a remarkably clear idea of the distance religious liberty had traveled, the distance it had yet to go, and the welcome results for free government that the final victory would secure. They saw that the course of religious liberty was doubly important for such government—important for the political liberties it dragged in its wake, important because religious liberty was itself a political liberty. Their own experience and the recent history of America, England, and Europe told them that the union of church and state was an inherently autocratic arrangement, and that those who achieved religious freedom were about two thirds of the way to political and social freedom as well. They believed with a famous North Carolina radical: "It is a most certain fact . . . that the blending of civil and religious offices, sacred and secular things, has been an introduction to slavery in all nations where arbitrary government has been introduced." [85]

It is hard to overstate the political importance of pioneers in religious liberty like Williams, Clarke, Calvert, Penn, and Davies, for the devotion of these eminent men and of their thousands of co-workers helped smooth the course of government in the future republic. By demanding that the state cease supporting one religion at the expense of all, they helped return government to its legitimate sphere of operation. By encouraging men of one religion to show respect for men of other religions, they brought light and reason to political as well as religious controversy. In managing to do all this with a minimum of bloodshed and persecution, they put the vast majority of America's churches on the side of political liberty. And in insisting that each church stand on its own feet without secular support, they purified and strengthened religion itself. Yet we must remind ourselves again that the physical and social environment was one in which prophets of freedom could preach with maximum efficiency. The total American environment worked massively and inexorably for religious as well as political liberty.

By the coming of the Revolutionary era America's religious future had been fixed. America would be a land of religious freedom, and American politics would be conducted accordingly. Yet true religious feeling was, if anything, more widely and strongly held than in many European countries where conformity and establishment remained state policy. The principles of the awakening American democracy were to be thoroughly moral, if not indeed religious, in character. The men of 1776 believed that the good state would rise on the rock of private and public morality, that morality was in the case of most men and all states the product of religion, and that the earthly mission of religion was to set men free. It was no mere pose when they justified resistance to oppression as obedience to God and an appeal to heaven.

CHAPTER THREE

The Colonial Economy and the Rise of Liberty

THROUGH all recorded history man's primary concern has been to "make a living," to acquire and use food, shelter, clothing, and physical comforts. Several notable cultures have existed in which the worship of God, the study of war, or the playing of politics seemed to consume most of the time of most people, but even in these societies the dominance of religion, war, or politics was made possible only by a peculiar conjunction of economic forces. Although economic determinism has been grossly overworked in certain conspicuous efforts to rewrite the past, the value of this technique is beyond dispute. Certainly in a study like this an understanding of the economic pattern is of fundamental importance.

The paramount influence of economic motives, conditions, and institutions in the shaping of America, and thus in the shaping of American political thought, is apparent at every stage of colonial history.[1] The decline of feudalism and rise of commercial capitalism inspired the great explorations that opened up the Western hemisphere. A host of economic motives—the search for gold and silver, the demand for raw materials, the quest for new markets, the desire for private profit—promoted the settlement of North America and the West Indies.[2] A longing for economic betterment was the compelling force that brought most colonists over the seas, whether from East Anglia in 1630, the Rhineland in 1700, or Ulster in 1720. And the powder-train of events that set off the American Revolution was fired and fanned by a series of decisions on commercial policy.

A few words of caution may serve as helpful guides to this compressed but complex investigation of the colonial economy. First, this chapter will concentrate on the more strictly economic problems and developments of the period. Such socio-economic factors as slavery, indentured servitude, class conflict, and the social results of economic variety will be given primary treatment in Chapter 4. Second, this chapter will concentrate on the eighteenth century. The pioneer economy of the seventeenth century was simply a prologue to the more expanded economy of the eighteenth. It was in the quarter century just before 1765 that the economic development of the American colonies was most pronounced. Third, it should be made clear at the outset that the influence of economic forces on the rise of political liberty was mixed in character and results. Many economic arrangements and theories—for example, the web of laws, customs, and pressures that controlled the acquisition and tenure of land—seemed often to be working just as powerfully against liberty, self-government, and political equality as for them. In general, however, the story of the colonial economy is one of expansion—in freedom of choice, equality of opportunity, level of productivity, and vitality of competition. It is the story of the origins of the fabled economic system that has shaped the destiny of modern America.

THE COLONIAL ECONOMY

The economy of the continental colonies exhibited several features that influenced the course of political thought and action:

THE OLD COLONIAL SYSTEM. The most obvious characteristic of the early American economy was the fact that it was a colonial economy, that these thirteen political entities were commercial accessories of a burgeoning empire. The colonial period of American history coincided with the highest development of the English mercantile system; from beginning to end the colonies existed primarily for economic support of the mother country.

Mercantilism, it will be remembered, was a many-sided condition rather than a coherent theory,[3] a species of economic nationalism nourished on the assumption that the states of Europe were engaged in perpetual commercial war with one another. Although there were as many varieties of mercantile theory as there were mercantilists, the economists of seventeenth- and eighteenth-century England were united in their insistence that the state must control economic organization and method in the interest of national power and aggrandizement. Internally, this called for elaborate regulation of production and labor. Externally, it called for a fantastic apparatus of law and policy designed to achieve a favorable balance of trade, "to sell more to strangers yearly than wee consume of theirs in value": [4] protective tariffs, embargoes, bounties, prohibitions, navigation acts, treaties, and monopolies. Most important for American history, mercantile doctrine called for settlement and exploitation of overseas colonies.[5]

In the old colonial system a colony was to be a colony in the most obvious sense of the word: a perpetually subordinate agricultural and extractive area expected to serve the mother country as a source of raw materials, a safety-valve for excess or unwanted population, and a market for finished goods. The perfect colony under the mercantile system was one in which "the inhabitants . . . wear not a rag of their own manufacturing; drive not a nail of their own forging; eat not out of a platter or cup of their own making; nay . . . produce not even bread to eat," [6] but rather grow staples for export to and through the mother country. The perfect colony, of course, never existed, nor were English colonial policy and English mercantilism always synonymous. Yet the general assumptions of mercantilism governed the mother country's policy throughout the decisive period of American development. England always feared and often frustrated the rise of an American economy that would compete with rather than supplement her own economy. The legislative and administrative techniques through which this policy was converted into a working reality will be described and evaluated at a later stage in this chapter.

COLONIAL MERCANTILISM. A corollary of this first characteristic is the interesting and oft-forgotten fact that the colonists, too, were mercantilists. The men of Massachusetts and Virginia, like the men of London and Bristol, were products of a social heritage that looked upon government control of economic activity as an ethical and practical necessity. The attempt of certain defenders of "rugged individualism" to project laissez-faire capitalism back to Plymouth and Jamestown is historical nonsense. The early colonists, whose economic theories were a compound of declining medievalism and rising mercantilism,[7] acknowledged government intervention as the one sure cure for the plague of economic problems besetting their infant communities. Their descendants shook off the medieval but not the mercantile doctrines of economic surveillance, and not until the middle of the eighteenth century did laissez-faire policies begin to challenge this long-standing tradition of public regulation of business. The Revolution touched off a major revival of economic controls,[8] thereby demonstrating that the colonists were not opposed to mercantilism except of the imperial variety.

Evidences of domestic mercantilism fill the records of town and province. Among the subjects regulated at one time or another by law and ordinance were: the price and quality of commodities like bread, meat, bricks, firewood, and leather; [9] fares charged by public conveyances, storage and wharfage rates, and fees for such public services as corn-grinding and slaughtering; licenses, fees, and wages of millers, carmen, porters, draymen, and smiths; prices of food, drink, and lodging in taverns; and market practices in general, a survival of medieval prohibitions on forestalling, engrossing, regrating, and monopolizing the necessities of life. The assemblies passed a multitude of laws governing commerce and manufacturing: tonnage duties, import and export taxes,[10] inspection laws, port regulations, and embargoes, not to mention bounties, monopoly privileges, and subsidies.[11]

Nor was this intervention, as is often assumed, confined to the Puritan colonies. Although Massachusetts experimented most purposefully in wage- and price-controls, Virginia and Maryland regulated their major undertaking, the tobacco industry, with force and ingenuity.[12] The attempt to raise agricultural prices by restrictions on production is a legacy from colonial America, not a New Deal invention.

The intentions of the colonial mercantilists far outran the effectiveness of their laws and ordinances. The people of the colonies, like people all through history, were extremely adept at evading economic controls. Nature was too grand, conditions too primitive, government too meager, society too increasingly fluid and secular to permit these controls to be enforced with vigor or continuity. Yet it is a fact to remember that throughout the colonial period government regulation and stimulation of the economy were regarded as part of the natural order of things.[13]

THE SWAY OF AGRICULTURE. The colonial economy was predominantly agrarian, which is exactly what English merchants wanted it to be. Something like eight in ten colonists took their living from the soil.[14] One of ten was engaged in one of the closely allied extractive industries—fishing, lumbering, fur-trading, and the production of naval stores. So completely did soil and forest dominate the lives and occupations of men that in 1765 only five places on the American continent had populations in excess of eight thousand. These cities—Boston, New York, Philadelphia, Newport, Charleston—had probably eighty thousand inhabitants, less than five per cent of the total. Commerce, of which there was a great deal, and manufacturing, of which there was very little, were both mere extensions of the great pursuit of agriculture. Many merchants, fishermen, and craftsmen were themselves part-time cultivators of the soil.

The implications of an agrarian economy for the development of the colonies and their habits of thinking were many. The dominance of agriculture had these social effects: The land itself was the most important single economic factor in early American history; the colonies would have to pass through a long period of dependence on the mother country before they were able to strike out for themselves; a people quite unprepared for the "curses and vexations" of eighteenth-century urban life were largely spared its ill effects; the land was celebrated as the sure foundation of wealth, virtue, and freedom;[15] politics took on a decidedly rural flavor; the native aristocracy, except in parts of commercial New England, was a landed aristocracy; and the colonial economy was a simple affair in which emphasis rested on self-sufficiency, hard work, and personal independence.

SIMPLICITY. This last point, the simplicity of the colonial economy, demands separate attention. The techniques employed in field,[16] forest, shop, or counting-house were often so simple as to verge on the primitive. Technology and research had done little in 1650 and not much more in 1750 to distinguish farmer, fisherman, laborer, craftsman, or merchant from his counterpart in feudal times. Only the broadest outlines of specialization and of division of labor were marked out in colonial America. Men were by necessity jacks-of-all-trades, and most of them spent their lives in ceaseless toil. One important result of this general concentration on the struggle for existence was the fact that ordinary men were left with little time or energy for politics or political thinking, which therefore remained largely in the keeping of gentry and preachers. The latter, it should be remembered, were toiling pretty hard themselves.

The context of law, custom, and theory [17] in which men carried on this economy of long hours and few rewards was correspondingly simple.[18] However perplexing the rules and problems of commerce may have seemed to a Virginia planter or Boston lawyer-merchant, they exhibited none of the complexity of modern or even of nineteenth-century economic society. The patterns and social results of taxation are example enough of this state of affairs. Although the deceptively low taxes of 1653 or 1753 were just as hard for a man to pay as those of 1953, the system that taxed him was certainly easier to understand and control.[19]

THE LACK OF MANUFACTURING. A corollary of agrarian simplicity was the absence of manufacturing on any but the most restricted and primitive scale.[20] This should occasion no surprise, for the industrial revolution had not come to England itself. Yet the level of manufacturing enterprise divorced from the household was, until the end of the colonial period, far lower in the colonies than in the mother country. Ironworking, flour-milling,[21] wood-preparing, shipbuilding, glassmaking, and other such undertakings were carried on in small and localized units. Nothing resembling a modern factory, not even Peter Hasenclever's ill-fated iron works in New York and New Jersey, existed in colonial times. Since there was no industry, there were no industrial problems, and economic, social, and political theory remained simple, pure, and comprehensible.

The reasons usually advanced to explain the retarded condition of manufacturing offer an instructive impression of the colonial economy. Among these were: English laws encouraging agrarian and extractive pursuits and discouraging manufacturing; the difficulties of transportation and communication within the colonies and with the rest of the world, which frustrated the rise of stable markets; a chronic shortage of coin and specie, and the instability and inadequacy of the many forms of paper issues and barter that were employed as substitutes;[22] a lack of surplus capital, and the preference of colonial investors for such traditional ventures as shipping, slaves, and land; the sovereignty of the natural environment, of sea, forest, and soil; the tradition of agriculture as a business and way of life; the high cost and scarcity of labor, the result of an environment in which few men could command wages attractive enough to divert them from the lure of cheap land; the assumption of agrarian thinkers that manufacturing and poverty went always hand in hand; and the absence of socio-economic compulsions that might have led a little sooner to improved methods of craftsmanship, labor-saving machinery, and the beginnings of technology.

Household manufactures,[23] individual crafts, and small and widely dispersed ventures in converting iron ore, wood, and wheat to commercial use—this was the extent of "industry" in colonial America. In the final reckoning, not English policy but colonial conditions retarded American industrial development. Toward the end of the colonial period the pace of industrial progress began to quicken, but the units established were tiny by modern standards.

THE IMPORTANCE OF COMMERCE. From inception to independence the colonies were partners in a strongly commercial civilization. Agriculture was the primary pursuit, but except in the pioneering stages it was commercial rather than subsistence farming that occupied most colonists, whether on large farms or small. The purpose of the colonial farmer was no different from that of his present-day descendant: to produce surpluses for sale in the domestic or foreign market. The purpose of his countrymen in town and port was to pay him cash or barter for these surpluses, convert them or package them, and ship them off at a profit.

The lifeblood of the colonial economy was trade—in agricultural surpluses and other commodities as well—within the colonies and over the seas.[24] Foreign commerce in particular was a more vital element in the life of this economically underdeveloped area than it would have been in an older, more self-sufficient community. Indeed, the welfare of the colonies depended on foreign commerce to a degree hardly understandable to later generations.[25] The merchants of Boston, Newport, New York, Philadelphia, and Charleston, standing as they did at the meeting-point of the countercurrents of American agricultural products and English finished goods, were thus the most important persons in the colonial economy.[26] Their profits and their leadership in politics and society are not difficult to explain.

ELEMENTS OF CAPITALISM. The tradition of government regulation of the economy was part of the colonial way of life; laissez-faire arguments were rarely heard in economic debate; manufacturing on any but the most primitive scale was unknown to the American continent. Yet it would be a mistake to overlook the elements of capitalism that had developed in the colonies by 1765, for example, virtually universal private ownership of the means of production, the primacy of the profit motive (in Peter Faneuil's Boston, if not in John Winthrop's), and the use of credit and the wage system. Mercantilism, after all, was not hostile to individual ownership and enterprise. It merely insisted that men, while pursuing their own destinies, keep in mind the larger purposes of the sheltering state. Within those purposes there was a considerable amount of economic elbow-room. Especially in the colonies, where conditions befogged the watchful eye of government, most men were engaged in what was essentially free enterprise. The colonies had been founded through private initiative acting in response to national needs, and such initiative continued to power the American economy throughout the colonial period. The farmer and merchant were undoubted capitalists, and their agrarian-commercial capitalism was a plainly marked way-station on the road to industrial capitalism. Although by the time of the Revolution the theory of laissez-faire had become more current in England than in the colonies, the conditions favoring laissez-faire were hardly less developed in the latter area.

AN EXPANDING ECONOMY. Finally, the long-run trend of the colonial economy was one of expansion—in population, productivity, capital accumulation, opportunity, social mobility, goals of enterprise, and openmindedness of economic thought. An extra element of economic freedom had always been present in the American adventure. Feudal land-tenure, the guild system, the efficient state, and communal agriculture had failed to take hold in the wilderness; and, once the pioneer period was past, the economy moved steadily forward under the goad of private initiative. The economic picture in 1765 had plenty of blotches—the exhaustion of soil and credit in Virginia, the growth of monopoly and land speculation, the failure to solve the currency problem, and the curse of slavery—but there can be no doubt that the American economy was, to an astounding degree, an expanding one. For all its difficulties and its organization into localized units, the American iron industry produced one seventh of the world's supply in 1775.

These, then, were the broad features of the colonial economy: mercantilism abroad, mercantilism at home, simplicity of economic organization, the dominance of agriculture, the absence of manufacturing, the importance of commerce, the presence of many elements of capitalism, and the steady expansion of production, wealth, and opportunity. The question now arises: Just what did the colonists do for a living?

THE THREE SECTIONS AND THEIR ECONOMIES

Colonial America was divided economically into three distinct and integral units: New England, an area of small farms and far-ranging commerce; the South, an area devoted to the growing of staples for export to England; and the middle colonies, an area of more conspicuous diversity and opportunity for expansion than either of the other groups of colonies.[27] The economy of each of these three sections should be examined with care, for out of the economy grew many features of the society, and out of the society grew habits of life and thought that proved decisive for the political future of the colonies.

NEW ENGLAND.[28] The key economic fact about colonial New England was that it was an area fitted by nature for commerce rather than agriculture. New Hampshire, Connecticut, Rhode Island, and Massachusetts formed the most unsatisfactory group of colonies, "the most prejudicial Plantation to this Kingdom," from the English point of view, for they produced no important staple for export. The narrow and sandy coastal plain, the hills and valleys, and the boulder-strewn soil could be farmed for subsistence, but there was little incentive for growing surplus crops. Agriculture was diversified, and as elsewhere most people gained their livelihood from the soil: "Yet were the greater part of the people wholly devoted to the Plow." [29] Among the leading products of the small farms of New England were corn, oats, barley, rye, buckwheat, fruits, vegetables, dairy products, sheep, horses, cattle, and swine.[30] In several of these items the farmers of Massachusetts and Connecticut produced surpluses for export, especially to the West Indies, but the cash value of this trade was trifling when compared with that carried on in the staples of Virginia or the Carolinas.

Unable to rely on one or two major staples for export, yet unwilling to live without the finished goods that England alone could supply, the resourceful men of New England turned with a will to redressing the unfavorable balance of trade. Although the bulk of Northern manufactures was produced in households and other small units and was intended largely for domestic consumption, extractive industries produced surpluses for export to half the world. Fish, rum, and ships were New England's chief cash-producing exports, while whale products,[31] lumber,[32] and to a lesser extent furs,[33] iron, and naval stores also helped swell the current of New England commerce.

The main business of New England, as the fisherman of Marblehead said, was always "to catch fish." The cod achieved sainthood in Massachusetts for perfectly sound economic reasons.[34] Hundreds of ships and thousands of men were kept busy carrying cod to the Catholics of southern Europe (who welcomed it) and "refuse fish" to the slaves of the West Indies (who did not). Rum, the second support of New England's economic health, was manufactured in prodigious quantities. In 1774 more than sixty distilleries in Massachusetts alone produced 2,700,000 gallons from West Indian molasses and thereby contributed decisively to the success of the slave trade, the debauching of the Indians, the sustaining of patriotic morale, and the coming of the Revolution. "I know not why," wrote John Adams in 1818, "we should blush to confess that molasses was an essential ingredient in American independence." [35] As for shipbuilding, the fact that one third of the seven-thousand-odd ships engaged in English commerce were built in American yards, most of them in the small yards of the New England coast, attests the importance of this native industry. Seventy-five per cent of all colonial commerce was carried in colonial bottoms. Shipbuilding was one American undertaking consistently smiled upon by the English authorities.

Ship, wharf, distillery, and counting-house were the foundations of New England prosperity. Massachusetts, Rhode Island, New Hampshire, and Connecticut were the only colonies in which commerce was more important than agriculture. The coastwise trade and various triangular trades, in all of which rum was the magic potion that made the Yankee thrice welcome, poured back into New England a variety of products and forms of money which could then be shipped off to old England in payment for hardware, dry goods, small luxuries, and household furnishings. Forbidden to ship such products as fish and grains to England, the New Englanders engaged in a measure of ocean-going commerce that seems fantastic for an essentially self-sufficient economy. The geography of New England and the compulsions of English mercantilism sent the men of Massachusetts down to the sea in ships.[36]

SOUTHERN COLONIES. The economies of Maryland, Virginia, Georgia, and the Carolinas were of a character that responded more satisfactorily to the demands of mercantilism. The key economic fact about these colonies was that they were able to concentrate on a handful of staples for consumption in or reshipment by the mother country: tobacco in Maryland, Virginia, and North Carolina, rice and indigo in South Carolina and Georgia. These colonies produced other articles for export—naval stores,[37] wheat, corn, furs,[38] deerskins, flax, hemp, fruit, livestock, iron, and lumber—but extant statistics prove that the constant test of economic well-being for each colony was its ability to grow, ship, and claim a decent price for one or two staples.

The South was therefore a thoroughgoing agrarian region.[39] Plantations dominated the economy of the tidewater; small farms flourished in the back country of Virginia and the Carolinas. Only Charleston, which in 1765 counted some five thousand white and five thousand Negro souls, could be classified as a city.[40] Elsewhere, especially in Virginia, the configuration of the coast made it possible for many planters to load their produce aboard ships—other men's ships, of course—that came up the river to the planters' docks. Such manufacturing or extraction as did exist—ironmaking in Maryland and Virginia,[41] production of naval stores in the Carolinas, the activities of the ever-present sawmills and flour mills—were subordinate to and integrated with the main business of growing staples for export. Most articles manufactured in the South were produced and consumed on self-contained plantations.

From the beginning Southern agriculture was conducted on a commercial basis.[42] The desire of the Virginia Company for profit, the climate and soil of Virginia and Maryland, the growing European penchant for smoking and snuffing, and the dictates of mercantilism, which could not long tolerate the outward flow of specie for Spanish tobacco, combined to make production of the "sot-weed" the consuming business of Virginia, Maryland, and North Carolina.[43] The Southern colonies could and did grow other crops, for export as well as for home consumption: by 1750 Virginia and Maryland led all other colonies in the export of Indian corn. But it was "king tobacco" that made or broke these colonies throughout early American history. Even as late as 1770, when the urge for diversification was becoming stronger in the tobacco-producing colonies, more than one fourth the total value of all American exports could be counted in tobacco.

The social and political results of this one-crop economy—the growth of large plantations, the amassing of fantastic debts, the creation of a genuine landed aristocracy, the spread and consolidation of human slavery, soil exhaustion and abandonment, land speculation—are examined in other parts of this chapter or in Chapter 4. Our concern here is economic results: the capitalist nature of this staple-producing type of enterprise; the over-sensitivity of the planter's economy to the world price of his staple; his subservience to the dictates of the mercantile system; the curse of the "invisible charges" (freight payments, commissions, interest, extremely high duties, insurance premiums, cooperage, cartage, rent, and what not), which lined the pockets of the English merchants;[44] and the consequent existence, with little hope of redress, of an unfavorable balance of trade. Whatever prosperity seemed to exist in Virginia and Maryland was a bogus gloss over an essentially rotten economic condition. And the reforms that might have corrected this situation—crop restriction, lower duties, scaling-down of debts, suppression of the slave trade, thorough changes in the marketing system—were flatly opposed by the English merchants and government. Toward the close of the colonial period many planters achieved a more healthy financial position by building up self-sufficient plantations and by branching out into other profitmaking ventures, principally speculation in western lands. Yet the sway of tobacco had hardly been challenged, except by occasional writers to the press who complained of "eternal Piddling about that sovereign Weed Tobacco." [45]

Capitalist agriculture and the plantation system were likewise characteristic of rice- and indigo-production in the colonies south of Virginia.[46] Rice was first successfully cultivated at the turn of the eighteenth century. By the outbreak of the Revolution 165,000 barrels a year were moving through Charleston and Savannah, a good fraction of this total directed, by grudging permission of Parliament, to ports in Europe south of Cape Finisterre. This gave the staple-producing economies of South Carolina and Georgia an element of strength that the economies of Maryland and Virginia needed badly. Indigo was first shipped out of the southernmost colonies in the 1740's. In a very few years England was taking more than one million pounds annually from Southern plantations.

All this time the back country of these colonies was filling up with men who had less capital and different ideas. The result was an expanding agrarian economy, which produced livestock, grains, naval stores, and tobacco for export, and avoided the pitfalls of the tidewater system through diversification, smaller units, and increased production for home consumption.

MIDDLE COLONIES. The region lying between Albany and Baltimore supported the best-balanced economy in colonial America. Like New England a booming commercial area, it was far less dependent on circuitous trading to pile up remittances to England. Like the South a famous agricultural belt, it grew crops less subject to price fluctuations and less destructive of the soil than the tobacco of Virginia and Maryland. And toward the middle of the eighteenth century it took the lead from New England in the number and productivity of its manufacturing enterprises. Climate, soil, topography, and ingenuity combined to make the middle colonies, especially Pennsylvania, the soundest economic unit in the entire imperial structure.

The expanding economy of the four middle colonies could be most readily observed in its two leading ports, Philadelphia and New York. The former served as the natural market or throat of export for Pennsylvania, Delaware, and West Jersey,[47] the latter for East Jersey, the Hudson valley, and western Connecticut. This hinterland, like those to the north and south, was a largely self-sufficient agricultural area. Unlike that to the north, it was also able to grow large surpluses of cereals for export to southern Europe, the West Indies, New England, and even to the British Isles. Wheat, whether unprocessed or converted into flour or bread, totaled well over one half the value of exports from both New York and Pennsylvania in the period 1760-1770.

The farms that grew this wheat and gave the region the name of "the bread colonies" were larger and more scattered than those of New England, smaller and less scattered than those to the south. Although overextended units could and did prosper with the aid of tenancy and servitude, small units were equally capable of producing wheat for the mills of the Brandy-wine and Raritan. In addition, the farmers of this favored region grew cattle, sheep, hogs, and horses, and shipped them or their products in the West Indies trade. Pennsylvania, New York, and Connecticut contributed a major proportion of the six thousand horses, three thousand oxen, and eighteen thousand hogs and sheep exported to the West Indies in 1770. Whether its acres were few or many, its labor free or indentured, its crop wheat or potatoes or flax, the farm of the middle colonies was conducted on a thoroughly commercial-capitalist basis.

The growing and shipping of wheat and livestock by no means absorbed all the energies of the multinational middle colonies. Flour-mills for grinding wheat, sawmills for cutting lumber, bloomeries and forges for producing and working iron,[48] yards for building ships, and tiny factories for making paper, glass, stockings, cloth, pottery, bricks, potash, and other articles for domestic or foreign consumption dotted the banks of the rivers leading to Philadelphia or New York. In the region around Philadelphia colonial manufacturing reached its peak of development. By the middle of the eighteenth century ever-increasing amounts of surplus capital, amassed in the first instance from trade in staples, were flowing into these miniature industrial enterprises. A Swedish traveler wrote of Germantown in 1748, "Most of the inhabitants are Manufacturers, and make almost everything in such quantity and perfection, that in a short time this province will want very little from *England*, its mother country." [49]

THE FACTORS OF FREEDOM: I

The influence of economic forces on the rise of liberty in the colonies was mixed in character and results. Most of these forces were working silently and powerfully for ultimate independence, the prime condition for the flowering of authentic freedom, but at the same time they were working against as well as for liberty and equality within each colony. Four basic forces will be singled out for investigation: the land systems of the colonies; the growth of capitalism; wages and conditions of labor; and the clash of English and American interests. No one of these was an unmixed blessing to the cause of American democracy, but the preponderance of their total influence favored the growth of human freedom.

THE LAND SYSTEMS. The most important feature of the American economy was the land itself—and how it was acquired, held, worked, and alienated. To a civilization in which land was the basis and badge of wealth and status the American colonies alone offered this treasure in abundance. Most people who came to the colonies were in search of land on which to plant and prosper. The possession of land was an absolute requirement for political participation in seven of the thirteen colonies, and everywhere it was recognized as the one indisputable stake in society. If the ease with which it could be acquired, especially by well-placed officials and their favorites, released torrents of greed that made a mockery of equality, it also released the energies of tens of thousands of men who were willing to sweat for the good life. The extent and richness of the soil, the laws and customs governing its acquisition and use, the hunger of men for it, and the consequent sway of agriculture were the elements to which we must pay constant attention in judging the influence of this first great economic factor of political freedom.

The land systems of New England and of the middle and Southern colonies were sufficiently different from one another, and therefore productive of sufficiently different social results, to merit separate description. A few details about the American land common to all colonies may serve as an introduction.

Despite the fact of ultimate possession in the Crown and the existence of vast and often long-lived proprietary schemes, the forms and spirit of feudal tenure never took hold in America. Land was too cheap and abundant, the settlers too impatient of restrictions, England itself too advanced, and the proprietors too distant and misinformed ever to have permitted the successful transplanting of the manorial system.[50] The bestowal of lands in "free and common socage," the most liberal grant the Crown could have made, was a decisive factor in the development of the colonies.[51]

The enfeebling of feudalism and complete failure of the few attempts at communism—not to be confused with modern attempts of the same name—resulted in the triumph of private ownership as the method of land-holding. Outside New England the quit-rent, a fixed yearly payment to Crown or proprietor in recognition and conversion of the ancient obligations of tenantry, continued to be demanded of otherwise free and unencumbered land-holders. Yet for most of those who paid quit-rents the burden was small; in one famous instance the tenant's obligation was discharged by "one red rose forever." And upon those who ignored payments or fell into arrears, chiefly in New York and several proprietary colonies, retribution was rarely visited. The leading authority on quit-rents has estimated "conservatively" that at the time of the Revolution the rent rolls in Crown and proprietary colonies totaled £37,500, collections £19,000.[52]

In most colonies land could be acquired with ridiculous ease by purchase or grant. The policies of Crown, colony, and speculator alike were directed to encouraging settlement and cultivation. As the colonies became more thickly settled, unspoiled land in the older areas grew more difficult to obtain. Yet there was always the frontier, especially from Pennsylvania southward, and few were the resolute and land-hungry men who failed to acquire acres of their own. Only in ill-managed New York, where tenantry, speculation, and a manorial system flourished in unholy alliance,[53] was it difficult for the plain man to obtain land. As a result, New York lagged well behind other colonies in immigration.

This and the following description give too much order and simplicity to a fantastically complicated situation. The digger into land laws, deeds, and records turns up a dozen exceptions to every one rule, and the total picture often appears as one vast jumble of clouded titles, rent wars, law-suits, feudal remnants, and cross purposes in official policy. Yet it would be a mistake not to recognize the final sovereignty of these determinants: the failure of feudalism, the triumph of private ownership, and the ease of ac-quisition.

The land system of New England put simultaneous emphasis on the gen-eral purposes of the community and the special needs of the individual.[54] The result was a pattern of land-holding in Massachusetts, Connecticut, and Rhode Island, and to a lesser extent in New Hampshire, with these dis-tinguishing features: stability of law and custom in the older settlements, orderliness in the course of westward expansion, and almost everywhere a condition of relative equality marked by small farms held in fee simple. Provisions in the various charters for tenure in free and common socage were the chief blow at feudalism, but the determination of the first New Englanders to have done with past oppressions and inequities are evident in these clauses from the Massachusetts "Body of Liberties" (1641):

> 10. All our lands and heritages shall be free from all fines and licenses upon Alienations, and from all hariotts, wardships, Liveries, Primer-seisins, yeare day and wast, Escheates, and forfeitures, upon the death of parents or Ancestors, be they naturall, casuall, or Juditiall.
> 81. When parents dye intestate, the Elder sonne shall have a doble por-tion of his whole estate reall and personall, unlesse the General Court upon just cause alleadged shall judge otherwise.
> 82. When parents dye intestate having no heires males of their bodies their daughters shall inherit as Copartners, unles the General Court upon just reason shall judge otherwise.[55]

Thus at a stroke did Massachusetts abolish feudal obligations and primo-geniture.

Most of New England was settled initially on a community basis.[56] A group desiring to head west or north petitioned the colonial assembly for a grant of land. After the new township had been surveyed and "safety, Christian communion, schools, civility, and other good ends"[57] had been satisfied by reserving plots for these purposes, the settlers, within certain limits, distributed the land among themselves.[58] The amount any one man might obtain varied according to his means and needs, but rarely was gross inequality permitted by law or custom. In time the close-knit agricultural town and its system of house lots, upland fields, and commons gave way to a more dispersed, individualistic pattern. By 1750, thanks to progressive liberalization of the laws of tenure and alienation,[59] the New England farmer was master of his own land. And by 1750, thanks to the nature of the region and the stern wisdom of the early settlers, New England was an area of small, compact farms. The eighteenth century was marred by speculation in frontier lands and by unseemly squabbles between proprietors and new-comers in some of the older settlements, but the system survived these rude shocks with comparatively little damage.[60]

It would be wrong to point with uncritical pride to the land policies of

f settlement,
t who would
o trouble ac-
: "headright"
by importing
cheaply from
nies that had
, corrupt, or
: for himself.
ish of Penn-
several other
authority for
answer:

ws of God
 Christians

was a system
an under the
e progressive
ntry reached
st Jersey, an
nexhaustible
s, and quit-
d only with
abolition of
 established.
nomic insti-
lthough the
iscontent, it
deterrent to

concentra-
ntation held
umbers. The
as that made
s than poor
polies.[68]
lonies on a
peculators,[69]
was a mis-
1 man hun-
pital invest-
 settlement
s instances.
eat fortune

ual abuses, frauds, quarrels, monopolies, and
f even the most sensible communities. Yet
ed in most towns toward a condition of
stability. In contrast to conditions in Eng-
d systems of Massachusetts and Connecticut
om.[61] Though surcharged as usual with pa-
rds of Daniel Webster describe the colonial
id make plain the significance of the system
id spirit of government:

wer, the nature of government must essen-
n which property is holden and distributed.
belonging to property, whether it exists in
n the rights of property that both despotism
nce ordinarily commence their attacks. Our
government here under a condition of com-
vealth, and their early laws were of a nature
ality.

nment rests not more on political constitu-
regulate the descent and transmission of prop-
uld not have been maintained, where property
principles of the feudal system; nor, on the
constitution possibly exist with us. Our New
ther no great capitals from Europe; and if
productive in which they could have been
m the whole feudal policy of the other con-
new country. There were, as yet, no lands
rendering service. The whole soil was unre-
y were themselves, either from their original
ty of their common interest, nearly on a gen-
ty. Their situation demanded a parcelling out
it may be fairly said, that this necessary act
m of their government. The character of their
ermined by the fundamental laws respecting
estates divisible among sons and daughters.
at first limited and curtailed, was afterwards
all freehold. The entailment of estates, long
s for fettering and tying up inheritances, were
n of society, and seldom made use of. On the
id was every way facilitated, even to the sub-
of debt. The establishment of public registries,
ms of conveyance, have greatly facilitated the
ne proprietor to another. The consequence of
eat subdivision of the soil, and a great equality
most certainly, of a popular government.[62]

various land systems were directed to economic
ls.[63] The land was generally held of the Crown
m of tenure. The individual secured his own
id, especially in the latter case, was pledged to

an annual quit-rent. Since official policy favored the process
grants and sales were liberal and quit-rents small. An immigra
actually settle down and work a piece of land generally had
quiring all he could use. Through such devices as the famou
system of the Southern colonies he could get additional land
one or more immigrants. Moreover, he could always buy land
the government or from one of the many speculative comp
purchased vast tracts of land or had been granted them by laz
conniving authorities. In some areas he might simply strike o
Squatting was a way of life among the impoverished Scotch-
sylvania and North Carolina, and the governments of these and
colonies in time came to recognize this practice by law. As to
pre-emption, the squatters of Pennsylvania had a memorable

> In doing this by force, they alleged that it was against the
> and nature that so much land should be idle while so man
> wanted it to labor on and to raise their bread.[64]

The result of this laxity in the middle and Southern colonies
in which disorder, fraud, and inequity were more prevalent t
New England way. Although conditions were somewhat mo
in the middle than in the Southern colonies, engrossing and ten
a peak in New York [65] and utter confusion rock bottom in
area of "so many doubtfull titles and rights that it creates an
and profitable pool for the lawyers." [66] Primogeniture, enta
rents disappeared generally in the region south of New Engla
the Revolution, although here and there—as in the case of
primogeniture in Pennsylvania—more liberal techniques we
The quit-rents are a clear example of the way in which an e
tution can work both for and against the course of liberty.
quit-rent was a relic of feudalism and cause of much social
was also, wherever collected with any efficiency, a powerfu
large holdings and arrant speculation.

The eighteenth century witnessed a lamentable trend towa
tion in all the Southern colonies. Even in areas where the p
firmest sway, however, the small farmer was present in sizable
lax methods of the South had mixed social results.[67] The conditi
land cheaper and easier to acquire for poor men in the Caroli
men in Connecticut also made possible more abuses and mo

We must not end this discussion of land systems in the
sour note. A shocking amount of land passed into the hands of
yet many of these people played a valuable promotional role.
fortune of the colonial period that the thing for which the pl
gered and thirsted was also the thing from which returns on
ment were most spectacular. Yet it cannot be said that eith
or liberty was held back by speculation except in a few notor
A gentleman in Philadelphia could report in 1768 that "Every

made here within these 50 years has been by land," [70] but he could also
have reported that for every great fortune made by a Quaker in Philadelphia
a hundred good livings had been made by Germans and Scotch-Irish in the
valleys to the west and north. This was essentially the state of affairs through
most of colonial America. Despite a distressing catalogue of inequity, speculation, greed, class conflict, and downright corruption, land was easier to acquire, keep, work, sell, and will in the colonies than in any other place in
the Atlantic world. By the middle of the eighteenth century the land was
supporting a hardy yeomanry whose children and grandchildren were to
provide the decisive spirit and substance of the Revolution, Jeffersonian
Democracy, and Jacksonian Democracy. Land for the brave man's asking,
"free land . . . open to a fit people," [71] was the paramount economic factor
of freedom in colonial America. Thus might tens of thousands of Americans
have mused:

> The instant I enter on my own land, the bright idea of property, of ex-
> clusive right, of independence exalt my mind. Precious soil, I say to myself,
> by what singular custom of law is it that thou wast made to constitute the
> riches of the freeholder? What should we American farmers be without
> the distinct possession of that soil? It feeds, it clothes us, from it we draw
> even a great exuberancy, our best meat, our richest drink, the very honey of
> our bees comes from this privileged spot. No wonder we should thus cher-
> ish its possession, no wonder that so many Europeans who have never been
> able to say that such portion of land was theirs, cross the Atlantic to realise
> that happiness. This formerly rude soil has been converted by my father
> into a pleasant farm, and in return it has established all our rights; on it is
> founded our rank, our freedom, our power as citizens, our importance as
> inhabitants of such a district. These images I must confess I always behold
> with pleasure, and extend them as far as my imagination can reach: for this
> is what may be called the true and the only philosophy of an American
> farmer.[72]

THE GROWTH OF CAPITALISM. The American climate, writes Louis Hacker,
"has always been capitalist." [73] We have already had occasion to inquire into
the validity of this bold assertion and have discovered that many of the
elements of capitalism—private ownership of means of production, the primacy of the profit motive, and the use of credit and the wage system—
flourished within the context of colonial mercantilism. The growth of this
commercial and agrarian capitalism prepared the way for the triumph of
industrial capitalism, which in turn shaped the destiny of modern America.

The development of capitalist institutions in the colonies was, of course,
a related phase of the rise of capitalism in Europe. Throughout the colonial
period enterprise in America was tied in tightly to the economy of the
mother country, and not until long after the great political break did England's former colonies strike out radically on their own line of economic
development. If the colonies exhibited certain unique details of developing
capitalism, they nevertheless conformed faithfully to the broad outlines of
the European economy. As Mr. Hacker also reminds us, "The growth of

our economic institutionalism, that is to say, the various phases of capitalism, has been the growth of Europe's. Capitalism was a European phenomenon; and we inherited it." [74] It does Americans no harm to remember these things; to recall, for example, that the industrial revolution in America came after and was spurred by the industrial revolution in England.

Yet the colonists made important contributions to capitalism, especially to the fact of economic individualism, and thereby created an economy with a flavor all its own. The techniques and assumptions of mercantilism never did flourish as vigorously in America as in England. The state was not, and in the nature of things could not be, the bureaucratic triumph that it was in England and Europe. Mercantilism as a system of internal regulation was always in a condition of gradual decline, although the revival of controls during the Revolution proves that its basic principles had by no means fallen into the disrepute of later times. Mercantile legislation remained on the books and mercantile assumptions in the air, but by the end of the colonial period laissez-faire practices were prevalent in commerce, manufacturing, and agriculture.

Theories of laissez-faire did not keep pace with the progress of capitalism. Certain doctrines of economic individualism attained a vogue in the colonies. The common-sense creed of "industry and frugality" was proclaimed by preachers like Samuel Whitman and laymen like Franklin.[75] A tentative belief in free trade and the profit motive persuaded the minds of several far-seeing colonists.[76] Yet a full-blown faith in laissez-faire did not take hold until after the Revolution. The colonists were far more neutral in matters of economic doctrine than their ancestors or descendants. Few of them asserted for publication that this or that economic system was an absolute prerequisite of national power or human freedom. Economic thought in the colonial period was traditional, self-contradictory, primitive, and generally quite nebulous.

Whatever the state of economic theory in colonial America, the realities of economic fact pointed toward the future. The instruments of developing capitalism inherited from the mother country were put to work in virgin soil. Commercial feudalism, like agrarian feudalism, proved exceedingly short-lived amid the primitive bounty of the American continent. Most important for the rise of liberty in the colonies, the elements of capitalism favored the release of the pent-up energies of thousands of men with whom America alone could swap freedom and security for sweat and resolution. The farmer, merchant, mariner, and craftsman were all capitalists who, like those of modern America, pursued their own destinies within the limiting but not frustrating framework of a mixed economy. The colonies were not dedicated officially to free enterprise, but they were full of free-enterprisers.

If for some men the transition from feudalism to capitalism meant only the supplanting of one form of serfdom by another, for many more it was the opening of the great doors of opportunity. If the evolution of colonial capitalism carried with it a spate of class conflicts over land and currency, these conflicts, too, hastened the day of liberty. Forest,[77] sea, and soil[78]; the resolute men who worked them; the Anglo-European legacy of capitalist arrangements and methods—these were the ingredients of opportunity and individualism, which were in turn the gifts of colonial capitalism to American social and political liberty.

THE FACTORS OF FREEDOM: II

WAGES AND CONDITIONS OF LABOR. Most men in most societies work with their hands for a living. The wages and conditions of labor are therefore a major·determinant of the extent and tenacity of human freedom. It was a fact of huge moment for the rise of American liberty that the price of labor was higher in the colonies than in England or Europe and that conditions of work were more humane and pleasant. Wage-earners, in the modern sense of the phrase, were comparatively few in the colonies, except in certain ports, cities, and northern villages. Yet by 1765 they constituted an important class, one in which many part-time farmers could also be counted. The progress of this class toward a "democracy of labor"—a general pattern of employment marked by decent wages and working conditions, protections against arbitrary employers, a philosophy preaching the dignity of labor, opportunities for advancement, and legal cushions against disaster— was an important economic factor of freedom. By no means were all these advantages realized, but colonial labor had come a long way from England and mercantilism.

In the mercantile system the place of labor was designedly mean and subordinate. "It was the fate of the workers to be poor that the nation might be rich, and to be ceaselessly diligent that the nation might be powerful." [79] The ideal laborer shunned idleness, raised a large family, lived in poverty, and received his pittance with a smile. The real laborer, as Defoe wrote in echo of all mercantilists, was "saucy, mutinous, and beggarly." [80] It was therefore the business of the state to regulate him thoroughly. Maximum- not minimum-wage legislation was characteristic of mercantilism, for only thus could the hated "forraigners" be undersold in the struggle for markets. Government intervened in capitalist enterprise not to raise the poor man up but to keep him down.

Mercantilist doctrines of labor, which were supported at crucial points by the medieval notions of the Puritans, were brought with official approval to Massachusetts and Virginia. Most early colonies took a hard stab at legislation designed to control high wages,[81] and the journals of the gentleman adventurers are full of complaints against "excessive rates of laborers' and workmen's wages" [82] and "great extortion used by divers persons of little conscience." [83] Massachusetts and her towns enacted laws and orders that set maximum wages and minimum hours, made labor compulsory under certain circumstances, punished idleness and vagrancy, impressed certain classes for labor on public works, and dealt severely with strangers. The other colonies were not far behind.[84] Had the ruling class in the ʼearly colonies had its way, low wages and long hours would have been the perpetual lot of the American workingman.

The land rather than the ruling class had its way in the end. Dear land and cheap labor depressed the common man in Europe; cheap land and dear labor raised him up in America. The existence of vast tracts of land and of schemes for their settlement drew a constant stream of workers away from wage-earning and into agricultural self-support. The economic history of the colonies is marked by a chronic scarcity of all types of labor, and thus by a consistently high scale of wages. Mercantilism and medievalism alike were undermined by the American environment. Regulation of wages and of other problems of labor was gradually abandoned, first by the colonies, then by the towns. A great mass of early legislation went unenforced, and further attempts at regulation were discouraged. Dozens of diaries and official reports pay tribute to the lure of uncultivated lands. Wrote Governor John Wentworth of New Hampshire in 1768:

> The people are by no means inclined to any sort of manufacture. Scarcely a shoemaker, a joiner, or silversmith but quits his trade, as soon as he can get able to buy a little tract of land and build a cottage in the wilderness.[85]

Governor Henry Moore of New York echoed this observation in a letter to the Board of Trade (1767):

> The Price of Labour is so great in this part of the World, that it will always prove the greatest obstacle to any Manufactures attempted to be set up here, and the genius of the People in a Country where every one can have Land to work upon leads them so naturally into Agriculture, that it prevails over every other occupation. There can be no stronger Instances of this, than in the servants Imported from Europe of different Trades; as soon as the Time stipulated in their Indentures is expired, they immediately quit their Masters, and get a small tract of Land, in settling which for the first three or four years they lead miserable lives, and in the most abject Poverty; but all this is patiently borne and submitted to with the greatest chearfulness, the Satisfaction of being Land holders smooths every difficulty, and makes them prefer this manner of living to that comfortable subsistence which they could procure for themselves and their families by working at the Trades in which they were brought up.
>
> The Master of a Glass-house; which was set up here a few years ago, now a Bankrupt, assured me that his ruin was owing to no other cause than being deserted in this manner by his servants, which he had Imported at a great expence; and that many others had suffered and been reduced as he was, by the same kind of Misfortune.[86]

The author of *American Husbandry* spoke of the paradoxical fact that "nothing but a high price will induce men to labour at all, and at the same time it presently puts a conclusion to it by so soon enabling them to take a piece of waste land." [87] Other factors, too, such as the cost of transportation from Europe, kept wages high.

The result was, as William Penn testified, that America was "a good poor Man's country." [88] Not only were nominal wages two or three times those prevalent in England, but real wages, according to the most competent testimony, "exceeded by 30 to 100 per cent the wages of a contemporary English workman." [89] The differences between colonial and English wages became less pronounced in the eighteenth century, but the real price of labor was always higher in the colonies.[90] The Royal Navy had to be especially on guard against desertion from ships in colonial ports.[91]

As wages were higher, so were conditions of work better. The laborer, who knew as well as his master of the existence of cheap land, must certainly have been a freer spirit than his hemmed-in British brother. Part-time subsistence agriculture gave thousands of wage-earners an added measure of security. The absence of any remnants of the guild system gave other men the security that goes with being a jack-of-all trades. "If any one could or would carry on ten trades," wrote a German traveler, "no one would have a right to prevent him." [92] And apparently many colonists did carry on at least a half dozen at a time. Even the apprentice system seems to have been more easy-going,[93] since it was often directed to purposes other than the maintenance of craft traditions and monopolies.

In our terms, of course, conditions of labor were hard and primitive. The great panoply of protective legislation that cushions the shock of industrial capitalism had only a meager counterpart in colonial statutes. No unions emerged to give the colonial worker the strength of collectivity.[94] No strike of workingmen took place in the colonial era.[95] No labor-saving machinery was installed on a large scale—to be welcomed or resisted. The worker in America, as everywhere in the Western world, had to shift for himself. Yet it could be said of America, as of nowhere in the Western world, that cheap land, high wages, short supply, and increasing social mobility permitted the worker to shift for himself with some hope of success. By our standards his life was "poore, nasty, brutish, and short." By the standards of seventeenth- and eighteenth-century England or Germany his life was free and productive.

The high price of labor had ill effects as well as good. An abundance of land and a scarcity of free labor drove profit-seeking planters and farmers to the easy but unhappy solution of unfree labor. Whatever the price or quantity of free labor, slavery and the indenture system would have developed in the colonies; yet the thriving condition of slavery in the South and of bonded servitude in the middle colonies was nourished substantially by the dearness of free labor. The indenture system was, all things considered, a workable and not-too-baneful solution to one of the hard problems of a new country in a rough age, but slavery was a curse for which we have not yet paid the full price. If the colonial system of labor made many men free, it made other men slaves or, what is often worse, slave-owners. And in the end it was the skilled white artisan who suffered as much as anyone in the South, for the slave artisan replaced him almost completely in rural areas.[96] Some other social results of slavery will be mentioned in the chapter to follow.

In New England and the middle colonies the rise of a sizable body of skilled and unskilled free workers was a powerful impetus to political liberty. The colonial craftsman, as Carl Bridenbaugh has demonstrated, was a far more reputable person socially and politically than his counterpart in England.[97] Urban craftsmen were among the prime movers in the events of 1765 and 1775. The unskilled laborer, though still disfranchised, found his public voice in these headstrong years. The relative absence of poverty in the colonies had helped create a lower class ready for political emancipation. The Revolution did not free this class completely, but it stirred it to considerable activity.

THE CLASH OF ENGLISH AND AMERICAN INTERESTS. A final economic factor of freedom was the old colonial system itself. The seeds of independence were planted deep in a relationship in which one country assumed the role of eternal master over another that was peopled with some of its best stock and blessed with limitless opportunities for expansion. Englishmen in the American environment, and men of other proud breeds as well, would not always be satisfied with the short end of mercantilism. Few colonial writers echoed the elaborate mercantilist justification of colonies by remarking how pleasant it would be to remain forever a source of raw materials and market for finished goods.

The old colonial system was not just a figment of the ripe imaginations of Daniel Defoe, John Cary, Malachy Postlethwayt, and Sir Josiah Child. It existed in fact as well as theory—most concretely in the enforcement of the celebrated Navigation Acts, which governed England's commercial policy from 1651 to 1849. Of the three-hundred-odd instances of commercial legislation enacted in these two centuries, three laws in particular were directed toward the colonies: the Navigation Act of 1660 (re-enacted in 1661), the Staple Act of 1663, and the Act of Frauds of 1696.[98] For the colonies these laws laid down three controlling principles: (1) Trade between Britain and the colonies was barred to all but English or colonial ships manned by crews three-fourths Englishmen or colonials. (2) All colonial imports from Europe, except wine and salt from southern Europe and (before the Act of Union of 1707) servants, horses, and provisions from Scotland, had to pass through England. (3) Many colonial products were placed on the "enumerated" list—including, at one time or another, tobacco, sugar, indigo, rice, cotton, molasses, naval stores, spices, dye woods, pig- and bar-iron, pot- and pearl-ashes, hides, whale fins, and numerous other commodities England could not produce herself. These articles could be exported by the colonies only to Britain, Ireland, or other English colonies.

The Navigation Acts and their many modifications were plainly designed for mercantile ends. Through them England intended to secure a monopoly of the trade of the colonies: to take from them, pretty much at her own price, whatever colonial products she needed; to ship them, again largely at her own price, surpluses of her own finished goods; and to make sizable additional profits by acting as the mandatory entrepôt for colonial exports to and imports from Europe. At the same time, the colonists were left free to trade with the West Indies and southern Europe in such products as flour and fish, in order to pile up specie and credits to pay for still more English wares.

These acts guaranteed to English merchants the richest fruits of colonial commerce. The bounty system and other favoring legislation spurred the production of needed raw materials and staples. The only remaining problem for mercantilist concern was the potential threat of colonial manufacturing. The English manufacturers persuaded Parliament to meet this threat with three isolated but thoroughly imperial statutes: the Woolens Act of 1699, the Hat Act of 1732, and the Iron Act of 1750.[99] Each of these was designed to frustrate the growth of a colonial industry that was threatening to poach on the privileged preserve of a group of English manufacturers. The Woolens Act forbade the export of wool and wool products from one colony to another or to a foreign country. The Hat Act forbade the export of hats and limited each hatmaker to two apprentices. The Iron Act forbade the erection of ironworking establishments, and at the same time removed all duties on colonial pig- and bar-iron shipped to England.[100]

One final statute aimed at the overweening colonists was the result of the pressures of a uniquely vested interest. The Molasses Act of 1733,[101] which imposed prohibitive duties on rum, molasses, and sugar imported into the colonies from the non-British West Indies, was passed by Parliament under the whip of an organized minority group. In the French West Indies the Northern merchants had found a cheaper, more plentiful source of raw materials for New England rum, and the planters of Jamaica and the sugar islands—many of whom lived in England and sat in Parliament—were determined to ruin the French even if this meant ruining the New Englanders as well.

More important than the laws themselves was the manner of their enforcement. Generations of historians have sought to evaluate the administration of this array of legislation, and on these points general agreement now exists: The Navigation Acts were, all things considered, reasonably well enforced,[102] especially after the Act of 1696 incorporating governors in the administrative system and orders of 1697 standardizing procedures for vice-admiralty courts. The Woolens, Hat, and Iron acts were largely ignored by the colonists, since machinery for steady enforcement of this program did not exist.[103] The Molasses Act, as every schoolboy knows or used to know, was the most flagrantly disregarded law between the Seventh Commandment and the Volstead Act. The Molasses Act, not the Navigation Acts, made smuggling part of the early American way of life.[104] The extent of this practice is indicated in the fact that Rhode Island alone imported more molasses annually than the total output of the British West Indies. So vital was this trade to the commercial colonies that it persisted throughout the French and Indian War—an act of treason on an epic scale.[105] In an average year in the 1750's Massachusetts merchants imported 500 hogsheads of molasses legally from the British West Indies and 14,500 hogsheads illegally from the French.

The Privy Council, spurred and supported by the Board of Trade, did its part to keep the colonies in their proper place in the old colonial system.

It disallowed provincial laws that encouraged home industries, discriminated against English wares, scaled down the eternal and ever-mounting colonial debts, placed export duties on enumerated commodities or import duties on English merchandise, monopolized Indian trade, authorized payments of quit-rents in paper money, interfered with the transporting of convicts and slaves, or in any way smacked of possible independence rather than perpetual dependence.[106] Specific and circular instructions went out to governors advising them to exercise this or that power, especially the veto, for mercantile ends. Parliament was advised of the need for legislation to check colonial presumptions. In such defenses of the old colonial system as the fight against paper money, the Privy Council used all these methods—disallowance, instructions, and legislative recommendations—with vigor and success.

The economic results of this network of law and administration were not nearly so disastrous as some historians have insisted. L. A. Harper has estimated tentatively that the burdens of mercantilism cost the colonies something over three million dollars a year.[107] An example of how English merchants reaped extra profits from the system is the fact that in the 1760's they re-exported three fourths of the tobacco and rice imported from the Southern colonies.[108] Yet Harper is quick to point out that the imperial blessings of military and naval protection cannot be reckoned in statistical tables. Certainly the colonies received many benefits, the most important of which was their qualified inclusion in rather than total exclusion from a great commercial system. England was the natural monopolist of much of the colonists' trade and looked with favor, or at worst with neutrality, on much of the circuitous trade based on fish, flour, provisions, and rum. Although the Woolens, Hat, and Iron acts may have frightened some timid capital away from these infant enterprises, colonial conditions rather than English laws explain the absence of manufacturing. The industrial development of the colonies was just about where it would have been had Americans been allowed to determine their own policies. Until the middle of the eighteenth century colonial and world conditions were such that the Americans, especially the merchants of the North, gained more than they lost from the old colonial system.[109]

The political results of mercantilism were favorable to the growth of liberty and self-government. For all their benefits to the colonies, the Navigation Acts were a constant source of petty irritation to many colonial merchants, farmers, and consumers, causing them, as a Swedish traveler noted in 1748, "to grow less tender for their mother country." [110] The tension that existed between colonial and vice-admiralty courts was one major cause and effect of this irritation. The Woolens and Hat acts stirred up few political quarrels, but the Iron Act, which was aimed at the fastest-growing and most menacing colonial industry, was followed in due course by provincial laws encouraging new plants in New Jersey, Massachusetts, and Pennsylvania. The Iron Act was thus far more helpful to colonial propagandists than it was harmful to colonial merchants. The employment of gubernatorial veto and royal disallowance to slap down headstrong colonial legislation on subjects such as land, currency, and commerce evoked considerable protest. A healthy proportion of the political battles between governor and assembly were fought over economic problems. For example, behind the political squabbles over paper money stood the opposing economic camps of hard-money England and easy-money America. The Paper Money Act of 1751 was a portent of things to come. Most merchants begged for it; the rural debtors opposed it. Between them they managed to raise for the first time in years the question of Parliament's authority. The clash of colonial aspiration and imperial mercantilism was a constant spur to republicanism in thought and action.

After 1765, of course, the conflict of English and American economic self-interest became more intense and sharply defined. It is not the business of this chapter to weigh once again, as so many historians have weighed, the many causes of the American Revolution.[111] It should be sufficient to remark that for one compelling economic reason—the rise of the colonies to a level of population, ingenuity, and surplus capital at which the growth of apparent economic independence was about to begin—the determination of George III's government to tighten up the loose stays in the old colonial system was certain to lead to political trouble. The further determination of his government to restrict the few allowable outlets for colonial capital and initiative—western lands [112] and ocean-going commerce—did as much to hasten the final breach as did any other factor. Yet Part 1 of this book is the story of colonial development before 1765, and in this period economic forces helped create not a revolution but the makings of one. Forest, sea, and soil; commerce, agriculture, and manufacturing; free labor, servitude, and slavery; counting-house, mill, farm, and plantation; rum, tobacco, rice, and flour; private ownership, profits, speculation, wages, and credits; and above all the growth of economic opportunity, mobility, and individualism—these were the marks, not all of them exactly inspiring, of an economy that could not go on much longer in a state of political dependency. The wisest English heads were already convinced that the colonies, especially those to the north, "in respect of climate, soil, agriculture and manufactures, possess most of the requisites of an independant people." [113] Burke caught the flavor of American enterprise when he paid his famous tribute to the New England whalers:

> Whilst we follow them among the tumbling mountains of ice, and behold them penetrating into the deepest frozen recesses of Hudson's Bay and Davis's Straits, whilst we are looking for them beneath the arctic circle, we hear that they have pierced into the opposite region of polar cold, that they are at the antipodes, and engaged under the frozen serpent of the south. Falkland Island, which seemed too remote and romantic an object for the grasp of national ambition, is but a stage and resting-place in the progress of their victorious industry. Nor is the equinoctial heat more discouraging to them, than the accumulated winter of both the poles. We know that whilst some of them draw the line and strike the harpoon on the coast of Africa, others run the longitude, and pursue their gigantic game along the coast of Brazil. No sea but what is vexed by their fisheries. No climate that

is not witness to their toils. Neither the perseverance of Holland, nor the activity of France, nor the dexterous and firm sagacity of English enterprise, ever carried this most perilous mode of hard industry to the extent to which it has been pushed by this recent people; a people who are still, as it were, but in the gristle, and not yet hardened into the bone of manhood. When I contemplate these things; when I know that the colonies in general owe little or nothing to any care of ours, and that they are not squeezed into this happy form by the constraints of watchful and suspicious government, but that, through a wise and salutary neglect, a generous nature has been suffered to take her own way to perfection; when I reflect upon these effects, when I see how profitable they have been to us, I feel all the pride of power sink, and all presumption in the wisdom of human contrivances melt and die away within me. My rigour relents. I pardon something to the spirit of liberty.[114]

Such a people, it seems plain, were no longer colonials to be regulated and taxed for imperial purposes.

CHAPTER FOUR

Colonial Society
and the Rise of Liberty

THE sociology of the American settlements is a subject to which increasing numbers of colonial historians now devote their talents for tireless probing and prudent reconstruction. In recent years—thanks to the labors of men like Wertenbaker, Morris, Bridenbaugh, Adams, Jernegan, A. E. Smith, and a host of lesser scholars writing "in partial fulfillment of the requirements for the degree of Doctor of Philosophy"—we have learned a great deal we had only guessed at before about social problems in colonial times. We have learned, too, of the profound influence of social attitudes on the evolution of self-government and of a libertarian faith.

Social problems and attitudes and their influence on political liberty are the concern of this chapter. We shall confine it to a hard core of sociological topics, placing emphasis as usual on their significance for politics and political theory: the class structure of the colonies; the units of social organization—family, farm, plantation, town, and city; certain features and problems common to all societies, such as crime and punishment, status of women and children, and care of the unfortunate; and, once again, the factors of freedom, those broad social developments which made it possible for the colonists to think, act, and ultimately fight in terms of human liberty.[1] It should be noted that in each of the preliminary chapters we discussed questions that might easily have been included under this heading: in Chapter 1, political behavior, especially the extent of popular participation in politics; in Chapter 2, a variety of problems of individual belief and group behavior in an age when many men considered their religion a way of life; in Chapter 3, the economic forces that helped shape society. And we have yet to examine two further areas of sociological inquiry: in Chapter 5, certain aspects of culture and education, both of them subjects that the social historian counts as important districts within his spacious province, and, in the introduction to Part 2, the racial and national origins of the people of the colonies.

THE CLASS STRUCTURE

Each of the thirteen colonies in 1765 exhibited a class structure more developed and generally acknowledged than any we could imagine in modern America. In some areas classes existed from the very first settlement; in others they developed from an original condition of equality under circumstances that favored the growth of social divisions. Two circumstances in particular led to the formation of classes: the influence of a frontier economy, above all the fact that land and profits could be obtained by different men in grossly different quantities; and the inheritance from England and Europe of a tradition of social stratification. While the class structure was not so pronounced and rigid as that of England or Germany, it was well-defined enough to work a determining influence on political activity.

To define a class and distinguish it from other classes is no simple matter, especially when it rides the buoyant but treacherous waves of a pioneer society. Yet the thinking colonist, had he been asked about the "ranks" and "sorts" of people in his own experience, could have pointed with some accuracy to five separate classes of men who passed daily before his eyes: the "better sort," which in some times and places was merely the top class on the ladder but in others was a genuine aristocracy made up of large land-holders, crown officials, merchants, and allied lawyers and professional men; the "middling sort," the great body of small land-holders, independent artisans, shopkeepers, petty officials, and professional men of lesser pretensions; the "meaner sort," the free but depressed category of poor men who were laborers, servants, dependent artisans, sailors, unprosperous farmers, and nondescript drifters; the bonded white servants, an even meaner sort, who served some master under an indenture limited in time; and the very lowest elements of society, the Negroes, of whom only a few thousand had been delivered from the curse of perpetual bondage into a precarious condition of legal freedom. All five of these strata of men had an immense influence on the development of the colonies, but only the first two took an active part in the fermenting process of self-government. Wealth, occupation, learning, ancestry, religion, national origin, breeding, and pretensions [2] were the ingredients of class distinction, and as always in America wealth and pretensions led all the rest.

THE BETTER SORT. Popular belief in the existence of a better sort—distinguishable from ordinary men by dress, bearing, and speech, and entitled to leadership, respect, and even deference—prevailed almost everywhere throughout the colonial period.[3] In 1636 the ruling elders of Massachusetts Bay agreed with Lord Say and Sele that the politically active community "should consist of two distinct ranks of men"—"gentlemen of the country" and "freeholders." [4] In 1651 the General Court of Massachusetts declared its "vtter detestation & dislike that men or women of meane condition . . . should take vppon them the garbe of gentlemen, by the wearing of golde or silver lace, or buttons." [5] In 1674 a tailor in York County, Virginia, was punished for racing a horse, since "it was contrary to law for a labourer to make a race, being a sport only for gentlemen." [6] In the eighteenth century both Harvard and Yale used "family dignity" as the chief criterion in "placing" each student in his class.[7] And in 1775 the revolutionary Virginia Convention resolved that "the natural strength, and only security of a free government" was "a well regulated militia, composed of Gentlemen and Yeomen." [8] These official opinions were echoed in thousands of letters, diaries, newspaper articles, and books in which authors expressed or implied a belief in the gentry and its right to lead.[9] Who were these gentlemen who dominated the social, economic, and political life of every colony?

The New England aristocracy of the eighteenth century was for the most part the product of an expanding commercial capitalism. The leading members of the upper class were the wealthy merchants, around whose central position revolved their lawyers, their ministers, and an occasional master artisan or shopkeeper of impeccable lineage. Only in Rhode Island was there an upper class chiefly dependent on extensive holdings of land for wealth and status. The Narragansett Planters, with their stock-producing plantations, gangs of Negro slaves, fast and famous horses, and orthodox Church-of-England opinions, were a fascinating variant from the normal social pattern.[10] In Massachusetts and New Hampshire there was frosting on the cake in the person of the royal governor, his devoted retinue of officials, and those merchants who displayed an abnormal desire to be classed as English gentry. Only in Boston, where reigned the Hutchinsons, Olivers, Faneuils, Hancocks, Amorys, Boylstons, and Lechmeres, and in Newport, where reigned (and slaved!) the Redwoods, Eastons, Wantons, Bernons, Malbones, Ellerys, Paines, Ayraults, and Brinleys, did capital accumulation, polite manners, and the uses of conspicuous wealth reach proportions that permitted the favored few to behave and think like true American aristocrats. Daniel West, an English visitor to Boston in 1720, acknowledged "that a gentleman from London would almost think himself at home at Boston, when he observes the number of people, their houses, their furniture, their tables, their dress and conversation, which perhaps is as splendid and showy as that of the most considerable tradesmen in London" [11]—about as decent a compliment as an Englishman could afford to pay to an upper class so actively concerned with the sources of its wealth. The wealthy merchants of Portsmouth, Salem, Providence, New Haven, and a half-dozen lesser ports could perhaps also be classed as a native aristocracy, but in hundreds of New England towns the better sort occupied a position not too far removed from that of the celebrated yeomen.

The middle colonies harbored two remarkable aristocracies. In New York, in many ways the most stratified of all thirteen colonies, an authentic aristocracy grew quickly out of the maldistribution of land.[12] Schuyler, De Lancey, Livingston, Beekman, Philipse, Lloyd, Van Cortlandt, Smith, Heathcote, Morris, and Van Rensselaer were the names of the most prominent landholding families.[13] As the colony developed, members of these powerful clans joined Crugers, Van Horns, Van Dams, Floyds, Bayards, and Waltons in the city in wringing profits and leisure from commerce and the law.[14] In the meantime, merchant families sought additional wealth and prestige by themselves acquiring landed estates. A politically important characteristic of the New York aristocracy was the fantastic pattern of intermarriage among leading families. When Abram De Peyster died in 1767, Van Cortlandts, De Lanceys, Beekmans, Livingstons, Schuylers, Jays, Philipses, and many other aristocratic families crowded the church to see their relative off to heaven. Cadwallader Colden, in recommending to the Board of Trade that Judge Robert R. Livingston be removed from judicial office, pointed out that "no Cause of any Consequence can come before him in which . . . he or the Livingston Family are not interested." [15] No aristocracy dominated all phases of a colony's affairs so completely as did these children of England, Holland, and France the life of New York. They ruled with condescension and lived in splendor.[16]

Philadelphia's aristocracy was commercial in character. Norrises, Shippens, Pembertons, Hills, Logans, Carpenters, Dickinsons, and Merediths were some of the solid Quaker families with which other non-Quaker families allied themselves as the city progressed toward its pre-Revolutionary peak of culture and urbanity. The persistence of inherited notions of social stratification is most clearly visible in the social attitudes of the Quakers, who rarely preached or practiced egalitarianism.[17] Here in Philadelphia, too, was exhibited most ridiculously that peculiar trait of our peculiar aristocracy: Consisting entirely of the children and grandchildren of self-made men, the upper class looked upon recently self-made men with a contempt that would have done credit to a Spanish grandee.

In the South flourished the most memorable of provincial aristocracies. However disparate their English origins, the planters of eighteenth-century Virginia [18]—Carters,[19] Byrds, Lees, Corbins, Randolphs, Fitzhughs, Beverleys, Blairs, Blands, Masons, and Pages—formed a true aristocracy that derived its status from the land and ruled in the Whig tradition. Cheap and exploitable land,[20] a plentiful supply of slaves, and an easily grown staple were the economic supports of the Virginia aristocracy. The first gentlemen of Maryland—Tilghmans, Darnalls, Carrolls, Ringgolds, Snowdens, Addisons, Dulanys, Taskers, Goldsboroughs—were hardly less eminent; [21] the first gentlemen of South Carolina—Pinckneys, Draytons, Middletons, Manigaults, Izards, Rutledges, Ravenels, Bees, and Hugers—were if anything more cultivated, haughty, and jealous of their privileges. Charleston was to South Carolina what New York City was to the Hudson Valley: the focal point of culture of an aristocracy with interests in both commerce and land. Slavery, the Anglican Church, and close social and economic ties with England gave the upper class in the South a special feeling that it was a genuine aristocracy,[22] one that in Eliza Pinckney's words lived "very Gentile and very much in the English taste." [23]

THE MIDDLING SORT. Throughout the colonies, but especially north of Maryland, a class of families who considered themselves neither "mean" nor "gentle" increased and multiplied. These were the self-respecting ancestors of the great middle class to which some eighty to ninety per cent of the American people now claim to belong. Up from this class had climbed hundreds of the proudest families of the aristocracy, and up to it climbed, especially in prosperous times, thousands upon thousands of former servants, laborers, and other unpropertied men. The middle class flourished alike on the farm or in the city. This was particularly true of New England, New Jersey, and Pennsylvania ("this wonderful province"),[24] the happy lands of the middling sort. The hardworking, self-reliant, property-conscious farmers of Essex, Fairfield, Bergen, and Bucks counties found their social and political equals in the hardworking, self-reliant, property-conscious shop-keepers and independent artisans of Boston, New London, Burlington, and Philadelphia.

In New York and the Southern colonies the middling sort lacked the numbers, secure status, and influence they enjoyed in Pennsylvania and New England. The land policies of the aristocracy in New York and the cruel sway of slavery and soil exhaustion in Virginia and South Carolina made the sturdy yeoman a much rarer bird in these highly stratified colonies than was good for their economic and social health. Yet the social pyramid showed a layer between the upper and lower classes: Small farms and freeholds dotted the map of New York; overseers and factors performed important functions in the Southern colonies; many yeomen refused to be driven out or depressed in Virginia; artisans and small tradesmen offered their services in New York, Norfolk, Charleston, Wilmington, and Baltimore; and out into the Piedmont and the valleys of the west streamed thousands who had no hope of being "gentle" and no intention of being "mean." North Carolina was the healthiest of those parts of the South where the combined pressures of the upper and lower classes were unable to drive the independent yeoman down or out.

THE MEANER SORT (FREE). The large class made up of poor but free whites was in many ways the unhappiest in the colonies. The man of the upper or middle class had his reputation and property, the indentured servant or slave had his legally defined status and obligations, however degrading. The poor white was cast upon his own in a world where the man who drifted was generally considered "mean."

The free white man with too little property or no property at all could be found in most professions and all colonies. He was most likely to be a tiller of the soil, which was often his own and as often some other man's. Most tenants and all farm laborers were members of the lower class. The line between the middling and inferior freeholder was drawn by each community in terms of property and stability. In every New England town or Southern parish there were prosperous yeomen fixed in the middle class and grubbing peasants fixed in the lower. Between these two groups swung a mass of farmers whom bad times made "mean" and good times "middling." Since the prosperous middling farmers were fully conscious of their status and political rights, this lower group was generally classed as "mean."

The line between the middle and lower class was more sharply drawn in the city or large village, where occupation and economic independence had more to do with a man's position. Dependent artisans, free servants, laborers, sailors, and apprentices made up the meaner sort in Boston, New York, and Philadelphia. Good times or bad, in country or in city, thousands of free whites were anchored permanently in the lower class. These were the men who lacked the intelligence, luck, or perseverance to set up shop for themselves or to acquire and work successfully the land that was theirs for the asking. Only in the South, where many a capable person was ground between the upper stone of the planters and the lower of Negro slavery, was the man of the lower class more likely to be the victim of circumstance rather than of his own shortcomings. A good portion of the meaner sort was the residue of those dregs of English society transported under bond or court order to the colonies.

THE MEANER SORT (BONDED). At one time or another in the colonial period more than a quarter of a million persons were placed willingly or unwillingly in the status known as indentured servitude.[25] This status was a species of semislavery limited in time (four to seven years) by contract and in severity by the European rather than African origin of the bonded man or woman. The indentured servant had in effect sold a number of years of labor in return for passage across the sea and the promise of certain limited benefits at the time of release. Most men and women of this class were bound before their departure to masters in America or to a ship captain or agent who would sell them and their contract upon arrival. A large number, particularly among the German families of Pennsylvania, came as "redemptioners" or "free-willers," with a chance to find a friend or relative to pay their passage before being turned back to the ship captain for auction to the highest bidder. A healthy fraction of the indentured class was in it willy-nilly: convicts, felons, and kidnapped persons, as well as debtors and other social unfortunates already in the colonies. The indentured white might serve in any capacity, even that of schoolmaster, but generally he was a farmhand or domestic servant.

Indentured servitude flourished most vigorously in seventeenth-century Virginia and Maryland [26] and in eighteenth-century Pennsylvania.[27] In Virginia in 1683 fully one sixth of the population was passing through the state of servitude.[28] Almost two thirds of the immigrants to Pennsylvania in the eighteenth century were indentured whites.[29] New England, suspicious of strangers and incapable of employing them in large numbers, received comparatively few of this class of men. South of New England, where cheap labor was a great and absorbing need, more than one half of all persons who migrated to the colonies were indentured servants. It is plain that, if only by weight of numbers, this fourth class was an important factor in the evolution of an indigenous American social pattern.

The indentured servant's lot was rough but endurable. Unlike the Negro slave, he was not completely dependent on the character of his master, for he had legal and property rights—and he was a white Christian. The age was one in which men were not unaccustomed to the notion of selling themselves or being sold. Indentured servitude was simply the English system of binding out the poor, young, and unemployed, reshaped to the insatiable needs of a frontier economy. Degraded men who entered or were forced into servitude were all the more degraded by this experience, but thousands of respectable Englishmen, Germans, and Scotch-Irish passed through servitude to liberty and often on to prosperity without any permanent loss of self-respect. Peter Kalm reported that many Germans in Pennsylvania preferred temporary bondage in order to learn the language and customs of the country and to "better be able to consider what they shall do when they have got their liberty." [30]

It would be pleasant to confirm the popular assumption that most indentured servants went on to become sturdy yeomen and independent artisans, but the harsh fact is, as A. E. Smith has proved conclusively,[31] that only a small fraction ever rose into the middle class. Most of these people were of humble origin, and most of them turned to humble occupations upon achieving their freedom. South of Connecticut the "meaner sort" were for the most part former bondsmen or convicts who had served their time. The vicious character of the time-serving convicts, the rise of a strong aristocracy, and the corrupting influence of slavery all contributed to the decline in status of the servant class in the later decades of the colonial period. Like all institutions geared to pioneer needs, indentured servitude was a mixed blessing for colonial society.[32]

THE SLAVES. Lowest of the social classes were the Negro slaves. Some idea of the importance of this miserable order of unwilling captives may be drawn from the estimated census of 1765: 1,450,000 whites, 400,000 Negroes. All but a tiny fraction of the latter were chattel slaves, fully seven eighths of them living in the five southernmost colonies. In South Carolina they outnumbered the white population by two to one.[33] And even in the North, especially in New York, Rhode Island, and Connecticut,[34] they were counted in thousands. Slavery existed in law and fact in each of the thirteen colonies.[35]

Negro slavery was the social product of many powerful forces. Among the most important were: the search for cheap labor by an economy devoted to the wasteful production of tobacco, rice, and indigo; the desire of slaver and planter for profits and more profits; [36] the mores and traditions of a coldblooded age; [37] and the crude facts that the Negro was strong, black, and primitive, though hardly more primitive than many poor whites. Slavery was not immediately established with the landing of the first Negroes but developed in response to circumstances of place and time. The social position of the Negro, if it can be called that, grew worse rather than better as the Southern colonies expanded and prospered.

The sorrowful story of Negro slavery has been too well and often told to be repeated here,[38] but attention should be called to two socially significant aspects of this institution: the attitudes of the four white classes toward this fifth order of men, and the total effect of slavery on colonial society.

Few white colonists ever regarded the Negro as even a very inferior and unfortunate brother. Most men were indifferent to his problems or fate, assuming that if and when freed he and his fellows would naturally constitute the lowest class. Only among the poor whites of the South was there a well-defined class attitude toward the Negro; and, as might be expected in an essentially competitive situation, it was one of veiled hostility or vicious hatred. The general colonial attitude toward slaves and slavery was essentially this: Until the very days of the Revolution few white men, even the most sincere friends of liberty, thought it anything but "natural" that such a condition should exist. The mental climate of the colonies was overwhelmingly hostile to the assumption that the Negro was a whole man. Advertisements hawking "several negro Girls and a negro Boy, and likewise good Cheshire Cheese" ran in the newspapers constantly.[39] Only in Pennsylvania and certain parts of rural New England did the Negro, slave or free, enjoy reasonably normal and intimate contacts with the white man. As a result, most speculation about natural rights and equality simply ignored the Negro. Evidence of this social attitude was the extremely restricted and degraded life led by the free Negro, even in New England.[40]

The influence of slavery on colonial society was terrible in consequence. If slavery helped develop the Southern colonies much faster than might otherwise have been expected, its total effect was a distressing catalogue of social ills: It exalted a few whites, degraded many more, permitted sinfully wasteful agriculture, created a miasma of fear in areas where Negroes were plentiful,[41] hardened class lines, stunted the growth of the Southern middle class, cheapened respect for labor, and dehumanized man's sympathy for man in an age already inhuman enough.[42] As for the slave himself, the sin against him was so colossal as to give most Americans the chills even to this day. The specious argument that the Negro was better off as a slave until he could be raised to the minimal standards of the white man's civilization was completely undercut by colonial laws that made slaves of the children of slaves. Neither economically nor spiritually was slavery seriously challenged at any time in the colonial period. There was no place for the Negro in the American definition of the rights of man.

In conclusion, these characteristics of the class structure were of major significance in shaping political attitudes: the inherited concept of stratification, which few colonists had any intention of rejecting completely; the indigenous and functional nature of the several classes, which were as much the product of the American environment as of the European heritage; the numerous criteria of class distinctions, of which property was the most decisive; the evolving content of these criteria, evidenced by the elevation of lawyers and doctors in the eighteenth century; the fluidity of membership in each class, with the Negro alone anchored permanently in his status; the softening of the twin attitudes of deference and condescension, at least by English standards; the relatively strong feeling of social solidarity, thanks to an expanding middle class and a rising standard of living; and the general acceptance of the doctrine of classes, a stultifying belief tempered considerably by the equally accepted doctrine that the individual should rise or fall by his own virtues and capacities. Then as now Americans were convinced that a fluid class structure was totally compatible with constitutional government and political liberty.

UNITS OF SOCIAL ORGANIZATION

Fully as important as the class structure was the manner in which the colonists were organized to pursue their economic, educational, spiritual, and cultural ends. Social organization in early America exhibited different aspects in different sections. In New England society was compact, communal, and cellular. In the South it was dispersed, particularized, yet also cellular. The element that held together the variants in different areas was the basic unit of organization, the family. We shall inspect this unit briefly, then turn to the larger units through which it fulfilled its many functions.

THE FAMILY. It is hard for modern Americans to realize how dominant a role the family played in the lives of their colonial ancestors.[43] Tradition, circumstance, and law united to give the family a prime responsibility for the successful functioning of society. In response to the burdens thrust upon it, the colonial family was highly patriarchal in organization.[44] The head of the family, however kindly, was a near-absolute master within the unit; at the same time, he was its exclusive representative to the larger community in political, economic, and religious affairs. The family as a social unit not only incorporated parents, children, and all manner of dependent relatives, but also included freed and bonded servants, slaves, and boarders. An average family might easily number twenty or thirty people. Few were the colonists who would or could "live alone and like it." "The selfish luxury of solitary living" was looked upon with suspicion. In early New England law and custom made life particularly uncomfortable for the unmarried and unattached man or woman. A New Haven law of 1656 ordered:

> That no single person of either Sex, do henceforward board, diet, or Sojourn, or be permitted so to do, or to have lodging; or house room within any of the Plantations of this Jurisdiction, but either in some allowed Relation, or in some approved Family licensed thereunto, by the court, or by a Magistrate, or some Officer, or Officers in that Plantation, appointed thereunto, where there is no Magistrate; The Governor of which Family, so licensed, shal as he may conveniently, duly observe the course, carriage, and behaviour, of every such single person, whether he, or she walk diligently in a constant imployment, attending both Family duties, and the publick worship of God, and keeping good order day and night, or otherwise.[45]

As for the South, Colonel Byrd wrote that "an Old Maid or an Old Bachelor are as scarce among us and reckoned as ominous as a Blazing Star." [46] The often ludicrous haste with which widows and widowers sought remarriage attests to the intrinsic nature of the family tie.[47]

The family served society in a half-dozen essential capacities. It was the key agency of human association, the leading instrument of education,[48] and an important secondary center of religious life and instruction. In addition, whether occupied primarily in farm or shop, it was a virtually self-sustaining economic unit and, in its developed stage, the leading producer of food and manufactured articles.[49]

The influence of the family upon society at large was visited forcefully upon the field of politics. Its focal position made the father a special person in the eyes of the world and thus helped justify the fact of limited suffrage. The family was a principal agent in diffusing those virtues out of which colonists thought the good society would rise: industry, frugality, humility, piety, honesty, charity, and that famous American blend of self-reliance and communal spirit. And finally, it was a powerful force for social stability in a society that was becoming progressively more "open."

THE ISOLATED FARM. Although the family was the cell of three larger forms of social organization—plantation, town, and city—it also existed as a self-contained unit, with no buffer except a poorly organized county between it and the colony. This was especially true of the family engaged in limited and freehold farming in the South in the seventeenth century and almost everywhere outside settled New England in the eighteenth.[50] The consuming purpose of families in this category was plain: to farm for subsistence and if possible for exchange. To this paramount task each member of the family contributed his or her efforts. Few were the American farms that had even a single hired man or bonded servant. The only person to have contact with the larger world—and he only rarely—was the father. The family itself lived, loved, suffered, and toiled in a state of isolation almost impossible to comprehend. Thousands of families were denied even the occasional diversions of a crossroads settlement or a church.

The social attitudes generated by this life of narrow toil and isolation were understandably mixed. Certainly it encouraged crudity, ignorance, slovenliness, immorality, violence, shiftlessness, and incredible parochialism; [51] yet fierce independence, lack of concern for social standing, voluntary co-operation, and inquisitive friendliness to strangers [52] were other qualities the open country bred more generously than the built-up settlement. And the gathering resentments harbored by this class of men—who were often in debt, under-represented or ignored in the developing process of self-government, plagued by rents and taxes, and exposed without support to the ravages of Indian warfare—proved a powerful force for the coming of real democracy.

THE PLANTATION. The rural isolation of the farm was matched by that of the plantation, but in most other particulars the latter was a quite different type of social institution. Here the family was the center of a group that might easily number fifty to one hundred relatives, tenants, hired workers, and slaves. The line between the large farm and small plantation was often quite difficult to trace, but there was no mistaking the true plantation. Some of its distinguishing marks were: a large tract of land; an economic pattern on one hand quite self-contained, on the other devoted to growing a staple for export; a numerous and servile working force; a master and mistress who worked hard but avoided menial labor; and a family that strove consciously to live in gentle style, importing many of its props and ideas from England.[53]

The plantation family refused to be provincialized by its distance from other plantations and from centers of population and culture. Its members, especially the head, were a hundred times more mobile than the poor farming family. An area of plantations therefore produced a more sociable, cultivated, worldly, and public-spirited class of men than an area of small and struggling farms.[54] The gulf between planter and yeoman yawned twice as large in those counties where they lived side by side. One of the consuming purposes of the planter was to make it possible for his children to live on the same high level he had occupied. He therefore spent considerable time finding proper husbands for his daughters and adequate lands for his sons. This attitude of class consciousness and social aspiration distinguished the planter from the lesser men about him. The colonial plantation, whether devoted to indigo in Georgia, rice in the Carolinas, tobacco in Virginia and Maryland, or stock-raising in southwestern Rhode Island, was the fertile nursery of America's landed aristocracy. The New York manor, an overextended rural unit built on tenantry rather than slavery, also produced a ruling attitude of caste, culture, and conservatism. It is interesting to note that the Church of England took firmest root in those areas where the plantation was an essential unit of the social pattern.

THE TOWN. The New England town was the most highly developed unit of communal organization in the colonies.[55] Like most early American institutions it was a product of the interaction of an English inheritance and a wilderness environment. In the close-knit settlements of New England, and in their early offshoots in New York and New Jersey, the family joined with other families of like mind and purpose in a planned pattern of community living quite removed from that of the Southern colonies. We have already examined or will examine shortly the techniques through which the men of the towns achieved their common ends in politics, land distribution, religion, and education. In each of these matters they placed constant emphasis on the larger purposes of the community rather than the wishes or whims of the individual. A newcomer or would-be purchaser had to meet the standards of the community before he could settle in a New England or Long Island town. The records are full of entries like these:

It is ordered yt whosoever shall take up a lot in Towne shal live upon it himselfe and also yt no man shal sell his alotment or any part thereof unless it be to such as ye Towne shall aprove of and give consent to ye sale thereof.

It is ordered that Daniel Turner shall within the space of ffortnite eythe sojurne in some ffamily or bee a servant to some or else Depart the towne.

at a towne meeting the 6th of June 1664 is was voted and agreed by the magar vot that Jery Wood shall have liberty to perchas heare in this towne and to be reseved as an inhabitante.[56]

The townsman was made constantly aware that he could enjoy his measure of freedom only as part of a more important whole:

at a towne meeting it was voeted and agread vpon that the fence be maed vp at the end of the ould feeld fence and thay that doe not com to help about it the next Thursday every man that is wanting shall pay five shillens.[57]

He was permitted isolation or eccentricity in many affairs that we would find important, but in all matters of vital concern to the community he was asked for public service and for conformity in thought and action. The social result was a mixture of individualism and communal feeling that boded well for the democratic future. The town resolved the conflicting claims of liberty and authority more sensibly than any other institution in colonial America. If it bred provincialism, it also bred ordered liberty.

A famous son of a famous town explained why New Englanders found New England superior to "every other colony in America and, indeed, of every other part of the world that I know anything of":

1. The people are purer English blood; less mixed with Scotch, Irish, Dutch, French, Danish, Swedish, etc., than any other; and descended from Englishmen, too, who left Europe in purer times than the present, and less tainted with corruption than those they left behind them.

2. The institutions in New England for the support of religion, morals, and decency exceed any other; obliging every parish to have a minister, and every person to go to meeting, etc.

3. The public institutions in New England for the education of youth, supporting colleges at the public expense, and obliging towns to maintain grammar schools, are not equaled, and never were, in any part of the world.

4. The division of our territory, that is, our counties, into townships; empowering towns to assemble, choose officers, make laws, mend roads, and twenty other things, gives every man an opportunity of showing and improving that education which he received at college or at school, and makes knowledge and dexterity at public business common.

5. Our law for the distribution of intestate estates occasions a frequent division of landed property, and prevents monopolies of land.[58]

Some years later he entered in his diary:

Major Langbourne dined with us again. He was lamenting the difference of character between Virginia and New England. I offered to give him a receipt for making a New England in Virginia. He desired it; and I recommended to him town meetings, training days, town schools, and ministers, giving him a short explanation of each article. The meeting-house and school-house and training field are the scenes where New England men were formed. Colonel Trumbull, who was present, agreed that these are the ingredients.

In all countries and in all companies, for several years, I have, in conversation and in writing, enumerated the towns, militia, schools, and churches, as the four causes of the growth and defence of New England. The virtues and talents of the people are there formed; their temperance, patience, fortitude, prudence, and justice, as well as their sagacity, knowledge, judgment, taste, skill, ingenuity, dexterity, and industry.[59]

Adams always spoke as a loyal advocate for his section and way of life, yet his rendering of the causes of New England's unusual measure of stability, solidarity, and well-being was essentially sound. He might also have mentioned several other major influences: the tavern, which rivaled the church and town-meeting as a centripetal force; the developing highway-system, which made it possible for the family far from the main part of town to discharge its political, religious, and social duties; [60] the twin institutions of "inhabitancy" and "warning-out," [61] which were symbols of the central position assigned to the family by custom and law; and the unusual proportion of people who could be classed as the middling sort. Far more significant politically than the silly notions and rules of stratification entertained in many towns was the profound leveling effect of small land-holdings and a stable way of life. Thanks to the town and the habits and virtues it rewarded, New England was the first great home of the American middle class.

THE CITY. Five concentrations of population, all of them seaports, could be classed as cities in 1765: Boston (15,500), Newport (8,000), New York (18,000), Philadelphia (30,000), and Charleston (10,000).[62] In addition, such ports as Salem, Portsmouth, Providence, New Haven, New London, Perth Amboy, Annapolis, Baltimore, Norfolk, Wilmington, and Savannah, and such country towns as Lynn, Hartford, Albany, Burlington, Princeton, Lancaster, Germantown, and Williamsburg had taken on some of the characteristics of urban living. These cities and large settlements had an influence out of all proportion to their population on the struggle for free society, self-government, an independent economy, social maturity, and an American culture.

The growth of an indigenous class-structure was visibly hastened by circumstances of urban living. The city environment was especially favorable to the rise of an aristocracy. Profits could be made more quickly and reinvested more imaginatively; occupation, thanks to specialization of labor, was a more definite criterion of status; and the gentle pleasures, whether of the club or the dancing-class, could be pursued without excessive effort and in any season. Conditions also favored the firm establishment of a shopkeeping middle class and laboring lower class. Yet the class structure, if more obvious than that of the country, was at the same time more fluid. Men in the bustling city moved up and down the ladder more rapidly than men in the conservative country.

Popular participation and public interest in political affairs were much keener in urban than in rural areas. Here in the city were the visible instruments of provincial government: the chambers of the assembly and the residence of the governor. Here, too, was the home of the printing press, that new engine of politics. Where participation lagged, as in tightly run

Philadelphia and badly governed Charleston, interest was kept alive by the club, tavern, weekly, pamphlet, broadside, and public concourse. Internecine warfare among the established classes brought the observant lower orders ever nearer to political emancipation.

The city was the narrow throat of the main streams of commerce that flowed to and from the productive American land, and as such it led the way toward an ever more bountiful, rewarding, and free-wheeling economy. The economic pattern of the city was diverse and fast-moving; it held out opportunities to the industrious and frugal man that could not be surpassed anywhere in the Atlantic community. The momentous clash between the old world of mercantilism and the new world of economic individualism was largely decided in the colonial cities.

The city came to grips long before the country did with the problems of a growing society. It was forced by necessity to take public action and use public funds in such matters as care of the poor, punishment of crime, regulation of markets, and prevention of fire. At the same time, the men of the city learned that private initiative and voluntary action were likewise workable methods for solving common problems. The association of free men for social, economic, and political purposes got its first real test in Boston and Philadelphia. While the country remained in a condition of social infancy, the city pushed upward, thanks to men like Franklin, toward new levels of communal co-operation.

Finally, the city was the crucible of a new culture. The great cultural achievement of the colonial age, the reception and conversion of English and European tastes and ideas, was largely the work of the upper and middle classes in the cities. Education, literature, science, and the arts flourished most vigorously in the cities. At the same time, an influential process of cultural exchange went on among the leading seaports. Carl Bridenbaugh writes that by the 1740's "it was possible for an educated gentleman like Dr. Alexander Hamilton to travel the length of the colonies with letters in his pocket to the cultural leaders in each community, to converse and exchange ideas with them, and enter into discussions, activities and amusements. Nothing better indicates the emergence of a definite urban society." [63] Nothing better indicates the emergence of centers of social and economic power that would provide the necessary leadership in the pre-Revolutionary decade. Boston rather than Lexington and Concord led the way to independence.

FEATURES AND PROBLEMS OF
COLONIAL SOCIETY

Most colonists shared a common set of assumptions and prejudices about such matters as the status of women and care of the unfortunate. A review of the colonial approach to problems found in all societies will lead to several conclusions about the level of social consciousness in these pioneering communities.

WOMEN AND CHILDREN IN THE COLONIES. In law, custom, and practice colonial women occupied a position well below that status of near-equality enjoyed by the women of modern America.[64] The sphere in which they moved was severely limited by the traditions of a civilization dedicated to male superiority. The common law subjected both the person and property of a married woman almost completely to her husband's control; and since the pressures of colonial society forced most women to marry young and stay married, the law as inherited and applied recognized two different ranks of people. Women played no part in government and only a small part in business.[65] Except for the brave widow who carried on with her late husband's shop, inn, press, or plantation, woman's place was by the hearth. The fact of social and legal inferiority was rationalized by the assumption of intellectual inferiority.[66] Education for women was elementary and, except among the better sort, wholly utilitarian.[67]

Their value as wives, housekeepers, and mothers was, of course, recognized by all. The institution of marriage was held in high esteem.[68] Indeed, in a society with too many men and with laws forbidding bonded men to marry, the marital tie was a badge of respectability. Once married and set down in her new home, the wife entered upon a regimen of labor that would appall the modern woman. In middle- and lower-class homes she was cook, baker, nurse, teacher, seamstress, laundress, and manager of the economy. Wives of poor farmers devoted their odd hours to the fields. In the upper-class home the wife was more manager than doer.[69] The mistress of the plantation was perhaps the most responsible and hardworking woman in the colonies.[70] Women in all stations were, as an English nobleman observed, "in general great Breeders." [71] Whether the help her children gave her compensated for the hardship of bearing and raising them is a question on which no colonial woman has left any clear testimony. Toil and parturition were her lot, yet she was not heard to complain any louder than modern woman. Unaware that her descendants would have waffle irons and anesthesia, she got along surprisingly well without most of the comforts that even husbands consider the basic necessities of modern women.

The status of women improved slowly but measurably throughout the colonial period. If they did not attain anything like equality with men, they nevertheless won—thanks to their scarcity [72] and high value—more respect, freedom, and legal recognition than their sisters in England and Europe. Conditions made it possible for many women, especially former indentured servants, to marry well above them. In many colonies the legal rights or capacities of women in property, conveyance of land, marriage and divorce, inheritance, contracts, torts, and testimony were expanded well beyond the reactionary confines of the common law.[73] And everywhere, as many a traveler attested, they enjoyed a measure of freedom in coming and going that set older women to shaking their heads. This improvement in status was an inevitable result of the enhanced bargaining-power bestowed on women by a surplus of men.

The total contribution of women to the development of the colonies has never been adequately acknowledged, except by women historians. Not only did they labor at a hundred essential tasks that men would or could not perform, not only did they procreate the race with unexampled fertility, but they acted as a powerful stabilizing influence in the evolution of society. Violence, religious primitivism,[74] alcoholism, and shiftlessness were noticeably less prevalent in those areas where settled homes and decent women were most numerous. The women of colonial America were inferior in status but not in influence.

The status of children was comparable to that of their mothers: They might be loved and cherished, but they were clearly more subject to discipline and authority than children of later times.[75] Obedience without delay or question was the cardinal virtue in colonial children. We shall take notice in Chapter 5 of the poverty and practicality of their education, which was shaped by the plain economic truth that they were valued highly for the assistance they could bring the family, even at an early age—the boys as helpers in field, barn, woodshed, and shop, the girls as comforts to overworked mothers. And if there were no place for them in the home economy, they could be bound out as apprentices. In general, what was true of women was true of children: They were subject to the command of the master of the house, finding scant refuge from severity or cruelty in either law or custom; they were welcomed particularly for their contributions of an economic nature; and they endured an existence that to us seems unbelievably hard and cruel, yet to them, in an age of limited knowledge and horizons, must have seemed about as secure and happy as a child's life today.

CRIME AND PUNISHMENT. The criminal record of the colonies was better than might have been expected of a frontier society that had inherited some of the more vicious notions and people of the parent country. Convictions for arson, rape, robbery, infanticide, murder, and other crimes are to be found in the records of every colonial court, but life and property seem to have been more secure in America than in England. Few colonists ever found things so bad as to resort to murder. Between 1663 and 1775 only twelve murders, five of them premeditated, were committed by white men in Connecticut. The famous English highwayman had no counterpart in America, and even the footpads of the cities, where crimes were more numerous and vicious, were pale imitations of British models. "The organized shame of such districts as London's Whitechapel, the accretion of generations of outlawry and vice," [76] was nowhere to be found, even in the most worldly seaports. The better economic conditions of the meaner sort had much to do with this noticeably lower level in the number and brutality of crimes.

The sex habits of the colonists, especially those of the Puritans, have received much attention from popular historians. Since there was no Dr. Kinsey to inquire and report, the total picture of sexual behavior is quite confused; an excellent case can be made for or against the virtue of the colonists, depending on the manner in which available statistics and contemporary judgments are handled.[77] For example, no one ever will determine finally whether bundling was an open invitation to lechery or the final test of the purity in Puritanism.[78] It is reasonably safe to conclude that sex habits and morals were neither better nor worse than those of later times. Considering the coarseness of the age, the low character of many immigrants, and the lack of recreational outlets of a more wholesome character, we might even say that the record was excellent. The whole number of perversions and illicit acts recorded in ever-watchful, ever-curious New England must be reckoned quite normal when spread over 150 years. What Bradford said of early Plymouth was probably true of most times and places in the colonies: "hear . . . is not more evills in this kind, nor nothing nere so' many by proportion, as in other places; but they are hear more discovered and seen." [79] Morbid publicity about sexual misconduct was to be expected in an age that had little else exciting to discuss, bemoan, or envy.

As to the level of morality in the relations of man to man and to society, the sense one gets of colonial conduct is once again confused and contradictory. The more one reads old church-records, court minutes, sermons, and newspapers, the more convinced he is that nothing ever really changes, at least nothing in the peculiar world of business and political ethics. Men in the colonies were honest and dishonest, open and sly, highminded and sneaky, law-abiding and law-breaking. If public morals were less corrupt than in England, this could be ascribed to the obvious truth that the stakes were not so high. The colonist demonstrated, in his blithe disregard of the Molasses Act of 1733, that he, like his descendants, would ignore any law contrary to the general sense of the community. Smuggling and speakeasies are only two famous manifestations of the American refusal to obey "impossible" laws.

Many colonists were disturbed by evidence of lowered standards of public ethics. Letters bewailing civic corruption in the *New-York Gazette* of 1753 are hardly distinguishable from similar letters to the *New York Times* in 1953.[80] Colonial Americans of a certain type, like modern Americans of the same type, thought the country was "going to hell in a bucket," and very soon at that. It should be mentioned in passing that the lottery, now generally regarded as corrupting and deplorable, was the favorite method of raising money in the colonies. Lotteries were conducted under both public and private auspices. They were extremely popular with all ranks and were used to raise funds for schools, colleges, charities, bridges, forts, and roads, as well as for churches of just about every denomination. They were rarely attacked on any grounds, never on grounds of being destructive of public virtue.[81]

The punishment of crime and immorality was, of course, severe and callous. Imprisonment, except of debtors and persons awaiting trial, was virtually unknown.[82] Convicted men paid their debt to society in one installment—by execution, fine, exposure to ridicule or shame, mutilation, or corporal punishment. Penology was a social science unknown to the colonies. English traditions and frontier conditions rendered the responsible authorities wholly devoid of concern over the rehabilitation of the criminal or of interest in how he became one in the first place. Yet here, too, the trend was toward more humanitarian methods. The death penalty was progressively restricted to only the most serious crimes, such as piracy, murder, and arson. Branding and mutilation, if not whipping, were inflicted less and less frequently. Criminal codes remained severe but were less vindictively enforced. Pennsylvania offers the most interesting case study for the social historian.[83] An original code of unusual mildness was made considerably more severe in the early eighteenth century, so severe indeed as to call forth vetoes from the Privy Council; yet the cruel and unusual penalties seem to have been designed to frighten rather than punish. It was, however, totally characteristic of the age for the government to react to an increase in crime by stiffening old penalties and devising new ones.

ALCOHOL. The modern historian, as he observes his colonial ancestors, is all but overcome by the fumes of alcohol, by the aroma of sack, brandy, beer, hard cider, port, punch, and "kill-devil" rum.[84] The colonists had other outlets of recreation—hunting, fishing, horse-racing, cock-fighting, bowling, ball-playing, boating, cards, and dancing [85]—but the drinking of spirituous liquors seems to have swamped them all.

No important event was complete without heavy drinking, be it a wedding, funeral, baptism, house-raising, ship-launching, election, college commencement, or training day. No town or settlement was complete without one or more taverns. Contemporaneous accounts of eighteenth-century Boston listed one house in eight as a drinking-place.[86] And every household did its share of home brewing and distilling. One European visitor after another was amazed that even the "peasants" in America had fruit trees,[87] not always realizing that apples and cherries were for drinking rather than eating. Most Americans seem to have spent their leisure hours "tyed by the Lipps to a pewter engine," [88] as Madam Knight observed of the citizens of Dedham in 1704. Drunkenness was probably the leading vice, or avenue of release, in colonial America—all of which led a gentleman in York County, Virginia, to declare in his will:

> Having observed in the daies of my pilgrimage the debauches used at burialls tending much to the dishonour of God and his true religion, my will is that noe strong drinks be provided or spirits at my buriall.[89]

Pulpit and press [90] took continual notice of the scandalous amount of drinking at public functions and in solitude, but there was no concerted move toward prohibition or temperance in colonial times, whether through public law or private co-operation.[91] Cotton Mather might deliver *A Serious Address to those who unnecessarily Frequent the Tavern, and Often spend the Evening in Publick Houses*, George Whitefield might preach of *The Heinous Sin of Drunkenness*, and Increase Mather might prophesy *Wo to Drunkards*,[92] but the tavern-frequenters and drunkards went right on drinking. Even these strong attacks were aimed at individual excesses rather than root causes. Provincial legislation dealt with the drinking problems of Indians, slaves, servants, and apprentices, not with those of the public in general.[93]

The incidence of intoxication in colonial times is of interest to the social historian for three reasons. It shows once again the influence of English social habits upon those of the colonists. It gives us some idea of a way of life so rough and narrow that it forced men into violent methods of forgetting their troubles. And its unchallenged sway illustrates the general lack of a crusading spirit in the social attitudes of the first Americans.

THE POOR, INSANE, AND ENSLAVED. Colonial methods in dealing with unfortunate members of society were thoroughly in keeping with the English inheritance and pioneering environment. Little time, thought, or money was or could be devoted to care and protection of the poor and insane. Such people were looked upon as social nuisances rather than sociological problems, and methods of handling them were rough if not often downright heartless.

Although many travelers and diarists agreed with Andrew Burnaby—"America is formed for happiness. . . . In a course of 1,200 miles I did not see a single object that solicited charity"[94]—the records of town and parish reveal that the poor were also with us in the colonies. Their peculiar problem was handled in a number of ways, all of them crude.[95] New England towns relied heavily on the harsh technique of "warning-out." Several cities built almshouses and then showed what they thought of the "honest poor" by also housing criminals in them. All colonies subscribed as best they could to the principles of the Elizabethan Poor Laws of 1601, which placed responsibility on local authorities—"every towne providing for their owne poore."[96] Funds were raised through the property tax, and the poor who could not be dispatched or set to labor in workhouses were cared for by families under agreement with town or parish. Poor children were usually bound out as apprentices. Cities and larger settlements turned increasingly to institutional care and to a differentiation between paupers and "sturdy beggars," but early Americans never could rid themselves of the notion that poverty was somehow criminal, that it was wrong to fight "against the order of God and Nature, which perhaps has appointed want and misery as the proper punishments for, and cautions against, as well as necessary consequences of, idleness and extravagance."[97]

The accepted methods of treating the insane were "punishment, repression, and indifference."[98] Ignorance, superstition, lack of public funds, and tradition helped maintain an attitude of cruelty, ridicule, and carelessness toward the feebleminded. The Pennsylvania Hospital, founded in 1751, was the first in America to give the insane any sort of institutional treatment; not until 1773 did a colony (Virginia) erect a separate establishment to house and care for them. The New England way was for the most part the American way: take them into private homes or drive them out of town. This entry of November 10, 1742, in the Boston records is worth pages of commentary on colonial methods of handling social problems:

> Complaint being made by Mr. Cooke that Mr. Samuel Coolidge formerly chaplain of the Castle, is now in this Town & in a Distracted Condition & very likely to be a Town Charge.
> Voted, That Mr. Savell Warn him out of Town according to law.[99]

We have already had cause to examine Negro slavery in the colonies and have discovered that indifference toward the plight of the slave and presumption of his permanent inferiority were the common attitudes of the white man. It need only be added that protests against slavery on humanitarian grounds and organized movements to free, protect, or educate [100] the Negro were few and feeble before 1765. The protests of John Woolman, Anthony Benezet, Elias Neau, Samuel Sewall, George Keith, John Hepburn, the Germantown Mennonites of 1688, the missionaries of the Society for the Propagation of the Gospel, and the Society of Friends were saintly voices in a callous wilderness.[101]

This review of colonial attitudes toward women and children, crime and punishment, the use and abuse of liquor, and the care of the unfortunate is evidence that the level of social feeling was low yet steadily rising. It was low in the colonies principally because it was low in the countries from which the colonists had come, because they, too, were children of a world that was crude, callous, ignorant, and indifferent in matters that concerned man's relations with man. It was rising for the very same reason, because all over the Atlantic world prophetic voices were being raised ever louder in protest against brutality and apathy. Some of these voices spoke from England to America, some from America to England and the rest of the Western world. All foretold a day when organized humanitarianism would bring law and social action to the support of a new sense of compassion and concern for troubled man.

THE FACTORS OF FREEDOM: I

Institutional and doctrinal developments in colonial society were, like those in the economy, working both for and against liberty, self-government, and political equality. So basic an institution as the militia was in some times and places a leveling, democratizing influence, in others a breeder of class distinctions.[102] So widespread a social outlook as that of the middle class, in which a disingenuous mania for rank vied with an invigorating spirit of independence, was likewise a mixed blessing. Yet for the most part these developments were creating an environment in which free government and libertarian ideas could prosper. Four broad social developments were especially influential for the rise of liberty: the firm establishment of a middle class; the emergence of a native aristocracy; the increasingly fluid character of the social structure; and the periodic eruption of social grievances into class and sectional conflict.

ESTABLISHMENT OF A MIDDLE CLASS. American democracy has always been middle-class democracy, a celebrated scheme of society and government from which aristocracy and proletariat, to the extent that each has existed, have alike been excluded from full reception and participation. Since our own bourgeoisie has been a large one, counting (according to various modern estimates) up to eighty or ninety per cent of the population, American identification of democracy with the political rule and social habits of the middle class has not been so fraudulent as many foreign observers would have us believe. In any case, free government in the United States has been a reasonably faithful reflection of the virtues and faults of the middle class. The rise of this class in the colonial era and its struggle for the stakes of political and economic power were one of the great determinants of early American history.

The rise of the middle class was neither so steady nor so massive as might easily have been the case. At least one healthy society of self-respecting yeomen, that of seventeenth-century Virginia, was sapped and stratified by conditions peculiar to the tobacco colonies. In another province, New York, a neo-feudal land system based on greed and corruption obstructed the natural process that had taken place in early Virginia. Yet even in these colonies the middling sort could not be wiped out or totally suppressed, and in Pennsylvania ("the heaven of the farmers, the paradise of the mechanics"),[108] New Jersey, New England, and the western counties in the South the yeoman became so common a species as to share heavily in government and set the tone of society. Among the forces that sustained the advance of the middling sort were the importance of this class and its principles in England, the middle-class background of many thousands of immigrants, the infinity of opportunities open to the industrious and frugal, and the long rise, despite temporary setbacks, of the productive capacity of the colonies and of the prices paid by the world for their staples and wares. The very conditions that helped create a class structure were at the same time hastening the triumph of the one class whose virtues and attitudes could vitiate most of the evil effects of stratification.

These virtues and attitudes were for the most part welcome supports to liberty and self-government. If the average farmer or shopkeeper had too much respect for the gentry, too little compassion for the meaner sort, and too lively a concern for the symbols and privileges of his own substratum in the middling band, these attitudes, especially the first two, were a good deal less pronounced than those of the middle class in England. And on the credit side of the ledger, the middle class could count several imposing contributions to ordered liberty.

First, the middling sort provided the chief stabilizing influence in religion, politics, economic affairs, and human relations. No people, however virtuous and politically talented, can make a success of free government unless it rests on a broad floor of social and economic stability. The small farmers, independent artisans, and shopkeepers of the American colonies—most of them men who were sensible in religion, diligent in business, steady in politics, and law-abiding in social attitude—gave a measure of strength to society which neither the fancies of the aristocracy nor the abasement of the lower class could shake. If thousands went off after Whitefield like men slapping bees, tens of thousands stood fast in the ancient ways. A certain measure of conservatism is necessary to the proper functioning of free society, and the healthy conservatism of the eighteenth century was largely a middle-class product.

Second, the middle-class philosophy [104] became the dominant element in the colonial mind. Industry, frugality, honesty, and self-reliance were celebrated not only for the rewards they brought yeoman and artisan, but also for the support they gave free government and fluid society. The colonial middle class first gave expression to the peculiar mixture of individualism and co-operation that has characterized the American psychology through most of our history. We shall learn more of the political influence of the virtues and beliefs of the middling sort when we salute their great expounder, Benjamin Franklin.

Finally, the middle class was both product and crucible of the process of "leveling" to which so many foreign observers bore friendly or unfriendly witness. An English officer said of the New Englanders in 1759, "They came out with a levelling spirit, and they retain it." [105] Lord Adam Gordon, observing the same section in 1765, spoke of "that ancient rugged Spirit of Levelling, early Imported from home, and successfully nursed, and cherished." As to Boston, "The levelling principle here, every where Operates strongly, and takes the lead, every body has property, and every body knows it." [106] A writer in the *Pennsylvania Journal* in 1756 declared:

> The People of this Province are generally of the middling Sort, and at present pretty much upon a Level. They are chiefly industrious Farmers, Artificers or Men in Trade; they enjoy and are fond of Freedom, and *the meanest among them* thinks he has a right to Civility from the greatest.[107]

The better sort might moan that politics was fast becoming the province of "mechanicks and ignorant wretches, obstinate to the last degree," [108] but the average man of the middling sort felt himself neither ignorant nor wretched. The meaner sort might lament their degraded and voteless station, but the average man believed that no wall but their own laziness barred them from the broad plateau of middling equality he occupied so proudly. The drive toward social equality, which was to come to fruition in the Jacksonian era, was well under way in the colonial period. It was the middling not the meaner sort that was engaged in this process so important for the establishment of true political democracy. The fact that this class was still comparatively small in 1765—perhaps one fifth to one fourth of the white population—shows how far American democracy had yet to travel.

EMERGENCE OF AN ARISTOCRACY. The self-creation of an indigenous aristocracy was a mixed blessing for the cause of liberty and self-government in the colonies.[109] The acquisition of wealth and pretensions by a small group of hard-driving commercial capitalists made the existence and labors of the meaner sort a social necessity. As the upper class pulled itself up, the lower classes were forced lower. The result was a class structure in which the gaps between classes were a constant threat to social solidarity. And since in most societies, especially young ones, political power flows toward the centers of social and economic power, the new American aristocracy became in time a tight-fisted, even oligarchic ruling class in almost every colony. In the end, however, because of circumstances over which it had little control, the aristocracy was to go along with and even lead the procession moving fitfully toward self-government. Even the most democratically oriented historians consider this class to have been an essential ingredient of early American liberty.

A clear recognition of the origins, pursuits, and political attitudes of the colonial gentry will help toward an understanding of its sometimes voluntary, more often involuntary, contributions to this liberty. Few of the leading families in Boston, New York, Philadelphia, or even Virginia could lay claim to gentle ancestry. Cadwallader Colden of New York was only exaggerating for the sake of emphasis when he wrote in 1765 that "the most opulent families, in our own memory, have arisen from the lowest rank of the people." [110] Indeed, it can be argued that the better sort in the colonies were a self-seeking plutocracy rather than a duty-conscious aristocracy. The records speak of an upper class, whether situated in Salem or Prince George County, that was more consistently devoted to business management and capital investment than to culture, sports, and the other pursuits of refined leisure. The first American aristocracy was a working aristocracy. The planter hunted profits more often than foxes; the merchant drove bargains more often than blooded horses. For few American gentlemen, no matter how many generations removed from the founder of their fortunes, was leisure an end in itself.

The one attitude that saved the better sort from the harsh label of plutocracy was their devotion to political affairs and public service. The colonial gentleman did not flee from political activity; he sought office avidly and held it tenaciously, because of the prestige and profits attached to it, and because of the inherited belief that public service was a duty of the gentry. Governor's council, assembly, provincial judiciary, county court, vestry, and often even the machinery of town government were largely in the hands of the upper class. The way in which the aristocrat made his contributions to the rise of liberty is testimony to the great truth that democracy is the work of all manner of men, not just of good-hearted democrats.

The office-holding aristocracy took the lead in the struggle between provincial assembly and royal governor. If some members of the ruling class rallied around the governor and supported his attempts to apply prerogative to a stiff-necked people, many more championed the designing measures that sought to exalt the assembly as the guardian of colonial rights and profits. It is a question open to debate whether the gentlemen of tidewater Virginia were more anxious to make the House of Burgesses a genuine legislature at the expense of the royal prerogative, or to keep it their own instrument at the expense of the under-represented western counties. In any case, the protesting assemblies of 1765, the key instruments of self-government and schools of political thought, had been largely shaped and were now largely manned by men who considered themselves the better sort. No assembly made a more resolute protest against the Stamp Act than that of South Carolina; yet eligibility for this body that spoke of "the freedom of a people" was limited to men with five hundred acres of land, ten slaves, or property valued at £1,000!

At the same time that colonial aristocrats were bringing new vitality to inherited institutions of self-government, they were helping to popularize a liberal political philosophy. Although the country party in the assembly struggled chiefly to improve its own position in a high-level war with the governor and his party, it wanted to believe, for purposes of morale, that it fought for the whole province against executive encroachment. And since it needed the support of the middle class and even of the lower classes, its arguments were couched in the language of Pym, Hampden, Sidney, and Locke. The lower orders of men, who were supposed to sit by quietly and await the outcome of this internecine political strife, could hardly be blamed for coming to believe some of the things they read and heard about the rights of Englishmen and the common weal.

The workings of this strange process of education in liberal political theory were especially apparent in New York, where Livingstons assaulted De Lanceys in the provincial press as if they themselves were apostles of pure liberty and their opponents agents of blackest oppression.[111] Zenger's *New-York Weekly Journal* and the short-lived *Independent Reflector*, two of the most radical journals in colonial America, were simply journalistic outposts of the country wing of the New York aristocracy. If these aristocrats were, as one historian has observed, a "dilettante democracy . . . equally anxious to clip the pinions of ambitious royalty and to curb the insolence of the unfettered mob," [112] they nevertheless chose to battle the agents of royalty with phrases and theories that had a special appeal to the "mob." The pre-1765 popularity of radical Whig doctrines in New York was largely the work of men who were aristocrats to the core, the eminent triumvirate of William Livingston, William Smith, jr., and John Morin Scott.[113] Here as elsewhere the lasting results of the assembly's campaign against the governors were the strengthening of elective institutions and popularizing of a progressive political theory.

We must be careful not to hold in ridicule the colonial aristocrat's devotion to liberty and justice, however much he might have defined these words to his own advantage. Certainly among the planting aristocracy of the South the spirit of liberty was vigorous and sincere. Real or imagined attempts by the Crown to restrict the processes of self-government evoked some of the most "leveling" and "republican" protests of the colonial period—not from the democratic Cohees but from the aristocratic Tuckahoes. Said Burke of the Southern colonies:

> There is, however, a circumstance attending these colonies, which . . . makes the spirit of liberty still more high and haughty than in those to the northward. It is, that in Virginia and the Carolinas they have a vast multitude of slaves. Where this is the case in any part of the world, those who are free, are by far the most proud and jealous of their freedom. Freedom is to them not only an enjoyment, but a kind of rank and privilege.

Not seeing there, that freedom, as in countries where it is a common blessing, and as broad and general as the air, may be united with much abject
toil, with great misery, with all the exterior of servitude, liberty looks,
amongst them, like something that is more noble and liberal. I do not mean,
Sir, to commend the superior morality of this sentiment, which has at least
as much pride as virtue in it; but I cannot alter the nature of man. The
fact is so; and these people of the southern colonies are much more strongly,
and with a higher and more stubborn spirit, attached to liberty, than those
to the northward. Such were all the ancient commonwealths; such were our
Gothic ancestors; such in our days were the Poles; and such will be all
masters of slaves, who are not slaves themselves. In such a people, the
haughtiness of domination combines with the spirit of freedom, fortifies it,
and renders it invincible.[114]

A keen observer on the spot had already voiced similar observations:

> The public or political character of the Virginians, corresponds with their
> private one: they are haughty and jealous of their liberties, impatient of
> restraint, and can scarcely bear the thought of being controuled by any
> superior power. Many of them consider the colonies as independent states,
> not connected with Great Britain, otherwise than by having the same com-
> mon king, and being bound to her by natural affection.[115]

While both these Englishmen were speaking of the planters of the South,
their remarks could be extended to a healthy portion of the aristocracy
everywhere. For men like the New York triumvirate "liberty" was something more than a helpful word with which to bolster arguments against the
royal prerogative.

Finally, we need mention only in passing the memorable part played by
the pro-American wing of the aristocracy in the period between the Stamp
Act and the Declaration of Independence. It was to this class of men—the
only class with a common outlook and with acquaintances that bridged
the gaps of intercolonial rivalry, mistrust, and ignorance [116]—that the great
mass of Americans turned for leadership in this decade. In the third part
of this book we shall learn more of the political activities of the upper class
at the zenith of its career in America, particularly of its assistance in broad-
casting the doctrines of natural law and rights. Mere mention of the names
of Washington, Jefferson, Lee, Mason, Carroll, Rutledge, Pinckney, Otis,
Hancock, Trumbull, Ellery, Morris, Livingston, Dickinson, and Schuyler
should be enough to remind us of the role of the landed and merchant
aristocracy in the Revolution. James Logan had written of the New England
colonies in 1732 that "while there are no noble or Great and Ancient Families . . . they cannot Rebel." [117] If an authentic aristocracy was a prerequisite to true self-government in the colonies, then by 1765 this prerequisite
was in being. The colonies could not possibly have resisted or revolted
without these men and their unique training in the school of political leadership.

THE FACTORS OF FREEDOM: II

THE INCREASING FLUIDITY OF SOCIETY. A third broad development that favored the growth of political liberty was an increase in fluidity throughout the social structure. Slowly but massively the colonies were beginning to move toward that bumptious spirit and condition of equality that was to characterize the American social order in the first half of the nineteenth century and to eliminate property as a condition for political activity. Like most other major sociological trends in American history, the loosening up of colonial society had bad effects as well as good. Yet it seems clear in retrospect that it was both a confirmation and a cause of the long-range movement toward political democracy.

We have already noted one instance of this increasing fluidity: the fact that classes in the colonies, however well defined and accepted, were in no sense closed corporations denying admittance to those born in other classes. Passage from one class to another grew progressively more possible throughout the eighteenth century, except perhaps in semifeudal Virginia and South Carolina. In the cities, where fortunes could be more easily won or lost, the social ladder seemed as much a challenge as an obstruction to the ambitious tradesman. Since wealth was the chief criterion of social status, the general increase in economic opportunity in the eighteenth century was matched by an increase in social mobility. Observant Americans were well aware of this development. Said a writer to a Philadelphia newspaper in 1776:

> Is not one half of the property in the city of Philadelphia owned by men who wear LEATHER APRONS?
> Does not the other half belong to men whose fathers or grandfathers wore LEATHER APRONS? [118]

He need only have added some remark about "leather aprons to leather aprons in three generations" to have given a generalized picture of the class structure in Philadelphia and most of America.

Another sign of a society growing ever less rigid was the change in attitudes among the different classes. In particular, the lower-class attitude of deference and upper-class attitude of condescension were slowly being converted into a more healthy relationship, one of respect that worked both ways on the social scale.[119] This, of course, was a more selective attitude, in which the person, not his station, was the primary determinant. Contempt rather than respect continued to mark the feelings of the better sort about "rioting sailors and mechanicks"; bitter hatred rather than respect often marked those of the meaner sort about the class that often left them no outlet but rioting. The middle class remained steadfast in its familiar attitude of friendly mistrust toward the class above and the class below.

Still another sign of increased fluidity—many would have called it a sign of social disintegration—was the improved status of women, children, and dependents everywhere, and of servants in the North. Women became less subordinate, children less exposed to discipline, dependents less put upon, and servants less subject to the master's whims. This, of course, is a very general observation, for the shift toward more tenderness and trust was at best one of emphasis. Yet the evidence of diaries and letters points unmistakably to a freer and more pleasant pattern of social intercourse within the family and out of doors. This trend was matched, as we have already seen, by a rise in concern over social problems and in compassion for the unfortunate.

The New England towns, of which there were more than 550 in 1776, are ideal laboratories in which to observe the trend toward a more open, undisciplined, flexible society.[120] Frontier and city were environments in which mobility was part of the natural order of things, but the changes that took place during the eighteenth century in the monolithic structure of the older towns reveal the sweep of this third major trend. The New England towns were unable to withstand the combined impact of the expansion of population, secularization of life, and growth of commerce which molded all social developments in eighteenth-century America. The growth of interest in the world outside, the sharpening of class antagonisms, the decline of clerical leadership, the emigration of offshoots of the best old stock, the easier influx of "strangers," the increasing frivolity of training day, the appearance of new and other-minded churches, the proliferation of household manufactures, the unflagging popularity of the tavern, the upswing in sexual immorality—not all these were welcome developments; indeed, some were most unfortunate. Yet they indicate relaxation of the rigid communalism that all towns had aspired to and many had achieved.

The changes in old towns were reflected in altered methods of settling new ones. Grants were now made to individuals rather than to congregations, and the resulting patterns of settlement were dispersed rather than communal. The New England town did not disintegrate under the pressures of the eighteenth century. It was far too tough and functional a social organism to collapse that easily. Yet it did undergo an extensive modification that can best be described as the rise of self-centered as opposed to community-minded individualism. Much that was good sank slowly into discard, but so, too, did much that was outmoded and intolerant. The residuum of unity that persisted was relatively unforced, rising from the plain man at the bottom rather than imposed by the gentleman at the top.

American society in the eighteenth century continued to exhibit three prominent features that had appeared in the seventeenth to distinguish it from England and Europe: first, there were relatively fewer people in both the upper and lower classes—always excepting, in the latter instance, the Negro slaves; second, passage from one class to the next, and especially from both directions into the middle class, was easier; and third, the colonies were well on the way to achieving a revolutionary compromise between the new demands of the individual for a life of his own and the old demands of the group for social unity. Unfriendly visitors and officials could sneer as they pleased about "leveling," but most Americans agreed with the greatest American, "I see no Country of Europe where there is so much general Comfort & Happiness as in America." [121]

CLASS AND SECTIONAL CONFLICT. Controversy is the life-thrust of the open society. The groups that develop within such a society must inevitably come into conflict over the stakes of social, economic, and political power. Particularly in an active and growing community will parties, economic interests, churches, sections, and classes squabble among themselves for preferment. The mature society is one that has recognized this condition by creating institutions that foster the spirit of compromise and techniques that make possible the peaceful resolution of serious differences. Colonial America, an active and growing community, had its full share of controversy, especially of a class or sectional character. We have already noted the contesting classes. The basic sectional cleavage was between the settled seaboard and pioneering back-country. Since the former was the realm of the aristocracy and the latter the haven of the small farmer, sectional and class conflict often went hand in hand.

The seventeenth century set the style for the eighteenth. From the first settlement in each colony, groups and sections argued bitterly over land, economic policy, religion, and political power. At times antagonisms erupted into riots that exposed the depth of certain cleavages in society; and once, on the occasion of Bacon's Rebellion in Virginia in 1676,[122] the scourge of civil war was visited upon the land. Other instances of class and sectional hostility in the seventeenth century were the anti-proprietary revolts in Maryland (1652-1689), similar outbreaks in South Carolina (1685-1691) and North Carolina (1677-1679), the long struggle between aristocratic and popular forces in New York that came to a climax in Leisler's Revolt (1689-1691), and a volley of spats over land and government in New Jersey. Most participants in these large and small revolts were Englishmen or the sons of Englishmen, and as such were trustees of a tradition of law and order. Their outbursts of violence, most of which were motivated by antagonisms within a colony rather than between colony and home authorities, were therefore especially convincing proof of the growing complexity of American society.

Six bones of contention fed the controversies of the eighteenth century: land, currency, religion, representation, government activity, and simple class-antagonism. In most instances, grievances in three or four of these categories worked together to incite an oppressed class or section to protest and an oppressing class or section to reprisal. And generally there was something to be said for each side in the dispute.

We have already noted, in Chapter 2, the unfortunate circumstance underlying most conflicts over land in the colonial period: the fact that it was the one thing for which the common man longed and the most rewarding type of capital investment. The result was a perpetual, protean struggle between settler and speculator, the one seeking productive and unencumbered land at the cheapest possible price, the other seeking the largest possible return on his risk capital. Quit-rents, conflicting titles, squatting, timber-cutting, land-engrossing, and tenantry only added to a confusion of rights and purposes out of which social conflicts grew naturally. In Pennsylvania, Virginia, the Carolinas, western New England, New York,[123] and above all New Jersey, disputes flourished between settlers and proprietors, debtors and collectors, farmers and speculators, squatters and landlords, and between settlers armed with conflicting titles. Courts, assembly, council, and units of local government were all cockpits of contention over disputed titles and claims; and when the men with the more basic claim, those who actually worked the land, could get no satisfaction from petition and litigation, they resorted to rump meetings, riot, and armed resistance. Class conflict over the land reached its bitter peak in New Jersey.[124] The attempt of the proprietors of East Jersey to assert their legal rights was met head-on by the determination of the settlers to resist all oppressive rents and claims. The result was a decade (1745-1755) of rioting, squatting, political anarchy, legal and political maneuvering, and appeal to "the Rules of natural Justice."[125] Eventually almost the entire northern part of the colony was in an uproar against the landlords; the uproar did not, however, prevent the steady rise of economic prosperity!

The demand for easy money has divided Americans for more than 250 years. Not a single colony in the eighteenth century could escape the tensions that lead to and derive from the issuance of paper money. The conflict between the agrarian debtor of the middle class and the mercantile creditor of the upper class was bitter, for it was essentially a struggle over the price the latter should pay the former for the fruits of his labor. For the most part, the forces that favored either a contracted or expanded currency carried on their vendetta in legislature and press. The Crown, which had a monetary policy harder than any that was popular in the colonies, intervened repeatedly to demolish the schemes of debt-ridden farmers and their allies among the lesser merchants. Occasionally, however, these differences in opinion over the necessity and effects of promissory notes, bills of credit, and land banks threatened to erupt into open violence. During the memorable land-bank controversy in Massachusetts in 1741, the struggle between the farmers, who controlled the assembly, and the merchants, who rallied around the governor, came near to tearing the province apart.[126] Only the determined action of Governor Belcher and his supporters prevented a riotous march of the farmers on Boston; and only a naked display of imperial power, an act of Parliament extending the Bubble Act of 1720 to the colonies, forced the inflationist party to abandon the land-bank. The outlawing of the land-bank left a heritage of radical agrarian antipathy toward the merchants of Boston that was of huge consequence for the future course of Massachusetts politics. In Rhode Island, to the contrary, the Newport merchants took the most severe beating, since they were constantly forced to accept payment of country debts in paper currency "Esteemed upon the worst footing of any in North America." [127] Only another act of Parliament (in 1751) could halt the riotous inflation resulting from the creation of nine land-banks in forty years. By this and subsequent acts Parliament effectively outlawed all but the most sober issues of paper currency in New England and the other colonies. This did nothing to relieve the tension between debtor and creditor in America.

There is little that need be added to the discussion in Chapter 2 of the class and sectional antagonisms aroused by the Great Awakening. As was said in that context, the upsurge in religious feeling was generally quite primitive in character, appealing primarily to the poor and despised, revolting the well-born, well-educated, and well-to-do. The splitting of Congregational, Reformed, and Presbyterian churches into camps that conformed generally to class lines was a staggering blow to many a hitherto peaceful village society.[128] The excesses of enthusiasm caused even liberal spirits like Jonathan Mayhew to speak in acid language of "the meaner sort," [129] and conservatives, convinced that the whole social order was in danger, adopted attitudes toward the "giddy, ignorant people" that were crude and contemptuous. The enthusiasts, on the other hand, did as much to quicken the spirit of social equality as to revive the spirit of true religion.

A fourth grievance that did much to stir up social controversy was the problem of representation in the assemblies. In many colonies the western counties, largely inhabited by small farmers, were kept deliberately underrepresented by the old counties, largely controlled by conservative merchants or land-holders. In 1760 Lancaster County in Pennsylvania was nearly twice as heavily populated as Bucks County, yet it sent only four representatives to the assembly against eight from the older area. Discrimination against newly settled areas was even more flagrant in Virginia and the Carolinas.[130] The persistent petitions of frontier counties for more equitable representation and the persistent refusal of tidewater counties to pay heed added fuel to the fires of bitterness between sections and classes.

Still another bone of contention was the refusal of the ruling class in several colonies to adjust or operate the machinery of government in favor of the newer sections. One example was eastern hostility to schemes to raise farm prices and scale down debts. Another was the lukewarm attitude of settled counties toward frontier demands for protection against Indian warfare. The infamous riot of the "Paxton Boys" in 1764 was the bitter fruit of this type of contention in Pennsylvania. A third instance was the intolerable difficulty, travel, and expense involved in going to law in the newer counties. In many of these counties sheriffs, judges, and lawyers were simply agents of the eastern ruling class whom small farmers denounced as "cursed hungry Caterpillars, that will eat out the very Bowels of our Commonwealth, if they are not pulled down from their Nests in a very short time." [131] Many sober, hardworking pioneers were convinced that the provincial government was working against rather than for their protection and welfare.

Not all class antagonisms were sectional in nature. Classes could also exist side by side with little respect or affection for one another. This was especially true in the developing cities, where wealth had accumulated in amounts grand enough to permit many aristocratic families to engage in ostentatious display. The widening economic gulf between the gentry and the meaner sort had a disruptive effect on class relations. There is a great deal of evidence of simple antagonism between rich and poor in New York, Charleston, and Philadelphia; and even in supposedly stable Boston, poor rioted in resentment of rich and rich despised poor.

The basic sectional division during this period was between west and east within each colony rather than between one group of colonies and another. The west—such counties as Lancaster, York, and Cumberland in Pennsylvania, Frederick in Maryland, Augusta in Virginia,[132] Orange and Anson in North Carolina, and Orangeburg and Ninety-Six Precincts in South Carolina—was the area of protest; the east was the area of indifference and reaction. Mixed in national origin (with the Scotch-Irish giving the mixture its special flavor), dissenting in religion, democratic in politics, and leveling in social attitudes, the men of the "Old West" felt entitled to a better deal in representation, religious freedom, prices, taxation, debts, protection, and the administration of justice. In many a colony in 1764 civil war seemed more likely than war with Britain. Only once, however, did the grievances of the back country explode into sustained and organized violence—the famous Regulator movement in North Carolina (1768-1771),[133] an uprising of yeomen settlers against the office-holding, privileged class and its agents. An inequitable tax-system, corrupt and oppressive officials, callous land-engrossing, excessive judicial fees, and under-representation were the wrongs that touched off this display of mob violence. The Regulators interfered bodily with the operation of courts, raided jails to release imprisoned fellows, resisted evictions and collections, and launched attacks on homes and offices of hated county officials. The showdown took place at Alamance in May 1771, when Governor Tryon's militia, topheavy with officers from the planter class, routed the Regulator army of some two thousand men. This show of force and the execution of seven ringleaders brought the movement to collapse. Hundreds of Regulators moved on to the west; the others submitted and were granted amnesty. But hate between east and west was now part of life in North Carolina—as it was in several other colonies to the north and south. Alamance was not the first battle of the Revolution but the last and largest sectional uprising of the colonial period.

The importance of class and sectional controversy for the rise of political liberty should be obvious to even the most casual student of the colonial period. Group antagonism was a sign of a growing society, a cause of major readjustments within it, and a spur to political participation. An English observer remarked in 1760 that "a spirit of party is universally prevalent in America." [134] He might have remarked more accurately that the colonists seemed to be coming to life politically. And he might have remarked, too, that as the men of the west and lower classes came to think and talk politically, they were only too pleased to borrow from eastern aristocrats the language of Whiggery and natural rights.

✦

There is little to add in conclusion to this selective description of colonial society. The politically significant features of that society are manifest: It was stratified, simple, callous, and communal; it was also becoming more fluid, complex,[135] humane, and individualistic. Most important, it was plastic and self-directing. The colonists were restricted by imperial design and inherited traditions, yet the design was shadowy and the traditions quite malleable when detached from their institutional expressions in England.

Despite instructions and influences that flowed continually from home, the colonists were able to build a society that answered their own needs and understandings. The early years in Georgia are proof of this truth.[136] The Trustees wanted small land-holdings in tail male, free labor, a prohibition on rum, and paternal government; the settlers wanted large land-holdings in fee simple, slavery,[137] rum, and an assembly. It took a few years, but the settlers got what they wanted, even if much that they wanted was bad. Slavery and land-grabbing would not be the last grave social mistakes Americans would commit. The path to social democracy would prove rocky and unending, but at least it would be one of their own making.

CHAPTER FIVE

The Colonial Mind
and the Rise of Liberty

THE rise of liberty in colonial America owed as much to the unfolding of spiritual and intellectual forces as to the interaction of transplanted institutions and native environment. The spirit of liberty—whether political, social, religious, or economic—was more deeply imbedded in the colonial mind than in colonial institutions. It would seem proper to close out this extended survey of the circumstances of early American life by exploring this mind and discovering what it believed, what it inherited or imported from England and Europe, what it learned in the wilderness, how it was trained, and through what agencies of cultural interchange it expressed and improved itself.

It may be quite misleading to speak about "the colonial mind." Although there was an ultimate unity to intellectual life, it was probably no more important, and was certainly less striking, than the sharp contrasts in thought and culture which arose out of diversities of time, section, proximity to sea or frontier, religion, national origin, occupation, property, and status. Yet we can use this term as a convenient label for these aspects of colonial life: education, science, literature, the arts, academic and practical philosophy, and political theory.[1] We shall examine each of these slices of the colonial mind primarily as an expression of the intellect or spirit, remembering always that ideas cannot be considered apart from the institutions that express or condition them. Before we proceed to this task, let us set down several capital facts about thought and culture in colonial America.

The historian of ideas must constantly bear in mind these principal diversities of circumstance: the three major regions (New England, middle colonies, Southern colonies) and the important subdivisions within the limits of each; the three broad periods of social and therefore intellectual and cultural development (1607-1675, the age of transfer; 1675-1725, the "dark ages" of the colonial mind; 1725-1765, the age of expansion, mobility, and enlightenment); and the four or five clear-cut levels within the class structure. Although we will concentrate on the culture and learning of the Northern towns, the upper and upper-middle classes, and the eighteenth century, we must not forget the plantations and frontier, the lower classes, or the first two ages of colonial development. Yet we do not flaunt history by concentrating in this manner. Rarely in any society have the upper and upper-middle classes been so manifestly the chief vehicle of liberating ideas. And it was in the Northern towns, in the last three or four decades of the colonial period, that the ideas prophetic of the American future achieved their most memorable pre-Revolutionary triumphs.

For all its importance in our scheme of historical values, the colonial mind can lay only a tiny claim to serious consideration in the intellectual history of Western man. The general level of literary and artistic achievement or comprehension was low; and, except for Jonathan Edwards and Benjamin Franklin, the colonies did not produce a single intellect worthy of universal contemplation. Many colonists were well aware of their shortcomings and hopeful of correcting them. Their oft-expressed sense of inferiority had the ring of challenge rather than despair. Americans looked forward confidently to the rise of an indigenous culture. "After the first Cares for the Necessaries of Life are over," wrote Franklin, "we shall come to think of the Embellishments. Already some of our young Geniuses begin to lisp Attempts at Painting, Poetry and Musick." [2]

The starkness of early American culture was as much a result of the colonists' struggles with the wilderness as of their dependent relationship with England. "How can he get wisdom that holdeth the plow and that glorieth in the goad, that driveth oxen, and is occupied in their labors and whose talk is of bullocks?" asked Governor Lewis Morris of the New Jersey Assembly in 1745. [3] "How indeed?" the assembled plowmen might have asked in rebuttal. We shall never know how many Newtons and Lockes, or at least Hoadlys and Addisons, might have arisen even in New Jersey had there been less need to talk of bullocks and more chance to talk of buskins. When we consider the work that had to be done in America simply to prepare the ground for the growth of a culture, especially to amass the surplus of wealth that makes it possibly for society to support poets and artists, we may well conclude that the general level of culture and the incidence of genius were both remarkably high. As one hopeful gentleman wrote to James Franklin's *Rhode Island Gazette:*

> In the Rise of States, the Arts of War and Peace, Agriculture, and the like, are of necessity more attended to than Erudition and Politeness, that comes on of course afterwards, when the *Golden Age* succeeds the *Iron.* So that instead of wondering why our Country has produced so few good

Writers, and why those which have been produced, have not always given a general *Satisfaction*, we may rather admire at the contrary.[4]

The paramount external influence in the intellectual development of the colonies was always that of England. Education, science, theology, philosophy, literature, journalism, manners, art, architecture, and political theory were largely English in origin and expression. Whether the process of transfer was largely unconscious, as in the seventeenth century when most colonials were transplanted Englishmen, or largely conscious, as in the eighteenth when fourth- and fifth-generation Americans still looked eastward for inspiration, the influence of English thought and culture was so commanding as to make the phrase "the American mind" almost a courtesy title. The processes of inheritance and importation were, to be sure, selective.[5] The colonists absorbed those elements of English culture which they found rational and serviceable; they rejected many that appeared outworn or corrupting or ill-adapted to the wilderness. Yet as one reads colonial newspapers, studies the curriculum of the colleges, browses in the libraries of Cotton Mather and Robert Carter, and hears in his imagination the debates of the assemblies, he must admit that the adjective "English-American" rather than "American" describes the dominant culture, even as late as 1765. The colonial mind was largely derivative and often downright imitative.

The colonial mind was thoroughly Christian in its approach to education, philosophy, and social theory. At the same time, it was constantly in a state of evolution, and the most interesting development was the secularization of thought, aspirations, and culture. This process, which was attended and intensified by the advance of individualism, rationalism, skepticism, and humanism,[6] can be traced in almost every province of intellectual life: in education, literature, art, science, philosophy, political and social thought, and even in religion itself. The Christian religion grew less influential as the colonies moved toward maturity and liberty. Yet this decline in influence was only relative; the variants of Christianity remained a primary determinant of the culture of every class and section.

Finally, a third great force, the idea of human liberty, worked with Christianity and the English heritage to bring an ultimate unity to the deep-seated intellectual and cultural diversities in early America. Liberty, in one guise or another, was the aspiration of most men and the characteristic of most currents of thought that moved westward to America. The total environment was one in which prophets of freedom, exponents of a rising humanism, could preach with maximum efficiency, and in which prophets of perdition, defenders of a dying obscurantism, could delay but not prevent the coming of a new order. Liberating systems of thought and culture—Whiggery, rationalism, the new science—were welcomed with acclaim, especially in the eighteenth century. Harsh systems like Puritanism grew steadily more humane. The individualistic, rationalistic, and popular elements in this great way of life seemed to thrive in American soil, while the authoritarian, dogmatic, and aristocratic elements bore withered fruit. The total colonial mind of 1765 still retained many ingredients of dogma and despair, but it had absorbed many more of reason and optimism. The most powerful single factor of freedom in early America was the devotion to liberty in the colonial mind.

EDUCATION IN THE COLONIES

The first subject of concern in any assessment of the colonial mind must be the character, purposes, instruments, and achievements of the system of education. Although the total picture of this phase of colonial life, as of so many others, is one of confusion compounded by lack of reliable contemporary statistics and observations, the outlines are sufficiently distinct to permit a number of generalizations.[7]

Two attributes of colonial education are especially alien and therefore intriguing to the modern mind: the manner in which it conformed to the demands of the class structure, and the extent to which it was motivated and directed by institutionalized religion. Class and religion are still important forces in certain phases of American education, but they are by no means so important as two centuries ago. We have already noted, in Chapter 4, the significance of the class structure in colonial America; it should come as no surprise that the pattern of education conformed to assumptions of social inequality. The character and duration of a child's education were determined by the acknowledged status of his parents. Most children were cut off completely by custom and economic necessity from secondary and higher education. And most men who gave any thought to the subject agreed with William Smith of Philadelphia that each social group—the "gentlemen," those "design'd for the Mechanic Professions," and "all the remaining People of the Country"—should receive a different type of education.[8] Neither the fact nor the ideal of educational democracy had any standing in early America.

Religion and education were closely associated in the colonial mind. Although education, even in early Massachusetts, attempted to teach many things—knowledge of the world, "good literature," virtue, manners, civic consciousness, and business and professional skills[9]—its chief purpose was to support revealed religion. Most institutions of education were begun and maintained by religious groups for religious ends. The Puritan ministers of New England[10] and the Anglican missionaries of the Society for the Propagation of the Gospel[11] are the best-remembered educators of the colonial era.

The secularization of social aims in the eighteenth century did much to weaken the dominance of religion. New currents from abroad and new challenges of the environment turned men's thoughts to the secular, public, and utilitarian aspects of education. Yet religion, thanks in part to the tenacity of inherited assumptions about class structure and education, remained the central consideration. Even men so fundamentally skeptical as Colden and Franklin considered the inculcation of the Christian ethic to be the common element of education for every class and the marrow of education for the poor. They agreed with most other men of the period that education had a higher, more social purpose than the improvement or salvation of the individual. Indoctrination, the active inculcation of values—whether designed to reinforce true religion or "to form the Minds of the Youth, to Virtue, and to make them useful Members of the Society" [12]—was the distinguishing mark of educational method in early America.

Education was largely a result of private solicitude and a function of private enterprise. Too much has been made of the Massachusetts laws of 1642 and 1647 and their Connecticut counterparts.[13] Although they specified community responsibility and hinted at universality and compulsion at the primary level, they were far from establishing free public education in any form that we can comprehend. Indeed, it is impossible to speak of a "system" of schools, either public or private, in the colonies. An astounding percentage of persons, even in New England, received their small ration of education at home rather than in an organized school. South of Connecticut the chief agencies of education were the home, church, shop, and field. Most laws concerning education dealt with the special problem of preparing poor children for a gainful occupation. Free education was closely identified with povery. This was especially true in Virginia, where the legislature enacted at least ten important laws dealing with primary education of the poor, orphaned, and illegitimate.[14]

The cultural heritage from England and the conditions of wilderness living were both unfavorable to the growth of an educational system exhibiting scope or depth. The class structure, the slow progress of pedagogy, political oligarchy, the high economic value placed on children, the ravages of border warfare, the pattern of rural settlement, the difficulties of transportation, the decline of learning and culture in the middle period, excesses of religious enthusiasm—all these were obstructions to the growth and refinement of instruments of formal education. The insatiable demands of soil and sea, which made extended leisure a will-o'-the-wisp for men of all classes, was especially responsible for the utilitarian complexion that permeated even upper-class education.

In addition to the home itself—the principal unit of primary education in all sections and among all classes—a variety of persons and institutions offered instruction in the rudiments: the semipublic writing schools of New England,[15] the parochial schools of New York and Pennsylvania,[16] the "old-field" schools of Virginia,[17] and the parsons, masters,[18] tutors, and private schools of every section. The quality of a child's primary education varied with his religion, class, section, and proximity to settlement. The child of an Anglican or Congregational merchant in Boston [19] received a training far more intense than that of the child of a Quaker farmer in Rhode Island or a Calvinist family on the Virginia frontier. Yet the many instruments of basic education did have two common features: they ladled out their lessons with the spoon of authority and paid primary devotion to the five R's—Reading, 'Riting, 'Rithmetic, Rules of Conduct, and Religion.

Comparatively few young people reached the level of education we class as secondary. Such education had two main purposes: to prepare a limited group for college and to teach a somewhat larger group the skills, learning, and manners that distinguished the merchant and planting classes from the mass of men.[20] The chief instruments of class education were the urban private schools, some of which became sufficiently large and stabilized to be known as "academies." The academy, a major development in eighteenth-century education, continued to offer Latin and Greek to those youths whose families intended them for college and at the same time provided a more utilitarian bill of fare—mathematics, composition, geography, modern languages, science, accounting, and bookkeeping—for those entering business and the professions. Training in good manners, genteel accomplishments, and polite learning was offered to all young men of the upper or would-be-upper class. Substantial rural families sent their sons to board in the city or employed tutors or ministers to educate them at home. Some of the best-educated men in America never saw the inside of a schoolhouse. The family, though less important than it was at the primary level, was also an essential unit of secondary education.

The colleges responded conspicuously to the pressures of a society more actively concerned than ours with religion and status. Of the seven colleges in the colonial period—Harvard (1636), William and Mary (1693), Yale (1701), New Jersey, now Princeton (1747), Philadelphia, now Pennsylvania (1749), King's, now Columbia (1754), and Rhode Island, now Brown (1764) [21]—all but Pennsylvania were creatures of sectarian impulse, and all remained, despite the trend toward broader educational horizons, primary supports of the Christian order. Although then as now poor boys with talents and courage could fight their way up to a college education, most students were from the upper or upper-middle classes. Curriculum and methods were based on the practices of Oxford and Cambridge and thus, more remotely, on those of the great universities of medieval Europe. The ancient languages, rhetoric, and philosophy were the core of the curriculum in the early period. Mathematics, moral literature, modern languages, and science made inroads on the classical subjects in the eighteenth century. The facts and fancies of political theory, history, geography, and other more worldly subjects entered the student's mind along the indirect routes of the classical writers and orthodox philosophers. Entrance into the ministry, the stated goal of a majority of students, gave a Christian cast to all parts of the curriculum.

It is easy to smile at the dull, rigid, crabbed methods that prevailed in colonial colleges, but if we judge the vineyards by the fruit they brought forth, we must acknowledge them a fertile ground of learning, science, reason, and liberty. They may not have taught young men enough useful knowledge, but they did teach them—in their own tradition-ridden way—to think, communicate, and lead.[22] These tiny seminaries were worthy ancestors of the modern university. The roll-call of Harvard and William and Mary men in the Revolution should be evidence enough that Latin, logic, and metaphysics were not such poisonous fertilizer after all in the cultivation of reason, liberality, virtue, honor, and love of liberty.[23]

Although numerous Yale and Harvard alumni in the more conservative New England pulpits would have disagreed violently, these excerpts from the public prospectus advertising the opening of King's College in 1754 render with some accuracy the ideals of higher education in the third quarter of the eighteenth century:

> III. And that people may be the better satisfied in sending their Children for education to this College, it is to be understood, that as to Religion, there is no Intention to impose on the Scholars, the peculiar Tenets of any particular Sect of Christians; but to inculcate upon their tender Minds, the great Principles of Christianity and Morality, in which true Christians of each Denomination are generally agreed. . . .
>
> IV. The chief Thing that is aimed at in this College is, to teach and engage the Children to *know God in Jesus Christ,* and to love and serve him, in all *Sobriety, Godliness,* and *Righteousness* of Life, with a *perfect Heart, and a willing Mind;* and to train them up in all virtuous Habits, and all such useful Knowledge as may render them creditable to their Families and Friends, Ornaments to their Country and useful to the public Weal in their Generations. . . .
>
> V. And, *lastly,* a serious, *virtuous,* and *industrious* Course of Life, being first provided for, it is further the Design of this College, to instruct and perfect the Youth in the Learned Languages, and in the Arts of *reasoning* exactly, of *writing* correctly, and *speaking* eloquently; and in the Arts of *numbering* and *measuring;* of *Surveying* and *Navigation,* of *Geography* and *History,* of *Husbandry, Commerce* and *Government,* and in the Knowledge of all *Nature* in the *Heavens* above us, and in the *Air, Water,* and *Earth* around us, and the various kinds of *Meteors, Stones, Mines,* and *Minerals, Plants* and *Animals,* and of every Thing *useful* for the Comfort, the Convenience and Elegance of Life, in the chief *Manufactures* relating to any of these Things: And, finally, to lead them from the Study of Nature to the Knowledge of themselves, and of the God of Nature, and their Duty to him, themselves, and one another, and every Thing that can contribute to their true Happiness, both here and hereafter.[24]

Another indication of the advance of higher education was this passage from the charter of Rhode Island College:

> And furthermore, it is hereby enacted and declared, That into this liberal and catholic Institution shall never be admitted any religious tests: But on the contrary, all the members hereof shall forever enjoy full, free, absolute, and uninterrupted liberty of conscience: And that the places of Professors, Tutors, and all other officers, the President alone excepted, shall be free and open for all denominations of Protestants: And that youth of all religious denominations shall and may be freely admitted to the equal advantages, emoluments, and honors of the College or University; and shall receive a like fair, generous, and equal treatment, during their residence therein, they conducting themselves peaceably, and conforming to the laws and statutes thereof. And that the public teaching shall, in general, respect the sciences; and that the sectarian differences of opinions shall not make any part of the public and classical instruction: Although all religious controversies may be studied freely, examined, and explained by the President,

Professors, and Tutors, in a personal, separate, and distinct manner, to the youth of any or each denomination: And above all, a constant regard be paid to, and effectual care be taken of the morals of the College.[25]

By 1764, the year of this liberal but still not quite liberated announcement of educational policy, the colleges were well up in the movement toward a more humane and open, if not yet democratic, society.

Adult education reached its peak of formal development in the seaports of the eighteenth century. Libraries circulated books among a growing proportion of the population; the books themselves grew more practical in content and instructive in method. Newspapers, of which there were none in 1700 and twenty-three in 1765, offered moral and scientific instruction as well as news of commercial and dynastic doings. Evening schools advertised courses in mathematics, navigation, surveying, bookkeeping, languages, and other useful subjects.[26] The public lecture illustrating the magic of electricity was hardly less popular than Addison's *Cato* or Gay's *Beggar's Opera.*[27] And as Franklin and dozens of lesser men proved conclusively, self-education in the home and club did as much as any formal institution to raise the level of knowledge and curiosity.

If there is any one phase of colonial life to which it is unwise, unjust, and unreal to apply present-day standards and values, it is the area of education. The one question we may properly ask of the total system of education is this: In the light of the environment in which it operated and the heritage upon which it was building, did it answer the needs of the people satisfactorily? The answer would seem to be an admiring yes. Despite a legion of obstacles to expansion and refinement, not the least of these being the inherent conservatism of education itself, the system was surely as good as could have been expected. Indeed, thanks to the earnest faith in education that dominated the colonial mind even in the dark days of the middle period,[28] the system could stand comparison with those of England and Europe. The vigor of this faith is one of the principal keys to the colonial mind. It was strong in 1636:

> After God had carried us safe to *New-England,* and wee had builded our houses, provided necessaries for our liveli-hood, rear'd convenient places for Gods worship, and setled the Civill Government: One of the next things we longed for, and looked after was to advance *Learning* and perpetuate it to Posterity; dreading to leave an illiterate Ministery to the Churches, when our present Ministers shall lie in the Dust. And as wee were thinking and consulting how to effect this great Work; it pleased God to stir up the heart of one Mr. *Harvard* (a godly Gentleman, and a lover of Learning, there living amongst us) to give the one halfe of his Estate (it being in all about 1700. l.) towards the erecting of a Colledge, and all his Library: after him another gave 300. l. others after them cast in more, and the publique hand of the State added the rest: The Colledge was, by common consent, appointed to be at Cambridge, (a place very pleasant and accomodate) and is called (according to the name of the first founder) *Harvard Colledge.*[29]

It was no less strong in 1753 and 1754:

Nothing has a more direct Tendency to advance the Happiness and Glory of a Community, than the founding of *publick Schools* and *Seminaries of Learning*, for the *Education of Youth*, and adorning their Minds with useful Knowledge and Virtue.[30]

The Right Education of Youth has ever been esteemed, by wise Men, one of the chief cares of the best constituted States; and it is a Truth, confirmed both by Reason and Experience, that *Societies* have more or less flourished, in all that exalts or embellishes human Nature, in Proportion as they have taken more or less Care in this important matter.[31]

The ideals of colonial education outran the reality. Then as now men lamented publicly the "contemptuous Treatment of, and parsimonious Provision for, the Support of the Learned," and the seeming willingness of the community "to extinguish Learning, by starving its Propagators." [32] Yet rarely in history has a pioneer people given so much thought and support to education. Conservative and impoverished as the system may seem to us, it taught the mass of men to get along on their own and the best of men to think and lead.

CULTURE IN THE COLONIES

Culture—which we will define for present purposes as the enjoyment, criticism, and production of literature, music, drama, and the graphic arts—was the stepchild of colonial society.[33] It was urban, centered for the most part in seaports like Boston and Philadelphia and capitals like Annapolis and Williamsburg; [34] derivative, taking much of its inspiration and model from the culture of the mother country; [35] passive, emphasizing enjoyment and imitation rather than creation; late-blooming, waiting perforce on the rise of an indigenous aristocracy with sufficient wealth, leisure, and aspirations to elegance; and class-conscious, supported on the narrow base of the upper and upper-middle classes. We cannot emphasize too strongly as factors in cultural development the primary role of the towns, the dominance of conscious ties with England, and the sponsorship of the merchant aristocracy. Nor should we forget, as we shake our heads over the pitifully small production of art and literature of lasting value or universal interest, the impediments that geography, religion, and the level of the economy offered to the rise of a culture worthy of the times. Most colonists would probably have agreed smugly or reluctantly with a New England author, "The Plow-man that raiseth Grain is more serviceable to Mankind, than the Painter who draws only to please the Eye. The Carpenter who builds a good House to defend us from the Wind and Weather, is more serviceable than the curious Carver, who employs his Art to please the Fancy." [36] Let us examine the record of cultural achievement and see to what extent art and literature were able to surmount these obstacles.

LITERATURE.[37] Prose and poetry, especially when instructive and hortatory, were both held in high esteem throughout the colonial period. Printing-houses grew ever more numerous and productive. By the middle of the eighteenth century some twenty presses were printing several hundred separate titles and nearly twenty newspapers and magazines a year, all of which led one cynic to observe, "Letters (I don't mean Learning) grow upon us daily." [38] Books and periodicals were imported in astounding numbers from England, and booksellers and subscription libraries did a thriving business. The Library Company of Philadelphia, the Charleston Library Society, and the New York Society Library were the most successful examples of a movement that did much to lift the level of culture and understanding in the colonies.[39] Private libraries, too, played an essential part in this advance,[40] for in a pioneer society eager for knowledge the lending of books was a public duty. Franklin's tribute to the colonial libraries is well worth hearing:

> These libraries have improved the general conversation of the Americans, made the common tradesmen and farmers as intelligent as most gentlemen from other countries, and perhaps have contributed in some degree to the stand so generally made throughout the colonies in defence of their privileges.[41]

Theological disputation, the classics,[42] history, moral essays, and heroic verse were the forms of literature most generally imported and enjoyed. Although it is impossible to judge the popularity of each of the scores of English, Continental, and classical authors whose works appear repeatedly in library lists, wills, and advertisements, we can say with certainty that the urban culture of the eighteenth century prized two writers above all others: Joseph Addison (and to a lesser extent Richard Steele) for *The Spectator*, Alexander Pope for *An Essay on Man*.[43] Both the style and content of these products of eighteenth-century England appealed strongly to the colonial mind. The prose of *The Spectator* and the poetry of the *Essay on Man* were the arbiters of style. When newspapers were not filled with actual excerpts from these authors, they were overfilled with essays imitative of the one and verse imitative of the other. The *Essay on Man* was reprinted in America five times before 1765.[44] Bacon, Locke, Butler, Shakespeare, Bunyan, Milton, Watts, Defoe, Rapin, Swift, Dryden, Burnet, Richardson, Dodsley, and Smollett were perhaps the next most popular literary figures. Montaigne, Voltaire,[45] Buffon, Rabelais, and Montesquieu all won substantial followings, but the most popular single item of French origin was Fénelon's *Télémaque*, a political novel advertising the doctrine that kings exist for people rather than the other way around. This list of authors provides a useful guide to colonial tastes and aspirations.[46]

The bulk of the literature produced by the colonists themselves consisted of theological tracts, political pamphlets, and histories. Jonathan Edwards and John Woolman did the best-remembered work in the first category, although the fantastic outpourings of the Mathers and their colleagues can also be panned for a few semiprecious gems. Political pamphleteering became a popular pastime in the eighteenth century, reaching its artistic zenith in some of the great tracts to be discussed later in this book. The works of

Bradford, Winthrop, Johnson, Mather, Prince, Stith, Byrd, Beverley, Smith, Douglass, Colden, and above all Hutchinson form a highly respectable body of historical literature. Several of these histories were published in colonial times to edify, inspire, and exhort the colonists themselves. The majestic theme of the American Mission raises some of them to heights of colonial self-consciousness not reached in any other branch of our early literature. As to poets, the colonies spawned dozens of imitators of Pope like Mather Byles and producers of doggerel like Michael Wigglesworth, but not one who could be taken seriously in England. Anne Bradstreet, Edward Taylor of Massachusetts, the unknown author of "Bacon's Epitaph," and Francis Hopkinson of Philadelphia are the most interesting representatives of the handful of poets who receive passing mention in modern anthologies.

The literature of early America was wholly a product of men busy with the affairs of life. No man of letters ever earned his bread in the colonies. Yet for all the stultifying effects of environment and dependence, a literature of astonishing quantity and at least moderate quality did manage to flourish. In Franklin's descriptions of his experiments, Byrd's entertaining comments on the men of the frontier, and the "captive narratives" of plain people like Mary Rowlandson the beginnings of a true American literature are plainly visible. Historians of our literature have no cause to apologize for the colonial period.

MUSIC AND THE THEATER. Music as an art form labored under especially discouraging handicaps.[47] Not until well into the eighteenth century were the tastes and fortunes of any group of colonists sufficiently advanced to promote the staging of a formal concert; the first such affair took place under Anglican auspices, and amid prophecies of hellfire, in Boston in 1731. Well before this date, especially in the more easy-going and gentle-minded South, a few men of polite aspirations were performing on imported instruments in their own homes. As the eighteenth century progressed, private enjoyment and public performance both quickened noticeably. The latter was largely confined to urban centers, where the composers in favor in London were treated with respect if not entire fidelity. American composers did not exist. The sonatas of Scarlatti and suites of Handel vied with the ever-welcome *Beggar's Opera* for first rank in cultivated hearts.[48] The peak of artistic performance and popular enjoyment was reached among the Germans, especially in the Moravian settlement at Bethlehem. Yet a high wall of cultural isolation separated these people from the aristocracy of the urban centers. The laboriously imitative chamber concerts staged in the governor's palace at Williamsburg were unfortunately more representative of the quality and popularity of serious music in colonial America.

The theater was, if anything, even more dependent on alien plays and players for the modest success it achieved.[49] The old prejudices against the drama, like those against music and dancing, gave way slowly in some places and not at all in others. In this instance, too, the English-conscious gentry of the cities led the way in defying an active tradition that exulted in the absence of "Masquerades, Plays, Bells, Midnight Revellings or Assemblies to

Debauch the Mind or promote Intrigue." [50] Despite the deep hostility that continued well past 1765 in Quaker-Presbyterian Philadelphia and in Puritan Boston,[51] the theater took strong hold in the few places that could support it. New York, Charleston, and Williamsburg were treated to isolated performances and "seasons." Shakespeare (unadulterated or as "altered by Colly Cibber, Esq."), Steele, Rowe, Lillo, Congreve, Farquhar, Garrick, Gay, Dryden, and Otway were all welcomed with acclaim, but Addison's *Cato*, which appealed to Whiggish hearts even more strongly than Fénelon's *Télémaque*, was the prime favorite of American audiences. Thomas Godfrey, jr.'s *Prince of Parthia*, which was presented at Philadelphia in 1767, was the first American play to be performed in public. It was noticeably faithful to English models in form, plot, language, and mood. And although colonists staged amateur plays in club, home, and college, and filled minor roles in professional productions, the best roles in the best performances were generally spoken by Englishmen. The traveling company of Englishmen organized by Lewis Hallam and continued by David Douglass was the one bright ornament of the colonial theater. Douglass fooled no one but the patriots when he changed the name of his troupe to "The American Company" in 1766.

PAINTING AND ARCHITECTURE. Far less dependent and derivative than the theater, and therefore far more successful in expressing creative impulses in the colonial mind, was the art of painting.[52] Many painters in the colonies, such as Smibert, Theus, and Hesselius, were transplanted Europeans; many more were native limners who were willing slaves to the latest English style. Yet in Robert Feke, Benjamin West, John Singleton Copley, and Charles Willson Peale, the colonies bred artists of genuine merit. In his American phase Copley raised the genre of bourgeois realism to a high level of beauty and maturity. He was unquestionably early America's most notable artistic genius. Yet his removal to England is more instructive for our purposes than a critical appraisal of *Mrs. Michael Gill* or the wonderful *Boy with Squirrel*. Early American painting was for the most part portrait-painting under the sponsorship of the aristocracy, and far too much of it was in an inappropriate "court style." The limits of such sponsorship were plainly too narrow for men with the genius of Copley and West. America could not yet give the artist enough of the things he needed except majestic themes and the exciting sense of identification with a brave new world. Yet in cutting himself loose from these elements in his native surroundings, each of these estimable painters lost his chance for universal acclaim.

American architecture was peculiarly the prisoner of England.[53] Except for Peter Harrison of Newport,[54] himself an immigrant from England, the colonies did not produce a single architect who could challenge the dictatorial sway of the construction guides of Englishmen like Inigo Jones and James Gibbs. On the frontier and among the plain people architecture could be functional, shrewd, and expressive of solid values. But wherever wealth accumulated and men aspired, deliberate imitation of English patterns was the rule. The great houses of the eighteenth-century aristocracy were almost all Georgian. The Warner house in Portsmouth and the Hammond house in Annapolis are visible reminders that while the taste of our ancestors was good as far as it went, it went straight to England whenever it had the chance. If there is much that is American about Nassau Hall and Westover, there is, we must admit, much more that is English.

A word might well be added about the minor arts in America.[55] The range of imaginative power and degree of technical skill necessary to produce lasting achievements in the primary arts could not yet grow in American soil, but in such crafts as furniture-making and silversmithing colonial craftsmen, once again following the lead if not the dictation of English masters, achieved a high level of professional competence. The cabinetmakers and silversmiths of Philadelphia could have made a handsome living in London. An insight into the character and aspirations of colonial society is the fact that these creators of objects both useful and beautiful were rewarded with large incomes and high social standing.

The folk culture of the colonies was more legend than fact. Honest searchers for genuine examples of colonial folk-art—whether in furniture, sign-painting, balladry, gravestones,[56] or frontier narratives—are quite certain to meet frustration. Except among the culturally isolated Germans of the western valleys the art, music, and literature of the people was extremely sterile. Much has been made of the almanacs of Franklin, Ames, and their lesser imitators as vehicles of folk culture, but only by those who confuse instruction with creation. The almanacs are a phenomenon of early American mass-culture that fully deserve the attention they get, but as media that dispensed the imported wisdom of Newton and secular morality of Franklin downward to the plain people rather than channeling the native wisdom of the plain people upward to the cultivated world. In time the almanacs became small magazines that offered lectures on astronomy, practical hints on farming, political thoughts, capsuled history, jokes, poems, recipes, distance tables, medical advice, moral essays, and calculations.[57] The almanac was, next to the Bible, the most active ingredient in the culture of the people; as such it provides a rewarding glimpse of the practicality and sterility that characterized the mass mind.

The culture of the colonies, like that of later America, was a jumble of contradictions: good taste and bad taste and no taste at all; slavish imitation, intelligent selection, and bold experiment; erudition, common sense, and base ignorance. The creation of an indigenous culture was regarded as the next great task of this ingenious people, yet it was already being argued that they would be led astray rather than set free by the accumulation of surplus capital. Liberty, respect for learning and artistic achievement, and the broadening of educational opportunity were factors highly favorable to the building of an American culture, but materialism had already begun its tireless assault on sound values and the creative impulse. "The only principle of Life propagated among the young People is to get Money," growled Cadwallader Colden in 1748, "and Men are only esteemed according to . . . the Money they are possessed of." [58] The struggle of the artist and scholar to gain the respect and encouragement of their fellow citizens was already under way in the colonial period.

SCIENCE IN THE COLONIES

The colonial mind had a peculiar respect and affinity for science.[59] The opening of America to settlement and the birth of modern science were cognate developments of Western civilization. Science and its philosophical corollaries were perhaps the most important intellectual force shaping the destiny of eighteenth-century America, and the men of America were quick to acknowledge and eager to repay the debt. It is not entirely coincidental that in this instance the westward current of ideas should have been at least partially reversed. Colonial influence on English and European thought scored its one modest success in the field of science. The reasons for the vigor of colonial science are not easy to unravel, but it is certainly possible to point to the overpowering presence of nature, the practical needs of the colonists, and the fascination of the natural world for minds grown weary of the supernatural as factors that recommended it strongly to Americans of all classes and sections.

Science in colonial America was not just science but Newtonian science, an inquiry into the phenomena of the natural world in the spirit and with the methods of Sir Isaac Newton. The influence of this great man, which extended well beyond the bounds of science, was a determining element in the relationship of the colonial mind to the world about it.[60] Through Newton's writings the whole new approach to nature of Bacon, Copernicus, Harvey, Kepler, Brahe, Galileo, Descartes, and Boyle was impressed on colonial minds. Precious few colonists ever so much as saw the cover of the *Principia*, but the assumptions and attitudes of Newtonian science, made palatable to the learned few in dozens of explanatory books and to the people in almanacs and newspapers, took strong hold upon their imaginations. As Carl Becker has written, "It was not necessary to read the *Principia* in order to be a good Newtonian, any more than it is necessary to read the *Origin of Species* in order to be a good Darwinian."[61] Empiricism, rationalism, induction, the mechanical explanation of natural phenomena—all these techniques and postulates of the new science found favor in the inquiring colonial mind. And since Newton insisted stubbornly that he had come not to destroy but to fulfill the teachings of revealed religion, Cotton Mather could take him to his bosom no less warmly than Franklin or Colden. Mather extended Newton the ultimate accolade when he called him "the perpetual Dictator of the learned World."[62] Most Americans were ready to sing right along with William Livingston to

> IMMORTAL NEWTON; whose illustrious name
> Will shine on records of eternal fame.[63]

Science in the colonies was divided into two broad categories: natural philosophy, in which physics and astronomy were the most important special fields, and natural history, in which botany aroused the keenest interest. The mind of the colonial scientist was not, of course, given to making careful distinctions; the man we now remember for work in electricity or astronomy was probably no less concerned with botany, medicine, mechanics, oceanography, agriculture, and meteorology. Students of the colonial mind must use modern divisions and subdivisions of science with extreme care, for the ideal of the whole man, certainly in the field of science, still had meaning in the eighteenth century.

A goodly company of Americans made contributions to the accumulating body of knowledge of the natural world. The great man of colonial science, Benjamin Franklin, whose career as natural philosopher we shall describe in Chapter 11, was always quick to acknowledge the co-operation and discoveries of the many other Americans with whom he worked and corresponded. John Winthrop of Harvard, second only to Franklin in the muster of colonial scientists, repaid his debt to Newton with brilliant work in astronomy and sound investigation in a half-dozen other fields.[64] Thomas Brattle of Harvard, some of whose observations were used by Newton in the *Principia*, and David Rittenhouse of Philadelphia, whose orreries at Princeton and Philadelphia were wonders of the age,[65] were other pioneers in a field that had a strong appeal for colonial minds.[66] Electricity, hardly less popular than astronomy after the diffusion of Franklin's great experiments, numbered such votaries as James Bowdoin of Boston, John Lining of Charleston, Philip Syng of Franklin's Junto, and Ebenezer Kinnersley, the popularizer of electrical knowledge. All these men were willing workers in other vineyards of natural philosophy. Franklin had a correspondent worthy of his fellowship in Cadwallader Colden, the nearest thing to the whole man New York has ever offered. Colden, who turned his hand to at least as many divisions of science as Franklin, is of particular interest as the first scientific mind in America more devoted to theory than to practical experiment. His ambitious *Principles of Action in Matter*, which was published in American, England, and on the Continent,[67] was a bold if bewildering attempt to enlarge upon Newton.

Natural history attracted several first-rate minds. John Clayton's *Flora Virginia*, Jared Eliot's experiments in scientific agriculture, James Logan's study of sex in plants, Alexander Garden's classification of plants, and above all John Bartram's work in collection and cross-fertilization were contributions to botany which received the acclaim of the best European natural scientists. William Douglass, John Banister, William Byrd II, Dr. John Mitchell, and Colden were other close observers of the flora of the new world. Douglass, Winthrop, and others looked hard for the natural causes of earthquakes. Bartram, Colden, Mitchell, and Lewis Evans pioneered in descriptive anthropology. Medicine, a time-honored battlefield of superstitious traditionalism and scientific procedure, made few advances in the colonies,[68] and most of these were the work of men trained in Europe. John Tennent, Zabdiel Boylston, Colden, Garden, Lining, Douglass, Mitchell, John Kearsley, Thomas Bond, and John Morgan were men whose knowledge and methods were more prophetic than typical. It has been estimated that only 200 out of 3,500 persons practicing medicine in the colonies just before the Revolution had medical degrees,[69] and little that even these 200 advised would be classed today as sound medicine.[70]

The men who have been mentioned here were only the most prominent of colonial scientists. Dozens of other searchers of the wonders of the world, from John Winthrop, jr., of Connecticut through Thomas Robie of Harvard to William Small of William and Mary, are also due a measure of credit for the development of this uniquely successful branch of learning.

Whatever the object of their inquiries and however primitive their methods, colonial scientists had three traits in common: They showed a special interest in the natural world immediately about them, whether it took the form of rattlesnakes, corn, lightning, Indians, or earthquakes; they were, with one or two obvious exceptions like Colden the theorist and Bartram the pure lover of nature, quite utilitarian in outlook or motivation, hoping consciously that their work would prove a "benefit of mankind in general"; [71] and they were imbued with the spirit of the new science, with the conviction that openminded observation was the only proper technique with which to come to grips with nature. Their knowledge of mathematical tools may have been limited and their hypotheses few, but they were an enthusiastic band of brothers in their devotion to nature and her laws. Another characteristic common to most colonial scientists was the pursuit of full careers in other fields. Bartram was able to support himself by selling plants and seeds to other botanists; Winthrop, Small, and Isaac Greenwood of Harvard earned livelihoods as teachers. The others were at best what we would call elegant amateurs.

Only a small fraction of the advances in science registered in this era were inspired or supported by the colleges. Yet the colleges were unusually friendly to science.[72] Even in the seventeenth century Harvard was offering some instruction in natural philosophy; there is evidence that Copernicus had conquered the young Turks of the faculty as early as 1659.[73] Late in the century began a shift to the new science which was brought to a revolutionary if somewhat alcoholic climax in the professorship of Isaac Greenwood (1727-1738). While Harvard and William and Mary led the way, the others were not far behind. By 1750 science claimed a sizable portion of the student's time at each of the old colleges, and at the Philadelphia Academy he might be giving up to forty per cent of his hours to mathematics, physics, mechanics, astronomy, botany, agriculture, and other scientific studies. The methods of teaching were dull, primitive, and didactic by modern standards, but they were well on the road to liberation from the scholastic past. Jefferson's tribute to William Small—"To his enlightened and affectionate guidance of my studies while at college, I am indebted for everything" [74]—was also a tribute to academic science in the colonies. If it did little to discover, it did much to receive, disseminate, and inspire.

We must salute the Royal Society of London for its assistance to colonial science. The leadership of this great institution reminds us that the eminence of American science was only relative, that in this area, too, the colonies were still a provincial outpost of European learning. The learned society rather than the college was the key institution in the advance of scientific learning in the Age of the Enlightenment,[75] and the fact that colonists like Franklin were willing but unable to inaugurate a genuine learned society before 1765 is evidence of a social order not yet ready for intellectual independence.[76] In the absence of a colonial corresponding society, the Royal Society was the channel through which new discoveries and hypotheses were sped to America and American contributions were advertised to England and the continent. The *Philosophical Transactions* carried several score important papers originating in the colonies, and a full eighteen Americans were elected to fellowship in the Society before 1776.[77]

The currents of science flowing in from England and Europe and the freshets of science arising in the colonies gave a notable swell to the onward course of political liberty. The new freedom in science and the new freedom in government were, of course, collateral developments in the unfolding of the Enlightenment. It would be hard to say which freedom, political or scientific, was more instrumental in fostering the other. We may point to at least three ways in which Newtonian science quickened the advance toward free government. First, it helped break down the wall of superstition and ignorance which blocked the road to the open society. We have learned already of the importance of humanistic religion in the rise of political liberty; the new science was historically and logically a major element in this religion. The repressive alliance of authoritarian religion and the monolithic state fought savagely, but in vain, against the massive infiltration of the new alliance of science, rationalism, and libertarian political thought. In America as in Europe science released men's minds from bondage to the "false truths of revelation," then encouraged these minds to believe that truth, in any field of human endeavor, could be discovered by impartial observation and fearless application of reason. A decisive majority of the best minds in eighteenth-century America considered the use of reason an essential prop of free government,[78] and science had done as much as any other intellectual force to advertise the beauties of reason to their minds.

The advance of science popularized other methods and assumptions that were essential to the conduct of free government. Franklin was only one of a number of forward-looking colonists who recognized the kinship of scientific method and democratic procedure. Free inquiry, free exchange of information, optimism, self-criticism, pragmatism, objectivity—all these ingredients of the coming republic were already active in the republic of science that flourished in the eighteenth century.

Finally, the new science had a direct influence on the development of American political and constitutional thought. Basic to the Newtonian system were the great generalizations of a universe governed by immutable natural laws and of harmony as the pattern and product of these laws. The first of these gave new sanction to the doctrine of natural law; the second had much to do with the growing popularity of the Whiggish principle of balanced government. It is going a bit too far to look upon the American Constitution as a monument to Sir Isaac Newton,[79] but certainly the widespread acceptance of his theory of a harmonious universe helped create an intellectual atmosphere in which a system of checks and balances would have a special appeal to constitution-makers. If John Winthrop could thank immortal Newton for discovering the law of attraction and repulsion, "the fundamental law which the alwise CREATOR has established for regulating the several movements in this grand machine," [80] certainly John Adams could thank him for supporting the law of checks and balances, the fundamental law of the machine of constitutional government.

We must not overstate either the progress or influence of colonial science. America produced no Newton or Boyle, and science was but one of many intellectual forces that encouraged men to think in terms of human liberty. Yet we cannot ignore the influence of the scientific spirit in generating an attitude of optimism and openmindedness, an attitude that the almanacs [81] and newspapers [82] helped to spread among the plain people. Science had done much to improve man's lot, and the end was by no means in sight. The feeling of pride in the advances of the age and of confidence in those yet to come was best expressed by an anonymous writer in the *Virginia Gazette:*

> The World, but a few Ages since, was in a very poor Condition, as to Trade, and Navigation. Nor, indeed, were they much better in other Matters of useful Knowledge. It was a Green-headed Time, every useful Improvement was hid from them; they had neither lok'd into Heaven nor Earth; into the Sea, nor Land, as has been done since. They had Philosophy without Experiment; Mathematics without Instruments; Geometry without Scale; Astronomy without Demonstration. . . . They went to Sea without Compass; and sail'd without the Needle. They view'd the Stars without Telescopes; and measured Latitude without Observation. . . . They had Surgery without Anatomy, and Physicians without the Materia Medica. . . . As for Geographic Discoveries, they had neither seen the North Cape, nor the Cape of Good Hope. . . . As they were ignorant of Places, so of Things also; so vast are the Improvements of Sciences, that all our Knowledge of Mathematics, of Nature, of the brightest Part of humane Wisdom, had their Admission among us within the last two Centuries. . . . The World is now daily increasing in experimental Knowledge, and let no Man flatter the Age, with pretending we are arrived to a Perfection of Discoveries.[83]

PHILOSOPHY IN THE COLONIES

Philosophy in the formal sense of metaphysical speculation hardly existed at all in colonial America.[84] Those men with enough learning to think philosophically were too much concerned with theological disputation or the affairs of life to help build up an environment in which a Hobbes or Locke, or even a Shaftesbury or Berkeley, could arise and prosper. Dr. Samuel Johnson of Connecticut was a devoted exponent of Berkeley's subjective idealism; his *Elementa Philosophia,* written for his students at King's, was the only formal defense of a philosophical system produced in the colonies.[85] Cadwallader Colden wrote a number of books and letters in which he came close to a philosophy of pure materialism.[86] In his ever-charming *Journal* John Woolman brought mysticism to a pitch of intensity rarely if ever matched in this country. And Jonathan Edwards, in his defense of the old faith, worked out a memorable exposition of unreconstructed Puritanism touched with idealism and mysticism. But these were at best the gropings for truth of men who, except for Johnson, cannot be considered philosophers in the technical sense.

Philosophy in the broader sense of an outlook on life or a system of practical ethics found a happy home in the colonial mind. Most educated colonists seem to have searched consciously for fixed principles of moral wisdom, and many of little or no education also had a "philosophy" of their own. Three patterns of thought claim the attention of the student of the colonial mind: Puritanism, rationalism, and middle-class morality. Most men of standing in early America subscribed to one or another, or to a prudent combination, of these working philosophies. All were highly derivative in character, finding their law and prophets in the mother country. All had a formative impact on the developing American mind and thus upon the rise of political liberty.

PURITANISM. The Puritan way of life is an earnest reminder that religion, especially the Christian religion as it emerged from the magnificent mind of John Calvin, was the ascendant element in the working philosophies of most colonists. Puritanism as a way of life was in its prime an extension of a system of theology that held to the austere doctrines of an unknowable and omnipotent God who intervenes constantly in the unfolding of nature and lives of men; of men corrupt and depraved, for whom salvation through grace was the only need and goal; of a world created from nothing and destined for nothing; and of knowledge, true knowledge, as a gift of God to be received through revelation rather than reason.[87] The triumph of orthodox Puritanism as a theology was the signal of its failure as a way of life. It embraced too much, it dug too deep, it speculated too minutely. Most important, it made too much of piety among a people quite unready to renounce the world. Yet "reconstructed Puritanism," the less austere but highly moralistic brand that developed in the colonies, was a leading way of life in eighteenth-century America.

We have learned or will learn of the significance of colonial Puritanism in religion, science, education, economics, politics, and sociology. We may therefore limit ourselves here to a discussion of Puritanism as a system of practical ethics, and to an examination of those elements in it which helped convert it to a faith in which reason triumphed over revelation and good works over grace.

The moral teachings of Puritanism, the principles of individual conduct that it pressed so insistently upon unregenerate man, were just those rules which one might expect to hear proclaimed by a Christian movement burning to reform the world and yet live in it. Piety, sobriety, industry, honesty, frugality, simplicity, order, silence, resolution—these were the instrumental virtues through which men might yet build here on earth a reasonable imitation of the city of God. The practice of them brought Puritan saints no nearer to the arbitrarily bestowed gift of salvation and eternal life, but the man who displayed them in his dealings with other men could consider himself an expediter of God's great plan to reform the world. And although he could not in his orthodoxy subscribe to a covenant of works, it was hard for the good Puritan to believe that he was predestined to eternal torment. The virtuous life was, if not the means, certainly the sign of salvation, and the practice of the Puritan virtues became in itself a consuming purpose.

Both as theology and way of life Puritanism was constantly in evolution. Perhaps the most interesting development, or rather pair of developments, was the splitting of the apparent monolith of Puritanism into the neo-orthodoxy of Jonathan Edwards and Thomas Clap, sons of austere Yale, and the Christian rationalism of Jonathan Mayhew and Charles Chauncy,[88] sons of latitudinarian Harvard. These two lines of development in Puritan thought can be traced back to the dichotomy of revelation and reason in the systems of the great saints like Hooker and Cotton, to the decisive fact of intellectual history that the Puritans, scholastics all, were overly anxious to demonstrate logically the coherency and consistency of revealed dogma. In seeking to bolster revelation with reason, to "make a philosophy out of their piety and objective knowledge out of a subjective mood," [89] they laid open their whole rugged creed to the incursions of rationalism. The liberal theology and moral teachings of Mayhew, which we shall examine at length, were as legitimate descendants of seventeenth-century Puritanism as were the magnificent apologia of Edwards [90] or the reactionary gospel of Clap.[91] Thanks to its historic insistence on reason and disapproval of enthusiasm, Puritanism moved into enlightened rationalism more gracefully and naturally than any other denomination in the Protestant left wing.

The plans of the Puritan fathers for a holy commonwealth in the new world never did stand much chance of success. The wilderness environment was a treacherous foundation, the men of the great migration defective materials. Yet the Puritan system of practical ethics, which called upon responsible, rational, virtuous, self-reliant men to pursue their busy lives within a system of ordered liberty, was the first and, it may certainly be argued, the greatest of all American ways of life.

RATIONALISM. Rationalism was a way of thinking which cherished reason as the source of valid knowledge; assumed the worth and dignity of man, as well as his ability to use reason in the search for happiness and truth; proclaimed a benevolent, dependable, gentlemanly God; and therefore stood forth in its most developed form as an enlightened protest against tradition, dogma, superstition, and authority. Rationalism moved into the colonial consciousness on the heels of Newtonian science,[92] but it found the ground already prepared for it by Puritanism [93] and Anglicanism. The colonial rationalists found their chief sources of inspiration among men of the latter faith: in the writings of such latitudinarians as John Tillotson, Archbishop of Canterbury; Samuel Clarke and William Wollaston, Anglican ministers; and John Locke and Sir Isaac Newton, by their own admission devoted sons of the Church. Those who went one step further, with Lord Shaftesbury and Anthony Collins, to deprive religion entirely of dependence on revelation were dangerously near to embracing all-out deism,[94] but this logical extension of the rationalist position made slow headway among the conservative and practical-minded colonists.[95] Rationalism in colonial America was Christian rationalism, not least because the rich and well-born to whom these ideas appealed were unwilling to sap the most solid foundation of a stable, stratified society.[96] Even so skeptical a thinker as Franklin thought organized Christianity a necessary support of free and ordered government.

Rationalism, like its offspring deism, was more class-conscious than most other systems of thought: It made its deepest inroads into the educated upper class, which was also, be it noted, the carrier of Newtonian science. It made hardly any impression at all on the mass of men, for whom tradition, superstition, and indifference remained determining spiritual influences. The planters, merchants, and liberal preachers who welcomed rationalism to their bosoms were leaders in action as well as thought, and through their good offices rationalism worked considerable influence on the colonial mind. First, it helped liberalize all those religions, especially Congregationalism and Anglicanism, which made room for reason. Second, as the creed of men who labored the distinction between the religion of the Gospels and that of the priests, it reintroduced the moral teachings of Jesus to many upper-class minds. Third, by elevating reason into "an universal rule, as well in religious, as civil affairs," [97] it played a part in ridding educated minds of dependence on tradition and dogma. Next, it gave added impetus to the upward trend of humanitarianism, for it was obsessed with the notion that wicked institutions alone prevented the flowering of the inherent decency of all men. So far as the rationalist was concerned, the most acceptable service to God was kindness to God's children. Fifth, since it drew much of its inspiration from the Newtonian concept of a harmonious universe governed by immutable laws, it advertised the notions of mechanistic society and balanced government, both of them corollaries of the doctrine of higher law. Finally, rationalism placed emphasis on virtuous living and thus contributed to the vogue of morality and moralizing in eighteenth-century America. Most colonial rationalists would have agreed with an author in the Boston *American Magazine* that reason was "speculative Virtue" and virtue "practical Reason." [98] We shall learn more of this liberating doctrine when we meet John Wise, Jonathan Mayhew, and Benjamin Franklin.

MIDDLE-CLASS MORALITY. Few people in history have been more given to public moralizing, to proclaiming a catalogue of virtues and exhorting one another to exhibit them, than the American colonists. Practical morality was an important by-product of Puritanism and rationalism as well as of the actual experiences of the colonists. Yet so prevalent was this pattern of thought, so universal and self-generating was the urge to preach the solid virtues, that we may consider it an independent working-philosophy to which thousands of colonists subscribed directly. We have prefixed the adjective "middle-class" because the virtues most loudly sung and vices most loudly damned were those that the man "on the make," the man so representative of eighteenth-century America, would be especially eager to display or shun. Even the conscious Virginia aristocrat, the devoted reader of Allestree's *A Gentleman's Calling* and Peacham's *The Compleat Gentleman*, was infected with the desire to preach and practice virtues that a genuine Cavalier would have refused to admit to his list.

A thorough check of newspapers and magazines, the chief purveyors of this morality, shows these virtues to have been the most repeatedly discussed: wisdom, justice, temperance, fortitude, industry, frugality, piety, charity, sobriety, sincerity, honesty, simplicity, humility, contentment, love, benevolence, humanity, mercy, patriotism, modesty, patience, and good manners.[99] The columns of newspapers in every part of the colonies were filled with original essays, letters, and London reprints praising one, several, or all of these virtues.[100] The virtues themselves, as can be plainly seen, were an ill-assorted mishmash of Greek, Roman, Christian, and latter-day English qualities, some of them ends and others means, some of them gentle and others quite vulgar in origin and appeal. The vices most often warned against were, of course, the opposites of the cherished virtues: ignorance, injustice, intemperance, cowardice, laziness, luxury, irreverence, selfishness, drunkenness, deceit, fraud, covetousness, vanity, ambition, hate, violence, flattery, ingratitude, and bad manners. The regularity and virulence with which authors assaulted these vices is evidence enough that middle-class morality was more an ideal than a widespread reality in the colonies.

Just how a man was to practice the one and shun the other was never made entirely clear in these thousands of essays. Just why he should do so was proclaimed again and again by imitators of Addison, Pope, Mather, and Franklin: because at the end of the high road of virtue lay the precious goals of individual freedom and national well-being, of liberty and prosperity for a man and his country. By such well-worn devices as the horrible example, the dream, the success story, the portrayal of the good and honest man,[101] the appeal to ancient Rome (the most virtuous country that ever existed),[102] the Greek or Roman oration,[103] and the straightforward promise of prosperity, the men of America bid one another be good.

The ultimate sanction of virtue, to which the moralist appealed repeatedly, was religion. Few men who cherished virtue as the foundation of liberty ever doubted that religion was in turn the foundation of virtue. Said a favorite London reprint:

> Remember, Posterity! that Virtue is the Soul of Liberty, and Religion is the Soul of Virtue; and therefore, to see a People, whose Virtue is departed, exert the Powers invested in them by their Laws, for the Defence of Liberty, would be to the full as great a Miracle, as if a rotten Carcase, the Relic of a departed Soul should rise up, and, unanimated by its former

Inhabitant, perform the ordinary Functions of Life. So that if you will be free, you must be virtuous; and if you will be virtuous, you must be religious. Let me then most seriously and earnestly recommend to you, the earliest and most careful Instruction of Youth, in the Belief of God and the Christian Religion.[104]

Virtue was hardly less dependent on the diffusion of knowledge:

It has been the constant Observation in all Ages and Nations, that as *Learning* and *Knowledge* increased, so did the *Virtue, Strength* and *Liberty* of the People; and where the same has decreased by the like Degrees, the People have degenerated into *Vice, Poverty*, and *Slavery. Ease* and *Plenty* are the natural Fruits of *Liberty;* and where these abound, *Learning* and the liberal Arts flourish.[105]

We may smile, we may weary at the endless moralizing of the colonists, but there can be no doubt that here was a working philosophy of huge consequence for the American future.

The common elements in these philosophies account for their peculiar appeal to the developing American mind. From reconstructed Puritanism, from Christian rationalism, and from the morality of the rising middle-class the colonist learned most of the valuable lessons that he was also learning, if he were any sort of pragmatist, from his efforts to get along in the American environment. All these philosophies sang of individualism, reason, self-improvement, activity, and a religion of good works; all were optimistic about man's nature and the nation's future; all were moralistic, and the morality they preached had its reward in this world as well as in the next; and all of them rejected the notion of infallibility in religion and politics, exalting in its place the great right of private judgment. The ways of life that held sway in the colonial period were uniquely suited to the needs of a vigorous, upstart people more intent upon the pursuit of happines than the storming of the gates of heaven.

POLITICAL THEORY IN THE COLONIES

Economic and social theory, which we touched upon in Chapters 3 and 4, were fields of speculation to which few colonists were attracted. The thinking American had little time or use for economic theory; unlike many of his twentieth-century descendants, he was not given to asserting that human liberty was contingent upon the existence of one particular economic system. His social theory was simply a bundle of unproved assumptions about social stratification, the patriarchal family, female inferiority, and the general hopelessness of improving the lot of the poor, sick, depraved, and enslaved. Economic and social theory both remained at an extremely primitive level throughout the colonial period.

It was quite otherwise with political theory.[106] If the seventeenth century had been an age of theology, the eighteenth was an age of politics. The pace of public life was slow; indifference rather than eager participation marked the average man's attitude toward government. Yet there were incidents—

the founding of an unorthodox newspaper in Boston, the trial of a popular editor in New York, an attack on an unpopular proprietary government in Pennsylvania, an arbitrary levying of a land fee in Virginia—that touched off political controversies of an intensely partisan nature. Men of opposing views rushed boldly into the lists, and arguments over specific issues were supported by appeals to general principles.[107] The resulting pamphlets, broadsides, and newspaper articles reveal that the thinking men of eighteenth-century America were peculiarly at home in political disputation. They reveal, too, the astonishing distance the colonial mind had traveled since the logic-chopping days of the New England saints. Theology still held prime interest for many colonists, as Dr. Hamilton learned in a Connecticut tavern:

> After dinner there came in a rabble of clowns who fell to disputing upon points of divinity as learnedly as if they had been professed theologues. 'Tis strange to see how this humour prevails, even among the lower class of the people here. They will talk so pointedly about justification, sanctification, adoption, regeneration, repentance, free grace, reprobation, original sin, and a thousand other such pritty, chimerical knick knacks as if they had done nothing but studied divinity all their life time and perused all the lumber of the scholastic divines, and yet the fellows look as much, or rather more, like clowns than the very riffraff of our Maryland planters. To talk in this dialect in our parts would be like Greek, Hebrew, or Arabick.[108]

But the colonist who counted, the preacher or merchant or planter who led his fellows in thought and action, devoted a healthy portion of his speculative moments to political thought. Although Parts 2 and 3 of this book will be given over entirely to the political theory of colonial and Revolutionary America, it would seem advisable to round out this discussion with a few general observations on this subject so appealing to the colonial mind.

The leading figures in political thought were educated men in the upper and upper-middle classes: the prophetic preachers of New England, the contentious merchants and lawyers of the middle colonies, and the less articulate but no less mettlesome planters of the South. The result of this monopoly of political disputation by men of affairs was a political theory more imitative than original, more opportunistic than profound, more propagandistic than speculative. The chief printed sources—the Massachusetts and Connecticut election sermons,[109] the essays and letters in such politically conscious journals as the New-England Courant (1721-1722), New-York Weekly Journal (1733-1736), Boston Independent Advertiser (1748-1749), and Independent Reflector (1752-1753),[110] and the pamphlets and public letters of such secular thinkers as Daniel Dulany, Richard Bland, Joseph Galloway, Benjamin Franklin, and William Livingston—show that political thought was the handmaiden of political action. The mission of colonial America was to carry a great political tradition to conclusion, not to create a great tradition of its own.

Political thought in the colonies was a proudly conscious extension of political thought in England. The more independent and self-assertive the colonists became, the more anxious they seemed to sound like true-born Englishmen. The prophets to whom appeals for support were most often and confidently directed were John Locke,[111] Algernon Sidney,[112] Bolingbroke,[113] John Somers,[114] Benjamin Hoadly,[115] Henry Care,[116] James Burgh,[117] Addison,[118] Pope, and the estimable team of Thomas Gordon and John Trenchard.[119] Americans were not in the habit of appealing to Americans, and Continental publicists like Grotius and Vattel and classical authorities like Plutarch and Cicero were valued chiefly as scouts for the English Whigs, the most noble warriors in the great army of libertarian political thought. The colonists stood, especially in their reception of natural law, at the end of a line of speculative development more than two thousand years old. They could very easily have imported all their essential theoretical notions straight from the Continent. The most attractive political thinker of the middle period, John Wise of Ipswich, found most of his explosive ideas in the *De Jure Naturae* of Baron Pufendorf. But most colonists preferred to go to the English writers in the Whig tradition for their lessons in political theory. Locke, Bolingbroke, Sidney, Addison, and Gordon and Trenchard were, so far as the colonists were concerned, the great men of this tradition, and the greatest of these were Gordon and Trenchard. No one can spend any time in the newspapers, library inventories, and pamphlets of colonial America without realizing that *Cato's Letters* rather than Locke's *Civil Government* was the most popular, quotable, esteemed source of political ideas in the colonial period.[120] The uncompromising Whiggery of "the Divine English Cato" was well calculated to stir colonial hearts. So long as Americans were more concerned with English rights than natural rights, Gordon and Trenchard were the witnesses most repeatedly called to support their pretensions to liberty.

The appeal of Gordon, Trenchard, Locke, and the other great defenders of English liberty was in no sense a narrow one. Except for a few lonely votaries of Tory conservatism, colonists of every political shade were dedicated wholeheartedly to the English constitutional tradition. Conservatives, middle-of-the-roaders, and radicals hammered at one another with the slogans of Whiggery. Rarely if ever in the history of free government has there been so unanimous a "party line" as that to which the colonists pledged their uncritical allegiance. And rarely if ever has the party line been so easily reduced to one comprehensible concept, even to one wonderful word: *Liberty*. Liberty, defined simply and unanimously as that "which exempts one Man from Subjection to another, so far as the Order and Oeconomy of Government will permit," [121] was the undefiled darling of colonial political thought. The fact that little attempt was made to go any further with this definition, except to make pious distinctions between liberty and license,[122] served only to strengthen the notion that liberty was the ultimate value toward which political speculation should be directed.[123] One of the authors of the *Independent Reflector* spoke for almost all colonial thinkers when he adopted as his "principal Design . . . opposing Oppression, and vindicating the *Liberty of Man*." [124]

In colonial as in English political thought the edifice of liberty was made to rest on three grand supports: natural law and natural rights, Whig constitutionalism, and virtue. Colonial political thought in the middle and late periods was dedicated almost exclusively to these three essentials of the "party line."

The ancient doctrine of natural law and its latter-day corollary of natural rights were staples of political theory.[125] We shall pay particular attention to colonial refinements of this noble philosophy in the chapters on Wise, Mayhew, and Bland, but it should be made clear now that almost all colonial publicists believed in a higher and controlling law, a scheme of moral absolutes to be discovered and understood principally through the use of reason.[126] The colonist who accepted the law of nature was more than likely to subscribe to these other teachings of this famous school: the concept of man as an essentially good, sociable, educable creature; [127] the historical or logical state of nature; [128] the formation of society and government through an act of will, specifically through the technique of compact or contract; [129] "Peace and Security," "the Publick Good," "the Happiness of the People," and "the preservation of the natural Rights of Mankind" as the chief ends of government; [130] the retention by men who have entered society of the largest feasible portion of their natural rights [131] (including the right to property) [132] and natural equality; [133] the instrument of majority rule as the one workable method of decision "among all Communities of civiliz'd Nations"; [134] public office as a public trust, the doctrine that magistrates are servants rather than rulers of the people; [135] the great right of resistance (rarely if ever styled "rebellion" or "revolution") against rulers bent on tyranny or violation of the law of nature.[136]

A favorite corollary of natural law was the concept of popular sovereignty. Colonial thinkers delighted to quote *Cato's Letters* on "the *sacred Priviledges of the People;* the *inviolable Majesty of the People;* the *awful Authority of the People,* and *the unappealable Judgment of the People.*" [137] No less favored was the belief that government was "of all human Things the most inestimable Blessing that Mankind enjoy." [138] The notion that government is at best a necessary evil found little if any response in colonial minds. Government, certainly free government, was good, beneficial, and popular, the product of purposeful men acting in pursuit of universal principles.

The second support of "Liberty, charming Liberty" was Whig constitutionalism. The principles and slogans of Whiggery were imported wholesale into colonial polemics and, until the very end of the colonial period, were more popular with the average colonist than were the principles of natural law and rights. The influence of English upon American political thought was in this instance overwhelming. The colonists sang continually these major themes of Whiggery: the English Constitution ("the best model of Government that can be framed by Mortals"); [139] English rights ("GOD be thanked, we enjoy the Liberties of England"); [140] balanced government ("the most compleat and regular, that has ever been contrived by the Wisdom of Man"); [141] jury trial ("that firmest Barrier of English Liberty"); [142] habeas corpus ("that inestimable jewel"); [143] limited monarchy ("under the mild and gentle Administration of a *limited* Prince, every Thing looks cheerful and happy, smiling and serene"); [144] the malignity of arbitrary power, a state in which the "Sovereign Power is directed by the Passions, Ignorance & Lust of them that Rule").[145]

They were equally pleased to sound the minor notes on rotation-in-office,[146] annual Parliaments,[147] free elections,[148] fear of standing armies,[149] liberty of the press,[150] the curse of "placemen," [151] the blessing of learned and upright judges,[152] and the "baleful influence of Party." [153] Political controversy in America before 1765 was carried on exclusively in the Whig idiom, with its devotion to the Glorious Revolution,[154] its hatred of the Jacobites,[155] and its consistent denunciation of the "popish doctrine of passive obedience and non-resistance." [156] Conservatives might lay extra emphasis on the principles of balanced government and property rights, but this did not make them any the less Whiggish in conviction.[157] "Before the revolution," wrote Jefferson, "we were all good Whigs, cordial in their free principles, and in their jealousies of the executive Magistrate." [158]

The colonist had no need or urge to fawn upon English sensibilities. He was entirely sincere and straight in his own mind when, in defiance of absolute monarchies, he cried:

> How much must an inhabitant of these Dispotick Governments envy an *English* man the Liberty he enjoys? . . . In such a Country, sure every Man in his right Senses would dwell if he could.[159]

This did not mean that he must go to England to find liberty and happiness, for the colonies were not only extensions but improved extensions of England.[160] Nor was English blood the condition of English liberty. A Pennsylvanian reminded his fellow freeholders:

> Whether you be *English, Irish, Germans,* or *Swedes,* whether you be churchmen presbyterians, quakers, or of any other denomination of religion, whatsoever, you are by your residence, and the laws of your country, freemen and not slaves. You are entitled to all the liberties of *Englishmen* and the freedom of this constitution.[161]

According to sound Whig doctrine, the antiquity of the English Constitution and liberties was their chief claim to devotion. As the colonists became increasingly conscious of natural law and rights, they began to set conformity to nature alongside antiquity as an explanation of the peculiar excellence of the English scheme. The printer of the *Connecticut Gazette* declared to his readers, "It is the glory of the British Government, that these natural Rights of Mankind, are secured by the Laws of the Land." [162] The English Constitution was the most accurate possible earthly model of the laws of nature; English rights were equally accurate reproductions of natural rights. The colonists could count no greater blessing, not even their natural situation, than their inheritance of the English form of government. A writer in one of the most American of newspapers asserted:

It has been a Question much controverted in the World, what Form of Government is best: And in what System . . . Liberty is best consulted and preserved. I cannot say, that I am wholly free from that Prejudice, which generally possesses Men in Favour of their own Country, and the Manners they have been used to from their Infancy: But I must needs declare for my own Part, there is no Form of Civil Government, which I have ever heard or read of, appears to me so well calculated, to preserve this Blessing, or to secure to its Subjects, all the most valuable Advantages of Civil Society, as the *English*. For in none that I have ever met with, is the Power of the Governors, and the Rights of the Governed, more nicely adjusted; or the Power which is necessary in the very Nature of Government to be intrusted in the Hands of some, by wiser Checks prevented from growing exorbitant.

This Constitution has indeed passed through various Emendations; but the principal Parts of it, are of very ancient Standing; and have continued through the several Successions of Kings to this Day; having never been in any great Degree attacked by any, but they have lost their Lives or their Crowns in the Attempt.

From this happy Constitution of our Mother Country, Ours in This is copied, or rather improved upon: Our invaluable CHARTER secures to us, all the English Liberties, besides which we have some additional Privileges, which the common People there have not. Our Fathers had so severely felt, the Effects of Tyranny, and the Weight of the *Bishops Yoke*, that they underwent the greatest Difficulties and Toils, to secure to themselves, and transmit to their Posterity, these invaluable Blessings:—And we their Posterity are this Day reaping the Fruits of their Toils.—Happy, beyond Expression! in the Form of our Government—In the Liberty we enjoy—if we know our own Happiness, and how to improve it.[163]

The author of this Whiggish piece went on to say:

But neither the wisest Constitution, nor the wisest Laws, will secure the Liberty and Happiness of a People, whose Manners are universally corrupt.—He therefore is the truest Friend to the Liberty of his Country, who tries most to promote its Virtue.—And who so far as his Power and Influence extends, will not suffer a Man to be chosen into any Office of Power and Trust, who is not a wise and virtuous Man. . . .

The sum of all is—If we would most truly enjoy this Gift of Heaven—Let us become a VIRTUOUS PEOPLE:—Then shall we both deserve and enjoy it: While on the other Hand—If we are universally vicious, and debauched in our Manners—Though the Form of our Constitution, carries the Face of the most exalted Freedom, we shall in Reality be the most ABJECT SLAVES.

Here he put his finger upon the third requisite of liberty, expressing a belief, shared by most colonial publicists, that "there is an inseparable connection between publick virtue and publick happiness," and that liberty, the essence of happiness, can exist only among a truly virtuous people.[164] The refinements of this aspect of political thought were many. Some colonists emphasized the dependence of virtue, and therefore of liberty, on the principles of religion.[165] Others called upon parents, educators, and public writers "to paint Virtue in its most beautiful Colours." [166] Still others, many of whom borrowed the idea consciously from *Cato's Letters,* asserted that "publick Men are the Patterns of Private; and the Virtues and Vices of the Governors become quickly the Virtues and Vices of the Governed." [167] A common theme was the arraignment of the most baneful public vices: luxury and corruption.[168] Readers of the newspapers were constantly reminded that "the Roman Virtue and the Roman Liberty expired together." [169] Even more common was the celebration of the great public virtues: patriotism,[170] public service,[171] industry and frugality,[172] justice,[173] and integrity.[174] Colonists were always delighted to hear, especially from English writers, that they were more virtuous than their elder brothers in England.[175]

A favorite practice was to delineate, especially just before election time, the character of the good ruler or representative.[176] In the last decade of the colonial period the ideal of the man of public virtue was made real in the person of William Pitt. The cult of this noblest of Whigs, "the Genius of England and the Comet of his Age," [177] was well advanced toward idolatry at least five years before the Stamp Act. The greatest of "the great men of England," the last and noblest of the Romans, was considered the embodiment of virtue, wisdom, patriotism, liberty, and temperance. The presence of such a man in high places proved that government was sound and just; his departure or dismissal proved that it had turned corrupt and vicious. The art of government was just as simple as that. Political liberty was nothing more than the presence in the body politic of a substantial proportion of virtuous, liberty-loving men.

The colonial belief that men who display, and encourage others to display, the Whig virtues can alone be trusted to rule in a free country [178] was matched by a collateral belief held by the royal governors. Instructed specifically to discourage vice and encourage "virtue and good living," they were constantly making proclamations "for the Encouragement of Piety and Virtue, and for punishing and suppressing Vice, Profaneness and Immorality." [179] The governors, of course, were more concerned with order than liberty, with obedience than justice. Virtue, in their definition, meant cheerful submission to royal authority. Whatever the motivation, it seems safe to say that no people in history was more dedicated to the notion that free government rests upon public and private morality. For our colonial ancestors human liberty was a problem in ethics rather than economics.

To close the circle on the three elements of liberty, we should note that virtue, like the English Constitution, was considered an earthly version of the law of nature. As one writer phrased it, virtue "in its most general sense, consists in an exact observance of the Laws of Nature," which command that we "contribute as much as we can . . . to the Preservation and Happiness of Mankind in General." Liberty, he continues, "is a natural Power of doing, or not doing whatever we have a Mind, so far as is consistent with the Rules of Virtue and the established Laws of the Society to which we belong." Here in one brief passage is the colonial "party line": liberty—the final goal and sweetest fruit of nature, virtue, and the English Constitution. "The End of Government therefore, and the chief business of all wise and just Governours, is, to inforce the Observance of the Laws of Virtue or Nature." [180]

Colonial political thinkers were English to the core, but this should not be taken to mean that they had no ideas or imagination of their own. The process of borrowing was highly selective. Trenchard, Gordon, Locke, Care, and Somers were imported and quoted because they answered the needs of the colonists; dozens of other writers, no less quotable and certainly no less English, were ignored or flatly rejected because they did not. Only the part of the whole English tradition that spoke of liberty got a warm welcome from this colonial people so intent upon liberty. And this part, too, was not accepted without changes in emphasis. Colonial thinkers paid special attention to principles that royal governors tended to play down: representation, freedom of press, equality, and jury trial.

At the same time, they came up with a few twists of their own. Agrarianism, the belief that the good men who make up the good state live and work in the country rather than the city, became increasingly popular in the eighteenth century. Long before Jefferson Americans were warning that the result of "clustering into Towns, is Luxury; a great and mighty Evil, carrying all before it, and crumbling States and Empires, into slow, but inevitable Ruin." [181] Long before John Taylor they were proclaiming that "Agriculture is the most solid Foundation on which to build the Wealth, and . . . the political Virtue of a Commonwealth." [182] A second interesting development was the trend toward what we may properly call political pragmatism. We shall discuss this point at length in the chapter on Franklin, but we should note here the peculiar American insistence that liberty was to be judged by its fruits rather than by its inherent rationality or conformity to nature, and that at least one of the fruits of liberty was economic prosperity.[183] A third variant was the American Mission, the belief that the colonies held a peculiar responsibility for the success of free government. The American version of the concept of the chosen people had its roots in Puritan Massachusetts. Said John Winthrop: "For we must consider that we shall be as a city upon a hill. The eyes of all peoples are upon us, so that if we shall deal falsely with our God in this work we have undertaken, we shall be made a story and a byword throughout the world." "God sifted a Whole Nation," cried William Stoughton in his election sermon of 1668, "that he might send Choice Grain over into this Wilderness." [184] By the eighteenth century this peculiar type of missionary complex had been secularized and amplified. Liberty rather than true religion was to be the burden of America's teaching to the world. The American Mission gave added dignity to colonial speculations about ultimate political truth.

Students of our intellectual history will never agree finally on the year, or even the decade, when the English-Americans in the continental colonies became more American than English in thought and culture. The rub, of course, is the definition of "American," which is often used to denote an idea or artistic creation produced, however imitatively, by someone living in America, and as often to denote an idea or creation that is original or at least indigenous, one that could not be exactly duplicated anywhere else. If we adopt, as we probably should, the latter definition, we must acknowledge that there was very little genuinely American in colonial thought and culture. The influence of England—a blessing to the extent that it lent the colonists a helping hand and kept them from excessive insularity, a disservice to the extent that it choked off native creative impulses—was paramount, never more so than at the moment when the colonists put on their first show of purposeful resistance to English imperial policy. Addison and Steele, Gordon and Trenchard, Locke, Newton, Pope—the roll-call of these great idols of the colonial mind is a measure of American intellectual dependence on England.

Yet the dependence was that of an imitative and fast-growing younger brother rather than of a servile and stunted child. It must be emphasized again that colonial borrowing of English institutions and ideas was selective, and that the chief criterion of selection was the usefulness of institution or idea to a people headed consciously in the direction of liberty. In all aspects of colonial thought, in science and education no less than in philosophy and political theory, the trend was to liberty, democracy, originality, and self-reliance. The men of the American settlements were a special breed of colonist, and theirs was accordingly a special brand of colonial culture.

Part 2

THE MEN

The American colonists were not completely at the mercy of the whims and dictates of their environment. Much of the environment was of their own making; and if circumstances were favorable to the rise of liberty, they did not relieve the colonists of the formidable task of winning it for themselves. The condition of liberty in 1765 was in large part the work of men determined to be free. The theory of liberty was even more positively their creation. Gifted leaders had received, reshaped, and proclaimed anew the principles of human freedom that were one of Western man's fairest possessions. The mass of men, who were unimaginative but stubborn in their notions of liberty, had accepted this revised version of an ancient faith and had thereby converted it into a popular creed.

Part 2 of this book is a testimony to that historic process, a reminder of the prime role that men have played in the growth of the American political tradition. It salutes the mass of men in the colonies by saying a few words about their national origins; it introduces the select group of representative leaders by recording the names of the other gifted men who had to be excluded from consideration.

NATIONAL ORIGINS OF THE COLONISTS

The attempt of historians and genealogists to decipher the national origins of the colonists has led to confusion and controversy, first, because of a manifest lack of statistics, and second, because of the temptation, apparently too strong even for some of our best-intentioned scholars, to magnify the numbers and accomplishments of one nationality at the expense of all others. Nevertheless, the development of more reliable historical techniques and a more equitable historical spirit has created a broad area of consensus on the composition and distribution of the population.

It is now generally agreed that almost all immigrants to the colonies came from the middle and lower classes. "The rich stay in Europe," wrote Crèvecoeur; "it is only the middling and the poor that emigrate." [1] The myths of aristocratic lineage die hard, especially in Cavalier country, but diaries, shipping lists, and court minutes tell us in no uncertain terms of the simple origins of even the most haughty families of New York and Virginia. This does not mean that early America was a land of rogues and poor servant-girls. England and the Continent sent over thousands upon thousands of substantial, intelligent, propertied men and women. Yet fully half the people who came to the colonies could not pay their own passage, [2] and gentleman immigrants, even in the seventeenth century, were amazingly few.

As a matter of fact, those twentieth-century Americans who like to go searching for an ancestor among the gentry of East Anglia may wind up with three or four among the riffraff of Old Bailey. Probably thirty to forty thousand convicts were shipped from England to the colonies in the eighteenth century, [3] a fact that inspired Dr. Johnson's famous growl: "Sir, they are a race of convicts, and ought to be content with anything we allow them short of hanging." [4] Their behavior in the colonies, especially in unhappy Virginia and Maryland, moved Franklin to offer America's rattlesnakes to England as the only appropriate return. [5] Not only did transported convicts commit a large proportion of the crimes recorded in eighteenth-century America, but their presence did much to degrade the servant class and make a callous society even more callous. The mother country's insistence on dumping "the dregs, the excrescence of England" [6] in the colonies was a major item in the catalogue of American grievances, especially since the Privy Council vetoed repeatedly the acts through which the colonies sought to protect themselves. [7]

Well before 1765 the colonies had begun to take on a pattern of national origins that was "characteristically American": They looked to one country for their language, institutions, and paramount culture, but to many for their population. [8] Americans were predominantly English in origin, but they were also Scotch, Irish, German, French, Swiss, Dutch, Swedish, and African. It is impossible to fix precisely the proportions of each nationality in the total white population of 1765; the necessary statistics are simply not available. These general percentages are about as accurate as can be expected: English, 65 to 70 per cent; Scots and Scotch-Irish, 12 to 15 per cent; Germans, 6 to 9 per cent; Irish, 3 to 5 per cent; Dutch 3 per cent; all others 3 to 5 per cent. [9] Out of a total population of 1,850,000, probably 400,000 were Negroes and mulattoes and a few thousand Indians (in the settled areas).

The eighteenth rather than seventeenth century was the era of immigration and expansion. The early migrations to Massachusetts and Virginia, astonishing as they must have seemed at the time, were trickles when contrasted with the flood of men that poured into the colonies in the peaceful stretches of the eighteenth century. The natural increase of population was also stepped up in the eighteenth century, a phenomenon to which Franklin called attention with a homely but trustworthy example: "Dr. Elliot writes me, that in their Town of Killingworth in which few or no Strangers come to settle, the People double every 15 Years, as appears by examining the Train band Lists taken annually." [10]

These approximate figures of the total population of the colonies are helpful to bear in mind: [11]

1650	50,000
1675	140,000
1700	240,000
1730	650,000
1750	1,150,000
1765	1,850,000

We may turn now to a brief reckoning of the major and minor national elements in this population.

ENGLISH. The fact that America's career as asylum of the oppressed of many nations was well under way in 1765 should not obscure the predominantly English character of the colonial population. Seven in ten were of English blood,[12] almost nine in ten were British. Although immigration from England tapered off sharply after 1689, the high rate of natural increase among the early families of New England [13] and the tidewater had by 1750 produced a basic stock of perhaps one million English-Americans. It was these people, of course, who controlled America—politically, linguistically, culturally, and institutionally. The Dutch, French, Germans, and Scotch-Irish were energizing transfusions, but the English were, from beginning to end, the body of colonial society. Even Pennsylvania, the most thoroughly cosmopolitan colony, had almost as many people of English descent as of all other nationalities put together.[14] This is a plain truth that historians of this or that national group would do well to keep in mind.

SCOTS AND SCOTCH-IRISH. From the North of Britain came two elements in the population: the Scots, who drifted in directly from their home country throughout the latter part of the colonial period, and the so-called Scotch-Irish, or the "Scots settled in Ireland," who had been living in the North of Ireland since early in the seventeenth century. The Scots,[15] a none too popular people in colonial days, came from both lowlands and highlands. The Scotch clergyman, factor, and schoolmaster from the lowlands—each a familiar figure in the colonies—were often quite English in character and outlook even before emigration. Highlanders, who left Scotland in largest numbers in the hard times after the rebellions of 1715 and 1745, were a more alien element, often preferring to settle in their own isolated communities. Wherever he came from and wherever he settled, the industrious Scot was a man who fitted naturally into the American scene.

The Scotch-Irish of Ulster, who numbered thousands of Englishmen and Irishmen along with the predominant Scots, began to come to America around 1715.[16] These people, for the most part lowlanders, had first been settled in northern Ireland in the reign of James I, had added to their numbers after 1685, and had prospered entirely too much for their own good. Harassed repeatedly by acts of Parliament that excluded their products, the Scotch-Irish were driven to seek a refuge in America. They came by tens of thousands, first to New England,[17] where they were not very enthusiastically welcomed,[18] then to Pennsylvania and the frontier counties to the south. The old colonists called them Irish, but they called themselves British. Said the inhabitants of Londonderry, New Hampshire, in 1720: "We were surprised to hear ourselves termed *Irish* people, when we so frequently ventured our all for the British Crown and Liberties against the Irish Papists." [19] It was a "Scot settled in Ireland" who first insisted that birth in a stable did not make a man a horse. Many Scotch-Irish came as indentured servants, but as servants who had every intention of ending up free, self-supporting farmers. By 1765 there were several hundred settlements in the western counties in which Scotch-Irish held sway. Natural-born frontiersmen, these hardy people were the most powerful national influence for western expansion, religious dissent, and democratic politics in the eighteenth century.

IRISH. Catholic or southern Irish, as distinguished from Calvinist or northern Scotch-Irish, were also to be found in every colony, but especially in Maryland and Pennsylvania. Most of them came as individuals or in families, often abandoning their religion in order to win a friendlier reception. The average southern Irish immigrant failed to preserve his national identity. The fact that the Scotch, Irish, and English strands of the total Irish migration of the eighteenth century will never be satisfactorily unraveled has persuaded some patriots [20] to make ridiculous claims for the "pure" Irish. Yet the claims of the Scotch-Irish must not be pushed too far in the other direction. At least twenty per cent of the "Irish" of the eighteenth-century migration must have actually been Irish in national origin.

GERMANS. The largest national element with a character distinctly alien to the dominant English strain was the German population in the middle and Southern colonies.[21] Poverty, war, and religious persecution drove so many thousands of Rhinelanders as redemptioners to Pennsylvania in the eighteenth century that Franklin and others predicted a Germanic future for their colony. In upstate New York,[22] the western counties of the South,[23] and above all in Pennsylvania,[24] Germans settled in great swarms, more often than not retaining their language, customs, and culture. Although they took a very small part in the political and social life of the colonies, their superior farming skill, thrift, and industry made them important in the economy, while their multiform Protestantism was a spur to religious liberty. Pennsylvania was the breadbasket of the American Revolution not least because it was one third German. Many a colonial official echoed the sentiments of

Governor Phipps, who recommended to the Massachusetts Assembly in 1750 that it encourage the immigration of a people so well fitted to "teach us by their Example those most necessary and excellent Arts for encreasing our Wealth, I mean Frugality and Diligence; in which at present we are exceedingly defective." [25]

SWISS. Perhaps fifteen to twenty thousand Swiss migrated to America from the German-speaking cantons between 1700 and 1765, fully half of this total arriving in the decade 1734-1744. [26] Pennsylvania and the Carolinas were the main destinations of these valuable immigrants, most of whom were regarded as another one of the numerous breeds of German immigrant. A few French-speaking Swiss were also in the colonies.

FRENCH. It has been variously estimated that between twenty and forty thousand French Protestants settled in the colonies after the revocation of the Edict of Nantes in 1685, most of them coming by way of England and Holland. Several features made this migration one of the most influential in colonial times: [27] the way in which the French scattered themselves throughout the colonies; the high proportion of gentle blood, intelligence, and professional skill they brought with them; and the almost effortless manner in which they were assimilated into the colonial population. In religion, speech, and culture the French Huguenot became an authentic English-American. Charleston [28] and New Rochelle in Westchester County, New York, are perhaps the most interesting places in which to study the assimilation of this people whose character was so well attuned to American methods and aspirations. It is fascinating to read the records of New Rochelle and see how easily the Huguenots took to the town-meeting form of government. *Visiteurs de fances, assesseurs, connestables,* and "Town Mens" all did their jobs as if they had been Yankees born. [29] The great names of Bowdoin, Revere, Bernon, Faneuil, Jay, De Lancey, Manigault, and Laurens are proof of the disproportionate influence of these few thousand exiles in the shaping of a new nationality. In addition to the Huguenots, perhaps five thousand Acadian French were deported and scattered along the coast in 1755, but their influence in the original colonies was negligible.

DUTCH. The story of New Netherland and New Amsterdam is such common American property that it is easy to overestimate the influence of Dutch blood and culture in the development of the colonies. [30] It is generally agreed that there were only ten thousand Dutch in the colonies in 1700, that perhaps fifty to sixty thousand persons had predominantly Dutch blood in 1765, and that in eighteenth-century New York and New Jersey, where this stock was concentrated, roughly fifteen to twenty per cent of the total white population could be classified as Dutch. Dutch immigration and influence were largely confined to the seventeenth century and the middle colonies. Dutch institutions were quickly scrapped after the English conquest of 1664, while the language, although some Hudson River farmers and Dutch Reformed pastors clung to it tenaciously, was in decline long before the end of the colonial period. The main contributions of the Dutch to the colonies were a good national stock, some expressive words, and a negative policy of colonization that made New York a cosmopolitan city from the beginning.[31] The first permanent settlers of New Netherland were thirty families of Protestant, French-speaking Walloons from the southern Netherlands. Comparatively few Dutch were prepared to leave home and settle permanently in the new world, yet those who did fathered a breed of typical colonists. An English nobleman observed in 1765, "The people of Albany are mostly descended of low Dutch, and carry down with them, the true and characteristick marks of their Native Country, Vizt an unwearied attention to their own personal and particular Interests, and an abhorrence to all superior powers." [32]

SWEDES. Some ten to fifteen thousand colonists in 1765 had predominantly Swedish blood.[33] Most of these were descendants of the few hundred settlers of New Sweden on the Delaware, which was founded as a fur-trading center in 1638 and was taken over by the Dutch in 1655. Although many of these sturdy farmers and traders migrated to other parts of the middle colonies,[34] the original area of settlement maintained cultural and ecclesiastical ties with the homeland until well into the eighteenth century. Over the years the Swedes proved to be a reasonably assimilable national element, as did also the small number of Finns and even smaller sprinkling of Danes who helped plant the tiny colony at Fort Christina.

JEWS. The total number of Jews in the colonies in 1765 could not have been more than 1,500, most of them Spanish or Portuguese in immediate origin.[35] Newport,[36] New York, Charleston, and Savannah were the principal havens of this trading people, but they could also be found in individual families or tiny groups through all the colonies. Jews suffered the expected social and political discrimination, but in the field of business they were first-class citizens. Many of them lived, as one traveler observed of the New York Jews, in highly respectable style.

> They have a synagogue and houses; and great country seats of their own property, and are allowed to keep shops in town. They have likewise several ships, which they freight, and send out with their own goods. In fine, they enjoy all the privileges common to the other inhabitants of this town and province.[37]

What Peter Kalm saw he reported correctly, but he did not see enough. The Jew was happy, but his was the limited happiness of a man held at arm's length.

NEGROES. We have already had occasion to discuss the Negro in colonial America, and need therefore mention only a few facts and figures: There were perhaps 400,000 Negroes in 1765, or slightly more than twenty per cent of the total population. All but forty thousand of this number were concentrated in the colonies south of Pennsylvania, and all but a handful were slaves. The Negro had in no way been assimilated into the population and had been integrated into the white man's society only on the white man's terms. Most important, he had been left by law and custom—and with little popular protest—in a state of ignorance, primitivism, and paganism, a state in which most colonists thought he naturally belonged. The total effect of slavery on the colonies was enormous, yet the white man's blood-lines and culture were hardly disturbed by the Negro's presence.

INDIANS. Only a few thousand Indians lived permanently within the settled areas in 1765.[38] Despite the pretty story of Pocahontas and John Rolfe, there was very little mixing of Indian and European blood. The white man's agriculture, commerce, road system, and language owed varying debts to the Indian tribes, but the chief influence of these native Americans was as a bar to easy westward expansion. Far too much blood was shed at the points of contact between these two contradictory ways of life to make the myth of the "noble savage" a part of colonial culture.

What was the total effect on society, culture, and government of this influx of nationalities into the American settlement? We have already tried to evaluate English influence at several points in Part 1. But what of the other nationalities, especially the Scotch-Irish and Germans? What did they do to reshape or improve the dominant English strain?

First, the melting-pot had only just begun to heat up in the latter part of the eighteenth century. Crèvecoeur's example of the English-French-Dutch family "whose present four sons have now four wives of four different nations"[39] was a phenomenon more prophetic of the Republic than typical of the colonies. The great process of national fusion had made little progress by 1765. Assimilation into the English stock rather than the creation of a new people was the result of such intermarriage as took place in colonial times. Nor were all the ingredients yet in the pot; the essential racial (Teutonic-Celtic) and religious (Protestant) unity of the population must not be overlooked.[40]

The mere volume of immigration from Germany and Ireland had a pronounced effect on colonial life. The swarming of these industrious peoples made possible the remarkable expansion in territory and population that marked the eighteenth century in America. If the Scotch-Irishman was America's typical frontiersman, the German was its typical farmer; and between them they made it possible for cities like Philadelphia and towns like Lancaster to grow and flourish. Though they were men of different natures, both sought the same blessing. "And what but LIBERTY, charming LIBERTY, is the resistless Magnet that attracts so many different Nations into that flourishing Colony?"[41]

Third, the arrival of non-English immigrants did much to weaken the hold of the mother country.[42] The newcomer wanted to be as loyal as any one else, but it was inevitable that his allegiance to the Crown should have little real emotional content. The Germans were inclined to be conservatively neutral about English dominion; the Scots and Irish were, for all the loyal humility that oozed from their petitions, innately hostile to the Georges and their agents. They lacked, as one traveler put it, the "same filial attachment" to England "which her own immediate offspring have."[43]

The influx of aliens did much to strengthen the Protestant, dissenting, individualistic character of colonial religion. The Presbyterian, Lutheran,

Baptist, and German Pietist churches were the chief beneficiaries of this immigration. The numbers and enthusiasm of these dissenting groups gave a tremendous lift to the cause of religious liberty in the colonies south of Pennsylvania.

Finally, the eighteenth-century immigrants helped democratize the political institutions that had been brought over from England and put to work in the wilderness. This was especially true of the Scotch-Irish, whose only quarrel with the representative governments of their adopted colonies was that they were not representative enough. The Germans were inclined to be politically passive; their major contribution to the coming democracy was the support they brought to the middle-class creed of industry, frugality, and self-reliance. The Scotch-Irish, on the other hand, were more politically conscious. If the controlling groups of the coastal counties refused to honor their legitimate claims for participation in public life, this rebuff served only to make their radicalism more insistent. They had little intention of altering the English-American scheme of government, but they did mean to show the world how democratic it could be. The sentiments of "leveling republicanism" were especially active on the Scotch-Irish frontier.

The selection of the six representative thinkers—Thomas Hooker, Roger Williams, John Wise, Jonathan Mayhew, Richard Bland, and Benjamin Franklin—was, all things considered, not too difficult an undertaking. Williams, Wise, and Franklin were automatic choices, the first two because of the democratic fervor of their writings, the third because he was at once the greatest man and greatest democrat to live in colonial America. Hooker and Mayhew, too, were relatively easy selections. The former was the most notable popularist within the authentic Puritan tradition; the latter was the most eloquent representative of American Whiggery. Bland was brought in only after a long and otherwise frustrating search for an articulate Southerner,[44] but once included he seemed entirely worthy to stand with the others.

At least fifty other prominent colonists who lived or spoke in the libertarian tradition were examined with rigor and rejected with reluctance. Some of them—Dr. Robert Child of Massachusetts (1613-1653), Nathaniel Bacon of Virginia (1647-1676), Jacob Leisler of New York (1640-1691), Dr. Johne Clark of Rhode Island (1609-1676), David Lloyd of Pennsylvania (1656?-1731), Josias Fendall of Maryland (1620?-1687), James Alexander of New York (1691-1756), and Andrew Hamilton of Pennsylvania (?-1741)—were men of action rather than of speculation. No one of these attractive and important figures left a large enough body of ideas in writing to be judged a serious political or social thinker. Others—John Woolman of New Jersey (1720-1772), Anthony Benezet of Pennsylvania (1713-1784), Christopher Sower (Sauer) of Pennsylvania (1693-1758), Francis Daniel Pastorius of Pennsylvania (1651-1720), and Samuel Davies of Virginia and New Jersey (1723-1761)—were simply not political enough in their approach to the great problems they declaimed upon so nobly. Still others—George Mason,

Patrick Henry, Thomas Jefferson, the Lees, Stephen Hopkins, James Otis, James Wilson, Samuel Adams, John Adams, Joseph Hawley, James Iredell, William Henry Drayton, John Dickinson, Charles Carroll—were only beginning their intellectual and political careers in the 1760's. They must be classed as Revolutionary rather than colonial thinkers; their political writings are more properly considered in Part 3 of this book.

Another class of men who did not have the necessary qualifications, principally because they served as purveyors of other men's ideas, were the liberty-minded journalists: Thomas Fleet of the *Boston Evening-Post*, James Franklin of the *New-England Courant* and *Rhode-Island Gazette*, Gamaliel Rogers and Daniel Fowle of the Boston *Independent Advertiser*, John Peter Zenger of the *New-York Weekly Journal*, Andrew Bradford of the *American Weekly Mercury*, William Bradford of the *Pennsylvania Journal*, and the patriotic team of Benjamin Edes and John Gill of the *Boston Gazette*. William Penn, too, was studied at length. He was finally and reluctantly discarded as an Englishman who, like Dean Berkeley, spent too little time in America to be considered a colonist. The liberal New England preachers of the eighteenth century, at least a half dozen of whom could have been given a full and loving presentation, are adequately represented by Wise and Mayhew.

Had considerations of space and art made it necessary or possible to include a seventh man, he would have been William Livingston of New York (1723-1790). Although he did not hit his full stride as a public figure until after his removal to New Jersey in 1772, this bold son of New York's most distinguished family had been in enough rousing political battles before 1765 to satisfy any three ordinary men. In the course of such incidents as the struggle over the founding of King's College, Livingston gave literary vent to a well-rounded political theory. In the end, three considerations blocked his inclusion: the difficulty in distinguishing his writings from those of his comrades-in-arms in the "New York Triumvirate," John Morin Scott and William Smith, jr.; the large proportion of his writings published after 1765, a fact that classes him with Otis and Samuel Adams rather than with Bland and Mayhew; and the clinching point that his principal ideas were expressed in the letters and pamphlets of Mayhew, Franklin, and Bland.

One other and more regrettable omission must be noted: the absence of any man who spoke for the advancing frontier. Although one or the other of the chosen six expounded every important doctrine in colonial political theory, it would have been useful and fitting to have heard some of these ideas from an authentic frontiersman. But a minute examination of the public and private literature of the colonial frontier led to these ineluctable conclusions: that the political voice of the early West never did speak clearly through any one outstanding man, and that when it did speak—through petitions, declarations, and letters to the newspapers—it adopted a tone of loyal deference that either belied the true sentiments of the men of the frontier or proved them far less radical than is commonly supposed.[45] The nearest thing to a frontier political thinker was Hermon Husband of North

Carolina (1724-1795), the penman of the Regulator movement. His literary remains are too sketchy to support his claim—not that he ever made one—to be considered a political thinker.[46] His writings were entirely characteristic of the frontier: straightforward recitals of grievances, tearful descriptions of the horrid excesses of "arbitrary power," and deferential pleas for lower fees, more equitable laws, and friendlier officials.

The men of the frontier, like most men of the tidewater, believed in an uncritical way in higher law, natural rights, the covenant, and constitutional government, but these beliefs were never once carefully expounded by any man or group. While we must regret the absence of one clear voice out of the old West, we can be satisfied that Williams, Wise, and Franklin expressed all the ideas that are properly identified with frontier democracy.

CHAPTER SIX

Thomas Hooker

ONCE upon a time in Hartford, Connecticut, lived a wonderful man named Thomas Hooker. The undisputed facts of his life are so few that many accounts of him seem almost like fairy-tales. No one knows what he looked like, but two splendid statues of him gaze out sternly over the bustling of the insurance peddlers. No one knows where he rests in dust, but a gravestone proclaims his triumphs and talents.

Historians agree upon the crowning act of his life, that he was "the chief instrument" in the founding of Connecticut, and upon the quality of his character, that he was "a person who while doing his master's work, would put a king in his pocket." [1] They do not agree, however, on the thoughts he entertained or the nature of the government he helped establish. One line pictures Hooker as the first American democrat, Connecticut as the first American democracy, and the Fundamental Orders of 1639 as "the first written constitution of modern democracy." [2] John Fiske and the loyal sons and daughters of Connecticut [3] have been the most devoted of this school, but such respectable scholars as Parrington, J. T. Adams, and J. M. Jacobson are also charter members. Let Professor Johnston of Princeton speak for this group:

> It is on the banks of the Connecticut, under the mighty preaching of Thomas Hooker and in the constitution to which he gave life, if not form, that we draw the first breath of that atmosphere which is now so familiar to us. The birthplace of American democracy is Hartford. [4]

Other historians, less eloquent and more critical, have challenged these high-flown claims. The most outspoken has been Perry Miller, who insists that the representation of Hooker as democrat "rests upon a misreading of two or three of his utterances," and asserts that Hooker's "religious and political opinions were thoroughly orthodox." [5] As for Connecticut, C. M.

Andrews pictured it as "a Puritan state, of the same flesh and blood as Massachusetts, and in her beginnings [representing] even better than her neighbor the Puritan ideal of a Heavenly City of God." [6]

The truth lies somewhere between these extremes, neither of which does full justice to Hooker and Connecticut nor expresses their significance for the rise of liberty in colonial America. Hooker was certainly no democrat in our sense of the word, nor can we look upon Connecticut as a genuine democracy. On the other hand, he was not quite so orthodox as Professor Miller would have us believe, and it is exactly here that his life and philosophy thrust themselves upon the student of American thought. If he stood fast in orthodoxy, he faced toward freedom and even took several steps into the democratic future. For this reason—that he represents the forces of liberty inherent in Puritanism more vividly than any other colonist of the seventeenth century—Hooker's life affords "a pattern well worthy of perpetual consideration." [7] Let us once again summon "the famous servant of Christ, grave godly and judicious Hooker," that he may testify to the virtues of New England Puritanism.

Come, Hooker, come forth of thy native soile.[8]

FROM ENGLAND TO MASSACHUSETTS

Thomas Hooker, noblest of the New England Puritans, was born in 1586 in the hamlet of Marfield, Leicestershire, England.[9] The few faint facts we know of his parentage point convincingly to an origin in yeoman stock.[10] Although Mather tells us that Hooker's mother and father "were neither unable, nor unwilling to bestow upon him a liberal education," [11] their chief service was to stand out of the way of a gifted child intent upon rising, at least intellectually, above his ancestral surroundings. Hooker achieved his education through scholarships and self-help, first at the grammar school in Market Bosworth where Samuel Johnson was later to serve as an unhappy usher, then at Cambridge where he made his way by waiting on fellow students at table. His college was Emmanuel, that "mere nursery of Puritans," where John Cotton and Nathaniel Ward also learned of new and sterner religious doctrine.

Having taken his B.A. in 1608 and M.A. in 1611, Hooker lingered on at Cambridge for a number of years as catechist and lecturer. This was the critical period of his life. He underwent a religious experience of soul-shattering intensity and body-racking duration, and he began a regimen of meditation and rhetoric which was to earn him a reputation as one of the most learned and powerful preachers of old and New England. We have the testimony of the illustrious William Ames "that though he had been acquainted with many scholars of divers nations, yet he never met with Mr. Hooker's equal, either for preaching or for disputing." [12] It is worth noting in this regard that most of Hooker's twenty-seven extant works were actually transcriptions from his sermons, in several instances the work of persons who "wrote after him in short-hand." Whatever their other merits as literary works, they are pre-eminent in Puritan literature for shrewdness of imagery.[13]

The record of Hooker's English ministry was one of huge popular and scant ecclesiastical success. He was first, from about 1620 to 1625, minister of a tiny country parish in Esher, Surrey. Already a preacher of marked nonconformist sympathies, he was able to occupy this position only because its living was "donative"; that is, dependent upon a patron and therefore not requiring presentation to a bishop and induction by his order. Some time during his stay at Esher he married the "waiting-woman" to his patron's wife—Susanna Garbrand, companion of all his years and mother of his several children, a woman about whom we know nothing more.

In 1625 Hooker removed to Chelmsford in Essex, where he served four years as lecturer in St. Mary's Church. His learning and eloquence, his talent for the kind of preaching that silences hecklers and torments doubters, made him one of the most conspicuous nonconformists in all England. By the time that William Laud removed to the See of London in July 1628, Hooker was marked for early suppression. The lecturers, "the people's creatures," who "blew the bellows of their sedition," were now to be brought to orthodox heel. The most famous of the lecturers in Laud's own diocese was one of the first to feel the heavy hand of that truculent bishop who, in his own perverse and unwitting way, had so much to do with the settling of America. A letter from Samuel Collins, Vicar of Braintree, to Chancellor Duck, Laud's zealous accessory in uprooting dissent, tells why Hooker could not be left to pursue his nonconformist labors in peace:

> Since my return from London I have spoken with Mr. Hooker, but I have small hope of prevailing with him. . . . All would be here very calme and quiet if he might depart. . . . If he be suspended its the resolution of his friend and himself to settle his abode in Essex, and maintenance is promised him in plentifull manner for the fruition of his private conference, which hath already more impeached the peace of our church than his publique ministry. His genius will still haunte all the pulpits in ye country, where any of his scholers may be admitted to preach. . . . There be divers young ministers about us . . . that spend their time in conference with him; and return home and preach what he hath brewed. . . . Our people's pallats grow so out of tast, yt noe food contents them but of Mr. Hooker's dressing. I have lived in Essex to see many changes, and have seene the people idolizing many new ministers and lecturers, but this man surpasses them all for learning and some other considerable partes and . . . gains more and far greater followers than all before him. . . . If my Lord tender his owne future peace . . . let him connive at Mr. Hooker's departure.[14]

Late in 1629 Hooker was forced to retire from his position at Chelmsford, and a few months later, having unsuccessfully sought refuge from Laud as a schoolmaster at Little Baddow, he fled to Holland and the fellowship of many other dissenting exiles. His attention had already been called to America. We have proof, in letters to John Winthrop,[15] that Hooker was wanted badly for the Massachusetts experiment and was being importuned as early as 1628 to go over with the first emigrants. In 1632 a band of people left Essex for America and settled near Boston under the expectant label of "Mr. Hooker's company." Finally, in July 1633, having returned to England and narrowly escaped capture by the King's officers, Hooker sailed for America on the *Griffin*, in company with John Cotton, John Haynes, and Samuel Stone, his own *fidus Achates*. Stone was to serve at Hooker's side until the master's death and then succeed him in the pastorate of the church at Hartford. Hooker and Cotton were fugitives from religious persecution in the most obvious sense, for "they gat out of England with much difficulty." [16] Unlike some of their less fortunate brothers-in-dissent, they "gat out" with uncropped ears and unslit nostrils.

In Winthrop's *Journal* there is this entry for October 11, 1633: "A fast at Newtown, where Mr. Hooker was chosen pastor, and Mr. Stone teacher, in such a manner as before at Boston." [17] Thus was solemnly founded what is today the First Church of Christ in Hartford, and thus did "noble Hooker" mount to the pulpit in which he at last, through his fourteen remaining years, found the peace and opportunity for service he had always sought in vain.

The ordinations of Hooker and Cotton ("before at Boston") were an event of great moment for the course of New England's ecclesiastical and political history. Neither of these great Puritans had been a separatist in England, yet each, when he finally took up the leadership of his American congregation, was ordained in a manner that was separatist, primitive, and essentially democratic. What the humble folk of the Scrooby-Leyden-Plymouth congregation had done out of conviction in 1620, the proud elders of Boston and Newtown, and of the eight or nine other churches in the Bay colony, did out of necessity between 1629 and 1633: They built their new churches on the Congregational principle of the competency of each body of believers to form its own church-estate and to choose and ordain its own officers. This had been done at Salem in 1629, to the dismay of many Puritans still in England, and it was done repeatedly in the founding of the other wilderness churches. In the very act of crossing the Atlantic, these nonseparatist Puritans became separatist Congregationalists. However vigorous their protests against the brand of "Brownism," we can read in Winthrop's own words what took place "before at Boston": [18] an act of pure, though yet unacknowledged Congregationalism. At the outset of his ministry in America Hooker found himself the pastor of a covenanted church, one that was separate from the Church of England, and indeed from all other churches in the world, in everything but the inconsistent theories of a few of its members.

FROM MASSACHUSETTS TO CONNECTICUT

In May 1634 there resounded through the tiny colony the first noticeable rumble of collective discontent. The point of origin was Newtown on the Charles, where Hooker had been installed only seven months before. The method of expression was a petition of the inhabitants complaining of "straitness for want of land" and asking "leave of the court to look out for enlargement or removal." [19] After a scouting party had explored the Agawam and Merrimac regions with the General Court's permission and had failed to discover what the Newtown congregation was seeking, another party explored Connecticut without permission and discovered it in abundance: rich meadow-lands at a comfortable distance from Massachusetts. The next step in the founding of Connecticut is most honestly related in Winthrop's spare and hardy style:

September 4 (1634). The general court began at Newtown, and continued a week, and then was adjourned fourteen days. Many things were there agitated and concluded. . . . But the main business, which spent the most time, and caused the adjourning of the court, was about the removal of Newtown. They had leave, the last general court, to look out some place for enlargement or removal . . . and now they moved, that they might have leave to remove to Connecticut. This matter was debated divers days, and many reasons alleged pro and con. The principal reasons for their removal were, 1. Their want of accomodation for their cattle, so as they were not able to maintain their ministers, nor could receive any more of their friends to help them; and here it was alleged by Mr. Hooker, as a fundamental error, that towns were set so near each to other.

2. The fruitfulness and commodiousness of Connecticut, and the danger of having it possessed by others, Dutch or English.

3. The strong bent of their spirits to remove thither.

Against these it was said, 1. That, in point of conscience, they ought not to depart from us, being knit to us in one body, and bound by oath to seek the welfare of this commonwealth.

2. That, in point of state and civil policy, we ought not to give them leave to depart. 1. Being we were now weak and in danger to be assailed. 2. The departure of Mr. Hooker would not only draw many from us, but also divert other friends that would come to us. . . .

Upon these and other arguments the court being divided, it was put to vote; and, of the deputies, fifteen were for their departure, and ten against it. The governor and two assistants were for it, and the deputy and all the rest of the assistants were against it, (except the secretary, who gave no vote;) whereupon no record was entered, because there were not six assistants in the vote, as the patent requires. Upon this grew a great difference between the governor and assistants, and the deputies. They would not yield the assistants a negative voice, and the others (considering how dangerous it might be to the commonwealth, if they should not keep that strength to balance the greater number of the deputies) thought it safe to stand upon it. So, when they could proceed no farther, the whole court agreed to keep a day of humiliation to seek the Lord, which accordingly was done, in all the congregations, the 18th day of this month; and the 24th the court met again. Before they began, Mr. Cotton preached, (being desired by all the court, upon Mr. Hooker's instant excuse of his unfitness for that occasion). . . . And it pleased the Lord so to assist him, and to bless his own ordinance, that the affairs of the court went on cheerfully; and although all were not satisfied about the negative voice to be left to the magistrates, yet no man moved aught about it, and the congregation of Newtown came and accepted of such enlargement as had formerly been offered them by Boston and Watertown; and so the fear of their removal to Connecticut was removed.[20]

This memorable passage from the most priceless original narrative of American history tells us a great deal about the standing of Hooker among his contemporaries. Certainly the only man who could have challenged his superiority in the qualities and gifts by which the world judges its preachers was John Cotton, and not until well after Hooker's departure did the Boston teacher make secure his ascendancy in the Bay area. Until then it was Hooker before all other ministers who was sought out for advice and support, especially in the squabbles that seem to have made up at least half the early history of the colony.[21] Even after his removal he was several times importuned, not always successfully, to return to Massachusetts to provide guidance for those less resolute. He was the common property of the New England churches. The roster of preachers upon whom Hooker had a decided, often decisive influence is an honor roll of New England Puritanism: John Cotton, John Davenport, Thomas Shepard (his son-in-law), John Norton, Samuel Stone, John Eliot (his assistant in Little Baddow), Nathaniel Rogers, John and Francis Higginson, Richard Mather, and many others.

We can only speculate about the reasons for the removal of the Newtown congregation to Connecticut. The first two arguments put forward by the petitioners seem substantial enough. The promise of plentiful and fertile land was to beckon Americans westward from security for generations to come. But this does nothing to explain why these particular congregations should have been the first to move out, since they were certainly no more straitened "for want of land" than several others in the Bay. The evidence, which has been examined and re-examined by generations of historians, sifts down in the final winnowing to two main conjectures: that there were personal rivalries between Haynes and Winthrop, and between Hooker and Cotton, carried on in a more or less polite character but steadily building up to a major civil feud; and that the people of these restless congregations, paced in this as in other affairs by their beloved Hooker, were becoming increasingly dissatisfied with the oligarchic tendencies of the ruling element in the Bay colony. We have the testimony of William Hubbard that "after Mr. Hooker's coming over, it was observed that many of the freemen grew to be very jealous of their liberties." [22]

In either case—whether emphasis be placed on the simple economic motive of land hunger or the more complex human motives of personal jealousies and of impatience with an oppressive religious and political order [23]—the founding of Connecticut was an event of profound historical import, both as fact and symbol. Factually, a new colony established itself one farther step removed from English oversight, a colony in which the fermenting process of self-government could take place with the least possible interference from the home country. Symbolically, the removal of "Mr. Hooker's company" was the first overt indication of the popular urges beneath the apparently integral autocracy of New England Puritanism, as well as the first of the westward migrations within America itself. For those who interpret the rise of American democracy in terms of never-ceasing pressure on the frontier, the bold exodus of these few families is an epic of American history. "Westward the course of empire takes its way."

The westward course of these first pioneers was not exactly imperial in sweep. Temporarily restrained by the cajoling of the General Court and the grant of additional lands, the men of Newtown—and soon of Dorchester, Watertown, and Roxbury as well—would not be still. Through the summer of 1635 little bands of impatient inhabitants of these towns, some with permission from the Court and some without, moved westward to the Connecticut. And finally, in late May 1636, with the Court's permission, and indeed under its commission,[24]

> Mr. Hooker, pastor of the church of Newtown, and the most of his congregation, went to Connecticut. His wife was carried in a horse litter; and they drove one hundred and sixty cattle, and fed of their milk by the way.[25]

Thus were founded the river towns of Hartford, Windsor, and Wethersfield, and with them the colony of Connecticut. Within a year almost eight hundred people were settled in the new Zion.

THE GOVERNMENT OF CONNECTICUT

Granted that Hooker was no democrat, Connecticut no democracy, and the Fundamental Orders no constitution in the modern sense of these words, the fact remains that the Connecticut experiment was dissimilar enough from the Massachusetts oligarchy to constitute an evident step in the direction of free society and popular government. Before investigating Hooker's political ideas, we must examine the government to which he gave his support and blessing.

The first government of Connecticut, which preceded the arrival of the main body under Hooker, was simply the rudimentary pattern of "government by the acknowledged elders" that was to guide hundreds of other frontier bands and settlements. The extent of formal government was a single constable appointed and sworn by the General Court of Massachusetts for the protection of the settlers.[26] On March 3, 1636, the Court issued a commission bestowing broad powers of government for one year on eight selected members of the emigrating congregations. This commission included a provision for convening the "inhabitants of the towns" into a general assembly "to procede in executing the power and authority" granted to the commissioners.[27] Regular government may be said to have begun in April 1636, two months before Hooker's coming, with the gathering of five of the commissioners in Connecticut to swear in constables and pass a few orders. The first General Court met at Hartford in 1637 and resolved almost quixotically "that there shalbe an offensive warr agt the Pequoitt." [28]

Finally, in 1638, with "the Pequoitt" thoroughly butchered and their threat to the colony erased, the settlers turned to the business of erecting their own government.

The Fundamental Orders of Connecticut were adopted by the General Court on January 14, 1639. The architects of this celebrated document were probably John Haynes, the leading member of Hooker's congregation,[29] Roger Ludlow, the keenest legal mind in all New England,[30] and Hooker himself, whose sermons and wise counsel pointed out the path for the others to travel. We can only guess at the mechanics of formation and adoption, for there is a complete gap in the public records of the colony from April 5, 1638, to April 11, 1639. The weight of evidence points to the establishment of a small committee by the General Court, then a series of informal consultations to which Hooker was called, and finally the writing of a draft by Roger Ludlow. The form of government thus set in motion was simply an extension of the informal government of the first two years of the colony. In most, but not all, important respects the Fundamental Orders were a faithful model of the charter government that had been left behind in Massachusetts Bay.[31]

The preamble is in essence a civil compact in which "we the Inhabitants and Residents" of the three towns did "assotiate and conioyne our selues to be as one Publike State or Commonwelth." The purposes of the government were two: "to mayntayne and presearue the liberty and purity of the gospell of our Lord Jesus"; and "to order and dispose of the affayres of the people," for which "an orderly and decent Gouerment" was declared to be necessary.

Eleven short articles then describe in barest detail the manner of government these good Englishmen found orderly and decent. The central organ was the General Court, which met twice a year: in April primarily for elections, in September for legislation and general business. The Court consisted of the governor (as moderator, with a tie-breaking vote), six assistants (or "Magestrats"), and four deputies from each town. The governor, who had to be a church member and former magistrate, was elected yearly by the "admitted freemen" of the colony. He could not succeed himself. The magistrates were also elected yearly by the freemen. The deputies, who had to be freemen themselves, were the choice of the "admitted Inhabitants in the seuerall Townes."

In the General Court was lodged "the supreme power of the Commonwelth"—executive, legislative, judicial, military, electoral, consultative, and constituent. It could make and repeal laws (including the provisions in the Fundamental Orders), levy rates, dispose of lands, appoint and remove the "publike Officers" necessary to execute the laws, and in general "deale in any other matter that concerns the good of this commonwelth." Neither the governor nor the magistrates had a "negative voice," nor could the Court be adjourned, prorogued, or dissolved except by its own vote. Specific provision was made for the Court to convene itself in the event the governor and magistrates should neglect or refuse to call it. Finally, the Court decided which inhabitants were to be admitted as freemen and thus made first-class citizens.

It should be clear that the primitive form of government ordained in the Fundamental Orders of 1639 was in no sense a democracy, constitutional or otherwise. The generations of patriotic historians and provincial orators who have insisted that Hooker and his companions did establish the first American democracy have distorted the minds and purposes of these excellent men. More than that, they have robbed them of their proper position in the long process through which American democracy came finally to fruition. The cardinal point about democracy in the colonies, which bears endless repeating every time a historical society meets to hallow the great men of old, is this: Democracy was never established in colonial America, except perhaps in the Rhode Island of Roger Williams; democracy, wherever and to whatever extent it existed before 1765, evolved. Here is the true significance of the Connecticut adventure of Hooker, Haynes, Stone, and Ludlow: the fact, less spectacular but more meaningful than the fancies of Fiske and Johnston, that they built a plainly marked way-station on the road from seventeenth-century England to nineteenth-century America.

In short, the Fundamental Orders are to be remembered and studied, not because they were democratic, but because they were half-aristocratic and half-popular—a curious and thoroughly English amalgam of Puritan authoritarianism, Congregational liberalism, corporate flexibility, incipient Whiggery, and Connecticut experimental popularism. In most particulars, the government of Connecticut was like that of Massachusetts, but at least four arrangements were clearly and designedly more liberal than those which had been imposed on the Bay colony. First, no religious qualification for the suffrage was fixed upon freemen or inhabitants.[32] Second, definite restrictions were placed upon the authority of the magistracy—for example, the provision for convening the General Court with or without gubernatorial and magisterial approval, and that permitting the deputies to meet before the regular court "to aduise and consult of all such things as may concerne the good of the publike" and to judge the validity of their own elections. Third, the "inhabitants," if not possessed of full political rights, were nevertheless empowered to elect deputies to the Court. Fourth, the governor was limited in power and forbidden to seek immediate re-election. Finally, not even a passing reference to any outside authority is found in the Fundamental Orders. Massachusetts was ignored; so, too, was Charles I. The origin of government in Connecticut was a clear-cut instance of free political association.[33]

In practice as in fundamental law the early government of Connecticut was more popular than that of Massachusetts. The absence of a religious test for the right to participate in political affairs, the moderate conduct of the magistrates, the clear reluctance of the clergy to push too far into the civil domain—these were signs of a more tolerant, less controversial manner of conducting public business than the ways of the oligarchy in Massachusetts. The steps forward—such as an order of October 1639 setting up a committee to codify and publish the laws, and one of April 1646 requesting Ludlow to draw up a complete "body of Lawes" [34]—and the steps to the rear—such as an order of February 1644 giving the magistrates a "negative voate" over the legislative activities of the General Court [35]—were taken with a minimum of civil commotion. The people of Connecticut were more homogeneous, to be sure, and thus more easily governed than the troublemakers of Massachusetts. Yet the beginnings of Connecticut's legendary "steady habits" date from a period when the stewardship of the Puritan elite was moderately and conscientiously discharged and the plain people given more voice than they had ever enjoyed in Massachusetts or England.

After Hooker's death there were several instances of reversion to more aristocratic government, instances that call our attention more explicitly to the popular character of the original Fundamental Orders. In 1657, as climax to an upsurge of aristocratic displeasure over the laxity of the towns in admitting inhabitants to the franchise, a property qualification was fixed in the laws.[36] In 1660 the prohibition against an incumbent governor's seeking re-election was abandoned.[37] Finally, in 1660, the authority of the restored monarchy was recognized, as of course it had to be. The scheme of government set out in the royal charter secured by John Winthrop, jr., in 1662 was simply an extension of what had developed under the Fundamental Orders. The charter was to serve until 1818.

Here, then, is evidence that Connecticut under Hooker, if not a democracy pure and simple, was a distinctly less autocratic civil society than Massachusetts. The spirit of political liberalism was lighted in America during the first years of the wilderness settlements, in but one or two places more brightly than in early Connecticut. And in a very real sense this early experience was a reflection of the popular leanings of the great New England Puritan, Thomas Hooker.

HOOKER AS POLITICAL THINKER

We turn now from the primitive self-government of the first western settlement to the political ideas of the preacher who contributed abundantly to its success. In approaching "incomparable Hooker," we must again take note that here was no hot rebel against the New England Way, no Williams or Hutchinson or Child or Morton. Rather, he was a man of commanding influence within the Puritan system, a man of whom Cotton Mather could write, "I shall now invite my reader to behold at once the *wonders of New England*, and it is [in] one *Thomas Hooker* that he shall behold them." [38] Hooker was the matchless representative of the virtues of early New England—a man whose life refutes the easy assumption that Endicott and Norton were the authentic Puritans and proves that within Puritanism itself were the seeds of political liberty.

The attempt to revive Hooker as a seventeenth-century Jefferson has led to confusion about his ecclesiastical views. Just as J. T. Adams strained the facts to set him up as the political antithesis of Winthrop, so Parrington ignored them to set him up as the ecclesiastical antithesis of Davenport and Cotton.[39] Nothing could be further from the truth. Hooker was orthodox to the marrow of his rugged old bones.[40] The timeworn diaries and histories that defended the New England Way, and the tracts from old England that assaulted it, are choked with references to Thomas Hooker. They make plain the conviction of friend and foe that here indeed was the great man of the western churches. None but an orthodox minister would have been called on to lead the face-to-face scrimmage with Roger Williams and "Mistris Hutchison," to preside over the early synods, and to compose New England's Reproof Valiant to the "many books coming out of England . . . against the congregational way." [41] Hooker was at least as proper a Puritan as Cotton and Winthrop.

That Hooker was a Puritan of the Puritans is simply another way of saying that we must stretch the point to the limit to speak of him as a political thinker. His references to matters political and social were few and scattered. A feeling of piety flooded his heart and mind so completely that he rarely contemplated man or society except as instruments of God's great plan. His prime, almost exclusive, intellectual concern was with ecclesiastical organization and religious doctrine.[42] The observations he registered about the type of political institution best suited to man's earthly needs were projections of his thoughts about the structure of the true church. The few unblended political ideas that we can quarry from the massive pit of Hooker's religious writings are little more than offhand references to "that resemblance" which church polity "hath with all other bodies politick." [43] The few political ideas that appear in the handful of his extant letters and sketchily reported sermons on civil affairs were efforts to deal with political organization in the same terms in which he had dealt with church organization.

It is therefore imperative to note that Hooker, though he stood like the Charter Oak itself on the same stern ecclesiastical ground as Cotton and Davenport, faced in a somewhat different direction. The discrepancy between Hooker's orthodoxy and Cotton's was primarily one of emphasis. Hooker's *Summe of Church-Discipline* and Cotton's *Way of the Congregational Churches Cleared* appeared as peas in the Puritan pod to detractors and defenders of the New England churches. But in his differences of emphasis the popular tendencies in New England Puritanism received their initial impetus. Hooker's differences with Cotton were differences of degree, but in time these often become differences of kind.

In placing a little more emphasis on the covenant of man to man than on that of man to God, on the congregation than on the elders, on the "right hand of fellowship" than on the discipline of the synod,[44] on the reason in man than on his sinfulness, on practice than on doctrine, on evangelism than on speculation, on the New Testament than on the Old, Hooker pried open a door that later generations of New England churchgoers swung wide for liberty. Miller has admitted that Hooker had "perhaps a greater feeling for the inner meaning of the Congregational tradition." [45] The "perhaps" is gratuitous, for he was clearly the better Congregationalist. He would have no truck, even in his orthodoxy, with the open Presbyterianism of Rutherford or the unavowed presbyterianism of Cotton.

The sum of Hooker's political ideas is found in four dissimilar sources: (1) the Fundamental Orders of 1639, which Ludlow drafted but Hooker inspired, and which contained nothing contrary to his political tastes; (2) *A Survey of the Summe of Church-Discipline*, which was famous for generations in Massachusetts and Connecticut as a defense of New England Congregationalism; (3) a letter to John Winthrop, written probably in November 1638, in which Hooker's political disagreements with the Massachusetts leaders are most positively asserted; and (4) the sermon of May 31, 1638, to the Connecticut General Court, preserved in the form of a listener's notes.

Hooker wrote *The Summe of Church-Discipline* much against his will and only at the urgent request of his fellow ministers. It was in substance a reply to that excellent Scottish churchman, Samuel Rutherford, whose *Due Right of Presbyteries* (1644) had been the most bone-rattling salvo fired by the Presbyterians in their barrage against the New England churches. Hooker's manuscript, along with another by Davenport, was dispatched to England in early 1646 on a ship that disappeared into the Atlantic wastes never to be seen again—except by certain sack-consuming citizens of New Haven on a thundery June evening several years later. [46] When Hooker had become convinced of the loss of his manuscript, he turned even more reluctantly to producing a substitute. *The Summe* was unfinished at his death and was seen to the London printer by other hands. Even in this form it was a brilliant exposition of Congregationalism. Although Hooker deals specifically with ecclesiastical organization, he several times makes clear that his ideas of the nature of the covenant, the power of the elders, and the role of the people are equally applicable to civil society. Here and there in the thorny thickets of *The Summe* are observations on "law, nature, and reason" which reveal the political ideas of liberal Puritanism. The search is wearying but altogether rewarding. [47]

The immediate occasion of the letter to Winthrop was a falling-out between Massachusetts, proud of her status as the leading New England colony, and Connecticut, jealous of her newly won independence, over a plan of confederation put forward by Winthrop and the Massachusetts magistrates in 1638. Winthrop worried the chief bone of contention in the pages of his *Journal*, belaboring Connecticut for refusing to trust their commissioners to the confederacy with "absolute power" to make important decisions, for asserting that the people at home should be constantly informed and requested for advice, and—here Winthrop makes a rare show of petulance—for choosing "divers *scores* men, who had no learning nor judgment." [48] This brought to the surface the disagreement between Hooker and Winthrop over the relative importance of people and magistrates in the conduct of civil affairs. In an exchange of letters, each of these worthy men seized the opportunity to express his basic philosophy. What we have of this historic debate is Winthrop's summary of an opening letter to Hooker, the full text of Hooker's reply, and a rough draft of Winthrop's conciliatory answer.[49] Winthrop, as generations of historians will happily attest, saved his correspondence; Hooker, as they will sadly lament, did not.

Had Hooker thought more consciously in a political vein, he might well have written out for publication the sermon to the General Court of May 1638. The few precious scraps of information that we possess of this lecture have come down to us in the form of ciphered notes in the manuscript notebook of Henry Wolcott, jr., of Windsor. This treasure was discovered in the nineteenth century and was deciphered by the noted Hartford antiquarian, J. Hammond Trumbull. Wolcott's outline of Hooker's sermon reads thus:

BY MR. HOOKER, AT HARTFORD, MAY 31, 1638

Text: Deut. i:13. "Take you wise men, and understanding, and known among your tribes, and I will make them rulers over you." Captains over thousands, and captains over hundreds—over fifties—over tens, &c.

Doctrine. I. That the choice of public magistrates belongs unto the people, by God's own allowance.

II. The privilege of election, which belongs to the people, therefore must not be exercised according to their humours, but according to the blessed will and law of God.

III. They who have power to appoint officers and magistrates, it is in their power, also, to set the bounds and limitations of the power and place unto which they call them.

Reasons. 1. Because the foundation of authority is laid, firstly, in the free consent of the people.

2. Because, by a free choice, the hearts of the people will be more inclined to the love of the persons [chosen] and more ready to yield [obedience].

3. Because, of that duty and engagement of the people.

Uses. The lesson taught is threefold:

1st. There is matter of thankful acknowledgment, in the [appreciation] of God's faithfulness toward us, and the permission of these measures that God doth command and vouchsafe.

2dly. Of reproof—to dash the conceits of all those that shall oppose it.

3dly. Of exhortation—to persuade us, as God hath given us liberty, to *take* it.

And lastly—as God hath spared our lives, and given us them in liberty, so to seek the guidance of God, and to choose *in* God and *for* God.[50]

This election sermon, surely one of the most influential ever preached in New England, set the stage for the adoption of the Fundamental Orders.

There is little to be said about the sources of Hooker's thought, which were almost exclusively theological. Like other leading exponents of early New England Congregationalism, he had gone to school with Augustine, Calvin, Beza, Parker, and Ames, and especially with the Continental logician, Petrus Ramus.[51] At the same time, he did a good deal of digging on his own into Scripture; many passages in his sermons are plainly those of an original mind. He was apparently untouched by winds of political doctrine. What little politics he expressed was transcribed ecclesiasticism. Charles M. Andrews once implied that Roger Williams might have had a good deal of influence on Hooker during the latter's visit to Providence in 1637, and confessed himself "tempted to believe" that some of the ideas later expounded by Williams in *The Bloudy Tenent* found their way into the election sermon.[52] The notion that Hooker was loosened up politically by the Rhode Island subversive is tempting indeed, but must ever remain in the realm of pleasant speculation.

THE COVENANT

The core of Hooker's political theory was the core of all speculation about the structure of church and state in Puritan New England: the covenant. He could no more have escaped from the grasp of this concept than he could have from a belief in hellfire and damnation. Yet there were several notable differences between Hooker's version of the covenant and that of Cotton and Winthrop, and for these differences we hail him as the leading spokesman for this idea in seventeenth-century America. For one thing, the covenant was for Hooker a living concept in a way that it was not for Winthrop. The Fundamental Orders of 1639, in whatever light we care to read them, were a long and popular step forward from the Massachusetts charter of 1629. For another, what was in Hooker's philosophy an article of faith was in many another Puritan's a convenient hypothesis with about as much popular substance as the contract of Hobbes. And in *The Summe of Church-Discipline* Hooker went a good deal further than any of his contemporaries in discussing the covenant as the basis for all forms of social organization.

Hooker's theory of the covenant was quite unsophisticated. Had he ever been asked directly to account for the formation of civil society, he might have drawn on his scriptural and historical knowledge for such explanations as that of conquest or of the expanding family. When he was asked directly how such a society *ought* to be formed—as he apparently was at least once in his life—he replied, "In the free consent of the people." Let us hear of the covenant from Hooker himself. Though the style is primitive, the spelling casual, the logic opaque, and the issues long dead, the meaning of *The Summe of Church-Discipline* cannot be misread. Hooker could have written Chapters 7 and 8 of Locke's *Second Treatise*.

> Mutuall covenanting and confoederating of the Saints in the fellowship of the faith according to the order of the Gospel, is that which gives constitution and being to a visible Church. . . .
> Its free for any man to offer to joyn with another who is fit for fellowship, or to refuse. Its as feee for another to reject or receive such who offer, and therefore that they do joyn, it is by their own free consent and mutuall ingagement on both sides; which being past, that mutuall relation of ingage-

ment, is as it were the sement, which soders the whole together: or like the mortising or brazing of the building, which gives fashion and firmnesse to the whole.

Whence it is evident, First, that it is not every relation, but such an ingagement, which issues from free consent, that makes the covenant.

Secondly, This ingagement gives each power over another, and maintains and holds up communion each with other, which cannot but be attended, according to the termes of the agreement.

And lastly it being of persons, who were wholly free, each from the other. There can no necessary tye of mutuall accord and fellowship come, but by free ingagement, free (I say) in regard of any humane constraint. . . .

This Covenant is dispensed or acted after a double manner.

Either { Explicitly,
       or
       Implicitely.

An Explicite Covenant is, when there is an open expression and profession of this ingagement in the face of the Assembly, which persons by mutuall consent undertake in the waies of Christ.

An Implicite Covenant is, when in their practice they do that, whereby they make themselves ingaged to walk in such a society, according to such rules of government, which are exercised amongst them, and so submit themselves thereunto: but doe not make any verball profession thereof. . . .

3. Its most according to the compleatnesse of the rule, and for the better being of the Church, that there be an explicite covenant. . . .

3. *The reasons of the Covenant.*

I.

The first is taken from that resemblance which this policy hath with all other bodies politick. . . .

The first part of the Argument, hath reason and common sense to put it beyond gainsaying. Each whole or intire body, is made up of his members, as, by mutuall reference and dependence they are ioyned each to the other. . . .

Its that sement which soders them all, that soul as it were, that acts all the parts and particular persons so interested in such a way, for there is no man constrained to enter into such a condition, unlesse he will: and he that will enter, must also willingly binde and ingage himself to each member of that society to promote the good of the whole, or else a member actually he is not. . . .

3. Amongst such who by no impression of nature, no rule of providence, or appointment from God, or reason, have power each over other, there must of necessity be a mutuall ingagement, each of the other, by their free consent, before by any rule of God they have any right or power, or can exercise either, each towards the other. This appears in all covenants betwixt Prince and People, Husband and Wife, Master and Servant, and most palpable is the expression of this in all confoederations and corporations. . . .

Mutuall subjection is, as it were the sinewes of society, by which it is sustained and supported.[53]

In Hooker's homely passages there were several rough deviations from the orthodox theory of the covenant which later generations were to refine into a philosophy of liberty. These points might be noted in support of Hooker's position as an important precursor of democratic political theory: (1) the flat affirmation of ecclesiastical equality; (2) the equally flat affirmation of the doctrine of free consent, of the unprejudiced liberty of every man "to joyn . . . or to refuse" to join in the covenant; (3) the distinction between the explicit and implicit covenant, and Hooker's popular preference for the former; (4) the attempt to justify the church covenant through its "resemblance . . . with all other bodies politick," as well as through "reason and common sense"—all this in rare anticipation of the democratic notions of John Wise; (5) the emphasis on the covenant as one of man to man, at the expense of the covenant between man and God; [54] (6) the reminder of the duties that "mutuall ingagement" lays upon all participants; (7) the clear assertion that "the good of the whole" is the chief purpose of a covenanted polity; and (8) the constant reiteration of the explosive doctrine, destined to be thundered from hundreds of pulpits:

> Mutuall subjection is, as it were the sinewes of society, by which it is sustained and supported.

We can now see the touch of Hooker's mighty hand in the preamble to the Fundamental Orders. Whatever else this primitive charter may have been, it was certainly one of the most outspoken plantation covenants in colonial New England. The counsel of the master was writ large in its words:

> Forasmuch as it hath pleased the Allmighty God by the wise disposition of his diuyne providence so to Order and dispose of things that we the Inhabitants and Residents of Windsor, Harteford and Wethersfield are now cohabiting and dwelling in and vppon the River of Conectecotte and the Lands thereunto adioyneing; And well knowing where a people are gathered togather the word of God requires that to mayntayne the peace and vnion of a such people there should be an orderly and decent Gouerment established according to God, to order and dispose of the affayres of the people at all seasons as occation shall require; doe therefore associate and conioyne our selues to be as one Publike State or Commonwelth; and doe, for our selues and our Successors and such as shall be adioyned to vs att any tyme hereafter, enter into Combination and Confederacōn togather. . . .

THE PEOPLE AND THEIR MAGISTRATES

Hooker was the most constructive exponent among orthodox Puritans of two other foward-looking doctrines that proceeded from the concept of the covenant: the sovereignty of the people, which is the logical foundation of the theory of free association, and limited magisterial authority, which is its most logical extension. On these two issues he parted company with Winthrop and thereby heralded the democratizing of the New England Way. And on these two issues he showed himself to be a more genuine

Congregationalist than Cotton. Again we must recall that the disagreements among these men were a matter of emphasis—especially over the relative importance to be accorded elders or magistrates on one hand, and congregation or citizenry on the other. Hooker never in his life gave countenance to straight-out democracy. Yet he did stress the ultimate power of the whole congregation, and he did oppose the autocratic notion of a magistracy elected for life and unrestricted by written law. He was the more influential because he chose to speak within the system of Puritan orthodoxy, if not within the borders of Massachusetts.

A passage in the preface to *The Summe of Church-Discipline* expresses Hooker's advanced definition of "the people": the congregation in the visible church, the "Inhabitants and Residents" in the civil community.

> But whether all Ecclesiasticall power be impaled, impropriated and rightly taken into the Presbytery alone: Or that the people of the particular Churches should come in for a share, according to their places and proportions; This is left as the subject of the inquiry of this age, and that which occasions great thoughts of heart of all hands. . . .
>
> These are the times when people shall be fitted for such priviledges, fit I say to obtain them, and fit to use them. . . .
>
> And whereas it hath been charged upon the people, that through their ignorance and unskilfulnesse, they are not able to wield such priviledges, and therefore not fit to share in any such power. The Lord hath promised: To take away the vail from all faces in the mountain, the weak shall be as David, and David as an Angel of God. The light of the Moon shall be as the Sun, and the Sun seven times brighter, when he hath not only informed them, but made them to be ashamed of their abominations, and of all that they have done, then he will shew them the frame of his house, and the patern thereof, the going out thereof, the coming in thereof, the whole fashion thereof, and all the ordinances thereof, all the figures thereof, and laws thereof. . . .

These are the words of a man with faith in the right and capacity of the whole congregation to exercise the sovereign authority that God has bestowed upon it. To be sure, Hooker's ecclesiastical democracy was a democracy of the Saints, who were apparently few in early Connecticut, just as his political democracy was restricted to the godly, sober, and respectable. "The people" in Hooker's theory was a limited body, yet not nearly so limited as in Winthrop's or Endicott's. And surely he hoped that all men in time would deserve full ecclesiastical and political citizenship. Despite his orthodox persuasion concerning predestination, despite his eloquent despair with the crudeness and ignorance in men, he stressed repeatedly the reasonableness present in every man's mind and soul. There was nothing in this preacher's theology that made him, like some of his colleagues, *want* to believe that most men never could be Saints; there was nothing in his politics that led him to believe that participation in government would always be the responsibility of the few. In announcing the sovereignty of all those who had subscribed to the compact, in proclaiming that ecclesiastical and political authority should come from below and not from above, Hooker prepared the way for later messengers of the belief that all men are qualified for free association. He was a better prophet than he realized of the Revolutionary doctrine of popular sovereignty.

Hooker's opinion of the authority of the magistrates in civil affairs and of the elders in the church is most plainly read in the letters that he exchanged with Winthrop in 1638-1639. The sweeping and discretionary power of the magistracy was the marrow of the noble governor's political theory. Although Winthrop, too, was imbued with the covenant idea, his version of this Puritan belief was free of any popular taint. The reins of a decent form of government were firmly in the hands of ruling magistrates, just as the government of a true church was in the safekeeping of elders. With consistency and courage Winthrop proclaimed his doctrine of magisterial oligarchy to the restless inhabitants of Massachusetts. In his famous lay sermon to the company aboard the *Arbella—A Modell of Christian Charity* (1630)—he declared that God had called some people to be "highe and eminent in power and dignitie; others meane and in subieccion." Fifteen years later, in the "little speech" to the General Court that had just acquitted him of a charge of exceeding his magisterial authority, he could still maintain with dignity and candor that the only true liberty of man was his liberty "quietly and cheerfully [to] submit to that authority which is set over" him.[55] In his letter to Hooker, Winthrop expounded his doctrine of the stewardship of a hand-picked magistracy over a people charged by heaven to obey cheerfully and submit permanently. In his notes the chief argument is summarized thus:

> I expostulated about the unwarrantableness and unsafeness of referring matter of counsel or judicature to the body of the people, quia the best part is always the least, and of that best part the wiser part is always the lesser. The old law was, choose ye out judges etc. and thou shalt bring the matter to the judge etc.

Winthrop also warned, as we learn from a passage in Hooker's letter, that "to referr the dicision of a civill quaestion or controversy to whole churches cannot be safe."

To this blunt dismissal of the people's claims to political participation Hooker made a testy and unequivocal rejoinder. The revealing portions of his letter are these:

> I fully assent to those staple principles which you sett downe: to witt: That the people should choose some from amongest them: that they should referr matter of counsell to ther counsellours, matter of Judicature to ther iudges: Only the quaestion here growes: what rule the Judge must have to iudge by: 2ly who those counsellors must be.
> That in the matter which is referred to the iudge the sentence should lye in his breast, or be left to his discretion according to which he should goe: I am afrayd it is a course which wants both safety and warrant: I must confesse I ever looked at it as a way which leads directly to tyranny, and so to confusion, and must playnly professe: If it was in my liberty, I should

choose nether to live nor leave my posterity vnder such a government: Sit liber judex as the Lawyers speake: 17 Deut. 10, 11: Thou shalt observe to do according to all that they informe according to the sentence of the Law Thou shalt seek the law at his mouth: not ask what his discretion allowes, but what the law requires: And therfore the Apost[les] when the rulers and high preist passed sentence agaynst ther preaching as preiudiciall to the state, The Apost[le] Peter made it not daynty to professe and practise contrary to ther charge, because ther sentence was contrary to law, though they might have pretended discretion and depth of wisdom and policy in ther charge.

And we know in other Countryes, had not the law overruled the lusts of men, and the crooked ends of iudges many tymes, both places and people had beene in reason past all releif in many cases of difficulty: you well knowe what the Heathen man sayd by the candell light of common sense: The law is not subiect to passion, nor to be taken aside with self seeking ends, and therfore ought to have cheif rule over rulers them selves.

Its also a truth that counsell should be sought from counsellors: but the quaestion yet is, who those should be: Reserving smaller matters, which fall in occasionally in common course to a lower counsell: In matters of greater consequence, which concern the common good, a generall counsell chosen by all to transact businesses which concerne all, I conceave vnder favour most sutable to rule and most safe for releif of the wholl This was the practise of the Jewish church directed by God Deutr. 17:10:11; 2 Cron: 19 and the approved experience of the best ordered states give in evidence this way: Salomons one wise man, and the one wise woman in Abell that delivered the city showes the excellency of wisdome and of counsell where it is, but doth not conclude that one or few should be counsellors, since in the multitude of counsellors ther is safety.

Here is evidence, which can hardly be misread, that Hooker was well launched on the course from autocracy to liberty. He rejected flatly the essence of Winthrop's politics, the doctrine that government is most wisely committed to the very few, who must be allowed to govern according to their own discretion. He had already proved the earnestness of his resolve "nether to live nor leave my posterity vnder such a government," and he now made clear why it was in Connecticut, which was about to adopt the Fundamental Orders and a definite code of laws, that he was pleased to live. "If I was to choose I would be where I am."

Hooker's thinking about the magistrates was at odds with Winthrop's in at least four essentials: They were to be chosen by the people at regular intervals; they were to govern not at their own discretion but in accordance with written law; they were to consult the people and defer to their measured judgment in all "matters of greater consequence, which concern the common good"; and they were to act subject to the authority of the people "to set the bounds and limitations of the power and place" to which they had been called. If we add to these tenets the generous definition of "the people" toward which Hooker assuredly looked, we have arrived at an acceptable definition of representative, constitutional democracy.

"THE LIGHT OF THE WESTERN CHURCHES"

Hooker died at Hartford July 7, 1647, the victim of "an epidemical sickness" that had swept the northern colonies.[56] His eleven years in Connecticut had been devoted in full measure to the needs of his people, and in all his labors he had been generous and self-effacing. It is almost unbelievable how few scraps of direct or even hearsay evidence we have of his ministry in Hartford. The Connecticut records scarcely acknowledge his existence, except in such passages as this:

> Walter Gray, for his misdemeanor in laboring to inueagle the affections of Mr. Hoockers mayde, is to be publiquely corrected the next lecture day.[57]

In this light, it is somewhat amusing to read the eighteenth-century jeer of Samuel Peters, "Hooker reigned twelve years high-priest over Hertford," [58] or the twentieth-century observation of Perry Miller and T. H. Johnson, "For the rest of his life he was the virtual dictator of Connecticut." [59] These remarks do little justice to the character of men like Ludlow, Haynes, Wolcott, Hopkins, Steele, Stone, and, if I may be pardoned the gesture, Dr. Rossiter of Windsor. Hooker was neither high priest nor dictator, but a preacher whose fusion of benevolence and eloquence sustained the colony through the first awkward decade. The fact that only one person in his church was excommunicated during his ministry bears witness to the tenacity of his lifelong conviction that, "If men would be tender and careful to keep off offensive expressions, they might keep some distance in opinion, in some things, without hazard to truth or love." [60] When he did go out of his way to keep dissent in check, he did it in the knowledge that one ill-tempered controversy like those provoked by Roger Williams and Anne Hutchinson would have been enough to rend asunder the infant experiment. Stability, too, has its uses for freedom.

There is little else to add to this account of the masterful life and selfless preaching of "the Light of the Western Churches." [61] He was neither democrat nor constitutionalist but a child of his time and place. He was not an advocate of religious freedom or toleration but a staunch believer in the oneness of church and state.[62] Certainly he had no such modern notions as that of "the state as a public-service corporation," which Parrington bestowed on him in a giddy transport of liberal rapture.[63] Yet in his primitive encounters with the magnificent theories of the social compact, the sovereignty of the people, and the authority of the electors to set limits upon the elected, Hooker took such a conspicuous step toward the democracy of the future that he must always be celebrated in the annals of American liberty. He first planted in New England soil the seeds of liberty hidden away in the brittle pod of Puritanism. He first proved, all unwittingly, that the New England Way contained the means of its own liberation.

CHAPTER SEVEN

Roger Williams

IN THE year 1654, a certain windmill in the Low Countries, whirling round with extraordinary violence, by reason of a violent storm then blowing; the stone at length by its rapid motion became so intensely hot, as to fire the mill, from whence the flames, being dispersed by the high winds, did set a whole town on fire. But I can tell my reader, that above twenty years before this, there was a whole country in America like to be set on fire by the rapid motion of a windmill, in the head of one particular man.[1]

With these quaint words Cotton Mather of Boston paid his orthodox respects to Roger Williams of Providence. Since Mather was the chief apologist for the Massachusetts oligarchy and Williams the "first rebel against the divine church-order established in the wilderness," we might have expected the author of the *Magnalia* to be more caustic in his sketch of the great heretic. Yet Mather, like many another orthodox New Englander, could not help paying this remarkable man a grudging compliment. Of Williams's life in Providence he remarked:

> It was more than forty years after his exile that he lived here, and in many things acquitted himself so laudably, that many judicious persons judged him to have the root of the matter in him, during the long winter of his retirement.[2]

Modern writers, too, have had trouble putting Williams in his place and have found him the most slippery of candidates for definitive biography. He has, of course, long since received his due from the historians, theologians, orators, and school children of a grateful nation. He has been depicted, quite properly, as the founder or at least chief colonist of Rhode Island, one of the noblest white friends of the Indians, the "apostle of complete religious liberty," and the rod and staff of the most popular system of government in the colonial period. Yet he remains a puzzling figure; before him the

modern mind stands for a while in wonder, then retreats into shameless
hyperbole.

This chapter makes no attempt to bring perfect order out of the per-
plexities of Williams's life and mind. Rather, it is a severely limited evaluation of his political thought and practice that may perhaps help others to
present him as a whole man. It pictures him as the embodiment of certain
ideas and techniques that were to take fast root in American soil. And it
salutes him, without hyperbole, as the first great democrat of the colonial
era.

FROM ENGLAND TO MASSACHUSETTS

The story of Roger Williams begins exactly as that of an authentic folk-
hero should begin: in a pall of uncertainty about his ancestry and origin.
The records of his birth and early years went up in the smoke of the great
London fire of 1666,[3] and it has required the most intense application of
antiquarian scholarship to dispel a good deal of nineteenth-century misin-
formation about him. It is now agreed that he was born in 1603 in the parish
of St. Sepulchre's, London, the third of four children of James Williams,
"citizen and merchant tailor," and his wife Alice Pemberton of the "lesser
landed gentry." [4] As a boy he lived with his well-established parents in
Cow Lane, witnessed some of the stirring events of the reign of James I,
and, by his own testimony, was "persecuted even in and out of my father's
house" for early and unexpected dissent from accepted religious ideas.[5] We
know nothing of his early education, except for the providential fact that
he somehow acquired a skill that was to change the whole course of his life.
Like many a famous American of later times, young Roger Williams attracted the attention of a distinguished public figure because he had learned
to take shorthand. Years later an English lady testified:

> This Roger Williams, when he was a youth, would, in a short hand, take
> sermons and speeches in the Star Chamber and present them to my dear
> father. He, seeing so hopeful a youth, took such liking to him that he sent
> him in to Sutton's Hospital . . . full little did he think that he would have
> proved such a rebel to God, the king, and his country.[6]

The "dear father" whom Williams served as court stenographer, and
who "was often pleased to call" him "his son," was that great man of the
law, Sir Edward Coke. James I himself could hardly have been a more
eminent and useful patron to a young man anxious to be something more
than a merchant tailor. From "Sutton's Hospital," where he was a scholar
of celebrated Charterhouse, Williams went in 1624 as pensioner to Pembroke
Hall, Cambridge. Having received his bachelor's degree in 1627, he passed
two additional years at Cambridge as a graduate student in theology, where
he was doubtless stuffed with the mixed fare of scholasticism, classicism,
and Puritanism that the tutors of Cambridge were serving up in his college
days. Already a person of pronounced nonconforming views, and therefore

excluded from preferment in the England of Charles and Laud, he withdrew from the university before completing requirements for his second degree and took a position as chaplain to Sir Edward Masham, a leading Puritan gentleman of Otes in Essex.

His short residence with this family was almost as fortunate a turn of events as his service with Coke, for he made the solid acquaintance of several men who were later to rule England and support Rhode Island in her struggles with greedy neighbors. Cromwell, Hampden, and Whalley were all relatives of Lady Masham. The young minister flew a little fast and high, it would seem, for he sued unsuccessfully for the hand of Whalley's sister. Rebuffed by the maiden's guardian, although not by the maiden,[7] he found a lifetime of solace and devotion in Mary Barnard, a young lady of his own class, whom he married at High Laver December 15, 1629.[8]

The call to New England had already sounded. In the summer of 1629 Williams had attended a meeting at Sempringham of persons interested in the Bay enterprise. He had ridden there in the memorable company of Thomas Hooker and John Cotton and had doubtless been asked to cast his lot with the prospective emigrants. Finally, in late 1630, still too young and unimportant to invite Laud's close attention, yet old and knowing enough to imagine what would befall him when his own turn came due, he made for Bristol and Massachusetts. Winthrop's *Journal* has this entry for February 5, 1631:

> The ship *Lyon*, Mr. William Peirce, master, arrived at Nantasket. She brought Mr. Williams, (a godly minister), with his wife. . . .[9]

The arrival of Williams was an event of some importance, for most of the famous men of God who were to hold sway in Massachusetts and Connecticut had not yet come over. We have testimony of the esteem in which he was held in the fact that he was asked shortly to be teacher to the first church at Boston. He was forced to refuse this position by a conscience already far stronger than any desire for worldly preferment, "because I durst not officiate to an unseparated people, as, upon examination and conference, I found them to be."[10] Dismayed that a dissenting congregation would cling so stubbornly to the Church of England, Williams withdrew to the more amiable atmosphere of Salem. Here, too, he was "called to the office of a teacher," and here, too, he found himself out of step with the elders. Under pressure from the oligarchs in Boston, who were further appalled by Williams's opinion "that the magistrates might not punish . . . a breach of the first table,"[11] the Salem congregation retracted its offer. Once again Williams withdrew, this time to Plymouth.

For two years Williams lived quietly at Plymouth and "wrought hard at the hoe" for his bread. Bradford set him down as "a man godly and zealous, having many precious parts, but very unsettled in judgment," who "exercised his gifts among them" by teaching in a manner somewhat unsettling yet "well approved."[12] In late 1633 Williams returned to Salem, there to assist the pastor, Samuel Skelton, "by way of prophecy," and

Cotton arrived in Boston, there to accept the position that Williams had refused.[18] Winthrop tells the story of the next two years:

(November, 1633) The ministers in the bay and Sagus did meet, once a fortnight, at one of their houses by course, where some question of moment was debated. Mr. Skelton, the pastor of Salem, and Mr. Williams . . . took some exception against it, as fearing it might grow in time to a presbytery or superintendency, to the prejudice of the churches' liberties.

(December 27, 1633) The governor and assistants met at Boston, and took into consideration a treatise, which Mr. Williams (then of Salem) had sent to them, and which he had formerly written to the governor and council of Plymouth, wherein, among other things, he disputes their right to the lands they possessed here, and concluded that, claiming by the king's grant, they could have no title, nor otherwise, except they compounded with the natives.

(November 27, 1634) It was likewise informed, that Mr. Williams of Salem had broken his promise to us, in teaching publickly against the king's patent, and our great sin in claiming right thereby to this country, etc., and for usual terming the churches of England antichristian.

(April 30, 1635) The governor and assistants sent for Mr. Williams. The occasion was, for that he had taught publicly, that a magistrate ought not to tender an oath to an unregenerate man, for that we thereby have communion with a wicked man in the worship of God, and cause him to take the name of God in vain. He was heard before all the ministers, and very clearly confuted.

(July 8, 1635) At the general court, Mr. Williams of Salem was summoned, and did appear. It was laid to his charge, that, being under question before the magistracy and churches for divers dangerous opinions, viz. 1. that the magistrate ought not to punish the breach of the first table, otherwise than in such cases as did disturb the civil peace; 2, that he ought not to tender an oath to an unregenerate man; 3, that a man ought not to pray with such, though wife, child etc.; 4, that a man ought not to give thanks after the sacrament nor after meat, etc.; and that the other churches were about to write to the church of Salem to admonish him of these errors; notwithstanding the church had since called him to [the] office of a teacher. Much debate was about these things. The said opinions were adjudged by all, magistrates and ministers, (who were desired to be present,) to be erroneous, and very dangerous, and the calling of him to office, at that time, was judged a great contempt of authority.

(July 12, 1635) Salem men had preferred a petition, at the last general court, for some land in Marblehead Neck, which they did challenge as belonging to their town; but, because they had chosen Mr. Williams their teacher, while he stood under question of authority, and so offered contempt to the magistrates, etc., their petition was refused till, etc.

(August, 1635) Mr. Williams, pastor of Salem, being sick and not able to speak, wrote to his church a protestation, that he could not communicate with the churches in the bay; neither would he communicate with them, except they would refuse communion with the rest; but the whole church was grieved herewith.

(October, 1635) At this general court, Mr. Williams, the teacher at Salem, was again convented. . . . Mr. Hooker was appointed to dispute with him, but could not reduce him from any of his errors. So, the next morning, the court sentenced him to depart out of our jurisdiction within six weeks, all the ministers, save one, approving the sentence, and his own church had him under question also for the same cause; and he, at his return home, refused communion with his own church, who openly disclaimed his errors, and wrote an humble submission to the magistrates, acknowledging their fault in joining with Mr. Williams in that letter to the churches against them, etc.[14]

Here are set down the facts of Williams's expulsion from Massachusetts: the "divers new and dangerous opinions" with which he challenged the authority of magistrates and ministers; the attempts, in which the best minds in the colony joined, to argue him into submission; the extent to which many plain people had been "much taken with the apprehension of his godliness"; the calculating manner in which the church at Salem was threatened and bribed in an effort to turn it against Williams; [15] his final decision to separate from all churches and stand alone and unyielding before the General Court; the sentence of banishment; and the reduction of the Salem recalcitrants.

Here, too, is evidence of the confusion that has marked the controversy whether Williams was "enlarged" out of Massachusetts primarily for religious or for political reasons. He was enlarged for both: for subverting the peace and order of a community in which state and church, religion and politics, were thoroughly and deliberately merged in one ideal and institutional pattern. In challenging the authority of Winthrop, he denied the teachings of Cotton; in questioning the logic of Hooker, he undermined the position of Haynes. In flouting the majesty of an untrustworthy king, several of whose highborn subjects had already moved in hostile array against the charter, he tampered capriciously with the unreliable but essential foundation of the holy experiment. And in proclaiming the sinful doctrine of unqualified separatism, in asserting as a practical consequence that the state might not punish errors and shortcomings in religion, he questioned not only the essence of the Puritan purpose but one of the most ancient assumptions of Christendom itself. His ideas were none too ordered in his own mind, but the danger they offered to the Bay colony was clear and present. Though we like to applaud Williams and hoot at his persecutors, we must agree that one outspoken man proclaiming separation, the invalidity of the patent, and civil immunity of breaches of the first table—all this from a prominent pulpit—was just one rebel too many for a Bible commonwealth. He was neither the first nor the last, but simply the most famous, to be ordered out of the Bay for what must have appeared to the elders as calculated subversion.[16] In our light, they were guilty of bigotry and persecution; in theirs, which burned as brightly and a good deal more fiercely, they were engaged in an act of simple self-preservation.

FROM MASSACHUSETTS TO RHODE ISLAND

Since Williams was too sick to travel and his wife was pregnant, the magistrates granted him leave to remain in Salem until spring, under severe injunction "not to go about to draw others to his opinions." The gesture was lost on Williams, however, for word soon filtered back to Boston that he was preaching the same old heresy to "company in his house." More dangerous still, "he had drawn about twenty persons to his opinion, and they were intended to erect a plantation about the Narragansett Bay, from whence the infection would easily spread" into Massachusetts. "Whereupon," writes Winthrop,

> . . . a warrant was sent to him to come presently to Boston, to be shipped, etc. He returned answer, (and divers of Salem came with it,) that he could not come without hazard of his life, etc. Whereupon a pinnace was sent with commission to Capt. Underhill, etc., to apprehend him, and carry him aboard the ship, (which then rode at Natascutt;) but, when they came at his house, they found he had been gone three days before; but whither they could not learn.[17]

Winthrop must have set down these last words with a dissembling pen, for the outcast was later to give "that ever honored Governor" full credit for advising him "to steer [his] course to Narragansett Bay and Indians, for many high and heavenly and public ends." [18] From Salem Williams and one or two companions fought their way through the wilderness snows to the half-starved hospitality of the Indians to the south. Some time in May,

> I first pitched, and began to build and plant at Seekonk, now Rehoboth, but I received a letter from my ancient friend, Mr. Winslow, then Governor of Plymouth, professing his own and others love and respect to me, yet lovingly advising me, since I was fallen into the edge of their bounds, and they were loath to displease the Bay, to remove but to the other side of the water, and then, he said, I had the country free before me, and might be as free as themselves, and we should be loving neighbors together.[19]

Once more he moved on, leaving the year's planting behind, and came by canoe in June 1636 to a spring near the meeting of the Moshassuck and Woonasquetucket rivers. Here at last he found the refuge of his years, in a place that he named Providence, "in a Sence of Gods mercefull providence unto me in my destresse." [20] By winter perhaps eight families had been settled in houses, a pattern of farming, trading, and hunting had begun, and a primitive form of town democracy had been instituted for regulating their few public affairs. With the planting of Portsmouth in 1638, Newport in 1639, and Shawomet (Warwick) in 1643 by other heretics, troublemakers, and backsliders from the Bay area, another English colony had become a visible if not yet legal reality. All four settlements were legal in Williams's sight, however, for in each instance the white man had made good his occupation with a solemn deed from Canonicus and Miantonomo, great sachems of the Narragansett.[21]

Here in Rhode Island and Providence Plantations, removed in space and doctrine from the two worlds he had tilted at in vain, Williams lived strenuously for almost a half century. Except for two excursions to England in behalf of friends and neighbors, he wrought his legendary deeds within the bounds of this tiny colony, which at his death in 1683 counted not more than four thousand persons. The record of his life in and about Providence bears striking witness to the truth that great men not only can live in small places, but often must. Williams and his colleagues were able to break radically with centuries of doctrine and build their new society without bloodshed only because their lands were spare and remote. Rhode Island could not have been much larger and richer and still have served as laboratory for the democratic future.

Despite the studied refusal of early New England historians to give the first rebel his due, we know a surprising number of well-documented facts about his life and deeds—as planter, proprietor, statesman, envoy and friend to the savage, religious pioneer, and visitor to England. His years in Rhode Island remind us that the famous men of early New England, with few exceptions, spent most of their days in backbreaking toil. Williams was first of all farmer and trader. "I know what it is to Study, to Preach, to be an Elder, to be applauded; and yet what it is also to tug at the Oar, to dig with the Spade, and Plow." [22] He could honestly say that he had "digged as hard as most diggers in Old and New England for a living." He knew what it was, too, to provide for a wife and six children.

As first proprietor of the lands about Providence Williams showed unique solicitude for the needs of those who arrived with him and after him to seek refuge from intolerance and autocracy. His historic services in more dramatic affairs have obscured his actions and agitations in behalf of a liberal land policy. He spiked the schemes of land-grabbers like William Harris and Humphrey Atherton, and at the same time ceded graciously, with scant compensation, his prior rights to the land conveyed to him as an act of "love and favor" by Canonicus and Miantonomo. Although he was not altogether successful in stemming the onrushing tide of speculation, he did achieve conspicuous victories in applying his doctrine of "liberty and equality, in land and government." [23] There is no more impressive evidence of his generosity and foresight than his solemn protest, delivered some time around 1662, against the plans of his forgetful neighbors in Providence to divide among themselves certain lands still held in common:

> I have one only motion and petition, which I earnestly pray the town to lay to heart . . . it is this, that after you have got over the black brook of some soul bondage yourselves, you tear not down the bridge after you, by leaving no small pittance for distressed souls that may come after you.[24]

Williams participated in the political affairs of town and colony from his first days as proprietor to his last as simple citizen. He was called upon repeatedly by his fellow outcasts to discharge some office of the greatest or smallest trust. As arbitrator, moderator, constitution-maker, town councilor, assistant, "chief officer" (1644-1647), president (1654-1657), peacemaker, captain of the trainband, committeeman, special envoy to red man and white, scribe, and general handyman for Providence and the colony, he gave years of his many-sided life to public service. Few political thinkers have had so many practical opportunities to test their theories, or have drawn so many new ideas from experience. Not content to spin out fine notions and watch them float off to agitate Massachusetts and England, he put the doctrines of popular republicanism and religious liberty to work in the Rhode Island commonwealth. Not content to draw all his ideas out of books and "right reason," he arrived at some of his most cherished beliefs along the hard road of experience.

His chief visible services, not only to his own colony but to all New England, were his labors for peace and order among and with the Indians. The story is an old one, well and often told. It should be enough to sum up his half century as the leading white man in the world of Narragansett and Wampanoag under these three headings: his Indian diplomacy, which he pursued at tremendous cost to his health and wealth and often in peril of his life;[25] the publication, in London in 1643, of the justly famed *Key into the Language of America;*[26] and his shrewd but honest activities as a trader who refused to traffic with the savage in liquor and guns. Williams achieved his most notable triumph in Indian diplomacy in his first year in Providence, when "the Lord drew the bow of the Pequod war against the country." In successfully detaching the Narragansetts from an alliance with the Pequots, he may well have saved New England from war to the knife.[27]

Williams is best remembered as religious pioneer,[28] as one who roamed from Anglicanism through Puritanism and Baptism to Seekerism, spending his last forty-odd years in search of the religious truth that he probably never expected to find on earth. A thoroughgoing Calvinist in his personal theology, Williams was none the less sufficiently unsure about the five points—and completely unsure about problems of church organization—to find Seekerism the most comfortable platform on which to take his stand. Through all his years, and largely because of him, Rhode Island clung in law and spirit to the doctrines of absolute separation and liberty of individual conscience. The acid test of the sincerity of Williams's views came with the arrival after 1657 of large numbers of Quakers. Although he shrank in disgust from their excesses and debated caustically with their leaders,[29] never by word, deed, or counsel did he lend the slightest dignity to the common cause of persecution that harried these difficult people in England and the colonies. Rather, he joined with his fellow colonists in spurning the peremptory demand of the United Colonies that Rhode Island cast out her Quakers.[30] Later in his life, when they had become so numerous as to capture the government, he withdrew not an inch from his consistent submission to the doctrine of majority rule. His public record in connection with the Jews is no less liberal and honorable. Williams helped persuade

Cromwell in 1652 to readmit them to England and called upon rulers "to break down that superstitious wall of separation (as to Civil things) between us Gentiles and the Jews." [31] When the first Jews came to Rhode Island in 1658, he welcomed them as he did all victims of oppression. For the elders of Boston this was just one more reason to look upon Rhode Island as a pit of anarchy and bestiality.[32]

A word should be said about his two visits to England. The first, on which he embarked at New Amsterdam in early 1643 and from which he returned (with the aid of a safe-conduct) through Boston in late 1644, was occasioned by the struggling colony's need of legal sanction for union and independence. Thanks to his wide and sympathetic acquaintance among the parliamentary party, Williams was able to secure a patent from the Warwick commission which strengthened the hand of Rhode Island against her traducers without and seducers within.[33] He also published several important books and engaged heavily in the religious and political controversies that were shaking all England. He was gone from Providence a second time, from November 1651 to the summer of 1654, to petition the council of state to confirm the patent of 1644 and vacate a damaging commission it had granted William Coddington in April 1651. In this quest, too, he made shrewd diplomatic use of his friendship with the great men of England and their distaste for the "lord brethren" of Massachusetts to score a victory for Rhode Island.[34] During this visit he apparently saw a good deal of Cromwell, Milton, and Vane, and again took advantage of his presence in civilization to publish tracts on issues of great moment.[35]

In all these trials and exploits—in the fields at home, the meeting-houses at Portsmouth and Newport, the public places of England, and the "filthy smoky holes" of the Indians—Williams displayed an extraordinary character. All the adjectives that we like to pin on our great men—generous, sincere, decent, public-spirited, honest, brave, warmhearted, unselfish—applied to him as to few other persons of prominence in colonial America. That he was human, too, and could complain, quarrel, boast, and beg is likewise evident in the records and letters that remain. Perhaps the most important visible trait of his triumphant character was his perpetual search for truth and willingness to argue openly and freely about it. If there was any single event in his wonderful life that tells us of the way he chose to live it, it was the occasion in 1672 when he rowed with his "old bones" from Providence to Newport to debate with three leading Quaker orators before a hostile audience.

THE GOVERNMENT OF RHODE ISLAND

We cannot understand Williams's political theory without some knowledge of the government of seventeenth-century Rhode Island,[36] a political theater in which his principles had profound influence, and in which they in turn were tried and found good. The vicissitudes of Rhode Island government during this first half-century in the wilderness are significant in their own right: They provide an interesting case-study in the interaction of English habits and frontier conditions, and they prove that it was no easy matter to set up a polity dedicated to the reconciliation of liberty and order.

Through most of Williams's life Rhode Island was in political difficulties. It was repeatedly menaced from within by disunion, treason, and straightout anarchy, and from without by the grasping schemes of powerful neighbors who hated its principles and coveted its lands and harbors. More often than not, internal dissension and external encroachment went hand in hand, for its malcontents learned early to appeal to Boston or London for support against Williams. Other factors that frustrated orderly government were the intense land-hunger of certain inhabitants, most notoriously the testy William Harris of Providence and Pawtuxet,[37] and a reputation, carefully nurtured by all the old wives and preachers of Boston and New Amsterdam, as the "sewer" of New England, where riffraff ran wild and women gave birth to horned monsters.[38] The despised colony was several times denied admittance to the New England Confederation on the ground that it lacked a stable government. Yet Rhode Island managed to endure through all this turmoil, slander, and isolation with surprisingly little damage to the principles of religious liberty, equality in land, and popular government on which it was founded.

The political chronology of early Rhode Island is roughly this: the establishment of Providence (1636) as a primitive form of householders' democracy; the establishment of Portsmouth (1638), Newport (1639), and Warwick (1643) according to various political impulses ranging from democracy to neo-feudalism, yet all like Providence on the basis of a compact; the union of these autonomous towns in the patent of 1644; the creation, after three more years of separatism, of the first real government, which lasted until the secession of Aquidneck (Portsmouth and Newport) in 1651; the re-establishment of the union in 1654; and the winning in 1663 of a royal charter, which altered a few but preserved most of the techniques the Rhode Islanders had created for their own governing.

The first rude government in Providence was shaped almost completely to the notions of Roger Williams. It was based squarely on two explicit compacts—one among the first heads of families, the other, adopted a year or two later, admitting certain newcomers and single men.[39] The authority of the rulers extended "only in civill things." The core of government was the town meeting, which began when "the masters of families . . . met once a fortnight and consulted about our common peace, watch, and planting." [40] The executive and judicial machinery was extremely simple—hardly more than a clerk, a treasurer, and, after 1640, five "Disposers," who were elected every three months to settle disputes by arbitration. This primitive pattern of popular government was grounded upon an unusually liberal land policy, for which Williams fought without respite. Under it newcomers were to be admitted "into the same fellowship and privilege" with the first inhabitants. The stake-in-society principle underpinned and limited the democracy of Providence, but it was one town in which the stake was open to all on equal terms.

The other towns were established on principles that varied from general accord with those of Williams to flat contradiction.[41] The island of Aquidneck was purchased with his aid from the Narragansetts and settled by several leading Antinomians who had departed or been banished from Boston —most notably William Coddington, John Clarke, and William Hutchinson. The first government at Portsmouth was a curious combination of theocracy and feudalism, in which principal authority was lodged in a single "Judge," the former Boston oligarch, Coddington. The arrival of such malcontents as Anne Hutchinson and Samuell Gorton [42] and the example of Providence conspired shortly to upset Coddington's little dictatorship. In early 1639 he withdrew in anger with his followers to found a new town at Newport. The popular-minded yeomen remaining at Portsmouth entered into a second compact for a "civill body politicke." In 1640 the two Aquidneck settlements united for certain general purposes, and a year later a new popular movement forced the adoption of these forward-looking orders:

> It is ordered and unanimously agreed upon, that the Government which this Bodie Politick doth attend unto in this Island, and the Jurisdiction thereof, in favour of our Prince is a DEMOCRACIE, or Popular Government; that is to say, It is in the Powre of the Body of Freemen orderly assembled, or the major part of them, to make or constitute Just Lawes, by which they will be regulated, and to depute from among themselves such Ministers as shall see them faithfully executed between Man and Man.
>
> It was further ordered, by the authority of this present Courte, that none bee accounted a Delinquent for *Doctrine:* Provided, it be not directly repugnant to ye Government or Lawes established.[43]

Thus were two of Williams's great principles, popular government and religious liberty, established in the towns about Narragansett Bay. They were likewise established, although with more interference from outside detractors, at Warwick in 1643.

The colony of Rhode Island began its formal existence in March 1644, when Williams secured his precious patent from the Commissioners of Plantations. Unlike Massachusetts, Plymouth, and Connecticut, Rhode Island was formed in the union of independent towns. What had brought them together to send Williams to England was exactly what has brought discordant autonomies together since the beginning of history: fear of designing and more powerful neighbors. The patent itself was all that Williams could have asked for, except in the loose delineation of the colony's boundaries. It incorporated Providence, Newport, and Portsmouth as an independent and united plantation; gave them authority to rule themselves and future settlers by whatever "Form of Civil Government, as by voluntary consent of all, or the great Part of them, they shall find most suitable to their Estate and Condition"; recognized therewith the principle of separation of church and state; ordered that laws "be conformable to the Laws of England," but only "so far as the Nature and Constitution of the place will admit"; and reserved to England the right to supervise external relations between Rhode Island and the other colonies.[44]

Not for another three years did the necessities of union become sufficiently pressing to force the organization of government under the patent. Then, in May 1647, at a meeting of the three older towns and Warwick at Portsmouth, the charter was accepted and a popular type of government adopted.[45] The most interesting features of the new government were these: (1) it was adopted by an assembly attended by "the major parte of the Colonie" and was thus one of the few constitutions in history to proceed directly from the people; (2) it was couched in the language of an explicit civil compact; (3) the form was declared to be "DEMOCRATICALL; that is to say, a Government held by ye free and voluntarie consent of all, or the greater parte of the free Inhabitants;" (4) it recognized the rights of the originally independent towns by establishing a pattern of incipient federalism that was strengthened by subsequent laws and town charters; [46] (5) it made further concessions to the towns by inaugurating a primitive system of initiative, referendum, and recall; [47] and (6) it instituted an extensive code of laws and liberties based directly on those of England.

The code in turn embodied several notable features: an affirmation of Chapter 29 of Magna Charta, the concept of public office as not only a trust but a duty, a strain of leniency not found in the codes of neighboring colonies, a careful organization of courts to enforce the laws, and finally this noble statement:

> These are the Lawes that concern all men, and these are the Penalties for the transgression thereof, which by common consent are Ratified and Established throwout this whole Colonie; and otherwise than thus what is herein forbidden, all men may walk as their consciences perswade them, every one in the name of his God.

The officers of the new government, all elected annually by the court of election, were a president, four assistants (one to each town), recorder, treasurer, and sergeant. The duties of president and assistants were both executive and judicial, but in no sense were they "magistrates" on the Massachusetts model. The core of government remained, of course, the General Court, which became a representative body for legislative purposes—with six "commissioners" chosen from each town—but remained a primary gathering when convened as court of election.

This popular scheme of government continued until 1663 with several changes and one conspicuous break. The changes were the addition of several new executive officials, the further liberalization of many fundamental laws, the repeated use of Williams's cherished principle of arbitration, and the institution of ad hoc committees for executive duties.[48] The break lasted from 1651 to 1654 and was chiefly the work of that dissident aristocrat, William Coddington, who did everything in his power, including overtures to the New England Confederation and a trip to England for a commission to govern Aquidneck for life, to frustrate the patent of 1644.

Only after the joint voyage to England of Williams and John Clarke, emissary of the anti-Coddington forces in Newport and Portsmouth, was Coddington finally brought to earth.[49]

The restoration of Charles II in 1660 presented a new threat to Rhode Island's independent status. Thanks, however, to the quick submission of the colony and devoted diplomacy of John Clarke,[50] a royal charter of astounding liberality was passed through the seals July 8, 1663. It confirmed the scheme of government existent in Rhode Island, with some change in the number and title of officials and with provisions looking to a stronger central government. Most important, Clarke had included in his petition a specific request "to hold forth a lively experiment, that a flourishing civill State may stand, yea, and best be maintained, and that among English spirits, with a full liberty in religious concernments." [51] Charles II, whose persecuting tendencies were softened in this instance by a desire to make his colonies attractive to would-be settlers, granted this request with a gallant sweep that must have stunned the elders of Massachusetts.[52]

> Our royall will and pleasure is, that noe person within the sayd colonye, at any tyme hereafter, shall bee any wise molested, punished, disquieted, or called in question, for any differences in opinione in matters of religion, and doe not actually disturb the civill peace of our sayd colony; but that all and everye person and persons may, from tyme to tyme, and at all tymes hereafter, freelye and fullye have and enjoye his and theire own judgments and consciences, in matters of religious concernments, throughout the tract of lande hereafter mentioned; they behaving themselves peaceablie and quietlie, and not useing this libertie to lycentiousnesse and profanenesse, nor to the civill injurye or outward disturbeance of others.

This charter endured as the foundation of government in colony and state for almost two centuries.

The record of Rhode Island politics in Roger Williams's lifetime is obviously spotty, especially when contrasted with the stability of Massachusetts or Connecticut. Yet those historians who have concluded that government in Rhode Island was a failure have been noticeably wide of the mark. When we recall the factors that militated against its success—the pre-existence of the towns,[53] the open hostility of its neighbors, the speculative schemes of Harris and Atherton that Williams refused to suffer gladly, the designs of Coddington, the lack of geographic unity, the virtual nonexistence of a hortatory clergy, the leniency of the code, the free play accorded all manner of heterodoxies, and the general spirit of democracy and independence which several times erupted in barefaced anarchy—we may wonder how it survived at all to win its independence within the British colonial system. Yet it did survive, with no more actual bloodshed than a few battered heads and with its libertarian principles in a remarkable state of preservation. Nor should it be forgotten that while Harris agitated, Gorton posed, Coddington plotted, and overheated zealots ran naked about the streets, most of the colony's good people tilled their lands and plied their

trades with no interference from magistrates, preachers, or other persecuting oligarchs.

"Possibly," wrote Williams to Vane in 1654,

> a sweet cup hath rendered many of us wanton and too active, for we have
> long drunk of the cup of as great liberties as any people that we can hear
> of under the whole heaven.[54]

Possibly, yet no more wanton and active than could be expected of men
who had hardly suspected that orderly government could exist without
severe regulation and legalized inequality. The colonial records testify that
Rhode Island was the closest thing to democracy in seventeenth-century
America. And they testify also that Roger Williams was the one man most
responsible for this triumph of liberty.

WILLIAMS AS POLITICAL THINKER

Williams stands alone and unchallenged among colonial thinkers. Populist,
libertarian, skeptic, and seeker, advocate of a future that is yet to come,
he was by all odds the most exciting character in the story of colonial
liberty. We must not be surprised or chagrined to learn that he was also
the most lonely.[55] It is the business of prophets to be lonely.

Several facts about Williams's political philosophy should be established
at the outset. First, an unusually close connection between theory and practice marked both his mind and career. It is popular among historians to
eulogize him as thinker and write him off as practitioner, but this is to un-
derestimate grossly the success with which he converted doctrine into fact.
He stamped his personality emphatically upon the society in which he lived,
and the society in turn gave form and support to some of his most finespun ideas. It also taught him a few hard truths that he would never have
learned in England or Massachusetts.

Although Williams produced a sizable body of doctrine, he was no doctrinaire. In politics as in religion he was always the seeker. As sponsor of
an actual political experiment he could speak with a good deal more authority than other seventeenth-century republicans, yet he shied away from
proclaiming political and social dogma. Although he arrived at many of his
basic ideas at an early date and championed them loudly to the end of his
life, he stood always ready to abandon them should more workable principles
be found to take their place.

Williams serves as a reminder that the first settlers were not only English
but English-minded, men who had worked up their theories in the mother
country and had brought them over to be tested in a strange land. Only by
courtesy, and for the sake of national pride, can we call a man like Williams
an American. The debate between Cotton and Williams over the nature of
church and state was carried on in England, through the medium of English
presses, and as an attempt to influence English rather than colonial opinion.

Williams did not expound a systematic political theory, and we must search at length through his tracts and letters for ideas that can be properly termed political in character. His writings were occasional, polemic, and framed in the idiom of his age, all of which is another way of saying that he was the father of all American political thinkers. Although he had an inclusive political philosophy, he never attempted to present it in an organized, discriminating manner.[56]

We must look in two categories of Williams's writings for his political ideas: the numerous books and pamphlets that he contributed to the great Anglo-American debate on the nature of church and state, and a handful of extant letters, especially four public lectures to the town of Providence on the manner in which his fellow citizens were disregarding the noble purposes of the original settlement.[57] The most important of his formal writings were:

Mr. Cottons Letter Lately Printed, Examined and Answered (London, 1644), in which Williams first proclaimed in print his doctrines of separatism, sectarianism, and freedom of conscience.

Queries of Highest Consideration (London, 1644), a direct contribution to the presbyterian controversy then agitating England.

The Bloudy Tenent of Persecution for Cause of Conscience (London, 1644), his most celebrated and influential work, in which he launched an all-out assault on the closely related ideas of a national church and persecution of religious nonconformity. Williams addressed *The Bloudy Tenent* to Parliament, which repaid the unsolicited compliment by ordering the common hangman to burn the book. Three years later Cotton published a reply, *The Bloudy Tenent Washed White in the Blood of the Lambe* (London, 1647), which justified the ways of Massachusetts against the disruptive nonsense of religious liberty.

The Bloody Tenent Yet More Bloody (London, 1652), Williams's answer to Cotton's "Fig-leave Evasions and Distinctions."

The Hireling Ministry None of Christs (London, 1652), a powerful indictment of the national church.

The Fourth Paper, Presented by Major Butler (London, 1652), a plea for liberty of conscience, even for non-Christians.

Experiments of Spiritual Life and Health (London, 1652), a tract on piety in which he evidenced an essentially humanistic opinion of the nature of man.

George Fox Digg'd out of his Burrowes (Boston, 1676), in which he made clear that there are limits to what men can do to disturb the peace in the name of religious liberty.[58]

In all these works, as their titles quaintly proclaim, Williams had the relationship of church and state as his primary concern. Yet in advancing his own revolutionary solutions to the problems this relationship had generated, especially in advocating rigid separation and freedom for all well-behaved religions, he was forced into an attitude toward political authority hardly less radical than his theology. His life and thought provide one more illustration of the historic manner in which the struggle against autocracy in the state followed naturally from, or even moved step by step with, the struggle against autocracy in the church. Although there have been several bold attempts to secularize Williams's thought, to draw a sharp line between his politics and ecclesiasticism and give primacy to the former,[59] these ignore the whole tenor of his writings and the limitations on speculation and debate characteristic of the age in which he lived. Not only were religious nonconformity and political liberalism inseparable parts of his total philosophy, but it was about the former that he thought first, hardest, and most influentially.

SEVENTEENTH-CENTURY REPUBLICANISM

The strictly political aspects of Williams's philosophy—which we consider "strictly political" at the risk of misreading his seventeenth-century mind —were so casually proclaimed that we would do him a disservice were we to regard them as either the hard core of his thought or his chief contribution to the evolution of democratic theory. Here and there in his writings he expressed his adherence to all well-known refinements of early republicanism, but he rarely if ever paused to explain any one of them. He saved his powers of analysis for the more pressing questions of persecution and "soul liberty." Though he was a devoted exponent of the liberating doctrines of popular sovereignty and the social compact, he had pondered neither profoundly nor originally about the noble philosophy that was in time to dominate the American mind. It should therefore be sufficient to list briefly, with the aid of a few quotations, the various elements of seventeenth-century republicanism that he carried across the sea, followed dutifully but not fanatically in his experiments at state-building, and flung at Cotton in an offhand manner in the debate over persecution.

Civil government, wrote Williams, though ultimately of divine origin, springs immediately from the body of the people, "who have fundamentally in themselves the Root of Power, to set up what Government and Governours they shall agree upon." [60] Agreement on the form of government is reached through explicit techniques of popular consent. The records of Providence and Rhode Island reveal that Williams regarded government, though not necessarily society, as the artificial creation of an open covenant. The purpose of government is altogether popular: "the preservation of the peace and welfare of the state" and of all the people in it.[61] Peace, which Williams defined in the broadest terms as liberty and security for all men, was the favorite word in his political lexicon. Civil government brings peace and is therefore good and necessary.

> If the sword and balances of justice (in a sort or measure) be not drawn and held forth, against scandalous offenders against civil state, that civil state must dissolve by little and little from civility to barbarisme, which is a wilderness of life and manners.[62]

It makes no difference, said Williams, what form of government the people decide upon so long as all those in authority look upon themselves as "eyes and hands and instruments of the people," [63] recognize that any "Minister or Magistrate goes beyond his commission, who intermeddles with that which cannot be given him in commission from the people," [64] and remain answerable to the unprejudiced power of recall vested in the community at large. The fundamental organ of government is the assembly of the citizens, primary or representative according to circumstance, and operating under the doctrine of majority rule.

Most of these principles are expressed in a famous passage from *The Bloudy Tenent:*

> That the Civill Power may erect and establish what forme of civill Government may seeme in wisedome most meet, I acknowledge the proposition to be most true, both in it self, and also considered with the end of it, that a civill Government is an Ordinance of God, to conserve the civill peace of people, so farre as concernes their Bodies and Goods, as formerly hath been said.
>
> But from this Grant I infer, (as before hath been touched) that the Soveraigne, originall, and foundation of civill power lies in the people, (whom they must needs meane by the civill power distinct from the Government set up.) And if so, that a People may erect and establish what forme of Government seemes to them most meete for their civill condition: It is evident that such Governments as are by them erected and established, have no more power, nor for no longer time, then the civill power or people consenting and agreeing shall betrust them with. This is cleere not only in Reason, but in the experience of all commonweales, where the people are not deprived of their naturall freedome by the power of Tyrants.[65]

Williams was extremely hazy about natural or fundamental law [66] and therefore about the whole concept of natural rights. He certainly cannot be cited as an early Anglo-American exponent of the right of resistance or revolution.[67] The rights that Williams emphasized in his writings were civil and English, not natural and universal. A notable passage from an admonitory letter to the town of Warwick in 1666 expresses this clearly:

> The whole summ and scope of his Majesties Royall graunt and charter to us is to bestow upon us 2 inestimable Jewells.
>
> The first is peace, commonly calld among all men the Kings peace (among) ourselues and among all the Kings subjects and Friends in this Countrey and wheresoeuer. . . .
>
> The 2 Jewell is Libertie: the first of our spirits which neither Old nor N. Eng: knowes the like, nor no part of the World a greater.
>
> 2. Libertie of our persons: no Life no Limbe taken from us: No Corporall punishment no Restraint, but by knowne Lawes and Agreements of our own making.
>
> 3. Libertie of our Estates, Howses catle, Lands, Goods, and not a peny to be taken by any rate, without euery mans free debate by his Deputies, chosen by himself and sent to the General Assembly.
>
> 4. Libertie of Societie and Corporacion: of sending or being sent to the

Gen: Assembly: of choosing and being chosen to all offices, and of making or repealing all Lawes and Constitutions among us.

5. A Libertie, which other Charters haue not, to wit of attending to the Lawe of Eng: with a favourable mitigacion viz: not absolutely but respecting our Wilderness Estate and Condicion.[68]

RELIGIOUS LIBERTY

Roger Williams made his chief contribution to liberty with brave new solutions to bitter old problems that had been agitating Christendom since the beginning of the Reformation. By proclaiming in *The Bloudy Tenent* and underwriting in Rhode Island the doctrines of religious liberty that he had dimly perceived at Cambridge and was still groping for at Salem, Williams swept away, almost too impudently, a formidable barrier to political liberty; at the same time, he furnished an object lesson that men of good will in other Christian countries could ponder and apply. The portrait of Williams as religious figure has been painted and repainted in so many hundreds of books and articles [69]—often faithfully and as often too heroically—that we may confine this exposition to the political implications of his explosive teachings. More precisely, we must examine two related aspects of his religious doctrines: where they fixed the line between authority of state and liberty of individual, and what their formulation and successful application actually contributed to the rise of American liberty.

Williams's religious teachings were essentially negative in character, for he denied just about every important principle of church and state that men had been asserting for more than a thousand years: that there was one true religion, that there was one true church, that the central purpose of the divinely ordained state was to defend the church, that prince and bishop or minister and magistrate must support each other with the sanctions at their command, that the civil power must protect the true religion by punishing errors of doctrine and shortcomings of religious performance, and that it might rightfully persecute for cause of conscience. In short, Williams rejected categorically the unity of church and state that had dominated the Middle Ages and was even then dominating Massachusetts and Connecticut, "that commonly received and not questioned opinion, viz. That the civill state and the spirituall, the Church and Commonweale, they are like Hippocrates twinnes, they are borne together, grow up together, laugh together, weepe together, sicken and die together." [70]

In practical terms, this meant that church and state were to be cleanly separated, that no religion was to be preferred or nourished by the civil power, that each church was to be treated as just another private organization with the usual corporate rights, that liberty of conscience was to be guaranteed to each individual, and that no man was to be molested by his government or fellow citizens for his religious opinions—so long as he did not express them in such manner as to disturb the civil peace. The purpose of government was "the preservation of the peace and welfare of the state," not the propagation of one religion or all. The authority of the state was to extend only to a man's behavior, never to his conscience.

Williams's own words, however archaic they may seem to us, expressed these ideas with an intensity that must have amazed the General Court in Boston and Parliament in London.

> All Civill States with their Officers of justice in their respective constitutions and administrations are . . . essentially Civill, and therefore not Judges, Governours or Defendours of the Spirituall or Christian State and Worship.
>
> It is the will and command of God that (since the comming of his Sonne the Lord Jesus) a permission of the most Paganish, Jewish, Turkish, or Antichristian consciences and worships, bee granted to all men in all Nations and Countries: and they are onely to bee fought against with that Sword which is only (in Soule matters) able to conquer, to wit, the Sword of Gods Spirit, the Word of God.
>
> God requireth not an uniformity of Religion to be inacted and inforced in any civill State; which inforced uniformity (sooner or later) is the greatest occasion of civill Warre, ravishing of conscience, persecution of Christ Jesus in his servants, and of the hypocrisie and destruction of millions of souls.
>
> The permission of other consciences and worships then a state professeth, only can (according to God) procure a firme and lasting peace, (good assurance being taken according to the wisdome of the civill State for uniformity of civill obedience from all sorts.) . . .
>
> The government of the civill Magistrate extendeth no further then over the bodies and goods of their subjects, not over their soules, and therefore they may not undertake to give Lawes unto the soules and consciences of men.
>
> The Church of Christ doth not use the Arme of secular power to compell men to the true profession of the truth, for this is to be done with spirituall weapons, whereby Christians are to be exhorted, not compelled.[71]

His most famous and oft-quoted words were these:

> Hence it is that so many glorious and flourishing cities of the World maintaine their Civill peace, yea the very Americans and wildest Pagans keep the peace of their Towns or Cities; though neither in one nor the other can any man prove a true Church of God in those places, and consequently no spiritual heavenly peace: The Peace Spiritual (whether true or false) being of a higher and farre different nature from the Peace of the place or people, being meerly and essentially civill and humane.
>
> The Church or company of worshippers (whether true or false) is like unto a Body or Colledge of Physitians in a Citie; like unto a Corporation, Society, or Company of East-Indie or Turkie-Merchants, or any other Societie or Company in London: which Companies may hold their Courts, keep their Records, hold disputations; and in matters concerning their Societie, may dissent, divide, breake into Schismes and Factions, sue and implead each other at the Law, yea wholly breake and dissolve into pieces and nothing, and yet the peace of the Citie not be in the least measure impaired or disturbed; because of the essence or being of the Citie, and so the wellbeing and peace thereof is essentially distinct from those particular Societies;

the Citie-Courts, Citie-Laws, Citie-punishments distinct from theirs. The Citie was before them, and stands absolute and intire, when such a Corporation or Society is taken down.[72]

It is plain to see what Williams thought about the authority of the state in religious matters. He opened up a whole new field of liberty for the individual, or rather set up a fence between ruler and ruled that the former had no power—from nature, Scripture, principle, or expediency—to break down or push beyond. At the same time, he did not advocate that the state adopt a completely laissez-faire attitude toward religion. It could punish outrages against the civil peace by persons whose religion moved them to violence or obscenity. It could defend one person professing an unpopular faith against the active intolerance of another.[73]

Through his bold advocacy of the twin doctrines of separation of church and state and liberty of conscience, and through his endorsement of their trial-by-ordeal in despised Rhode Island, Williams reached two centuries or more into the American future. He asserted and proved that a moral, stable society could exist without the support and sanctions of a national church. With one bold stroke—by thrusting them out of the area of political intervention—he disposed of several questions that had muddied and bloodied Western society for generations and had repeatedly fractured the peace so necessary for the effective working of free institutions. He added new dignity and meaning to individualism by telling men that they could think and teach as they pleased, even irreligiously and anti-Christianly,[74] without answering to any earthly authority. And he gave impetus to good government by reminding those in authority of their proper and primary tasks. In short, he solved the most perplexing political problem of his age by demonstrating that it was not political at all. And he did all this, as good Americans have done ever since, with the help of arguments that were derived from expediency. He assaulted *The Bloudy Tenent* with a benumbing array of citations from Scripture and applications of reason, but his most telling accusation was that "there is no Doctrine, no Tenent so directly tending to break the Cities peace, as this Doctrine of persecuting or punishing each other for the cause of conscience or Religion." [75] Contrary to the opinions of the persecutors of old and New England,

> The free permitting of the *consciences* and *meetings* of *conscionable* and *faithful people* throughout the *Nation*, and the free permission of the *Nation* to frequent such *assemblies*, will be one of the principal Means and expedients (as the present state of Christianity stands) for the propagating and spreading of the Gospel of the Son of God.[76]

There is a surprisingly modern and utilitarian note in Williams's case for separation and "soul liberty."

Williams was not, as many writers and orators have loosely insisted, an advocate of toleration. This concept implies the superiority of one belief over others, and the willingness of those who hold it to tolerate those who refuse to conform. Williams pushed well beyond the boundaries of mere toleration to proclaim religious liberty as the consequence of the essential equality of all faiths.[77] Here again he made little sense to most men of his age, the less because he was in fact "pious with a fervor and passion that went beyond most of his contemporaries," and not, like Jefferson, "a man to whom theology and divine grace had become stuff and nonsense." [78]

As first theoretical and practical exponent of the American doctrine of religious liberty, Roger Williams is rightly considered an authentic folk-hero. Ideas and realities of this sweep are the gift of many men, but Williams surely comes as close as any American to being the embodiment of a fundamental principle of democracy.

THE ANVIL OF EXPERIENCE

Williams is well and wisely celebrated for his doctrines of popular republicanism and religious liberty. In discussing these two categories of his thought, we have done little more than recall and reshape the paramount facts in a record that has long been public property. Yet there was a third category that his biographers do not touch upon with sufficient emphasis or enlightenment: a half-dozen tenets of political authority and organization which he neither brought with him out of England nor deduced from first principles, but rather hammered out on the anvil of experience during his long public service. These were the lessons in political science that he found through experience to be helpful or essential to free and orderly government:

Free inquiry and free expression of the results. Speaking, in *The Bloody Tenent Yet More Bloody*, to "the several respective General Courts, especially that of the Massachusetts in N. England," Williams noted with sorrow that "Liberty of searching out Truth [was] hardly got, and as hardly kept." [79] In this writing, of course, he was concerned primarily with the search for religious truth, but excerpts from his letters and incidents in his career prove that he was as much the seeker in politics as in religion. He came to the conclusion that in statecraft as in theology authority grounded in doctrine would harden into tyranny grounded in dogma, and that open-minded investigation was therefore the only trustworthy technique for reaching adequate solutions to social problems. Free men, argued Williams, must have free minds, and he spent his life convincing friends and neighbors that Rhode Island's unique government and way of life depended for continued success on their cultivation of the habits of intellectual freedom.

At the same time, he made clear that a man must be prepared to discuss his conclusions openly and responsibly with his fellow citizens—without fear of official interference or private intolerance. "Free Conferrings, Disputings and Preachings" were, as he testified in his debates with the Quakers at the end of his life, the main cog in the mechanism of freedom.

> None shall see the Truth but the Soul that loves it, and digs for it as for treasures of gold and silver, and is impartial, patient, and pitiful to the opposers.[80]

Williams was uniquely anxious to accord freedom of expression to opinions that he found stupid or even dangerous. The only "ism" against which he set his face intolerantly seems to have been that interesting practice of certain early Quakers, nudism.[81] Williams learned from experience in the wilderness—at the assembly in Portsmouth, the town meeting in Providence, and the council fire in the Narragansett country—what he could only have assumed in England and Massachusetts: that men who will search openly for the truth and talk freely and humbly about their conclusions with their fellows are the stuff of political liberty.

ARBITRATION. In keeping with his everlasting emphasis on peace among men, Williams put a high value on the spirit of compromise. He had learned to recognize this spirit as the magic wand that turns license into liberty and thus brings stability to free society. Writing to the inhabitants of Providence in 1648, he had this to say about the squabbles then convulsing the Rhode Island towns:

> WORTHY FRIENDS, that ourselves and all men are apt and prone to differ, it is no new thing. In all former ages, in all parts of the world, in these parts, and in our dear native country and mournful state of England, that either part or party is most right in his own eyes, his cause right, his carriage right, his arguments right, his answers right, is as woefully and constantly true as the former. . . . And since, dear friends, it is an honor for men to cease from strife; since the life of love is sweet, and union is as strong as sweet and since you have been lately pleased to call me to some public service and my soul hath been long musing how I might bring water to quench, and not oil or fluid to the flame, I am now humbly bold to beseech you . . . to be willing to be pacifiable, willing to be reconcilable, willing to be sociable, and to listen to the (I hope not unreasonable) motion following: To try out matters by disputes and writings, is sometimes endless; to try out arguments by arms and swords, is cruel and merciless; to trouble the state and Lords of England, is most unreasonable, most chargeable; to trouble our neighbors of other colonies seems neither safe nor honorable. Methinks, dear friends, the colony now looks with the torn face of two parties, and that the greater number of Portsmouth, with other loving friends adhering to them, appear as one grieved party; the other three towns, or greater part of them, appear to be another: Let each party choose and nominate three . . . let authority be given to them to examine every public difference, grievance, and obstruction of justice, peace and common safety: let them, by one final sentence of all or the greater part of them, end all, and set the whole into an unanimous posture and order, and let them set a censure upon any that shall oppose their sentence.[82]

Here is a tribute to arbitration, the technique that Williams considered the most sensible way for free men to solve their problems and compromise their differences. "Agreed," stated the plantation covenant adopted by Providence in 1640, "that after many Considerations and Consultations of our owne State and alsoe of States abroad in way of government, we apprehend, no way so suitable to our Condition as government by way of arbitration. But if men agree themselves by way of arbitration, no State we know of disallows that, neither doe we." [83] This was a clear recognition of the efficacy of a procedure that Williams had learned something of in Massachusetts [84] and had made one of the most dependable props of the Rhode Island way. All his life he clung to a conviction that peacefully minded men could settle their own differences without recourse to governmental sanctions, by referring them to fellow citizens who were prepared to examine the facts objectively and give reasoned judgment.

THE NECESSITY OF AUTHORITY. It has been written that in the beginning Massachusetts had law without liberty and Rhode Island liberty without law. This is, as we have seen, a gratuitous insult to the people of seventeenth-century Rhode Island, most of whom tilled their fields, paid their taxes, and discharged their duties faithfully as citizens of a free state. Nevertheless, there were some who found any kind of authority distasteful and preached the gospel of all-out anarchy. "We enjoy liberties of soul and body," lamented Williams in a letter to John Winthrop, jr., "but it is license we desire." [85] To them and to all others who would wreck free government by defying even the most legitimate and needful authority, Williams made answer in 1655 through a public letter to the town of Providence. In it he made clear that it was the civil liberty of men under a government of their own making, not the irresponsible license of beasts in a jungle, that he had always championed.

> That ever I should speak or write a tittle, that tends to such an infinite liberty of conscience, is a mistake, and which I have ever disclaimed and abhorred. To prevent such mistakes, I shall at present only propose this case: There goes many a ship to sea, with many hundred souls in one ship, whose weal and woe is common, and is a true picture of a commonwealth, or a human combination or society. It hath fallen out sometimes, that both papists and protestants, Jews and Turks, may be embarked in one ship; upon which supposal I affirm, that all the liberty of conscience, that ever I pleaded for, turns upon these two hinges—that none of the papists, protestants, Jews, or Turks, be forced to come to the ship's prayers or worship, nor compelled from their own particular prayers or worship, if they practice any. I further add, that I never denied, that notwithstanding this liberty, the commander of this ship ought to command the ship's course, yea, and also command that justice, peace and sobriety, be kept and practiced, both among the seamen and all the passengers. If any of the seamen refuse to perform their services, or passengers to pay their freight; if any refuse to help, in person or purse, towards the common charges or defence; if any refuse to obey the common laws and orders of the ship, concerning their common peace or preservation; if any shall mutiny and rise up against their commanders and officers; if any should preach or write that there ought to be no commanders and officers, because all are equal in Christ, therefore no masters nor officers, no laws nor orders, nor corrections nor punishments;—I say, I never denied, but in such cases, whatever is pretended, the commander or commanders may judge, resist, compel and punish such transgressors, according to their deserts and merits.[86]

This was the courageous message of a persecuted individualist to those of his fellow refugees who, perhaps understandably, could not rid themselves of the notion that all authority was evil and oppressive. Not only was it an important contribution to the working theory of one of our first free governments, but it stands even today as a uniquely toughminded testament of a man who had learned through the hardest kind of experience that liberty without law and government without authority are swamps in which true freedom sinks without a trace.

RIGHTS AND DUTIES. Along with this clear-eyed apology for authority went another of Williams's pragmatic beliefs about the place of the individual in the political community, one that was not to be acknowledged officially outside Rhode Island until the French constitution of 1792: the idea of reciprocity of rights and duties. Williams's individualism was surprisingly modern in flavor. His writings stressed the social fact that men found the fullest expression of their liberty in fulfilling their functions in the community. A free man had duties as well as rights; indeed, he had no claim to the latter unless he was prepared to execute the former.

Again we read in the record of Williams's years in Providence that he came to this unusual notion through saddening experience, and again we have evidence that the colony itself accepted the great man's teaching. The Acts and Orders of 1647 embody the concept of reciprocal rights and duties. For example,

> In case a man be called unto Office by a lawfull Assemble, and refuse to beare office, or be called by an officer to assist in the execution of his office, and refuse to assist him, he shall forfeit as much again as his wages would have amounted unto, or be otherwise fined by the judgment of his Peers, and to pay his fine or forfeiture. . . . But in case of eminent danger, no man shall refuse.[87]

The trials of friendless Rhode Island, menaced by white enemies and red from without, weakened by anarchists and Quakers from within, taught Williams and his co-workers the necessity of individual participation in public life.

EQUALITY. Three centuries ago in Providence Roger Williams practiced another belief that many Americans are still content to preach: the principle of equality, perhaps the firmest spiritual and practical foundation of democratic society. If Williams had a less exalted notion of equality than some of the natural-law philosophers of the eighteenth century, he had a far more intimate working knowledge of its prime importance for the merging of liberty and order through free institutions. He arrived first at a belief in religious equality, in the parity of all faiths in the eyes of the state. In time and through experience he moved further in the direction of democracy by extending this concept to at least three other essentials: equality in law (which was realized in the code of 1647), equality in land (which he sponsored with a selflessness unmatched in colonial America), and equality in government (which spurred his relentless campaign against the pattern of feudalism that Coddington insisted on transplanting to America). There were limits to his understanding of equality—for example, the status of inferiority in which he seemed content to leave women—but he could hardly have been expected to cast loose completely from his age. It is enough to point out that Williams, thanks to an overflowing humanity and a shrewd perception of conditions in England, Massachusetts, and his own colony, was far ahead of his age in proclaiming equality as both right and necessity in these four fundamentals—religion, law, land, and government. Most unusual, of course, was his insistence on land for all on equal terms—for the latecomer as well as for the original homesteader. The peculiar American doctrine of equality of opportunity has at least one of its roots in Williams's democratic land policy.

PLURALISM, ECONOMIC DETERMINISM, CHANGE? It is not at all surprising that many historians and political scientists have explained Williams's mind in overly modern terms, for it takes little imagination to picture him as the seventeenth-century prophet of several momentous twentieth-century principles. For one thing, there is evidence that in his comprehension of the workings of political, religious, and corporate institutions he came very close to the concept of pluralism. For another, he had a primitive understanding of the way in which economic arrangements shape political institutions, which explains his emphasis on "liberty and equality, both in land and government." [88] And he seems to have perceived, thanks to his freedom from dogma and from respect for prescriptive authority, that social and political institutions are ever in a state of change, and that it is therefore both inexpedient and unnatural to enforce a rigid pattern of law and government upon any society. "Nor can your most prudent Heads, and potent hands," he warned Parliament in 1652, "possibly erect that Fabrick, which the next Age (it may be the next Parliament) may not tumble down." [89] Actually, he did not say enough about these matters to justify our considering him their early expounder. It would be a mistake to read too much Laski, Beard, or Spencer into this searching colonial mind.

Yet it would be a mistake, too, not to recognize in Williams an early exemplar of the American tradition of political pragmatism. Even when he seemed to his contemporaries to be most hopelessly impractical, as in his enthusiastic advocacy of separation and "soul liberty," he was arguing from experience rather than contemplation of eternal verities. Some of his half-dozen working principles have been absorbed into the great body of American thought, some have not. But all were the product of a general technique that unnumbered Americans, most of whom never heard of Roger Williams, were to make the leading article of their political faith: No idea is sound until it has been tested through experience; if it has been learned through experience, so much the sounder. To this extent at least Williams was the first *American* political thinker

"ON EAGLES' WINGS, THROUGH
MIGHTY LABORS"

Roger Williams died in Providence some time between January 27 and March 15, 1683, survived by his wife and six children. Although he was mourned by his friends and neighbors, who buried "the Venerable remaines of Mr.

Roger Williams, the Father of Providence, the Founder of the Colony, and of Liberty of Conscience" with "all the solemnity the colony was able to shew," [90] his passing stirred hardly a ripple of interest in old or New England. He left a living monument to political and religious liberty in Rhode Island, but not until almost two centuries later did his words and deeds become generally known in the United States and Europe.[91]

The reason is, of course, that his mind had far outrun the understanding of all but the most imaginative of his fellow colonials. His radical solutions to the great problems of the age, which to us seem eminently sound and workable, were looked upon by most of his contemporaries as sheerest nonsense. Yet we can see plainly that his books and letters, for all their thorny verbiage and interminable wranglings, were a memorable stage in the rise of a theory of liberty. In giving practical application to the concepts of popular sovereignty and social compact; in concluding almost pragmatically that reciprocity of rights and duties, the spirit of compromise, equality in land and government, and a certain minimum of order and authority were requisites of successful free government; and above all in proclaiming separation of church and state and liberty of conscience on grounds of social expediency, Williams left a legacy of ideas and accomplishments that persuades us to look upon him as the first American democrat.[92] Perhaps his finest achievement was that he came to know better than any man of his age—better than the autocrats in London and Boston, better than the nihilists in Providence and Pawtuxet—just where to draw the line between the freedom of the individual and the sanctions of the state. An English thinker has written, "If democracy . . . in its ultimate meaning be held to imply not only a government in which the preponderant share of power resides in the hands of the people, but a society based on the principles of political and religious freedom, Rhode Island beyond any other of the American Colonies is entitled to be called democratic." [93] The debt of Rhode Island the democracy to Williams the democrat is one that can hardly be overstated. If the colony, as it grew and prospered, retreated noticeably from Williams's original program for a popular government and equitable land-policy, it retreated hardly at all from his program for religious liberty. Thanks to Roger Williams and his "impractical notions," Rhode Island led all the world in the practice of this vital principle of human liberty.

Williams's life was heroic, and we are stirred by his triumphs. It was simple, and we are refreshed by his lack of pretension. Above all it was an act of faith, and we are astonished by his sense of destiny.

> It hath pleased the Most High to carry me on eagles' wings, through mighty labors, mighty hazards, mighty sufferings. . . . In my poor span of time, I have been oft in the jaws of death, sickening at sea, ship-wrecked on shore, in danger of arrows, swords and bullets: and yet, methinks, the most high and most holy God hath reserved me for some service to his most glorious and eternal majesty.[94]

CHAPTER EIGHT

John Wise

THE seventeenth century in America has been described as a *saeculum theologicum,* the eighteenth as a *saeculum politicum.*[1] No one is likely to cavil at this neat bisection of colonial intellectual history. An immense gulf separates the crabbed fields of the Puritan divines from the lush meadows of Otis, Jefferson, and Hamilton. At the same time, this generalization, like others of its type, demands qualification. We must remember that there were many bridges across the gulf, that one age passed into the other without too rough a detour in our social and literary development. These two centuries did, after all, have an intellectual unity.

Of all the bridges from the age of theology to that of politics, the most convenient and plainly marked is the life and writings of John Wise, pastor of a church in Chebacco (then part of Ipswich, now of Essex) in Massachusetts. The dates of Wise's ministerial career, 1675 to 1725, are symbolic of the manner in which his thinking spanned the two ages. A relentless warrior for both ecclesiastical and political democracy, he was a companion-at-arms to all the Separatists who had gone before and to all the Revolutionists who were to come after. A fellowship with Wise brings Samuel Adams and Jonathan Mayhew into company with Robert Browne and John Robinson; his life and work persuade us to look upon the debate between Daniel Leonard and John Adams as a projection of the debate between John Cotton and Roger Williams. From the Cambridge Platform to Wise and "from Wise to the Declaration of Independence is a clear and inevitable progress." [2]

Yet Wise is an obscure figure. Although there have been several brilliant efforts to bring him forward to the front rank of the champions of American liberty, he continues to receive only passing mention in the histories of our political thought and none at all in the histories of our democracy.

He has not been without witnesses to his "valor and great deeds." His own generation looked upon him as a public figure of special stature:

> He was of a Generous and Publick Spirit, a Great Lover of his Country, and our happy Constitution, a studious Assertor, and faithful Defender of its Liberties and Interests.[3]

Moses Coit Tyler called Wise "the first great American democrat." The eminent Congregational theologian, Williston Walker, not to be outdone by an ex-Congregationalist from the West, presented his spiritual forebear as "the first conspicuous American opponent of taxation without representation," and Parrington thought that Wise had "the keenest mind and most trenchant pen of his generation of New Englanders." [4] Yet Charles E. Merriam ignored him completely in his *History of American Political Theories*, and for even the most perceptive historians he remains the forgotten saint in the hagiology of American democracy.

Wise was a far too noble democrat in practice, a far too compelling democrat in theory, to be forever indulged the oblivion that has been his usual lot. His life is a rare testament to all that is good and decent in human hearts and minds; his political philosophy is a sure sign that the essentials of liberty were taking fast hold in the New England villages. Let us therefore turn to a brief account of his life and a more extended analysis of his political ideas.

PREACHER AND DEMOCRAT

John Wise, as befits a man nominated for the title of "the first great American democrat," was of humble, even plebeian origin. He was born in Roxbury, Massachusetts, probably in July 1652, the fifth of thirteen children of Joseph Wise. His father had come to Massachusetts Bay about 1635 as an indentured servant of Dr. George Alcock. The death of the master in 1640 gave freedom to the servant. Alcock's will bequeathed to Joseph Wise "my young heifer, and the rest of his time from after mid-somer next." [5] Joseph celebrated his good fortune by marrying Mary Thompson, probably of Braintree, on December 3 of his first year of freedom.[6]

After receiving his early education in the "Free Schoole" in Roxbury and the church of John Eliot, apostle to the Indians, John Wise entered Harvard in 1669, the first son of an indentured servant to be admitted to the college.[7] He took his first degree in 1673, his second in 1676, maintaining as his commencement part the affirmative of the spacious question: *"An impossibile sit Mundum fuisse ab aeterno?"* He apparently loved good fun (college style) as much as philosophical debate, for he was arrested and censured along with several of his friends for feasting on a turkey stolen from Captain Daniel Gookin.[8]

Following brief intervals of preaching in the Connecticut towns of Branford and Hatfield,[9] Wise came to Ipswich, one of the leading settlements in the Bay colony, as minister of the Second Church. The good people who lived in the part of Ipswich known as Chebacco had been finding it increasingly difficult to travel the six or seven miles to meeting in Ipswich, and in 1677 had petitioned the town for liberty to call a minister to preach among them. After a lengthy struggle with the Saints of Ipswich, the Saints of Chebacco finally won permission from the General Court to establish a church of their own.[10] With the gathering of the church and final withdrawal of the objections of the Ipswich meeting, Wise was formally ordained August 12, 1683.[11] With him to his new parish he brought his wife, Abigail Gardner of Roxbury, whom he had married December 5, 1678. Wise had seven children, three of whom were graduates of Harvard.

Until his death in 1725 Wise labored for the Lord in this single vineyard. Without pretension to fame or ambition for power, he was content to live and work in relative obscurity, leaving to others, notably the Mathers, the questionable glory of provincial leadership. From our point of view, he carried his quest for oblivion too far. It is regrettable that he declined the General Court's invitation to deliver the election sermon in 1719,[12] even more regrettable that he left no diary to complement those of Samuel Sewall and Cotton Mather. Only on rare occasions does Wise's noble figure suddenly appear in the pages of colonial histories. We see him for a moment taking vigorous sides in an issue that agitates the colony; then, just as suddenly, we see him no more until several years have passed and a new issue has arisen. He was apparently uninterested in permanent leadership or power. His few appearances, however, were Homeric, for when he did decide to come forth from Chebacco and strike a blow for justice, he fought with brilliance and tenacity. It is remarkable and gratifying to find Wise so consistently right about the issues of his time, issues that found many a man no less intelligent and humane than he far over the wrong side of the fence and deep in the fields of error.

To his quiet life in Ipswich and occasional sallies into colonial prominence Wise brought a physical presence fully as powerful as his intellect, which was, as we shall see, unique in his time. We unfortunately have no likeness of him, but we have ample testimony that he was a man "of a majestic form, and of great muscular strength and activity."[13] Tyler writes, "He had almost every quality that gives distinction among men. He was of towering height, of great muscular power, stately and graceful in shape and movement; in his advancing years, of an aspect most venerable."[14] He was accounted by his fellow townsmen "a superior wrestler," this being a reputation, according to the town's nineteenth-century antiquarian, "much more respectable in his day than ours."[15] The story is told that late in Wise's life the leading sport of Andover, Captain John Chandler, came over to Ipswich to challenge him for the championship of the area. Wise, although at first pleading age and infirmity, finally agreed to grapple with Chandler. In a very few seconds he threw Chandler completely over his front wall, whereupon the champion of Andover arose and announced that he would be on his way just as soon as Mr. Wise threw his horse over after him. The connection between Wise's big body and big spirit was not missed by his friends and neighbors:

The graceful Structure of his Manly Body, Majestick Aspect, and sweet
Deportment, were but an Emblem of the mighty Genius & brighter Excellencies of his Superior Soul.[16]

His parishioners were convinced that the power of his prayer was equal
to that of his muscles. On one occasion a boat's crew from Chebacco fell
among pirates. At Sunday meeting Wise prayed for their deliverance, ending with an impassioned "Great God! if there is no other way, may they
rise and butcher their enemies." The next day the crew, having risen and
butchered their enemies. returned to Chebacco. The parish was persuaded
of the efficacy of prayer.

Wise's first sally into colonial affairs pitted him against Sir Edmund
Andros, royal governor of the Dominion of New England under James II.[17]
The plans of the Crown for a united, well-governed, subordinate New England failed to reckon with the spirit of self-government that animated many
of the Massachusetts towns. It was one thing for Sir Edmund simply to do
away with the General Court, quite another to exercise its powers by laying
a tax on the towns without legislative consent. In 1687 Andros and his council, acting pursuant to royal commission, re-enacted the old Massachusetts
revenue law. Included in this public levy was the "country rate," a tax of
one penny on one pound to be collected in the several towns by commissioners of their own choosing. The town of Ipswich, aroused to stubborn
rebellion by Wise, refused to elect a commissioner to collect the tax and
lectured the council "that no taxes should be levied upon the subject without the consent of an Assembly, chosen by the Freeholders for assessing the
same." [18] Wise, who seems to have been a spiritual forebear of Samuel Adams,
had won the leading citizens of Ipswich to this stand in an extraordinary
conclave the night before town meeting. The town's defiance was a preview
of things to come:

> At a Legall Towne Meeting August 23d 1687.
> Assembled by vertue of an order from John Usher Esq. Treas[er], for choos-
> ing a Commiss[er] to join wth y[e] Selectmen to assess y[e] Inhabitants, according
> to an act of his Excellency y[e] Governor & Counsill, for Levying rates.
> Then considering that the s'd act doth infringe their Liberty as Free
> borne English subjects of his Majes[tie], by interfearing w[th] y[e] statutory Laws
> of the Land, By w[ch] it is enacted, that no taxes shall be Levied on y[e] Sub-
> jects w[th]out consent of an assembly chosen by y[e] Freeholders for assessing
> y[e] same.
> They do therefore vote, that they are not willing to choose a Commiss[er]
> for such an end, w[th]out s'd previledges.
> And morover consent not that the Selectmen do proseed to lay any such
> rate, until it be appointed by a General assembly, concurring w[th] y[e] Gov-
> ern[er], and Counsell,—Voted by the whole assembly twisse.[19]

Sir Edmund was no man to brook interference with his application of
Stuart prerogative to Massachusetts Bay, especially since he realized that
a soft policy toward Ipswich would encourage the whole colony to resist.
He therefore seized Wise and twenty-seven others and, having grilled them

in council, placed six of them on trial before judges thoroughly prejudiced and a jury firmly packed. Wise led the defense, quoting Magna Charta, the statutes, and "the rights of Englishmen" in denial of the council's arbitrary assessment. For his pains in asserting his privileges before the council he was told, "Mr. Wise, you have no more privileges left you, than not to be sold for Slaves." And for his unyielding attitude in court he was punished with a fine of fifty pounds, suspension from the ministry, and payment of a £1,000 bond for one year's good behavior.[20] Wise was allowed to resume his preaching,[21] and after the expulsion of Andros the next year, he brought suit against his former fellow townsman Joseph Dudley, who as chief justice had denied him a writ of habeas corpus. Legend tells us that he collected damages.[22]

At this time Wise received evidence of the esteem in which he was held by town and colony. In 1689 he went as a representative from Ipswich to the meeting in Boston at which the General Court was reorganized, and in 1690 he marched against Quebec as chaplain of the ill-conceived expedition under Sir William Phips, having been appointed to this position of trust by the General Court itself. He carried himself with distinction throughout the unpleasant fiasco before Quebec, "where not only the Pious Discharge of his Sacred Office, but his Heroick Spirit, and Martial Skill and Wisdom, did greatly distinguish him." [23] Wise left a pungent account of the expedition and of the reasons for its failure. This document, discovered in Paris in the late nineteenth century, was in the form of a letter to Increase Mather, who was in England as agent for Massachusetts during the intercharter period.[24] Not so brilliant as Caesar, Trotsky, or Churchill in reporting the campaigns in which he took part, Wise is a good deal more humble and bluntly honest.

Wise's consistent stand for common sense in the witchcraft persecution of 1692 moves him even further toward the front rank of the tiny company of colonial democrats. The historian of the Salem craze, Charles W. Upham, wrote of him as "a learned, able, and enlightened man. He had a free spirit, and was perhaps the only minister in the neighborhood or country, who was discerning enough to see the erroneousness of the proceedings from the beginning." [25] Whether he was composing a petition to the Assistants to save John Procter's life,[26] commending Increase Mather's testimony against "spectral evidence," or signing an address to the General Court to remove "the infamy and reproach" from the names and posterity of those convicted of witchcraft, Wise demonstrated a total lack of fear of the persecutors of his time.

Other issues claimed Wise's attention. For example, he took part in the controversy over singing by note that excited the colony around 1720. He wrote to Thomas Symmes, the leader of the movement to substitute congregational singing for the primitive method of chanting a line at a time behind a precentor, "that when there were a sufficient number in a Congregation, to carry away a Tune Roundly, it was proper to introduce that Tune." Wise, like Symmes, was unimpressed by cries of "Popery!" A more serious affair was the question of inoculation against smallpox. Wise was one of a handful of ministers who advocated this radical innovation of which the Mathers were the chief proponents.[27] The currency problem was another of his interests. The arguments of Sewall and the rising merchant-aristocracy for the maintenance of a metallic currency found a cold reception among the country folk of Ipswich. Convinced, with his parishioners, of the merits of paper money, Wise entered the lists under the pseudonym "Amicus Patriae" with *A Word of Comfort to a Melancholy Country*, "Humbly Dedicated to the Merchants in Boston." [28] His economic musings were not altogether sound, but his sympathies were once again at the disposal of the rising agrarian democracy.

THE DEFENSE OF CONGREGATIONALISM

Despite his excursions into the political, economic, social, medical, and musical contentions of his time, Wise was first and last a minister. It is therefore not surprising that the controversy into which he plunged with the most vigor and consequence was primarily religious in character. Throughout the last twenty years of his life he carried on a running fight with the Mathers and others who sought to impose more order on the constitution of the New England churches. This skirmish was, of course, only one episode in the long struggle in the Congregational churches between "Barrowism," the semi-presbyterianism advanced by Henry Barrowe, and "Brownism," the doctrine of virtual autonomy in the local church. Although not exactly an uncritical follower of Robert Browne and his extreme views, Wise was a zealous believer in democracy in the church, which to him meant church government in the hands of the individual congregation and only loose bonds of "mutual watch and brotherly helpfulness" between the churches of the colony.

The decline of the Puritan oligarchy, symbolized and made certain by the withdrawal of the charter in 1684, ushered in a period of unrest in the affairs of the New England churches. The clergy, feeling political power slipping from its fingers, did what most clergies have done under similar circumstances: It set out to bolster its ecclesiastical power. Specifically, it became the avowed purpose of the Mathers and their sympathizers to effect a closer union of the churches and to institute active control of the different congregations through the so-called Ministerial Convention of Massachusetts. This was an annual gathering of the ministers of the province at the time of the May General Court, "which had begun in the informal coming together of the ministers in the earliest days of the colony, and had crystallized sufficiently by about 1680 to have a moderator, a dinner, and a sermon." [29] In addition to the Convention, several ministerial associations, voluntary groupings of the ministers of a particular area, had arisen in the Bay colony.

The most significant action of the "Presbyterian Party" was that of nine prominent ministers—among them Samuel Willard, Ebenezer Pemberton, and

Cotton Mather—who met in Boston in September 1705 and drew up sixteen proposals. These proposals, which would have imposed a synodal form
of government upon hitherto autonomous churches, were transmitted to
the various associations November 5, 1705, and were approved by the
Ministerial Convention that met in Boston in May 1706. There can be no
question that the centralizing plans of the Mather group, quite innocuous
when viewed from our secular age, would have worked substantial alterations in the Congregational polity of colonial New England. They were
a pronounced step toward union and conciliar control, and thus were hostile
to the principle of autonomy in the local churches. The threat was the more
pronounced because of the excellent persons who had originated or approved
the sixteen proposals. A majority of the Massachusetts pastors, many of
them perhaps unwittingly, had signified acquiescence in this plan.

Not John Wise, however. As two gentlemen of Gloucester were later to
point out, "All our Watchmen were not asleep, nor the Camp of Christ
surprized and taken, before they had Warning." [30] Wise thought that the
proposals "smelled very strong of the infallible chair," and his warning to
the camp was immediate and vociferous. The New England method of
ministerial licensure may be said to date from these recommendations of
1705, and certainly the ministerial associations were further stimulated.
Otherwise the proposals, especially those looking to the establishment of a
standing council with power to discipline the member churches, were received with hostility or disdain and had little success in altering the government of the churches.

Wise spoke out sharply to his parishioners and correspondents in defiance
of this scheme, but apparently had nothing immediate to say for publication.
The opposition of the more radical churches hardly needed stimulation.
When, however, the churches of Connecticut embarked in 1708 on a similar
presbyterian adventure—by adopting the Saybrook Platform, a series of
elaborate articles based on the Massachusetts proposals of 1705—he took up
his pen and advanced to do battle for democracy in the churches. Here was
"mischief, mischief in *summo gradu;* yea exorbitant mischief," and Wise
would have none of it.

His contribution to this decisive contest consisted of two small volumes.
The first, *The Churches' Quarrel Espoused* (1710), was a "Reply in Satire"
to the sixteen proposals of the Mather faction. Printing the proposals without comment in the first pages of his book, Wise proceeded to destroy
them one by one with shrewd, witty, even abusive satire. He wrote a
limited treatise for a limited purpose, and the whole production was purely
occasional. Nevertheless, it was a superlative exposition of ecclesiastical
democracy and a convincing rejection of the presbyterian idea as unsuitable
for the churches of Christ, "especially in such a country and climate as
this."

In 1717 Wise returned to combat with a second book, *A Vindication of
the Government of New-England Churches.* This work, the product of
several years of painstaking reading and reflection, was his most brilliant

literary performance. Indeed, it was probably the outstanding piece of polemical writing in the first 150 years of the American settlements. As a systematic defense of ecclesiastical democracy *A Vindication* was several cuts above *The Churches' Quarrel Espoused*. Where the first book had been negative, destructive, and satirical, *A Vindication* was positive, constructive, and sober. Since the day of its publication it has been a powerful force in Congregational thought.[31]

A Vindication was something more than an ecclesiastical tract. Wise was not content to base his defense of congregational autonomy on the Word of God alone. Although he was careful to find support for his arguments in Scripture, the "Providence of God," and the example of the primitive churches, his case for democracy in the church rested most heavily upon its similarity to democracy in the state. Wise reversed completely the line of argument of those who had praised political democracy as a reflection of ecclesiastical democracy and had championed the social contract as the logical extension of the church covenant. The spectacle of a Puritan minister examining "the Light of Nature" to discover that democracy was the form of government most favored by the precepts of natural law, then grounding his case for democracy in the church on "the near affinity our constitution holds" with political democracy, was truly astounding—not least to Cotton Mather, who had already branded Wise "a furious Man"[32] and had preached against his attitude as a "Satanick insult, twice over."[33] Wise's approach was a revolution in our intellectual history, for he was the first New England preacher to free himself from the restrictions of the *saeculum theologicum* and enter into literary controversy without primary reliance on the weapons of Scriptural disputation or Ramean logic. Thus, whatever Wise may have set forth to prove, his second book is a work in political rather than ecclesiastical theory.

WISE AS POLITICAL THINKER

Wise was not an original political thinker. He would have been the first to admit that his argument from the law of nature, uncommon as it must have seemed to many of his adversaries, was simply a reshaping to his own purposes of a system of thought that had long since swept over Europe, and that he had read for himself in the writings of one of its leading exponents. Nevertheless, he must be accorded full credit for applying the principles of natural law to the problems of New England and for phrasing them in language that his compatriots could understand and repeat.

Wise himself acknowledged his primary debt: "And I shall principally take Baron Puffendorf for my chief guide and spokesman."[34] The baron, of course, was the eminent German jurist Samuel von Pufendorf (1632–1694), a major figure in the natural-law school. His great work, *De Jure Naturae et Gentium*,[35] a persuasive exposition of natural law, particularly in its application to international law, had been published in 1672 and republished many times over. An English translation had been printed in London in 1703. It is impossible to determine the year in which Wise first came upon Pufendorf's work, or to discover whether his copy was in the Latin original or English translation. A careful comparison of the language of Wise's two books suggests that he first studied Pufendorf thoughtfully after 1710. By the time he came to write *A Vindication*, he had absorbed completely the philosophy and phraseology of the natural-law school.

Wise did not rely on Pufendorf alone. He was a learned man, and his pages are spiced, but fortunately not cloyed, with quotations and lessons from all manner of writers and schools—the ancients (Plato, Aristotle, Virgil, Plutarch, Cicero, Cato); the church fathers (especially Tertullian and Eusebius of Caesarea); the early and late leaders of the Reformation (Luther, Benedict Turretin, William Ames, John Owen); fellow New Englanders (the Mathers, Nicholas Noyes, Cotton); such diverse political and philosophical figures as Boethius, Ulpian, Machiavelli, Richard Hooker, and Sir Edward Coke (whose name he also gives, with the cavalier disregard of his age for the niceties of spelling, as Cook and Cooke); Greek, Roman, church, and English history; and Aesop's fables. Despite this impressive list of authorities, his books owe a good deal to his own reasoning about the conformity to nature of the New England churches. He could say with Hobbes that he had used his brains more than his bookshelves. He did not, it should be noted, cite Calvin or Locke.

Wise's style merits some mention. The substance of his two books was muscular enough to overwhelm the arguments of his presbyterian adversaries, but when clothed in the mailed fist of his vivid prose its effect was positively crushing. A contrast of *The Churches' Quarrel Espoused* with such thorny offerings as Williams's *Bloody Tenents*, Hooker's *Survey of the Summe of Church-Discipline*, Cotton's *The Way of the Congregational Churches Cleared*, or any of the many hundred items in the Mathers' well-padded bibliography would make an instructive study in American literary development. The prose of his occasional or unpublished writings—the complaint against Andros, the account of the expedition to Quebec, the paper-currency tracts, his *Instructions for Emigrants from Essex County, Mass., to South Carolina* (1697) [36]—was loose and undistinguished, brilliant only in flashes and spelled with abandon. It was still a great improvement over Hooker or Williams. The two major works are of a far different order. His imagery is fresh and far-ranging; intensive order marks the progression of his arguments; and he alternates sobriety and satire, learning and wit, eloquence and plain talk, with a skill that would be exceptional in any time and place. Considering his time and place, it is evidence of natural genius.

Examples of his forceful prose will fill the pages from here on. A few other phrases, not particularly germane to his political theory, should be recorded here in testimony to his skill and for the delight of the reader. Of controversy he writes: "I neither desire, nor design to hurt any man, no, not so much as a hair on his head, but I solely aim at *error*, that is the butt I level for." Of order and disorder: "Order is both the beauty and safety of the universe; take away the decorum whereby the whole hangs together, the great frame of nature is unpinned and drops piece from piece; and out of a beautiful structure we have a chaos." Of duty: "The dream of an embroilment can never counterpoise duty; if men are trusted with duty, they must consult that, and not events. If men are placed at helm to steer in all weather that blows, they must not be afraid of the waves or a wet coat." Of the state of New England: "There is no want in this country, unless it be the want of good and honest hearts." Of Harvard: "That artillery garden from whence we receive our most expert soldiers in Christ." At another point he cautions his readers against "an implicit faith in the stark naked *ipse dixits* of any men." [37] This sort of writing, many times more striking when read in the context of Wise's two books than when sifted here, led Tyler to acclaim Wise as "the one American who, upon the whole, was the most powerful and brilliant prose-writer produced in this country during the colonial time." [38] With this judgment we can warmly agree.

Wise's political philosophy was as simple as it was unusual. There was nothing of the Mephistopheles in this country pastor, and we do not have to rummage through piles of confused verbiage for his few direct and comprehensible ideas. Although Wise in his modesty warned, "I shall go out of the common road, and take into an unusual and unbeaten path, wherein possibly I may fall into some thickets now and then, and be somewhat entangled," [39] the reader is never for a moment led astray. Let us turn to the chief tenets of his political theory.

MAN AND HIS RIGHTS

NATURAL LAW. A simple, even artless faith in the existence of higher law was the foundation of Wise's political thought. So comfortably at home was he with this ancient doctrine that he hardly paused to explain its significance or content. He seems to have assumed that his readers would understand exactly what he was talking about, and that they, too, would subscribe to the concept of a law of nature "written on men's hearts." This law of nature, wrote Wise, could be discovered and applied to current problems. It was for man, who was "most properly the subject of the law of nature" and "the favorite animal on earth," to employ "right reason" in the search for its principles.

> That which is to be drawn from man's reason, flowing from the true current of that faculty, when unperverted, may be said to be the law of nature, on which account, the Holy Scriptures declare it written on men's hearts. For being endowed with a soul, you may know from yourself, how, and what you ought to act. (Rom.2:14.) These having not a law, are a law to themselves. So that the meaning is, when we acknowledge the law of nature to be the dictate of right reason, we must mean that the understanding of man is endowed with such a power, as to be able, from the contemplation of human condition to discover a necessity of living agreeably with this law; and likewise to find out some principle, by which the precepts of it,

may be clearly and solidly demonstrated. The way to discover the law of
nature in our own state, is by a narrow watch, and accurate contemplation
of our natural condition and propensions.[40]

And to what final definition of natural law would the application of
recta ratio lead Wise's average man? The Golden Rule—this was for Wise
the sum of nature's rules for human conduct.

> Others say this is the way to find out the law of nature, namely, if a man
> any way doubts, whether what he is going to do to another man be agree-
> able to the law of nature, then let him suppose himself to be in that other
> man's room, and by this rule effectually executed. A man must be a very
> dull scholar to nature not to make proficiency in the knowledge of her laws.[41]

The law of nature, as it appeared in Wise's system, was of divine origin.
He might have agreed with Grotius that God, once he had established the
law of nature, could not alter its content or terms—"Just as even God, then,
cannot cause that two times two should not make four, so He cannot cause
that that which is intrinsically evil be not evil" [42]—but as a Puritan divine he
could not have subscribed to a secularized version of the higher law.

> God has provided a rule for men in all their actions, obliging each one
> to the performance of that which is right, not only as to justice but like-
> wise as to all other moral virtues, the which is nothing but the dictate of
> right reason founded in the soul of man.[43]

THE NATURE OF MAN. The contrasting philosophies of Hobbes and Locke,
or of Calhoun and Jefferson, demonstrate that any particular system of
political theory is a reflection of the opinion held by its author about the
nature of man. It should come as no surprise, then, that Wise, like Locke
and Jefferson a believer in popular government, considered man to be
inherently good and reasonable. Although "a principle of self-love and self-
preservation is very predominant in every man's being," he is also possessed
of "a sociable disposition" and "an affection or love to mankind in general." [44] Wise seems to have freed his thinking completely from the harsh
compulsions of the Calvinistic view of human nature. He would not even
be drawn into a discussion of this matter.

> In this discourse I shall waive the consideration of man's moral turpitude,
> but shall view him physically as a creature which God has made and fur-
> nished essentially with many ennobling immunities, which render him the
> most august animal in the world, and still, whatever has happened since his
> creation, he remains at the upper end of nature, and as such is a creature
> of a very noble character.[45]

The most important of man's qualities was "sociableness"; if he lacked this
characteristic, "every government would soon moulder and dissolve."

> Man is a creature extremely desirous of his own preservation; of him-
> self he is plainly exposed to many wants, unable to secure his own safety
> and maintenance without assistance of his fellows; and he is also able of
> returning kindness by the furtherance of mutual good; but yet man is often

found to be malicious, insolent, and easily provoked, and as powerful in effecting mischief as he is ready in designing it. Now that such a creature may be preserved, it is necessary that he be sociable; that is, that he be capable and disposed to unite himself to those of his own species, and to regulate himself towards them, that they may have no fair reason to do him harm; but rather incline to promote his interests, and secure his rights and concerns. This then is a fundamental law of nature, that every man as far as in him lies, do maintain a sociableness with others, agreeable with the main end and disposition of human nature in general. For this is very apparent, that reason and society render man the most potent of all creatures. And finally, from the principles of sociableness it follows as a fundamental law of nature, that man is not so wedded to his own interest, but that he can make the common good the mark of his aim; and hence he becomes capacitated to enter into a civil state by the law of nature; for without this property in nature, namely, sociableness, which is for cementing of parts, every government would soon moulder and dissolve.[46]

No statement of Wise's was more central to his political theory than this observation "that man is not so wedded to his own interest, but that he can make the common good the mark of his aim." Again and again he returned to acclaim this quality as the basis of popular government, often calling it "sociableness" and as often "fraternity." It is good to hear from this son of the wilderness settlements so powerful an exposition of the fraternal attitude. In our latter-day efforts to proclaim liberty and equality through all the lands—or to sit at home and ponder the fundamental contradiction of these two requisites of democracy—we have tended to forget that there is a third element in the celebrated trinity, fraternity, without which democracy would be little better than a mediocre anarchy. A century and a half before Walt Whitman, Wise bore witness to the need for fraternal sympathy in free society, and with a good deal less beating of his breast.

NATURAL RIGHTS. Wise was an enthusiastic believer in natural rights. Man in a state of nature was "a free-born subject under the crown of heaven, and owing homage to none but God himself." To him belonged "an original liberty enstamped upon his rational nature." Wise, like the other writers of his time and school, did not attempt to catalogue the contents of this liberty. It was enough for him to define man's natural liberty as the "faculty of doing or omitting things according to the direction of his judgment," with the qualification that "this liberty does not consist in a loose and ungovernable freedom, or an unbounded license of acting." [47]

Such license is disagreeing with the condition and dignity of man, and would make man of a lower and meaner constitution than brute creatures, who in all their liberties are kept under a better and more rational government by their instincts. Therefore, as Plutarch says: Those persons only who live in obedience to reason, are worthy to be accounted free: they alone live as they will, who have learned what they ought to will. So that the true natural liberty of man, such as really and truly agrees to him must be understood, as he is guided and restrained by the ties of reason and laws of nature; all the rest is brutal, if not worse.[48]

These were notions that Wise had taken from Pufendorf. From the *De Jure Naturae*, too, came Wise's radical assertion of natural equality, a doctrine of no particular currency in colonial New England. This concept was a corollary of the idea of natural rights, just as the latter was in its turn a corollary of the law of nature.

> The third capital immunity belonging to man's nature, is an equality amongst men; which is not to be denied by the law of nature, till man has resigned himself with all his rights for the sake of a civil state, and then his personal liberty and equality is to be cherished and preserved to the highest degree, as will consist with all just distinctions amongst men of honor, and shall be agreeable with the public good. . . . Since, then, human nature agrees equally with all persons, and since no one can live a sociable life with another that does not own or respect him as a man, it follows as a command of the law of nature, that every man esteem and treat another as one who is naturally his equal, or who is a man as well as he.[49]

And to his support he called Boethius by name and Horace by implication. One of his most forceful sentences appears to have been a literal translation of that magnificent

> *Pallida Mors aequo pulsat pede pauperum tabernas*
> *regumque turris.*

CIVIL RIGHTS. In Wise's thinking there was a close identity of natural and civil rights, the second being simply that portion of the first which men retained upon entrance into government, with adaptions to meet the conditions of organized society.

> It is certainly a great truth, namely, that man's original liberty after it is resigned (yet under due restrictions) ought to be cherished in all wise governments; or otherwise a man in making himself a subject, he alters himself from a freeman into a slave, which to do is repugnant to the law of nature. Also the natural equality of men amongst men must be duly favored; in that government was never established by God or nature, to give one man a prerogative to insult over another, therefore, in a civil, as well as in a natural state of being, a just equality is to be indulged so far as that every man is bound to honor every man, which is agreeable both with nature and religion, (1 Pet.2:17); Honor all men.[50]

In turn, civil rights were for Wise "the rights of Englishmen." The Ipswich minister was a loyal colonial, and the pages of his books are full of laudatory remarks about Magna Charta and "the ancient liberties of the English nation."

> All Englishmen live and die by laws of their own making . . . they are never pleased with upstart law-makers.
> Englishmen hate an arbitrary power (politically considered) as they hate the devil.
> The very name of an arbitrary government is ready to put an Englishman's blood into a fermentation; but when it really comes and shakes its

whip over their ears, and tells them it is their master, it makes them stark mad.[51]

Wise, needless to say, considered himself very much an Englishman. Yet he was also a zealous New Englander. He could have cried with Stoughton, "God sifted a Whole Nation that he might send Choice Grain over into this Wilderness," for he found on every side evidence of the particular solicitude that God indulged for Massachusetts and her sisters. Later American statesmen and writers were to assert that God had singled out this country for peculiar blessings, but in bestowing His grace had also bestowed a particular responsibility for the success of free government. Wise, no less proud and hortatory of New England than they were to be of all America, called upon his readers to give "recognition of what God has done for these famous English colonies" by following His way and that of nature with reverence and good example.

CIVIL GOVERNMENT

THE CONTRACT. We have already noted that Wise considered "sociableness" to be a dominant trait of natural man. It was this "inclination to society" that caused men, acting in obedience to the dictates of nature, to seek out one another for mutual protection and support.

> Every man, considered in a natural state, must be allowed to be free and at his own disposal; yet to suit man's inclinations to society, and in a peculiar manner to gratify the necessity he is in of public rule and order, he is impelled to enter into a civil community, and divests himself of his natural freedom, and puts himself under government, which amongst other things, comprehends the power of life and death over him, together with the authority to enjoin him some things to which he has an utter aversion, and to prohibit him other things for which he may have as strong an inclination— so that he may be often, under this authority, obliged to sacrifice his private for the public good; so that though man is inclined to society, yet he is driven to a combination by great necessity. For that the true and leading cause of forming governments and yielding up natural liberty, and throwing man's equality into a common pile to be new cast by rules of fellowship, was really and truly to guard themselves against the injuries men were liable to interchangeably; for none so good to man as man, and yet none a greater enemy.[52]

Still following Pufendorf, but simplifying him greatly, Wise continues:

> Let us conceive in our mind a multitude of men, all naturally free and equal, going about voluntarily to erect themselves into a new commonwealth. Now their condition being such, to bring themselves into a politic body they must needs enter into divers covenants.
>
> 1. They must interchangeably each man covenant to join in one lasting society, that they may be capable to concert the measures of their safety, by a public vote.
>
> 2. A vote or decree must then nextly pass to set up some particular species

of government over them. And if they are joined in their first compact upon absolute terms to stand to the decision of the first vote concerning the species of government, then all are bound by the majority to acquiesce in that particular form thereby settled, though their own private opinions incline them to some other model.

3. After a decree has specified the particular form of government, then there will be need of a new covenant, whereby those upon whom sovereignty is conferred engage to take care of the common peace and welfare; and the subjects, on the other hand, to yield them faithful obedience; in which covenant is included that submission and union of wills by which a state may be conceived to be but one person.[53]

Here is as precise a rendition of the social contract as any political theorist has ever presented. Certainly Locke, who was later to get most of the credit for popularizing this notion, never expressed it in such plain terms as these. The contract as an explanation of the nature of government and society has long since been driven from the stage of political philosophy under a hail of ridicule and abuse. We now seek other, more sophisticated explanations of political obedience. Yet we should not impute to Wise too much naïveté in his political thought. Far more "subtile" men than he—Plato, Epicurus, Cicero, St. Augustine, Althusius, the Monarchomachs, Grotius, Locke, Hobbes, and Pufendorf—had subscribed to some version of this antique concept. And for Wise, it must be remembered, the mutual agreement of free men to form a community was no mere figment of the imagination. He had known men who had come in the beginning and had actually signed their names to church and plantation covenants. When the Mayflower company undertook to "covenant and combine our selves togeather into a civill body politick, for our better ordering and preservation," they were putting this theory to practical use. Moreover, the covenant was the foundation of the New England churches. All in all, it was for Wise a concept of compelling historical and logical force. And it is still, for all its *lacunae*, the noblest answer ever made to the perplexing question: Why should men who call themselves free owe their allegiance, obedience, and even their lives to government? If only for the purposes of our democratic dialectic, it is comforting to think of the "consent of the governed" as the foundation of government. Wise, in this instance, was a true American democrat, one who pointed ahead to the Revolution by asserting that "English government and law is a charter-party settled by mutual compact between persons of all degrees in the nation." [54]

Since all men were naturally free and equal, and since they had contracted one with another to form a society for the protection of an important residuum of that freedom and equality (so much as "shall be agreeable with the public good"), all political power rested in the keeping of the people. They could commission others to exercise it for them, but they alone could be said to possess it. "The first human subject and original of civil power is the people." [55] Respectfully aware of the presence of God at all levels of human endeavor, Wise nevertheless refused to have anything to do with the Puritan fiction of God as the repository of political sovereignty. He could say, "It must needs be allowed as a fundamental principle relating to government, that (under God) all power is originally in the people," [56] yet God was no part of the mechanics of establishing and maintaining civil government. The people were the focus of Wise's attention.

THE FORMS OF GOVERNMENT; DEMOCRACY THE BEST. Many Puritan ministers, most prominently Wise's old pastor John Eliot in *The Christian Commonwealth*, expressed a belief that God had ordained a definite type of government, although not all of them could agree on the identity of the divinely favored form. Wise did not share this point of view. "Nothing can be God's ordinance, but what he has particularly declared to be such; there is no particular form of civil government described in God's word, neither does nature prompt it. The government of the Jews was changed five times." [57]

His own catalogue of the types of civil polity was the time-honored trinity—democracy, aristocracy, monarchy:

> The forms of a regular state are three only, which forms arise from the proper and particular subject in which the supreme power resides. As,
>
> 1. A democracy, which is when the sovereign power is lodged in a council consisting of all the members, and where every member has the privilege of a vote. . . .
>
> 2. The second species of regular government is an aristocracy, and this is said then to be constituted when the people or assembly, united by a first covenant, and having thereby cast themselves into the first rudiments of a state, do then by common decree devolve the sovereign power on a council consisting of some select members; and these having accepted of the designation, are then properly invested with sovereign command, and then an aristocracy is formed.
>
> 3. The third species of a regular government is a monarchy, which is settled when the sovereign power is conferred on some one worthy person. It differs from the former, because a monarch, who is but one person in natural as well as in moral account, and so is furnished with an immediate power of exercising sovereign command in all instances of government; but the forenamed must needs have particular time and place assigned, but the power and authority is equal in each.[58]

He also recognized that there could be "mixed governments." Indeed, being a loyal if colonial Englishman, he had kind words for the British Constitution:

> Mixed governments, which are various and of divers kinds (not now to be enumerated), yet possibly the fairest in the world is that which has a regular monarchy, settled upon a noble democracy as its basis; and each part of the government is so adjusted by pacts and laws that render the whole constitution an elysium. It is said of the British empire, that it is such a monarchy as that, by the necessary subordinate concurrence of the lords and commons in the making and repealing all statutes or acts of parliament, it hath the main advantages of an aristocracy and of a democracy, and yet free from the disadvantages and evils of either. It is such a monarchy as, by most admirable temperament, affords very much to the industry, liberty,

and happiness of the subject, and reserves enough for the majesty and pre-rogative of any king who will own his people as subjects, not as slaves. It is a kingdom that, of all the kingdoms of the world, is most like to the king-dom of Jesus Christ, whose yoke is easy and burden light.[59]

For pure monarchy or aristocracy, in church or state, Wise had nothing but contempt. A constitutional monarchy, one in which the king "will own his people as subjects, not as slaves," and will rule in association with popular institutions, held no fears for him. But as for an absolute monarchy, of which the Papacy was this New England Puritan's horrid example, "God and wise nature were never propitious to the birth of this monster." He could conceive of excellent rule by a "select company of choice persons," but he saw clearly the inherent danger of aristocratic government: the fact that a small ruling group must eventually be corrupted by power and sub-stitute "private will" for common weal as "the rule of their personal and ministerial actions."

> For what is it that cunning and learned men cannot make the world swal-low as an article of their creed, if they are once invested with an uncon-trollable power, and are to be the standing orators to mankind in matters of faith and obedience? [60]

And so, Wise concluded, "Considering how great an interest is embarked, and how frail a bottom we trust," we must shun the monarchical and aristo-cratic solutions to the problems of ecclesiastical and civil polity, "especially if we can find a safer way home." The way, of course, was democracy. Wise was by experience and reason a true democrat. With his training in the town meeting and his belief in popular sovereignty, he could not have been other-wise. "A democracy in church or state is a very honorable and regular government according to the dictates of right reason." [61] Equally important:

> This form of government appears in the greatest part of the world to have been the most ancient. For that reason seems to show it to be most probable, that when men (being originally in a condition of natural free-dom and equality) had thoughts of joining in a civil body, would without question be inclined to administer their common affairs by their common judgment, and so must necessarily, to gratify that inclination, establish a democracy; neither can it be rationally imagined that fathers of families, being yet free and independent, should in a moment or little time take off their long delight in governing their own affairs, and devolve all upon some single sovereign commander; for that it seems to have been thought more equitable that what belonged to all should be managed by all, when all had entered by compact into one community.[62]

Democracy for Wise was, of course, a simple concept, the philosophical reflection of a simple form of government, the town meeting.

> A democracy is then erected, when . . . the right of determining all mat-ters relating to the public safety is actually placed in a general assembly of the whole people; or by their own compact and mutual agreement, deter-mine themselves the proper subject for the exercise of sovereign power.

And to complete this state, and render it capable to exert its power to answer the end of a civil state, these conditions are necessary.

(1) That a certain time and place be assigned for assembling.

(2) That when the assembly be orderly met, as to time and place, that then the vote of the majority must pass for the vote of the whole body.

(3) That magistrates be appointed to exercise the authority of the whole for the better despatch of business of every day's occurrence, who also may, with more mature diligence, search into more important affairs; and if in case any thing happens of greater consequence, may report it to the assembly, and be peculiarly serviceable in putting all public decrees into execution, because a large body of people is almost useless in respect of the last service, and of many others as to the more particular application and exercise of power. Therefore it is most agreeable with the law of nature, that they institute their officers to act in their name and stead.[63]

Wise seems to have had little grasp of the idea of representative democracy. It is safe to say, however, that he looked upon the General Court, if not the royal governor, as an instrument of popular government, since its members were the elected representatives of the town meetings. As a matter of dialectic, Wise was in no position to argue too warmly for representative democracy. His primary concern was to defend congregational autonomy. The General Court may have been an essential part of civil government, but he did not want, indeed wrote his books directly against, an ecclesiastical version of this provincial assembly.

The Natural Aristocracy. Wise was no leveler or doctrinaire populist. Like Jefferson, he not only conceded but pointed with satisfaction to the existence of an *aristoi*. Yet the "best men" were not best by reason of wealth or blood; the only aristocracy that a democrat could recognize was that of learning or virtue or wisdom. Wise went back to Aristotle for support of the principle that "nothing is more suitable to nature, than that those who excel in understanding and prudence, should rule and control those who are less happy in those advantages." [64] Yet he, again like Jefferson, left it to the people to determine by free suffrage whether or not such men were actually to govern, and he granted them the power of recall along with that of election. "Nor does natural fitness for government make a man presently governor over another. . . . It would be the greatest absurdity to believe, that nature actually invests the wise with a sovereignty over the weak." Wise developed this point even further by insisting that it was the business of society to keep the road open for others, to preserve a real equality of opportunity. Himself a natural aristocrat who had risen from the bottom of a stratified society, Wise could write with sincerity, "The parity of our descent inclines us to keep up the like parity by our laws, and to yield the precedency to nothing but to superior virtue and wisdom." [65]

Majority Rule. We have heard enough from Wise to know that he was a strong advocate of "the venerable major vote." The simplicity of his political thought is manifest in his uncritical acceptance of this doctrine and apparent incapacity to comprehend its dangers. But Locke, too, was oblivious to the perils that John Adams, Hamilton, and Calhoun—all of them staunch conservatives, it should be noted—never wearied of voicing. In a political entity as homogeneous as that of colonial Ipswich there was little danger of a tyranny of the majority. Even Calhoun, it must be remembered, considered majority rule a sufficient support of constitutional government "if the whole community had the same interest." [66] Wise had one splendid passage concerning majority rule, in which he made clear his democratic dedication to the rule of "one person, one vote":

> But in every distinct house of these states, the members are equal in their vote: the most ayes make the affirmative vote, and most noes the negative. They do not weigh the intellectual furniture, or other distinguishing qualifications of the several voters, in the scales of the golden rule of fellowship; they only add up the ayes and the noes, and so determine the suffrage of the house.[67]

THE BENEFICENT NATURE OF CIVIL GOVERNMENT. At one point at least Wise disagreed sharply with the more radical adherents of the natural-rights school of the late eighteenth century. Paine, for example, believed that "Society in every state is a blessing, but Government, even in its best state, is but a necessary evil." [68] Wise, to the contrary, took a more traditional view of the character of civil government. So necessary, such "an incomparable benefit to mankind" was government, that natural man was "driven" into it willy-nilly. Yet this was no hardship, for:

> Government is the greatest blessing in the world, of a worldly nature; it is felony, cheaper by far to the loosers, to plunder men of their estate and wealth, nay, and of their lives too, than to despoil them of government; for by the latter you harass and worry them in the world with plagues and miseries, worse than death itself, that the basest is far better than no government; a churlish tyranny is better than an insolent anarchy, where men are without law, and all hail fellows, not well, but badly met.[69]

THE PURPOSE OF GOVERNMENT. Every defender of a particular political theory must be prepared to answer the question: What are the true ends of the government you advocate? Wise had a reply that arose naturally from his theories of compact and consent, and it was a far cry from that of the Puritan oligarchy. The protection of the free man and preservation of his freedom and equality, not the maintenance of the true religion, were the purposes for which government was instituted. In this respect Wise echoed Locke and anticipated the Declaration of Independence.

> The end of all good government is to cultivate humanity, and promote the happiness of all, and the good of every man in all his rights, his life, liberty, estate, honor, etc., without injury or abuse done to any.[70]

THE CORPORAL ANALOGY. One of the oldest devices in political theory is the comparison of the state with the human body. Wise presented his version thus quaintly:

A civil state is a compound moral person . . . which may be conceived as though the whole state was now become but one man; . . . And by way of resemblance the aforesaid being may be thus anatomized.

(1) The sovereign power is the soul infused, giving life and motion to the whole body.

(2) Subordinate officers are the joints by which the body moves.

(3) Wealth and riches are the strength.

(4) Equity and laws are the reason.

(5) Counsellors the memory.

(6) *Salus Populi*, or the happiness of the people is the end of its being, or main business to be attended and done.

(7) Concord amongst the members and all estates, is the health.

(8) Sedition is sickness, and civil war death.[71]

THE RIGHT OF RESISTANCE. This principle had an inferior standing in Wise's political theory. This was certainly not true of most prominent writers of the natural-law school. Locke, for example, devoted his longest chapter to "The Dissolution of Government," and the right of resistance, even of revolution, is openly proclaimed in the Declaration of Independence. But Wise, who had come forth to defend an established church-democracy against an encroaching aristocracy, was neither by nature nor purpose a revolutionary political thinker. If anything, he was an unabashed traditional-ist. Had he been questioned about his purpose, he would have proclaimed simply: *stare super antiquas vias*. And for him the ancient ways upon which New England stood were the ways of pure ecclesiastical democracy. In his interpretation of the Cambridge Platform of 1649 as the foundation of democracy in the New England churches he was reading a few too many popular principles into a theocratic constitution, yet he was apparently quite sincere in his belief that it sponsored congregational autonomy. "And this is our constitution, and why cannot we be pleased?" [72]

His conception of the right of resistance or revolution was therefore not at all well defined. Like others of his school he maintained that "the prince who strives to subvert the fundamental laws of the society is the traitor and rebel," [73] but he made no attempt to fix standards for determining when the contract had been broken and the people thus entitled to reassert their con-stituent power. Wise cannot be cited as an authority in favor of the right of resistance. Had he written his tracts in 1688, he would doubtless have given more attention to this important corollary of the contract theory. Had he written them in 1765 or 1776, he might have outdone Paine and Jefferson in proclaiming the necessity of resistance and revolution. Like all American political thinkers he shaped theory to fact.

"A STAR OF THE FIRST MAGNITUDE"

All these major and minor principles add up to a coherent and impressive theory, the more impressive by reason of the time and place in which it was expounded. Writing in defense of a form of ecclesiastical government that he considered the established order, Wise ranged far afield from his original purpose and ended up by rendering a magnificent apologia for political democracy. Like Hooker and Williams, he saw clearly what Cotton, Winthrop, Davenport, and the Mathers refused to acknowledge: the bridge leading from the church covenant to the social contract, from congregational autonomy to self-government, from democracy in the church to democracy in the state. Unlike his liberal or radical predecessors, he retraced the course their minds had traveled and justified Congregationalism by its similarity to the first and most "natural" of civil governments—democracy. In doing all this—in linking up ecclesiasticism and politics and arguing from the latter toward the former—he made a notable contribution to American intellectual history, one that has never been properly acknowledged.

Wise claims the attention of the historian of ideas for at least three other reasons. First, he was not just a libertarian but a thoroughly democratic thinker. No other colonist, whether writer or man of affairs, was so bold in his use of words like "democracy" and "equality" or so genuinely willing to champion the radical concepts they expressed. Second, he was the model for all the hundreds of New England preachers who received and reaffirmed the liberating principles of natural law and rights. His books are evidence that the political theory of the Revolution had been part of men's thinking for several generations before 1765. Few men moved so far as Wise into the radical wing of the natural-law school, but many of his ideas about higher law and the contract were widely accepted articles of political faith. Finally, the fact that Wise, the most prominent of early American exponents of natural law, went to Pufendorf rather than Locke for his lessons in political theory, proves that the latter was not, after all, the exclusive oracle of the American libertarians. They were heirs of a great tradition of which Locke was only one of many eminent apostles.

It would be pleasant to report that Wise's teachings, even if forgotten today, were a vital force in the American Revolution. The fact is that his ideas were quite without effect, even upon the minds of the Massachusetts patriots. Although his two books were reprinted in 1772 and purchased in large quantities by such celebrated Revolutionary figures as Timothy Pickering (6 copies), Ebenezer Dorr (3), William Dawes (100!), Artemas Ward (6), Rev. Edward Emerson of Concord (24), John Scollay (4), and Tapping Reeve of Litchfield,[74] rarely do we find Wise's name quoted in the leading tracts and pamphlets of the time. Rarely, of course, do we find the rebellious colonists calling any of their fellow countrymen to witness, for they were far too pleased with the advice tendered by Locke, Sidney, Cicero, and St. Paul to pay much attention to native prophecy. There were two special reasons for Wise's oblivion. First, his books were out of print until 1772, while those of the others, especially Locke's *Civil Government*, were available in numerous editions. Even when reprinted, Wise's works seem to have been invoked largely for Congregational purposes. Second, the point has already been made that Wise's purpose, the defense of the Congregational principle, persuaded him to say as little as possible about the right of resistance. For this reason more than any other he was ignored by a people for whom the most useful principle of the natural-rights theory was the right of resistance.

Forgotten by the late eighteenth century, Wise has been forgotten ever since. That he will remain a shadowy figure in the political and intellectual history of American democracy, a noble person with a lesser reputation than he doubtless deserves, seems altogether probable. History plays strange jokes, and just as we will never celebrate July 2 as Independence Day, so we will never see Wise taught in high school. This is unfortunate, for he has as valid a claim to our patriotic attention as Roger Williams or any other figure in colonial history. There were brave democrats before Samuel Adams and Thomas Jefferson, none braver than John Wise.

Wise died on April 8, 1725, less than two months after the death of his wife. He remained strong to the end in the principles he had so passionately embraced. "He told me in the beginning of his Sickness," said his son-in-law, John White, "that he had been a Man of Contention, but the State of the Churches making it necessary; upon the most serious Review, he could say he had *Fought a Good Fight;* and had comfort in reflecting upon the same." [75] Wise was buried in the yard of his church and rests there to this day under a stone that proclaims:

> For Talents, Piety and Learning he shone
> As a Star of the first magnitude.

Since Wise never did care for praise, it would be more to his liking were we to conclude with his own words of good cheer for his and this and every other generation of American democracy:

> Hold your hold, brethren! *Et validis incumbite remis,* pull up well upon your oars, you have a rich cargo, and I hope we shall escape shipwreck; for according to the latest observation, if we are not within sight, yet we are not far from harbor; and though the noise of great breakers which we hear imports hazard, yet I hope daylight and good piloting will secure all. [76]

CHAPTER NINE

Jonathan Mayhew

IN HIS last doughty years John Adams of Quincy was much given to
reminiscing about the coming of the Revolution, particularly with Southern correspondents who refused to acknowledge gracefully the primacy of
Massachusetts. Although the old man of 1818 is not always to be trusted as
he recreates the events of 1765 and 1776, many of his observations have
stood up bravely under the battering of modern scholarship. One such musing about men long dead and events forgotten was this enumeration of the
men of Massachusetts chiefly responsible for the "awakening and revival of
American principles and feelings" in the early 1760's:

> The characters the most conspicuous, the most ardent and influential in
> this revival, from 1760 to 1766, were, first and foremost, before all and above
> all, James Otis; next to him was Oxenbridge Thacher; next to him, Samuel
> Adams; next to him, John Hancock; then Dr. Mayhew.[1]

The most instructive lesson that we learn from this heroic muster is one
that Adams himself apparently overlooked: the fact that of the five Massachusetts colonials most prominent in the first overt phase of the Revolution four were men of affairs (two lawyers, a politician, a merchant) and
only one a man of God—and he the fifth in line. Had any such roll of Commonwealth leaders been drawn up in 1650 or 1700, or even so late as 1750,
the influence of the pulpit would surely have been more pronounced. The
first and second of these names indicate a major transformation in the character of colonial leadership which took place in the decades immediately
preceding the Revolution. By 1760 the pulpit had lost much of its direct
political influence, for a variety of reasons upon which most historians agree:
the growth of science and humanistic learning, the expansion of trade and
population, the establishment of the popular press, and the abrupt rise of
the legal profession. The day of the preacher was at an end; the day of

the lawyer had dawned. Yet at least one minister stood fast in the great tradition.

Another gentleman, who had great influence in the commencement of the Revolution, was Doctor Jonathan Mayhew, a descendant of the ancient governor of Martha's Vineyard. This divine had raised a great reputation both in Europe and America, by the publication of a . . . sermon in 1750, on the 30th of January, on the subject of passive obedience and non-resistance, in which the saintship and martyrdom of King Charles the First are considered, seasoned with wit and satire superior to any in Swift or Franklin. It was read by everybody; celebrated by friends, and abused by enemies. During the reigns of King George the First and King George the Second, the reigns of the Stuarts, the two Jameses and the two Charleses were in general disgrace in England. In America they had always been held in abhorrence. The persecutions and cruelties suffered by their ancestors under those reigns, had been transmitted by history and tradition, and Mayhew seemed to be raised up to revive all their animosities against tyranny, in church and state, and at the same time to destroy their bigotry, fanaticism, and inconsistency. . . . To draw the character of Mayhew, would be to transcribe a dozen volumes. This transcendent genius threw all the weight of his great fame into the scale of his country in 1761, and maintained it there with zeal and ardor till his death, in 1766.[2]

This is high praise, yet Mayhew surely earned it. For nineteen years his pulpit was the storm center of Boston theology, and for almost as long the religious outpost of colonial resistance to British political and ecclesiastical encroachment. One of the last of the great colonial preachers, he was at the same time the rough-voiced herald of a new day for religious and political liberty. Rationalism and Whiggery had no more outspoken an exponent.

THE WEST CHURCH IN BOSTON

Jonathan Mayhew was born at Chilmark, Martha's Vineyard, October 8, 1720. He was the third of four sons of the Reverend Experience Mayhew and his wife Remember, daughter of Shearjashub Bourne of Sandwich.[3] The Mayhews of the Vineyard were a family "respectable in all its stages." [4] Jonathan's great-great-grandfather, Thomas Mayhew, had acquired title to Martha's Vineyard in 1641 under both the Stirling and Gorges patents and had lived there from 1646 to 1682 as proprietor, magistrate, and missionary. His son, Thomas, Jr., had come to the island from the mainland in 1642 as the first permanent settler and had served, even before John Eliot, as an apostle to the Indians. Their immediate descendants, John and his son Experience, were like them tillers of the soil and converters of the "salvages." The last of this line was rewarded for his labors in 1720 with one of the first Harvard honorary degrees.[5]

The education of Jonathan Mayhew came from three sources: his father, Harvard, and himself. From Experience (and doubtless from Remember, too) proceeded the better part of his early schooling, in which he acquired a satisfactory acquaintance with Greek and Latin, an astonishing knowledge of "the inspired writings," and a profound mistrust of religious and political Calvinism. From Harvard in 1744 he received his degree, the outward sign of an intense formal education for which he had paid dearly. A lack of funds several times interrupted his residence at Cambridge,[6] and the effort to make up for lost time and studies played havoc with his health. (It did not, on the other hand, seem to interfere with his youthful relish for alcoholic sport.[7]) This was the Harvard of Edward Holyoke, that "polite Gentleman, of a noble commanding presence," called "Guts" by his devoted students and worse things by the orthodox clergy, for whom the college, especially after Leverett's noble presidency (1708-1724), was a liberal thorn in the side of expiring Calvinism. Holyoke, who reigned for thirty-two years (1737-1769), had an abiding influence on his students. The roll of those who learned of truth and freedom from this eminent divine is a *dramatis personae* of the Massachusetts phase of the American Revolution: Samuel and John Adams, James Otis, James Bowdoin, Oxenbridge Thacher, John Hancock, Timothy Pickering, Joseph Warren, Robert Treat Paine, and Jonathan Mayhew. Finally, from himself Mayhew received a continuing education that ceased only with death. Throughout his career he studied with peculiar intensity, ranging the fields of polite and polemic learning from Hebrew grammar to the latest sermons from London, from Harrington to Voltaire, from Genesis to Revelation. At one stage in his ministerial progress he studied himself into a state of physical collapse.

In March 1747 the West Church in Boston, which had already achieved some notoriety for liberal tendencies in its ten-year existence, invited Mayhew to become its second pastor. In the interval since his graduation from Harvard he had been moving steadily away from the five points of Calvinism, thanks to study of Samuel Clarke and Locke at Cambridge and a mutually fruitful and liberalizing residence with the celebrated Dr. Ebenezer Gay of Hingham. Mayhew's reputation had run before him: Although eleven ministers, including Mayhew's father and Dr. Gay, assembled from the country churches to welcome the new minister at his ordination, no representative of a Boston church put in an appearance. Mayhew eventually came to cordial social and even ecclesiastical terms with several of the city's clergy, but he was always catalogued as an "amiable heretic." He never joined the Boston Association of Congregational Ministers.

Mayhew's pastorate was short but honorable. For nineteen years he served his large and distinguished congregation with warmth and imagination, and his passing was mourned with unforced grief. "In this Charge he continued 'till his death, loving his people, and by them beloved." [8] However much his more peace-loving parishioners might have protested against the advanced and acid observations that he delivered almost every Sunday, they recognized in him a man of superior attainments as pastor, teacher, and friend. At his death it was written:

In him, *it may be truly said,* his disconsolate Widow has lost a kind and
affectionate Husband, his children a tender and faithful Parent, his Family
a humane and indulgent Master; the Poor *of all Denominations* a charitable
and constant Friend; his Church a worthy, learned, social, virtuous and religious Pastor; this Continent a resolute and strong Defender of its religious
Independency; and Mankind a bold and nervous Assertor of their rights,
and that Liberty wherewith Christ has made them free.[9]

Mayhew's congregation supported him loyally in his daring forays into
unexplored ecclesiastical country. He could write his father without cant
or conceit, "My people are united, attentive, and kind." [10] His character
shines through his sermons and letters in a pattern that cannot be miscon-
strued, and what his own words withhold those of his friends and enemies
convey. Here was a man quite comprehensible to the modern mind—candid,
sincere, diligent, amiable, publicity-conscious, supremely aware of his many
powers and few limitations, and constantly "on the run." To the meek,
mild, and decent he was a gentle friend and counselor; to the "hypocritical,
and the dogmatical and censorious" he was "bold and severe," at least in
print.[11] More than one literary antagonist came through a joust with Mayhew feeling that Old Nick himself had thrown acid in his face.[12] His style
is straightforward if not exactly dazzling, while from all accounts he was
a speaker of genuine eloquence.

From his first day in the West Church pulpit Mayhew was a man with
a name and mission. His liberal preaching and pamphleteering won him
immediate fame. His very first book, *Seven Sermons . . . Preached as a
Lecture in the West Meeting House,*[13] brought him an Aberdeen D.D., in
February 1750. As a conscientious and effective member of the Harvard
Board of Overseers he won the respect if not always the approval of such
colleagues as Thomas Hutchinson. He corresponded widely with persons
in England sympathetic to the causes of independency and colonial liberty,
most notably from 1759 to his death with the third of those gentlemen
named Thomas Hollis who were so pleasantly and purposefully philan-
thropic to Harvard College.[14] To James Otis, Samuel Adams, James Bowdoin, R. T. Paine, John Winthrop, Stephen Sewall, and Harrison Gray he
was a valued friend. His radical theology and liberal politics made him one
of the most controversial yet respected figures in all New England.

BISHOPS AND TAX COLLECTORS

Mayhew's lifelong campaign against New England orthodoxy was little more
than a series of opportunistic raids on a once-mighty army left defenseless
by desertion. Another of his ecclesiastical struggles, waged in 1763-1764
over a definite issue with a proudly armed band of adversaries, was at once
more dramatic and historically significant. This was the celebrated literary
debate between Mayhew and certain Anglican apologists over the Church
of England's designs upon the American colonies. The "Mayhew Contro-

versy," as it is known in the history of the Episcopal Church in America,[15] was actually three battles in one. At first simply an exchange of broadsides over the activities of the Society for the Propagation of the Gospel in Foreign Parts, it soon turned to a more fundamental issue: the propriety of establishing an American episcopate. And at bottom, of course, it was yet another phase of the conflict between American political independence and British authority.

A word of background will set the stage of the Mayhew Controversy. For almost a century and a half the most awesome bogey under the Puritan bed had been the vision of an Anglican Bishop of Boston. Even such elementary attempts to bring the Church of England to New England as the scheme of Governor Andros to use the South Meetinghouse for Anglican worship were enough to give the Puritan clergy nightmares of an American Laud. Most of the time this issue lay dormant, but only because conditions in the colonies and England rendered impractical any general extension of the episcopal system. By the middle of the eighteenth century, however, the establishment of an American episcopate seemed a distinct possibility. Leading colonial Episcopalians, beset from the North by the never-flagging hostility of independence and from the South by the growing autonomy of their own parishes, were outspoken in their desire for one or more bishops. At the same time, the Society for the Propagation of the Gospel, established in 1701 to carry on missionary work in those corners of the King's dominions where provision for a ministry was inadequate, had aroused much anxiety in New England by settling its missionaries in populated regions rather than on the frontier. By 1760 there were thirty Anglican ministers propagating their own version of the gospel in New England towns. Finally, many New Englanders of 1760 suspected that schemes for strengthening the colonial position of the Church of England were tied in with the Crown's determination to reassert its power over the increasingly headstrong Americans. From 1763 to the outbreak of Revolution this question was paramount in the minds of many Americans, for whom an Anglican bishop and a Stamp Tax collector were co-villains in a plot to subvert their ancient liberties. Actually, the threat from this quarter was not half so perilous as Mayhew and his colleagues believed. But this is a judgment made with the assistance of hindsight.

The principal stages in the Mayhew Controversy were these: (1) a newspaper article published in Boston in February 1763, which seized upon the death of an Anglican missionary in Braintree as an excuse for attacking the practice of the Society for the Propagation of the Gospel of placing its missionaries in settled towns; [16] (2) a return to these aspersions by the Rev. East Apthorp, missionary in Cambridge, entitled *Considerations on the Institution and Conduct of the Society;* (3) a quick retaliation by Mayhew, *Observations on the Charter and Conduct of the Society;* (4) a series of replies to Mayhew,[17] one of them from England; (5) two further rejoinders by Mayhew, *A Defence of the Observations* in reply to the most important American attack, and *Remarks on an Anonymous Tract* in reply to the

British pamphlet; (6) a final pamphlet by Apthorp,[18] in which he reviewed the entire controversy and got in a few last blows for the Church of England and the Society. Mayhew thought it unworthy of an answer and put an end to this war of words by ignoring it.[19]

He is a brave scholar indeed who can read over these mildewed pages with any feeling other than exasperated boredom. Both Mayhew and his opponents are guilty a thousand times over of all the sins of eighteenth-century pamphleteering, especially the practice of endless repetition of a simple and easily stated major premise. Only the British *An Answer to Doctor Mayhew's Observation*, which was eventually traced back to Thomas Secker, Archbishop of Canterbury, and Mayhew's *Remarks* are sufficiently well-ordered and well-mannered to merit modern consideration. In this tract Mayhew rose above the secondary questions whether the Society had, as he claimed, misread its charter, misapplied its funds, and misrepresented the state of religion in New England, for he challenged the Anglican hierarchy to deny that the real purpose of planting bishops in America was to establish the Church of England. In his *Remarks* he asked in more polite and therefore more convincing fashion what he had already asked with passion in the *Observations:*

> Will they never let us rest in peace, *except where all the weary are at rest?* Is it not enough, that they persecuted us out of the old world? Will they pursue us into the new to convert us here?—*compassing sea and land to make* us *proselytes,* while they neglect the heathen and heathenish plantations! What other new world remains as a sanctuary for us from their oppressions, in case of need? Where is the COLUMBUS to explore one for, and pilot us to it, before we are consumed by the flames, or deluged in a flood of episcopacy? [20]

We cannot pass this off as the fulmination of a New England dissenter ready to believe anything of Canterbury or Rome. For Mayhew, even in his most detached moments, the danger of the established church was clear and present, and he echoed faithfully the fears of like-minded countrymen. Again we hear from John Adams:

> Where is the man to be found at this day, when we see Methodistical bishops, bishops of the church of England, and bishops, archbishops, and Jesuits of the church of Rome, with indifference, who will believe that the apprehension of Episcopacy contributed fifty years ago, as much as any other cause, to arouse the attention, not only of the inquiring mind, but of the common people, and urge them to close thinking on the constitutional authority of parliament over the colonies? This, nevertheless, was a fact as certain as any in the history of North America. The objection was not merely to the office of a bishop, though even that was dreaded, but to the authority of parliament, on which it must be founded. . . . All sensible men knew that this system could not be effected but by act of parliament; and if parliament could do this, they could do all things; and what security could Americans have for life, liberty, property, or religion? [21]

In this passage the discerning old patriot gives the most plausible explanation for the intensity of Mayhew's loudly voiced convictions: the tight connection between the aspirations of the Anglican bishops and designs of the Tory ministers. Certainly it was known to all men that the established church was heavily committed to the prerogative state, that it had supported various plans to subject corporate and proprietary governments to the control of the Crown, and that Parliament claimed the final power to legislate religions in and out of the colonies (as it demonstrated in 1774 with the passage of the Quebec Act). Mayhew was perhaps more vocal than the people about him, but not much more alarmed. If we smile at him for baiting the Church of England, we must also smile at Otis for assailing the writs of assistance, at Samuel Adams for bombarding the Boston press, and at Henry for striking his poses in the House of Burgesses.

One joke that history played on Mayhew is too edifying to be consigned to a footnote. Elizabeth Mayhew, his daughter and only surviving child, was married after the Revolution to Peter Wainwright of Liverpool. Their son, who bore the proud dissenting name of Jonathan Mayhew Wainwright, was from 1852 to 1854 Episcopal Bishop of New York. This grandson of the man who had no use for bishops answered Rufus Choate's remark that the Pilgrims had founded "a state without a king and a church without a bishop" with the lofty rebuke, "There cannot be a church without a bishop."

There is little that need be said of Mayhew's other labors for religious and political freedom except to point out that no controversy with British authority was too trifling to enlist his tongue and pen. Twice he was at the front of those struggling for colonial liberties. In 1762 he was the penman, orator, and chief strategist of the Harvard Board of Overseers in its successful resistance to the establishment of a second college in Hampshire County. This was an engagement particularly to Mayhew's liking, for he was able to deliver stout blows to both Calvinists, who had begun the movement for a new college out of discontent with Harvard's "liberal" tendencies, and Anglicans, whose natural leader, the newly arrived Governor Bernard, seized this heaven-sent opportunity to embarrass and even undermine the citadel of Congregationalism.[22]

The resistance of Massachusetts to the ill-begotten Stamp Act needed no Mayhew to goad it into action. Indeed, had the Boston mob listened more attentively to the strong but moderate counsels of men like Mayhew, this exciting affair would have made a far prettier chapter in the history of American patriotism. In any case, the kind of leadership offered by Otis and Adams on the political front was matched by the exhortations of Mayhew, Chauncy, and Cooper from their famous pulpits. No sermon did more to stiffen resistance than Mayhew's memorable discourse of August 25, 1765, on Galatians v, 12-13. ("I would they were even cut off which trouble you. For, brethren, ye have been called unto liberty; only *use* not liberty for an occasion to the flesh, but by love serve one another.") No sermon expressed more exultantly yet humbly the sense of popular relief over the repeal of the Stamp Act than *The Snare Broken*, May 23, 1766, which Mayhew, always thoroughly respectful of the power of the press, had in print within six days of delivery. The first of these won Mayhew an undeservedly bad reputation among those ready to believe the worst of him. A leader of the mob that sacked Hutchinson's house August 26, 1765, dropped an offhand remark to the effect that he had been aroused by Mayhew's sermon; and although Mayhew and the Lieutenant-Governor immediately exchanged cordial letters of sympathy and respect, the outspoken minister was tarred with the brush of inciting mob violence.[23]

MAYHEW AS RELIGIOUS THINKER: PRIVATE JUDGMENT

The fact that most of Mayhew's friends were secular in vocation and political in taste tells us a great deal about his life, work, and thought. He saw more clearly than any other man in New England that the fight for "private judgment" in religion and for personal liberty in politics was one grand battle in which all patriots could join with a will. Mayhew's political philosophy was the natural corollary of the liberal gospel he preached. Before we can explore his politics we must understand his religion.

Mayhew's place in theology is most precisely fixed by saluting him as an important forerunner of American Unitarianism. Samuel A. Eliot devoted the first volume of his history of Unitarianism, *Heralds of a Liberal Faith*, to the "period of Protest," which he found "to begin with the ordination of Jonathan Mayhew in 1747 and to last until the election of Henry Ware to the Hollis Professorship of Divinity at Harvard in 1805." [24] John Adams wrote to Ebenezer Morse in 1815, "Sixty years ago my own minister, Rev. Lemuel Briant, Dr. Jonathan Mayhew, of the West Church in Boston, Rev. Mr. Shute, of Hingham, Rev. John Brown, of Cohasset, and, perhaps equal to all, if not above all, Rev. Dr. Gay, of Hingham, were Unitarians." [25] Whether Gay or Briant or Mayhew was the first Unitarian is impossible to state, for Unitarianism was the outgrowth of a historical process to which many men contributed their doubts and talents. In any case, within a few years of his ordination Mayhew was recognized as New England's most outspoken Arian, as a preacher who, if he could never satisfy his own mind and soul concerning the identity of Jesus Christ and his relation to God, could none the less insist with conviction that "God was ONE and SUPREME." In a note to a volume of sermons published in 1755 he rejected—somewhat obliquely, to be sure—the doctrine of the trinity.[26]

The impact of Mayhew's religious teachings was felt far beyond the confines of Unitarianism. For most men, after all, the nature of the trinity was a question of doctrinal disputation, and Mayhew's active beliefs would have been the same, and enjoyed the same widespread influence, whether he thought God to be one or three. Mayhew was important because he preached a gospel that rejected flatly the five points of Calvinism. The tenets of orthodox Puritanism—predestination, limited atonement, total depravity, irresistibility of grace, and perserverance of the saints—had no place in his theology. The God of the Mathers, and especially the God of Jonathan Edwards's harrowing Enfield sermon, *Sinners in the Hands of an Angry God*, was not the God of Jonathan Mayhew. Nor did he care for the Calvinism of the Great Awakening any more than for that of the Great Migration. He wrote his father that he had heard George Whitefield preach a sermon "which was a very low, confused, puerile, conceited, ill-natur'd, enthusiastick, etc. Performance as ever I heard in my Life." [27]

Not satisfied with rejecting and ridiculing orthodoxy, Mayhew developed a substitute creed that seemed to him the only plausible religion for the free and thinking man in the good society. First among his principles was his exposition of the nature of God, who for him was as much a God of love and reason as He was for orthodox Puritans a God of anger and whim. He is "a merciful and faithful Creator; a compassionate Parent; a gentle Master," [28]

> who governs his great family, his universal Kingdom, according to those general rules and maxims which are in themselves most wise and good, such as the wisest and best kings govern by. . . . Perfect goodness, love itself, is his very essence, in a peculiar sense; immeasurable, immutable, universal and everlasting love.[29]

As God is a "gentle Master," so is he a "righteous Judge" who "inspects our conduct" not with the "malice of an *Inquisitor*" but with "the bowels of a parent." [30] There is a "natural" difference between right and wrong— "Truth and moral rectitude are things fixed, stable and uniform, having their foundation in the nature of things"—and each of us is fully capable, thanks to a rational nature and free will, to choose the one over the other.[31] Man's covenant with God is one of grace *and* works: He who strives consciously to be good and kind, in the image of Christ, has within him a full measure of divine grace. The reward, of course, is eternal life, and there is no man who cannot win it. Indeed, most of us can expect it, for we aim at eternity from this point of vantage: We are all disposed by nature to follow the Christian ethic. In defiance of the very core of the orthodox creed, Mayhew proclaimed the rank absurdity of the doctrine of total depravity. Man for him was essentially good. This belief permitted him to engage in preaching that was profoundly moralistic. He expected his listeners to behave as circumspectly as their Puritan ancestors because it was the reasonable rather than necessary thing to do. In sum, Mayhew expounded a humanistic, liberal, rational, "natural religion." Only his calling, and an ultimate faith in the God of his New England fathers, restrained him from passing over into an attitude of outright deism. He was showered with Newtonianism but drenched with Scripture.

Students of religious philosophy get little satisfaction from Mayhew, for he was, as his Episcopal contemporary Samuel Johnson observed, a "loose thinker." [32] Yet he could hardly have been otherwise—by the nature of his task, which was to grope through the dark fog of centuries of scholastic authoritarianism for a few simple truths about man and God, and by the

nature of his religion, which placed emphasis on practice rather than speculation. His opinion of the *cymini sectores*, the splitters of doctrinal hairs, is
plain in this passage from one of his first sermons:

> It is infinitely dishonorable to the all-good and perfect Governor of the
> world to imagine, that he has suspended the eternal salvation of men upon
> any niceties of speculation; or that any one, who honestly aims at finding
> the truth, and at doing the will of his Maker, shall be finally discarded, be-
> cause he fell into some erroneous opinions.[33]

In rejecting authority in religion, Mayhew rejected the stuff upon which
authority feeds: speculation. The important thing was not to meditate on
the size of God's angels but to love God by doing good. What that meant,
any man could understand through the use of his own reason and the
revealed word, each of which counsels us to love one another. What
Morison has written of Boston Unitarianism, that it "was not a fixed dogma,
but a point of view that was receptive, searching, inquiring, and yet de-
vout," [34] may with peculiar emphasis be written of the religion of this early
Boston Unitarian. We are bound to take him as he was, in the words of
his friend Harrison Gray, "a great advocate for primitive Christianity." [35]
His faith was not expressed in a body of doctrine but in an attitude of
mind. And the core of this attitude, the prime rule of action for man in
search of God, was the fundamental right of "private judgment."

> Did I say, we have a *right* to judge and act for ourselves? I now add—it
> is our *indispensable duty* to do it. This is a right which we cannot relin-
> quish, or neglect to exercise, if we would, without being highly culpable.
> . . . God and nature and the gospel of Christ injoin it upon us a duty to
> maintain the right of private judgment.[36]

Since judgment was a private matter, this meant an end to priestly dictation. Mayhew's religious man was a free individual.

MAYHEW AS POLITICAL THINKER: POWER AS A TRUST

Mayhew's political philosophy is nowhere expressed in direct, methodical
form. He consistently adopted a self-deprecating attitude concerning his
right and ability to discuss political problems. Again and again he would
approach a point of controversy, go to the root of the matter with a few
brilliant observations, and suddenly, with some such remark as, "But these
are matters out of the way of my profession," turn off into ten or twelve
pages of Scriptural exhortation. As if to refute the accusation of Anglican
and Calvinist that he was one of those advanced preachers "who can scarcely
be accounted better christians than the Turks," [37] he rarely if ever discussed a subject of secular interest except in terms of Christian principle.
The results are extremely irritating to the modern reader, especially when
he sees how fertile and influential Mayhew's political ideas actually were.
Yet the circumstances under which he announced these ideas were so

memorable that he won for himself a solid reputation among America's pre-Revolutionary political thinkers.

Three sermons in particular brought Mayhew a full measure of respect or notoriety in New England and the mother country. The first and most celebrated, *A Discourse Concerning Unlimited Submission and Non-resistance to the Higher Powers*,[38] was delivered less than three years after his ordination, the Sunday after January 30, 1750. It was a dissenting preacher's refractory answer to the Tory-Anglican attempt to memorialize the anniversary of the death of Charles I and elevate him to "saintship and martyrdom." [39] It is for this discourse that Mayhew is chiefly remembered as political thinker and patriot, for it was the first responsible public expression in colonial America of the sacred right and duty of resistance to tyranny, the "MORNING GUN OF THE REVOLUTION, the *punctum temporis* when that period of history began." [40] In his second important lecture on political subjects, the Massachusetts Election Sermon of 1754, Mayhew expounded to Governor Shirley and the General Court his conception of political power as something held in trust for the sovereign people.[41] And finally, on the occasion of the repeal of the Stamp Act, only a few short weeks before his unseasonable death, he preached *The Snare Broken*,[42] a sermon of rejoicing dedicated to America's great friend Pitt.

The deliberate manner in which Mayhew confused politics with religion and larded all observations on the one with rambling references to the other becomes especially evident in an attempt to decipher his sources. On one hand, he was conversant with the great men of England, many of whose works had been sent him by Thomas Hollis—Harrington, Sidney, Milton, Hoadly, *Cato's Letters*, and Locke. On the other, he rarely quoted one of these secular writers without supporting him with a passage from the Bible, without attempting "to examine into the Scripture account of this matter"—at least into those parts that confirmed his rationalistic politics. Each of his three major pronouncements on political matters was in the form of a sermon preached on a particular text. To his listeners, of course, and even to most of his readers, this technique made a great deal more sense than it does to modern minds. It was in this period that Locke and others were elevated to the status of major prophets by the clergy of Massachusetts and Connecticut, and Mayhew did as much as any other preacher to introduce their ideas to the colonial audience. He was able to do this without upsetting his congregation by serving these rationalistic doses in a Scriptural spoon. Mayhew is an illuminating example of the affinity between the philosophy of natural rights and the postulates of that "primitive Christianity" which had reason for its guide. He was an agreeable synthesis of Locke and St. Paul.

Central to Mayhew's political philosophy was his patristic-medieval-Lockean doctrine of political authority as something held in trust for the people and exercised in their behalf. This in turn rested squarely upon his opinion of the nature of man, and of the basis, purpose, and character of government. Mayhew's natural man we have already met, and we have found him to be an essentially good, moral, reasonable, sociable person dwelling at the opposite end of the spiritual-psychological spectrum from total depravity. Since God is benevolent and asks not for fear but love, "The love of God is the love of the divine perfections; 'tis the love of truth, goodness, justice, holiness, and all moral excellencies." [43]

On men with these qualities rest the good society and free government, and to both they must be assumed to have given their consent. "From man, from common consent, it is that lawful rulers immediately receive their power." [44] Although Mayhew nowhere expresses a precise theory of the social contract, it is clear that he entertains no other view of the ultimate source of power in his kind of polity. "All besides is mere lawless force and usurpation; neither God nor nature having given any man a right of dominion over any society independently of that society's approbation and consent to be governed by him." [45] As for the assertions of the apologists for the divine right of kings, "These notions are not drawn from the holy scriptures, but from a far less pure and sacred fountain. They are only the devices of lawned parasites, or other graceless politicians, to serve the purposes of ambition and tyranny. And though they are of late date, yet being traced up to their true original, they will be found to come, by uninterrupted succession, from him who was a politician from the beginning" [46]—a saucy statement indeed to deliver to Governor Shirley's face.

The purpose of government in this Lockean's philosophy is, of course, the "happiness of society," or "human felicity," or the "common good of all, and of every individual, so far as is consistent therewith." In the election sermon of 1754 Mayhew expressed his humanistic concept of the "sole end" of political institutions:

> In the SECOND place, we are just to mention the great end of government. And after the glory of God, which we usually consider as the end of all things in general, that can be no other than the good of man, the common benefit of society. This is equally evident whether we consider it as a divine, or an human institution.
> As it is God's ordinance, it is designed for a blessing to the world. It is instituted for the preservation of men's persons, properties and various rights, against fraud and lawless violence; and that, by means of it, we may both procure, and quietly enjoy, those numerous blessings and advantages, which are quite unattainable out of society.[47]

The nature of civil government is in keeping with these ends: It is good, "sacred," in its proper form a "blessing" to all men. Mayhew was no more a friend to the "necessary evil" theory of government than was John Wise. He believed firmly in the inestimable benefits of a well-ordered civil polity. Following faithfully in Locke's footsteps, he found it "a thing of no consequence at all what the particular form of government is" [48] so long as it produced "good laws—laws attempered to the common felicity of the governed." At the same time, he was sure that "no form of government seems so unlikely to accomplish this end as absolute monarchy." Like other

good Americans of 1750 he eulogized the English pattern of mixed government, which was "justly the envy of most other nations." [49]

On these sound foundations Mayhew built his doctrine of governmental
power, expounding at unusual length an idea that most natural-rights thinkers
tossed off briskly or merely assumed. The core of his doctrine was this:
Public office, and any authority or function or privilege that may adhere to
it, is a public trust, to be exercised exclusively for the people who created
it. The king or magistrate or legislator, the temporary and conditional pos-
sessor of authority, must consider himself only as steward of the people.
As such he is to live an exemplary public and private life. These notions
are plain in the unvarnished words of Mayhew's election sermon, which
was preached, be it noted, on the parable of the talents.

> But it is not to be thought merely an office of generosity and charity, for
> Rulers to exert themselves in the service of the public. This is an indis-
> pensable duty of justice which they owe to it, by virtue of their station.
> They have taken the care and guardianship thereof upon themselves: yea
> they are commonly laid under the solemn obligation of an oath, to study
> and pursue its interest. And why are they honoured? why, rewarded by
> the public, but that the public may receive benefit from them? . . .
> Rulers, surely, even the most dignified and powerful of them, should not
> be so elevated with the thoughts of their power, as to forget from whom it
> comes; for what purposes it is delegated to them; whose impartial eye it is
> that surveys all their counsels, designs and actions; and who it is that will,
> one day, exact an account of their stewardship. . . .
> As the happiness of men in society depends greatly upon the goodness of
> their morals, and as morals have a close connection with religion, the latter
> as well as the former, ought doubtless to be encouraged by the civil mag-
> istrate . . . by his own pious life and good example.[50]

In his sermon against *Unlimited Submission* Mayhew also considered the
problem of obedience to those in authority:

> And here is a plain reason also why ye should pay tribute to them,—for
> they are God's ministers, exalted above the common level of mankind,—not
> that they may indulge themselves in softness and luxury, and be entitled to
> the servile homage of their fellowmen, but that they may execute an office
> no less laborious than honorable, and attend continually upon the public
> welfare.[51]

Mayhew's meaning is as clear today as it was two hundred years ago
when he went to war against the insolence of authority: There are standards
of good behavior for governments as well as individuals. Freedom and
order are impossible to achieve except in the *good* society. Mayhew's government was above all a moral government, derived from and conducted
by moral men. Lest it be thought that he was content to deal in diffident
generalities, it should be recorded that near the end of the election sermon
he turned to Shirley and hoped out loud, "You will never forget, Sir, whose
minister you are," [52] and that in his sermon of 1750 he took a slap at half

of Boston by scolding "all Christians concerned in that common practice of carrying on an illicit trade and running of goods." [53]

THE RIGHT OF RESISTANCE

Mayhew was a courageous if not entirely clear-headed political thinker. Certainly he never pulled up short of a logical conclusion simply because it was likely to be uncommon or unpopular. For him, therefore, as for the noble republicans and Whigs with whom he went to school, the natural consequence of a popular theory of the origin and purpose of government was the doctrine of popular resistance to abuses of public trust. Twenty-five years before Lexington and Concord Mayhew laid down the theoretical premises upon which the Revolution was to be justified, something few other preachers of Lockean principles were yet prepared to do. His clear expression of this doctrine is the more remarkable when set in its historical context, a time of peace, prosperity, and general satisfaction with British suzerainty.

Mayhew began by asserting that under ordinary circumstances obedience to authority is both a natural and Christian duty. He was no radical impatient of all governmental restraints, but a man preaching moderation and civic duty whose text was Romans xiii, 1-8 ("Let every soul be subject unto the higher powers. . . ."), and whose constant admonition was that "a decent regard be paid to those in authority." [54] Such obedience was dictated not only by the Apostle but by reason itself. It was the normal pattern of behavior for any man who had voluntarily surrendered his original freedom in return for the protection of government. "The true ground and reason of our obligation to be subject to the higher powers is, the usefulness of magistracy (when properly exercised) to human society, and its subserviency to the general welfare." [55] Even in 1766 we find Mayhew reminding his audience to adopt "a respectful, loyal and dutiful manner of speech and conduct, respecting his majesty and his government," and to support "his majesty's representatives, the civil magistrates, and all persons in authority, in the lawful exercise of their several offices." [56]

The word "lawful" is the key to the next stage in Mayhew's theory. He was "not in favor of submission to all who bear the title of rulers in common, but only to those who actually perform the duty of rulers by exercising a reasonable and just authority for the good of human society."

> If those who bear the title of civil rulers do not perform the duty of civil rulers, but act directly counter to the sole end and design of their office; if they injure and oppress their subjects, instead of defending their rights and doing them good, they have not the least pretence to be honored, obeyed, and rewarded. . . .
>
> When once magistrates act contrary to their office, and the end of their institution,—when they rob and ruin the public, instead of being guardians of its peace and welfare,—they immediately cease to be the ordinance and ministers of God, and no more deserve that glorious character than common pirates and highwaymen.[57]

In fine, "Rulers have no authority from God to do mischief," and citizens have no duty to submit to them if they persist in doing it. Mayhew rejected peremptorily the absolutist doctrines of unlimited submission and non-resistance, which had been bluntly expressed by such thinkers as Luther, James I, and Filmer, and which were to be just as bluntly expressed by Boucher and Leonard on the eve of the Revolution. Instead he asserted the citizen's right not only to ignore and disobey but actively to resist the commands of unlawful authority. He proclaimed it "warrantable and glorious" for the people

> to disobey the civil powers in certain circumstances, and in cases of very great and general oppression, when humble remonstrances fail of having any effect; and, when the public welfare cannot be otherwise provided for and secured, to rise unanimously even against the sovereign himself, in order to redress their grievances; to vindicate their natural and legal rights; to break the yoke of tyranny, and free themselves and posterity from inglorious servitude and ruin.[58]

To Mayhew's practical way of thinking there were two kinds of tyranny that might evoke resistance:

> We may very safely assert these two things in general, without undermining government: One is, that no civil rulers are to be obeyed when they enjoin things that are inconsistent with the commands of God. All such disobedience is lawful and glorious; particularly if persons refuse to comply with any *legal establishment of religion.* . . . Another thing that may be asserted with equal truth and safety is, that no government is to be submitted to at the expense of that which is the sole end of all government— the common good and safety of society.[59]

Mayhew agreed heartily with two of the most venerable refinements of the right of resistance—that in those cases in which resistance is justified it is not only a right but a duty, and that the real rebels are the tyrants who have violated their mandate, not the people who are bound to resist them.

> If it be our duty, for example, to obey our king merely for this reason, that he rules for the public welfare . . . it follows, by a parity of reason, that when he turns tyrant, and makes his subjects his prey to devour and destroy, instead of his charge to defend and cherish, we are bound to throw off our allegiance to him, and to resist. . . . Not to discontinue our allegiance in this case would be to join with the sovereign in promoting the slavery and misery of that society, the welfare of which we ourselves, as well as our sovereign, are indispensably obliged to secure and promote, as far as in us lies. . . .
>
> The king is as much bound by his oath not to infringe the legal rights of the people as the people are bound to yield subjection to him. From whence it follows, that as soon as the prince sets himself up above law, he loses the king in the tyrant. He does, to all intents and purposes, unking himself by acting out of and beyond that sphere which the constitution allows him to move in; and in such cases he has no more right to be obeyed than any inferior officer who acts beyond his commission. The subject's obligation to

allegiance then ceases, of course; and to resist him is no more rebellion than to resist any foreign invader.[60]

Mayhew is no more successful than Locke or Jefferson in being scientific about this unscientific theory, particularly in establishing the degree of illegality or despotism that would call for unpremeditated resistance or concerted revolution. The abuse must be real and "habitual," and arouse a virtually "unanimous" will to resist. Actually, there is little danger that the people will embark on open resistance for trifling causes, for "mankind in general have a disposition to be as submissive and passive and tame under government as they ought to be." [61] In the words that Jefferson borrowed from Locke, a "long train of abuses" is necessary both to incite and to justify active rebellion. In his sermon of 1750 Mayhew did precisely what Jefferson was to do twenty-six years later in the Declaration of Independence: He listed specifically, without too fine a regard for historical truth, the "repeated injuries and usurpations" of the monarch against whom he was affirming the necessity of revolution.[62]

In the end, of course, the people alone could decide on the necessity for resistance, subject only to the opinion of mankind and the judgment of God. Mayhew defended stoutly the capacity of the people to do the correct and natural thing that circumstance might dictate—obey gladly, submit sullenly, resist passively, or revolt violently.

> To say that subjects in general are not proper judges when their governors oppress them and play the tyrant, and when they defend their rights, administer justice impartially, and promote the public welfare, is as great treason as ever man uttered. 'Tis treason, not against one *single* man, but the state—against the whole body politic; 'tis treason against mankind, 'tis treason against common sense, 'tis treason against God. And this impious principle lays the foundation for justifying all the tyranny and oppression that ever any prince was guilty of. The people know for what end they set up and maintain their governors, and they are the proper judges when they execute their trust as they ought to do it.[63]

It is hardly necessary to point out that Mayhew added very little to the great body of political theory. By 1750 the right of resistance or revolution was heavy with age and respectability. Essentially medieval in origin, it had been strengthened and refined by a host of theorists and men of action—Aquinas, Knox, the Huguenots, Buchanan, Mariana, Althusius, and finally Milton and Locke—until it was available and acceptable to any person or community suffering under real or imagined oppression. Nevertheless, Mayhew's place is secure in the development of American political ideas. It was a remarkable accomplishment to have proclaimed a full quarter-century before the Declaration of Independence that a people "really oppressed in a great degree by their sovereign" had the right to have done with him. A thousand orators were to echo these words of Mayhew:

> For a nation thus abused to arise unanimously and resist their prince, even to the dethroning him, is not criminal, but a reasonable way of vindicating

their liberties and just rights: it is making use of the means, and the only means, which God has put into their power for mutual and self defence.[64]

"LIBERTY . . . THE DELIGHT OF THE WISE, GOOD AND BRAVE"

The fiduciary nature of governmental authority and the right of resistance to those who abuse it are the political principles for which Mayhew is best remembered. To these may be added a third major tenet, which rounds out the circle of his libertarian theory: the unbending belief in personal freedom and accountability that he called "private judgment" in religion and "liberty" in politics, and that we can recognize today as one of the first clear expressions of American individualism. Two passages from sermons delivered in the full vigor of his life will illustrate the intensity of his belief in individual freedom. In the dedication to a volume of eight sermons on *Christian Sobriety* preached to the young men of his church, Mayhew spoke of Cicero as a friend of liberty:

> And though he did not fall at last as a martyr directly for true religion; yet he fell as one of the most glorious advocates for LIBERTY, that the world ever saw: An honor next to that of suffering martyrdom for religion; and, in some sort, the same thing; true religion comprising in it the love of liberty, and of One's country; and the hatred of all tyranny and oppression.[65]

And in his sermon on the repeal of the Stamp Act he turned aside to make this autobiographical salute to liberty:

> If I may be indulged here in saying a few words more, respecting my notions of liberty in general, such as they are, it shall be as follows. Having been initiated, in youth, in the doctrines of civil liberty, as they were taught by such men as Plato, Demosthenes, Cicero and other renowned persons among the ancients; and such as Sidney and Milton, Locke and Hoadley, among the moderns, I liked them; they seemed rational. Having earlier still learned from the Holy Scriptures that wise, brave and virtuous men were always friends to liberty; that God gave the Israelites a king (or absolute monarch) in his anger, because they had not sense and virtue enough to like a free commonwealth, and to have himself for their king; that the Son of God came down from heaven to make us "free indeed," and that where the spirit of the Lord is, there is liberty; this made me conclude, that freedom was a great blessing. Having, also, from my childhood up, by the kind providence of my God, and the tender care of a good parent now at rest with Him, been educated to the love of liberty . . . I would not, I cannot now, though past middle age, relinquish the fair object of my youthful affections, Liberty . . . the delight of the wise, good and brave; the protectress of innocence from wrongs and oppression, the patroness of learning, arts, eloquence, virtue, rational loyalty, religion! [66]

Again we see the kinship in Mayhew's philosophy of things religious and political—of piety and patriotism, of private judgment and civil liberty, of impatience with speculating bishops and mistrust of overweening kings.

The teachings of Clarke and Locke fitted together neatly in his humanist mind. In his quest for truth in theology he stripped the savage husk of Puritanism with the knife of reason and revealed the latent fruit of private judgment. In his quest for sanity in politics he rejected the simple solutions of Stuart or Puritan authority and embraced with enthusiasm the momentous doctrine of natural rights.

The political and religious liberty that Mayhew preached had a boldly individualistic stamp to it. For him man was above all an individual, free to bring his own reason to the search for political truth and religious peace, accountable for his politics only to his fellow citizens and for his religion only to God. Society was necessary, natural, even beneficial; but it was all these things only when it liberated the powers of the people who composed it. Mayhew's American, like Mayhew himself, was impatient of pomp, privilege, and legalized inequality. Indeed, it is plain that in 1750 Mayhew had caught sight of "the American, this new man," whom Crèvecoeur and Tocqueville were to observe with wonder and Jefferson and Jackson to lead with pride.

Other aspects of Mayhew's political philosophy may be disposed of briefly. He may certainly be counted among the foremost colonial advocates of separation of church and state, and of religious toleration. He made clear his disapproval "of the ancient laws made in the colony, which bore hard on the members of the church of England," [67] and even recommended to the General Court that it consider "whether we have not some laws in force, hardly reconcilable with that religious liberty which we profess." He confessed to Hollis his deep distress that "bigotry in religious matters has far too much place among us; so much, as almost makes one ashamed of my country." [68] It would be asking too much of a dissenting minister of his time and place to criticize him for not extending the hand of friendship to Catholics [69] and for making such a fuss over the dangers of an Anglican invasion. Nevertheless, we may be sure that he was perfectly sincere when he wrote that "persecution and intolerance, are not only unjust, and criminal in the sight of God; but they also cramp, enfeeble, and diminish the state." [70]

He was an early and imaginative herald of the American Mission, of our own version of the concept of the chosen people. He believed that his own state and country held in trust for all nations a peculiar responsibility for the maintenance of political liberty. And he went even further in prophecy of America's destiny by proposing, in *The Snare Broken*, that Americans make ready to offer an asylum to the oppressed and, if ever called upon, to mount a rescue party for freedom in the mother country. Two passages from this great sermon are worth quoting in this regard. In his apostrophe to liberty, he ends with the hope:

> And if any miserable people on the continent or isles of Europe, after being weakened by luxury, debauchery, venality, intestine quarrels, or other vices, should, in the rude collisions, or now uncertain revolutions of kingdoms, be driven, in their extremity, to seek a safe retreat from slavery in some far distant climate, let them find, O let them find one in America

under thy brooding, sacred wings, where our oppressed fathers once found it, and we now enjoy it, by the favor of Him, whose service is the most glorious freedom!

And in almost the very next breath:

The great shock which was lately given to our liberties, may end in the confirmation and enlargement of them. As it is said, the stately oaks of the forest take the deeper root, extend their arms the farther, and exalt their venerable heads the higher, for being agitated by storms and tempests, provided they are not actually torn up, rent in pieces, or quite blasted by the lightning of heaven. And who knows, our liberties being thus established, but that on some future occasion, when the kingdoms of the earth are moved, and roughly dashed one against another by him that taketh up the isles as a very little thing, we, or our posterity, may even have the great felicity and honor to "save much people alive," and keep Britain herself from ruin.[71]

Concerning the emerging constitutional issues of the day Mayhew was not nearly so precise and emphatic as his lawyer friends. He assumed that there were limits to the power of Parliament to legislate for the colonies but never found it necessary to draw the line.[72] He has occasionally been cited as a prophet of judicial review, but the few hints of this doctrine in *The Snare Broken* are pale imitations of Otis's assault upon the writs of assistance. He was an early advocate of some sort of colonial union. One of the last messages from his patriot pen was a letter to Otis in which he urged the formation of committees of correspondence and a "communion of colonies."[73] Finally, Mayhew's plural devotion to the larger communities of which he was a member is an illustration of the three- or even four-fold patriotism of the eighteenth-century colonials. Passage on passage may be plucked from his political sermons to prove him a loyal American, a stout son of England, a zealous New Englander, and a man with abiding "faith in Massachusetts." To him, as to his friends, this confusion of loyalties was wholly natural.

"FOR THIS GREAT TRUTH HE BOLDLY LED THE VAN"

Such was the life, character, and teaching of the last of the great colonial preachers. How important a patriot leader he would have been in 1774-1776 we can only guess, for he died July 9, 1766, of "an obstinate nervous disorder in his Head."[74] We may be certain that he would have moved forward step by step with his political friends, for there is evidence enough in his sermons that he looked upon war and independence as justifiable techniques in the struggle for religious and political liberty. And we may be equally certain that he would have won a place, along with Otis, the Adamses, and Hancock, in the brightest galaxy of Revolutionary heroes. As it was, by 1775 his words and deeds were all but forgotten except by his friends. Just after Mayhew's death Edmund Quincy, jr., had expressed his sure hope that God would "send us other Mayhews, as we need them." [75] God sent them, more than enough of them, and the ironic result was to bury Mayhew in undeserved obscurity.

The importance of Mayhew for American political and intellectual history lies as much in what he represented as in what he did or said. First, with his career, and those of Chauncy and Cooper, we bid a sad but preordained farewell to the ancient glory of the Puritan ministry, to that precious band of men who, whether they fought for the future like Hooker or Wise or for the past like Cotton and the Mathers, were leaders of public thought and action as few American ministers have been since the Revolution. Second, Mayhew is easily the most striking representative of the dissenting preachers who from the 1740's onward proclaimed Locke and Sidney from their pulpits and prepared the mind of New England for the Revolution. Like most of these preachers he was a tireless sower of the ideas of English constitutionalism, in John Adams's opinion "a whig of the first magnitude." [76] And surely in his life and thought the tenacious American belief in the interdependence of religious and political freedom, of "democracy in church and state," reached its peak of conviction and candor.

In his own right, too, Mayhew may lay claim to a lasting place among our religious and political thinkers. What he lacked in profundity he redeemed in timing and intensity. It was a memorable achievement for a youthful Boston preacher to have advertised the right of resistance in 1750 and the essentials of Unitarianism in 1755. Even more significant and praiseworthy was his repeated emphasis on the right of private judgment and the use of reason in the solution of all personal and social problems. For this, after all, is the basic postulate of the American intellectual tradition, this optimistic, rationalistic, pragmatic, and ultimately democratic belief that "free examination is the way to truth." This is the rejection of the feudal past, of the right of king or bishop to proclaim dogma to the people, and the assertion of the American future, of the duty of the people to think for themselves.

> While Britain claim'd with laws our rights to lead,
> And faith was fetter'd by a bigot's creed.
> Then mental freedom first her power display'd,
> And called a MAYHEW to religion's aid.
> For this great truth he boldly led the van,
> *That private judgment was a right of man.*[77]

CHAPTER TEN

Richard Bland

THE institutions and values of American democracy are a rich inheritance to which all manner of men have contributed their lives and talents. Some of our most effective institutions and liberating values have been the gifts of men who were not democrats at all. Perhaps the most convincing evidence of this historical truth is the legacy of law and liberty willed to the new Republic by the men of the thirteen colonies. In our delight over discovering in early Virginia and New England a few lonely democrats born several centuries too soon, we have given them too much credit for the ultimate triumph of their splendid doctrines. Roger Williams, John Clarke, John Wise, and Nathaniel Bacon were prophets of freedom full worthy of veneration, but other men than these, men who had no truck with notions of social and political equality, were the real builders of the half-finished structure of liberty inherited by the Americans of 1776 and altered by their descendants to ever more democratic uses.

The provincial assembly of the eighteenth century was the workshop in which the colonists hammered out the tools of liberty. The Whig gentlemen who filled the benches in each assembly—and few of them thought of themselves as anything but Whigs—sought freedom and power for themselves only, displayed undisguised oligarchical tendencies, and certainly found nothing unjust in property qualifications that limited the suffrage to one man in four. Yet in their ceaseless, ill-tempered, often narrow-minded encroachments on the authority wielded by governor and council, they made use of institutions and arguments that were to prove readily convertible to democratic purposes. Their institutions were elective, representative, secular, constitutional, and limited by law; their arguments were framed in terms of "liberty" and "the people." If they knew not what they wrought, they nevertheless wrought well.

The key operator in the shift in the balance of political power in the eighteenth century was the representative in the lower house of the assembly—an aristocratic, liberty-loving, lawmaking moderate rather than a democratic, equality-seeking, stability-shattering leveler. Just such a man was Richard Bland of Virginia, for decades the most active member of America's oldest legislature. Whether in action in the House of Burgesses or in meditation in his library, he was the embodiment of a notable political way of life. His career and philosophy deserve more attention than they have hitherto received, for he was the very model of the American Whig.[1]

AN AMERICAN ARISTOCRAT

Richard Bland was an eighteenth-century Virginia aristocrat and was thus about as authentic an aristocrat as America has produced. Birth, inheritance, and training placed him at the topmost level of a stratified society. Character, intelligence, and performance kept him there throughout a long and useful life.

The Blands were one of Virginia's leading families, and as such were bound by ties of blood and affection to dozens of other leading families. The immigrant founder of the line was Theodorick Bland of Westover,[2] who came to Virginia from England in 1654 and prospered economically, politically, and socially until his death in 1671. Successful planter, eminent squire, Speaker of the House of Burgesses, and seven years a member of the Governor's Council, Theodorick Bland "was both in fortune and understanding inferior to no person of his time in the country." [3] His wife, Ann, daughter of Governor Richard Bennett, presented him with three sons who survived his untimely end.

The second of these, Richard Bland, Sr., was born at Berkeley in 1665 and died at Jordan's, Prince George County, in 1720, having sold the family lands at Westover to William Byrd I in 1688. He, too, was a public-spirited Virginia gentleman, serving in his time as burgess and justice of the peace of both Charles City and Prince George, vestryman of Bruton Parish, and visitor of the College of William and Mary.[4] After the death of his first wife and all their six children (a harsh reminder of the touch-and-go life led by even the "better sort" in colonial America), Bland married Elizabeth Randolph, daughter of William Randolph I of Turkey Island.

To them was born on May 6, 1710, the second Richard Bland, the subject of this chapter. His father a Bland, his mother a Randolph, his birthplace a large and successful plantation on the James, young Richard Bland was marked from birth for social and political leadership. His goodly inheritance, the estate at Jordan's, came to him earlier than he might have expected. Elizabeth Bland died in January 1720, her husband less than three months later. Young Richard, an orphan at nine and now master of Jordan's, was placed by his father's will in the guardianship of his eminent uncles, William and Richard Randolph.[5]

We know next to nothing of the quality of Bland's training and education, although the character and learning of the end-product are evidence enough that it was the best Virginia had to offer. From his father and uncles he learned to manage his affairs and serve his country; from his mother and the rector of Martin's Brandon he learned the rudiments; from a succession of roving tutors, or perhaps like his father at a small private school, he got a good enough classical education to gain admission to William and Mary; and from the president and six professors of the college he acquired the training in rhetoric, science, mathematics, and classical studies that launched him on his career as one of the most learned men in colonial Virginia. It has been repeatedly asserted that Bland's course at William and Mary was topped off by residence at the University of Edinburgh, but there is no evidence in the records to support this belief.

Self-education must have been a particularly important ingredient in Bland's training, as indeed it was in that of any man of his time who was eager for knowledge and alert to the deficiencies in the bare-bones system of formal education. He taught himself enough law to qualify for admittance to practice in 1746 and enough history to become a notable collector of old Virginia documents. John Adams of Massachusetts, a man who knew what he was talking about in such matters, described Bland in his diary as "a learned, bookish man," [6] and at the end of his own life Washington remembered him as "a man of erudition and intelligence." [7] Bland could learn from experience as well as from his library: He acquired much more liberal views than did many of his fellow planters on the questions of paper currency [8] and slavery. We have Jefferson's testimony on the latter issue:

> In the first or second session of the Legislature after I became a member, I drew to this subject the attention of Col. Bland, one of the oldest, ablest, & most respected members, and he undertook to move for certain moderate extensions of the protection of the laws to these people. I seconded his motion, and, as a younger member, was more spared in the debate; but he was denounced as an enemy of his country, & was treated with the grossest indecorum. [9]

Eighteenth-century Virginia was a land of status and stratification, but it was also one of opportunity, adventure, and increasing mobility. A man, if his skin was white, could rise in his lifetime from the lowest to the highest class; conversely, he could enter the world at the top and leave it a financial wreck and social cipher. Though birth, inheritance, and training were all in Bland's favor, they by no means guaranteed him a permanent grip on the top rung of the ladder. That he died as well as he was born—leaving rich lands, thirty Negroes, large herds of livestock, a fine library, and an unrivaled reputation—was a reasonably stiff measure of his character, ability, and intelligence.

Again we must acknowledge that we know a good deal less of Bland than we should like to know. If this chapter had set out to portray a representative Virginian in the role of planter or family man or soldier, it would have passed over Bland and seized upon any one of a dozen men about whose private lives and characters we have considerable documentary information.

Since our concern is with the political beliefs and attitudes of the Virginian, and since Bland was the most articulate political thinker active in the years before Jefferson, the Lees, and Mason, we must give what substance we can to his shadowy figure. The extant records, never especially satisfactory for the Southern colonies, are in this instance distressingly spare. The total number of private and public letters we can assign to Bland is exactly ten. The colonial records of his parish, Martin's Brandon, have vanished completely.[10] Most of his library and collection of old documents, which were purchased after his death by Jefferson, went up in the fire that gutted the Library of Congress in 1851. The surviving records of his county, Prince George, consist of one order book (1714-1720), one minute book (1737-1740), one book of deeds (1713-1729), and one of land entries. And every scholar in colonial history is sadly aware of the huge gaps in the files of the *Virginia Gazette* for the years when it must have carried news and letters of Bland. Even his portrait has been lost to posterity, slashed by British soldiers in 1781 and quite possibly carried off by one of Ben Butler's boys in 1864.

From scattered sources comes our knowledge of Bland's character. He was honorable, capable, dependable, public-spirited. He seems to have been more eloquent with pen than in debate, and indeed was often so intent upon the business at hand as to have experienced difficulty speaking out. On occasion he could show himself to be thoroughly human, for example, as a behind-the-scenes politician and a careless borrower of books.[11] He was not overly ambitious[12] and cared not in the least for show. A Virginia historian writes, "In personality Bland was of that type of Virginian which is best illustrated by the figure of George Mason, that type considered characteristically Virginian,—half practical farmer, half classical scholar and lawyer; genial, well-mannered, personally somewhat untidy and careless of clothes."[13]

Certainly he was a man whom no one could afford to treat lightly, for the pages of the only surviving minute book of Prince George County Court are full of litigations involving "Richard Bland, Gent."[14] And in a letter to a friend in England he could give a vinegary account of the rise and character of one of his godly adversaries.[15] Although spare of build he must have enjoyed good health and have had energy to burn. The records of the House of Burgesses show him to have been a faithful attendant and a horse for work. Moreover, he had three wives and twelve children, which is better than average for learned, bookish men. His wives were Anne Poythress, the mother of all twelve children; Martha Macon, widow of William Massie; and Elizabeth Blair, daughter of John Blair and widow of John Bolling.[16]

Bland's learning was apparently matched by his sense of fair play and clarity of mind. In a letter of Jerman Baker to Duncan Rose, dated February 16, 1764, appears this neat compliment to his intelligence:

Indeed you may remember that in Virginia I was constantly amongst the Enemies to a paper Currency, and expressed myself often so warmly on that subject as to bring upon myself some warm altercation with many Blockheads, & some men of Senses among the latter I recon Col⁰. R. Bland.[17]

Roger Atkinson wrote of Bland in 1774 that he was

a very old experienced veteran at ye Senate or ye Bar—staunch & tough as Whitleather—has something of ye look of musty old Parchen'ts w'ch he handleth & studieth much.[18]

Taken all in all, Bland seems to have been an admirable representative of the Virginia aristocracy. Messrs. Dixon and Hunter were probably not far from the truth when they saluted his death with this terse but warm accolade:

In short, he possessed all the inestimable qualifications that could render him dear to society—all that could form the virtuous upright man.[19]

THE MODEL BURGESS

Bland's performance as public figure was equaled by few and surpassed by no Virginians of the mid-eighteenth century. The dazzling exploits of Washington, Henry, Jefferson, R. H. Lee, Mason, and other great Virginians of the Revolution have all but wiped out the memory of Bland and his contemporaries, the men who came to power two or three decades before the Stamp Act and who, in their own way and time, did their share to prepare the colonies for ultimate freedom. A brief review of Bland's public life will therefore serve us doubly: It will provide a solid background against which to project and study his political ideas, and it will remind us that there were brave men before Washington, freedom-loving men before Jefferson, and irritating men before Henry.

The business of governing men occupied Bland's energies from his coming of age until his sudden death in Williamsburg October 26, 1776. At each of the three levels of Virginia government he filled the office that was his both as matter of right and as reward of ability: vestryman of his parish, Martin's Brandon; [20] justice of the peace of his county, Prince George; [21] and for more than thirty years (1742-1775) one of the two burgesses representing Prince George in the lower house of the Virginia Assembly. His hold on the reins of Prince George politics must have been especially tight. In 1745 Bland accepted an unidentified "Place of Profit," whereupon the Assembly asked the governor, as was routine in such cases, to issue a writ of election for a burgess to serve in his stead. The electors of Prince George promptly re-elected Richard Bland.[22] And for one five-year period, 1761-1765, the delegation from Prince George was Richard Bland and Richard Bland, jr.

He was commissioned in the county militia in 1739 [23] and in due season gained the expected rank of colonel. In the events leading to the Revolution he served, as we shall see, in a dozen or more positions of trust and honor.

For years he was, like his father before him, a visitor of William and Mary.[24] And through all these decades he devoted a good part of his time to the private pursuits of the landed aristocrat: keeping his plantation a going concern; speculating, like all men of his rank and age, in western lands;[25] and engaging in small enterprises (such as contracting to make improvements in the church of a neighboring parish)[26] to help reduce the debts that even a levelheaded planter could run up with his London agents.

Bland was one of the busiest and most important members of the House of Burgesses. He was especially in demand as historian, parliamentarian, and draftsman. Hugh Blair Grigsby had this to say of him:

> His great learning lay in the field of British history in its largest sense; and especially in that of Virginia. With all her ancient charters, and with her acts of Assembly in passing which for nearly the third of a century he had a voice, he was familiar; and in this department he may be said to have stood supreme. What John Selden was in the beginning of the troubles in the reign of Charles the first to the House of Commons, was Richard Bland to the House of Burgesses for thirty years during which he was a member. During that time on all questions touching the rights and privileges of the Colony he was the undoubted and truthful oracle.[27]

In all colonies, nowhere more purposefully than in Virginia, the assembly tried to place the execution of as many laws as possible in the hands of its own members, acting as individuals or in groups. The reasons for this common practice should be easy to understand: Government was simple and had little use for the specialist; the doctrine of the separation of powers had not yet become an article of blind faith; and this was a splendid device for keeping power out of the hands of the royal governor and his lieutenants. A random listing of some of Bland's varied services indicates the extent of this practice as well as the nature and scope of governmental activity in a world far simpler than any we could possibly imagine. It indicates, too, the confidence placed in Bland by his fellow burgesses.

These were some of the executive tasks for which Bland was singled out:[28] to act as commissioner for Virginia's Indian trade; to serve on a delegation to meet with envoys of other colonies to discuss the Indian trade; to settle the accounts of claimants suffering losses of tobacco in the burning of a public warehouse; to value a glebe; to act as trustee of "docked" lands; to direct the spending of £10,000 "for the encouragement and protection of the settlers upon the waters of the Mississippi"; to contract for the deportation of undesirable aliens (neutral French!); to spend a sizable sum for "the improving of arts and manufactures" in Virginia; to manage an official lottery to raise funds for improving navigation on the Potomac; and to perform a number of tasks vital to the prosecution of the French and Indian War.

Bland was for years the man whose constant attendance was most necessary to keep the legislative machinery of Virginia's government in motion. The records of the House of Burgesses are full of Richard Bland. From his first days as burgess he was drafting and reporting bills that dealt with such important subjects as taxation, proceedings of the county courts, distribution of estates of persons dying insolvent, currency adjustment, and revision of the laws; [29] acting as one of the managers of the lower house in conference with the Council; [30] and generally serving as the workhorse of a body not always given to hard and painstaking work. Later, at the height of his career, he was chairman and reporter of each of the chief committees through which the house did its business: Privileges and Elections, Propositions and Grievances, and Public Claims. In several sessions he sat—the only man to do so—on all three committees, as chairman of one and senior member of the other two. [31]

The house piled other work on him, apparently without compunction. It called on him again and again to help draw up an address to the Governor or the King (or to that soldier of the King, Jeffrey Amherst), sent him to act as its go-between in its dealings with Council and Governor, rarely if ever left him off the important special committees to examine enrolled bills and inspect the Treasurer's accounts, set him to testing the claims of several "quacks," and for years entrusted him alone with the delicate business of drafting the bill "for paying the Burgesses Wages in Money, for this present Session." [32] No job was too big or little for Bland to tackle. In his last years he held the vital post of chairman of the committee of the whole house, yet he also found time to draft and present "a Bill, To prevent Hogs running at Large in the Town of Port Royal" and "a Bill for destroying Crows and Squirrels in the County of Accomack." [33] Finally, he served almost as a matter of course on *ad hoc* committees of the House of Burgesses set up to meet such crises in the life of the colony as the posthumously discovered defalcation of Treasurer John Robinson, the prosecution of a member of the Council for offending the honor of the House of Burgesses, and the battles over the Two-Penny Act and the Stamp Act. [34]

Bland's record as burgess has been spread upon these pages for two good reasons: first, because it was a microcosm of political life in eighteenth-century America; second, because there could be no more convincing evidence of his integrity, learning, sense of duty, assiduity, and prominence. If he was the model of a colonial legislator, it was the very finest model. [35]

A TAX AND A WAR

Bland was a thoroughly committed participant in at least six incidents or controversies in the course of his career: the affair of the Pistole Fee (1753-1755), the French and Indian War, the storm over the Two-Penny Act (1758-1764), the fight against the establishment of an American episcopate (1771), the Stamp Act crisis (1764-1766), and the series of events that led Virginia to rebellion and independence. In each of these episodes his pen was active, expressing a body of principles and prejudices that was in outline and detail the guiding political faith of the men who ruled eighteenth-century Virginia.

The affair of the Pistole Fee was a minor incident in the course of colonial politics, yet it was just this sort of "minor incident" that spurred the growth of an independent American spirit.[36] Shortly after his arrival in Virginia, Governor Dinwiddie decided to put a stop to the loose methods of granting lands which had been allowed to develop over the years. To this end he issued orders that no land was to be granted except by patent, the fee for which was set at one pistole (about $3.60 in Virginia). In this action, which came at the end of a session and took the House of Burgesses completely by surprise, Dinwiddie had the consent of the Council. Since more than a thousand patents were ready for issue, and since several thousand more would now have to be sought for lands already held under warrant of survey, the Governor was set to reap a bountiful harvest. So, too, was the Crown, for Dinwiddie was determined to collect back quit-rents on lands obtained by warrant of survey and not subsequently patented.

When the Assembly reconvened for its next session several months later, a storm of protest broke on Dinwiddie's viceregal head. From six frontier counties, one of them just named Dinwiddie in the new Governor's honor, came petitions against the fee, whereupon the lower house, in an unusual display of the new colonial temperament, asked the Governor "to acquaint us with the Authority that impowers you to demand" this "extraordinary Fee." The Governor's reply, which in effect informed the burgesses that it was none of their business, was met by this Whiggish rejoinder:

We do humbly, but in the strongest Terms, represent to your Honour, that it is the undoubted Right of the Burgesses to enquire into the Grievances of the People: They have constantly exercised this Right, and we presume to affirm, that the drawing it into Question, in any Manner, cannot but be of dangerous Consequence to the Liberties of his Majesty's faithful Subjects, and to the Constitution of this Government.

The Rights of the Subject are so secured by Law, that they cannot be deprived of the least Part of their Property, but by their own Consent: Upon this excellent Principle is our Constitution founded, and ever since this Colony has had the Happiness of being under the immediate Protection of the Crown, the Royal Declarations have been, "That no Man's Life, Member, Freehold or Goods, be taken away or harmed, but by established and known Laws."

But the Demand of a Pistole, as a Fee for the Use of the Public Seal, being not warranted by any known and established Law, is, we humbly conceive, an Infringement of the Rights of the People, and a Greivance highly to be complained of.[37]

Again the Governor stuck to the letter of the law as read in England—that grants of land were "a Matter of Favour from the Crown, and not a Matter relative to the Administration of Government"—and again the house used phrases that smacked of Pym and Hampden:

Resolved, That the said Demand is illegal and arbitrary, contrary to the Charters of this Colony, to his Majesty's, and his Royal Predecessors Instructions to the several Governors, and the Express Order of his Majesty King William of Glorious Memory, in his Privy-Council, and manifestly tends to the subverting the Laws and Constitution of this Government.

Resolved, That whoever shall hereafter pay a Pistole, as a Fee to the Governor, for the Use of the Seal to Patent for Lands, shall be deemed a Betrayer of the Rights and Privileges of the People.[38]

The unexpected vigor of these resolutions led Dinwiddie to make sour comments to his private correspondents about "republican Principles." He could hardly have realized how good a seer he was, for this whole affair—with its confusion of rights and wrongs and its cast of overbearing royal agents and oversensitive colonials—was a prophetic miniature of things to come.

The House of Burgesses sent Attorney General Peyton Randolph to London with authority to prosecute an appeal to the Crown, as well as to hire a permanent agent to represent the colony's interests as understood by the colonists. The end result of the usual complicated maneuvering in the Privy Council and Board of Trade was a compromise that sustained Dinwiddie in principle but set important limits to the use of the fee. Since the burgesses, if not the petitioning settlers, were primarily concerned with the principle rather than the amount of the fee—which they insisted on regarding as a tax—the real issue was left for the future to resolve.

Bland was a key participant in this squabble, thanks to his pen, his knowledge of land tenures and charters, and his concern for Virginia's liberties. He sat on each of the committees created to study the problem and draw up resolves and addresses; he acted as one of the managers of the proceedings in the house; and he composed a piece, *A Modest and True State of the Case,* a fragment of which is the only surviving example of public comment on this issue.[39] A comparison of the official addresses and resolutions with Bland's arguments leaves little doubt of the identity of the chief penman for the burgesses. His arguments for the inseparability of taxation and representation and for the peculiar competency of the legislative power were Whiggish to the core.

Bland was a strong supporter of Virginia's exertions in the great war with the French for North America. In a political-military situation marked by extravagant contrasts of conduct—heroism and cowardice, highmindedness and pettifogging, selfless patriotism and feckless provincialism—Bland proved himself one of the most resolute, generous-spirited members of the House of Burgesses. He was chosen along with such stalwarts as John Robinson, Charles Carter, George Wythe, and Peyton Randolph to serve on a series of extraordinary committees to spend the sums appropriated for the defense of the colony.[40] He acted as commissioner for Indian trade in a broadly conceived scheme to lure untrustworthy tribes into friendship or at least benevolent neutrality. When ticklish occasions arose, such as the necessity to appoint committees to settle the accounts of the militia, his known integrity made him a certain choice. And when more pleasant duties beckoned, such as waiting upon a hero like Captain Robert Stobo with the thanks of the House of Burgesses, Bland joined George Washington, Richard Henry Lee, and Robert Carter Nicholas in a delegation that must have flavored gratitude with the salt of manly charm.

He acted as chief draftsman of statutes like "the Act for the better Regulating of the Militia," various levies of money "for the Protection of his Majesty's Subjects in this Colony, against the Insults and Encroachments of the French," and "an Act for the Defense of the Frontiers of this Colony." [41] When the lower house stopped battling Dinwiddie long enough to call his attention to a need upon which all could for once agree (a guard for the magazine at Williamsburg),[42] Bland seemed just the right man to wait upon the governor—which he did with success.

Finally, Bland had a good deal of active contact with the forces in the field. He was one of a five-man committee appointed "to enquire into the Conduct of the Officers and Men lately sent out upon an Expedition" that had turned out a miserable failure. Never too busy to see a small task left undone, he headed another committee to determine whether an Indian fighter was entitled to a reward for having "killed and scalped four *Shawnese Indians* in *Augusta*." As "Lieutenant of the County of Prince George" he armed "the Men draughted out of that County, at his own Expence," later being repaid to the penny.[43] And on the occasion of the notorious newspaper attack launched against Washington and the Virginia regiment ("The Virginia Centinel, No. X"),[44] Bland stood forth as an eloquent defender of the unhappy young colonel and his sorely taxed officers and men. He had foreseen such an attack and had previously written Washington:

> As I have some tho'ts of writing an account of our transactions which I desire to communicate to public view in order to wipe off all reflections from my country and the several persons concerned in the conduct of our military enterprizes so far as they can be justified, I shall take it as a particular mark of friendship if at your leisure hours, if you have any, you would send me short heads of such things relative to the French invasion with the dates when they happened as you judge most interesting and proper for such a work. I will speak the truth with boldness, and I hope with approbation from every honest and good man, amongst whom I assure you without flattery, I place you in the first rank.[45]

Bland apparently made good his promise, for in Washington's papers there is a hard-hitting rejoinder to the "Virginia Centinel," endorsed in Washington's hand as "written, it is supposed, by Col° Rich⁴ Bland, 1756." [46] Internal evidence leaves small room for doubt that Bland was the author of this piece and that it appeared in one of the lost issues of the *Virginia Gazette*. In this writing, as in all his actions during this trying period, Bland showed himself an advocate of unstinted measures at home and on the frontier.

PARSONS AND BISHOPS

Historical interest in the Two-Penny Act centers today in the "Parsons' Cause," the occasion for Patrick Henry's first bold appearance in colonial politics. Yet this affair had more significance than as the debut of any one man, even Patrick Henry, and it had other participants than the fiery Hanoverian. The facts of the episode make clear that it was yet another strain upon "the bond between the King and the colonists, and was the prelude to the great contest which snapped that bond asunder." [47]

In 1758, because of a sharp rise in the price of tobacco, the Assembly passed and the Governor approved a law, to be in force one year, permitting debts, contracts, levies, rents, and fees due in tobacco to be paid either in that staple or "in money, at the rate of sixteen shillings and eight pence for every hundred pounds of nett tobacco." [48] The price of tobacco was on the way up to six pence per pound, and the Assembly, in reducing its value as a circulating medium to the normal two pence per pound, was making a reasonably sincere attempt to prevent creditors and salaried persons "from taking advantage of the necessities of the people." Although the law was general in provision, the ministers of the established church were the only colonial claimants to raise an outcry. For generations their yearly pay had been sixteen thousand pounds of tobacco. This sum had been fixed by law as recently as 1748, and they liked not at all to be deprived of the pleasure of having their salaries tripled by the circumstances of war, speculation, and a bad crop.

Royal instructions insisted categorically that no law approved by the King could be repealed by a colonial assembly unless the repealing law contained a suspending clause. The purpose of such a clause was to delay the execution of the repealing law until the King's pleasure could be made known. Seizing upon the notorious fact that the Two-Penny Act had incorporated no suspending clause, the clergy attacked it as not only unjust but unconstitutional. Rev. John Camm of York-Hampton Parish went to England in behalf of the clergy in 1759 and there obtained an order of the Privy Council disallowing the Two-Penny Act. [49] Neither Camm nor any other minister ever got much satisfaction from his vestry. Camm's suit to recover the full market-value of his salary was kicked about for years by the stubborn Virginia courts and was finally dismissed on a technicality in 1767 by a calculating Privy Council. The suits of other ministers were being given much the same treatment in Virginia when Henry's eloquence and the jury's award of one penny to Rev. James Maury in Hanover County (December 1762) ended the contest in a rout of the clergy.

There can be no question that the heat of this controversy quickened the self-governing urges of the ruling Virginians. By no means were the members of the clergy entirely in the wrong, for they, too, had been hit hard by inflation. Moreover, the Assembly seemed to recognize no limits to its capacity to tamper with these salaries. The Assembly had begun to appear in exactly the same unfavorable light as the vestry: Each in its own way was claiming supremacy for the state over the church. Yet the shortsighted manner in which the clergy cut themselves loose completely from all other groups in Virginia and appealed for relief to the royal prerogative did much to weaken the control of the mother country in political as well as ecclesiastical affairs. In any event, we can agree with a Virginia historian that "the conflict was probably inevitable on account of the incongruousness of a church establishment dependent, in a final sense, upon a foreign and monarchical power, in a state every day growing more republican and more self-conscious." [50]

Henry's burst of eloquence has deprived Bland of the recognition due him as champion of the popular cause. In fact, the records would seem to show that Bland was the chief instigator of the whole affair. A petition of the inhabitants of Prince George County first called attention to the need for action, and Bland was what later and less polite generations would have labeled the Ed Flynn of Prince George County. He then acted as a committee of one in preparing a bill to meet "the Prayer of the said Petition" and saw it to successful enactment by Assembly and Governor. [51] A committee of correspondence was set up by the two houses in February 1759. [52] The business of this committee, of which Bland was a faithful member from its beginning in 1759 to its decline in 1770, was to correspond generally with an agent chosen to "represent the affairs of this colony" in London, but the clergy's appeal to the Privy Council to void the Two-Penny Act was the prime cause of its creation. The committee served the colony faithfully as an instrument of Virginia autonomy and reminded all Englishmen (who had eyes to see) that the people of Virginia had interests peculiarly their own.

When members of the clergy, taking heart from a letter of the Bishop of London to the Board of Trade recommending that the Two-Penny Act be voided, [53] attacked the act in public print, Bland became the chief pamphleteer for the popular cause. Three of his writings, *A Letter to the Clergy of Virginia* (1760), a letter printed in the *Virginia Gazette*, October 28, 1763, and *The Colonel Dismounted* (1764), [54] state all the arguments—factual, historical, political, ecclesiastical, and constitutional—for the Assembly's point of view. *The Colonel Dismounted* was a first-rate performance, combining as it did a satirical attack on Camm under pretense of defending him and a line of argument for colonial self-rule unprecedented for the time and place of publication.

The strength and unanimity of popular reaction to the tactics of the clergy in the Two-Penny affair convinced most Virginia ministers that they would do well to swim with the tide of colonial autonomy. As a result, the campaign of the Anglican clergy in the Northern colonies for an American episcopate found surprisingly little clerical support in Virginia. The one direct attempt was made in 1771 by a splinter group led by Commissary James Horrocks and the irrepressible John Camm, which met in Williamsburg in June and resolved somewhat lamely to petition the King for an episcopate. [55] Bland, who had been accused by spokesmen for the clergy of bringing all Virginia to a high "pitch of insolence" with his tracts on the Two-Penny Act, [56] was ready once again to help the popular cause. Two Anglican ministers from the faculty at William and Mary, Samuel Henley and Thomas Gwatkin, wrote so convincingly against any such scheme that Bland and other veterans of battles with the clergy could afford to stand at ease.[57] It is altogether possible that Bland did write a pamphlet on this issue that has since been lost.[58] The evidence of his standing among the opponents of the episcopate is to be found in a modest but firm letter to Thomas Adams in London (August 1, 1771),[59] some bitter remarks by Camm during the debate in Dixon and Hunter's *Virginia Gazette*, and the unanimous resolution of the House of Burgesses (July 12, 1771), which called on Bland and R. H. Lee to thank the anti-episcopal clergymen for their "wise and well-timed Opposition" to a project "by which much Disturbance, great Anxiety and Apprehension, would certainly take Place among his Majesty's faithful American Subjects." [60]

In the letter to Adams appears a statement by Bland that captures almost perfectly the blend of secularism, independence, dislike of old-world pomp, and yet simple faith that marked the attitude toward religion of the Virginia gentleman, of the dutiful squire who had led many services in the absence of the parish minister.

> I profess my self a sincere Son of the Established Church; but I can embrace her Doctrines without approving of her Hierarchy, which I know to be a Relick of the Papal Incroachments upon the Common Law.[61]

The plan for an American episcopate could not possibly have succeeded in these troubled times. The self-governing Virginians had got in the habit of controlling their church, and, as Bland made plain in his letter to Adams, the imposition of a bishop would have abrogated most of the statutes regulating ecclesiastical affairs. In his opposition to any sort of hierarchy, Bland, an Anglican to the bone, was acting out of political rather than religious principle.

STAMP ACT AND REVOLUTION

The Stamp Act roused Bland to his best literary effort, *An Inquiry into the Rights of the British Colonies*.[62] Once again his urge to pamphleteer came at the end of a train of public events in which he was an active participant. From the arrival of the shocking news of Parliament's mind to tax the colonies until the last drunken huzzah for the repeal of the Stamp Act, Bland was at the storm center of Virginia politics.[63] For the first time in his career he was associated with men who were more willing than he to break a lance with champions of prerogative and imperial power. A new breed, personified by that "Pillar of Fire" Patrick Henry, was coming to prominence in Virginia, and Bland was to be known in his last ten years as a warm but conservative friend to liberty.

In June 1764, immediately upon receiving news of Parliament's intentions, the committee of correspondence drafted a letter to their agent in London calling upon him to lobby against any sort of stamp tax.[64] The first reaction of the House of Burgesses, which came together October 30, was to appoint a committee of eight to draw up an address to the King and memorials to Lords and Commons. The committee was established November 14; six days later, as if to get it moving, Bland was added; and on December 18, after considerable give-and-take between the two houses, the General Assembly adopted an address and two memorials politely but manfully informing King and Parliament that they had no right to lay taxes upon a people unrepresented in the taxing legislature.[65] The authorship of these protests has never been conclusively fixed. Bland, R. H. Lee, Wythe, Carter, Pendleton, and Peyton Randolph have all received primary credit for one or more of them.[66]

An obstinate King, ministry, and Parliament were only hardened in their purpose by colonial lectures on the British Constitution. The news that the Stamp Act had become a reality was the call to arms for Patrick Henry and the rising radical party. Bland's position in the session of May 1765 was that of the prudent conservative. Jefferson was later to write of the passage of the Stamp Act resolutions:

> The famous stamp act was, however, past in Jan., 1765 and in the session of the Virgi assembly of May following, mr. Henry introduced the celebrated resolns of that date. These were drawn by George Johnson, a lawyer of the Northern neck, a very able, logical and correct speaker. Mr. Henry moved and Johnston seconded these resolns successively. They were opposed by Randolph, Bland, Pendleton, Nicholas, Wythe & all the old members whose influence in the house had till then been unbroken. They did it, not from any question of our rights, but on the ground that the same sentiments had been at their preceding session expressed in a more conciliatory form to which the answers were not yet received. But torrents of sublime eloquence from mr Henry, backed up by the solid reasoning of Johnston prevailed. The last however, & strongest resoln was carried but by a single vote. The debate on it was most bloody.[67]

This would seem a fair representation of Bland's motives for opposing this sudden salvo. He could agree wholeheartedly with Henry's resolves, even those which were rejected, for he had said no less about the rights of the colonists in his attack on the Pistole Fee and defense of the Two-Penny Act. But he was getting older, and Henry was a man he could not quite understand; and so he could take the position that these were very poor tactics. We know nothing of Bland's part in Virginia's out-of-doors protest against the arrival of the stamps, although we can be sure he had no intention of ever using stamped paper.

In March 1766, two months before the colony would know of the repeal of the Stamp Act, Bland's *Inquiry* was published by Alexander Purdie in Williamsburg.[68] It was reprinted twice in London in 1769, in the *Political Register* and in a separate edition by John Almon, and seems to have won a wide and thoughtful audience. Purdie and Dixon's *Gazette* printed a letter from London dated April 25, 1769, which said:

> I assure you no argument or pains have been omitted by the Agents for the colonies; they have taken their instructions from the best writers: If the Parliament will not hear BLAND and DICKENSON, neither will they be persuaded if one rose from the dead.[69]

This comment attests the importance attached by Virginians to Bland's pamphlet and at the same time explains why it has never since received much attention. Dickinson's "Letters from a Farmer in Pennsylvania," which appeared in all but three or four American newspapers in late 1767 and early 1768, were from the moment of their publication the scripture of the colonists. Bland was not the only political author forgotten by the colonists in their wild scramble to offer devotion to Dickinson and his finespun legalities. In this regard it is interesting to hear what Jefferson had to say to William Wirt fifty years later:

> Your characters are inimitably and justly drawn. I am not certain if more might not be said of Colonel Richard Bland. He was the most learned and logical man of those who took prominent lead in public affairs, profound in constitutional lore, a most ungraceful speaker, (as were Peyton Randolph and Robinson, in a remarkable degree.) He wrote the first pamphlet on the nature of the connection with Great Britain which had any pretension to accuracy of view on that subject, but it was a singular one. He would set out on sound principles, pursue them logically till he found them leading to the precipice which he had to leap, start back alarmed, then resume his ground, go over it in another direction, be led again by the correctness of his reasoning to the same place, and again back about, and try other processes to reconcile right and wrong, but finally left his reader and himself bewildered between the steady index of the compass in their hand, and the phantasm to which it seemed to point. Still there was more sound matter in his pamphlet than in the celebrated Farmers' letters, which were really but an *ignis fatuus,* misleading us from true principles.[70]

Jefferson's criticism had a good deal of truth in it but was not altogether fair to Bland. If Jefferson meant, as he probably did mean, that the analysis of the power of Parliament in his own *Summary View of the Rights of British America* was more precise and bold than that worked out by Bland, he was unquestionably corect. But when we remember that Jefferson wrote his tract in 1774 with earlier efforts like the *Inquiry* to steer by,[71] and in a time of far less concern for English sensibilities, we may excuse Bland for some of the backing and filling that dismayed Jefferson. In any case, in 1766 Bland's pamphlet was acclaimed by the popular party as the finest piece of political writing to have come out of Virginia. Nor were local partiots unaware that Bland was occupying high ground. Said the Sons of Liberty in Norfolk in a resolution of thanks to Bland:

> When the LIBERTY of a State is in Danger, the Man surely deserves well of his Country, who is instrumental in removing the impending Evil; but as the Means are various, we believe none preferable to reasonable Conviction.[72]

Bland in return saluted the Sons of Liberty for having championed "the glorious Cause of LIBERTY" against "the detestable Stamp-Act," and spoke eloquently of the "lasting Monuments of their patriotic Spirit and Love of Country."

Bland's part in the events leading to independence was of a piece with his actions in the Stamp Act crisis. He was handed a dozen difficult jobs and did all of them well; he remained a constant friend to the patriotic cause; but he showed his age and his inability to keep pace with the radicals by counseling conservatism at several critical junctures.[73]

With the repeal of the Stamp Act Virginia politics settled back into the usual routine. The next step toward ultimate independence was taken in 1768 upon arrival of news of the Townshend Acts. Again the bolder counties petitioned the House of Burgesses, and again the lower house decided to speak directly to the sovereign authorities at home. Bland was the key figure at every step of this new protest against arbitrary power. He chaired the committee of eleven set up to address King and Parliament; he wrote all three messages, reshaping in his own words the arguments of the past decade; and he succeeded in persuading the Council to go along with the memorials as reported to the lower house.[74]

These protests, of course, were given exactly the same ice-cold reception in England as those of 1764. When the newly arrived Governor, Lord Botetourt, dissolved the Assembly May 17, 1769, only eleven days after he had called it together, the time had come for something more communicative than words. The result was the unprecedented, extra-constitutional meeting of the burgesses at the house of Anthony Hay on the afternoon of the dissolution. On May 18 this group, which included all important members of the popular party, adopted some profoundly anti-British resolutions, the cutting edge of which was a mutual pledge to refrain from purchasing a long list of imported goods. Third in the list of 108 signers of the Williamsburg Association of 1769 was Richard Bland.[75] The non-importation resolutions of 1769 were in practice pretty much a failure, and a new Association was organized June 22, 1770, each signer pledging himself to have nothing to do socially with any individual who refused to join or live up to the articles of agreement. Again Bland's name was at the top of the list.[76]

For three years Virginia simmered without major incident, while events in the other colonies moved toward inevitable bloodshed. On March 12, 1773 the House of Burgesses took a fateful step when it appointed "a standing Committee of Correspondence and inquiry,"

> whose business it shall be to obtain the most early and Authentic intelligence of all such Acts and *Resolutions* of the *British Parliament*, or proceedings of Administration, as may relate to or affect the British Colonies in America, and to keep up and maintain a Correspondence and Communication with our Sister Colonies, respecting these important Considerations; and the result of such their proceedings, from Time to Time, to lay before this House.[77]

Bland was an active member of the Virginia Committee of Correspondence from this first establishment to its decline in 1775.[78] Although the kind of daring leadership he had offered in 1753 and 1758 was now exhibited by the Lees, Henry, Washington, and others, Bland was still a useful man for the radicals to have at their side, especially since he seemed willing in the end to go along with their every step. The record of his service in the critical years is a virtually inclusive listing of those committees, conventions, and delegations which guided Virginia to final independence: member of the Committee of Correspondence (1773-1775); signer of the Association of 1774; [79] a leader of the patriot party in the last House of Burgesses; deputy from Prince George County to the five Virginia Conventions of 1774-1776, which gradually supplanted the General Assembly as the colony's legislature and finally took on the duties of a constitutional convention; member of the Virginia Committee of Safety (1775-1776), which was the executive arm of the colony in the period between the departure of Lord Dunmore and establishment of state government; [80] delegate with Randolph, Washington, Henry, R. H. Lee, Pendleton, and Harrison to the first Continental Congress in 1774; and delegate with the same immortal band to the second in May 1775. [81] John Adams wrote of the Virginians and Bland at Philadelphia in 1774:

> These gentlemen from Virginia appear to be the most spirited and consistent of any. Harrison said he would have come on foot rather than not come. Bland said he would have gone, upon this occasion, if it had been to Jericho. [82]

Purdie's *Gazette* of June 16, 1775 carried news that Bland had returned from Congress "charged with some important business from that august body to be laid before the Assembly of this colony." Actually, Bland was beginning to show his age and had left Philadelphia because of ill health. He was elected to Congress a third time August 11, 1775, but the next day declined in an exchange that the Journal of the Convention describes in these words:

> RICHARD BLAND, Esq. returned the Convention his most grateful acknowledgements for the great honour they had pleased a third time to confer on him, by appointing him one of the deputies to represent this colony in General Congress, and said this fresh instance of their approbation was sufficient for an old man, almost deprived of sight, whose greatest ambition had ever been to receive the plaudit of his country, whenever he should retire from the public stage of life; that the honorable testimony he lately received of this approbation, joined with his present appointment, should ever animate him, as far as he was able, to support the glorious cause in which America was now engaged; but that his advanced age rendered him incapable of taking an active part in these weighty and important concerns, which must necessarily be agitated in the great council of the United Colonies, and therefore begging leave to decline the honor they had been pleased to confer on him, and desiring that some person more fit and able might supply his place.
>
> *Resolved unanimously,* That the thanks of this Convention are justly due to the said *Richard Bland,* Esq. one of the worthy deputies who represented this Colony in the late Continental Congress, for his faithful discharge of that important trust; and this body are only induced to dispense with his future services, of the like nature, on account of his advanced age.

The President accordingly delivered the thanks of the Convention to the said *Richard Bland*, Esq. in his place, who expressed the great pleasure he received from this distinguished testimony of his country's approbation of his services.[83]

Bland's refusal was greeted by Henry and the others with mixed feelings of regret and relief—regret because he was one of the last of the old colonial fighters for Virginia's rights and privileges, relief because the policy of no compromise would now go forward more smoothly. True to his desire for peaceful settlement of this imperial dispute, Bland had opposed Henry's resolution to arm the colony passed by the convention of March 1775.[84]

There was life in Bland yet, it would seem, for he remained active in Virginia's temporary legislature, discharged faithfully his duties with the Committee of Safety, served on a committee to encourage domestic manufactures, and performed a number of the small executive tasks he had learned to do so well in the French and Indian War.[85] He seems to have put up some of his own money to encourage manufacture of saltpeter for gunpowder, practicing what he had preached to a relative, "I fear supineness possesseth all ranks among us; why do we talk, and not act?"[86] In the Convention of 1776 he served on the committee that drew up the Declaration of Rights and the first constitution of the State of Virginia. And as if all these duties were not enough for "an old man, almost deprived of sight," he kept his grip on the home county by heading its Committee of Intelligence.[87]

In July 1775 Bland was given a dose of the same bitter medicine that America has always reserved for some of its most honorable public servants: He was accused of disloyalty and secret correspondence with the enemy. Bland, unlike some of those so recklessly denounced in 1951 and 1952, was able to face his accuser publicly and spit the medicine right back in his face. On his return from ordination in England in 1775, Rev. Samuel Sheild undertook to repay Bland for his anticlerical activities by spreading a cock-and-bull story that Bland had promised to support the colonial policies of the Crown in return for an appointment as collector of duties on tea. After Bland had demanded proof and Sheild had offered it,[88] the tough old patriot went straight before his peers. The Journal of the Convention carries these entries:

> For July 22, 1775,
> RICHARD BLAND, Esq. a member of this Convention, and one of the deputies appointed to represent this colony in General Congress, informed the Convention, that certain false and scandalous reports, highly reflecting on him in his publick character, had been propagated; to wit, that he had made application to the earl of *Dartmouth*, or some of the ministry, for an appointment to collect the taxes imposed on *America* by parliament; and that, as an inducement to them to grant the same, had promised to promote the designs of the ministry against this country; and also, that his conduct in General Congress had been such that he was obliged suddenly to decamp from the city of *Philadelphia*:

That he had served as a member of the General Assembly for upwards of 30 years, and hoped the part he had always publickly taken would have secured him, in his age, from an imputation so injurious to his character: That he earnestly requested a full and publick inquiry should be made into the truth of the said reports, and that the Rev. *Samuel Shield* [*sic*], the Rev. *John Hurt*, and *Samuel Overton*, and *Joseph Smith* who, he understood, had propagated the said reports, should be summoned to attend the said inquiry; and that every other person who had heard any thing of the said reports would also attend, that the fullest examination might be made into the truth thereof.

Resolved, That this Convention will, on *Friday* next, examine into the truth of the reports mentioned in the said information.

For July 28,

The Convention, according to the order of the day, went into an examination of the reports said to have been propagated to the prejudice of *Richard Bland*, Esq. a member of this Convention, and one of the deputies appointed to represent this Colony in General Congress; and, after examination of the Rev. *Samuel Shield*, and the Rev. *John Hurt*, and many other witnesses, and a full inquiry into the same, do find the said reports to be utterly false and groundless, and tending not only to injure the said *Richard Bland* in his publick character, but to prejudice the glorious cause in which *America* is now embarked.

Resolved unanimously, That this Convention do consider it as their duty to bear to the world their testimony that the said *Richard Bland* hath manifested himself the friend of his country, and uniformly stood forth an able asserter of her rights and liberties.[89]

A week later Bland read a full report of his triumph in the newspapers [90] and two weeks later was re-elected to Congress. Having been thus dramatically vindicated, he resigned his seat.

How important was Bland in the movement toward independence? H. J. Eckenrode once insisted that he "more than any other man was the author of the Revolution in Virginia," adding on another occasion: "The role enacted by western Virginia was not the creation of a movement but the precipitation of it. Patrick Henry was not the father of the Revolution but the heir of Richard Bland and his political executor." [91] If Eckenrode's salute was to Bland the man, it was plainly a case of overenthusiasm. But if, as seems more likely, it was a tribute to the historical primacy of the tidewater region and to Bland as its representative political figure, there can be little argument with the historian or his rhetorical device. The Revolution, like the earlier struggles for self-government, was largely the handiwork of the planter aristocracy, aided to be sure by the awakening democracy of the western counties. For Bland, the veteran of a half-dozen tussles with the Crown and several score with the Crown's agents, the Revolution was the climax to a life spent defending Virginia. All honor to the men of the west, who had their own troubles with the tidewater aristocracy, but all honor, too, to an aristocracy that was willing to hazard its fortunes in an authentic rebellion. Bland was not "more than any other man . . . the author of the Revolution," but he was a leader of the class of men in whose keeping the destiny of Virginia rested. He journeyed to Philadelphia with Washington, Henry, and Lee, and that should be glory enough for any one man.

BLAND AS POLITICAL THINKER: NATURAL LAW

Bland's writings are an accurate representation of the dominant political and constitutional theory of eighteenth-century Virginia. His thoughts about civil liberty, the right of resistance, the royal prerogative, and the competence of the Assembly were the thoughts not only of Robinson, Randolph, Wythe, and the entire House of Burgesses, but of planters and yeomen everywhere, even in the newly settled regions. Eighteenth-century Virginia, indeed eighteenth-century America, was dedicated with astounding unanimity to a "party line." Virginia planter, Boston merchant, Jersey farmer, and Pennsylvania printer might have different notions about the location of hell or purpose of an aristocracy, but as children of England they spoke the same political language. The principles of Whiggery, altered to American requirements, claimed the allegiance of all but a reactionary or radical handful of the colonists. These pages present the political faith of Richard Bland, but it is essential to recall that all Virginia agreed with Bland and most of America with Virginia.

Bland probably wrote at least seven pamphlets, a literary output altogether unique in the political history of the Southern colonies. Each of these efforts, or at least each that has survived, was an occasional contribution to a political controversy in which he was an active combatant. His arguments were therefore largely immediate in appeal, and the political theory supporting them was tossed off casually rather than worked out carefully. Bland's political, social, economic, and religious ideas were, like those of the other gentlemen with whom he governed Virginia, matters of faith rather than of reasoned conviction. They were all the more authoritative for being self-evident truths.

Bland's surviving works are *A Modest and True State of the Case* (1753), of which only a fragment remains, *A Letter to the Clergy of Virginia* (1760), *The Colonel Dismounted* (1764), and *An Inquiry into the Rights of the British Colonies* (1766). The lost works included a study of land tenure in Virginia, a treatise on water baptism written to refute the Quakers, and probably, although the evidence is less convincing, a tract on the subject of an American episcopate.[92] In addition, we learn something of Bland's ideas from his letters to the *Gazette* and to friends, from the protests of 1768 against the Townshend Acts, and from the laws, resolves, and addresses he penned for the House of Burgesses. If all this seems a skimpy production, especially when contrasted with the flood of political tracts in old and New England, we must remember that we have almost nothing else political from a Virginia pen in this period. If the style seems rough and the logic circuitous, we must remember that, when words are few, content rather than artistry has first claim to the listener's attention.

A word should be said about the sources of Bland's political and historical learning. For the most part, they were the writings with which any Virginia gentleman would become acquainted if he paid attention to his parents, the tutor and rector, the professors at the college, and the first page of the *Gazette*. Bland gives evidence of familiarity with Locke, Vattel, Domat, and Wollaston; Coke, Holt, and Sir William Temple; Bacon, Shaftesbury, Cervantes, Milton, Swift, and Pope; Hakluyt, Salmon, and Brady; and such classical writers as Thucydides, Lactantius, and Cicero. He was also conversant with contemporaneous political writing, a good deal of which he found reprinted in the various *Gazettes*, especially after the political awakening of the colonial press in 1765. And since he was the recognized oracle of Virginia history, he must have had a rare knowledge of the original sources, of the charters and documents that granted Virginia her liberties.

What did Bland, the archetype of the American Whig, believe to be rock-bottom political truth? His creed—and it was more a creed than a philosophy—had four principal articles of faith: the eternal validity of the natural-law doctrines most cogently stated by John Locke; the superiority over all other forms of government of the English Constitution, of which an uncorrupted model or extension was the peculiar property of the Virginians; the like superiority of those unique rights and liberties which were the heritage of the freeborn Englishman; and the conviction that the good state rests on the devotion of men of virtue, wisdom, integrity, and justice. Let us examine Bland's testimony to each of these beliefs.

The magnificent principles of natural law and natural rights were the common property of the American colonies. This doctrine was made to order for a proud colonial people on the way to independence through various stages of self-government. Bland, like his fellow colonists of every section, accepted these principles at face value; there is no indication at any place in his writings that he considered them even a little inconsistent, unhistorical, or illogical. A representative passage from Bland's *Inquiry into the Rights of the British Colonies* shows him a faithful adherent of the natural-law philosophy:

> Men in a State of Nature are absolutely free and independent of one another as to sovereign Jurisdiction, but when they enter into a Society, and by their own Consent become Members of it, they must submit to the Laws of the Society according to which they agree to be governed; for it is evident, by the very Act of Association, that each Member subjects himself to the Authority of that Body in whom, by common Consent, the legislative Power of the State is placed: But though they must submit to the Laws, so long as they remain Members of the Society, yet they retain so much of their natural Freedom as to have a Right to retire from the Society, to renounce the Benefits of it, to enter into another Society, and to settle in another Country; for their Engagements to the Society, and their Submission to the publick Authority of the State, do not oblige them to con-

tinue in it longer than they find it will conduce to their Happiness, which they have a natural Right to promote. This natural Right remains with every Man, and he cannot justly be deprived of it by any civil Authority.[93]

Here in a narrow compass are most of the ancient ideas that Locke had refined so persuasively in his famous treatise: the historical and logical state of nature, in which men are possessed of absolute freedom; the impulse to enter society in search of protection; the act of voluntary consent or compact, in which some freedom is renounced so that the remainder may be sure; the contingent retention of enough natural freedom to withdraw from the compact for sufficient cause; and the promotion of men's happiness as the chief end of society and government. If Bland did not expand on any of these concepts, it was probably because he thought it completely unnecessary. He might as well have expanded on the Sixth Commandment.

The core of this philosophy was, of course, the contract or compact, the notion that political obligation originates in the freely given consent of the individual. For Bland and his contemporaries the compact was no idle abstraction but a reality visible in the form of their ancient charters. However the Stuarts and early Virginians had looked upon the charters and confirmations, the descendants of the early Virginians, for whom Bland was the oracle, considered them voluntary compacts between a king in search of subjects and subjects in search of a king. But it was not so much the compact that interested Bland and his fellow colonials as the manner in which it might be abrogated by those who had, for more than trivial reasons, become dissatisfied with its terms. Bland put forward two solutions to this problem: the right of resistance and the right of migration, each a necessary theoretical support to the practical arguments of the colonial apologists. The free individual could oppose and refuse obedience to unlawful acts of the sovereign power, or he could choose "to retire from the Society, to renounce the Benefits of it . . . and to settle in another Country."

Bland had little of a positive nature to say about the right of resistance. He was not, like Jonathan Mayhew or Patrick Henry, the sort of man to go around shouting about rebellion before it was plainly necessary to rebel. Yet he did say enough in the *Inquiry* and *The Colonel Dismounted* to make clear his Whiggish disdain for the principles of passive obedience and Whiggish belief in the natural right to resist unlawful statutes and exertions of prerogative. An example of arbitrary action that would justify resistance is presented in the *Inquiry*:

> The Colonies are subordinate to the Authority of Parliament; subordinate I mean in Degree, but not absolutely so: For if by a Vote of the *British* Senate the Colonists were to be delivered up to the Rule of a *French* or *Turkish* Tyranny, they may refuse Obedience to such a Vote, and may oppose the Execution of it by Force.[94]

And another:

> If a Man invades my Property, he becomes an Aggressor, and puts himself into a State of War with me: I have a Right to oppose this Invader; If I have not Strength to repel him, I must submit, but he acquires no Right to my Estate which he has usurped. Whenever I recover Strength I may renew my Claim, and attempt to regain my Possession; if I am never strong enough, my Son, or his Son, may, when able, recover the natural Right of his Ancestor which has been unjustly taken from him.[95]

And much closer to home, in *The Colonel Dismounted*:

> I have, replied the Colonel, a high Reverence for the Majesty of the King's Authority, and shall upon every Occasion yield a due Obedience to all its just Powers and Prerogatives; but Submission, even to the supreme Magistrate, is not the whole Duty of a Citizen, especially such a Submission as he himself does not require: Something is likewise due to the Rights of our Country, and to the Liberties of Mankind. . . .
>
> I do not deny but that the Parliament, as the stronger Power, can force any Laws it shall think fit upon us; but the Inquiry is not what it can do, but what Constitutional Right it has to do so: And if it has not any Constitutional Right, then any Tax respecting our INTERNAL Polity, which may hereafter be imposed on us by Act of Parliament, is arbitrary, as depriving us of our Rights, and may be opposed. But we have nothing of this Sort to fear from those Guardians of the Rights and Liberties of Mankind.[96]

As conciliatory as the last sentence may have sounded—and we must remember that it was written in 1763—there should have been no doubt in the minds of Bland's readers that he and his fellow burgesses claimed an ultimate right to resist the commands of an arbitrary sovereign or Parliament. Bland never did make clear just how far the British ministry would have to go in oppressing the colonies before armed resistance would be justified, but like all subscribers to Lockean principles he believed that the amount of resistance would be determined by the extent of oppression. The passage of one oppressive law would justify opposition to that law alone. The passage of a number of such laws would justify general resistance. Absolute oppression would justify absolute rebellion, but in 1763 and 1765 no colonist was talking in these terms.

The natural right of migration was a handy colonial doctrine. It permitted Americans to argue that their ancestors had left England as free agents, that they had therefore been in a position to bargain for a new compact with the sovereign they were leaving behind, that each generation of colonists consented anew to this compact, and that any attempt to violate it could be openly resisted. The right of migration, the compact, and the right of resistance were closely associated in colonial argument. "I have observed before," writes Bland,

> that when Subjects are deprived of their civil Rights, or are dissatisfied with the Place they hold in the Community, they have a natural Right to quit the Society of which they are Members, and to retire into another Country.

Now when Men exercise this Right, and withdraw themselves from their Country, they recover their natural Freedom and Independence: The Jurisdiction and Sovereignty of the State they have quitted ceases; and if they unite, and by common Consent take Possession of a new Country, and form themselves into a political Society, they become a sovereign State, independent of the State from which they separated. If then the subjects of *England* have a natural Right to relinquish their Country, and by retiring from it, and associating together, to form a new political Society and independent State, they must have a Right, by Compact with the Sovereign of the Nation, to remove into a new Country, and to form a civil Establishment upon the Terms of the Compact. In such a Case, the Terms of the Compact must be obligatory and binding upon the Parties; they must be the Magna Charta, the fundamental Principles of Government, to this new Society; and every Infringement of them must be wrong, and may be opposed.[97]

A passage like this should be evidence enough of the American Whig's unquestioning dedication "to the Law of Nature, and those Rights of Mankind which flow from it," to a set of fundamental principles "applicable to every Sort of Government, and not contrary to the common Understandings of Mankind." [98] Bland's faith in the teachings of Locke and Wollaston was like his faith in the teachings of Jesus. They were "true, certain, and universal," not to be improved upon and certainly not to be fretted over. They were the pikes and cutlasses in a gentleman's intellectual armory, to be stored away when things were going well and to be dragged out and brandished when things went wrong.

"THE BLESSINGS OF A BRITISH CONSTITUTION"

Throughout the colonial period and right down to the last months before the Declaration of Independence, politically conscious Americans looked upon the British Constitution rather than natural law as the bulwark of their cherished liberties. Practical political thinking in eighteenth-century America was dominated by two assumptions: that the British Constitution was the best and happiest of all possible forms of government, and that the colonists, descendants of freeborn Englishmen, enjoyed the blessings of this constitution to the fullest extent consistent with a wilderness environment.

The British Constitution, we learn from Bland's writings, had at least four honorable claims to superiority over all other charters or systems of government: First, "the Laws of the Kingdom," the working rules of the Constitution, were "founded upon the Principles of the Law of Nature." [99] The Constitution was as pure a distillation of those "true, certain, and universal" principles "applicable to every Sort of Government" as mortal men could be expected to enjoy. Newton's laws of attraction were no more valid than the common law of England. Second, the British Constitution was founded, unlike many constitutions, in "the common consent of the People." [100] Third, this consent had been given repeatedly "from time immemorial;" it went back at least as far as the coming of the Saxons.[101] The antiquity of the British Constitution was as important a quality as its conformity to nature. And finally, it was peculiarly designed to promote liberty and justice, by protecting the subject from that old bugaboo "arbitrary power" and by governing him through techniques of "mildness and equity." [102] Bland put his faith in the Constitution in these guileless words:

> Under an *English* Government all Men are born free, are only subject to Laws made with their own Consent, and cannot be deprived of the Benefit of these Laws without a transgression of them. To assert this is sufficient, to demonstrate it to an *Englishman* is useless: He not only KNOWS, but, if I may use the Expression, FEELS it as a vital Principle in the Constitution, which places him in a Situation without the reach of the highest EXECUTIVE Power in the State, if he lives in an Obedience to its laws.[103]

The content of this best of constitutions was apparently so well known as to require no particular exposition. It included the common law, Magna Charta and other hard-won documents of the past, and the nexus of customs and understandings which brought balance to government and protection to the people. The most notable of these was, of course, the still-inchoate doctrine of the separation of powers. Although Bland was apparently unaware of Montesquieu's magnificent misinterpretation, he was nevertheless committed in a general way to the concept of three great branches of government, each with powers and a life of its own.

The key institution of government in this good Whig's philosophy was the legislative assembly. Government should be balanced and the powers separated, but Bland, following in the inconsistent steps of Locke and the other heroes of the Whig tradition, had a special affection for the legislature, "the natural Guardians of [the] Liberties" of the people.[104] The early American disposition to look to the legislature rather than to the executive or judiciary for care and protection, a disposition deriving from experience as well as tradition, is plain in the writings of the model burgess.

> If then the People of this Colony are free born, and have a Right to the Liberties and Privileges of *English* Subjects, they must necessarily have a legal Constitution, that is, a Legislature, composed, in Part, of the Representatives of the People, who may enact Laws for the INTERNAL Government of the Colony, and suitable to its various Circumstances and Occasions; and without such a Representative, I am bold enough to say, no law can be Made.[105]

The meridian of Bland's dedication to the legislative way of life is reached in *The Colonel Dismounted*. Throughout his argument runs a feeling of loyal enthusiasm for the competence and dignity of the Virginia Assembly.

Bland had little to say about the importance of an independent judiciary, principally because he was a writer on immediate topics, which in his time were the powers of King and Parliament or of Governor and Assembly. Though he used the sacred word "unconstitutional" and asserted that "the Constitution cannot be destroyed . . . by any Act of the General Assembly" or of Parliament,[106] he did not go on to place the final guardianship of the Constitution in the courts. The doctrine of judicial review was unknown to Bland and his colleagues. Yet the independent judiciary and the great popular institution associated with it—the jury of peers—were certainly regarded as essentials of the Constitution.

The existence of a monarch—pledged to protect the people under the terms of the compact, yet wielding a prerogative of whose limits he was the only short-range judge—was a basic assumption of Whig constitutionalism. Again and again Bland acknowledged the necessity of a king, not because he was anxious to play the dutiful subject but because he believed sincerely that a visible sovereign governing through the consent of the governed brought stability, dignity, effectiveness, and legitimacy to the best of all possible constitutions. Bland must have regarded as utter nonsense the charges of "republicanism" hurled at the Virginians by frustrated royal agents, for he meant what he said when he composed addresses that spoke of "the best of Kings" and of "our Loyalty and Attachment to his [Majesty's] Royal and Illustrious Person and Family." [107] A special committee headed by Bland said this to the Governor at the opening of the critical session of May 1755:

> We His Majesty's most dutiful and loyal Subjects, the Burgesses of *Virginia*, now met in General Assembly, return your Honor our sincere Thanks for your Speech at the Opening of this Session.
>
> The many Instances we have received of His Majesty's paternal and tender Concern for the Protection and Happiness of this Colony, do justly demand from us, the strongest Testimonies of the most inviolable Fidelity to his sacred Person and Government; and it would argue the highest Ingratitude, if we did not acknowledge ourselves truly affected with the Benefits which must arise to us by his Royal Care and Munificence, in sending to our Assistance, at the Expence of the Crown of *Great-Britain*, a Body of regular Forces, with a large Train of Artillery, under the Command of an able and experienced General.
>
> We beg Leave to assure your Honor, that we will take the important Matters, recommended to us by your Honor, under our most serious Consideration, and that His Majesty's Interest, and the public Good of our Country, which are inseparably united, shall govern us in all our Resolutions.[108]

Here was the essence of the Whig doctrine of a constitutional king: the inseparability of the interest of the monarch, the welfare of the country, and "the Rights of the Subjects." [109] The Glorious Revolution had once again reminded Englishmen and their kings that, while the rights of the people were sheltered by the throne, the throne rested on the rights of the people. Bland rejected categorically Filmer's theories of royal authority,[110] especially when these theories were dredged up by the ministers in their defense of the prerogative in the Two-Penny crisis. The point at issue, it will be remembered, was the right of the Assembly to ignore the royal instruction concerning suspending clauses. Said Bland in explaining the absence of such a clause in the act of 1758:

> To say that a royal Instruction to a Governour, for his own particular Conduct, is to have the Force and Validity of a Law, and must be obeyed without Reserve, is, at once, to strip us of all the Rights and Privileges of British Subjects, and to put us under the despotic Power of a *French* or *Turkish* Government; for what is the real Difference between a *French* Edict and an *English* Instruction if they are both equally absolute? The royal Instructions are nothing more than Rules and Orders laid down as Guides and Directions for the Conduct of Governours. These may, and certainly ought to be, Laws to them; but never can be thought, consistently with the Principles of the *British* Constitution, to have the Force or Power of Laws upon the People.
>
> The Royal Prerogative is, without Doubt, of great Weight and Power in a dependent and subordinate Government: Like the King of *Babylon's* Decree, it may, for aught I know, almost force the People of the Plantations to fall down and worship any Image it shall please to set up; but, great and powerful as it is, it can only be exerted while in the Hands of the best and most benign Sovereign, for the Good of his People, and not for their Destruction.[111]

The King, acting through the person of the royal governor, was an indispensable element of the British Constitution as extended to the colonies. He was, however, an agent of popular consent, deserving of "the deepest Loyalty" only so long as he acted as "the Father of his People." [112] It was in this sense that the Virginians appealed to him in 1764, out of "a Confidence that the Royal Benignity would never suffer them to be deprived of their Freedom (that sacred Birthright and inestimable Blessing)." [113] Not until the monarchy had been stripped of the aura of benignity by Thomas Paine and the course of events did Americans reluctantly turn republican. Few colonists—certainly not Bland—believed they could do without the divinity that doth hedge a king.

Toward the end of the colonial period, Americans became more and more convinced that they, not the English, were the trustees and beneficiaries of the British Constitution. The English people, it was asserted, had fallen on evil days, and their manifest lapse in morality had infected the best of all possible constitutions. Said Bland in the *Inquiry:*

> If what you say is a real Fact, that nine Tenths of the People of *Britain* are deprived of the high Privilege of being Electors, it shows a great Defect in the present Constitution, which has departed so much from its original Purity; but never can prove that those People are even *virtually* represented in Parliament. And here give me Leave to observe that it would be a Work worthy of the best patriotick Spirits in the Nation to effectuate an Alteration in this putrid Part of the Constitution; and, by restoring it to its pristine Perfection, prevent any "Order or Rank of the Subjects from imposing upon or binding the rest without their Consent." But, I fear, the Gangrene has taken too deep Hold to be eradicated in these Days of Venality.[114]

Although there was little hope that the English could restore the Constitution to its original purity, this did not mean that the Constitution had no home. In an address to the Governor in 1756, Bland and Peyton Randolph, a committee of two, spoke of the Virginians as men "who enjoy the Blessings of a *British* Constitution, reduced to its original Purity, and breathing nothing but Freedom and Justice." [115] The colonists believed that the ancient, pure, uncorrupted Constitution was their peculiar possession and trust.

The distinctive "Blessings of a *British* Constitution" were the celebrated rights and privileges flowing from it, and to these the Americans, "the Heirs and Descendants of free born *Britons*," [116] laid positive claim. The time had not yet come for them to talk of "natural" rights. The rights for which they contended were "constitutional," "civil," "ancient," and "British." These were, to be sure, especially precious because they, like the Constitution, were uniquely conformable to nature, the most perfect conceivable earthly reproductions of the rights that belonged to all men everywhere. Yet their particular attraction for pre-Revolutionary Americans like Bland was their British pedigree. The fact that these rights were ancient and had been bought with the blood of secular martyrs recommended them especially to colonial minds. The Saxons had brought them, the Angles had absorbed them, the first Virginians had transported them, Hampden ("that Great Man") had defended them, King William "of Glorious Memory" had confirmed them— and now they were safe in the keeping of the colonists, a people as uncorrupted as the early Britons and therefore worthy of this noble heritage. Bland never doubted that the colonists were "in full Possession of the Rights and Privileges of *Englishmen*." [117]

Like most other Whigs, Bland placed the defense of British rights in the legislative assembly. Although all branches of government existed primarily to protect the rights of the subject—King, courts, and House of Lords—the lower house of the legislature, the House of Commons (or House of Burgesses), had the chief responsibility for transmitting them unspoiled to future generations. Unless we recall the peculiar feeling of trusteeship that guided Bland and many of his colleagues, they often appear like so many posers, hypocrites, and babblers. It was hard for a good Whig to be anything but a member of the popular house; once called to membership, his first duty was clear.

Bland wrote at one time or another in explanation or defense of all the well-known rights to which Virginians laid claim: representation, "a Right without which, by the ancient Constitution of the State, all other Liberties were but a Species of Bondage"; [118] taxation only by elected representatives, "an essential Part of *British* Freedom"; [119] and property, perhaps the best example of a right both natural and British. The intimate association of these three freedoms in the mind of the good Whig is clear in Bland's writings. In the memorial of 1768 to the House of Lords he said of the Virginians:

> They presume not to claim any other than the natural Rights of *British* Subjects; the fundamental and vital Principles of their happy Government, so universally admired, is known to consist in this: that no Power on Earth

has a Right to impose Taxes upon the People or to take the smallest Portion of their Property without their Consent, given by their Representatives in Parliament; this has ever been esteemed the chief pillar of their Constitution, the very Palladium of their Liberties. If this Principle is suffered to decay, the Constitution must expire with it, as no Man can enjoy even the shadow of Freedom; if his property, acquired by his own Industry and the sweat of his brow, may be wrested from him at the Will of another without his own Consent.

This Truth is so well established that it is unnecessary to attempt a Demonstration of it to *Englishmen*, who feel the Principle firmly implanted in them diffusing through their whole frame Complacency and Chearfulness.[120]

And in his argument against the Pistole Fee he wrote:

The Rights of the Subjects are so secured by Law that they cannot be deprived of the least part of their property without their own consent. Upon this Principle of Law, the Liberty and Property of every Person who has the felicity to live under a British Government is founded. The Question then ought not to be about the smallness of the demand but the Lawfulness of it. For if it is against Law, the same Power which imposes one Pistole may impose an Hundred, and this not in one instance only but in every case in which this Leviathan of Power shall think fit to exercise its authority.

LIBERTY & PROPERTY are like those precious Vessels whose soundness is destroyed by the least flaw and whose use is lost by the smallest hole. Impositions destroy their Beauty nor are they to be soldered by patch-work which will always discover and frequently widen the original Flaw.

This shews the Iniquity of every measure which has the least tendency to break through the legal Forms of government and the expediency, nay the necessity of opposing in a legal way every attempt of this sort which like a small spark if not extinguished in the beginning will soon gain ground and at last blaze out into an irresistable Flame.[121]

The purpose of this vigilance was to guarantee to all men "the Fruits of their own Labour, with a Security which Liberty only can impart." [122]

Bland also mentioned a half-dozen other liberties that he found essential to a Whig society. Of freedom of speech and press he wrote to Washington:

If what I may say should give Offence to any, for I give you free Liberty to communicate it, tell them, that I have the Honour to be a British Subject, and, under that glorious Character, enjoy the Privileges of an Englishman, one of which is to examine with Freedom, our public Measures, without being liable to the Punishments of French Tyranny; and, if I think proper, to expose those public Errors which have had to[o] long a Course, and which have been blindly embraced by many, as the most true Opinions.[123]

Bland was only one of many Virginians who used the columns of the *Gazette* to expand on all manner of controversial topics. Although he several times mentioned the necessity of speaking and writing "with a proper Deference to Persons in High Office," [124] he could be tart and testy in his comments on certain public men. Yet he never forgot that the responsibility to argue "with Candour and Integrity" went along with the freedom to argue at all.

Freedom of petition, trial by jury ("fair, open and publick"),[125] and freedom of religion were other privileges Bland found imbedded in the Constitution. The first was essential because it permitted men to advertise their grievances and government to redress them.[126] Trial by jury was hardly less important than representation itself, although Virginians did not get wrought up over it until the ministry proposed to remove certain American offenders to England for trial. Freedom of religion was, of course, the kind of freedom guaranteed by the Act of Toleration, which Bland considered to have been extended to Virginia.[127] At other times he seemed to define freedom of religion as the power of the vestry to ignore the Bishop of London or the happy fact that Virginia harbored no "Papists." [128] In any case, Bland held a firm belief in the practical necessity of a live-and-let-live attitude toward religious doctrines. "For let me tell you," he wrote in 1771, "a Religious Dispute is the most Fierce and destructive of all others, to the peace and Happiness of Government." [129]

VIRTUE AND EMPIRE

No people since the Romans have done more talking about virtue than the Whigs of eighteenth-century England and their immediate ancestors. The Americans, Whigs to the core, filled their papers and pamphlets with salutes to the noble virtues: wisdom, justice, temperance, courage, honesty, frugality, sincerity, modesty, integrity, calmness, benevolence, sobriety, piety, simplicity, and a dozen other admirable qualities. At the same time, they made clear their belief that men who displayed these virtues would be free and that men who did not would be slaves. The free state and all its accessories—constitutional monarchy, the legislature, representation, trial by jury, freedom of religion, freedom of expression, security of property— depended for existence on men of wisdom and integrity. This had been true of republican Rome, the most glorious state in all recorded history; this was true of England, the Rome of the modern world; this was especially true of America, the Rome of the future, to which Virtue was even now moving her seat.

Bland did not express this interesting refinement of Whig political theory as clearly as he might have, principally because he had no immediate use for that sort of argument. Yet through all his writings there runs a strain of high morality. He assumed, as did a thousand writers to the English and American press, that a certain proportion of men (never precisely fixed) with a sincere belief in "the Roman virtues" was the first requisite for the existence of free government, and he acknowledged the intimate association of public virtue and private morality.[130] Truth, ingenuity, wisdom, candor, integrity, decency, industry, honesty, frugality, and "good manners" were the particular virtues to which Bland paid tribute.

On the statue of Lord Botetourt at the entrance to the College of William

and Mary are carved these words, which Bland composed at the request
of the Assembly:

LET WISDOM AND JUSTICE PRESIDE IN ANY COUNTRY
THE PEOPLE WILL REJOICE AND MUST BE HAPPY.[131]

Public virtue and private morality, carefully learned in youth and actively
cultivated in maturity, were far more essential to the preservation and advancement of human liberty than was any law or institution or constitutional
technique. Indeed, the great Constitution itself could not be worked except
in an atmosphere of integrity and morality, one in which the Whiggish
distinction between *power* and *right* would be known to all men and violated
by none.[132]

Two aspects of Bland's thought remain to be examined briefly: his reliance
on facts and history for support of his major arguments,[133] and the nature
and originality of the theory of the British empire worked out in his writings
on the Two-Penny and Stamp acts.

Bland the oracle used history rather than logic to confute the defenders
of parliamentary supremacy, while Bland the country lawyer used facts
rather than dogmas to harry the minions of ecclesiastical aristocracy. Although he never found time to carry through his projected history of Virginia, he was generally acknowledged to be the colony's chief intellectual
link with its past. Jefferson saluted Bland as "a great antiquarian," and
there is little doubt that his own interest in documentary materials was
stimulated by friendship with this wise old man. Bland's career as collector
of the basic documents of Virginia history would have been enough in itself
to establish him as a leading figure of the colonial period. If Bland was a
descendant of Englishmen in his devotion to history and its uses, he was
a forerunner of later Americans in his blunt assertion that "opinion shall
never influence my Judgment; I will examine Facts, and from them discover
Truths." [134] Bland, like later Americans, could never free himself completely
from the sway of opinion, but certainly his writings are loaded with enough
hard facts to give them a decidedly modern flavor. Two examples of his
practical approach to political problems will be sufficient to illustrate this
truth. To those burgesses obsessed with doctrinaire Whig notions about the
menace of a standing army Bland wrote:

In a British Government, where the Laws controul even the Sovereign's
Power, it is impossible that military Enterprizes can be carried on with Advantage without a proper Assistance from those who are intrusted with the
Disposition of the People's Money. If the Supplies, necessary to give Life
and Vigour to our Arms, are refused or granted with too much Frugality,
we must never expect to succeed against an Enemy subject to a despotic
Prince, who can dispose of the Lives and Fortunes of his Subjects as he
pleases.[135]

And to those ministers who proclaimed the inviolability of the royal instructions:

When, therefore, the Governour and Council . . . find, from the Uncertainty and Variableness of human Affairs, that any Accident happens which general Instructions can by no Means provide for; or which, by a rigid Observation of them, would destroy a People so far distant from the Royal Presence, before they can apply to the Throne for Relief; it is their Duty as good Magistrates, to exercise this Power as the Exigency of the State requires; and, though they should deviate from the strict Letter of an Instruction, or perhaps, in a small Degree, from the fixed Rule of the Constitution, yet such a Deviation cannot possibly be *Treason*, when it is intended to produce the most salutary End, the Preservation of the People: In such a Case it deserves Commendation and Reward.

The Royal Instructions ought certainly to be obeyed, and nothing but the most pressing Necessity can justify any Person for infringing them; but, as *salus populi est suprema lex*, where this Necessity prevails, every Consideration must give Place to it, and even these Instructions may be deviated from with Impunity: This is so evident to Reason, and so clear and fundamental a Rule in the *English* Constitution, that it would be losing of Time to produce Instances of it.[136]

This justification of an admittedly questionable action on the plea of "the most pressing Necessity" has few counterparts in early American political writing. Bland, who was fond of pointing to such ineluctable facts as the distance of the colonies from England,[137] was an interesting example of the growing American tendency to argue politics in practical terms. When he wrote that "Facts can be known and Truth discovered," he put his finger on one of the vital assumptions of the American tradition. When he paid a high tribute to common sense, he sounded almost like a Southern Franklin.[138]

The thinking of the colonists on the nature of the British empire is a subject to which we shall pay special attention in Chapter 12. It should be enough at this point to indicate the content of Bland's ideas and establish the primacy of his contribution.

The whole trend of colonial argument on this crucial constitutional point was away from loyal confusion and toward radical precision. In 1764-1768 men talked of difficult distinctions between internal and external taxation, internal and external legislation, taxation for revenue and taxation for regulation of trade. In 1775-1776 they were content to deny the power of Parliament completely and to point to the Crown as the tie that bound. Franklin, John Adams, James Wilson, and Jefferson now get most of the credit for this embryonic dominion theory, but the crude spadework of men like Bland raised a foundation on which they could build their polished dialectical structures.

Bland's ideas on this subject were never entirely coherent, for he wrote his most important tracts at a time when even the keenest colonial minds were floundering about in the swamps of "loyal confusion." If in his theory of parliamentary power there are inconsistencies between one time and another, or even between pages 25 and 26 of the same pamphlet, we must remember that his was a pioneer attempt to grapple with a problem never before examined carefully by colonial minds, a problem whose only practical solutions were the slavish alternative of total submission or the visionary alternative of dominion status. Bland the Whig would have none of the former; Bland the loyal colonial would take time to digest the latter. Hence we discover that Virginia was and was not dependent on England, that the colonies were both sisters and daughters of the home country, and that Parliament could and could not regulate intercolonial affairs.

Yet these points should be noted in support of a Virginia Tyler's claim that Bland wrote "the great initial paper of the American Revolution," and a Yankee Tyler's acknowledgment that he was the first expounder of a "prodigious innovation in constitutional doctrine": [139] his sharp denial, first stated in 1764 and stated again in 1766, that Parliament had the right to lay "any Tax respecting our INTERNAL Polity"; [140] his slightly more timid denial, for here he walked on eggs, that Parliament could even *legislate* on internal concerns of the colonies; [141] his historical argument, so necessary to the American case, that the first colonists had exercised the natural right of migration, had expended their own treasure in settling the colonies, and had thereupon made a voluntary compact with the King of England; [142] his blunt insistence in the *Inquiry* that the Navigation Acts, however venerable, "deprived the Colonies . . . of the *Privileges* of English Subjects, and constituted an unnatural Difference between Men under the same Allegiance, born equally free, and entitled to the same civil Rights"; [143] his absolute rejection of the sophistry of virtual representation; [144] and his interesting observation, which he did not carry through to its logical conclusion, that Charles II "was King in *Virginia* some Time before he had any certain Assurance of being restored to his Throne in *England*." [145]

Bland expounded ideas that were in every thinking colonist's mind, and the course of thought on this constitutional problem would have wandered in the same direction had he never lived at all. Yet his gropings of 1764 and 1766 came early enough in the battle to give him a reasonable claim to primacy among the hundreds of defenders of colonial self-government. *The Colonel Dismounted*, in which Bland first set down his ideas, was written in 1763 as the climax to the Two-Penny crisis. Bland denied Parliament's authority to lay internal taxes months before the Stamp Act was even proposed. He first among Americans stated clearly and boldly:

> Any Tax respecting our INTERNAL Polity, which may hereafter be imposed on us by Act of Parliament, is arbitrary, as depriving us of our Rights, and may be opposed.[146]

THE WHIG IN AMERICA

Bland died as he probably wanted to die: suddenly, painlessly, and on active political service. In the fall of 1776 he had come down the river to Williamsburg as one of Prince George's delegates to the first state legislature. There, in a gathering of men only four of whom had been in the old House of Burgesses when he had attacked the Pistole Fee, he plied his trade with the same skill and learning he had shown for thirty-five years. He was still the oracle, still the cautious progressive. He was chairman of the special committee that reported Jefferson's bill "to enable tenants in taille to convey their lands in fee simple" and a member of the small committee set up to revise the laws.[147] While walking the streets of Williamsburg October 26, probably on his way to the first session of the week, he collapsed and was taken to the house of his friend, John Tazewell. In a few hours he was dead.

Bland's name passed quickly from the memories of a people who were even then surfeited with heroes. His was not a life to excite or a personality to intrigue. He had fought no battles, cleared no forests, suffered no tortures; he had swamped no assemblies with torrents of eloquence. And Americans then as now liked their heroes to go off half-cocked. Yet in his own quiet and persevering manner he was more representative of a memorable way of life than any of the great Virginians who come so readily to mind. His career is a case study in the development of representative government. His writings are an accurate indication of the political values of the governing class in colonial America. His service in each of Virginia's three legislatures reminds us that in one colony at least the transition from subordination to independence was marked by precious little social upheaval. And his whole performance, in 1775 as in 1753, proves that we owe something to our aristocrats as well as to our democrats.

The tradition for which Bland was the penman and politician came to flower in Jefferson, Mason, and Madison.[148] What finer tribute could we pay this American Whig than to acknowledge him the elder brother of men like these?

CHAPTER ELEVEN

Benjamin Franklin

CAN any new thing be written of Benjamin Franklin? Is there a corner of his magnificent mind or an aspect of his towering influence that is not the most familiar public property? He has had a dozen or more notable biographers and a legion of faithful investigators of one or another of his activities and interests.[1] In his own writings, public as well as private, he examined himself with discrimination and revealed himself with candor.

Yet much remains to be hypothesized and verified in what Carl Van Doren liked to call "the Franklin science." We need a new and revised edition of his complete writings,[2] an expanded bibliography, a scientific biography, additional calendars of his papers, and a Franklin dictionary. We need a fuller biography than Van Doren's, something "half again as long";[3] and we need a fuller one even than that, something with the sweep and detail of the Freeman *Washington*. And while all this work proceeds, every writer who looks anew at a topic that Franklin touched with his kaleidoscopic genius must interpret the great man for himself and fit him into his own pattern.

The subject of this book is a case in point. Although an essay on Franklin as colonial democrat must go over ground that has been worn to ruts, it may also bring new insight to his thought and career. It is in the character of influential and representative colonial democrat|that we shall observe Dr. Benjamin Franklin. We shall try to confine him rigidly—as if he could be confined at all—to his years as colonial (1706-1765) and his significance as political thinker. If the narrative runs over into 1770 or 1775 or even 1785, it is because the Revolution was for Franklin the dramatic climax to his colonial career. If the talk of politics runs over into economics, science, religion, social problems, and a dozen other fields, it is because we deal with no ordinary man, but "a harmonious human multitude."[4] And since thought and action, the idea and the fact, were tied closely together in Franklin's scheme of life, we must say a few words about his public career before we can probe his public mind.

"BENJAMIN FRANKLIN, OF PHILADELPHIA, PRINTER"

Puritan Boston bred Benjamin Franklin. Dr. Holmes was only exaggerating when he poked fun at other people's civic pride by endorsing Franklin as a "citizen of Boston who dwelt for a little while in Philadelphia." He was born in Milk Street January 17, 1706, the tenth son and seventeenth child of Josiah Franklin, tallow chandler and soap boiler. His father had come from Northamptonshire, England, some time around 1683. His mother Abiah, Josiah's second wife, was a Folger from Nantucket. The Franklins were plain people—poor, pious, hardworking—but apparently well respected in the town of ten thousand that looked upon Joseph Dudley, Increase and Cotton Mather, and Samuel Sewall as its leading citizens. In 1694 Josiah had been stamped with the seal of righteousness that but one man in five could carry: church membership. The day Benjamin was born he was whisked across the street to be baptized in Old South Church—a likely beginning for a noted skeptic.

Even in infancy Benjamin displayed extraordinary aptitude. As an old man he told his son, "I do not remember when I could not read." Josiah intended him, "as the tithe of his sons, to the service of the Church," but after less than two years of schooling he was set to work making soap and candles. Apprenticed to his brother James, a printer, at the age of twelve, he began that famous regimen of labor at desk and press that made him the most skilled producer and printer of the written word in colonial America.

Franklin's life is America's most gratifying and widely known success story. The early exercises in reading and writing, the frustrated yearning for the sea, the difficulties with brother James, the escape by land and water to distant Philadelphia, the charming encounter with the "three great puffy rolls" and his future wife, the misguided but edifying trip to England to buy printing equipment, the return to his trade in Philadelphia—these are tales of his youth that millions of Americans know as well as their own lives. Rather than retrace his steps to prosperity and fame, let us discuss briefly the various careers he pursued, five or six at a time, between 1730 and 1765. From each of his major activities he drew important elements of his working philosophy. In each he exhibited one or more of those qualities of mind and habit that made him "the Father of all the Yankees," "the first American," "the essence of eighteenth-century America"—in short, the most important figure in the colonial experience. Let us consider Franklin as printer-businessman, scientist-inventor, author-moralist, community organizer, and politician-diplomat.

Franklin's will, dated 1788, began with the words, "I, Benjamin Franklin, of Philadelphia, printer, late Minister Plenipotentiary from the United States of America to the Court of France, now President of the State of Pennsylvania." [5] It was not false humility that led one of the most famous men in the world to style himself "printer," but solid pride in seventy years of skill and success in every line of an honorable trade. "He that hath a Trade," said Poor Richard, "hath an Estate." It was not caprice that led him to set up his private press at Passy in 1777, but the need of a sea-anchor for a storm-tossed old shell. "He that hath a Calling, hath an Office of Profit and Honour." Franklin the printer was more than an adept artisan. He was a successful businessman—the most notable self-made man in colonial America, the ancestor and patron saint of millions of other hardworking, clear-thinking, risk-calculating Americans. He did not gamble or speculate wildly, yet was willing to take a chance on something less than a sure bet. He cut no illegal corners, yet played the competitive game with some show of toughness. And while he pursued an accepted trade with skill, imagination, and hard work, he owed much of his success to the fact that in business as in diplomacy he was always alert to the main chance and willing to seize it.

The course of Franklin's career moved steadily onward: self-education in the printing trade in Boston, Philadelphia, and London; experience in a Quaker merchant's shop, where "I attended the business diligently, studied accounts, and grew, in a little time, expert at selling"; his first partnership in 1728; sole ownership of the business at twenty-four; and then eighteen years of increasing fame and fortune, to which the *Pennsylvania Gazette*, the almanac, public printing contracts, a stationer's shop, bookselling, partnerships with journeymen printers, and a dozen other ventures contributed handsomely. His own talents as author fitted neatly into his scheme for prosperity. In 1729,

> I wrote and printed an anonymous pamphlet . . . entitled *The Nature and Necessity of a Paper Currency*. It was well received by the common people in general; but the rich men disliked it, for it increased and strengthened the clamour for more money; and they happening to have no writers among them that were able to answer it, their opposition slackened, and the point was carried by a majority in the House. My friends there, who considered I had been of some service, thought fit to reward me by employing me in printing the money—a very profitable job and a great help to me. This was another advantage gained by my being able to write. [6]

Another element in Franklin's success was his shrewd understanding of the profits that come from a good reputation. In one of the most celebrated passages of the *Autobiography* he confesses:

> In order to secure my credit and character as a tradesman, I took care not only to be in *reality* industrious and frugal, but to avoid all *appearances* of the contrary. I dressed plain and was seen at no places of idle diversion. I never went out a fishing or shooting; a book, indeed, sometimes debauched me from my work, but that was seldom, snug, and gave no scandal; and to show that I was not above my business, I sometimes brought home the paper I purchased at the stores, thro' the streets on a wheelbarrow. Thus being esteemed an industrious, thriving, young man, and paying duly for what I bought . . . I went on swimmingly. [7]

So swimmingly indeed that by 1748 he had had enough of active business, whereupon with a characteristic display of well-ordered values and business acumen he entered into partnership with his foreman, David Hall, and retired to other and more interesting careers. Under the terms of this bargain he was relieved "of all care of the printing office" and assured an income of quite livable proportions. In this partial break with his calling Franklin showed himself a good deal wiser than most of the millions of Americans who were to follow his every step but the last. Few men have been able to withdraw so gracefully, seasonably, and profitably from a business in which they have tired of everything but the money it brings.

Franklin's real purpose in retiring from active business at an early age was to devote his best energies to science, to what his age called "natural philosophy." "I flattered myself that, by the sufficient tho' moderate fortune I had acquired, I had secured leisure during the rest of my life for philosophical studies and amusements." [8] Unfortunately for science, but fortunately for the future Republic, this period of "leisure" was to last only six years, until the Albany Congress of 1754 drew him off into a career of diplomacy. Nevertheless, in this short time Franklin pushed so far into unknown territory that he achieved lasting fame as one of America's great men of science.

Just why a colonial tradesman in his early forties, with practically no formal education or contact with the learned world, should suddenly have presented mankind with experiment-tested explanations of ancient mysteries is itself a mystery that no Franklin scholar will ever answer to our complete satisfaction. We must be content with the partial answers that his mind was vast and curious, that he could master thoroughly or perform adroitly anything to which he would devote even a fraction of his attention, and that from the day he met "natural philosophy" as a young printer in England he never ceased to tinker and ruminate, no matter how exhausting the press of business or diplomacy.

His reputation as scientist rests largely on his experiments in electricity, and no one should be misled by their apparent simplicity. Working with kite, pump handle, salt cellar, vinegar cruet, lightning rod, "electric tube," and "Muschenbroek's wonderful bottle" (the Leyden jar), he converted electricity from a curiosity to a science. A measure of his influence may be found in these electrical terms he first used in print in English: armature, battery, brush, charge, condense, conductor, discharge, electrician, electrify, minus and plus, and shock.[9] The "single fluid" theory, a description of the essential phenomena of the condenser, and the legend-making identification of electricity and lightning were his principal legacies to this field of science.[10]

In other fields his mind was hardly less active. Any instance of natural phenomena was sure to claim his attention and produce an idea to be tested by experiment. Oceanography (his pioneer work in locating the Gulf Stream), meteorology [11] (his discovery that northeast storms come from the southwest), heat physics (his measurements of heat absorption with regard to color), and medicine [12] (his invention of a flexible metal catheter and musings on the cause of colds) are a few of the sciences in which his influence was felt. And he has at least an arguable claim as America's pioneer social scientist. His *Observations concerning the Increase of Mankind* (1751) and *The Interest of Great Britain Considered* (1760) made brilliant use of vital statistics in the scientific study of problems of population.[13]

The sudden and surprising fame that Franklin's "philosophical studies and amusements" brought him in Europe and America—fame that was attested by unnumbered memberships in royal societies, honorary degrees, popular accolades, friendly epigrams, and malicious attacks—tried him exhaustively and found him sound in mind and heart. Forty years of honors were to flatter but not corrupt, and the most eminent American of his day remained always the humane and democratic person that the world came to identify with America itself. Because Franklin was an eminent scientist he could "stand before kings" and get a hearing for the colonies in high places; and because he stood before each king without forgetting that he was "Benjamin Franklin, of Philadelphia, printer," he got a much wider and more sympathetic hearing among the king's subjects. He played the part of the honest colonial with unswerving fidelity and introduced a new nationality to the courts and people of curious Europe. American independence and American democracy owe a massive debt to the manner in which Franklin handled his glories as scientist.

If Franklin had any major limitation in his character as scientist, it was the overly practical, utilitarian, unspeculative mood in which he approached his experiments, which is another way of saying that he was a notable representative of the developing American mind. His character as scientist was limned most sharply by Sir Humphry Davy:

> The experiments adduced by Dr. Franklin . . . were most ingeniously contrived and happily executed. A singular felicity of induction guided all his researches, and by very small means he established very grand truths. The style and manner of his publication on electricity are almost as worthy of admiration as the doctrine it contains. He has endeavoured to remove all mystery and obscurity from the subject; he has written equally for the uninitiated and for the philosopher; and he has rendered his details amusing as well as perspicuous, elegant as well as simple. Science appears in his language in a dress wonderfully decorous, the best adapted to display her native loveliness. He has in no case exhibited that false dignity, by which philosophy is kept aloof from common applications, and he has sought rather to make her a useful inmate and servant in the common habitations of man, than to preserve her merely as an object of admiration in temples and palaces.[14]

Franklin is remembered as tinkering inventor—of stove, lightning rod, bifocals, and clock—more often than as conscious scientist. He is also remembered as an inventor who, out of regard for the human race, refused to seek patents for his own devices.

Finally, Franklin was one of the first Americans to recognize that the elements of scientific method are more than coincidentally similar to basic democratic procedures. His approach to natural science had a profound influence upon his approach to political and social science. In the one as in the other he could see the necessity of free inquiry, free exchange of information, optimism, pragmatism, and humility. For him it was a logical step from the free republic of science to the free Republic of the United States.

PEN AND POLITICS

Franklin pursued devotedly the calling of author-moralist from the age of seven (a poem to his uncle in London) to eighty-four (a satire on the slave trade). In all these years his pen was rarely at rest, as he examined, recorded, or publicized his every interest in a style that is generally regarded to have been the most forceful in colonial America. He wrote influentially in several dozen fields, as a few titles will bear witness: *Dissertation on Liberty and Necessity, Pleasure and Pain; A Modest Enquiry into the Nature and Necessity of a Paper Currency; Proposals Relative to the Education of Youth in Pensilvania; On the Causes and Cure of Smoky Chimneys;* and *Information to Those Who would Remove to America.*

We run into all manner of difficulty in seeking to assess Franklin as a man of letters,[15] principally because his life was so much more memorable than anything he could possibly have written about it. Were his writings flat and dreary they would none the less be read widely, for they were the ponderings of the great man of a great age on some of its most basic problems. The happy fact is, of course, that they were nothing of the sort. Franklin was an author of unusual clarity, force, discipline, and charm; he was uniquely skilled in fitting style to subject. Whether he wrote satire for the press, sweet nonsense to a lady, bagatelles for his circle, propaganda for the populace, messages of state to a high-toned foreign minister, advice to the poor and humble, or descriptions of his experiments to be read before the Royal Society, he rarely missed the goal for which the rest of us strive in vain: perfect communication. Although he never wrote a full-sized book (and projected only one, the stillborn *Art of Virtue*),[16] it is plain from his letters and pamphlets that he could easily have written half a hundred. It is remarkable that his style should have been so consistently artistic and exciting in its own right, for he was one of the most "occasional" authors in American literature.

Franklin the author is best remembered for his moral tracts. Although they form only a fraction of his public writings and present only a sliver of his fabulous character, the *Autobiography*, the prefaces to *Poor Richard*, and *The Way to Wealth* were the first American contributions to universal literature. These lessons in bourgeois morality, the written record of his rage for self-improvement and for transmitting his experience to those who might profit from it, have worked a far-reaching influence on the character of American democracy. The legendary Franklin—frugal, industrious, shrewd, practical, ingenious, self-sustaining and self-reliant—is still praised or damned as the specimen American. The fact that his thirteen "virtues" were listed merely for instruction, and were a catalogue of commandments—chastity, for example—that he himself had trouble enough obeying, has long since been swallowed up in the uses to which Americans have put his advice. In the teachings of Poor Richard "the American, this new man" was to find at least half his character. That he often found the whole of it and saw no reason to inquire about or imitate the other Franklin—the cultured, traveled diplomat retired from his trade—is the measure of Franklin's genius as preceptor to "the middling people."

Had eighteenth-century Philadelphia been moved to commemorate Civic Virtue, the statue would surely have been one of Benjamin Franklin. His adopted city remembers him most warmly for his achievements as community organizer and supporter of good causes. He could always be counted on to help his fellow citizens—and to organize his fellow citizens to help themselves. Among the results of Franklin's civic energy were the city police; clean, paved, and lighted streets; the first organized militia in Pennsylvania; and the famous volunteer fire companies that made Philadelphia heaven for thousands of small boys. He was then a leading instigator, and is now a hallowed founder, of the American Philosophical Society, the Pennsylvania Hospital, and the University of Pennsylvania. Skeptic and deist, he nevertheless gave support to all the churches "for building their new Places of Worship." [17] As early as 1731 he conceived and organized the first circulating library in America, later to be known as the Library Company. His press, too, was always in public service—sometimes for pay, sometimes not. The *Pennsylvania Gazette* was an institution in itself, and it must be regretted that so promising a journalist should have devoted so little time and pains to this public service. Franklin's activities as journalist were clearly subsidiary to his careers as printer, author, and community organizer. Even the unsuccessful *Philadelphische Zeitung* (the first German-American newspaper) and *General Magazine* were civic undertakings set in motion by the outward-turning of his inner drive toward self-improvement. Franklin was also an early and enthusiastic Mason, a fact of considerable importance for his intercolonial and European reputations.[18]

Franklin's performance as community organizer is a significant chapter in the rise of American liberty. Voluntary action, the fruit of what we too often mock as "public spirit," has been one of the glories of free society, important alike in the material benefits and mental stimulation it has brought to thousands of American communities. Even today, when men turn ever more confidently toward government for solutions to community needs, the area for voluntary action is practically boundless. In Franklin's day civic improvements came from the people or came not at all. The war against civic indolence may seem endless and futile, but the day it ceases will mark the end of free society. Present-day "good citizens" can take heart and lessons from Benjamin Franklin, who knew how to use tact, imagination, perseverance, and democratic sympathy to help his friends make their city "a good place to live."

Franklin's key career was that of politician-diplomat. Entering provincial politics in 1736 as clerk to the Assembly, intercolonial politics in 1753 as deputy Postmaster-General for North America, and imperial affairs in 1757 as special agent of the Assembly in London, he became a wise and able practitioner at every level of public life. He knew what it was to stump for office, palaver with Indians, correspond with governors, wheedle appointments, administer important enterprises, convert popular sentiment, dicker with lords and gentlemen, write laws and constitutions and, finally, to stand before kings as a master diplomat. In all this, being Franklin, he was constantly engaged in self-education, putting principles to the test and finding new principles in the testing. We cannot estimate the vigor of his political faith unless we recall the variety of experience on which it drew.

In Pennsylvania he was clerk of the Assembly (1736-1751), deputy postmaster at Philadelphia (1737-1753), printer to the province, common soldier and colonel of the Pennsylvania militia,[19] representative in the Assembly (1751-1764), and Speaker (1764)—and in addition filled a half dozen other offices from alderman to Indian commissioner. In a muddled political situation [20] that found the Assembly appealing to the Crown for conversion from a proprietary to a royal colony, Franklin was a shrewd leader of the popular party. The struggle between Governor and Assembly in Pennsylvania was little different in character from the legislative-executive battles in other capitals of North America. The fact that the Governor represented Penns rather than Hanovers only sharpened popular resentment against privilege and legalized inequality. Lingering feudalism was the issue in Pennsylvania, and against it Franklin was a shrewd and relentless warrior. The chief proprietor paid him an unwitting compliment in his private correspondence:

> He broaches a Doctrine . . . that Obedience to Governors is no more due than protection to the People. . . . It is not fit to be always in the heads of the unthinking Multitude. . . . He is a dangerous Man and I should be glad he inhabited any other Country, as I believe him of a very uneasy Spirit, however as he is a Sort of Tribune of the People, he must be treated with regard.[21]

As North American Franklin filled two important posts. Although he shared the postmaster-generalship with William Hunter of Virginia, his own energy and Hunter's ill health combined to lodge in Franklin the chief responsibility. His success in improving this long-neglected service and in making it pay revenues to the mother country was one of his most satisfying achievements.[22] He introduced uniform accounting-methods, selected new routes, speeded deliveries, instituted the penny post and dead-letter office, and generally astounded the post office in London with his efficiency and zeal. More important, he helped draw the colonies more closely together and in his tours of inspection won a unique comprehension of their common problems.[23] His knowledge of the population, geography, products, and sentiment of North America was unsurpassed. Franklin's second service to all the colonies was his performance as commissioner from Pennsylvania to the Albany Congress of 1754. His farsighted but rejected "Plan of Union" shows how his mind was running on before those of his fellow Americans. Had colonists or Crown heeded his prophetic voice, the course of British-American relations might have run in stiller channels.

Franklin's progression from politician to statesman and from colonial administrator to imperial diplomat was effected during his first mission to England. Dispatched in 1757 to plead the popular cause against the proprietors, particularly to persuade the Privy Council to permit the proprietary estates to be taxed like other lands, Franklin achieved the purpose of his mission, reaped the first rich harvest of his fame, and after five happy years returned home a citizen of the world. By the time of his next two adventures abroad—in England (1764-1775) as a sort of ambassador extraordinary from the colonies, and in France (1776-1785) on the most famous of all American diplomatic missions—Franklin's and America's colonial phase had drawn to an abrupt close.

Through all these years, colonial and Revolutionary, Franklin never wandered from the libertarian faith that he had first proclaimed publicly in 1722: "I am . . . a mortal Enemy to arbitrary Government and unlimited Power. I am naturally very jealous for the Rights and Liberties of my Country." [24] Even when assailed by bitter enemies and misguided friends, he clung to a belief in the capacity of plain people to govern themselves. In fame as in obscurity Franklin showed himself a convinced democrat. It was America's incredible fortune to be represented at the points of decisive diplomacy by a man not only wise, famous, and infinitely able, but also benevolent, good-humored, and thoroughly democratic. The tune of Franklin's diplomacy was pitched almost scientifically to the aspirations and attitudes of the rising American multitude.

FRANKLIN AS POLITICAL THINKER

Franklin's political theory is as perplexing as it is intriguing, as elusive as it is important. He was an able and productive political pamphleteer. He reflected with peculiar accuracy the changing political moods of eighteenth-century America, and was looked upon as the representative colonist by the keenest observers of his time. He helped introduce to the American mind four or five fundamental assumptions about government and society. Yet he was never in the ordinary sense a theorist or philosopher in the field of political science.

The proof of this observation lies in Franklin's own writings: The sum total of his strictly philosophical musings about government and politics would fill, quite literally, about two printed pages. He wrote authoritatively about scores of events and problems that had persuaded other men to philosophize at length about the nature and purpose of government, but his arguments were descriptive, statistical, propagandistic, and totally lacking in any appeal to fundamentals.[25] He was the one American patriot to write influentially about the events of 1763-1776 without calling upon natural law, the rights of man, and the social contract.

If ever Franklin expressed a clear and conscious thought on such matters as the origin of government or the nature of authority, the research for this chapter, which has led through a half-dozen libraries and several hundred letters, pamphlets, and rough scribblings, has been unable to find it. He seems to have been constitutionally incapable of the kind of writing done by Williams, Wise, Mayhew, Otis, and almost every other political figure in colonial or Revolutionary America. If one small trickle of theory had leaked through somewhere out of the vast structure of his political writings, we might rejoice to have found the sure source of his ideas. The amazing fact that he never once permitted this to happen leaves us wondering if this refusal to philosophize was not the result of a calculated, rigidly observed rule of political argument.

His early and unhappy venture into speculation about the cosmos could well have conditioned his subsequent thinking about politics. "The great uncertainty I found in metaphysical reasonings disgusted me, and I quitted that kind of reading and study for others more satisfactory." [26] The nature of his task should also be remembered: Most of his mature political arguments were letters to the English press, not speeches to the American assemblies. He could hardly have rung the changes on natural rights and revolution in the *London Chronicle* or *Public Advertiser*. And certainly one piece like his *Rules by which a Great Empire may be reduced to a Small One* was worth a hundred passionate appeals to God and nature in the attempt to sway British opinion.[27] In any case, there is no acceptable explanation why Benjamin Franklin, of all people, should have been one of the least philosophical statesmen in American history.

Were the person under analysis anyone but Franklin, this chapter would end here. Yet we are dealing with the great democrat of colonial America, and we must somehow wring from his practical arguments the political faith that he doggedly refused to make articulate. One method of accomplishing this task is to describe Franklin's beliefs as other men saw them. This technique is not ordinarily to be trusted, but in a case like this it is the only alternative to no technique at all. And we have reasonable evidence, drawn particularly from Franklin's consistent actions in support of the popular cause, that he did espouse the principles ascribed to him by friend and foe. These principles may be reduced to two major headings: natural law and radical Whiggery.

It is impossible to evaluate the extent of Franklin's dedication to natural law and natural rights. As scientist, skeptic, and unprejudiced student of universal history, he could not have missed the inconsistencies and historical distortions in Locke's *Civil Government*. On the other hand, his pragmatic mind, which was always more concerned with the effects of a political philosophy than with its logic or symmetry, would have been the first to recognize the usefulness to the popular cause of a system that was based on the notion of government by the consent of the governed. Among the bits of evidence proving that Franklin accepted the dominant theory of his time and class are these: He studied and admired "the great Mr. Locke's" philosophical writings and was hardly less devoted to Algernon Sidney; [28] as a member of the Committee of Five he read over and endorsed Jefferson's rough draft of the Declaration of Independence; [29] and he was widely credited, especially in England, with the authorship of *Common Sense*, which Paine had published anonymously in Philadelphia. It was even rumored that the Queen had caught the Prince of Wales redhanded with "Dr. Franklin's pamphlet Common Sense." [30]

Scattered through Franklin's pamphlets, letters, and notes are other witnesses to his tacit conformity to the "party line," phrases and sentences that glimmer here and there in the great gray mass of his practical arguments. To quote these out of context would be unfair to Franklin, and indeed quite misleading. It must therefore suffice to state the impression they leave: that Franklin endorsed as useful doctrines the state of nature (in which all men are free and equal), the social contract, natural law, natural rights (including "life, liberty, and property," as well as freedom of inquiry, expression, petition, religion, and migration), and the happiness and security of the people as the purpose of government.[31] As the most conspicuous Revolutionary of 1776, Franklin could hardly have doubted the right of resistance and revolution, but we may search his writings in vain for any clear statement of this doctrine.[32]

The only elements in the natural rights-natural law theory that Franklin seems to have enlarged upon were property and equality. Although he shared generally the popular view of the sanctity of property—"Does not *every Man's Feelings* Declare that his Property is not to be taken from him without his Consent?" [33]—he seems to have entertained a somewhat more radical, socially minded view of the relation of any one man's possessions to the common weal. The Franklin touch is manifest in this passage:

> All Property, indeed, except the Savage's temporary Cabin, his Bow, his Matchcoat, and other little Acquisitions, absolutely necessary for his Subsistence, seems to me to be the Creature of public Convention. Hence the Public has the Right of Regulating Descents, and all other Conveyances of Property, and even of limiting the Quantity and the Uses of it. All the Property that is necessary to a Man, for the Conservation of the Individual and the Propagation of the Species, is his natural Right, which none can justly deprive him of: But all Property superfluous to such purposes is the Property of the Publick, who, by their Laws, have created it, and who may therefore by other Laws dispose of it, whenever the Welfare of the Publick shall demand such Disposition. He that does not like civil Society on these Terms, let him retire and live among Savages. He can have no right to the benefits of Society, who will not pay his Club towards the Support of it.[34]

Franklin's belief in equality was the obverse of his well-known impatience with "places, pensions, and peerages," with the stupidity and injustice of legalized inequalities of any description.[35] He came to this belief gradually, for in his earlier years he flirted with the doctrine of the stake-in-society. In the end, his naturally democratic sympathies triumphed resoundingly. Near the close of his life, in arguing against property as a qualification for the suffrage, he had this to say to the proponents of aristocracy:

> The Combinations of Civil Society are not like those of a Set of Merchants, who club their Property in different Proportions for Building and Freighting a Ship, and may therefore have some Right to vote in the Disposition of the Voyage in a greater or less Degree according to their respective Contributions; but the important ends of Civil Society, and the personal Securities of Life and Liberty, these remain the same in every Member of the society; and the poorest continues to have an equal Claim to them with the most opulent, whatever Difference Time, Chance, or Industry may occasion in their Circumstances.[36]

Franklin believed in natural rights and natural law as much as he could believe in any body of doctrine, and he subscribed with extra fervor to the basic Lockean belief in "a Society in which the Ruling Power is circumscribed by previous Laws or Agreements." [37] Like all men of his time he put his faith in limited government, government in which the rulers were the servants of the people.[38]

In considering Franklin a radical Whig the men about him were recognizing his kinship with scores of other representatives of the popular party in the colonial assemblies. With Pitt and King William as their heroes, the Glorious Revolution as their golden age, and the uncorrupted British Constitution as their idea of a perfect governmental system,[39] the colonial Whigs were preparing the ground in which American democracy was to grow. The battle cry of the good Whig, in the colonies as in England, was "Liberty!"—by which he meant constitutionalism, representation, government by "the people" (those who had some property), "the rights of Englishmen," [40] and a system of balanced government in which the legislature was actually dominant. Through most of his life, indeed through all of it as colonial, Franklin was in the van of the liberty-loving Whigs, hoping always to settle his colony's constitution "firmly on the Foundations of Equity and English Liberty." [41] Not all colonial Whigs—Franklin's friend Joseph Galloway, for example—were able to make the transition to independence, fewer still from there to democracy. Franklin seems to have had no trouble. He was a notable specimen of that uncommon species, the man who grows more democratic with age, fame, respectability, and the gout.

Among Franklin's literary remains was a printed paper, endorsed in his hand with the statement, "Some Good Whig Principles." In point of fact, these principles pushed well beyond sound Whiggery into radical country, which explains why he found them especially "good." These could easily have been his own words as he arrived in the mother country in 1764:

> It is declared,
> First, That the government of this realm, and the making of laws for the

same, ought to be lodged in the hands of King, Lords of Parliament, and Representatives of *the whole body* of the freemen of this realm.

Secondly, That *every man* of the commonalty (excepting infants, insane persons, and criminals) is, of common right, and by the laws of God, *a freeman*, and entitled to the free enjoyment of *liberty*.

Thirdly, That liberty, or freedom, consists in having *an actual share* in the appointment of those who frame the laws, and who are to be the guardians of every man's life, property, and peace; for the *all* of one man is as dear to him as the *all* of another; and the poor man has an *equal* right, but *more* need, to have representatives in the legislature than the rich one.

Fourthly, That they who have *no* voice nor vote in the electing of representatives, *do not enjoy* liberty; but are absolutely *enslaved* to those who have votes. . . .

And, sixthly and lastly . . . that it is *the right* of the commonalty of this realm to elect a *new* House of Commons once in *every year*, according to the ancient and sacred laws of the land. . . .[42]

Two more preliminary observations, and we shall be ready to outline Franklin's special contributions to the American tradition. The first touches upon his habits of thought. The methods Franklin employed in weighing political issues were hardly less significant than the decisions he reached. We will have a good deal less trouble with his political mind if we will remember that he was pragmatist, insisting that all ideas be judged by their effects; scientist, distrusting dogma and prizing free inquiry; skeptic, doubting all certainty and never "wholly committed" to any cause or truth; [43] and generalist, ranging through all disciplines and integrating them masterfully into one grand comprehension of human knowledge.

The second point concerns the location of his recorded ideas. For the most part, they are the same as for the other great figures of his time, who wrote copiously, influentially, and with absolutely no system. Pamphlets on current issues, letters to the press, private correspondence, and formal papers are the categories of authorship in which his contributions are to be sought. Hardly less important are the so-called "marginalia," notes made by Franklin in the margins of his copies of other men's pamphlets. Some of these notes are testimony to a universal human urge, the urge to scribble "This Wiseacre," "No!", "Childish," "All mere Quibbling," and "A Falsity!" alongside the brash paragraphs of enemy pamphleteers. Most of them, however, were written in a serious, searching vein, for they were one of his favorite methods of preparing retorts to the press. Although his most important editor, Albert H. Smyth, considered these scribblings "crude and fragmentary," "never intended for publication," and therefore not worth printing,[44] other scholars have valued them highly. These precious indications, in Franklin's own hand, of his innermost thoughts on the great issues of the 1760's are preserved in the Library of Congress, the New York Public Library, the Yale Library, the Philadelphia Athenaeum, and the Historical Society of Pennsylvania. They are a unique source of his political ideas.

Franklin's specific contributions to the aggregate of libertarian principles inherited by the Revolutionary generation were a patchwork of utility, reason, and warm human sympathy. Some of his offerings were directly and consciously bestowed on his fellow citizens. Some were working principles of method and attitude that he was content to practice and to let other men spin out into theories of liberty. All were essential supports of the new way of life and thought that he represented so magnificently before the rulers and people of Europe. Political pragmatism, conciliation and compromise, freedom of speech and press, economic individualism, and federalism were the elements of American democracy to which Franklin devoted special attention.

POLITICAL PRAGMATISM

Pragmatism as a rule of conscious political action has never had a more eminent exponent than Benjamin Franklin.[45] There were great pragmatists before this greatest of pragmatists. The political history of colonial America was written by men who had "the attitude of looking away from first things, principles, 'categories,' supposed necessities; and of looking towards last things, fruits, consequences, facts." [46] But in Franklin's life and political arguments this method became an acknowledged if yet nameless American fundamental. William James, in his lectures on pragmatism in 1906 and 1907, described this philosophy as "a new name for some old ways of thinking." Franklin might have been perplexed by the label, but he would certainly have recognized his own ways of thinking. No man could have been less concerned with origins and first principles or more concerned with consequences and facts. The character of his natural science left its mark on his political science. He was perhaps the most thoroughgoing utilitarian America has produced.

Franklin's political pragmatism was simply one influential expression of his general attitude toward life and its problems. He was not a political philosopher; he was not a philosopher at all. He was prepared to investigate every principle and institution known to the human race, but only through practical and unspeculative methods. He limited his own thought-process to the one devastating question: *Does it work?*, or more exactly, *Does it work well?* Most men who call themselves pragmatists, especially in politics, examine the evidence of consequences and facts from a predetermined observation-post constructed out of strongly held articles of faith. They are pragmatists within limits, within a context that itself may not be put to the test and may well be an irrational inheritance or a rationalized faith. Not so Franklin, who seemed willing to subject even his most basic beliefs, if they could be called that, to the test of experience. He was democrat, radical Whig, and friend of liberty because democracy, Whiggery, and liberty had demonstrated themselves to his uncommitted mind to be the best practical solutions to the problems facing men in society. He had proved and found solid the very context of his pragmatism.

An example of Franklin's consistent devotion to political pragmatism was his well-known attitude on the social usefulness of organized religion. Himself a pagan skeptic with no need for pastoral intervention, he nevertheless had pronounced and favorable views of the value of religion to a free and stable society. He had decided, after much observation in Boston and Philadelphia, that one of the essentials of self-government was a high level of public morality. He had decided further that such a condition of public morality was largely the product of organized religion. The churches and sects of New England and the middle colonies had helped create a collective state of mind conducive to habits of self-reliance and self-government. It had nourished the way of life that his other observations had already pointed out as the most blessed for the average man. Organized religion had worked, and worked well, in the colonies. It must therefore be supported, even by the skeptic. Franklin went to church, when he went to church, because it was "decent and proper," not because he was a believer. In his proposals that led to the founding of the Academy, he advocated the teaching of history because it would "also afford frequent Opportunities of showing the Necessity of a *Publick Religion,* from its Usefulness to the Publick; the Advantage of a Religious Character among private Persons; the Mischiefs of Superstition, etc., and the Excellency of the CHRISTIAN RELIGION above all others antient or modern." [47] He abandoned logical deism because "this doctrine, though it might be true, was not very useful." He turned back to give support to Christianity because this doctrine, though it might be untrue, was highly indispensable to his kind of society.

Education, too, was important because useful. Franklin's faith in education had a dozen outlets. The American Philosophical Society, the Library Company, the University of Pennsylvania, and the Franklin Funds of Boston and Philadelphia are present-day reminders of his high regard for formal and informal education of all classes, ages, and conditions of men. The famous *Proposals Relating to the Education of Youth in Pensilvania* (1749) [48] are utilitarian to the core. The modern reader cannot suppress the pleasant suspicion that Franklin's ideal academy would be geared to turn out the maximum number of young Franklins.

The proprietary government of Pennsylvania, target of his early popularism, was likewise put to the test, but found wanting. Franklin could easily have based his mistrust of this system on principle alone; he preferred to condemn it for its harmful effects. In a characteristic passage from the aptly titled *Cool Thoughts on the Present Situation* (1764), he launched this pragmatic attack on the proprietary system:

> Considering all Circumstances, I am at length inclin'd to think, that the Cause of these miserable Contentions is not to be sought for merely in the Depravity and Selfishness of human Minds. . . . I suspect therefore, that the Cause is radical, interwoven in the Constitution, and so become of the very Nature, of Proprietary Governments; and will therefore produce its Effects, as long as such Governments continue. And, as some Physicians say, every Animal Body brings into the World among its original Stamina the Seeds of that Disease that shall finally produce its Dissolution; so the Political

Body of a Proprietary Government, contains those convulsive Principles that will at length destroy it.

I may not be Philosopher enough to develop those Principles, nor would this Letter afford me Room, if I had Abilities, for such a Discussion. The *Fact* seems sufficient for our Purpose, and the *Fact* is notorious, that such Contentions have been in all Proprietary Governments, and have brought, or are now bringing, them all to a Conclusion.[49]

A final example of Franklin's political pragmatism was his oft-repeated warning against laws that outrage a people's fundamental opinions. This was the sort of argument—calling attention to consequences rather than constitutional rights—with which he attempted to dissuade the advocates of harsh measures for the colonies. He even printed small cards describing "The Result of England's Persistence in Her Policy Towards the Colonies."

> History affords us many instances of the ruin of states, by the prosecution of measures ill suited to the temper and genius of their people. The ordaining of laws in favour of *one* part of the nation, to the prejudice and oppression of *another*, is certainly the most erroneous and mistaken policy. An *equal* dispensation of protection, rights, privileges, and advantages, is what every part is entitled to, and ought to enjoy; it being a matter of no moment to the state, whether a subject grows rich and flourishing on the Thames or the Ohio, in Edinburgh or Dublin. These measures never fail to create great and violent jealousies and animosities between the people favoured and the people oppressed; whence a total separation of affections, interests, political obligations, and all manner of connexions, necessarily ensue, by which the whole state is weakened, and perhaps ruined for ever! [50]

Franklin's supremely practical observation, "the *Fact* seems sufficient for our Purpose, and the *Fact* is notorious," has become a major working principle of this race of pragmatists, and to him and his popular writings must go at least some of the credit.

CONCILIATION AND COMPROMISE

Franklin placed extraordinary value on the spirit and techniques of conciliation and compromise. By nature and experience he was disposed to seek peace and harmony in whatever controversy he might have wandered into by design or accident. His nature was skeptical and undogmatic; he could even doubt his own opinions. The benign speech that James Wilson delivered for him on the last day of the Convention of 1787 was characteristic of a lifetime of active political argument.

> I confess that I do not entirely approve of this Constitution at present, but Sir, I am not sure I shall never approve it: For having lived long, I have experienced many instances of being obliged, by better information or fuller consideration, to change opinions even on important subjects, which I once thought right, but found to be otherwise. It is therefore that the older I grow the more apt I am to doubt my own judgment, and to pay more respect to the judgment of others. Most men indeed as well as most

sects in religion, think themselves in possession of all truth, and that wherever others differ from them it is so far error. Steele, a Protestant, in a dedication tells the Pope, that the only difference between our two churches in their opinions of the certainty of their doctrine, is, the Romish Church is infallible, and the Church of England is never in the wrong. But tho' many private persons think almost as highly of their own infallibility as of that of their Sect, few express it so naturally as a certain French lady, who in a little dispute with her sister, said, I don't know how it happens, Sister, but I meet with nobody but myself that's *always* in the right. *Il n'y a que moi qui a toujours raison.*

In these sentiments, Sir, I agree to this Constitution, with all its faults, if they are such; because I think a general Government necessary for us . . . I consent, Sir, to this Constitution, because I expect no better, and because I am not sure that it is not the best. The opinions I have had of its errors I sacrifice to the public good. I have never whisper'd a syllable of them abroad. Within these walls they were born, and here they shall die. . . .

On the whole, Sir, I cannot help expressing a wish, that every member of the Convention who may still have objections to it, would with me on this occasion doubt a little of his own infallibility, and to make *manifest* our *unanimity,* put his name to this Instrument.[51]

Experience confirmed his natural faith in conciliation. He was a shrewd observer of proceedings in the Junto, the Assembly, and a thousand public meetings. He noted the differing consequences of the differing ways in which men might hold and express the same opinions. Having decided that the spirit of compromise was an essential of political success and the basis of stable, peaceful, effective self-government, he acted in character by laying down rules that would improve himself and others in this important respect.

I made it a rule to forbear all direct contradiction to the sentiments of others and all positive assertion of my own. I even forbade myself . . . the use of every word or expression in the language that imported a fixed opinion, such as "certainly," "undoubtedly," etc.; and I adopted instead of them, "I conceive," "I apprehend," or "I imagine" a thing to be so or so, or "It so appears to me at present." When another asserted something that I thought an error, I denied myself the pleasure of contradicting him abruptly and of showing immediately some absurdity in his proposition; and in answering I began by observing that in certain cases or circumstances his opinion would be right, but that in the present case there "appeared" or "seemed to me" some difference, etc. I soon found the advantage of this change in my manners: The conversations I engaged in went on more pleasantly; the modest way in which I proposed my opinions procured them a readier reception and less contradiction; I had less mortification when I was found to be in the wrong, and I more easily prevailed with others to give up their mistakes and join with me when I happened to be in the right.[52]

The Junto conducted its discussions deliberately in this spirit.

Our debates were to be under the direction of a president, and to be conducted in the sincere spirit of enquiry after truth, without fondness for dis-

pute or desire of victory; and to prevent warmth, all expressions of posi-
tiveness in opinion or of direct contradiction were after some time made
contraband and prohibited under small pecuniary penalties.[53]

Franklin never made the mistake of identifying conciliation and compromise with democracy, of regarding this spirit as an end in itself. In the
Assembly and before the House of Commons his "desire of victory" was
keen and apparent, but he was certain that victory would be easier to gain
if "fondness for dispute" were erased from his nature or at least not betrayed
in debate. He could take a firm stand—even commit himself to an advanced
position, as he did with few qualms in subscribing to the Declaration of
Independence—but he was satisfied that first he had explored all possible
alternatives and had done his best to avoid the final break.

The significance of conciliation and compromise for successful democracy
has never been examined satisfactorily in philosophical terms. It is to be
deeply regretted that Franklin could never bring himself to theorize in
letter or pamphlet about this fundamental principle of his personal code and
public faith. It "worked well," and that was enough for him. Yet any
political theorist who attempts to fix with finality the place of conciliation
and compromise in the American tradition will be well advised to study
Franklin's political conduct. His life argues powerfully that democracy
depends on men with a nice feeling for the proper balance between faith
and skepticism, principle and compromise, tenacity and conciliation. Franklin was boasting, not complaining, when he wrote from London to his
American posterity:

> Hence it has often happened to me, that while I have been thought here
> too much of an American, I have in America been deem'd too much of an
> Englishman.[54]

He could hardly have given himself a finer compliment.

FREEDOM OF SPEECH AND PRESS

Franklin was an influential defender of the twin freedoms of speech and
press. As the leading printer and journalist of the middle colonies, as scientist
dedicated to free inquiry and international exchange of information, and
as politician convinced that discussion and compromise were the essence of
self-government, he had intense personal reasons for championing freedom
of expression.

Through seventy years he never wavered in his belief in the social usefulness of freedom of speech, nor ever shrank from active conflict with those
who would suppress it. In 1722, when Benjamin was only sixteen years
old, his brother James was "taken up, censured, and imprisoned for a month"
for printing in his *New-England Courant* a political piece that "gave offence
to the Assembly."

> During my brother's confinement, which I resented a good deal notwith-
> standing our private differences, I had the management of the paper, and

I made bold to give our rulers some rubs in it, which my brother took very kindly, while others began to consider me in an unfavourable light as a young genius that had a turn for libelling and satire. My brother's discharge was accompanied with an order from the House (a very odd one) that "James Franklin should no longer print the paper called the *New England Courant.*" There was a consultation held in our printing house amongst his friends in this conjuncture. Some proposed to elude the order by changing the name of the paper; but my brother seeing inconveniences in that, it was finally concluded on as a better way to let it be printed for the future under the name of "Benjamin Franklin." [55]

The piece in which the apprentice "made bold to give our rulers some rubs" was the eighth of his communications to the *Courant* from "Silence Dogood." In this letter he quoted at length the most famous of *Cato's Letters,* which he presented as an "Abstract from the London Journal." Even over a pseudonym it was a bold swipe at authority, and the wonder is that Benjamin did not follow James to jail.

WITHOUT Freedom of Thought, there can be no such Thing as Wisdom; and no such Thing as publick Liberty, without Freedom of Speech; which is the Right of every Man, as far as by it, he does not hurt or controul the Right of another: And this is the only Check it ought to suffer, and the only Bounds it ought to Know.

This sacred Privilege is so essential to free Governments, that the Security of Property, and the Freedom of Speech always go together; and in those wretched Countries where a Man cannot call his Tongue his own, he can scarce call any Thing else his own. Whoever would overthrow the Liberty of a Nation, must begin by subduing the Freeness of Speech; a *Thing* terrible to Publick Traytors. . . .

The Administration of Government is nothing else but the Attendance of the *Trustees of the People* upon the Interest and Affairs of the People: And as it is the Part and Business of the People, for whose Sake alone all publick Matters are, or ought to be transacted, to see whether they be well or ill transacted; so it is the Interest, and ought to be the Ambition, of all honest Magistrates, to have their Deeds openly examined, and publickly scan'd. . . .

Misrepresentation of publick Measures is easily overthrown, by representing publick Measures truly; when they are honest, they ought to be publickly known, that they may be publickly commended; but if they are knavish or pernicious, they ought to be publickly detested. [56]

Franklin carried these youthful beliefs through seventy years of political storms. To freedom of speech he was "wholly committed."

The publisher of the *Pennsylvania Gazette* had considerable influence upon the development of a free and responsible press. Like the best papers in London, the *Gazette* adopted a policy of neutrality in public controversies. Franklin refused to make his paper the organ of the antiproprietary party, but threw its columns open to opinions from all sides. At the same time, he kept constant watch on the political winds that blew and weathered several storms by discreetly reefing his sails. As long as freedom of the press was uncertain in Pennsylvania, he was careful merely to antagonize, not enrage, the proprietary party. Meanwhile he did his best to cement this freedom by printing a responsible journal, by calling attention to the value of differing opinions, and by publishing an account of the trial of John Peter Zenger.

By 1750 the press in England and the colonies had achieved a remarkable measure of freedom. Franklin, who wrote to the *Public Advertiser* that "Free Government depends on Opinion, not on the brutal Force of a Standing Army," [57] made full use in England of what he had helped create in America: an unlicensed, uncensored press in which the public could find all important issues thoroughly, even controversially debated.

Franklin's most influential statement on freedom of press was "An Apology for Printers," which appeared in the *Gazette* June 10, 1731.[58] This "apology" is worth quoting at length, for it is an accurate representation of the principles of a free press which governed popular thinking in eighteenth-century America.

BEING frequently censur'd and condemn'd by different Persons for printing Things which they say ought not to be printed, I have sometimes thought it might be necessary to make a standing Apology for my self, and publish it once a Year, to be read upon all Occasions of that Nature. . . .

I request all who are angry with me on the Account of printing things they don't like, calmly to consider these following Particulars.

1. That the Opinions of Men are almost as various as their Faces; an Observation general enough to become a common Proverb, *So many Men so many Minds.*

2. That the Business of Printing has chiefly to do with Mens Opinions; most things that are printed tending to promote some, or oppose others.

3. That hence arises the peculiar Unhappiness of that Business, which other Callings are no way liable to; they who follow Printing being scarce able to do any thing in their way of getting a Living, which shall not probably give Offence to some, and perhaps to many; . . .

5. Printers are educated in the Belief, that when Men differ in Opinion, both Sides ought equally to have the Advantage of being heard by the Publick; and that when Truth and Error have fair Play, the former is always an overmatch for the latter: Hence they chearfully serve all contending Writers that pay them well, without regarding on which side they are of the Question in Dispute. . . .

10. That notwithstanding what might be urg'd in behalf of a Man's being allow'd to do in the Way of his Business whatever he is paid for, yet Printers do continually discourage the Printing of great Numbers of bad things, and stifle them in the Birth. I my self have constantly refused to print anything that might countenance Vice, or promote Immorality; tho' by complying in such Cases with the corrupt Taste of the Majority I might have got much Money. . . .

To this shrewd and useful set of working principles should be added a reflection penned by Franklin in a private letter more than a half century later.

It is a pleasing reflection, arising from the contemplation of our successful struggle . . . that liberty, which some years since appeared in danger
of extinction, is now regaining the ground she had lost, that arbitrary governments are likely to become more mild and reasonable, and to expire by
degrees, giving place to more equitable forms; one of the effects this of the
art of printing, which diffuses so general a light, augmenting with the growing day, and of so penetrating a nature, that all the window-shutters despotism and priestcraft can oppose to keep it out, prove insufficient.[59]

The old man at Passy was not so lucid as he had been in London or
Philadelphia, but his faith in the power of truth and in the influence of the
printed word was as strong as ever. Franklin went to his republican grave
secure in the knowledge that he had done as much as any other man to
advertise freedom of expression to the American political consciousness.

INDUSTRY AND FRUGALITY

Many Americans would argue that Franklin's reputation as herald of democracy should rest in the first instance upon his contributions to economic
individualism. Certainly no one, whether friend or foe of the American
system, would deny that our political democracy is underpinned and shaped
by a well-defined set of economic principles and institutions. Our economic
and political systems, like our economic and political traditions, have always
been inseparable, mutually nourishing elements of "the American way of
life." American democracy has been, in the best and truest sense of the
terms, middle-class, bourgeois, free-enterprise democracy. The twentieth-
century trend toward government regulation and the welfare state has, if
anything, sharpened our comprehension of this historical truth.

In the light of this truth, Franklin's significance is unmistakable. As self-
made business success he represented to the world the rise to prominence of
the American bourgeoisie; as author and moralist he preached to "the
middling people" the personal virtues that a nation of businessmen was to
practice and cherish; as the best-known economist in colonial America he
was a respected foe of mercantilism and advocate of the liberating principles
of laissez-faire.[60]

The first and second of these points may be considered together, for
Franklin's moralizing was an unsolicited testimonial to his own "way to
wealth." Father Abraham's formula for worldly success—"*Industry* and
Frugality"—paired virtues that Franklin had not come by naturally. He
had cultivated these qualities consciously in order to win financial independence, and he saw no reason why they could not be cultivated by other
men in business. The unique features of the American democratic culture
owe a good deal to these words from *The Way to Wealth*:

It would be thought a hard Government that should tax its People one-
tenth Part of their *Time*, to be employed in its Service. But *Idleness* taxes
many of us much more, if we reckon all that is spent in absolute *Sloth*, or
doing of nothing, with that which is spent in idle Employment or Amuse-

ments, that amount to nothing. *Sloth,* by bringing on Diseases, absolutely shortens Life. *Sloth, like Rust, consumes faster than Labour wears; while the used Key is always bright,* as *Poor Richard* says. *But dost thou love Life, then do not squander Time, for that's the stuff Life is made of,* as *Poor Richard* says. How much more than is necessary do we spend in sleep, forgetting that *The sleeping Fox catches no Poultry,* and that *There will be sleeping enough in the Grave,* as *Poor Richard* says.

If Time be of all Things the most precious, wasting Time must be, as *Poor Richard* says, *the greatest Prodigality;* since, as he elsewhere tells us, *Lost Time is never found again; and what we call Time enough, always proves little enough:* Let us then up and be doing, and doing to the Purpose; so by Diligence shall we do more with less Perplexity. *Sloth makes all Things difficult, but Industry all easy,* as *Poor Richard* says; and *He that riseth late must trot all Day, and shall scarce overtake his Business at Night;* while *Laziness travels so slowly, that Poverty soon overtakes him,* as we read in *Poor Richard,* who adds, *Drive thy Business, let not that drive thee;* and *Early to Bed, and early to rise, makes a Man healthy, wealthy, and wise.*

So what signifies *wishing* and *hoping* for better Times. We may make these Times better, if we bestir ourselves. *Industry need not wish,* as *Poor Richard* says, *and he that lives upon Hope will die fasting. There are no Gains without Pains; then Help Hands, for I have no Lands,* or if I have, they are smartly taxed. And, as *Poor Richard* likewise observes, *He that hath a Trade hath an Estate; and he that hath a Calling, hath an Office of Profit and Honour;* but then the *Trade* must be worked at, and the Calling well followed, or neither the *Estate* nor the *Office* will enable us to pay our Taxes. If we are industrious, we shall never starve; for as *Poor Richard* says, *At the working Man's House Hunger looks in, but dares not enter.* Nor will the Bailiff or the Constable enter, for *Industry pays Debts, while Despair encreaseth them,* says *Poor Richard.* What though you have found no Treasure, nor has any rich Relation left you a Legacy, *Diligence is the Mother of Goodluck* as *Poor Richard* says *and God gives all Things to Industry. Then plough deep, while Sluggards sleep, and you shall have Corn to sell and to keep, says Poor Dick.* . . . 'Tis true there is much to be done, and perhaps you are weak-handed, but stick to it steadily; and you will see great Effects, for *Constant Dropping wears away Stones,* and by *Diligence and Patience the Mouse ate in two the Cable;* and *Little Strokes fell great Oaks,* as *Poor Richard* says in his Almanack, the Year I cannot just now remember.

Methinks I hear some of you say, *Must a Man afford himself no Leisure?* I will tell thee, my friend, what *Poor Richard* says, *Employ thy Time well, if thou meanest to gain Leisure; and, since thou art not sure of a Minute, throw not away an Hour.* Leisure, is Time for doing something useful; this Leisure the diligent Man will obtain, but the lazy Man never; so that, as *Poor Richard* says *A Life of Leisure and a Life of Laziness are two Things.* Do you imagine that Sloth will afford you more Comfort than Labour? No, for as *Poor Richard* says, *Trouble springs from Idleness, and grievous Toil from needless Ease. Many without Labour, would live by their wits only, but they break for want of Stock.* Whereas Industry gives Comfort, and Plenty, and Respect: *Fly Pleasures, and they'll follow you. The diligent Spinner has a large Shift; and now I have a Sheep and a Cow, everyBody bids me good Morrow;* all which is well said by *Poor Richard. . . .*

So much for Industry, my Friends, and Attention to one's own Business; but to these we must add *Frugality,* if we would make our *Industry* more certainly successful. A Man may, if he knows not how to save as he gets, *keep his Nose all his Life to the Grindstone,* and die not worth a *Groat* at last. *A fat Kitchen makes a lean Will,* as *Poor Richard* says; and

> Many Estates are spent in the Getting,
> Since Women for Tea forsook Spinning and Knitting,
> And Men for Punch forsook Hewing and Splitting.

If you would be wealthy, says he, in another Almanack, *think of Saving as well as of Getting: The Indies have not made Spain rich, because her Outgoes are greater than her Incomes.*

Away then with your expensive Follies, and you will not then have so much Cause to complain of hard Times, heavy Taxes, and chargeable Families; for, as *Poor Dick* says,

> Women and Wine, Game and Deceit,
> Make the Wealth small and the Wants great.

And farther, *What maintains one Vice, would bring up two Children.* You may think perhaps, that a *little* Tea, or a *little* Punch now and then, Diet a *little* more costly, Clothes a *little* finer, and a *little* Entertainment now and then, can be no *great* Matter; but remember what *Poor Richard* says, *Many a Little makes a Mickle;* and farther, Beware of little *Expences; A small Leak will sink a great Ship;* and again, *Who Dainties love, shall Beggars prove;* and moreover, *Fools make Feasts, and wise Men eat them.*[61]

Whether industry and frugality were qualities of Puritan origin—whether Franklin was, as many scholars have insisted, an ideological middleman between Cotton Mather and John D. Rockefeller—is a question of scant meaning for his status as prophet of American capitalism.[62] The young Franklin could easily have read about the pleasant consequences of industry and frugality in several non-Calvinistic writers, or could have learned them from the Quaker merchants of Philadelphia.[63] It is highly probable that this lesson, too, was learned pragmatically, out of his own experience. In any case, his unsophisticated, straightforward writings on the elements of business success—the prefaces to *Poor Richard, The Way to Wealth,* and after his death the priceless *Autobiography*—were translated and retranslated into a dozen languages, printed and reprinted in hundreds of editions, read and reread by millions of people, especially by young and impressionable Americans. The influence of these few hundred pages has been matched by that of no other American book.

Industry and frugality can hardly be called political principles. Yet as the central elements in the American creed of economic individualism their influence upon our politics has been pronounced and lasting. The character of a nation cannot be other than the aggregate of the characters of its citizens, and American democracy surely owes a healthy portion of its past and present character to the efforts of its citizens to imitate the Franklin of the *Autobiography*. The frugal, industrious, self-reliant, community-minded businessman and farmer—the typical American—lives even today in the image of "Benjamin Franklin, printer." Carlyle was not too far from the truth when he looked at Franklin's portrait and exclaimed, "There is the father of all the Yankees."

The Puritan virtues, if we may call them that, do not add up to an especially pleasant and well-rounded personality. Franklin, however, never intended that they should stand alone, and such persons as D. H. Lawrence [64] have done the great bourgeois no honor in confusing his full-bodied character with that of the mythical Poor Richard. All that Franklin was trying to tell his fellow Americans was that first things must be attended to first: When a man had worked and saved his way to success and independence, he could then begin to live a fuller or even quite different life. This is what Franklin had in mind when he had Father Abraham declare, "Be *industrious* and *free; be frugal* and *free.*" [65] The expansion of America is evidence enough that as elements of a larger tradition, as facets of a whole personality, industry and frugality have given fiber alike to nation and individuals. The American mind stands fast in the belief that these virtues are indispensable props of freedom and independence, for as Father Abraham observed, "A Ploughman on his Legs is higher than a Gentleman on his Knees."

We must be extremely cautious in presenting Franklin as an early advocate of laissez-faire. Like Jefferson and Lincoln he has been rudely appropriated and glibly quoted as the patron saint of some of our most reactionary movements and organizations. And like Jefferson and Lincoln he was a good deal more benevolent, progressive, and community-minded than those who now call him to judgment against all social legislation.

Franklin's most imposing service to the triumph of laissez-faire was his attack on the restrictive doctrines of mercantilism. He was a colonial tradesman who resented the assignment of America to an inferior economic position. He was a friend of liberty who disliked the efforts of any exploiting group—whether proprietors, princes, priests, or English manufacturers—to prevent the mass of men from realizing their full capabilities and impulses toward freedom. Small wonder that he had no use for mercantilist policies. His central position in the controversy over Parliament's power to legislate for the colonies and his cordial relations with the French Physiocrats [66] strengthened his earlier, provincial convictions that free trade among all nations and colonies was the way to peace and economic prosperity, and that mercantilism, like all unnecessary tampering with "the order of God and Nature," was unwise, unjust, unprofitable, and ultimately unworkable.[67] It is amusing and instructive to notice the very different thought-processes by which Franklin and the Physiocrats arrived at identical conclusions about the unwisdom of government regulation of the economy and the beauties of free trade. The Physiocrats regarded free trade as part of their "natural order"—"that order which seemed obviously the best, not to any individual whomsoever, but to rational, cultured, liberal-minded men like the Physiocrats. It was not the product of the observation of external facts; it was the revelation of a principle within." [68] Nothing could have been further removed from Franklin's pragmatic method of fixing his gaze upon effects and consequences.[69]

Perhaps the clearest evidence of Franklin's devotion to a free economy is to be found in a copy of George Whatley's *The Principles of Trade* in the Library of Congress. This anti-mercantilist tract was published in 1765 and was republished in 1774 with many new notes. The Library of Congress copy,[70] a second edition, bears this inscription on the flyleaf: "The gift of Doctr. B. Franklin to Th. Jefferson," and this note on page 2: "Notes marked B. F. are Doctr. Franklin's." Some of the most important notes in the book are marked "B. F." in Jefferson's hand, and there is little doubt that these were Franklin's contributions to Whatley's new edition. Whatley spoke in his preface of "some very respectable Friends" who had indulged him "with their Ideas and Opinions." The most significant of "B. F.'s" ideas was the note on pages 33-34, a hard-packed essay containing at least four phrases found elsewhere in Franklin's writings. The spelling is Whatley's, but the words are Franklin's:

> Perhaps, in general, it wou'd be beter if Government medled no farther wide Trade, than to protect it, and let it take its Cours. Most of the Statutes, or Acts, Edicts, Arets and Placaarts of Parliaments, Princes, and States, for regulating, directing, or restraining of Trade; have, we think, been either political Blunders, or Jobbs obtain'd by artful Men, for private Advantage, under Pretence of public Good. When Colbert asembled some wise old Merchants of France; and desir'd their Advice and Opinion, how he cou'd best serve and promote Comerce; their Answer, after Consultation, was, in three words only, *Laissez nous faire*. Let us alone. It is said, by a very solid Writer of the same Nation, that he is wel advanc'd in the Science of Politics, who knows the ful Force of that Maxim *Pas trop gouverner:* Not to govern too strictly, which, perhaps, wou'd be of more Use when aply'd to Trade, than in any other public Concern. It were therefore to be wish'd that Comerce were as fre between al the Nations of the World, as it is between the several Countrys of England.

In his own writings, too, Franklin was outspoken in his praise of the new principles of laissez-faire that were shortly to be more scientifically demonstrated by Adam Smith and others.[71] He did as much as any American to dig the grave of mercantilism. In an age when liberalism was strongly and naturally opposed to government regulation of the economy, a passage such as this was a hard blow for freedom:

> It seems contrary to the Nature of Commerce, for Government to interfere in the Prices of Commodities. Trade is a voluntary Thing between Buyer and Seller, in every Article of which each exercises his own Judgment, and is to please himself. . . . Where there are a number of different Traders, the separate desire of each to get more Custom will operate in bringing their goods down to a reasonable Price. It therefore seems to me, that Trade will best find and make its own Rates; and that Government

cannot well interfere, unless it would take the whole Trade into its own hands . . . and manage it by its own Servants, at its own Risque.

Franklin's limitations as laissez-faire economist should be clearly understood. In addition to the obvious and characteristic fact that he refused to draw together his scattered arguments against mercantilism into a balanced economic philosophy, several points should be considered by economic individualists who insist upon invoking his illustrious shade: his strong, quite Jeffersonian agrarian bias ("Agriculture is the great Source of Wealth and Plenty");[72] his community-minded views on the nature of private property; his perception of the social evils of emergent industrialism ("Manufactures are founded in poverty");[73] his vigorous opposition to government by plutocracy;[74] his consistent hostility to the erection of tariff barriers;[75] and his refusal to pursue the pound after 1748. Franklin was an economic individualist, not because he had any mystic faith in the utility of the profit motive or benefits of an industrial society, but because economic individualism led to personal independence, which in turn enabled a man to live virtuously and usefully. Franklin could hardly have foreseen the great concentrations of wealth and economic power which were to signal the successes of American free enterprise, but we may rest assured that he would have found them poisonous to the simple, friendly, free, communal way of life he hoped his countrymen would cultivate and cherish. In any case, he did much to shape the economy that in turn has helped shape the American governmental system.

THE PROBLEM OF FEDERATION

In most political theories or popular traditions federalism has been at best a convenient technique of constitutional organization; more often than not it has been passed over completely. In the United States of America it has been an article of faith. The Republic was founded upon the concept of limited government, and the existence of the states, semisovereign entities with lives and powers of their own, has always been considered the one trustworthy limit upon all urges toward centralized absolutism. The federal principle is something more fundamental and emotion-provoking than one more check in a system of checks and balances.

Franklin made rich contributions to the theory and practice of American federalism. Almost alone among Americans of the mid-eighteenth century he saw, as usual from a wholly practical point of view, the solid advantages that each colony would derive from a solemn union for well-defined purposes. He was far ahead of the men about him in abandoning provincialism for an intercolonial attitude—too far, it would seem, for his efforts to speed up the slow development of American federalism ended in a magnificent failure.

Franklin tells the story of his great adventure in intercolonial diplomacy so frugally and honestly that it would be absurd to hear it from anyone but him:

In 1754 war with France being again apprehended, a congress of commissioners from the different Colonies was by an order of the Lords of Trade to be assembled at Albany, there to confer with the chiefs of the six nations concerning the means of defending both their country and ours. Governor Hamilton having received this order, acquainted the House with it . . . naming the Speaker (Mr. Norris) and myself to join Mr. Thomas Penn and Mr. Secretary Peters as commissioners to act for Pennsylvania . . . we met the other commissioners at Albany about the middle of June. In our way thither, I projected and drew up a plan for the union of all the Colonies under one government, so far as might be necessary for defence and other important general purposes. . . . I ventured to lay it before the Congress. It then appeared that several of the commissioners had formed plans of the same kind. A previous question was first taken whether a union should be established, which passed in the affirmative unanimously. A committee was then appointed, one member from each colony, to consider the several plans and report. Mine happened to be preferred, and with a few amendments was accordingly reported. By this plan the general government was to be administered by a president-general appointed and supported by the Crown and a grand council to be chosen by the representatives of the people of the several Colonies met in their respective Assemblies. The debates upon it in Congress went on daily hand in hand with the Indian business. Many objections and difficulties were started, but at length they were all overcome, and the plan was unanimously agreed to, and copies ordered to be transmitted to the Board of Trade and to the Assemblies of the several provinces. Its fate was singular. The Assemblies did not adopt it, as they all thought there was too much *prerogative* in it; and in England it was judged to have too much of the *democratic*. The Board of Trade therefore did not approve of it; nor recommend it for the approbation of His Majesty. . . .[76]

The powers of the president-general and grand council in Franklin's plan were sharply limited by the purpose of the proposed union—defense of the frontier. They were directed to four specific problems: Indian treaties "in which the general interest of the colonies may be concerned"; war and peace with the Indians; purchases and settlement of western lands; and regulation of Indian trade. To these ends the union was authorized to "raise and pay soldiers," "build forts," and "equip vessels," as well as to "make laws, and lay and levy such general duties, imposts, or taxes, as to them shall appear most equal and just." Representation on the council was to be proportioned to each colony's contributions to the common treasury, and the council was protected against dissolution or prorogation by the president-general.[77] Finally, the interests of the mother country were secured by subjecting all laws to the scrutiny and possible veto of the King-in-Council.

The Albany Plan was not so much the creation of one man's lively genius as the product of several fine minds working toward a long-contemplated goal, with all arrangements conditioned sharply by the fear of offending shortsighted Crown and stubborn colonies. Yet Franklin's plan was preferred to all others and was adopted by the commissioners with very few changes. Although he did not yet have a well-developed understanding of the federal principle, he did recognize the advantages and delicacies of confederation for defense. The Albany Plan is a landmark on the rough road of union that leads through the first Continental Congresses and the Articles of Confederation to the Constitution of 1787. It was a notable expression of Franklin's faith in co-operative effort in a common cause. He never ceased to believe that in this matter at least he was right and other men wrong.

> I am still of opinion it would have been happy for both sides the water if it had been adopted. The Colonies so united would have been sufficiently strong to have defended themselves; there would then have been no need of troops from England; of course the subsequent pretence for taxing America and the bloody contest it occasioned would have been avoided. But such mistakes are not new; history is full of the errors of states and princes.[78]

In June 1775, as delegate to the second Continental Congress, Franklin proposed a plan, "Articles of Confederation and Perpetual Union" for the "United Colonies of North America," [79] which was based on his Albany Plan and several other instances of colonial federation. The Congress was not ready for any such radical step, but again Franklin had pointed the way for other men to follow. In the crucial matter of representation Franklin, a "large-state" man with no shred of provincial prejudice, was strongly opposed to the Articles of Confederation eventually adopted. Representation in his proposed Congress was to be proportioned to population.[80] He was not entirely satisfied with the solution adopted by the Convention of 1787, but he was strong in his final faith in federal union.

Franklin's opinions on imperial federation and the power of Parliament to tax and govern the colonies deserve brief mention. He, too, took part in the process of backing and filling through which leading colonists moved toward the dominion theory finally implied in the Declaration of Independence. Having passed and repassed through the intermediate stages—acknowledgment of Parliament's power to legislate for the colonies,[81] advocacy of colonial representation in Parliament (an old favorite of Franklin's),[82] assertion of the finespun distinction between internal and external taxation,[83] simultaneous and confusing assertion of the distinction between taxation for revenue and taxation for regulation of commerce,[84]—Franklin took final refuge in the useful conclusion that the colonies, as equals of the mother country, were united to her only "by having one common sovereign, the King." [85] Under this interpretation of the colonial system, the achievement of independence, at least on paper, involved nothing more than renouncing allegiance to a tyrannical king.

DEMOCRACY

One final observation must be made and supported before we can close the circle of Franklin's political philosophy: In thought, action, and argument he was a warmhearted democrat, in the best and fullest sense of the word. Origin, temperament, environment, and experience all helped produce the leading democrat of the age. The last of these, experience, was especially instrumental. The delightful fact that Franklin, as he saw more and more of the way the world did its business, grew more and more sour on the supposed merits of monarchy and aristocracy leads us to believe that his democracy, too, was of pragmatic origin. Whatever the explanation, there is ample proof of his ever-growing respect for the right and capacity of ordinary men to govern themselves. His faith in the judgment of the people was not completely uncritical, but it was a faith on which he was willing to act.[86]

One example was the manner in which Franklin refused to abandon the tenets of radical Whiggery, but rather refined and republicanized them into a profoundly democratic system of constitutional principles. Franklin was one of the few old Revolutionaries at the Convention of 1787 who did not embrace the new faith in the separation of powers. He signed the Constitution willingly, believing that it was the best obtainable under the circumstances, and hoping that it would not frustrate the natural course of democratic progress. Yet he would have preferred a constitution with these radically different arrangements: a plural executive, unsalaried and probably elected by the legislature; a unicameral legislature, with representation proportioned to population; annual elections for all holders of public office, including officers of the militia; universal manhood suffrage, with no bow to property; a straightforward, unqualified bill of rights; and an easy method of formal amendment.[87]

Since he practiced what he preached and "doubted a little of his own infallibility," he did not find it necessary to withdraw from the convention. Yet it is clear that he was much in sympathy with the opposition of the radicals to the Constitution. The one point at which he departed from their doctrine may well have been decisive: Having abandoned the provincial attitude before most of the anti-Federalists were born, Franklin had little sympathy for their anti-national point of view. The old imperialist had great faith in the advantages of a "general government." He hoped out loud that each member of the proposed Congress would "consider himself rather as a Representative of the whole, than as an Agent for the Interests of a particular State."[88] And he even supported a motion that "the national legislature ought to be empowered to negative all laws, passed by the several States, contravening, in the opinion of the national legislature, the articles of union . . . or any Treaties subsisting under the authority of the union."[89] Franklin's final political faith was as "national" as it was "democratical."

He was one of the few men in America unafraid to use both of these adjectives in public.

Another example of Franklin's progress toward an ever purer democratic faith was his change in attitude on the question of Negro slavery. Although the Junto had taken an early stand against slavery, the organizer of the Junto was not above dealing in "likely young Negroes" as a sideline. In time he came to see the monstrous injustice of the thing and gave full backing to several organizations devoted to freeing and educating the Negro slave. His last public act was performed as President of the Pennsylvania Society for Promoting the Abolition of Slavery, when he signed a memorial to the House of Representatives calling for measures to discourage the slave trade. His last public writing was a letter to the *Federal Gazette* satirizing the arguments of a Georgia congressman in defense of this traffic.[90] By the time of his death he had expressed all the fundamental economic and ethical arguments against slavery, asserting in particular that it was unjust, unnatural, and inhuman, and a corrupting menace to free institutions and love of liberty.

Finally, Franklin was firmly in the popular ranks in his sanguine opinion of political parties. He did not consider them "factions" but natural products of free government, ventilators of public issues, and effective instruments of the popular will. In *The Internal State of America*, an undated but late sociological musing, Franklin had these characteristic words to say on a problem that gave some framers sleepless nights:

> It is true that in some of our States there are Parties and Discords; but let us look back, and ask if we were ever without them? Such will exist wherever there is Liberty; and perhaps they help to preserve it. By the Collision of different Sentiments, Sparks of Truth are struck out, and political Light is obtained. The different Factions, which at present divide us, aim all at the Publick Good; the Differences are only about the various Modes of promoting it. Things, Actions, Measures and Objects of all kinds, present themselves to the Minds of Men in such a Variety of Lights, that it is not possible we should all think alike at the same time on every Subject, when hardly the same Man retains at all times the same Ideas of it. Parties are therefore the common Lot of Humanity; and ours are by no means more mischievous or less beneficial than those of other Countries, Nations and Ages, enjoying in the same Degree the great Blessing of Political Liberty.[91]

These are the thoughts of a wise, kindly, democratic old man who looked upon co-operation through organization as the motive power of free society.

"THIS IS MY COUNTRY"

Conclusions are dangerous, especially when they deal with great men, even more so when the great man in question has already been rounded off by Becker and Van Doren.[92] This conclusion will therefore be narrow and apposite. Skirting any evaluation of Franklin's complete character and accomplishments, omitting any further mention of his influence on the American tradition, it will confine itself rigidly to one date and place—February 13, 1766, in the British House of Commons—and one question: What political faith did Franklin express and represent as he stood before the members and answered their questions about British North America? [93]

First, he represented a pattern of popular political thought ancient in origin but new in sweep. The more perceptive gentlemen, among them Franklin's well-wishers, could look behind his spare phrases and see the mind of a whole continent in political ferment. Whiggery, under several names and guises, had swept America, and the ultimate Whig was now at the bar. It must have been an unsettling experience for some members to hear the blessed words "unjust," "unconstitutional," "liberties," "privileges," and "common consent" drop from the lips of this middling person. Here before them was walking evidence that the people of the colonies were beginning to think in terms, not only of the constitutional rights of Englishmen, but of the natural rights of all men.

Second, Franklin represented new habits of thinking about political and social problems. However legalistic and theoretical were most arguments out of Boston and Philadelphia, his brand of persuasion was more expressive of the average colonial mind. Franklin's method was an informed, hardheaded appeal to facts. "The *Fact* seems sufficient for our Purpose, and the *Fact* is notorious." His case for repeal of the Stamp Act could be compressed in the warning, "It doesn't work; it never will." America's favorite argument was seeing its first heavy duty.

He likewise represented the incipient fact of American federalism. Himself a uniquely *American* official—"I am Deputy Postmaster-General of North-America"—he breathed the continental spirit that was to power the final drive toward independence. He could tell the House that "every assembly on the continent, and every member in every assembly" had denied Parliament's authority to pass the Stamp Act. From this day forward, throughout the next nine years, Franklin was unofficial ambassador for all the colonies. The American union was hastening to be born, and the sign of union was Dr. Franklin.

Next, Franklin represented the growing American conviction that the colonies were marked for a future state of "glory and honor" that would dwarf that of the mother country. As early as 1752 Poor Richard had echoed the widespread belief that America was a God-ordained haven for the oppressed of every land:

> Where the sick Stranger joys to find a Home,
> Where casual Ill, maim'd Labour, freely come;
> Those worn with Age, Infirmity or Care,
> Find Rest, Relief, and Health returning fair.
> There too the Walls of rising Schools ascend,
> For Publick Spirit still is Learning's Friend,
> Where Science, Virtue, sown with liberal Hand,
> In future Patriots shall inspire the Land.

God's plans for America were even more challenging than that:

I have long been of opinion, that *the foundations of the future grandeur and stability of the British empire lie in America;* and though, like other foundations, they are low and little now, they are, nevertheless, broad and strong enough to support the greatest political structure that human wisdom ever yet erected.[94]

A different sort of empire, cast loose from the mother country, was to' rise on this foundation and satisfy the prophecies of destiny that Franklin had pronounced.

Finally, and most important, Franklin stood before Commons and the world as the representative colonial. This person who knew so much more about America than anyone else, who talked of rights and resistance so confidently, this was no Belcher or Hutchinson, no placeman or royal governor, but a new breed of man to be heard in high places. Although Franklin was actually the most extraordinary man of the century, on that memorable day he was the true colonist—self-contained, plain-spoken, neither arrogant nor humble, the visible expression of the new way of life and liberty which was to occupy the continent. And as men looked in wonder at him and America, so he and America looked in disbelief at England. The eyes of the colonists seemed open for the first time to the corruption and self-interest that cankered and degraded all British politics. The new world was at last face to face with the old and about to reject it for something more wholesome. The old world would realize too late that Franklin spoke for a multitude even then turning away to a faith of its own when he said of the British nation, "It knows and feels itself so universally corrupt and rotten from Head to Foot, that it has little Confidence in any publick Men or publick Measures." [95]

Now that these things have been written, now that Franklin has surrendered his identity to colonial democracy, perhaps it would be proper to rescue him and end this chapter with our attention fixed on him alone. He was, after all, Dr. Benjamin Franklin, the most amazing man America has produced, as untypical in the whole as he was typical in his parts. And in fixing our attention we must recall the one conviction that brought harmony to this human multitude: the love of liberty—in every land, in every time, and for every man.

God grant, that not only the Love of Liberty, but a thorough Knowledge of the Rights of Man, may pervade all the Nations of the Earth, so that a Philosopher may set his Foot anywhere on its Surface, and say, "This is my Country." [96]

Part 3

THE HERITAGE

On March 22, 1765, George III gave his royal assent to the Stamp Act, a stick of imperial dynamite so harmless in appearance that it had passed both houses of Parliament as effortlessly as "a common Turnpike Bill." Eleven years later, July 2, 1776, the Continental Congress resolved after "the greatest and most solemn debate":

> That these United Colonies are, and, of right, ought to be, Free and Independent States; that they are absolved from all allegiance to the *British* crown, and that all political connexion between them, and the state of *Great Britain*, is, and ought to be totally dissolved.[1]

In the tumultuous years between these two fateful acts the American colonists, at least a sufficient number of them, stumbled and haggled their way to a heroic decision: to found a new nation upon political and social principles that were a standing reproach to almost every other nation in the world. Not for another seven years could they be certain that their decision had been sound as well as bold; only then would the mother country admit reluctantly that the new nation was a fact of life rather than an act of treason. The colonists were to learn at Brooklyn and Valley Forge that it was one thing to resolve for independence and another to achieve it.

Yet the resolution for independence, the decision to fight as a "separate and equal" people rather than as a loose association of remonstrating colonials, was as much the climax of a revolution as the formal beginning of one. The American Revolution, like most uprisings that are something more than a quick change of the palace guard, was a major event in intellectual as in political and social history. The Revolution in fact and law recognized

313

by treaty in 1783 would never have taken place at all except for the revolution in mind and spirit between 1765 and 1776, and that revolution, as John Adams was later to point out,[2] was made possible only by the great advances of the colonial period.

The intellectual history of the American Revolution is therefore largely confined to the years 1765-1776. In this period the colonists carried on their critical debates, proclaimed their central ideas, and reached their one truly revolutionary decision: to strike out for themselves as an independent republic. If the years under Washington were those that tried men's souls, the years under Samuel Adams were those that searched their minds. The intellectual history of this great event can be narrowed in subject matter as well as in time, for it is chiefly a history of political ideas. The announced purpose of the Americans was to dissolve the political bands that had connected them with England. The central problem for the decade was largely political in nature, and the search for solutions was pushed along political lines. Political theory rather than economic, religious, or social theory was the chief beneficiary of the outpouring of speeches, sermons, letters, resolves, and pamphlets that greeted each new move of the British ministry.

The noble political faith that anticipated and justified the American Revolution will be the subject of concern throughout the rest of this book. We shall examine with care not only the articles of this faith, but the purposes, sources, techniques, and influence of the men who proclaimed it. Before we describe this great adventure in political theory, we should recall briefly the situation of fact out of which it developed: the total environment in which these men wrote and argued, and the chain of events that set and kept them in motion.

THE AMERICAN COLONIES, 1765-1776

Conditions in the continental colonies in the pre-Revolutionary decade were conducive to political thinking of a libertarian character. The colonies expanded noticeably in population, settled area, and wealth; they expanded even more noticeably in political, social, and religious liberty. Progress and freedom were the concerns of the time, and a political theory dedicated to progress and freedom was an inevitable result.

The visible progress of the colonies in these eleven years was nothing short of astounding. Thanks to the fecundity of American mothers and the appeal of the American land, population increased from 1,850,000 in 1765 to more than 2,500,000 in 1776. America's troubles seemed only to make America more alluring; immigrants arrived in especially large numbers between 1770 and 1773. The westward pressure of 650,000 new colonists was, of course, enormous, and many new towns and settlements were planted in frontier lands east of the proclamation line of 1763. The sharp increase in population of the continental colonies lent support to radical arguments, especially popular after 1774, that Americans would some day outnumber Englishmen, and that there was "something absurd in supposing a continent to be perpetually governed by an island." [3] Signs of increased wealth and well-being inspired other Americans to sing the glories of "a commerce out of all proportion to our numbers." [4]

Far more significant than this material progress was the quickened influence of all those forces we singled out in Part I as the "factors of freedom." The "forces behind the forces"—the English heritage, the ocean, the frontier, and imperial tension—never worked so positively for political liberty as in this decade of ferment. Until the last days before independence the colonists continued to argue as Englishmen demanding English rights. The more they acted like Americans, the more they talked like Englishmen. Heirs of a tradition that glorified resistance to tyranny, they moved into political combat as English Whigs rather than American democrats, reminding the world that "it is the peculiar Right of Englishmen to complain when injured." [5] The other basic forces were no less conducive to liberty. In a situation that called desperately for accurate information, firm decisions, and resolute administration, the very distance between London and Boston frustrated the development of a viable imperial policy. In a situation that called no less desperately for colonial understanding of the financial and imperial difficulties facing Crown and Parliament, the push to the frontier weakened the bonds of loyalty to an already too-distant land. And the Stamp Act and Townshend Acts forced most articulate colonists to reduce the old conflict of English and American interests to the simplest possible terms. Since some Englishmen proposed to consign other Englishmen to perpetual inferiority, was it not simply a question of liberty or slavery?

Political factors of freedom enjoyed the sharpest increase in visible influence. The ancient struggle between royal governor and popular assembly took on new vigor and meaning. The depths of ill feeling were plumbed in the maneuvers and exchanges of Governors Bernard and Hutchinson and the Massachusetts legislature. The colonial press engaged in more political reporting and speculation in the single year between June 1765 and June 1766 than in all the sixty-odd years since the founding of the *Boston News-Letter*. In early 1765 there were twenty-three newspapers in the colonies, only two or three of which were politically conscious; in early 1775 there were thirty-eight, only two or three of which were not. The spirit of constitutionalism and the demand for written constitutions also quickened in the course of the great dispute over the undetermined boundaries of imperial power and colonial rights. The word "unconstitutional," an important adjunct of constitutionalism, became one of America's favorite words. Most important, the Stamp Act was a healthy spur to political awareness among all ranks of men. Wrote John Adams in 1766:

> The people, even to the lowest ranks, have become more attentive to their liberties, more inquisitive about them, and more determined to defend them, than they were ever before known or had occasion to be; innumerable have been the monuments of wit, humor, sense, learning, spirit, patriotism, and heroism, erected in the several provinces in the course of this year. Their counties, towns, and even private clubs and sodalities have voted

and determined; their merchants have agreed to sacrifice even their bread
to the cause of liberty; their legislatures have resolved; the united colonies
have remonstrated; the presses have everywhere groaned; and the pulpits
have thundered.[6]

The thundering pulpit, an old and faithful servant of American freedom,
set out to demonstrate anew the affinity of religious and political liberty.
Bumptious Protestantism vied with temperate rationalism as spurs to disestablishment and liberty of conscience. Conditions for the final triumph
of unqualified religious liberty grew more favorable in this unsettled decade.
So, too, did conditions of economic independence. The over-all state of the
American economy lent impressive support to radical claims that the colonies would get along just as well, if not better, outside the protecting confines of British mercantilism. In wealth, resources, production, ingenuity,
and energy the Americans were fast approaching the end of the colonial
line.

The broad social trends described in Chapter 4 continued through the
pre-Revolutionary decade. In every colony the middle class formed the
nucleus of the patriot party, and in Boston it attained a position of commanding political influence. The aristocracy split into opposing camps, but the
Lees of Virginia and Livingstons of New York are reminders that a decisive
share of patriotic leadership fell to the American aristocrat. The political
storms of the decade, which deposited power in new hands in almost every
colony, did much to stimulate social mobility and class conflict. The career
of the Sons of Liberty attests the growing fluidity of colonial society; the
uprisings of the "Paxton Boys" in Pennsylvania and the Regulators in North
Carolina attest the heightened tensions of class and section.

Finally, the colonial mind took rapid strides forward in this period,
not alone in the field of political thought. Deism, rationalism, and the scientific spirit claimed ever-increasing numbers of men in positions of leadership. The cult of virtue enjoyed a vogue even more intense than in the
colonial period. The arts showed new signs of indigenous strength. The
sharp increase in the number of newspapers was matched by an even
sharper increase in the output of books and pamphlets. Three new colleges
opened their doors to eager students, and King's and the Philadelphia Academy instituted the first American medical schools. Despite all the shouting
about English rights and ways, the colonial mind was growing steadily less
English and more American. By the standards of the old world, it was a
mind not especially attractive, not least because it was setting out at last to
find standards of its own.

The American colonies moved fast and far between 1765 and 1776. While
the King fumed, the ministry blundered, assemblies protested, mobs rioted,
and Samuel Adams plotted, the people of the colonies, however calm or
convulsed the political situation, pushed steadily ahead in numbers, wealth,
self-reliance, and devotion to liberty. The political theory of the American
Revolution can be understood only within this context of material and

spiritual progress. It was a theory dedicated to ordered liberty, for liberty was something most Americans already enjoyed.

THE CHAIN OF POLITICAL EVENTS, 1765-1776

If the factors of freedom in the colonial environment were so deep-seated as to make unqualified home rule or even independence an historical inevitability, still it cannot be denied that British obliquity and colonial obstinacy speeded up the inevitable by some tens of years. It is important for two reasons to review the chain of political events that led beyond home rule to independence: first, to refresh our memories about the policies that persuaded the hitherto moderate and nonpolitical Americans to search eagerly for first principles of imperial organization, governmental authority, and human nature; and second, to construct a timetable against which to measure the progress of the intellectual revolution that made it possible for the colonists to resolve for independence.[7]

The last struggle between imperial England and colonial America was touched off by the successful conclusion of the Seven Years' War. The Peace of Paris brought victory to England, but victory came attended as usual by a host of troubles. Two problems in particular pressed for solution, one of them urgent: the need for revenue to reduce a massive national debt and to guard the new empire; the other less urgent but more substantial: the consolidation of this empire on principles more purposeful than those of "salutary neglect." The Americans in their turn had an immediate and a long-range objective: the former, to resist and seek repeal of each new instance of "ministerial injustice"; the latter, to find their proper place in the empire. At bottom, the struggle was one between a mother country resolved upon centralized control and colonies looking forward to an increasing measure of home rule.

As time went by and relations deteriorated, the contest of ill tempers obscured the larger issue almost completely. Crown, ministry, and Parliament blundered ahead with policies compounded of ignorance, incredulity, stupidity, and irritability, while the people of England looked on with indifference or approval. The fateful steps of the 1770's found clear support in British public opinion, which was angrily determined to force submission upon the colonists. Although continuing to the end to appeal to the people of England for help and understanding, leading Americans agreed privately with John Witherspoon "that it was not the king and the ministry only, but the whole nation that was enraged against America," [8] and with Franklin that "every man in England seems to consider himself a piece of a sovereign over America, seems to jostle himself into the throne with the King and talks of *our subjects in the colonies*." [9] By the 1770's most Englishmen considered the colonists at best an inferior breed of Britons, at worst "the scum or off scouring of all nations," "a hotchpotch medley of foreign, enthusiastic madmen" lacking culture, manners, and gratitude.[10]

Little wonder that the Americans struck back boldly at an imperial policy apparently shaped by contempt for the colonies. Unwilling if not indeed unable to present an imperial solution satisfactory to both countries, they held fast to the conservative objective of restoring the balance of political and economic power which had existed in 1763. The British, who considered this balance ill-defined, treacherous, and shifting constantly in favor of the colonies, made clear that the days of salutary neglect were gone forever; the Americans, who no longer needed protection against the "turbulent Gallics," made clear that they could be satisfied with nothing less. Until the end of the decade the purpose of all but the most radical Americans was to restore the happy days of virtual home rule and untidy imperial supervision. The delegates from New Hampshire to the first Continental Congress were charged in all seriousness

> to devise, consult, and adopt measures, as may have the most likely tendency to extricate the Colonies from their present difficulties; to secure and perpetuate their rights, liberties, and privileges, and to restore that peace, harmony, & mutual confidence which once happily subsisted between the parent country and her Colonies.[11]

American measures in pursuit of this conservative policy were not so much actions as reactions. Rarely did the colonists take the lead in formulating arguments and policies. Most of what they said and did was forced or at least enticed out of them by imperial action. Even Samuel Adams and Franklin, who could see, or were willing to see, a good deal further ahead than their fellow colonists, had to wait for the ministry to help them from one step to the next. The ministry, as Americans now gratefully acknowledge, was extremely obliging. Here in brief was the timetable of the first stage of the American Revolution, the period in which the colonists decided, much against their better judgment, that they could and should bring a new nation into existence:

The death of George II and accession of George III in October 1760: The colonists, who could hardly have guessed how much sorrow they would reap from a young monarch determined to "be a king," greeted their new sovereign with unqualified loyalty and unaffected enthusiasm.

The End of the War in 1763: The defeat of the French and their expulsion from Canada was for the colonists a glorious triumph of Protestantism and political liberty. Pitt, the best of ministers, was joined with George III, the best of kings, in the paeans and prayers of the exultant Americans.

The announcement of the Proclamation Line of 1763 and passage of the Sugar and Currency Acts of 1764: Of these first tentative measures designed to take up the slack of salutary neglect, the Sugar Act alone met with any sort of concerted protest. Most of the clamor overlooked the serious fact that it was a revenue act put through with general support rather than another narrow attempt by the hated West India planters to swell the profits from their plantations. Only a few far-seeing colonists like Samuel Adams and Oxenbridge Thacher branded the act for what it was, and even they made sparing use of constitutional arguments.[12] The merchants of the seaports were more concerned over the ministry's plan to use the navy to cut down on smuggling.[13]

The Stamp Act of 1765: The colonies had been warned a year in advance of this revenue scheme, but they had been unable to ward it off by presenting an acceptable plan of their own. The Americans themselves were astounded by the vehemence and near-unanimity of the reaction, not only against the act itself but against its revelation of ministerial intentions, which, they now told themselves, they should have recognized more clearly in the unfriendly legislation of 1764. Assemblies remonstrated, towns and counties resolved, mobs marched about and in a few instances rioted, newspapers sprang to life, and preachers vied with lawyers to argue the injustice and unconstitutionality of it all. More important, and more declarative of American feelings, the act went completely unenforced in the old continental colonies. The most dramatic instance of protest was the hotly contested passage of four out of seven of Patrick Henry's famous resolves in the Virginia House of Burgesses. Newspapers reported this incident in such a way as to leave the impression that the gentlemen of this ancient and loyal colony had accepted even the most radical of Henry's proposals. The most influential instance of protest was the meeting of representatives of nine colonies in the Stamp Act Congress at New York. The "Declarations of the Rights and Grievances of the Colonists in America" adopted by the Congress October 19, 1765, were an accurate expression of prudent American sentiment at this first great crisis in imperial relations:

> The members of this congress, sincerely devoted, with the warmest sentiments of affection and duty to his majesty's person and government; inviolably attached to the present happy establishment of the protestant succession, and with minds deeply impressed by a sense of the present and impending misfortunes of the British colonies on this continent; having considered as maturely as time would permit, the circumstances of the said colonies, esteem it our indispensable duty to make the following declarations, of our humble opinion, respecting the most essential rights and liberties of the colonists, and of the grievances under which they labor, by reason of several late acts of parliament.
>
> 1st. That his majesty's subjects in these colonies, owe the same allegiance to the crown of Great Britain, that is owing from his subjects born within the realm, and all due subordination to that august body, the parliament of Great Britain.
>
> 2d. That his majesty's liege subjects in these colonies are entitled to all the inherent rights and privileges of his natural born subjects within the kingdom of Great Britain.
>
> 3d. That it is inseparably essential to the freedom of a people, and the undoubted rights of Englishmen, that no taxes should be imposed on them, but with their own consent, given personally, or by their representatives.
>
> 4th. That the people of these colonies are not, and from their local circumstances, cannot be, represented in the house of commons in Great Britain.
>
> 5th. That the only representatives of the people of these colonies, are persons chosen therein, by themselves; and that no taxes ever have been, or

can be constitutionally imposed on them, but by their respective legislatures.

6th. That all supplies to the crown, being free gifts of the people, it is unreasonable and inconsistent with the principles and spirit of the British constitution, for the people of Great Britain to grant to his majesty the property of the colonists.

7th. That trial by jury is the inherent and invaluable right of every British subject in these colonies.

8th. That the late act of parliament, entitled, An act for granting and applying certain stamp duties, and other duties in the British colonies and plantations in America, &c. by imposing taxes on the inhabitants of these colonies, and the said act, and several other acts, by extending the jurisdiction of the courts of admiralty beyond its ancient limits, have a manifest tendency to subvert the rights and liberties of the colonists.

9th. That the duties imposed by several late acts of parliament, from the peculiar circumstances of these colonies, will be extremely burthensome and grievous, and from the scarcity of specie, the payment of them absolutely impracticable.

10th. That as the profits of the trade of these colonies ultimately centre in Great Britain, to pay for the manufactures which they are obliged to take from thence, they eventually contribute very largely to all supplies granted there to the crown.

11th. That the restrictions imposed by several late acts of parliament, on the trade of these colonies, will render them unable to purchase the manufactures of Great Britain.

12th. That the increase, prosperity and happiness of these colonies, depend on the full and free enjoyment of their rights and liberties, and an intercourse, with Great Britain, mutually affectionate and advantageous.

13th. That it is the right of the British subjects in these colonies, to petition the king or either house of parliament.

Lastly, That it is the indispensable duty of these colonies to the best of sovereigns, to the mother country, and to themselves, to endeavor, by a loyal and dutiful address to his majesty, and humble application to both houses of parliament, to procure the repeal of the act for granting and applying certain stamp duties, of all clauses of any other acts of parliament, whereby the jurisdiction of the admiralty is extended as aforesaid, and of the other late acts for the restriction of the American commerce.[14]

A good deal more advanced, and therefore prophetic of American political argument during the next eight to ten years, were the resolves drawn up by Samuel Adams for the Massachusetts Assembly:

Whereas the just rights of his Majesty's subjects of this Province, derived to them from the British Constitution, as well as the royal charter, have been lately drawn into question: in order to ascertain the same, this House do unanimously come into the following resolves:—

1. *Resolved*, That there are certain essential rights of the British Constitution of government, which are founded in the law of God and nature, and are the common rights of mankind;—therefore,

2. *Resolved*, That the inhabitants of this Province are unalienably entitled to those essential rights in common with all men: and that no law of so-

ciety can, consistent with the law of God and nature, divest them of those rights.

3. *Resolved*, That no man can justly take the property of another without his consent; and that upon this original principle, the right of representation in the same body which exercises the power of making laws for levying taxes, which is one of the main pillars of the British Constitution, is evidently founded.

4. *Resolved*, That this inherent right, together with all other essential rights, liberties, privileges, and immunities of the people of Great Britain, have been fully confirmed to them by Magna Charta, and by former and by later acts of Parliament.

5. *Resolved*, That his Majesty's subjects in America are, in reason and common sense, entitled to the same extent of liberty with his Majesty's subjects in Britain.

6. *Resolved*, That by the declaration of the royal charter of this Province, the inhabitants are entitled to all the rights, liberties, and immunities of free and natural subjects of Great Britain to all intents, purposes, and constructions whatever.

7. *Resolved*, That the inhabitants of the Province appear to be entitled to all the rights aforementioned by an act of Parliament, 13th of Geo. II.

8. *Resolved*, That those rights do belong to the inhabitants of this Province upon the principle of common justice; their ancestors having settled this country at their sole expense, and their posterity having approved themselves most loyal and faithful subjects of Great Britain.

9. *Resolved*, That every individual in the Colonies is as advantageous to Great Britain as if he were in Great Britain and held to pay his full proportion of taxes there; and as the inhabitants of this Province pay their full proportion of taxes for the support of his Majesty's government here, it is unreasonable for them to be called upon to pay any part of the charges of the government there.

10. *Resolved*, That the inhabitants of this Province are not, and never have been, represented in the Parliament of Great Britain; and that such a representation there as the subjects in Britain do actually and rightfully enjoy *is impracticable* for the subjects in America;—and further, that in the opinion of this House, the several subordinate powers of legislation in America were constituted upon the apprehensions of this *impracticability*.

11. *Resolved*, That the only method whereby the constitutional rights of the subjects of this Province can be secure, consistent with a subordination to the supreme power of Great Britain, is by the continued exercise of such powers of government as are granted in the royal charter, and a firm adherence to the privileges of the same.

12. *Resolved*,—as a just conclusion from some of the foregoing resolves,— That all acts made by any power whatever, other than the General Assembly of this Province, imposing taxes on the inhabitants, are infringements of our inherent and unalienable rights as men and British subjects, and render void the most valuable declarations of our charter.

13. *Resolved*, That the extension of the powers of the Court of Admiralty within this Province is a most violent infraction of the right of trials by juries,—a right which this House, upon the principles of their British an-

cestors, hold most dear and sacred; it being the only security of the lives, liberties, and properties of his Majesty's subjects here

14. *Resolved,* That this House owe the strictest allegiance to his most sacred Majesty King George the Third; that they have the greatest veneration for the Parliament; and that they will, after the example of all their predecessors from the settlement of this country, exert themselves to their utmost in supporting his Majesty's authority in the Province, in promoting the true happiness of his subjects, and in enlarging the extent of his dominion.

Ordered, That all the foregoing resolves be kept in the records of this House, that a just sense of liberty and the firm sentiments of loyalty be transmitted to posterity.[15]

To this radical but still loyal statement one of Henry's unsuccessful resolves might well be appended. If the colonists were unwilling to say this in 1765, they were certainly willing to think it:

Resolved, That his Majesty's liege people, the inhabitants of this colony, are not bound to yield obedience to any law or ordinance whatever, designed to impose any taxation whatsoever upon them, other than the laws and ordinances of the General Assembly.[16]

The citizens of New London, Connecticut, were even one step farther along the road than Henry when they resolved:

That it is the Duty of every Person in the Colonies to oppose by every lawful Means, the Execution of those Acts imposed on them,—and if they can in no other way be relieved to reassume their natural Rights, and the Authority the Laws of Nature and of God have vested them with.[17]

The repeal of the Stamp Act and passage of the Declaratory Act in March 1766: In their joy over repeal, all but a handful of colonists conveniently overlooked three adverse truths: The act was repealed in behalf of English rather than American interests; the program of 1764 was still in force; and the Declaratory Act had asserted in unvarnished language the authority of Parliament over the colonies "in all cases whatsoever." In sermons, resolutions, toasts, and songs the colonists reaffirmed their delight at being Englishmen. With George III upon the throne and Pitt at his right hand, even in the robes of a peer, Americans could at last "be easie in our minds, contented with our condition." [18]

The passage of an act in May 1767 suspending the New York Legislature: The legislative was to remain suspended until ready to comply with the Mutiny Act of 1765, which required the assemblies to provide barracks and certain provisions for British troops. The New Yorkers, who had been no more remiss in this matter than several other colonies, finally gave way in a most grudging and indirect manner, but English prestige in that pivotal province had suffered a serious loss.

The enactment one month later of Townshend's program laying import duties on lead, glass, paint, paper, and tea: The reaction of the colonies, thanks to the conservative leadership of the merchants, was at once more sober and purposeful than that which had greeted the Stamp Act. The American leaders refused to be taken in by Townshend's clever use of their own distinction between internal and external taxation and struck back with an intricate system of commercial boycott. What bothered them most about the Townshend Acts was the ministry's stated design to use the revenues not merely for purposes of defense, but also for "defraying the charge of the administration of justice, and the support of the civil government in such provinces where it shall be found necessary"—a plan that, resolutely pursued, would have altered disastrously the balance of power between governor and assembly.

The affair of the Massachusetts Circular Letter: On February 11, 1768, the Massachusetts Assembly, under the prodding of Samuel Adams and his friends, voted to send a statement of opinion on current problems to the other colonies. This circular letter, though couched in prudent phrases, aroused ministerial resentment out of all proportion to its potential influence, in part because it put the question "whether any People can be said to enjoy any degree of Freedom if the Crown in addition to its un-doubted Authority of constituting a Govr, should also appoint him such a Stipend as it may judge proper without the Consent of the people & at their Expence." [19] The English themselves now began to react. Lord Hills-borough shot off a petulant message calling upon the governors to instruct their assemblies to treat the Massachusetts letter with "the contempt it de-serves." [20] Far more ill-advised, he instructed Bernard to demand that the Massachusetts Assembly rescind its letter or be dissolved for refusal. The assembly refused, Bernard dissolved, and Massachusetts seethed. It was one of the worst blunders the ministry had yet committed. The result was to give the circular letter far more popularity than it could possibly have won for itself.

The partial repeal of the Townshend Acts in March 1770: The with-drawal of the duty on all items save tea made clear to discerning Ameri-cans that the ministry was now determined to tax the colonies as an affirma-tion of sovereignty rather than as a method of producing revenue. Most colonists seemed satisfied with this partial repeal, but not those of Samuel Adams's mind:

> We cannot think the doctrine of the right of Parliament to tax us is given up, while an act remains in force for that purpose, and is daily put in execution; and the longer it remains the more danger there is of the people's becoming so accustomed to arbitrary and unconstitutional taxes, as to pay them without discontent.[21]

The Tea Act of 1773: This was a scheme for relieving the miseries of the East India Company by granting it a monopoly of the tea trade to the colonies. Once again the ministry had struck at the colonists both politically and commercially, and once again they reacted with resolves and agree-ments. The fact that the tax on tea had been retained as part of this monopolistic scheme permitted merchants and radicals to unite on the broad platform of no taxation without representation. In most ports the tea ships were persuaded to sail home without landing their cargoes, but in Boston, thanks to the obtuseness of Governor Hutchinson and the bravado of Samuel Adams, the Tea Party ended all hopes for peaceful resolution. Now it was the ministry's turn to react, which it did with a show of spleen that shocked the American moderates.

The swift passage in early 1774 of the Coercive Acts: These shut down the port of Boston, altered the government of Massachusetts, tightened up regulations for quartering troops, and authorized the governor of Massachusetts to send persons accused of riot to England for trial. Although the third of these acts was the only one aimed at any colony but Massachusetts, the reaction of the Americans was on a continental scale. "The question now," wrote William Henry Drayton, "is not whether Great Britain has a right to tax America against her consent, but whether she has a constitutional right to exercise despotism over America!" [22] The threat to carry off Americans to be tried in England permitted the colonists to ring all the changes on "one of their most darling rights, that of trial by juries." [23] The Quebec Act of June 1774, which provided for nonrepresentative government, trial without jury, and the "free exercise of the religion of the Church of Rome" in a greatly expanded Quebec, permitted them further to raise the ancient cries of "popery" and "arbitrary power." But the time had passed for isolated resolves and agreements. The chief reactions to the Coercive Acts were the beginning of extra-legal government in Massachusetts and the meeting of the first Continental Congress in Philadelphia. From here the road went on to independence by stages too well remembered to need description.

All the while that British actions and American reactions were rending the imperial fabric further asunder, old grievances and new incidents kept turning men's minds away from conciliation and compromise. The presence of troops in cities like Boston and the activities of the navy were constant sources of irritation; the "massacre" of March 5, 1770, was only the most bloody of many passages-at-arms between the King's troops or cutters and American mobs. The mere publication of a book advocating an American episcopate was enough to touch off a violent controversy in the newspapers over the alleged threat of the Crown to dissenting religions. The debts of the planters, in the words of an unfriendly but not entirely untrustworthy witness, made them "deeply interested in picking a quarrel" with England. [24] The proclamation line of 1763, originally designed as a temporary expedient, took on the look of a permanent policy to thwart westward expansion. And the Navigation, Iron, Hat, and Woolens Acts, against which few colonists had ever protested in general terms, now began to weigh heavily on sensitive American minds. After the affair of the Stamp Act, complaints in this vein began to appear more frequently:

A colonist cannot make a button, a horse-shoe nor a hob-nail, but some sooty iron-monger or respectable button-maker of Britain shall bawl and squawl that his honor's worship is most egregiously maltreated, injured, cheated and robb'd by the rascally North American republicans. . . . Do your honors really believe that North-America was created for the sole emolument of your very respectable dinnerizing corporations? Is this country the property of the merchant tailors and woolen drapers? Have they or any other high born British mechanic, an indefeazible right to the agonies, toils, and bloody sweat of the inhabitants of this land and the profits and produce of all their labors? [25]

The British commercial system now seemed to an increasing number of Americans "an Ottoman policy . . . strangling us in infancy," a long-range plan to "crush [our] native talents and keep [us] in a constant state of inferiority." [26] The attempt of the ministry to tighten up a few loose bolts had laid the entire imperial structure open to colonial doubts.

With the circumstances of the period and the timetable of discord clearly in mind, we may now proceed to the main business of Part 3: to describe in detail the political thought of the American Revolution. Chapter 12 will present the leading publicists of the Revolution, and will also comment upon their agencies of communication, purposes, methods of argument, and sources. Chapters 13 and 14 will discuss the principles of political theory which persuaded men's minds in this decade. In all three chapters we shall quote extensively from the writings of the period. Workers of an intellectual revolution should be allowed to speak for themselves.

CHAPTER TWELVE

American Political Writing, 1765-1776

THE political theory of the American Revolution was not just an interesting array of speculative deductions, but a conspicuously useful servant of everyday argument. It existed not in a vacuum but in a highly charged political atmosphere. It is essential to recognize the close affinity of fact and theory, of practical purpose and philosophical justification, in the minds of the patriot leaders. For this reason, we turn first to a survey of the spokesmen, agencies, purposes, and characteristics of political debate in this period. Separated from this historical context, the political theory of the Revolution is a warmed-over hash of ancient platitudes; kept within this context, it is a magnificent invocation of first principles in support of human liberty and constitutional government.

THE AMERICAN SPOKESMEN AND THEIR AGENCIES OF COMMUNICATION

The political principles of the Revolution were so unsophisticated in expression and inclusive in appeal as to seem a declaration of faith rather than a body of theory. The uniquely popular nature of these principles is apparent in the status and calling of the men who expounded them to the people. The spokesmen of the preliminary decade arose from every class and occupation. The natural leaders of all parts of the population joined in political argument and, to a greater or lesser degree, in the common American practice of "recurring to first principles." Tavern-keeper, cartman, and village wit stood

, in general, to more important purposes than the
civil rights of human nature, being intended to
slavery of sin and Satan, to point out their escape
ugh faith in a crucified Jesus, and to assist them in
eternal blessedness. But still there are special times
ay treat of politics.[1]

ry decade was just such a special time and season.
reated of politics but played the game as well. A
attested the importance of the New England min-
use in these angry words:

e fact that previous to and during all these acts of
in the Colonies, especially to the eastward, the Presby-
d with the most wicked, malicious and inflammatory
ed by the favourite orators amongst that sect, spiriting
to the most violent opposition to Government; per-
the intention of Government was to rule them with a
make them all slaves; and assuring them that if they
man to oppose those arbitrary schemes, *God* would assist
y every *ministerial tool*, (the amiable name these wretches
tow on the professors of the Church) from the face of
w was the time to strike, whilst Government at home
n; together with a long string of such seditious stuff, well
ose on the poor devils their hearers, and make them run
of extravagance and folly.[2]

he clergy as leaders of political thought was equally im-
inisters been the only spokesmen of the rebellion, had
damses, and Otis never appeared in print, the political
Revolution would have followed almost exactly the same
ps a little more mention of God, but certainly no less of
the sermons of the patriot ministers, who were responsible
one fourth of the total output of political thought in this
expressed every possible refinement of the reigning political
ling thinkers among the ministers, for the most part sons
churches, were Mayhew, Chauncy, Samuel Cooper, Stephen
Clarke, Samuel Webster, and Samuel Cooke. A step behind
d of prophets was a small army—"the black Regiment," as
labeled it[3]—of staunch expounders of English and natural
m Gordon, Samuel West, Samuel Langdon, Judah Champion,
otion, Simeon Howard, Amos Adams, John Cleaveland, Phillips
Skillman, John Allen, Thomas Allen, Gad Hitchcock, John
rles Turner, Ebenezer Bridge, Eliphalet Williams, Edward
on Haven, Samuel Lockwood, and literally hundreds of others
skilled than Mayhew or Cooper in discussing resistance, un-
hts, and political consent.
New England the clergy was less accustomed to find its way
n political matters, but such names as John Witherspoon, William

as ready to d
Adams or Cha

Unfortunately
wits ever broke
was that they ha
variation of the r
of political and re
average man was
minister. Political t
sense that a group
people made these p

The remembered l
few exceptions, men
slowly forming contin
the next largest of prea
their first calling, their s
a figure of importance te
historian of ideas. This fa
some of its most obvious
appeal, its willingness to i
At least three colonial th
could have become first-rate
term, but the mere mention
James Wilson—reveals why t
designed for the type of abst
was later to engage.

The men from whom we sha
up a virtually complete roster
Revolution. The chief spokesme
from the upper or upper-middle
Adams, John Adams, Wilson, Blan
Parsons, Alexander Hamilton, Geo
less important as individual thinker
orators and pamphleteers were: Josi
Thacher, Daniel Dulany, Joseph Haw
Hopkins, the three Lee brothers of
Chase, James Iredell, Joseph Warren
Silas Downer, James Bowdoin, David K
Bancroft. Men like Thomas Mifflin, J
Lovell, and such staunch Whig publishe
Journal and Isaiah Thomas of the *Massac*
list without detracting one bit from its

Rev. William Gordon of Roxbury beg
with these words of apology and admoni

The pulpit is devoted
fate of kingdoms, or th
recover men from the
from future misery thr
their preparations for a
and seasons when it m

The pre-Revolutiona
The clergy not only
loyalist writing in 177
isters to the patriot ca

It is an indubitabl
violence, committed
terian pulpits groan
harangues, pronoun
their godly hearers
suading them that
rod of iron, and t
would rise as one
them to sweep awa
are pleased to bes
the earth; that n
was afraid of the
calculated to imp
into every degre

The work of t
pressive. Had m
Jefferson, the A
thought of the
line—with perha
John Locke. In
for one fifth to
decade, we find
faith. The lead
of the Puritan
Johnson, Jona
this select ban
Peter Oliver
rights: Willia
Ebenezer Dev
Payson, Isaa
Tucker, Ch
Barnard, Jas
hardly less
alienable rig
Outside
into print o

Smith, Jacob Duché, John Joachim Zubly, John Hurt, and William Tennent are evidence that there, too, men of God were keen participants in political argument. The incidence of loyalist ministers was somewhat higher in colonies where the Church of England held sway, but just as all dissenting preachers were not patriots, so all Anglicans were not Tories. It took a Tory, Peter Oliver, to pay the ultimate, if entirely hostile, compliment to the political and intellectual importance of those members of the American clergy who shunned neutrality as resolutely as passive obedience:

> As to their Pulpits, many of them were converted into Gutters of Sedition, the Torrents bore down all before them. The Clergy had quite unlearned the Gospel, & had substituted Politicks in its Stead.[4]

The political thinkers of the Revolution found their way to contemporary and future audiences through every possible outlet. The agencies of communication of the past, like those of the present, were co-operative instruments of public opinion. An important piece of political thought that appeared in one of these agencies was certain to be copied or mentioned almost immediately in three or four others. Yet each of these channels did have its own special audience:

THE PAMPHLET. The most effective weapon of political argument was the pamphlet. In our search for the dominant principles of the decade, we must turn first to the hundreds of examples of this near-forgotten art.[5] Otis's *Rights of the British Colonies*, John Adams's *Thoughts on Government*, Hamilton's *The Farmer Refuted*, Jefferson's *Summary View*, and Paine's best-selling *Common Sense* were perhaps the most influential instances of the use of this technique. Almost all important colonial pamphlets were reprinted immediately in London, where they were paid the honest compliment of a flood of opposing pamphlets.

THE NEWSPAPER ARTICLE. Several key figures of the Revolution favored the press as an arena in which to argue and theorize, principally because a well-written article or letter in a local weekly was certain to be reprinted in other Whig newspapers throughout the colonies. Dickinson's "Letters from a Farmer in Pennsylvania," which appeared first in the *Pennsylvania Chronicle*[6] and was reprinted in full in all but three or four journals in the colonies, is the most famous instance of political writing for the press. John Adams's "Dissertation on the Canon and Feudal Law" and "Novanglus," Arthur Lee's "Monitor," and Samuel Adams's "Vindex" were other pieces that appeared first in the newspapers.[7] Nor must we overlook the thousands of articles and letters whose unknown authors helped shape Revolutionary theory, articles signed Chronus, Rusticus, Junius, Cato, Verus, Sydney, Benevolus, Benevolentior, A Female American, A Whig, Ploughjogger, Yet a Free Citizen, Foresight, A Friend to Liberty and Property, Americanus, Solomon, Solomon Junior, Nil Desperandum de Patria, or any one of hundreds of other names and slogans that spoke of English and Roman liberty.[8] Even when we manage to identify crafty Sam Adams with twenty-five different pseudonyms in the *Boston Gazette* and *Massachusetts Spy*, we still can recognize in the pseudonymous articles and letters of the decade a groundswell of popular political thought. No one who has been through the files of the *Boston Gazette, Massachusetts Spy, New-York Journal, Newport Mercury,* and *Pennsylvania Journal*—or of such less celebrated weeklies as *Dunlap's Maryland Gazette* and the *Norwich Packet*—can fail to agree with a penman of the times that "the PRESS hath never done greater Service since its first Invention." [9] Its service to political thought was as imposing as its service to political action. A Tory writer in the *Boston Evening-Post* complained that the Whig press had made it possible for "the peasants and their housewives in every part of the land . . . to dispute on politics and positively to determine upon our liberties." [10] Pro Rege et Grege, Be Angry and Sin Not, a Patagonian, and Ichabod Snuffle have a very special place among the makers of American thought.

THE BROADSIDE. This channel of communication was used to call patriots to action rather than to discuss major issues with any show of depth or dispassion. Yet "The Alarm," a series of broadsides published in New York over the pseudonym Hampden during the tea crisis,[11] presented one of the best short treatises on property and the unalienable character of natural rights to appear in the pre-Revolutionary period. Even in these ephemeral throwaways, so often satirical, demagogic, or downright abusive, we find useful examples of the recurrence to first principles.

THE ALMANAC. The almanac held on to its mass audience in the years after 1765. The printer of the almanac, who was anxious to preserve his special slice of that audience by giving it what it wanted, followed the trend of the times by offering poems, essays, couplets, and slogans about liberty, taxation, and John Locke. The almanacs of Nathaniel Ames are a rewarding storehouse of common political notions.[12]

THE SERMON. The thundering pulpit, which through at least half the colonial period had been the only significant agency of communication, continued to reach tens of thousands who had no time or urge to read pamphlets and newspapers. While Mayhew, Chauncy, Cooke, and Cooper worked their chief influence in print, the forgotten ministers of hundreds of country churches proved once again the power of the spoken word. Requested by the Provincial Congress to "make the question of the rights of the colonies . . . a topic of the pulpit on week days," the Massachusetts clergy responded by making it the topic on Sundays as well. The theory of the Revolution had its broadest appeal in New England towns, and the eloquence of the clergy was more instrumental than the writings of Otis and the Adamses in bringing this about. At the same time, the printed sermon competed with the political pamphlet and newspaper article for first place in patriot affections. The annual election sermon in Connecticut and Massachusetts took on new meaning in these years of crisis. The election sermons of 1770—preached by Samuel Cooke in Massachusetts and Stephen Johnson in Connecticut—were among the best tracts in political theory in the whole Revolutionary era.

THE ORATION. The spoken and printed sermon had its lay counterpart in the oration, a formal address devoted to advancing the patriot cause. Commencement pieces of students at Harvard and the Philadelphia Academy are one fruitful source of contemporary political ideas; speeches of Sons of Liberty at the dedication of their famous poles and trees are another. The annual oration on March 5 in Boston, a patriot device to keep alive the memory of the Massacre, was designed, in the words of one of its sponsors, "to preserve in the Minds of the People a lively Sense of the Danger of standing Armies." [13] The student of Revolutionary attitudes toward civil and military power finds exactly what he is looking for in the March 5 orations of James Lovell, John Hancock, Joseph Warren, and Benjamin Church.

THE LETTER. In any study of an age in which few men had leisure or talent for formal political speculation, public and private letters of leading men of action are especially valuable as sources of political ideas. Public letters, those written designedly for publication, were a standard part of early journalism. Many private letters were also influential as agencies of communication, passed as they were from hand to hand among patriot leaders in a certain area. The letters of men like the Adamses, the Lees, James Iredell, and Franklin—whether public, private, or secret—are a welcome addition to and often a qualification of their more formal writings.

THE OFFICIAL PAPER. Petitions to King and Parliament, public letters to members of the English ministry, resolutions, remonstrances, statements of grievances, declarations of rights, instructions to representatives, exchanges with royal governors, charges to grand juries, and grand jury presentments—in these and other official papers the colonists agitated the ideas of the era. The interdependence of the agencies of communication is evident in the fact that Samuel Adams, Dickinson, and Jefferson based official documents on their own previous writings and that patriot publishers hurried the results into print in pamphlets and newspapers. A set of resolutions on the Stamp Act adopted by the town meeting of Little Compton, Rhode Island, or a charge to the grand jury delivered by a patriot judge like Drayton might find its way into a dozen newspapers throughout the colonies. An appeal of Congress to the people of England or Quebec was certain to be picked up by the London press.

Although many official papers were worded to fit the occasion or audience and were thus not always honestly expressive of the sentiments of their authors, they light up the common ground on which patriots of differing views could meet in harmony. The address of Congress to "the Inhabitants of the Province of Quebec" of October 26, 1774, offers a unique catalogue of those political and social rights which colonists held closest to their hearts.[14] Judge Drayton's charge to the grand jury in Charleston May 2, 1776, is one of the most illuminating statements of the decade about the right of the people to resist a tyrant king.[15] The *Essex Result*, a commentary on the proposed Massachusetts Constitution of 1778 written by Theophilus Parsons for a convention at Ipswich, is one of the three or four most profound pieces of general speculation in the entire Revolutionary period.[16]

Town meetings,[17] county courts, assemblies, and Continental Congresses were all contributors to American political thought. The memorable fact about their papers is not so much that Samuel Adams or Jefferson or Bland wrote them, but that official bodies were willing to express as their collective sentiments the political philosophies these penmen had worked out in their chambers. The official paper reached its zenith in the Declaration of Independence, the Virginia Declaration of Rights, and the best of the early state constitutions, all eminent expressions of the political theory of the Revolution.

The one type of writing missing from this outpouring of political literature was the lengthy, careful, speculative treatise. No Hobbes or Rousseau or Locke arose in America to pronounce in one glorious book a political theory worthy of an age of revolution and constitution-making. Americans would wait another ten years after 1776 even to read such treatises as *The Federalist* and John Adams's *Defence of the Constitutions*. In the meantime, they strove to make up in volume and popularity for what their theory lacked in depth and originality. It often seems that all America had taken to heart John Adams's exhortation of 1765:

Let us tenderly and kindly cherish, therefore, the means of knowledge. Let us dare to read, think, speak, and write. Let every order and degree among the people rouse their attention and animate their resolution. . . .

Let the pulpit resound with the doctrines and sentiments of religious liberty. . . . Let us see delineated before us the true map of man. Let us hear the dignity of his nature, and the noble rank he holds among the works of God,—that consenting to slavery is a sacrilegious breach of trust, as offensive in the sight of God as it is derogatory from our own honor or interest or happiness,—and that God Almighty has promulgated from heaven, liberty, peace, and good-will to man!

Let the bar proclaim, "the laws, the rights, the generous plan of power," delivered down from remote antiquity,—inform the world of the mighty struggles and numberless sacrifices made by our ancestors in defence of freedom. Let it be known, that British liberties are not the grants of princes or parliaments, but original rights, conditions of original contracts, coequal with prerogative, and coeval with government; that many of our rights are inherent and essential, agreed on as maxims, and established as preliminaries, even before a parliament existed. Let them search for the foundations of British laws and government in the frame of human nature, in the constitution of the intellectual and moral world. . . .

Let the colleges join their harmony in the same delightful concert. Let every declamation turn upon the beauty of liberty and virtue, and the deformity, turpitude, and malignity, of slavery and vice. Let the public disputations become researches into the grounds and nature and ends of government, and the means of preserving the good and demolishing the evil. Let the dialogues, and all the exercises, become the instruments of impressing on the tender mind, and of spreading and distributing far and wide, the ideas of right and the sensations of freedom.

In a word, let every sluice of knowledge be opened and set a-flowing.[18]

THE PROBLEM OF THE AMERICAN SPOKESMEN

American leaders, as we have already noted, had two ends in view as they maneuvered their way through this confusing decade: one immediate, to resist and seek repeal of each oppressive act of Parliament or related policy of the ministry; and one long-range, to find the proper place for the colonies within the protecting pale of the rising British empire. In the first instance, the prime constitutional issue was the power of Parliament to tax the colonies; in the second, and ultimately more important and perplexing, it was the power of Crown and Parliament together to govern them, whether by taxation, legislation, supervision, inspection, royal veto, or other means. The chief constitutional problem was therefore to find the line, if such there was, between the general authority of Parliament and special authority of each assembly, between total submission and independence. We cannot investigate the political theory of the Revolution unless we first recall this great problem in constitutional theory, the organization of the British Empire,[19] for at every stage of the imperial controversy the Americans appealed to first principles in support of their current constitutional stand. Political theory justified the first show of resistance; political theory was the final answer to the constitutional problem. Government by consent and the rights of man were the only theoretical foundation upon which independence could be based.

It is impossible to fix precisely the state of American opinion at any given time concerning the confused relationship between England and the colonies. Men who shared the same political views found themselves in clear if amiable disagreement over the central constitutional issue. Some shifted their opinions from one crisis to the next, driving one author to protest, "Shall we, Proteus-like, perpetually change our ground, assume every moment some new and strange shape, to defend, to evade?"[20] Others, notably James Otis and Richard Bland, expressed two or three different interpretations in one pamphlet. Few Americans voiced their opinions in words that meant the same thing to all men. The problem of locating the line was a formidable one, principally because few men had ever tried to locate it before except in terms of subjection or independence. The result was a discouraging confusion of language and opinion. The most we can say is that all patriots began with a hazy belief in home rule quite opposed to the assumptions of the Stamp and Declaratory Acts, and moved at different speeds in the direction of a dominion theory of the British Empire. At least seven different solutions to the problem of imperial organization were brought forward at one time or another during this period.

COMPLETE SUBJECTION AND VIRTUAL REPRESENTATION. The doctrine of the Declaratory Act—that the King in Parliament had "full power and authority to make laws and statutes of sufficient force and validity to bind the colonies and people of *America*, subjects of the Crown of *Great Britain*, in all cases whatsoever"[21]—was apparently acceptable to only one leader of American thought, James Otis, and even he was not entirely convinced

that the Parliament of Great-Britain hath a just, clear, equitable and constitutional right, power and authority, to bind the colonies, by all acts wherein
they are named.[22]

Nowhere else in patriot literature, certainly after 1765, was the Tory
dogma of complete subjection treated with any attitude but contempt.

The chief historical interest of this dogma lies in the corollary through
which ministerial supporters tried to make it palatable to colonial tastes:
virtual representation. This argument was designed to silence the cry of
"no taxation without representation" by reviving and extending the ancient
fiction that all Englishmen, whether enfranchised or not, were virtually
represented in Parliament. The colonies, asserted Tory writers, stood in the
same constitutional and practical position as the cities of Manchester and
Sheffield. That they elected no representatives did not mean they were
unrepresented and therefore taxed without their consent, for each member
of the House of Commons, whether from London or Old Sarum, represented the interests of all Englishmen.

> Our nation is represented in parliament by an assembly as numerous as
> can well consist with order and dispatch, chosen by persons so differently
> qualified in different places, that the mode of choice seems to be, for the
> most part, formed by chance, and settled by custom. Of individuals far the
> greater part have no vote, and of the voters few have any personal knowl-
> edge of him to whom they intrust their liberty and fortune.
> Yet this representation has the whole effect expected or desired; that of
> spreading so wide the care of general interest, and the participation of
> publick counsels, that the advantage or corruption of particular men can
> seldom operate with much injury to the Publick.
> For this reason many populous and opulent towns neither enjoy nor
> desire particular representatives; they are included in the general scheme
> of public administration, and cannot suffer but with the rest of the empire.
> It is urged that the *Americans* have not the same security, and that a
> *British* legislator may wanton with their property; yet if it be true, that
> their wealth is our wealth, and that their ruin will be our ruin, the parlia-
> ment has the same interest in attending to them, as to any other part of
> the nation. The reason why we place any confidence in our representatives
> is, that they must share in the good or evil which their counsels shall pro-
> duce. Their share is indeed commonly consequential and remote; but it is
> not often possible that any immediate advantage can be extended to such
> numbers as may prevail against it. We are therefore as secure against inten-
> tional depravations of government as human wisdom can make us, and upon
> this security the *Americans* may venture to repose.[23]

The American answer to virtual representation was a mixture of irritation
and contempt. "Our *privileges* are all *virtual*," shouted Arthur Lee, "our
sufferings are *real*." [24] Most writers rejected in just such a sentence or
paragraph the sophistry of virtual representation, refusing to dignify it
with lengthy rebuttal. James Otis spoke the colonial mind when he rattled
off his famous retort:

To what purpose is it to ring everlasting changes to the colonists on the cases of Manchester, Birmingham and Sheffield, who return no members? If those now so considerable places are not represented, they ought to be. . . . It may perhaps sound strangely to some, but it is in my most humble opinion as good *law* and as good *sense* too, to affirm that all the plebeians of Great-Britain are in fact or virtually represented in the assembly of the Tuskarora's, as that all the colonists are in fact or virtually represented in the honourable house of Commons of Great-Britain.[25]

A few colonists took the doctrine of virtual representation seriously enough to refute it with a careful show of history and logic. The most convincing objector was Daniel Dulany the younger, later to become a loyalist, who devoted some of the best pages of his early pamphlet on taxation to demolishing virtual representation. This doctrine, he asserted, "consists of Facts not true, and of Conclusions inadmissible," and "is a mere Cob-web, spread to catch the unwary, and entangle the weak." The key paragraph of his argument was this:

There is not that intimate and inseparable Relation between the *Electors of Great-Britain* and the *Inhabitants of the Colonies,* which must inevitably involve both in the same Taxation; on the contrary, not a single *actual* Elector in *England,* might be immediately affected by a Taxation in *America,* imposed by a Statute which would have a general Operation and Effect, upon the Properties of the Inhabitants of the Colonies. The latter might be oppressed in a Thousand Shapes, without any Sympathy, or exciting any Alarm in the former. Moreover, even Acts, oppressive and injurious to the Colonies in an extreme Degree, might become popular in *England,* from the Promise or Expectation that the very Measures which depressed the Colonies, would give Ease to the Inhabitants of *Great-Britain.* It is indeed true, that the Interests of *England* and the Colonies are allied, and an Injury to the Colonies produced into all its Consequences, will eventually affect the Mother Country, yet these Consequences being generally remote, are not at once foreseen; they do not immediately alarm the Fears, and engage the Passions of the *English* Electors, the Connection between a Freeholder of *Great Britain,* and a *British American* being deducible only through a Train of Reasoning, which few will take the Trouble, or can have an Opportunity, if they have Capacity to investigate; wherefore the Relation between the *British Americans,* and the *English Electors,* is a Knot too infirm to be relied on as a competent Security, especially against the Force of a present, counteracting Expectation of Relief.[26]

Richard Bland, Maurice Moore of North Carolina, Edward Bancroft, John Dickinson, Arthur Lee, and an anonymous pamphleteer who may have been Samuel Cooper were other dissenters from this doctrine.[27]

REPRESENTATION IN PARLIAMENT. One small band of patriots, for whom Otis and Franklin were spokesmen, proposed that the colonies be "represented in some proportion to their number and estates, in the grand legislature of the nation."[28] In his *Rights of the British Colonies* Otis wrote:

A representation in Parliament from the several Colonies, since they are become so large and numerous, as to be called on not to maintain provincial

government, civil and military among themselves, for this they have chearfully done, but to contribute towards the support of a national standing
army, by reason of the heavy national debt . . . can't be tho't an unreasonable thing, nor if asked, could it be called an immodest request. . . . Besides the equity of an American representation in parliament, a thousand
advantages would result from it. It would be the most effectual means of
giving those of both countries a thorough knowledge of each others interests; as well as that of the whole, which are inseparable.[29]

Neither Otis nor Franklin advanced this solution with any real show of
conviction, for it proved equally distasteful to leaders and led on both
sides of the ocean. The equity of American representation was not admitted
by Parliament, the advantages were not at all clear to the colonists. The
arguments of the Adamses were representative of an overwhelming colonial
opinion. Samuel Adams wrote to the colony's agent in 1765:

> We are far however from desiring any Representation there, because we
> think the Colonies cannot be equally and fully represented; and if not equally
> then in Effect not at all. A Representative should be, and continue to be
> well acquainted with the internal Circumstances of the People whom he
> represents. . . . Now the Colonies are at so great a Distance from the Place
> where the Parliament meets, from which they are separated by a wide
> Ocean; and their Circumstances are so often and continually varying, as
> is the Case in all Countries not fully settled, that it would not be possible
> for Men, tho' ever so well acquainted with them at the Beginning of a
> Parliament, to continue to have an adequate Knowledge of them during
> the Existence of that Parliament.[30]

And John Adams queried his readers in 1775:

> Would not representatives in the house of commons, unless they were
> numerous in proportion to the numbers of people in America, be a snare
> rather than a blessing?
> Would Britain ever agree to a proportionable number of American mem-
> bers; and if she would, could America support the expense of them?
> Could American representatives possibly know the sense, the exigencies,
> &c. of their constituents, at such a distance, so perfectly as it is absolutely
> necessary legislators should know?
> Could Americans ever come to the knowledge of the behavior of their
> members, so as to dismiss the unworthy?
> Would Americans in general ever submit to septennial elections?
> Have we not sufficient evidence, in the general frailty and depravity of
> human nature . . . that a deep, treacherous, plausible, corrupt minister
> would be able to seduce our members to betray us as fast as we could send
> them? [31]

Imperial federation was unacceptable to colonial minds on historical,
psychological, and practical grounds. To send a few representatives to
England would serve only to legalize parliamentary taxation, not prevent it.

INTERNAL AND EXTERNAL TAXATION. The threat and passage of the Stamp
Act evoked the first unsuccessful attempt to locate a fixed line between

parliamentary and provincial power: the distinction between excise taxes (internal taxation) and custom duties (external taxation). Although recent researches have demonstrated that this formula was neither so clear-cut nor popular as historians have hitherto assumed,[32] many Americans did subscribe to the general notion that Parliament had the right to pass the Sugar Act but not the Stamp Act. The protests and pamphlets of 1765-1766 did not express this distinction so clearly as they might have, principally because the colonists saw no reason to approve a bad act in order to destroy an evil one. They talked a great deal about internal taxation, since that is what they were denying. They talked very little about external taxation, since to approve it positively was not essential to their arguments and to deny it flatly was not yet essential to their liberties. Therefore, while they resisted the Stamp Act, attacking it on grounds of unconstitutionality, they acquiesced in the Sugar Act, attacking it on grounds of inexpediency.

Actually, the distinction was quite untenable, and many leading Americans shunned it from the beginning. Otis, the lone wolf who argued against British policies while conceding their constitutionality, asserted flatly that "there is no foundation for the distinction some make in England, between an internal and an external tax on the colonies," and added "that the Parliament of Great-Britain has a just and equitable right, power and authority, to *impose taxes on the colonies, internal and external, on lands, as well as on trade.*" [33] But English friends of America found this formula so useful that they converted it into a working principle of the imperial constitution. Enough had been said about "internal taxes" in official resolutions [34] and in pamphlets like Dulany's *Considerations*, Bland's *Inquiry*, and Stephen Hopkins's *Grievances* [35] to convince Pitt—and indeed Franklin [36]—that the colonists had adopted the distinction as their own key to the imperial relationship. The implications of Dulany's widely read argument, which did not even use the phrase "external taxes," were good enough for Pitt. Having cut through Dulany's confusion to an interpretation that suited his own ends, he could blow down an obstreperous but also more perceptive member with the annoyed remark, "If the gentleman does not understand the difference between internal and external taxes, I cannot help it." [37] Whether American or English in origin, the distinction was unworkable, as Charles Townshend was soon to demonstrate.

TAXATION FOR REVENUE AND TAXATION FOR REGULATION OF TRADE. In the course of his examintion before the House of Commons February 13, 1766, Franklin was asked if his countrymen had given much thought to the supposed distinction between internal and external taxation. "They never have hitherto," he answered, adding:

> Many arguments have been used here to shew them, that there is no difference, and that, if you have no right to tax them internally, you have none to tax them externally, or make any other law to bind them. At present they do not reason so; but in time they may possibly be convinced by these arguments.[38]

Franklin, the public Franklin, was behind the onward surge of American opinion. Many colonists were already convinced that there was no distinction between these two forms of taxation. The Townshend duties, which were based squarely on the distinction, forced them now to deny it positively.

Townshend's error, of course, had been to announce in the legislation itself that the revenues from these duties would be used for a specific and highly unpopular purpose. Many Americans now raised a new distinction, already implicit in numerous resolves and pamphlets, between taxation for revenue (unconstitutional) and taxation as part of a scheme for regulating imperial trade (constitutional). The area of unconstitutionality was expanded to include not only all internal taxes but those external taxes which were designed to produce revenue. The chief spokesman for this solution was John Dickinson. In his fantastically popular "Letters from a Farmer in Pennsylvania" he stated the new doctrine in these words:

> The parliament unquestionably possesses a legal authority to *regulate* the trade of *Great-Britain,* and all her colonies. Such an authority is essential to the relation between a mother country and her colonies; and necessary for the common good of all. . . .
>
> I have looked over *every statute* relating to these colonies, from their settlement to this time; and I find every one of them founded on this principle, till the *Stamp-Act* administration. *All before,* are calculated to regulate trade, and preserve or promote a mutually beneficial intercourse between the several constituent parts of the empire; and though many of them imposed duties on trade, yet those duties were always imposed *with design* to restrain the commerce of one part, that was injurious to another, and thus to promote the general welfare. The raising a revenue thereby was never intended. Thus the King, by his judges in his courts of justice, imposes fines which all together amount to a very considerable sum, and contribute to the support of government: But this is merely a consequence arising from restrictions, that only meant to keep peace, and prevent confusion; and surely a man would argue very loosely, who should conclude from hence, that the King has a right to levy money in general upon his subjects. Never did the *British* parliament, till the period above mentioned, think of imposing duties in *America,* FOR THE PURPOSE OF RAISING A REVENUE. . . .
>
> Here [in the Townshend Acts] we may observe an authority *expressly* claimed and exerted to impose duties on these colonies; not for the regulation of trade; not for the preservation or promotion of a mutually beneficial intercourse between the several constituent parts of the empire, heretofore the *sole objects* of parliamentary institutions; *but for the single purpose of levying money upon us.*
>
> This I call an innovation; and a most dangerous innovation.[39]

The difficulty with this distinction, as critics on both sides of the ocean were quick to point out, could be framed in the simple question: What if a trade regulation should produce revenue? To this Dickinson answered:

> The *nature* of any impositions laid by parliament on these colonies, must determine the *design* in laying them. It may not be easy in every instance

to discover that design. Wherever it is doubtful, I think submission cannot be dangerous; nay, it must be right; for, in my opinion, there is no privilege these colonies claim, which they ought in *duty* and *prudence* more earnestly to maintain and defend, than the authority of the *British* parliament to regulate the trade of all her dominions.[40]

The criterion of intent satisfied no one for long. Radical colonists were anxious to erect a constitutional barrier that left a good deal less scope to parliamentary discretion. Defenders of the English point of view asserted that it was "only a pretense under which to strip Parliament of all jurisdiction over the colonies."[41] Dickinson's legalistic attempt to give precision to a vague boundary was doomed to failure. Yet until the end of the decade patriot writers made use of the distinction between taxation for revenue and "impositions" for regulation of trade.[42]

DENIAL OF TAXATION; HOME RULE. The next step beyond Dickinson, to which less cautious men had already pushed, was a doctrine of home rule that denied taxation of any description and admitted legislation only for concerns clearly imperial in nature. Clear-sighted men in both camps had already pointed to the absurdity of considering internal taxation and internal legislation as two different things,[43] realizing that laws could do more than taxes to correct or impair the situation created by salutary neglect. Several toughminded legislatures had seized upon the Stamp Act to voice constitutional objections to parliamentary legislation "respecting their internal Polity,"[44] and some movers of these resolutions had gone on to expand upon this point in the first searching pamphlets. This, for example, was the general if confused position taken by Richard Bland in his *Inquiry*. It was a position implicit in many later resolutions and pamphlets, especially after such shows of force as the act suspending the New York Assembly;[45] it was the position finally adopted by conservative patriots like John Dickinson. His *Essay on the Constitutional Power*, published in July 1774, was the best and final statement of the doctrine of home rule, of exemption from Parliament's power to tax at all and to legislate on matters not clearly imperial in scope.[46]

A DOMINION THEORY OF THE BRITISH EMPIRE. By 1773 Governor Hutchinson of Massachusetts had lost both his good will and perspective. "I know of no line," he wrote to the Massachusetts legislature, "that can be drawn between the supreme authority of Parliament and the total independence of the colonies: it is impossible there should be two independent Legislatures in one and the same state."[47] "If there be no such line," answered the lower house, with the help of John Adams, "the consequence is, either that the colonies are the vassals of the Parliament, or that they are totally independent." But there was yet a third possibility: the union of the colonies and England "in one head and common Sovereign."[48] Thus, under pressure of events at home and abroad, the colonists arrived at a final theory of imperial organization that was still one step short of independence.

This dominion theory of the empire, which held simply and prophetically that the only tie between the colonies and England was a common sovereign, had been long in the making. As early as 1765 men were reaching out for this radical solution,[49] and in 1768 Franklin could reflect:

> The more I have thought and read on the subject, the more I find myself confirmed in opinion, that no middle doctrine can be well maintained, I mean not clearly with intelligible arguments. Something might be made of either of the extremes; that Parliament has a power to make *all laws* for us, or that it has a power to make *no laws* for us; and I think the arguments for the latter more numerous and weighty, than those for the former. Supposing that doctrine established, the colonies would then be so many separate states, only subject to the same king, as England and Scotland were before the union.[50]

By 1770 Franklin was no longer in doubt, nor, for that matter, were several other leaders of the American cause.[51] Not until 1774, however, was the dominion theory put forward without apologies or qualifications. John Adams's "Novanglus," Jefferson's *Summary View*, Hamilton's *The Farmer Refuted*, and James Iredell's "To the Inhabitants of Great Britain" all arrived simultaneously at these conclusions: that the power of Parliament to lay taxes or pass laws for the colonies was "none at all"; that the colonies had voluntarily, by "free, cheerful consent," allowed Parliament the "power of regulating trade"; and that the "fealty and allegiance of Americans" was due only "to the person of King George III, whom God long preserve and prosper."[52] The most brilliant statement of this radical position was James Wilson's *Considerations on the Nature and Extent of the Legislative Authority of the British Parliament.* The future justice of the Supreme Court rested the case for American equality not only on law and history, but on "natural right," "the principles of liberty," and "the happiness of the colonies" as well. Wilson's opening passage tells us graphically of the pains with which men like Wilson, Franklin, and John Adams groped in good faith for a line between parliamentary and provincial power:

> The following sheets were written during the late non-importation agreement: but that agreement being dissolved before they were ready for the press, it was then judged unseasonable to publish them. Many will, perhaps, be surprised to see the legislative authority of the British parliament over the colonies denied *in every instance.* Those the writer informs, that, when he began this piece, he would probably have been surprised at such an opinion himself; for that it was the *result*, and not the *occasion*, of his disquisitions. He entered upon them with a view and expectation of being able to trace some constitutional line between those cases in which we ought, and those in which we ought not, to acknowledge the power of parliament over us. In the prosecution of his inquiries, he became fully convinced that such a line does not exist; and that there can be no medium between acknowledging and denying that power in *all* cases. Which of these two alternatives is most consistent with law, with the principles of liberty, and with the happiness of the colonies, let the publick determine.

His closing paragraphs mark the abandonment of the attempt to admit Parliament to some sort of authority over the colonies. It was now considered "repugnant to the essential maxims of jurisprudence, to the ultimate end of all governments, to the genius of the British constitution, and to the liberty and happiness of the colonies, that they should be bound by the legislative authority of the parliament of Great Britain."

There is another, and a much more reasonable meaning, which may be intended by the dependence of the colonies on Great Britain. The phrase may be used to denote the obedience and loyalty, which the colonists owe to the *kings* of Great Britain. . . .

Those who launched into the unknown deep, in quest of new countries and habitations, still considered themselves as subjects of the English monarchs, and behaved suitably to that character; but it no where appears, that they still considered themselves as represented in an English parliament, or that they thought the authority of the English parliament extended over them. They took possession of the country in the *king's* name: they treated, or made war with the Indians by *his* authority: they held the lands under *his* grants, and paid *him* the rents reserved upon them: they established governments under the sanction of *his* prerogative, or by virtue of *his* charters: —no application for those purposes was made to the parliament: no ratification of the charters or letters patent was solicited from that assembly, as is usual with England with regard to grants and franchises of much less importance. . . .

This is a dependence, which they have acknowledged hitherto; which they acknowledge now; and which, if it is reasonable to judge of the future by the past and the present, they will continue to acknowledge hereafter. . . .

From this dependence . . . arises a strict connexion between the inhabitants of Great Britain and those of America. They are fellow subjects; they are under allegiance to the same prince; and this union of allegiance naturally produces a union of hearts. It is also productive of a union of measures through the whole British dominions. To the king is intrusted the direction and management of the great machine of government. . . .

The connexion and harmony between Great Britain and us, which it is her interest and ours mutually to cultivate, and on which her prosperity, as well as ours, so materially depends, will be better preserved by the operation of the legal prerogatives of the crown, than by the exertion of an unlimited authority by parliament.[53]

Even in this apparently clear-cut solution American spokesmen stood on confused ground, for in their anxiety to exclude Parliament from their affairs they had come dangerously near to a wholesale revival of the royal prerogative.[54] Had this solution actually been given a trial, could they conceivably have been satisfied? The next step had to be independence.

INDEPENDENCE. From the dominion status of 1774 to independence in 1776 was an easy road in political and constitutional theory. If history and natural law justified immunity from the authority of Parliament, so, too, did they justify deposing a wicked King. Up to 1774 Americans had done little thinking in this vein. The authority of Parliament had been the bone of contention, and the participation of the King in the exercise of that authority had been studiously or carelessly ignored. The only independence the colonists sought was independence of Parliament. The publication of Jefferson's *Summary View* gave a brand-new twist to the imperial tie. At the same time that it reduced the imperial problem to a simple question of personal allegiance to a common sovereign, it made clear that colonists were learning to distinguish the actions of the sovereign from those of Parliament. The Virginia radical made separate listings of Parliament's usurpations and George III's "deviations from the line of duty," and warned the King that persistence in these deviations could lead to denunciation of the last bond of empire.[55]

The final stage of American argument is, of course, most plainly read in the Declaration of Independence, in which the dominion theory and natural law were skillfully woven together to justify the bold decision to dissolve an empire.[56] Thanks to the dominion theory of 1774, the Americans could ignore Parliament almost completely and concentrate their fire on George III. Having already proved, largely through their own reading of history, that they were totally outside the jurisdiction of Parliament and were subjects of the King by free choice, they had only to prove to a candid world that the latter, not the former, had played the tyrant. And it was exactly here, at the moment when they renounced a covenanted monarch, that the whole theory of natural law proved its worth to a people who prided themselves on their political morality. This theory had been extremely helpful at every stage of the struggle since 1765. In this final stage it was absolutely essential.

THE CHARACTERISTICS OF POLITICAL WRITING

Political writing in the pre-Revolutionary decade was shaped by circumstances of time, place, purpose, and tradition. The kind of political commentary in which colonial authors indulged was an intriguing blend of old English and new American attitudes, beliefs, and prejudices. We must understand clearly the major characteristics of public disputation in this great decade of American political thought.

OCCASIONALISM. Much serious political writing in this period was occasional, even opportunistic in nature. The pamphlets, speeches, resolutions, and sermons supporting the American cause were the work of busy men with little time or appetite for long, hard thoughts, of men who, through no fault of their own, could no more seize the initiative in print than in action. Each political writing, like each political maneuver, was largely a reaction to English policy and argument. The ministry planned, Parliament legislated, and word of a new policy reached America; as if in conditioned response, pamphlets and resolutions poured from the presses, all bearing the stamp of the occasional performance. Few writers, however, were as honest as Rev. John Allen, who ended his *Beauties of Liberty* with the apology, "This Peice comes into the World, as Men go through it, with many faults."[57] The total impression one gets from the vast literature of the period is indeed one of many faults—of haste, superficiality, repetition, and ambiguity. Hardly a single example of political, economic, or constitutional argument was the work of a man who had approached his writing desk with deliberate tread. Wilson's *Considerations* and John Adams's *Dissertation* were two of the few exceptions to this broad statement. "The Centinel" was all too correct when he told his countrymen:

> There is scarce a man in the community, but what will tell you he is an Englishman, a freeman, and that he glories in the nature of that government under which he lives. But ask him what he means by being a freeman, desire him to explain to you the properties, and the eminently glorious principles which are contained in this constitution, and you non-plus him and find very few satisfactory answers to the enquiry. The bulk of the citizens, as they enjoy the happiness resulting herefrom, seldom take pains to examine the constituent principles, as perhaps business, avocations, and many other causes render it impracticable.[58]

A consequence of this occasionalism was the extravagant confusion that marred the discussion of imperial organization. Bland and Otis were surely not so confused in mind as they were in print, but consistency was apparently worth sacrificing to a printer's deadline. Another example was the indiscriminate appeal to any and every type of higher law against oppressive acts of Parliament: charters, common law, Magna Charta, the British Constitution, and "the law of God and nature." [59] But would it have aided the American cause had the colonists decided which of these defenses—"the immutable laws of nature, the principles of the English constitution, and the several charters or compacts" [60]—they proposed to rely upon most heavily? At least some of the confusion in colonial arguments must have been calculated to confuse.

PROPAGANDA.[61] Few American writers were entirely honest in method. Hyperbole, misrepresentation, and the appeal to fear were overworked techniques. Black and white were the shades most used in argument. The equation of the small evil with the big was a particular favorite.[62] Any show of ministerial determination was "arbitrary power." The slightest hint of obedience to the hated acts was "compleat slavery" or "Egyptian bondage." [63] George III was either the "best of Kings" or the "Royal Brute." It is not in disparagement of American pamphleteers, who wrote to win a great cause rather than the approval of critics yet unborn, to say that they rank with liberty's most effective and disingenuous propagandists.

Political argument reached heights of make-believe in the outcry against "Popery" and the "Papists." Fear and hatred of Catholicism were strong throughout the colonies, and no small service was rendered the American cause by authors who gave their audience no choice except "Liberty and Protestantism" and "Popery and arbitrary Power." [64] No doubt many colonists were profoundly concerned about the future of dissenting Protestantism under English rule, but they were hardly so many or so concerned as to justify the thousands of pages devoted to this issue. It must often have seemed to the newspaper reader of the day that the real goal of the British ministry was to extend Roman Catholicism rather than imperial control. The clamor about "Popery," in which many writers who should have known better joined with a will,[65] was most deafening in 1768-1769, at the time of the agitation over an episcopate, and in 1774, after the passage of the Quebec Act. Samuel Adams, the master propagandist, recognized the usefulness of this issue by penning a series of articles to the *Boston Gazette* in which he made statements about English designs that even he could not have believed for a moment.[66]

The Anson County Committee of Safety thought it had pushed the Catholic argument as far as it would go when it told a certain doubter that

> Lord North was a Roman Catholick, that the King's crown tottered upon his shoulders, for he had established the Roman Catholick Religion in the Province of Quebec, and that the King and Parliament did intend to establish Popery on all the Continent of America.[67]

But a Philadelphia patriot had already outdone them in a piece that reached this climax:

> We may live to see our churches converted into mass houses, and lands plundered of tythes for the support of a Popish clergy. The Inquisition may erect her standard in Pennsylvania and the city of Philadelphia may yet experience the carnage of a St. Bartholomew's day.[68]

The loose or designed use of "Communism" today has an exact counterpart in the use of "Popery" in the pre-Revolutionary decade. The way to dispose of General Gage was to brand him "a Papist in politicks." [69] What could have been easier, or more full of guile?

The catalogue of grievances against Crown or Parliament was another propaganda technique used to full advantage.[70] The Declaration of Independence was the best known of these statements which combined truth and distortion in amounts calculated to convince the irresolute of the evil designs of the mother country. This effective piece of propaganda was, like the Revolution itself, the work of a determined minority that could hardly have afforded to be more straightforward and moderate in statement. Propaganda was a faithful servant of liberty in this decisive decade.[71]

LEGALISM. In his speech on conciliation March 22, 1765, Burke spoke in evident admiration of a feature of American politics and political discussion. The fifth item in his list of the "variety of powerful causes" giving rise to the "fierce spirit of liberty . . . in the English Colonies" was education in the law:

> Permit me, sir, to add another circumstance in our colonies, which contributes no mean part towards the growth and effect of this untractable spirit. I mean their education. In no country perhaps in the world is the law so general a study. The profession itself is numerous and powerful; and in most provinces it takes the lead. The greater number of the deputies sent to the congress were lawyers. But all who read, and most do read, endeavor to obtain some smattering in that science. I have been told by an eminent bookseller, that in no branch of his business, after tracts of popular devotion, were so many books as those on the law exported to the plantations.

The colonists have now fallen into the way of printing them for their own use. I hear that they have sold nearly as many of Blackstone's Commentaries in America as in England. . . . This study renders men acute, inquisitive, dexterous, prompt in attack, ready in defence, full of resources. In other countries, the people, more simple, and of a less mercurial cast, judge of an ill principle in government only by an actual grievance; here they anticipate the evil, and judge of the pressure of the grievance by the badness of the principle. They augur misgovernment at a distance; and snuff the approach of tyranny in every tainted breeze.[72]

The pre-Revolutionary crisis marked the climax of an historic process that had been generations in the making: the seizure of political power by the legal profession. Otis, Wilson, Dickinson, John Adams, Dulany, Jefferson, Henry, Drayton, Iredell, and dozens of other American leaders were practicing lawyers; their assaults on English policy were therefore thoroughly legalistic in approach and expression. The argument from legal history—heavily laden with citations to Bracton, Coke, Blackstone, Hale, Holt, and other giants of English law—was a favorite not only with these sons of the common law, but also, as Burke pointed out, with those patriots who had only a "smattering in that science." While Dickinson's "Letters" and Wilson's *Considerations* were the most refined examples of the lawyer's brief,[73] hundreds of other pamphlets and letters exploited the widespread popularity of this type of argument. Small wonder Tories were so angry at the lawyers for "cultivating, with unwearied Pains, the Seeds of Infatuation and Tumult." [74] It must often have seemed to Grenville and North that they were dealing with a race of legal historians.

FACTS. "Let Facts be submitted to a candid World," commanded the delegates at Philadelphia July 4, 1776, thereby ending eleven years of debate in which the submission of facts, not all of them exactly candid, had been a major intellectual support of the American cause. The English-American had always been a handy man with economic and historical facts, with the appeal to common sense about the present and to common agreement about the past. Now in his time of trial and transition to independence he tried to ward off "ministerial vengeance" by showing its unworkability as well as its unconstitutionality. When every argument against the Stamp Act had been recited ten thousand times or more, the hardheaded replies of Franklin in the House of Commons proved the most persuasive of all:

Q. Are not the Colonies, from their circumstances, very able to pay the stamp duty?
A. In my opinion there is not gold and silver enough in the Colonies to pay the stamp duty for one year. . . .
Q. Can any thing less than a military force carry the stamp act into execution?
A. I do not see how a military force can be applied to that purpose.
Q. Why may it not?
A. Suppose a military force sent into America, they will find nobody in arms; what are they then to do? They cannot force a man to take stamps

who chuses to do without them. They will not find a rebellion; they may indeed make one.

Q. If the act is not repealed, what do you think will be the consequences?

A. A total loss of the respect and affection the people of America bear to this country, and of all the commerce that depends on that respect and affection.

Q. How can the commerce be affected?

A. You will find, that if the act is not repealed, they will take very little of your manufactures in a short time.

Q. Is it in their power to do without them?

A. I think they may very well do without them.

Q. Is it their interest not to take them?

A. The goods they take from Britain are either necessaries, mere conveniences, or superfluities. The first, as cloth, &c. with a little industry they can make at home; the second they can do without, till they are able to provide them among themselves; and the last, which are much the greatest part, they will strike off immediately. They are mere articles of fashion, purchased and consumed because the fashion in a respected country; but will now be detested and rejected. The people have already struck off, by general agreement, the use of all goods fashionable in mournings, and many thousand pounds worth are sent back as unsaleable.[75]

The calm recital of the harmful consequences of English policy—especially when harmful to England itself—was a powerful weapon of colonial argument. A pamphlet like the anonymous *Essay on the Trade of the Northern Colonies* (1764) [76]—cool, moderate, reasonable, and above all factual—was worth a dozen apostrophes to abstract justice or reviews of legal history in the attempt to sway American and English opinion.

The appeal to facts, the invitation to hardheaded consideration of economic results, proved most popular in the same months when the appeal to heaven reached a climax. Many colonists who were convinced that America was entitled by "reason and justice" to seek independence had also to be convinced that they would be as well if not better off commercially. Paine's recital of grievances, abuse of monarchy, and interpretation of the "voice of nature and reason" were crushing blows for independence, but the most crushing of all was his simple remark, "Our corn will fetch its price in any market in Europe." [77] The advantages of free trade with the world were played up by many authors with special earnestness.

What will be the probable benefits of independence? A free and unlimited trade; a great accession of wealth, and a proportionable rise in the value of land; the establishment, gradual improvement and perfection of manufactures and science; a vast influx of foreigners, encouraged by the mildness of a free, equal, and tolerating government to leave their native countries, and settle in these Colonies; an astonishing encrease of our people from the present stock. . . . WE CANNOT PAY TOO GREAT A PRICE FOR LIBERTY, AND POSTERITY WILL THINK INDEPENDENCE A CHEAP PURCHASE AT EIGHTEEN MILLIONS.[78]

Independence, wrote a canny Scot in Princeton to his native countrymen all over America, would prove "both honourable and profitable to this country." [79] Throughout this decade profit and loss vied with honor and dishonor as major themes of colonial polemics.

CONSERVATISM. Perhaps the most remarkable feature of the political literature of this decade was its essential conservatism. If the Americans were the most successful revolutionaries of all time, they were revolutionaries by chance rather than choice. Until the last few months before independence the steady purpose of their resistance was to restore an old order rather than to build a new one, to get back to "the good days of George the second. There was no junto, no backstairs business then; a Whig King and Whig minister, speaking to a Whig people." [80]

> The British Parliament is violently usurping the powers of our colony governments, and rendering our legal Assemblies utterly useless; to prevent this, the necessity of our situation has obliged us to depart from the common forms, and to adopt measures which would be otherwise unjustifiable; but, in this departure, we have been influenced by an ardent desire to repel innovations destructive to all good government among us, and fatal to the foundations of law, liberty, and justice: We have declared, in the most explicit terms, that we wish for nothing more, than a restoration to our ancient condition.[81]

The ingrained conservatism of even the most high-spirited sermons and pamphlets is evident in four major themes that were chanted without pause: the invocation of the first settlers, appeal to the ancient charters, veneration of the British Constitution and British rights, and homage to the monarchy. There is no reason to believe that until the Coercive Acts or even later the American writers were not entirely sincere in their conservative wish to be "restored to their original standing." [82] The ministry, not they, had changed the rules of the game. They stood fast in the great tradition, "Whigs in a Reign when Whiggism is out of Fashion." [83]

Americans in 1776 like Americans today were fond of invoking the example of "Ancestors remarkable for their Zeal for true Religion & Liberty." [84] "Let us read and recollect and impress upon our souls," wrote John Adams to the Boston public,

> the views and ends of our own more immediate forefathers, in exchanging their native country for a dreary, inhospitable wilderness. Let us examine into the nature of that power, and the cruelty of that oppression, which drove them from their homes. Recollect their amazing fortitude, their bitter sufferings,—the hunger, the nakedness, the cold, which they patiently endured,—the severe labors of clearing their grounds, building their houses, raising their provisions, amidst dangers from wild beasts and savage men, before they had time or money or materials for commerce. Recollect the civil and religious principles and hopes and expectations which constantly supported and carried them through all hardships with patience and resig-

nation. Let us recollect it was liberty, the hope of liberty for themselves and us and ours, which conquered all discouragements, dangers, and trials.[85]

"Look back, therefore," echoed Provost Smith of Philadelphia,

> with reverence look back to the times of ancient virtue and renown. Look back to the mighty purposes which your fathers had in view, when they traversed a vast ocean, and planted this land. Recal to your minds their labours, their toils, their perseverance, and let their divine spirit animate you in all your actions.[86]

The Pilgrim Fathers were whirling in their graves 165 years before the founding of the American Liberty League: In 1769 a society was formed to commemorate annually the landing at Plymouth, and a good part of every celebration was devoted to a comparison of odious present with glorious past.[87] Stephen Hopkins developed this theme in his account of the first settlers of Providence:

> Nothing but extreme Diligence, and matchless Perseverance, could possibly have carried them through this Undertaking; could have procured them the scanty Morsels which supported a Life of Want and of Innocence. Too much have we their Descendants departed from the Diligence, Fortitude, Frugality, and Innocence of these our Fathers.[88]

For the most part, however, the colonists called upon their ancestors to inspire rather than to chastise. "The famous Tools of Power are holding up the picture of Want and Misery," wrote Samuel Adams from beleaguered Boston in 1774, "but in vain do they think to intimidate us; The Virtue of our Ancestors inspires—they were content with Clams & Muscles." [89]

The appeal to the charter in defense of colonial rights, a usage popular even with residents of colonies without charters, was a second instance of the conservative orientation of the American mind. In law the charters were not much more sacred than medieval grants and were open to attack from Parliament, courts, and Crown. But in the eyes and arguments of the colonists, especially the men of New England, they were unassailable declarations of "the rights and privileges of natural freeborn subjects of Great Britain" and irrevocable recognitions of the authority of the assemblies to tax and govern without leave of Parliament.[90] Actually, the charter-rights argument was extremely weak, at least in terms of home rule for all colonies.[91] But so long as it made any sense, the New Englanders, for whom Otis was a typical spokesman, appealed repeatedly to their sacred charters.

> It would indeed seem very hard and severe, for those of the colonists, who have charters, with peculiar priviledges, to loose them. They were given to their ancestors, in consideration of their sufferings and merit, in discovering and settling America. Our fore-fathers were soon worn away in the toils of hard labour on their little plantations, and in war with the Savages. They thought they were earning a sure inheritance for their posterity. Could they imagine it would ever be tho't just to deprive them or theirs of their charter priviledges! [92]

A much broader yet equally conservative footing on which to stand and resist oppressive acts of Parliament was the British Constitution and British rights—the former still that "glorious fabrick," "that noble constitution—the envy and terror of Europe," [93] the latter still "the invaluable Rights of Englishmen. . . . Rights! which no Time, no Contract, no Climate can diminish!" [94] Not until the end of the decade did Americans waver in their allegiance to the government and liberties they enjoyed as "descendants of free-born Britons." Paine's open assault on "the so much boasted constitution of England" was perhaps the most radical section in *Common Sense*.[95] Almost all other colonists were proud to live under governments that were "nearly copies of the happy British original," [96] or of enjoying "the British constitution in greater purity and perfection than they do in England." [97] Magna Charta,[98] the Glorious Revolution,[99] and other memorable documents or events in the story of English liberty were called upon for support. The Bill of Rights, the Habeas Corpus Act, and the Petition of Right were reprinted widely for popular edification.[100] Nowhere was the conservative temper of colonial polemics more evident than in this loyal, desperate veneration of a form of government and pattern of rights whose chief distinction was their undoubted antiquity. Whether conservative or radical, few Americans ever disagreed with John Witherspoon's judgment:

> It is proper to observe, that the British settlements have been improved in a proportion far beyond the settlements of other European nations. To what can this be ascribed? Not to the climate, for they are of all climates; not to the people, for they are a mixture of all nations. It must therefore be resolved singly into the degree of British liberty which they brought from home, and which pervaded more or less their several constitutions.[101]

Finally, in their never-ending expression of "the warmest sentiments of affection and duty to his majesty's person and government" and attachment "to the present happy establishment of the protestant succession," [102] the colonists revealed their deep-seated conservatism. Not until months after the shooting war had begun did they turn away sadly from their sincere conviction that the house of Hanover was "amongst the choicest of God's providential gifts to Great-Britain and the British Colonies." [103] Rarely did a writer so much as hint that the oppressive acts of Parliament or coercions of the ministry could be laid at the King's door. In their anxiety to preserve the blessings of a cherished constitutional monarchy, the colonists ignored almost wilfully the plain fact of the King's eager association in the policy of tighter imperial control. Even after Lexington and Concord the Massachusetts Provincial Congress could declare:

> These, brethren, are marks of ministerial vengeance against this colony, for refusing, with her sister colonies, a submission to slavery; but they have not yet detached us from our royal sovereign. We profess to be his loyal and dutiful subjects, and so hardly dealt with as we have been, are still ready, with our lives and fortunes, to defend his person, family, crown and dignity.[104]

Colonial propagandists contributed materially to the show of unanimity on this issue. Yet the propagandists themselves would have been the first to admit that the depth of American feeling for the monarchy and its incumbent made possible their fabrication of "the very model of a patriot king." Simple folk and propagandists alike were careful to maintain the crucial distinction between King and ministry:

> Have we not repeatedly and solemnly professed an inviolable loyalty to the person, power, and dignity of our sovereign, and unanimously declared, that it is not with him we contend, but with an envious cloud of false witnesses, that surround his throne, and intercept the sunshine of his favor from our oppressed land? [105]

English Whigs were taken somewhat aback by the warmth of colonial fealty, especially when Hamilton, Wilson, and others seemed ready to grant the King wide powers of government. But Americans were Whigs, not Tories. They had no intention of blowing up the royal prerogative into a potential tyranny. The King so loved and exalted was a constitutional monarch. His chief business was to protect the Americans from parliamentary or ministerial oppression. His prerogative was a check on power rather than power itself.[106] And if ever he should step out of his constitutional role, the remedy was that reserved for all tyrant kings:

> Virginians, you have nothing to fear, for Centuries to come, while you continue under the Protection of the Crown. You are defended against its Encroachments by the Power you have derived from the People. Should the King of Britain ever invade your Rights, he ceases, according to the British Constitution, to be King of the Dominion of Virginia.[107]

Not until 1776 and *Common Sense* did Americans wake from their dream of a patriot king.

A conservatism in political speculation matched this conservatism in political debate. However radical Revolutionary principles may have seemed to the rest of the world, in the minds of the colonists they were thoroughly preservative and respectful of the past. The explanation is, of course, that the American past—at least as Americans liked to read it—displayed a condition of human liberty and constitutional government that the rest of the world could only long for or detest. The political theory of this revolution was designed to preserve a world that had already been made over.

SENSE OF DESTINY. Pamphleteers and orators had their eyes on the future as well as the past. Having called upon his listeners to "look back to the times of ancient virtue and renown," Provost Smith reminded them that they were ancestors as well as descendants. It was entirely up to them whether they should be venerated, despised, or forgotten:

> Look forward also to distant posterity. Figure to yourselves millions and millions to spring from your loins, who may be born *freemen* or *slaves*, as Heaven shall now approve or reject your councils. Think, that on you it may depend, whether this great country, in ages hence, shall be filled and

adorned with a virtuous and inlightened people; enjoing *Liberty* and all its concomitant blessings, together with the *Religion* of *Jesus,* as it flows uncorrupted from his holy oracles; or covered with a race of men more contemptible than the savages that roam the wilderness.[108]

All American writers sounded the note of destiny, reminding fellow countrymen that their deeds would determine the fate and their words inspire the hearts of generations of free men yet unborn. It was this sort of exhortation, repeated in thousands of sermons and letters, that raised a peevish quarrel over unpopular taxes to an epic struggle over the future of a continent:

> The Sun never shined on a cause of greater worth. 'Tis not the affair of a City, a County, a Province, or a Kingdom; but of a Continent—of at least one eighth part of the habitable Globe. 'Tis not the concern of a day, a year, or an age; posterity are virtually involved in the contest, and will be more or less affected even to the end of time, by the proceedings now. Now is the seed-time of Continental union, faith and honour.[109]

Faith in the transcendent importance of the American cause reached its peak of conviction and fancy in the concept of the American Mission. The leaders of the Revolution, like the prophets of ancient Israel, were convinced that God had singled out their nation for a destiny far higher than their own prosperity and greatness. "The Revolution," wrote John Witherspoon, was "an important aera in the history of mankind," [110] for it was now to be determined—in the best possible laboratory and with the best possible materials—whether free government could be made reality or must remain a cruel will-o'-the-wisp. America would have other missions: For one thing, it was "a country marked out by the great *God* of nature as a receptacle for distress." [111] But its central mission was to be the testing-ground of freedom. Washington caught the solemnity of this truth in his first inaugural address:

> The preservation of the sacred fire of liberty and the destiny of the republican model of government are justly considered, perhaps, as *deeply,* as *finally,* staked on the experiment intrusted to the hands of the American people.[112]

The American Mission was plainly a decisive factor in the shaping of Revolutionary political thought, for it drove the colonists beyond charter and Constitution to claim sanction for their actions in the great principles of natural justice. The appeal to the universal doctrines of natural law and natural rights came easily to a people who believed words like these:

> To anticipate the future glory of America from our present hopes and prospects is ravishing and transporting to the mind. In this light we behold our country, beyond the reach of all oppressors, under the great charter of independence, enjoying the purest liberty; beautiful and strong in its union; the envy of tyrants and devils, but the delight of God and all good men; a refuge to the oppressed; the joy of the earth; each state happy in a wise model of government, and abounding with wise men, patriots, and heroes;

the strength and abilities of the whole continent, collected in a grave and venerable council, at the head of all, seeking and promoting the good of the present and future generations. Hail, my happy country, saved of the Lord! Happy land, emerged from the deluges of the Old World drowned in luxury and lewd excess! Hail, happy posterity, that shall reap the peaceful fruits of our sufferings, fatigues, and wars! [113]

This conviction of a higher destiny had much to do with the popularity of American political thought among liberty-minded men in England and France. America became an influential center of political speculation in the last three decades of the eighteenth century because American writers took the grand view of their country's past and future.

THE RECOURSE TO FIRST PRINCIPLES; THE AMERICAN CONSENSUS

Occasional, propagandistic, legalistic, factual, conservative, conscious of destiny—these words catch the quality of political argument in the years that led to independence. One final characteristic, the most significant for our purposes, remains to be mentioned: the habit, in which most colonists indulged to excess, of "recurring to first principles," of appealing to basic doctrines of political theory to support legal, factual, and constitutional arguments. Few men were willing to argue about a specific issue—deny the wisdom of the Stamp Act, defend an editor against charges of libel, protest the landing of the tea, interpret the Massachusetts Charter, condemn the quartering of troops in New York—without first calling upon rules of justice that were considered to apply to all men everywhere.[114] These rules, of course, were the ancient body of political assumptions known as natural law and natural rights. The great political philosophy of the Western world enjoyed one of its proudest seasons in this time of resistance and revolution. If the Americans added few novel twists of their own to this philosophy, they gave it a unique vogue among men of all ranks and callings. Few people in history have been so devoted to a "party line" that had no sanction other than its appeal to free minds; few people have made such effective use of the recourse to first principles.

The reasons for the popularity of natural law and natural rights are not difficult to understand. This philosophy gave men of all colonies and national origins a common ground on which to stand and defy ministerial tyranny. It came naturally to colonial advocates who could see that they were getting nowhere with appeals to the charters, English rights, and simple expediency. "It has often mortified me," wrote a gentleman masquerading as "Benevolus" to the New Jersey Assembly in early 1775,

> to hear our warmest advocates for liberty (tho' with the best design) recurring to doubtful constitutions, charters, acts of Parliament, and public faith, as the foundations of our reasonable and rightful claims—These, at best, can be but declaratory of those rights—The true foundation of American liberty, is in human nature.[115]

The universality of natural law gave colonists a strong sense of fellowship with all men struggling to be free, while its antiquity placed them in a great chain of heroes and philosophers stretching back through their own ancestors to the beginnings of Western history. Natural law and rights, wrote John Adams, "are what are called revolution principles."

> They are the principles of Aristotle and Plato, of Livy and Cicero, and Sidney, Harrington, and Locke; the principles of nature and eternal reason; the principles on which the whole government over us now stands. It is therefore astonishing, if any thing can be so, that writers, who call themselves friends of government, should in this age and country be so inconsistent with themselves, so indiscreet, so immodest, as to insinuate a doubt concerning them.[116]

There were few deviationists from the American "party line." Some spokesmen for the patriot cause saluted natural law and natural rights only in passing; others demonstrated that the question was, after all, one of free choice by expressing irregular opinions of the nature of man or origin of government. But all American publicists—whether celebrated or anonymous, sophisticated or untutored, speculative or pedestrian—paid devotion of one sort or another to "revolution principles." [117] Nowhere in patriot literature is there a single direct suggestion that the essentials of this political theory were unhistorical, illogical, or unsound. Even the Tories, except for bold spirits like Jonathan Boucher, refrained from attacking it frontally, and even Boucher, if the tactical situation demanded such talk, could speak of "consent," "constitutional right," and "the great Hampden." [118] The warmest sort of enemy approval of the American consensus was expressed in Gentleman Johnny Burgoyne's famous letter to Charles Lee:

> I am no stranger to the doctrines of Mr. Locke and other of the best advocates for the rights of mankind, upon the compact always implied between the governing and the governed, and the right of resistance in the latter, when the compact shall be so violated as to leave no other means of redress. I look with reverence, almost amounting to idolatry, upon those immortal whigs who adopted and applied such doctrine during part of the reign of Charles the 1st, and in that of James IId.[119]

In political theory, if not in devotion to the patriot cause, "nine tenths of the people" were, as John Adams remarked, "high whigs." [120] To the political theory of high Whiggery the last two chapters of this book will be wholly devoted. As an introduction to these chapters we shall quote at length from two memorable expressions of the common faith. The first, "The Rights of the Colonists," written by James Otis and Samuel Adams and adopted by the Boston town meeting, is a reminder that men in the mass subscribed to these principles. The second, which needs no identification, is still the most historic, felicitous, and frugal statement of the political theory of the Revolution:

From "The Rights of the Colonists," November 29, 1772:

Among the Natural Rights of the Colonists are these First. a Right to *Life;* Secondly to *Liberty;* thirdly to *Property;* together with the Right to support and defend them in the best manner they can—Those are evident Branches of, rather than deductions from the Duty of Self Preservation, commonly called the first Law of Nature—

All Men have a Right to remain in a State of Nature as long as they please: And in case of intollerable Oppression, Civil or Religious, to leave the Society they belong to, and enter into another.—

When Men enter into Society, it is by voluntary consent; and they have a right to demand and insist upon the performance of such conditions, And previous limitations as form an equitable *original compact.*—

Every natural Right not expressly given up or from the nature of a Social Compact necessarily ceded remains.—

All positive and civil laws, should conform as far as possible, to the Law of natural reason and equity.—

As neither reason requires, nor religeon permits the contrary, every Man living in or out of a state of civil society, has a right peaceably and quietly to worship God according to the dictates of his conscience. . . .

The natural liberty of Men by entring into society is abridg'd or restrained so far only as is necessary for the Great end of Society the best good of the whole—

In the state of nature, every man is under God, Judge and sole Judge, of his own rights and the injuries done him: By entering into society, he agrees to an Arbiter or indifferent Judge between him and his neighbours; but he no more renounces his original right, than by taking a cause out of the ordinary course of law, and leaving the decision to Referees or indifferent Arbitrations. . . .

"The natural liberty of man is to be free from any superior power on earth, and not to be under the will or legislative authority of man; but only to have the law of nature for his rule. . . ."

In short it is the greatest absurdity to suppose it in the power of one or any number of men at the entering into society, to renounce their essential natural rights, or the means of preserving those rights when the great end of civil government from the very nature of its institution is for the support, protection and defence of those very rights: the principal of which as is before observed, are life, liberty and property. If men through fear, fraud or mistake, should *in terms* renounce and give up any essential natural right, the eternal law of reason and the great end of society, would absolutely vacate such renunciation; the right to freedom being *the gift* of God Almighty, it is not in the power of Man to alienate this gift, and voluntarily become a slave. . . .

A Common Wealth or state is a body politick or civil society of men, united together to promote their mutual safety and prosperity, by means of their union.

The *absolute Rights* of Englishmen, and all freemen in or out of Civil society, are principally, *personal security personal liberty* and *private property.*

All Persons born in the British American Colonies are by the laws of God and nature, and by the Common law of England, *exclusive of all charters from the Crown,* well Entitled, and by the Acts of the British

Parliament are declared to be entitled to all the natural essential, inherent & inseperable Rights Liberties and Privileges of Subjects born in Great Britain, or within the Realm. Among those Rights are the following; which no men or body of men, consistently with their own rights as men and citizens or members of society, can for themselves give up, or take away from others.

First, "The first fundamental positive law of all Commonwealths or States, is the establishing the legislative power; as the first fundamental *natural* law also, which is to govern even the legislative power itself, is the preservation of the Society."

Secondly, The Legislative has no right to absolute arbitrary power over the lives and fortunes of the people. . . .

Thirdly, The supreme power cannot Justly take from any man, any part of his property without his consent, in person or by his Representative.—

These are some of the first principles of natural law & Justice, and the great Barriers of all free states, and of the British Constitution in particular. It is utterly irreconcileable to these principles, and to many other fundamental maxims of the common law, common sense and reason, that a British house of commons, should have a right, at pleasure, to give and grant the property of the Colonists.[121]

From the Declaration of Independence:

We hold these truths to be self-evident, that all men are created equal, that they are endowed by their Creator with certain unalienable Rights, that among these are Life, Liberty, and the pursuit of Happiness. That, to secure these rights, Governments are instituted among Men, deriving their just Powers from the consent of the governed. That, whenever any form of Government becomes destructive of these ends, it is the Right of the People to alter or to abolish it, and to institute new Government, laying its foundation on such Principles, and organizing its Powers in such form, as to them shall seem most likely to effect their Safety and Happiness. Prudence, indeed, will dictate that Governments long established should not be changed for light and transient causes; and, accordingly, all experience hath shewn, that mankind are more disposed to suffer, while evils are sufferable, than to right themselves by abolishing the forms to which they are accustomed. But, when a long train of abuses and usurpations, pursuing invariably the same Object, evinces a design to reduce them under absolute Despotism, it is their right, it is their duty, to throw off such Government, and to provide new Guards for their future Security.[122]

Almost fifty years after the event, the author of the Declaration of Independence had this to say about his alleged lack of originality:

With respect to our rights, and the acts of the British government contravening those rights, there was but one opinion on this side of the water. All American whigs thought alike on these subjects. When forced, therefore, to resort to arms for redress, an appeal to the tribunal of the world was deemed proper for our justification. This was the object of the Declaration of Independence. Not to find out new principles, or new arguments, never before thought of, not merely to say things which had never been said before; but to place before mankind the common sense of the subject, in terms so plain and firm as to command their assent, and to justify ourselves in the independent stand we are compelled to take. Neither aiming at originality of principle or sentiment, nor yet copied from any particular and previous writing, it was intended to be an expression of the American mind, and to give to that expression the proper tone and spirit called for by the occasion. All its authority rests then on the harmonizing sentiments of the day, whether expressed in conversation, in letters, printed essays, or in the elementary books of public right, as Aristotle, Cicero, Locke, Sidney, &c.[123]

This statement serves us in two important ways: as explanation of the popularity of the American consensus, and as introduction to a few pages about the sources on which Jefferson and his colleagues drew.

THE SOURCES OF AMERICAN POLITICAL THEORY

American thinkers were conscious heirs of the noble tradition of natural law. Greece, Rome, Israel, the church, the continent, and England had all brought forth great men to affirm the reality of moral restraints on political power, and colonists turned eagerly to these prophets of freedom for philosophical support in the struggle against England. The consensus was part of almost everyone's intellectual equipment. No one really had to quote chapter and verse for ideas like the compact and right to property. But the rules of the game, especially as played in England, required political thinkers to cite their authorities, and this the colonists were entirely willing to do. Political theorists of the Revolution were not slaves to the past they adored; they were selective about the men they quoted and about the ideas they took from any particular man. They searched all literature for words of liberty and refused to let a man's reputation repel or dazzle them. Thus they seized upon Blackstone's homage to natural law and ignored Locke's comments on the supremacy of Parliament. We may separate their sources into four categories:

THE ANCIENTS. The Hebraic, Christian, and classical traditions [124] were all very much alive in the colonies. Spokesmen for liberty in each tradition saw heavy duty in the patriot cause. Dissenting ministers, of course, relied heavily on the great men of the Old and New Testaments. Out of the mouths of prophets and apostles they plucked encouraging words about resistance, liberty, equality, public virtue, patriotism, and higher law. John Allen saluted Micah as a "SON OF LIBERTY," [125] and Samuel Cooper traced the compact back to Joshua and his companions.[126] They did not, however, make much use of the church fathers. St. Thomas Aquinas might just as well never have written his expositions of higher law.

Among the Greeks to whom learned men like Jefferson and John Adams appealed for support were Herodotus, Thucydides, Plutarch, and Polybius. Aristotle enjoyed only a slight vogue, and Plato was virtually ignored. Although Dickinson could quote Sophocles on "the unwritten law divine, immutable, eternal" in a convincing manner,[127] most authors used the ancient Greeks for window-dressing. The history of the Greek leagues was more instructive to colonial writers than the arguments of Greek philosophers. The Romans were much more useful to the patriot cause, especially Cicero for his exposition of natural law, Tacitus for his defense of a simple, agrarian society, and the imperial lawyers for their continued insistence on higher law. But they, too, were men who confirmed the colonists in old convictions rather than taught them anything new. The Americans would have believed just as vigorously in public morality had Cato and the Gracchi never lived.

ENGLISH LIBERTARIANS. In no instance did the colonists prove themselves such faithful children of England as in their sweeping reliance on English political thinkers. Patriot spokesmen dug deep in the libraries of their fathers to find any Englishman who could be quoted in support of the cause. Common-law jurists, liberal ecclesiastics, seventeenth-century republicans, eighteenth-century Whigs, and even learned Tories were called to judgment. The one mildly surprising omission from the catalogue of English authorities was the complete boycott of the Levellers and Diggers of the seventeenth century. Lilburne, Winstanley, Overton, and the rest never appear in colonial literature. Those colonists who knew their work were probably aware that no purpose would be served by dragging them into the argument. And in any case, the American consensus was as far to the right of the Levellers as it was to the left of Jacobite exponents of divine right and passive obedience. Two other English thinkers whom the Americans refused to touch were Hobbes and Filmer. If they appear at all in colonial literature, it is only to serve as straw men for patriots to ridicule and knock down.[128] David Hume, on the other hand, was treated with some respect.[129]

It is not easy to separate the English libertarians into major and minor prophets of the American cause, but several men do stand out as thinkers whom the colonists seem to have read and pondered with special care: John Locke, of whom more in a few paragraphs; Algernon Sidney, still the *beau idéal* of the American republicans; [130] Sir Edward Coke, "that great luminary of the law," the human embodiment of common law, Magna Charta, and constitutionalism; [131] Lord Bolingbroke, of whom John Adams observed tartly, "[His] knowledge of the constitution will not be disputed, whatever may be justly said of his religion and his morals"; [132] and Gordon and Trenchard, whose *Cato's Letters* retained a wide audience in this nation of Whigs.[133]

In the second rank, according to actual use of their words and ideas, were such diverse British thinkers as Joseph Addison, the Marquis of Halifax, Lord John Somers, Henry Care, Richard Hooker, John Milton, Francis Hutcheson, Benjamin Hoadly, Marchamont Nedham, Henry Neville, Christopher St. Germain, George Buchanan, Thomas Bradbury, Robert Dodsley, John Knox, Sir John Hawles, Bishop Burnet, William Molineux, William Wollaston, and James Harrington. Works of Somers, Care, Buchanan, Bradbury, Dodsley, Knox, and Hawles were reprinted in the colonies in the pre-Revolutionary decade.[134] St. Germain's sixteenth-century legal treatise *Doctor and Student* was a favorite of Jefferson's, and Harrington's *Oceana* helped shape the mettlesome mind of John Adams.[135] Milton is worth mentioning only because of the rarity with which he was quoted; it would almost seem that a conspiracy had been raised against him. Jurists other than Coke who were used with regularity were Bracton, Fortescue, Hale, Holt, Kames, and Bacon.

The influence of John Locke's second treatise *Of Civil Government* must be more carefully weighed. Locke has always been considered the supreme if not indeed exclusive source of Revolutionary ideas. Other men's works may have been cited, we are told, but Locke's were studied: He was the one genuine philosophical ancestor of the Adamses, Jefferson, and the political preachers, the man acclaimed and echoed by all America as "the finest reasoner, and best writer on government, that this or any other age has produced." [136] Locke was hardly less the theoretical father of the American Revolution than Marx of the Russian. But is this true?

It is difficult to estimate the debt owed to Locke by patriot thinkers. But the unmistakable impression one gets from roaming through the entire range of Revolutionary literature is that he was definitely not so important a figure as we have hitherto assumed. [137] There is no evidence that his treatise sold any better than a half-dozen other books that said pretty much the same thing, [138] and until 1774 his name was mentioned only rarely in the columns of even the most radical newspapers. In hundreds of Whiggish pamphlets and letters he is not quoted at all; in other hundreds he appears as one of four or five English and Continental sources. Perhaps ninety per cent of the quotations from *Civil Government* are limited to a few overworked passages about property and legislation. His discussion of "the dissolution of government" is hardly used at all. Many thoughtful colonists turned away from his confusions and omissions to summon other thinkers to testify about the origin of government and substance of natural law.

This must not be taken to mean that Locke lacked stature with the learned or popularity with the public. He had a very special place in American affections. He was

> Sagacious *Locke*, by providence design'd
> T'exalt, instruct, and rectify the mind. [139]

Nathaniel Ames spoke the minds of a great many people when he wrote in his almanac: "As it is unpardonable for a Navigator to be without his charts, so it is for a *Senator* to be without HIS, which is Lock's 'Essay on Government.' " [140] A great many others, however, seemed to prefer the writings of Burlamaqui or Vattel or even Blackstone as master charts of the rights of man. The natural-law philosophy had long held sway in the Western world, and a colonist in search of first principles could have turned to any one of a score of political theorists and have been completely satisfied. John Wise, the most vocal and explicit of all natural-law thinkers in the colonial period, read his lessons with Pufendorf and never even mentioned Locke. If Locke looms above the other great men of this ancient school, if he is the one author whom Tories delighted to throw back at patriot publicists, [141] it is probably because of one very practical rather than philosophical reason: He was a famous, almost unassailable English philosopher who had glorified a rebellion of Englishmen against an English king. Despite his inconsistencies and omissions, despite his failure to give the ancient line any really new twist, he was therefore the most popular source of Revolutionary ideas. As such he was *primus inter pares*, not the lonely oracle of the American consensus.

CONTINENTAL LIBERTARIANS. Although many references in colonial litera-ture to European authors were window-dressing of the most obvious sort, at least four Continental philosophers were studied with care and quoted with confidence: Emmerich de Vattel, a name to be flung about as confidently as that of Locke or Sidney; [142] Baron Pufendorf, whose name turns up repeatedly in the most improbable places; [143] Jean Jacques Burlamaqui, a particular favorite of James Wilson and John Dickinson; [144] and Montesquieu, whom every literate colonist could quote to advantage, and whose exposition of the separation of powers was already making perfect sense to American minds. [145] It would be hard to fix the precise responsibility of any one of these men for any one leading principle of colonial theory, except in the case of Montesquieu's doctrine of the separation of powers and Burlamaqui's emphasis on happiness as a right of man and an object of government. They all had the same message for the men of the Revolution: that government could be limited, that men could be free, that kings could be unseated for playing the tyrant. Other Continentals who appear occasionally, but only occasionally, in Revolutionary tracts are Grotius, Jean Domat, Barbeyrac, Voltaire, and Beccaria. [146] John Adams was one of the few colonists who dared or cared to use Machiavelli. [147] Rousseau, far from being an important source of the Declaration of Independence, was a minor figure of whom precious few traces can be found. [148] Indeed, Rousseau's whole approach to man, society, and government ran counter to the basic principles of Ameri-can Revolutionary thought. The colonists went to the Continent to seek help for the English Whigs, not to learn any new and unsettling ideas.

CONTEMPORARY ENGLISHMEN. Revolutionary pamphleteers and orators drew heavy intellectual support from two classes of contemporary English-men: a small band of Whig statesmen who spoke up manfully for American rights, and an even smaller band of radicals who clung to the doctrine of natural rights in the face of a nation grown weary of Locke and Sidney. The most widely quoted in the first group were Edmund Burke, Colonel Barré, Lord Camden, Bishop Shipley, General Conway, Charles James Fox, Governor Johnstone, and above all the elder Pitt. [149] Men like Pitt and Barré looked upon the colonists' cause as their cause, and their speeches in the Whig tradition were reprinted, studied, and quoted wherever men debated their liberties in this decade. Pitt, "glorious and immortal," the "guardian of America," was the idol of the colonies. [150] His eloquent arguments against taxation without representation were repaid in full measure by a grateful people. Ships, towns, and babies bore the proud name of Pitt; preachers, orators, and poets celebrated his Roman virtues.

> I thank thee, Pitt, for all thy glorious Strife
> Against the Foes of LIBERTY and Life. [151]

A Son of Liberty in Bristol County, Massachusetts paid him the ultimate tribute of identification with English liberty:

> Our Toast in general is,—*Magna Charta,*—the *British Constitution,*—PITT and Liberty forever! [152]

The most prominent members of the second category were Richard Price, James Burgh, Joseph Priestley, Granville Sharp, Catherine Macauley, John Cartwright, David Hartley the younger, and the unknown authors of the *Letters of Junius* and *The Crisis.* Reprints of their works appeared everywhere in the colonies. Price's *Observations on the Nature of Civil Liberty* [153] and *The Crisis* [154] were especially popular with colonial debaters, the former for bringing Locke up to date, the latter for its savage attacks on King and Parliament and its justification of the right of revolution. John Wilkes [155] and the Irish patriot Dr. Charles Lucas [156] were other radicals whose words appeared repeatedly in colonial pamphlets and letters. Few American leaders knew just what to make of Wilkes as a man,[157] but many made a great deal of his arguments for parliamentary privilege and the liberty of the subject.[158] It should nevertheless be plain that one friendly observation of Pitt or Burke was worth more to American pamphleteers than a hundred pages of Price or the entire works of Wilkes. Not until the argument shifted substantially away from English rights and over to natural justice did Price and Priestley influence American minds.

One other contemporary Englishman, a man who defies easy classification, remains to be mentioned: Sir William Blackstone, the great Tory jurist. The publication of his *Commentaries* in Philadelphia in 1771 was a major event in American intellectual history. Blackstone's huge influence on American law is, of course, well known; what is not so well known was his high standing as political theorist with men like Wilson, Hamilton, Dickinson, and Otis.[159] Blackstone was almost as popular among colonial political thinkers as among colonial lawyers, probably because the one group included so many of the other—and vice versa. The Americans read the eclectic *Commentaries* in a shrewdly selective manner, citing this oracle repeatedly and effectively in support of all manner of Whiggish doctrines. Two of the most popular borrowings from English political literature were Blackstone's memorable salutes to natural law and natural liberty.[160] The *Commentaries* were also an important secondary outlet for the teachings of Locke and Burlamaqui.

The colonists went everywhere, even to the Koran,[161] for refinements of political theory and particulars of public dispute that would aid them in their struggle against parliamentary power—everywhere, that is to say, but to their own colonial ancestors. One may search in vain through the literature of the time for a single significant quotation from Hooker, Williams, or Wise. A few scraps from Hooker's desolate farewell sermon to England appeared in an issue of the *New-Hampshire Gazette,* a few offhand references to Williams in Stephen Hopkins's *Historical Account* in the *Providence Gazette.*[162] Wise's two tracts were reprinted in 1772—then ignored by the pamphleteers. Increase Mather's *Narrative of the Miseries . . . in the Tyranic Reign of Sir Edmund Andros*, Cotton Mather's *The Good Old Ways*, Zenger's *Brief Narrative* (which carried Andrew Hamilton's great speech), and Dummer's *Defence of the New-England Charters* were all reprinted for special audiences and obvious reasons,[163] but no American writer was ever called to bear witness to the sanctity of the compact or the right of resistance. Yet if men argued for religious liberty without summoning Williams, if they described the contract without quoting Wise, if they proclaimed the right to depose a tyrant without bowing to Mayhew, this did not mean that these early American thinkers and their lesser colleagues had written and preached in vain. Quite the contrary: John Wise and his fellows had helped create a nation of Whigs for whom the appeal to Locke and Burlamaqui was a completely natural performance. Thanks to the early colonial theorists, the men of the Revolution were devoted heart and mind to the great traditions of Whiggery and natural justice.

CHAPTER THIRTEEN

American Political Thought, 1765-1776: The Rights of Man

"NEVER was there a People," wrote a colonist in 1768, "whom it more immediately concerned to search into the Nature and Extent of their Rights and Privileges than it does the People of America at this Day." [1] Never was there a people for whom advice of this kind was less necessary. Americans searched eagerly into the nature and extent of their rights and privileges; they searched, too, for basic principles that would justify these rights and give them substance.

The principles in which they placed their special trust were those of the oldest of libertarian philosophies, the school of natural law. The practical purpose of the colonists was to limit the power of Parliament, and like all men with the slightest feeling for abstract justice, they sought limits more universal than those staked out in laws, charters, and constitutions. The great philosophy that preached the reality of moral restraints on power had always been a part of their Anglo-Christian heritage. Now, in their time of trial, the colonists summoned it to their defense. The eloquence of the patriot leaders changed this philosophy from "a commonplace of morality" to "a mass of dynamite," [2] and with this dynamite they proceeded to blow up an empire.

As we turn at last to the political theory of the Revolution, we must keep one fact clearly in mind: The progression of ideas through the next two chapters is the result of a modern attempt to bring order out of the writings of men who had neither time nor predilection for ordered exposition. No Revolutionary theorist presented his views in this particular form. Indeed, no one man even touched upon all the ideas that we are to discuss in these pages. The political faith that sustained the Revolution was the work of many men, and only through an intensely ordered rendering of a protean literature can we hope to make clear the principles upon which a majority agreed. The organization of the next two chapters follows the lead of the Revolutionary authors in presenting these principles in the two familiar contexts of man and government. The state of nature, the law of nature, and the nature and rights of man are the subjects of inquiry in the present chapter. The origin, purpose, nature, structure, and moral basis of government are the concern of Chapter 14. The many ideas that appear in both of these chapters are evidence of the Revolutionary assumption that man without government was almost impossible to imagine.[3]

THE STATE OF NATURE

The state of nature—the state of "men living together according to reason without a common superior on earth, with authority to judge between them" [4]—was the point of reference around which Revolutionary thinkers grouped the principles of their political theory. The state of nature was, of course, an old concept, and men raised in the tradition of natural law could accept and use it without feeling any urge to subject it to critical analysis. Most American thinkers were content to mention the state of nature in a sentence or two, then move on briskly to consider those rights which men could be said to enjoy because they had once lived in it. An author writing under the pseudonym "Spartanus" made one of the few attempts to describe this state:

> In the days of Adam and Noah, every man had an equal right to the unoccupied earth, which God said he had given to the children of men. The whole world was before them, there was much more land than they could occupy or enjoy.—Each man had a right to occupy new land where he pleased, and to take wild beasts by hunting. This was what civilians call a state of nature. In this state every man had a right to enjoy himself, a right to his enclosure, to what he took in hunting, and to feed his flocks where he pleased, so that in any of these, he did not interfere with any pre-occupant. In such a state every man had a right to defend himself and repel injuries, as he thought best. . . . Every man had an equal right to judge between himself & his neighbour, and to do that which was right in his own eyes.[5]

Samuel Cooke was another who elaborated upon the state of nature. Indeed, it would seem that he had two such states in mind:

> In a pure state of nature, government is in a great measure unnecessary. Private property in that state is inconsiderable. Men need no arbiter to determine their rights; they covet only a bare support; their stock is but the subsistence of a day; the uncultivated deserts are their habitations, and they carry their all with them in their frequent removes. They are each one a law to himself, which, in general, is of force sufficient for their security in that course of life.
> It is far otherwise when mankind are formed into collective bodies, or a

social state of life. Here, their frequent mutual intercourse, in a degree, necessarily leads them to different apprehensions respecting their several rights, even where their intentions are upright. Temptations to injustice and violence increase, and the occasions of them multiply in proportion to the increase and opulence of the society. The laws of nature, though enforced by divine revelation, which bind the conscience of the upright, prove insufficient to restrain the sons of violence, who have not the fear of God before their eyes.[6]

The true state of nature, that is to say, was simply that condition of no positive law and no formal government that preceded the organization of the political community. A few writers followed Hobbes in describing this state:

The miseries of the state of nature are so evident, that there is no occasion to display them; every man is sensible that violence, rapine, and slaughter must be continually practised where no restraints are provided to curb the inordinancy of self-affection.[7]

Most, however, agreed with Locke that it was "a state of peace, goodwill, mutual assistance, and preservation." [8] All were willing to go one step further with Locke and assert that, although most men in the state of nature were inclined to respect the persons and properties of other men, the want of a superior power to adjust honest differences of opinion and "restrain the sons of violence" rendered it a very precarious existence. The state of nature, like natural man, had much in it that was good, much that was bad. However pleasing the prospect, few men would refuse to abandon it, even fewer seek to return to it. It was a state perhaps "more excellent than that, in which men are meanly submissive to the haughty will of an imperious tyrant," [9] but men would go back to it only to clear the ground for a new government.

It is impossible to say just how seriously the colonists believed in the state of nature as a fact of history.[10] Certainly Americans had more right than most people to talk of the state of nature as if it had been or could be a real situation. Colonial theorists and debaters used this phrase to describe these situations of historical fact: the condition of no government in prehistoric or Biblical times; the situation facing the Pilgrim fathers in Provincetown harbor in 1620 and other unorganized or unauthorized settlements throughout the colonial period; [11] the state of the colonies in 1775, especially after the King had dissolved the compact by sending troops against them; [12] and, following Locke, the relations to one another of "governments all through the world." [13] This was, after all, long before the days of cultural anthropology and social history, and a belief in the state of nature as a fact in the past was perfectly consistent with learning or intelligence, especially since all but a tiny fraction of colonial thinkers seemed to consider this state a pre-political rather than pre-social phenomenon. For men as different in approach as James Otis and Rev. Samuel Cooke society without government—rather than men without society—was the real state of nature.

Most American theorists were more interested in the state of nature as logical hypothesis than as chronological fact. It was far more convenient for them to assume its existence than describe its outlines, and certainly such an assumption called for no explanation from men raised in the Anglo-Christian tradition. The state of nature served as a logical antecedent to at least five major principles of Revolutionary theory, since it permitted the colonists to:

(1) proclaim the prior existence and therefore prior validity of the law of nature, the system of natural justice that commands men to love, assist, and respect one another;

(2) describe man's basic nature, by calling attention to those qualities of character he possesses before and despite government or society;

(3) describe man's basic rights, which are therefore considered the gifts of God or nature and not of the community:

> In a state of nature, no man had any *moral* power to deprive another of his life, limbs, property, or liberty; nor the least authority to command or exact obedience from him.

> In a state of nature, every man had the sovereign controul over his own person. He might also have, in that state, a qualified property. . . . Over this qualified property every man in a state of nature had also a sovereign control.

> No man in the State of Nature can justly take Anothers Property without his Consent.

> Man, in a state of nature, has undoubtedly a right to speak and act without controul.[14]

(4) demonstrate the clear necessity of government based on principles of freedom:

> As in a state of nature much happiness cannot be enjoyed by individuals, so it has been conformable to the inclinations of almost all men, to enter into a political society so constituted, as to remove the inconveniences they were obliged to submit to in their former state, and, at the same time, to retain all those natural rights, the enjoyment of which would be consistent with the nature of a free government, and the necessary subordination to the supreme power of the state.[15]

(5) give a mechanistic explanation of the origin of government, in order to free men from the past and let them build new political institutions to suit themselves. "We often read," declaimed a Boston orator,

> of the original contract, and of mankind, in the early ages, passing from a state of nature to immediate civilization. But *what eye* could penetrate through gothic night and barbarous fable to that remote period. Such an eye, perhaps, was present, when the Deity conceived the universe and fixed his compass upon the great deep.

And yet the people of Massachusetts have reduced to practice the wonderful theory. A numerous people have convened in a state of nature, and, like *our ideas* of the patriarchs, have deputed a few fathers of the land to draw up for them a glorious covenant. It has been drawn. The people have signed it with rapture, and have, thereby, bartered, among themselves, an easy degree of obedience for the highest possible civil happiness.[16]

For men anxious to recur to first principles of natural justice the state of nature was a prime philosophical assumption. The dictates of a political theory concerned with limits on political power in behalf of individual liberty demanded that men and their rights be declared logically and chronologically anterior to the organized community. Whatever else it was, the pre-political state of nature was an extremely handy point of reference.

THE LAW OF NATURE

The Declaration of Independence was written, the Constitution adopted, and the Republic launched in an age when most men, whether subtle or simple, believed unequivocally in higher law, generally called "the law of nature." If a few men like Bentham doubted or denied, most political theorists—in America, all political theorists—assumed the existence and applicability of "the Laws of Nature and of Nature's God." Thinking colonists realized that they were the latest heirs of a political tradition unrivaled in age and universality. By the time the law of nature had come into their hands, it had assumed many different shapes in the service of many different peoples and purposes. Greek philosophers, Roman jurists, Church fathers, medieval scholastics, Protestant reformers, Continental and English liberals—all these and many others had made rich contributions to the doctrine of natural law. And all had agreed, no matter what their special interpretation of its content and dictates, that it placed some sort of moral restriction on political power, indeed on all human activity.[17] To understand the place of natural law in Revolutionary thought we must seek brief answers to these questions: What did the colonists consider to be its source? How did they define it? What did it actually mean in terms of their political theory?

Colonial opinion of the ultimate source of higher law divided into three fairly distinct categories. One group of men held it be of immediately divine origin. For them the higher law was, as Rev. Eliphalet Williams of Hartford told the Connecticut legislature, "the law of God, eternal and immutable." [18] New England preachers, at least the more conservative of them, were the leading members of this group, but it was by no means confined to clerical thinkers. James Otis, for example, considered the law of nature to be "the *unchangeable will of God*, the author of nature, whose laws never vary." [19] For most of these thinkers, if not necessarily for Otis, the commands of higher law were to be found primarily in Scripture.[20] Since the great men of Israel had commanded a variety of things, Eliphalet Williams's law of God was just about as flexible as Samuel Adams's law of nature.

A second group sought, in the tradition of Cicero and Grotius, to secularize higher law. Although they could not quite eliminate the touch of divinity, they were able to thrust God well into the background. Such rationalists in religion as John Adams and Jefferson were willing to concede that God—not necessarily the Christian God—had set the grand machine of nature in motion, but they added quickly that the laws governing this machine had by now become "natural" in the strictest sense: They were at once cause, effect, and expression of nature, an order of things that functioned without divine intervention. Even if God had decreed this order in his original omnipotence, he could no longer tamper with it. Indeed he, too, was bound to respect and follow its laws. The laws of nature that controlled the actions of men were as certain and imperative as those which controlled the movement of the spheres. They were part of the pattern of nature itself, to be discovered by men, whether Christians or pagans, through the use of right reason. Many thinkers, of course, appealed to both "God and nature," a sort of holy duality, but these must be classed finally as believers in natural as contrasted with purely divine law. Reason rather than revelation was their means of discovering the dictates of higher law.

A recent book has argued with some persuasiveness that a few key political theorists adopted a utilitarian rather than metaphysical approach to higher law. When men like James Wilson spoke of the law of nature, we are told, they "appear . . . to have meant, not a transcendental essence, but a practical plan . . . the plan to make possible individual, free, righteous development within a happy and prosperous commonwealth." [21] History, not God or nature, was the source of higher law; experience, not revelation or reason, taught men its commands and penalties. Whether Wilson or any other like-minded colonist was this much of a utilitarian is debatable, but it can be argued that one strong group of American thinkers looked upon the history of liberty and tyranny as the true source of those rules of natural justice which Parliament seemed bent on violating. The higher law that limited political power was simply an experience-proved boundary "built up in the minds of freedom-loving men—not always the same, perhaps, but always on the alert—beyond which it is not safe for governments to go." [22] *Weltgeschichte ist Weltgericht:* History had a way of punishing those men who disregarded its lessons in political freedom.

The colonists revealed the derivative quality of their political theory by quoting English and Continental definitions of the law of nature rather than seeking to define it for themselves. Locke, Pufendorf, Vattel, and Burlamaqui were all called into service for this purpose, but Sir William Blackstone's definition was probably the best known and most widely cited. No young man after 1771 could become a lawyer without reading these words:

> Man, considered as a creature, must necessarily be subject to the laws of his creator, for he is entirely a dependent being. . . . And consequently, as man depends absolutely upon his maker for every thing, it is necessary that he should in all points conform to his maker's will.
>
> This will of his maker is called the law of nature. For as God, when he created matter, and endued it with a principle of mobility, established certain rules for the perpetual direction of that motion; so, when he created

man, and endued him with freewill to conduct himself in all parts of life, he laid down certain immutable laws of human nature, whereby that freewill is in some degree regulated and restrained, and gave him also the faculty of reason to discover the purport of those laws.

Considering the creator only as a being of infinite *power*, he was able unquestionably to have prescribed whatever laws he pleased to his creature, man, however unjust or severe. But as he is also a being of infinite *wisdom*, he has laid down only such laws as were founded in those relations of justice, that existed in the nature of things antecedent to any positive precept. These are the eternal, immutable laws of good and evil, to which the creator himself in all his dispensations conforms; and which he has enabled human reason to discover, so far as they are necessary for the conduct of human actions. Such among others are these principles: that we should live honestly, should hurt nobody, and should render to every one his due; to which three general precepts Justinian has reduced the whole doctrine of law. . . .

This law of nature, being coeval with mankind and dictated by God himself, is of course superior in obligation to any other. It is binding over all the globe in all countries, and at all times: no human laws are of any validity, if contrary to this; and such of them as are valid derive all their force, and all their authority, mediately or immediately, from this original.[23]

The colonists could not possibly have accepted Blackstone's assertion of parliamentary supremacy, but they found his definition of natural law too satisfying to ignore.[24] Indeed, they were delighted to quote a high Tory for their purposes.

The law of nature, whatever its source and however defined, had at least four basic applications or meanings in colonial political theory. First, it was a set of moral standards governing private conduct. There were, it was generally believed, certain rules of human behavior discoverable through reason, experience, or revelation. Justinian had reduced these "immutable laws of good and evil" to three blunt commands; the colonists reduced them further to one: the Golden Rule.

For the greatest of all laws that respect mankind, is, to love our neighbours as ourselves, and do as we would be done by.[25]

Prosperity and happiness were the lot of men who obeyed this law, adversity and sadness the lot of men who did not. Since the good state, the state shaped to the laws of nature, rested on good men, men who obeyed the laws of nature, one of the duties of the political community was to encourage virtue and discourage vice. The cult of virtue, of which we have learned already and will learn again, was an intimate corollary of natural law. The virtuous life was the natural life, just as good government was natural government.

The laws of nature formed a system of abstract justice to which the laws of men should conform.[26] Positive law that ran counter to a community's inherited sense of right and wrong was not only bad law but no law at all, for had not Blackstone himself asserted that "no human laws are of any validity if contrary to . . . the law of nature"? The chief business of an assembly was therefore to search proposed legislation for clauses or commands that outraged accepted notions of abstract justice. A law was a good law, one that demanded obedience, if it was "founded on the law of nature." [27] The British Constitution was the greatest of all systems of government because it was "grounded on the eternal and immutable laws of nature." [28]

But the law of nature, at least in American opinion, was something more than a model of perfection to which positive law should conform. It was also a line of demarcation around the proper sphere of political authority. Governments that pushed beyond it did so at peril of resistance or even revolution. Since the greatest and freest of constitutions was an earthly replica of natural law, any violation of it was both unconstitutional and unnatural. The Massachusetts House of Representatives told the other assemblies "that in all free States the Constitution is fixed; & as the supreme Legislative derives its Power & Authority from the Constitution, it cannot overleap the Bounds of it without destroying its own Foundation." [29] This, of course, was Locke's great message: that government must respect the commands of natural law or release men from obedience. In time Americans came to regard natural law as the one clear restriction on Parliament's power to tax or govern the colonies. Since it was "repugnant to the Laws of Nature . . . for the Subjects of one State to exercise Jurisdiction over those of another," [30] the people of the second state, in this instance the immediate guardians of those laws, must apply whatever sanctions they had at their command.

Finally and most important, natural law was the source of natural rights. A truly free people, wrote Jefferson, would claim "their rights as derived from the laws of nature, and not as the gift of their chief magistrate" or of the community.[31] Thus it became necessary to establish the existence of natural law in order to provide an unbreachable defense for the rights of man. In the final reckoning, natural law came to be equated with natural rights. Most colonists were so intent upon proving that this law was the one great source and defense of their rights that they used these expressions interchangeably.

In basing their final campaign of resistance to imperial power on "the supreme and uncontrollable laws of nature," the American colonists stood firm in one of their greatest traditions. The higher law, whether proceeding from God or nature, had been part of men's thinking since the first settlements. By the time of the Revolution it was a universally accepted article of faith. If hundreds of New England preachers could declaim upon the law of God and nature, certainly their leading seminary of learning could make General Washington a "Doctor of Laws, the Law of Nature and Nations, and the Civil Law." [32] If a philosopher could invoke "the Laws of Nature and of Nature's God" in behalf of a whole people, certainly one of the least of this people, a runaway servant, could invoke them for release from his contract.[33] Bentham might blast natural law as "nothing but a phrase . . . the natural tendency of [which] is to compel a man by the force of conscience, to rise up in arms against any law whatever that he happens not to like," [34] but Americans seemed not the least bit bothered by its inherent inconsistencies and dangers. The mind of God as read by revelation, the plan of nature as analyzed by right reason, and the history of mankind as interpreted by the scholars of the nation all proclaimed the reality of moral limits on political power. If the rest of the world could not agree that certain truths were self-evident, then the rest of the world was simply ignoring the plain dictates of universal justice.

THE NATURE OF MAN

A political thinker's appraisal of man's basic character generally determines the direction of his entire line of thought. We have already had occasion to note this fact in the chapter on John Wise, calling attention to the contrasting views of man and consequent contrasting philosophies of Hobbes and Locke and of Calhoun and Jefferson. Revolutionary theorists devoted special attention to this question. Their sermons and pamphlets are full of assumptions and comments about the natural virtues and vices of the men about them. They were bothered not at all by a lack of scientific psychological data; the lessons of history, properly selected, gave support to all possible shadings of opinion.

The American consensus dictated no particular estimate of the nature of man. Patriot philosophers with identical opinions about the location of sovereignty could entertain the most divergent views about the reasoning powers of men, and a single thinker might advance two or three different estimates within the pages of one tract. A good deal depended, of course, upon the author's immediate purpose. An argument for home rule would lead him to sweeping generalizations about self-reliance and sociability. A tirade against the British ministry would evoke equally broad comments about man's vicious nature. We must remember that the colonists were heirs of several great and contradictory traditions. A son of the Puritans who was also a child of the Enlightenment could be indulged a little confusion on this crucial point.

We may reduce the wide range of opinion on the nature of man to three general attitudes. One small group of thinkers, of whom Jefferson was perhaps the boldest, took the "enlightened" view, considering man a naturally good, decent, friendly, capable person whose troubles were the bitter fruit of a world he had never made. Another, to which many Calvinist preachers belonged, clung to doctrines of sin and depravity, preferring to lay stress on "the ignorance, prejudice, partiality and injustice of human nature." [35] Most thinkers settled down, or oscillated, between these two extremes, finding much that was good and much that was bad in the character of every single man. Said the author of a piece entitled "Loose thoughts on GOVERNMENT":

In whatever situation we take a view of man, whether ranging the forests in the rude state of his primeval existence, or in the smooth situation of polished society; wheresoever we place him, on the burning sands of Africa, the freezing coasts of Labrador, or the more congenial climes of the temperate zones, we shall every where find him the same complex being, a slave to his passions, and tossed and agitated by a thousand disagreeing virtues and discordant vices.[36]

What exactly were those fundamental traits that Revolutionary theorists found ingrained in man? Which ones were most significant for political organization?

Four qualities that our culture considers "good" were given special stress in the literature of the Revolution: *sociability*, the impulse to associate and co-operate with other men in pursuit of common ends; [37] *love of liberty*, which makes it unnatural and therefore impossible for a man to submit to slavery; [38] *goodness*, the quality of basic human decency that inspires every man to "a love of truth, and a veneration for virtue"; [39] and *rationality*, or "*reasonableness*," the ability to read, understand, and apply "the eternal laws of natural justice, humanity and equity." [40] Five qualities that we would consider "bad" were stressed with equal vigor, as often as not by the same authors who extolled man's goodness: *selfishness*, the impulse to seek one's own happiness even in defiance of the common good; [41] *depravity*, the quality of sinfulness—of jealousy, injustice, anger, ignorance, deceit, vanity, and intemperance—that lurks in every human soul; [42] *passion*, the refusal to be rational, "as natural to men as reason" itself; [43] *moral laziness*, "Inattention to the real Importance of things," which brings men to slavery contrary to nature and their wills; [44] and *corruptibility*, the inevitable result of "the passion for acquiring power" which operates so "forcibly on the human mind." [45] All these "disagreeing virtues and discordant vices" were thought to be present to some degree in every man, no matter how lofty his station or low his character.

Perhaps the most politically significant of all these qualities was sociability, the urge man feels to associate with other men, even if this means surrendering a substantial part of his original freedom. So pointed was the emphasis placed upon "the social Principle in man" that many thinkers excluded the pre-social state of nature, and therefore natural man, from serious consideration. Man was clearly a social animal, a being "formed for social life." [46] If he had a natural state, that state was society, for " 'tis clear that men cannot live apart or independent of each other." [47] Society itself was therefore natural, and few men if any could be said to be in it by free choice. Colonial thinkers were understandably confused in this matter, but it seems clear that the most thoughtful of them made a distinction between society and government. The former was the "natural" result of the presence of a number of men in a certain area; the latter was the mechanistic if inevitable result of an act of will. In short, the contract in Revolutionary thought was governmental, not social.

The one other quality deserving special mention was the transformation that is more than likely to come over man when he is placed in a situation of power. Revolutionary theorists generally agreed with Hamilton that "a fondness for power is implanted in most men, and it is natural to abuse it when acquired." [48] "The history of mankind," wrote James Iredell, "unhappily justifies the strongest suspicion of men in authority." [49] "Every man by nature," echoed Rev. Thomas Allen of Pittsfield, "has the seeds of tyranny deeply implanted within him." [50] Although this belief in man's love of power was not nearly so strong or widely advertised as it was later to be in Federalist political theory, few authors failed to mention it as a human characteristic, and none went out of his way to deny it specifically. The universal American belief in constitutionalism and the rule of law—indeed in the necessity of a written, comprehensible constitution—derived from this suspicious appraisal of man in authority. No one ever spoke more succinctly to this point than Samuel Adams:

> All men are fond of Power. It is difficult for us to be prevaild upon to believe that we possess more than belongs to us. Even publick Bodies of men legally constituted are too prone to covet more Power than the Publick hath judgd it safe to entrust them with. It is happy when their Power is not only subject to Controul while it is exercisd, but frequently reverts into the hands of the People from whom it is derived, and to whom Men in Power ought for ever to be accountable.[51]

If man was a composite of good and evil, of ennobling excellencies and degrading imperfections, then one of the chief ends of the community was "to separate his virtues from his vices," [52] to help him pursue his better nature. The achievement of this called for two types of collective action: establishing or encouraging institutions, especially religious and political institutions, that would give free play to his virtues while controlling or suppressing his vices; educating him to recognize the sweet harvest of the one and bitter fruits of the other. True religion encouraged man to suppress his savage impulses; constitutional government forced him to think before acting; sound education taught him the delights of virtue and liberty.

The American colonists, as we learned in Chapter 5, had always placed special faith in the efficacy of education. The Revolutionists once again stood firm in the ancient ways by insisting almost unanimously:

> Let the people by all means encourage *schools* and *colleges*, and all the means of *learning* and *knowledge*, if they would guard against *slavery*. For a *wise*, a *knowing* and a *learned* people, are the least likely of any in the world to be enslaved.[53]

Whatever disagreement might have existed over man's other natural or social characteristics, all American thinkers conceded him a capacity for learning. Different men could acquire knowledge in different amounts, but all men could acquire the minimum necessary for survival and citizenship. Man was something more than a fortuitous complex of virtues and vices. He was *educable*—he could learn and be taught. More to the point, he could learn why to cherish virtue and shun vice, how to serve the community and defend liberty. Free government rested on virtue, virtue on knowledge, knowledge on regular techniques of education. It was therefore the business of government "to make provision for schools and all suitable means of instruction." [54] The exigencies of the economy, the weight of tradition, and the unsettled state of the times conspired against general acceptance of the doctrine of free and universal public education, but no political thinker doubted the imperative necessity of community action in this crucial area. The eloquent words of Rev. Phillips Payson expressed American thinking about education for liberty:

> The slavery of a people is generally founded in ignorance of some kind or another; and there are not wanting such facts as abundantly prove the human mind may be so sunk and debased, through ignorance and its natural effects, as even to adore its enslaver, and kiss its chains. Hence knowledge and learning may well be considered as most essentially requisite to a free, righteous government. . . .
> Every kind of useful knowledge will be carefully encouraged and promoted by the rulers of a free state. . . . The education of youth, by instructors properly qualified, the establishment of societies for useful arts and sciences, the encouragement of persons of superior abilities, will always command the attention of wise rulers.[55]

Political thinkers naturally emphasized the acquisition of political knowledge. Said John Jay on the inauguration of the New York Constitution of 1777:

> Let virtue, honor, the love of liberty and of science be, and remain, the soul of this constitution, and it will become the source of great and extensive happiness to this and future generations. Vice, ignorance, and want of vigilance, will be the only enemies able to destroy it. Against these provide, and, of these, be forever jealous. Every member of the state, ought diligently to read and study the constitution of his country, and teach the rising generation to be free. By knowing their rights, they will sooner perceive when they are violated, and be the better prepared to defend and assert them.[56]

Others called attention to the mutual dependence of liberty and learning. Education and knowledge were as much the effect as the cause of free government. The infant republic could look forward confidently to intellectual splendor. Dr. David Ramsay was one of many who prophesied:

> Every circumstance concurs to make it probable, that the arts and sciences will be cultivated, extended, and improved, in independent America. . . . Our free governments are the proper nurseries of rhetoric, criticism, and the arts which are founded on the philosophy of the human mind. In monarchies, an extreme degree of politeness disguises the simplicity of nature, and "sets the looks at variance with the thoughts;" in republics, mankind appear as they really are, without any false coloring: In these governments, therefore, attentive observers have an opportunity of knowing all the avenues to the heart, and of thoroughly understanding human nature. The great inferiority of the moderns to the ancients in fine writing, is to be referred

to this veil cast over mankind by the artificial refinements of modern mon-archies. From the operation of similar causes, it is hoped, that the free governments of America will produce poets, orators, critics and historians, equal to the most celebrated of the ancient commonwealths of Greece and Italy.[57]

Many Americans may have smiled at the grandeur of this hope, but few doubted the capacity of "this numerous, brave and hardy people"[58] to learn the rights and duties of citizenship in a free republic. No characteristic of man had more political significance than his innate capacity for instruction in virtue and freedom.

The natural character of man was an alloy of virtue and vice; his natural state was pure freedom and equality. "All men are, by nature, equal and free," wrote James Wilson; "no one has a right to any authority over another without his consent."[59] Revolutionary thinkers were in virtually unanimous accord on this point. Men might be grossly unequal in appearance, talents, intelligence, virtue, and fortune, but to this extent at least they were absolutely equal: No man had any natural right of dominion over any other; every man was free in the sight of God and plan of nature. The ranks and privileges of organized society were the result of unnatural usurpation, faulty institutions, the dead hand of an ignorant past, or the inevitable division of men into rulers and ruled.

The principle of natural equality was not incompatible with political, social, or economic stratification, but the burden of proof was squarely on advocates of artificial inequality.[60] It was for them to demonstrate that an unequal arrangement was essential to the stability, prosperity, or independence of the community. Conversely, the goal of political science was to discover a political pattern that would recreate the equality of rights and near-equality of property that had preceded the formation of government.[61] The glory of a free constitution was that it reduced these social inequalities to the barest minimum and preserved as much natural equality "as is compatible with the people's security against foreign invasion and domestic usurpation."[62]

It is important to note these two aspects of the doctrine of natural equality to which most Revolutionists subscribed: that equality among men existed within a limited sphere, but that within this sphere all men were created absolutely equal. Each had an equal claim to be free of any earthly power; each could be governed only with his consent. In this sense equality was both an essential feature of human relations and an essential principle of libertarian political theory. It was an article of faith, a challenge to constitution-makers, and the central arrangement of political organization. James Otis was not really joking when he wrote in support of natural equality:

> No government has a right to make hobby horses, asses and slaves of the subject, nature having made sufficient of the two former, for all the lawful purposes of man, from the harmless peasant in the field, to the most refined politician in the cabinet; but none of the last, which infallibly proves they are unnecessary.[63]

THE NATURAL RIGHTS OF MAN

No political theory, however detached or speculative, ever ranges in perfect symmetry over all great questions of power, organization, and obedience. The political theorist concentrates inevitably upon the problems of his own civilization. His theoretical structure is proportioned to "the felt necessities" of the age rather than to a standard, timeless pattern in which every possible question receives its just due. The political theorists of the Revolution were no exception to this rule. Heirs of a great tradition of personal liberty, children of an age concerned with the individual rather than the community, targets of a policy that seemed to defy the dictates of abstract justice, they used up most of their energy defining the rights of man and devising methods of protecting them. They were individualists because the individual was under fire, limitationists because a government had overleaped its limits, constitutionalists because the existence of their constitution hung in the balance. Above all, they were exponents of natural rights. A legislature claiming the power to bind them in all cases whatsoever had moved decisively against their liberty and property, and they meant to stand and fight this invasion on the broadest possible ground.

The doctrine of natural rights was therefore the hard core of Revolutionary political theory. Like almost all other exponents of higher law, Americans gave this law a content and meaning that suited their practical purpose. The natural rights of man were so useful, even essential, to this purpose that they were willing to equate them with natural law itself. The rights of man, that is to say, not only depended upon or sprang from natural law; they *were* natural law, at least so far as it could be understood by men. In the political theory of the American Revolution natural law was all but swallowed up in natural rights. The dictates, indeed the content, of "the supreme and uncontrollable laws of nature" became "the *absolute* rights of individuals." [64] If a man wished to follow the path of universal justice, he had only to understand and respect these rights. In our own effort to understand the doctrine of natural rights as expounded in the pre-Revolutionary decade we must seek answers to these questions: What exactly was meant by the phrase "natural rights"? What was the source of these rights? What specific rights of man were covered by this concept?

By natural rights the Revolutionists meant simply those rights which belong to man as man. They used several adjectives in addition to "natural" to express the special quality of these rights. They were *natural*, traceable directly to the great plan of nature if not indeed derived from "the great Legislator of the universe"; [65] *absolute*, belonging to man before, outside of, and quite without regard to organized government or society; [66] *eternal*, never varying in content or identity; *essential*, since necessary to man's existence as man; and *unalienable* (or inalienable), "of that importance, that no equivalent can be received in exchange." [67] Inherent, universal, unalterable, inestimable, sacred, indefeasible, fundamental, imprescriptible, divine, God-given, hereditary, and indelible were other adjectives used to stamp the natural rights of mankind with transcendent significance. In the heat of the struggle over the authority of Parliament, some American authors carelessly or designedly confused natural rights with civil or constitutional rights. But more serious thinkers like Otis, Hamilton, and Parsons expressed the true sense of the patriot school when they distinguished those rights which were natural, absolute, eternal, essential, and unalienable from those which were constitutional, civil, social, or relative.[68] The fact or fiction of the state of nature was especially serviceable in clearing up this confusion. In the last analysis, natural rights were different from civil or constitutional rights because they had belonged to man in the state of nature. He had brought them with him into society. He had brought them with him into government. And he would take them with him should he ever return to the state of nature or of natural society. In any case, a fundamental article of the American faith was the belief that every man—no matter what his station, calling, learning, and fortune—had certain natural, unalienable rights. These were "antecedent to all earthly government," [69] incapable of being surrendered to government, and identified with nature or with God himself. Perhaps most important to patriot purposes, they served as the ultimate standard for human laws and the ultimate check upon arbitrary power.

The sources of natural rights were the sources of natural law: God, nature, or history. For the most part colonial theorists were willing to merge God and nature into one magnificent and consecrated source. An occasional author, especially if he occupied a dissenting pulpit, might speak specifically of "natural liberty" as "a gift of the beneficent Creator to the whole human race," [70] but most would have agreed with John Dickinson's message to the Committee of Correspondence in Barbados:

> Kings or parliaments could not *give* the *rights essential to happiness,* as you confess those invaded by the Stamp Act to be. We claim them from a higher source—from the King of kings, and Lord of all the earth. They are not annexed to us by parchments and seals. They are created in us by the decrees of Providence, which establish the laws of our nature. They are born with us; exist with us; and cannot be taken from us by any human power, without taking our lives. In short, they are founded on the immutable maxims of reason and justice.[71]

Men like Hamilton and Jefferson might have wished to ignore or at least neutralize the hand of God, but they, like Dickinson, were always careful to mention both God and nature. No passage in Revolutionary literature is more justly famous than Hamilton's flamboyant escape from the trap of the Tory argument that New York had no charter and New Yorkers therefore no charter rights:

> THE SACRED RIGHTS OF MANKIND ARE NOT TO BE RUMMAGED FOR AMONG OLD PARCHMENTS OR MUSTY RECORDS. THEY ARE WRITTEN, AS WITH A SUNBEAM, IN THE WHOLE VOLUME OF HUMAN NATURE, BY THE HAND OF THE DIVINITY ITSELF, AND CAN NEVER BE ERASED OR OBSCURED BY MORTAL POWER.[72]

A few writers described the rights of man as "hard-earned." John Adams in particular went deep into the past to remind his readers that these rights, although traceable to God and nature, had in fact been secured in laws and constitutions only after the most bitter struggles against despotism and indifference. He who wished to identify those rights which no government should touch must look not only to "the nature of man" but to "the history of nations." [73] Throughout the political theory of this history-conscious people runs this implicit assumption: Natural and unalienable rights are those basic liberties which are enjoyed and respected wherever men are free, prosperous, and happy. Washington was thinking of rights as the legacy of history rather than the gift of God when he wrote the state governors:

> The foundation of our empire was not laid in the gloomy age of ignorance and superstition; but at an epocha when the rights of mankind were better understood and more clearly defined, than at any former period. The researches of the human mind after social happiness have been carried to a great extent; the treasures of knowledge, acquired by the labors of philosophers, sages, and legislators, through a long succession of years, are laid open for our use, and their collective wisdom may be happily applied in the establishment of our forms of government.[74]

What were these rights which man possessed as man and could never surrender? In the pamphlets, sermons, and documents of this decade almost every conceivable human right—including the right to brew beer at home—was proclaimed to be natural, unalienable, and essential to the good society.[75] But in works that were more political theory than propaganda we find these rights singled out as the legitimate possession of all men everywhere: life, liberty, property, conscience, and happiness.

The right to life was so far above dispute that authors were content merely to mention it in passing. Blackstone had not been able to say much more than that it was "the immediate gift of God, a right inherent by nature in every individual," [76] and no American was going to improve on that celebrated man of the law. The strategic importance of the right to life lay in its great corollary or defense: the law or right of self-preservation.[77] This secondary right made it possible for a single man or a whole nation to meet force with force, to resist all arbitrary invasions of life, liberty, and property.

The natural right to liberty was central to all other rights, and the literature of the Revolution is full of salutes to its blessings and excellencies.[78] "Liberty!" had been the American watchword for so many generations that no author, Whig or Tory, ever doubted in print that it was "in some degree . . . the right of every human creature." [79] Indeed, man without natural liberty was a contradiction in terms. "The god who gave us life," wrote Jefferson to George III, "gave us liberty at the same time." [80] Liberty was defined simply as the freedom and power of each individual to act as he pleased "without restraint or control." From this natural liberty, the freedom from "obligation to obedience," [81] flowed all other liberties that men enjoyed in society.

The colonists, of course, were concerned about specific liberties in the political community rather than the original liberty of man in the state of nature. Most of their discussions of liberty are therefore somewhat confused. Yet we can discover certain common ideas about natural liberty in even the most occasional apostrophes. A good example of the way in which the colonial theorist dealt with liberty is this communication to "The Sentinel" in the *New-York Gazette:*

> Liberty, as it is the honour and glory of a nation, so also it is their pleasure and happiness. There is not perhaps one temporal blessing bestowed by the supreme being on mankind that is more agreeable when enjoyed; more difficult to be parted with; or more desirable when absent. A love for Liberty seems interwoven with our very nature; and we are always ready to pronounce a people happy or miserable in proportion as they are possessed or destitute of it. . . . There is perhaps nothing in this life more essential to our happiness. It is the state for which we are naturally calculated. It is what we all desire. The absence of it produces positive pain, as well as the presence of it positive happiness. It is the fountain of wealth, and of all real honours. For I cannot conceive of any true dignity a Slave can enjoy; for although he commands a thousand or ten thousand others, he is yet but a Slave himself.[82]

Colonial theorists, even the holders of slaves, concurred generally with this author's assumption that all men were naturally free. Most arguments for abolition of Negro slavery advanced in this decade were based on the doctrine of natural, unalienable liberty.

Perhaps the most interesting subsidiary right that Revolutionary pamphleteers deduced from natural liberty was

> a right, which nature has given to all men, of departing from the country in which chance, not choice has placed them, of going in quest of new habitations, and of there establishing new societies, under such laws and regulations as to them shall seem most likely to promote public happiness.[83]

The natural right of migration was extremely useful to the cause, since it permitted colonists to argue that their ancestors had left England as free agents and had made a fresh contract with the sovereign left behind. Bland and Jefferson were the two most vocal exponents of this radical doctrine,[84] and each made clear that "the natural right of an individual to remove his person and effects wherever he pleases" was a direct corollary of the essential freedom stamped indelibly on man's nature.[85] The hardy migrants of Vermont placed this statement in their first Declaration of Rights:

> All people have a natural and inherent right to emigrate from one State to another, that will receive them; or to form a new State in vacant countries, or in such countries as they can purchase, whenever they think that thereby they can promote their own happiness.[86]

The right to acquire and enjoy property was universally acclaimed in the literature of the Revolution. "The law of nature," wrote "Sidney" in the Norfolk *Virginia Gazette*, "being founded in reason and justice admits of property." [87] Samuel Adams spoke for all American publicists when he told General Conway, "It is acknowledged to be an unalterable law in nature, that a man should have the free use and sole disposal of the fruit of his honest industry, subject to no controul." [88] And elsewhere:

It is observable, that though many have disregarded life, and contemned liberty, yet there are few men who do not agree that property is a valuable acquisition, which ought to be held sacred. Many have fought, and bled, and died for this, who have been insensible to all other obligations. Those who ridicule the ideas of right and justice, faith and truth among men, will put a high value upon money. Property is admitted to have an existence, even in the savage state of nature. The bow, the arrow, and the tomahawk; the hunting and the fishing ground, are species of property, as important to an American savage, as pearls, rubies, and diamonds are to the Mogul, or a Nabob in the East, or the lands, tenements, hereditaments, messuages, gold and silver of the Europeans. And if property is necessary for the support of savage life, it is by no means less so in civil society.[89]

Although Locke had several times used the word "property" in the broad sense of everything a man is or has, colonists limited their definition to ownership of things tangible or at least convertible to money.[90] Property in this sense was so essential to the fulfillment of man's promise and powers that it could almost be equated with liberty itself. If Locke included liberty in his definition of property, colonists included property in their definition of liberty. As one anonymous contributor to "The Weekly Dung-Barge" put it, "*Liberty* and *Property* are not only join'd in common discourse, but are in their own natures so nearly ally'd that we cannot be said to possess the one without the enjoyment of the other." [91] This was not because Americans were more materialistic than other people. Quite the contrary, their primary, long-range concern was with political and spiritual aspects of human freedom. But the crisis of the moment, to which their theorizing was directed, was an unprecedented invasion of the right to dispose of property without compulsion: that is, the right of men to be taxed only by representatives of their own choosing. The colonists were no more obsessed than their ancestors or descendants with the great right of "virtuous enjoyment and free possession of property honestly gained." [92] Few thinkers ever doubted, however, that it was a natural right of man, and not a right granted by society. The town of Newburyport spoke for all America when it lectured its representative to the General Assembly:

That a People should be taxed at the Will of another, whether of one Man or many, without their own Consent in Person or by Representative, is *rank* Slavery. For if their Superior sees fit, they may be deprived of their whole Property, upon any frivolous Pretext, or without any Pretext at all. And a People, without Property, or in the precarious Possession of it, are in no better State than Slaves; for Liberty, or even Life itself, without the En-joyment of them flowing from Property, are of no Value.[93]

Only two other rights—the right of conscience and the right to happiness—were ever placed by more than one or two authors at the same level of sanctity and universality with life, liberty, and property. In one sense, of course, each of these rights was simply a derivative of natural liberty. Yet, in another and more important sense, they were considered to have an existence of their own. Each was essential to the full expression of man's inherent nature; each was plainly antecedent to society and government. The right to happiness—or at least to pursue happiness without interfer-ence—was a logical assumption in the political theory of men to whom rationalism had made a triumphant appeal. Happiness rather than salvation seemed now to be man's chief obsession. Through all the writings of men like Wilson, R. H. Lee, Jefferson, Iredell, and Mayhew runs a firm belief that "the Creator surely wills the happiness of his Creatures," [94] that "God did not make men to be unhappy,"

> that mankind were intended to be happy, at least that God gave them the power of being so, if they would properly exert the means He has bestowed upon them.[95]

Or as Dickinson put it:

> It would be an insult on the divine Majesty to say, that he has given or allowed any man or body of men *a right to make me miserable*. If no man or body of men has *such a right*, I have a *right to be happy*. If there can be no happiness without freedom, I have a *right to be free*.[96]

Jefferson was more than a felicitous penman when he proclaimed the "pursuit of happiness" to be a natural right of man,[97] for by the time of the Declaration most thinkers agreed with him on this point. He was, however, something of a nonconformist in substituting this right for that of property. He alone flirted seriously with the advanced view that property was a social rather than natural right.[98]

The right of conscience, the right of each individual to reach out for God without interference or even assistance from other men, was naturally of prime interest to a people well on the way to full religious liberty. William Livingston reminded his fellow countrymen in these angry words that po-litical interference with a man's religious opinions was a violation of the commands of natural justice:

> Who, in a state of nature, ever deemed it an inconvenience that every man should choose his own religion? Did the free denizens of the world . . . ever worry one another for not practising ridiculous rites, or for believing things incredible? Did men in their aboriginal condition ever suffer perse-cution for conscience sake? The most frantic enthusiast will not pretend it. Why then should the members of society be supposed, on their entering into it, to have had in contemplation the reforming an abuse which never existed? [99]

The men of the Revolution may have been given to fantastic hyperbole and astounding ambiguity in discussing their rights and privileges, but there can be no doubt of their sincerity and conviction in placing special value on these five rights: life, liberty, property, happiness, and conscience.

THE CIVIL RIGHTS OF THE COLONISTS

If these rights belonged to man as man—to man, that is to say, in a real or or conjectured state of nature—what happened after the formation of government? What rights could man properly claim as a member of a free community? To answer these questions we must anticipate Chapter 14 by quoting a few famous words on the origin and purpose of government:

> We hold these truths to be self-evident, that all men are created equal, that they are endowed by their Creator with certain unalienable Rights, that among these are Life, Liberty, and the pursuit of Happiness. That to secure these rights, Governments are instituted among Men, deriving their just powers from the consent of the governed.

At this point colonial theorists ran full tilt into trouble. If the natural rights of man were really unalienable, how could a government be expected to secure them? In the act of escaping from the insecurities of the state of nature and entering an organized community, a man had to agree to certain restraints upon his original freedom. He could not possibly live in peace with his fellow men and retain the full measure of natural liberty. Yet how could he alienate that which was unalienable?

Most authors went blithely ahead in ignorance or disdain of this difficult question, but the best of them would have agreed to two correlative distinctions worked out by Theophilus Parsons: one between "the surrendering of a power to controul our natural rights" and the surrendering of the rights themselves, the other between rights alienable and rights unalienable in the former and more limited sense of alienation of control.[100] According to Parsons, only one natural right—the right of conscience—is completely unalienable: A man can surrender neither the right itself nor his original power to control it. The power to control the other natural rights, however, can be surrendered by a freely contracting individual—in return for a proper equivalent. "In a state of nature," said Parsons,

> every man had the sovereign controul over his own person. He might also have, in that state, a qualified property. . . . Over this qualified property every man in a state of nature had also a sovereign controul. And in entering into political society, he surrendered this right of controul over his person and property, (with an exception to the rights of conscience) to the supreme legislative power, to be exercised by that power, *when the good of the whole demanded it.* This was all the right he could surrender, being all the alienable right of which he was possessed. The only objects of legislation therefore, are the person and property of the individuals which compose the state.[101]

In the words of another thinker:

> Men in a state of nature were equal. Their actions were subject to no limitations but those which arose from the laws of God. But through want of a common judge finally to determine their respective rights, and power sufficient to vindicate them, injuries must often have remained unredressed, or been punished by private revenge, beyond the demand of justice. *Civil Society* remedies these evils, adjusting the rights of individuals by a common wisdom, and protecting the exercise of them by a common power. It restricts every man from acting in such a manner as to injure others, as it restrains others from injuring him.[102]

In short, men can surrender to the political community a certain amount of the original power to control their persons and properties. Just how much of this power they can and should surrender is a key question of political theory, to be answered in each instance according to the circumstances of the society and characters of the men who make it up. Every man must surrender enough control over his original liberty to permit government to maintain an organized, stable, peaceful pattern of human relations. No man should surrender so much that government dictates his every action. Between these two self-evident extremes the balance of liberty and authority must ever be in constant motion. The benefit of the doubt should be extended to liberty rather than authority:

> There is no doubt, but by entering into society, mankind voluntarily give up a part of their natural rights, and bind themselves to the obedience of laws, calculated for the general good. But, we must distinguish between authority and oppression; between laws and capricious dictates; and keeping the original intention of government ever in view, we should take care that no more restraint be laid upon natural liberty, than what the necessities of society require.[103]

It is the business of lawgivers and political theorists to search in good faith for the delicate balance between liberty and authority, between the desire and duty of the individual to retain as much control as possible over his person and property and the responsibility of government to maintain peace and order by "restrict[ing] every man from acting in such a manner as to injure others." In a free state the balance tips decisively in the direction of liberty. Men in such a state are generally virtuous; they make a conscious effort to use their freedom and property in a way that does not interfere with the freedom and property of men with whom they must live and do business. Government intervention is the exception rather than the rule. In autocratic states, where men are usually ignorant and immoral, the balance tips just as decisively toward authority. Government is arbitrary because men will not respect one another. The limits between liberty and political power in any particular community are set by the general state of morality, knowledge, and common agreement.

To this extent, then, colonial theorists withdrew from the untenable position that natural rights were absolute and unalienable: A man could alienate part of the original power to control his rights. It was possible and proper for government to take his life, qualify his liberty, regulate his property, direct his search for happiness—even forbid all antisocial outward manifestations of the inner drives of conscience—if this was done in fulfillment of a contract and in pursuit of known laws. The constitution and laws of every free state must recognize and protect man's natural rights. Whatever restrictions government places upon the free exercise of these rights must result from his freely given consent. The liberty that man retains is then properly styled *civil* or, if clearly acknowledged in fundamental law, *constitutional*. In Hamilton's words, which most American thinkers echoed, *"Civil liberty is only natural liberty, modified and secured by the sanctions of civil society."* [104] In the process of being modified in order to be secured, natural liberty becomes civil and civil liberty becomes constitutional.

We shall have a good deal to say in this and the next chapter about liberty, property, and the pursuit of happiness as civil or constitutional rights, but this would seem a convenient place to dispose briefly of religious liberty, the civil version of the natural right to conscience. Most American thinkers were in accord on these points: The right to conscience was absolutely unalienable, and government had no authority to enforce religious conformity. Government nevertheless did have authority to forbid and punish antisocial actions resulting from the pressures of a free conscience. Freedom of religion was a political freedom; political and religious liberty were "linked together in one indissoluble bond." [105] Few could agree on the exact measure of religious liberty that free men should enjoy under free government. The day of persecution and forced conformity was over, but the day of establishment and anti-Catholicism lingered on. Yet if Americans were not quite ready for complete disestablishment and liberty of conscience for all men, even "Papists," they had moved a long way, in theory as in fact, from the medieval union of church and state. The Virginia Declaration of Rights expressed the best sentiments of the time:

> Religion, or the duty which we owe to our Creator, and the manner of discharging it, can be directed only by reason and conviction, not by force or violence; and therefore all men are equally entitled to the free exercise of religion, according to the dictates of conscience; and it is the duty of all to practice Christian forbearance, love, and charity towards each other.[106]

In the state of nature all men possessed the five natural rights in equal degree. What became of this original equality in the process of transforming them from their natural to their civil character? Colonial theorists were in almost complete agreement that the contract could not alter the fact of natural equality to life, liberty (defined as liberty of action), conscience, and the pursuit of happiness. They were in less complete yet fairly general agreement that inequality was admissible in property and political liberty. In other words, all persons under a particular government had surrendered control of their rights to life and liberty of action to the same degree, but they had surrendered control of their rights to property and political liberty in varying degrees. Legal inequalities in property and political rights were, however, to be carefully restricted. They were permissible only if necessary to the preservation of peace, order, and independence.[107] This formula, of course, left room for bitter disagreement between proponents of property qualifications for political activity and heralds of manhood suffrage. Judge Drayton of Charleston and the unknown author of the New Hampshire tract *The People the Best Governors* spoke much the same political language, yet their comments on the right of plain people to govern themselves showed them to be poles apart on the question of democracy. Drayton complained that a faction in Charleston had

> consulted *De Arduis Reipublicae*, with Men who were never in a Way to study, or to advise upon any Points, but Rules how to cut up a *Beast in the Market* to the best advantage, to *cobble* an old Shoe in the neatest Manner, or to build a *necessary* House. Nature never intended that *such Men* should be *profound Politicians* or *able Statesmen*.[108]

To the contrary, rejoined the New Hampshire radical:

> God gave mankind freedom by nature, made every man equal to his neighbor, and has virtually enjoined them to govern themselves by their own laws. . . . The people best know their own wants and necessities, and therefore are best able to rule themselves. Tent-makers, cobblers, and common tradesmen composed the legislature at Athens.[109]

Colonial pamphleteers proclaimed at least seven other civil rights in addition to those believed to be natural and unalienable: the freedoms of speech, press, assembly, and petition; civil supremacy; representation and free elections; jury trial and its attendant safeguards. If these were not the inherent possession of all men everywhere, they were certainly the possession or aspiration of all men living under free government. The first four were not only individual rights but social necessities, conditions essential to the conduct of representative government. The last two, representation and jury trial, were not only rights but the means of defending all other rights. No man could consider himself truly free were his person and property subject to the control of a legislative or judicial organ in which he was not represented.

FREEDOM OF SPEECH, PRESS, ASSEMBLY, AND PETITION. Colonial pamphleteers seemed more anxious to proclaim than to analyze these political freedoms. They all concurred on several decisive points about the content and significance of these freedoms: that they were closely, indeed inseparably, connected; that they were derived from the natural right to liberty; and that they were as essential to the operation of free government as to the happiness of free men. Colonial thinking about each of these rights had a strong social rather than individualistic bias.

Freedom of speech was rarely discussed as an isolated phenomenon, and then only in such general and confused terms as these:

Man, in a state of nature, has undoubtedly a right to speak and act without controul. In a state of civil society, that right is limited by the law— Political liberty consists in a freedom of speech and action, so far as the laws of a community will permit, and no farther: all beyond is criminal, and tends to the destruction of Liberty itself.— That Society whose laws least restrain the words and actions of its members, is most free.— There is no nation on the earth, where freedom of speech is more extensive than among the English: This is what keeps the constitution in health and vigour, and is in a great measure the cause of our preservation as a free people: For should it ever be dangerous to exercise this privilege, it is easy to see, without the spirit of prophecy, slavery and bondage would soon be the portion of Britons.[110]

The social value attached to this liberty is also revealed in a comment of Samuel Cooke's that "freedom of speech . . . is essential to a free constitution, and the ruler's surest guide." [111]

Freedom of press, which as often as not was considered synonymous with the freedoms of speech, discussion, inquiry, thought, and communication, naturally received special attention in newspapers. For the most part, authors and editors placed emphasis on the social utility of this key political freedom. It was an "eminent instrument of promoting knowledge," "one grand means of promoting public virtue," and the "great palladium of the public liberty." [112] The last of these functions was perhaps the most important:

> Without this check, we should be liable to oppression, whenever a tyrant was in power; nay, an ambitious designing ruler, I dare to say, fears more the correction of the Press, than any other controul whatever; and it is to the freedom with which the conduct of the Great is scanned in England, that we are principally indebted for our glorious constitution.[113]

Letter after letter to and from colonial editors paid tribute to the restraints a free press imposed on dangerous extensions of arbitrary power. English reprints,[114] accounts of the Zenger trial,[115] and original pieces [116] were all ammunition for colonial batteries that never wore out saluting freedom of press as "one of the principal handmaids of liberty." "However little some may think of common newspapers," wrote a Virginian, "to a wise man they appear the Ark of God for the safety of the people." [117] Freedom of press was sorely tried in the harsh, confusing days following the passage of the Coercive Acts,[118] but American thinkers did their sincere best to defend the central position they had assigned to this freedom in the pattern of constitutional government.

The lively concern of Revolutionary journalists for the freedom their elders had wrung from reluctant politicians produced at least two laughs worth recording for history. The editor of the *New-Hampshire Gazette* ended an especially eloquent salute to the advantages of a free press with this piece of practical advice:

> The Conclusion of the whole is, That unless many of the Customers of this Paper make better Pay than they have for several Years past, they must

be deprived of these Advantages; and therefore it is hoped a *Word to the Wise* will be sufficient to induce them thereto: And many Persons who have been a long Time in Arrears for Advertisements, are desired also to discharge the same.[119]

And the printer of the Wilmington *North-Carolina Gazette* spoke for many another bedeviled editor when he told his public:

The Printer hereof cannot help observing to the Publick, that he is at present in a very disagreeable Situation. At the earnest Desire, or rather stern Command of the People, he has endeavoured, with great Difficulty, to carry on a News-Paper, well knowing, that that Province that is deprived of the Liberty of the Press, is deprived of one of the darling Privileges which they, as Englishmen, boast of.—The Consequence has been, that, for publishing a Letter from a Gentleman at Tarborough . . . he has been THREATENED with a Horse-Whipping;—and doubtless he would have run some such Hazard, had he refus'd inserting that very Letter—What Part is he now to act?—Continue to keep his Press open and free, and be in Danger of Corporal Punishment, or block it up, and run the Risque of having his Brains knocked out? Sad Alternative.[120]

The allied rights of assembly and petition were proclaimed in hundreds of town and county resolutions. The towns of Middlesex County, Massachusetts, acknowledged the importance of these rights in this representative statement:

Resolved, That every people have an absolute right of meeting together to consult upon common grievances, and to petition, remonstrate, and use every legal method for their removal.

Resolved, That the act which prohibits these constitutional meetings cuts away the scaffolding of English supremacy, and reduces us to a most abject state of vassalage and slavery.[121]

The rights of assembly and petition were especially important for the conduct of representative government. These ancient liberties existed primarily for the health of the community rather than for the happiness of the individual.

CIVIL SUPREMACY: NO STANDING ARMIES. The problem of civil-military relations weighed heavily on the minds of the colonists. By 1765 their Whig heritage and contacts with British troops had given rise to an almost doctrinaire tradition of civil supremacy. The events of the pre-Revolutionary decade, especially the Boston massacre, served only to harden the conviction that "military aid has ever been deemed dangerous to a free civil state, and has often been used as an effectual engine to subvert it." [122] Two of the most telling indictments in Jefferson's catalogue of kingly sins were: "He has kept among us, in times of peace, standing Armies without the Consent of our legislatures," and "He has affected to render the Military independent of and superior to the Civil power."

The Revolutionary tradition of civil supremacy, proclaimed most vocally by orators in and around Boston, found expression in three popular assumptions: the inherent danger of standing or "mercenary" armies, "a tremendous curse to a state" and "the scourge of mankind"; [123] the effectiveness, even superiority, of the militia; and the necessity of tight civil—that is, *legislative* —control over all military personnel at all times. The popular American solution was to do away completely with the military profession and make every able-bodied man both citizen and soldier. A few authors were willing to concede that regular armies might be necessary in time of war when all other means had failed,[124] but most men were prisoners of the Cincinnatus complex: No army of mercenaries could ever fight as bravely or successfully as a "well-regulated militia" defending hearth and home.[125] These notions, which were to govern American military policy for generations after the Revolution, were given typical expression in these passages:

Samuel Adams to the *Boston Gazette:*

It is a very improbable supposition, that any people can long remain free, with a strong military power in the very heart of their country: Unless that military power is under the direction of the people, and even then it is dangerous.—History, both ancient and modern, affords many instances of the overthrow of states and kingdoms by the power of soldiers, who were rais'd and maintain'd at first, under the plausible pretence of defending those very liberties which they afterwards destroyed. Even where there is a necessity of the military power, within the land, which by the way but rarely happens, a wise and prudent people will always have a watchful & a jealous eye over it; for the maxims and rules of the army, are essentially different from the genius of a free people, and the laws of a free government.[126]

Josiah Quincy, jr., at the time of the Coercive Acts:

No free government was ever founded or ever preserved it's liberty without uniting the characters of citizen and soldier in those destined for defence of the state. The sword should never be in the hands of any, but those who have an interest in the safety of the community. . . . Such are a well regulated militia composed of the freeholders, citizen and husbandman, who take up arms to preserve their property as individuals, and their rights as freemen.[127]

James Lovell, the "Massacre Orator" in 1771:

The true strength and safety of every commonwealth or limited monarchy, is the bravery of its freeholders, its militia. By brave militias they rise to grandeur; and they come to ruin by a mercenary army.[128]

And finally, the Town of Boston to its representatives, May 10, 1773:

Standing armies have for ever made shipwreck of free states. . . . The militia of the colony are its natural and best defence; and it is an approved maxim in all well-policed states, that the sword should never be entrusted but to those who combat *pro aris et focis;* and whose interest it is to preserve the public peace.[129]

No standing armies, a well-regulated militia, and unqualified legislative control—these were the essentials of the early American tradition of civil supremacy, a tradition as important for the defense of individual liberty as for the success of constitutional government. The free citizen of a free government had a manifest right to be protected against military power and supremacy. Yet this right carried with it a clearly defined duty: to serve in the militia, to combine the characters of citizen and soldier. On this point all colonists were agreed. Southerners might look askance at "the New-England levelling doctrine" of a citizen army "raised, *officered* and *conducted* by common consent," [130] but they were no less dedicated to the belief that "the natural strength, and only security of a free government" was "a well regulated militia." [131]

REPRESENTATION AND JURY TRIAL. In 1765 the Town of Boston informed its representatives in the General Court:

> The most essential Rights of British Subjects are those of being represented in the same Body which exercises the Power of levying Taxes upon them, & of having their Property tryed by Jurys: These are the very Pillars of the British Constitution founded in the Common Rights of Mankind.[132]

Representation in the supreme lawmaking and taxing legislature and trial by one's "peers of the vicinage, according to the course of [the] law" were the two "main Pillars of the British Constitution." [133] Indeed, since the Constitution was "founded in the Common Rights of Mankind," since "the Rights of Nature" were "happily interwoven" in its "ancient fabrick," [134] these two great liberties or methods of defending liberty were properly the birthright of free men everywhere. In order to enjoy and defend their natural liberties a people did not have to adopt an exact imitation of the English legislative and judicial pattern, but the solid foundation of all free governments was some form of equal representation and impartial trial.[135] Only through such instruments of popular control could the people consent to necessary restrictions on their liberty and property.

John Adams expressed the devotion of the colonists to these two major constitutional arrangements in a passage that must be quoted at length. In one of his celebrated letters from "The Earl of Clarendon to William Pym," Adams pointed to the "grand division of constitutional powers . . . into those of legislation and those of execution." Having justified the immediate participation of the people in the legislative power, he went on to say:

> This popular power, however, when the numbers grew large, became impracticable to be exercised by the universal and immediate suffrage of the people; and this impracticability has introduced from the feudal system an expedient which we call representation. This expedient is only an equivalent for the suffrage of the whole people in the common management of public concerns. It is in reality nothing more than this, the people choose attorneys to vote for them in the great council of the nation, reserving always the fundamentals of the government, reserving also a right to give their attorneys instructions how to vote, and a right at certain, stated intervals, of choosing

a-new; discarding an old attorney, and choosing a wiser and better. And it is this reservation of fundamentals, of the right of giving instructions, and of new elections, which creates a popular check upon the whole government. . . .

The other grand division of power is that of execution. And here the king is, by the constitution, supreme executor of the laws, and is always present, in person or by his judges, in his courts, distributing justice among the people. But the executive branch of the constitution, as far as respects the administration of justice, has in it a mixture of popular power too. . . . The people choose a grand jury, to make inquiry and presentment of crimes. Twelve of these must agree in finding the bill. And the petit jury must try the same fact over again, and find the person guilty, before he can be punished. Innocence, therefore, is so well protected in this wise constitution, that no man can be punished till twenty-four of his neighbors have said upon oath that he is guilty. So it is also in the trial of causes between party and party. No man's property or liberty can be taken from him till twelve men in his neighborhood have said upon oath, that by laws of his own making it ought to be taken away, that is, that the facts are such as to fall within such laws. . . .

These two popular powers, therefore, are the heart and lungs, the main-spring and the centre wheel, and without them the body must die, the watch must run down, the government must become arbitrary. . . . In these two powers consist wholly the liberty and security of the people. They have no other fortification against wanton, cruel power; no other indemnification against being ridden like horses, fleeced like sheep, worked like cattle, and fed and clothed like swine and hounds; no other defence against fines, imprisonments, whipping-posts, gibbets, bastinadoes, and racks.[136]

In this brilliant passage Adams set down most of the significant American refinements of the rights of representation and jury trial. As to representation, these points of general accord among the colonists should be noted:

The business of the supreme legislature was to make laws, lay taxes, redress grievances, and interpose "in the mal conduct of the executive." [137] No other instrument of government had the right or capacity to bind the people, since only through their representatives could they give consent to external control over their persons and properties. "The rights of a people to tax themselves, is essential to their liberties; and to submit to taxes in any other way, is compleat slavery." [138] Neither taxation nor legislation without representation was possible under free government. For this reason, the "right of Representation" was the basic right of political man, the right "on which all other rights essentially depend." [139]

The people's chief defense against executive misconduct or usurpation was the legislature rather than the judiciary. Article V of the Maryland Declaration of Rights of 1776 announced:

That the right in the people to participate in the Legislature is the best security of liberty, and the foundation of all free government.[140]

For this reason in particular, the legislature was entitled to meet frequently and for extended periods. "The necessity and importance of a legislative in being," wrote Samuel Adams, should resolve all conflicts between legislature and executive in favor of the former: that is, "in favor of the people." [141]

Representation should be "equal": that is, apportioned in such a way as to guard against giving "an undue influence to some parts of the community over others." [142] In the words of Theophilus Parsons:

> The rights of representation should be so equally and impartially distributed, that the representatives should have the same views, and interests with the people at large. They should think, feel, and act like them, and in fine, should be an exact miniature of their constituents. They should be (if we may use the expression) the whole body politic, with all it's property, rights, and priviledges, reduced to a smaller scale, every part being diminished in just proportion.[143]

And of John Adams:

> It [the representative assembly] should be in miniature an exact portrait of the people at large. It should think, feel, reason, and act like them. That it may be the interest of this assembly to do strict justice at all times, it should be an equal representation, or, in other words, equal interests among the people should have equal interests in it.[144]

The frontier towns and counties made excellent use of the doctrine of equal representation in their fight for seats in the provincial legislature.[145]

Representation should be direct and contractual, not indirect and virtual. Representatives should follow the wishes of their constituents so far as humanly possible; the latter should therefore give detailed and frequent instructions to the former. Colonial theories of representation were not especially subtle.[146] Burke's appeal of 1774 would have received even shorter shrift from the electors of Boston than it did from those of Bristol. Most colonial theorists agreed with "The Censor" of Philadelphia

> that the right of instructing lies with the constituents, and them only; that the representatives are bound to regard them as the dictates of their masters, and not left at liberty to comply with or reject them, as they may think proper.[147]

For this reason in particular, that it made a mockery of notions of instruction and accountability, virtual representation was anathema to colonial opinion.[148]

The elections on which equal and faithful representation was based were to be free and frequent. Free elections, where "no bribery, corruption, or undue influence . . . have place," [149] were in Wilson's words the "point of last consequence to all free governments." [150] Only through an uncorrupted and unintimidated suffrage could a people elect a legislature dedicated to the common weal. A Virginian attested the importance attached to free elections in these blunt words:

> The freedom of election is necessary for the well-being of the Laws and the liberties of the state, which would otherwise fall a sacrifice to the altars

of bribery and corruption, and party-Spirit. To this end, the representatives should be the unbiassed choice of the people, by ballot, in which no man should make interest, either directly or indirectly, for himself or his friend, under the penalty of a heavy fine, and an exclusion from the house of representatives for ever; for it is generally found, that the people will choose right, if left to themselves.[151]

Frequent elections, which in fact and principle meant annual elections, were the one sure way to secure almost continuous accountability. Not only was a short term the best possible guarantee that the legislature would remain "in miniature an exact portrait of the people at large," but it was a major bulwark against abuse and usurpation of power. "Elections may be septennial or triennial," wrote John Adams to John Penn,

> but, for my own part, I think they ought to be annual; *for there is not in all science a maxim more infallible than this, where annual elections end, there slavery begins.*[152]

Concerning "that firmest Barrier of *English* Liberty, THE TRIAL BY JURIES," [153] colonial authors had little to say of an analytical nature. Certainly no one ever questioned its justice and workability, and it is unusual to happen upon a writer who does not speak of "this inestimable jewel" in the most glowing terms.[154] The right to jury trial was generally considered to cover all other procedural rights, including "that great bulwark and palladium of English liberty," habeas corpus.[155]

It is difficult to exaggerate the esteem in which the colonists held the representative legislature and jury trial. The vehemence of their defense of these two bulwarks of freedom was, of course, a direct reaction to the ministry's assault upon them in the Sugar and Stamp Acts. Yet colonial devotion to these ancient techniques was more than just occasional. Few Americans believed that the representative assembly and jury trial could ever be improved upon as instruments of popular control of government. John Adams spoke for almost every American when he exclaimed:

> What a fine reflection and consolation is it for a man, that he can be subjected to no laws which he does not make himself, or constitute some of his friends to make for him,—his father, brother, neighbor, friend, a man of his own rank, nearly of his own education, fortune, habits, passions, prejudices, one whose life and fortune and liberty are to be affected, like those of his constituents, by the laws he shall consent to for himself and them! What a satisfaction is it to reflect, that he can lie under the imputation of no guilt, be subjected to no punishment, lose none of his property, or the necessaries, conveniences, or ornaments of life, which indulgent Providence has showered around him, but by the judgment of his peers, his equals, his neighbors, men who know him and to whom he is known, who have no end to serve by punishing him, who wish to find him innocent, if charged with a crime, and are indifferent on which side the truth lies, if he disputes with his neighbor! [156]

THE RIGHT OF RESISTANCE

Under normal operating conditions of free society and constitutional government, representation and jury trial formed the last and firmest line of defense against arbitrary power. Political conditions in the pre-Revolutionary decade were far from normal, however, and the practical-minded colonists shaped their theory to fit this imperative fact. Representation was no defense against a legislature in which they were represented only virtually or not at all; jury trial was no defense against an executive operating through courts of vice-admiralty. Led by their pamphleteers and prodded by their preachers, the colonists therefore went in search of an extraordinary line of defense, and they found it in the right of resistance to tyranny. American writers disagreed sharply over certain practical applications of this right, but none ever doubted its certain existence. "The most mischievous of all doctrines, that of passive obedience and non-resistance," [157] had no place at all in the American "party line." In the words of William Smith:

> The doctrine of absolute *Non-resistance* has been fully exploded among every virtuous people. The freeborn soul revolts against it.[158]

And of James Otis:

> He that would palm the doctrine of unlimited passive obedience upon mankind—is not only a fool and a knave, but a rebel against common sense, as well as the laws of God, of Nature, and his Country.[159]

And of "Camillus" in the *Pennsylvania Gazette:*

> Those ornaments of human nature, *Locke, Sydney, Hoadley,* and many other illustrious names, have so refuted these absurd doctrines of passive obedience and non-resistance; and they are so repugnant to the common sense and happiness of mankind, that it would be an affront to the understandings of my countrymen to suppose they could now admit of serious argument.[160]

Jonathan Boucher and his few colleagues in high Toryism were never so far from making sense to Americans as when they preached the gospel of unquestioning submission.[161] The very definition of a Tory was: "a maintainer of the infernal doctrine of arbitrary power, and indefeasible right on the part of the sovereign, and of passive obedience and non resistance" on the part of the subject.[162]

The essential conservatism of Revolutionary theorists is most clearly revealed in their handling of the doctrine of resistance, a doctrine, they were quick to point out, that was "far from being new." [163] Spokesmen of a people who denied indignantly that they were "big with disaffection, disobedience, sedition and treason," [164] the colonial pamphleteers were extremely guarded in their comments on this delicate subject. It is impossible to discover an important American author who wrote in defense of "the right of revolution" or acclaimed resistance as anything but a necessary and unpleasant evil. The whole effort of American thinkers was directed to restricting and qualifying—one might say *legalizing*—the extraordinary right of appealing to arms.

One example of this conservative position was the insistence of most writers on discussing resistance as a community right. Resistance to oppression was, to be sure, both a personal and community right. Hamilton reminded his countrymen in *A Full Vindication* that "self-preservation is the first principle of our nature," and other writers, following Blackstone and Grotius, asserted the unalienability of the great law of self-defense.[165] A man could not bargain away for any equivalent his ultimate right to use force to meet unlawful force, whether it be the pistol of a highwayman or the decree of a wicked judge.[166] For the most part, however, American theorists devoted their attention to the causes and techniques of large-scale, public resistance to arbitrary power and ignored the unalienable right of the individual to defend his life, liberty, and property against illegal force. A South Carolinian spoke of "those *latent*, though *inherent* rights of society, which *no climate, no time, no constitution, no contract*, can ever destroy or diminish," [167] and Jefferson wrote in his *Summary View* of "those sacred and sovereign rights of punishment, reserved in the hands of the people for cases of extreme necessity, and judged by the constitution unsafe to be delegated to any other judicature." [168]

The American theorists, constitutionalists all, placed special emphasis on the broken contract as justification for community resistance. The will of God, the Old and New Testaments, nature, history, and the British Constitution all sanctioned popular resistance to oppressive authority,[169] but the one clear occasion for exercising this right was the breaking of the original contract, "the overleaping the bounds of the fundamental law." The General Court of Massachusetts tied together the contract and resistance in its proclamation of January 23, 1776:

> As the happiness of the people is the sole end of government, so the consent of the people is the only foundation of it, in reason, morality, and the natural fitness of things. And therefore every act of government, every exercise of sovereignty, against, or without, the consent of the people, is injustice, usurpation, and tyranny. . . .
> When kings, ministers, governors, or legislators, therefore, instead of exercising the powers entrusted with them, according to the principles, forms and proportions stated by the constitution, and established by the original compact, prostitute those powers to the purposes of oppression—to subvert, instead of supporting a free constitution;—to destroy, instead of preserving the lives, liberties and properties of the people;—they are no longer to be deemed magistrates vested with a sacred character, but become public enemies, and ought to be resisted.[170]

The grand jury for 1776 in Georgetown, South Carolina expressed a similar notion:

> When a People . . . find that, by the baseness and corruption of their rulers, those laws which were intended as the guardians of their sacred and unalienable rights, are impiously perverted into instruments of oppression;

and, in violation of every social compact, and the ties of common justice, every means is adopted by those whom they instituted to govern and protect them, to enslave and destroy them: human nature and the laws of *God* justify their employing those means for redress which self-preservation dictates.[171]

And Chief Justice Drayton of the same colony identified the contract and the parties to it by stating:

The house of Brunswick was yet scarcely settled in the British throne, to which it had been called by a free people, when, in the year 1719, our ancestors in this country, finding that the government of the lords proprietors operated to their ruin, exercised the rights transmitted to them by their forefathers of England; and casting off the proprietary authority, called upon the house of Brunswick to rule over them—a house elevated to royal dominion, for no other purpose than to preserve to a people their unalienable rights. The king accepted the invitation, and thereby indisputably admitted the legality of that revolution. And in so doing, by his own act, he vested in those our forefathers, and us their posterity, a clear right to effect *another* revolution, if ever the government of the house of Brunswick should operate to the ruin of the people.[172]

From this identification of South Carolina's contract with the Kings of England Judge Drayton moved ahead to document fully—by comparing the actions of James II and George III—those breaches which permitted the colonists to renounce their allegiance.[173] In doing this he followed the lead of several more important thinkers, all of whom were anxious to prove that the King had "unkinged" himself by breaking the contract.[174] Although Drayton and the others agreed that God and nature had granted the right of resistance to every man and community for self-defense against arbitrary force of any kind, they preferred to treat this right as the whole people's final remedy against one specific show of force: the grossly unconstitutional actions of covenanted rulers.

Resistance to illegal authority, not rebellion or revolution, was the only right and purpose of the American colonists. The emphasis their spokesmen placed on the broken contract permitted them to deny absolutely that they were rebellious in nature or revolutionary in intent. It was all as simple as this: They had contracted away—not irrevocably—their original power to govern themselves. They were meeting the harsh fact of a major breach of the contract by resuming this power and granting it to others on new terms. The rulers who had exercised unlawful authority were the real rebels. The people were merely exercising "the right of saving themselves from ruin." [175] Scores of letters and pamphlets, of which the instances below are among the most eloquent, developed a theme especially appealing to American minds.

"Pacificus" to "Tranquillus" in the *Pennsylvania Gazette:*

I readily agree with you, Sir, that the crime of rebellion is of the deepest dye, and in every civil war, doubtless one side or the other are rebels; but if that be the only government pleasing to God or useful to man, which maintains the peace, safety and happiness of the people, and if no good reason can be assigned to induce any rational creature to become a member of that community which denies these blessings to its members, then I would ask, who are the rebels in any contest of the kind, the governors who abuse the trust reposed in them, and exercise the delegated power of the people to their hurt; or the governed, who attempt to protect themselves against the abuse of that power?

If subjection is only due to a legal exertion of power, and if power ought only to be employed for the good of the community, then he alone is chargeable with rebellion, who uses the power he possesses to the hurt of the people, and not the people, who oppose every illegal exertion of that power.[176]

"The Monitor" to John Holt's *New-York Journal:*

Our enemies falsely charged us with endeavouring to subvert the Constitution; but upon the fairest examination, it must be evident, that we are its truest supporters; while they are its most flagitious destroyers. . . .

If the Constitution is to be the touchstone of Treason and Rebellion, and the violators of it are the Traitors and Rebels, then will those appellations belong more properly to the Ministry and their instruments, who are labouring to overturn it, than to us, who are making every possible exertion in support of its purest principles? [177]

Virginians made excellent practical use of this distinction. When their last royal Governor, Lord Dunmore, proclaimed them to be in rebellion, they retorted immediately in public print that he was the rebel and they the saviors of the constitution.[178] "By the frame of our constitution, the duties of protection and allegiance are reciprocal." [179] Since the Governor had withdrawn his protection, Virginians could withdraw their allegiance.

Resistance to unlawful authority, to breaches of the original contract, was more than just a right and "a Virtue." [180] The Provincial Congress reminded the inhabitants of Massachusetts that it was "the Christian and social duty of each Individual," [181] and Rev. John Allen argued:

It is no rebellion to oppose any King, ministry, or governor, that destroys by any violence or authority whatever, the rights of the people. Shall a man be deem'd a rebel that supports his own rights? It is the first law of nature, and he must be a rebel to GOD, to the laws of nature, and his own conscience, who will not do it.[182]

In short, "the man who refuses to assert his right to liberty, property, and life, is guilty of the worst kind of rebellion; he commits high treason against *God*." [183] Hardly less important to this history-conscious people, he is a betrayer of generations yet unborn:

Honor, justice, and *humanity* call upon us to hold, and to transmit to our posterity, that liberty which we received from our ancestors. It is not our duty to leave wealth to our children; but it is our duty to leave liberty to them. No infamy, iniquity, or cruelty, can exceed our own, if we, born and educated in a country of freedom, entitled to its blessings, and knowing their value, pusillanimously deserting the post assigned us by Divine Providence, surrender succeeding generations to a condition of wretchedness, from which no human efforts, in all probability, will be sufficient to extricate them.[184]

American theorists revealed their conservative orientation in other refinements or qualifications of the right of resistance. First, they rejected flatly the stock Tory argument that to admit the right of resistance was simply to invite political and social instability. "Quite the contrary," replied an unknown author writing "For the Perusal of Lord NORTH":

> People are not so easily got out of their old forms as some are apt to suggest; they are hardly to be prevailed with to amend the acknowledged faults in the frame they have been accustomed to. . . .
> Such revolutions happen not upon every little mismanagement in public affairs. Great mistakes in the ruling party, and many wrong laws, and slips of human frailty, will be borne by the people; but if a long train of abuses and artifices, all tending the same way, make the design visible to the people, and they see whither they are going, it is not to be wondered that they should then rouse themselves, for specious names and forms are worse than the state of nature or pure anarchy.[185]

Jefferson emphasized this point in the preamble to the Declaration of Independence. He, too, made use of the Lockean phrase, "a long train of abuses," to describe the circumstances necessary to overcome mankind's disposition "to suffer, while evils are sufferable, than to right themselves by abolishing the forms to which they are accustomed." Far from being turbulent, restless, and seditious, the people, even though aware of their right to resist, were not half so likely to violate the terms of the contract as were their governors and magistrates. As Samuel Cooke put it:

> The history of past ages and of our nation shows that the greatest dangers have arisen from lawless power. The body of a people are disposed to lead quiet and peaceable lives, and it is their highest interest to support the government under which their quietness is ensured. They retain a reverence for their superiors, and seldom foresee or suspect danger till they feel their burdens.[186]

Therefore, added the aptly named "Pacificus," there must be

> a strong presumption against the supreme magistrate and his creatures, in every contest of this nature; for it is scarcely credible that the community would revolt from that power which they knew to be exerted for their good; or that they would withdraw their allegiance from the governor, who exercised the authority with which they had invested him, purely for their service.[187]

Second, the people had a solemn duty to be peaceful and law-abiding. Rev. Charles Turner spoke for a large majority when he warned:

> The people ought to have the end of government, the publick good, at heart, as well as the magistrate; and therefore, to yield all loyal subjection

to well regulated government, in opposition to every thing of a factious nature and complexion.[188]

Force was the people's final defense, but force, wrote "John Locke" to the people of Boston,

> is to be opposed only to unjust and unlawful force; whoever makes any opposition in any other case, draws on himself a just condemnation both from GOD and man.[189]

Third, the nature and extent of resistance was to be determined by the nature and extent of oppression. Petty tyranny called for passive resistance; premeditated despotism called for active resistance.[190] Resistance in the extreme sense of outright revolution—the "appeal to God by the sword," [191] as the Colony of New Hampshire labeled it—was never to be undertaken except by an overwhelming majority of a thoroughly abused people. There was no place in Revolutionary theory for the *coup d'état* of a militant minority dedicated to the building of a new order. Samuel West expressed this thought in his election sermon of 1776:

> If it be asked, who are the proper judges to determine, when rulers are guilty of tyranny and oppression? I answer, the publick; not a few disaffected individuals, but the collective body of the state must decide this question.[192]

Finally, all colonial writers agreed with Jefferson's assumption that any exercise of "the Right of the People to alter or to abolish" government would be followed almost immediately by an exercise of their associated right "to institute new Government." For all their flirtation with the state of nature, for all their loyalty to the mechanistic explanation of government, Americans could think of man only as a member of a political community. Men did not revolt against government to eliminate it entirely and return to a state of nature, but to organize a new one, "laying its foundation on such principles and organizing its powers in such form, as to them shall seem most likely to effect their Safety and Happiness." God granted men the right of resistance to help them preserve orderly constitutional government, not to induce them to fly from the tyranny of arbitrary power to the tyranny of no power at all.

The natural or God-given right of resistance to arbitrary power was the last resort of a people unable to protect their lives, liberties, and properties by normal constitutional methods. It was a right to be exercised only by an overwhelming majority of the community against rulers who had so completely ignored the terms of the original contract as to make further allegiance a crime against God and reason. The people could be counted on never to resist except under overriding compulsion and to temper their methods to the nature and degree of oppression. The only possible outcome of a full reversion of power to the people was a new contract with new rulers under new terms of reciprocal protection and allegiance. Resistance or revolution was not so much the right as the solemn, unpleasant duty of a betrayed people.[193] Thus did the conservative, law-abiding, constitutional Americans reason about the use of force in defense of liberty. Never have a people engaged in revolution been so anxious to convince themselves and the world that they were not really revolutionaries at all. Chief Justice Drayton of South Carolina expressed the legalism and conservatism of colonial thinking about the act of resistance when he announced to his grand jury that George III had "unkinged" himself:

> And thus, as I have on the foot of the best authorities made it evident, that George the third, king of Great Britain, has endeavored to subvert the constitution of this country, by breaking the original contract between king and people; by the advice of wicked persons, has violated the fundamental laws, and has withdrawn himself, by withdrawing the constitutional benefits of the kingly office, and his protection out of this country: From such a result of injuries, from such a conjuncture of circumstances—the law of the land authorises me to declare, and it is my duty boldly to declare the law, that George the third, king of Great Britain, has abdicated the government, and that the throne is thereby vacant; that is, HE HAS NO AUTHORITY OVER US, and WE OWE NO OBEDIENCE TO HIM.[194]

CONCLUSION: CONGRESS AND VIRGINIA PROCLAIM THE RIGHTS OF MAN

The rights of men—not just of Englishmen but of all men—were the one common interest of all American thinkers. The most important expression of Revolutionary political thought is therefore to be found in the declarations of rights adopted by several new states in the first years of independence. Life, liberty, property, happiness, and conscience; the freedoms of speech, press, petition, and assembly; civil supremacy, free and equal representation, and judicial safeguards; the power of the people to "reform, alter, or abolish" old governments and establish new ones—all these rights found eloquent acknowledgment in these imaginative and influential documents. We shall conclude this extended discussion of natural and civil rights by quoting first from an official message of the first Continental Congress, then from the most celebrated of the early state declarations of rights.

An extract from the famous "Letter to the Inhabitants of the Province of Quebec," drafted by John Dickinson and adopted by Congress October 26, 1774:

> The first grand right, is that of the people having a share in their own government by their representatives chosen by themselves, and, in consequence, of being ruled by *laws*, which they themselves approve, not by *edicts of men* over whom they have no controul. This is a bulwark surrounding and defending their property, which by their honest cares and labours they have acquired, so that no portions of it can legally be taken from them, but with their own full and free consent. . . .
> The next great right is that of trial by jury. This provides, that neither life, liberty nor property, can be taken from the possessor, until twelve of his unexceptionable countrymen and peers of his vicinage, who from that neigh-

bourhood may reasonably be supposed to be acquainted with his character, and the characters of the witnesses, upon a fair trial, and full enquiry, face to face, in open Court, before as many of the people as chuse to attend, shall pass their sentence upon oath against him. . . .

Another right relates merely to the liberty of the person. If a subject is seized and imprisoned, tho' by order of Government, he may, by virtue of this right, immediately obtain a writ, termed a Habeas Corpus, from a Judge, whose sworn duty it is to grant it, and thereupon procure any illegal restraint to be quickly enquired into and redressed.

A fourth right, is that of holding lands by the tenure of easy rents, and not by rigorous and oppressive services, frequently forcing the possessors from their families and their business, to perform what ought to be done, in all well regulated states, by men hired for the purpose.

The last right we shall mention, regards the freedom of the press. The importance of this consists, besides the advancement of truth, science, morality, and arts in general, in its diffusion of liberal sentiments on the administration of Government, its ready communication of thoughts between subjects, and its consequential promotion of union among them, whereby oppressive officers are shamed or intimidated, into more honourable and just modes of conducting affairs.

These are the invaluable rights, that form a considerable part of our mild system of government; that, sending its equitable energy through all ranks and classes of men, defends the poor from the rich, the weak from the powerful, the industrious from the rapacious, the peaceable from the violent, the tenants from the lords, and all from their superiors.

These are the rights, without which a people cannot be free and happy.[195]

The Virginia Declaration of Rights, drafted by George Mason and adopted by the Virginia Convention, June 12, 1776:

A Declaration of Rights, made by the Representatives of the good People of Virginia, assembled in full and free Convention, which rights do pertain to them and their posterity as the basis and foundation of government.

I. That all men are by nature equally free and independent, and have certain inherent rights, of which, when they enter into a state of society, they cannot by any compact deprive or divest their posterity; namely, the enjoyment of life and liberty, with the means of acquiring and possessing property, and pursuing and obtaining happiness and safety.

II. That all power is vested in, and consequently derived from, the people; that magistrates are their trustees and servants, and at all times amenable to them.

III. That government is, or ought to be, instituted for the common benefit, protection, and security of the people, nation or community; of all the various modes and forms of government, that is best which is capable of producing the greatest degree of happiness and safety, and is most effectually secured against the danger of maladministration; and that, when a government shall be found inadequate or contrary to these purposes, a majority of the community hath an indubitable, unalienable, and indefeasible right to reform, alter or abolish it, in such manner as shall be judged most conducive to the public weal.

IV. That no man, or set of men, are entitled to exclusive or separate

. emoluments or privileges from the community but in consideration of public
services, which not being descendible, neither ought the offices of magistrate,
legislator or judge to be hereditary.

V. That the legislative, executive and judicial powers should be separate
and distinct; and that the members thereof may be restrained from oppression, by feeling and participating the burthens of the people, they should, at
fixed periods, be reduced to a private station, return into that body from
which they were originally taken, and the vacancies be supplied by frequent,
certain and regular elections, in which all, or any part or the former members to be again eligible or ineligible, as the laws shall direct.

VI. That all elections ought to be free, and that all men having sufficient
evidence of permanent common interest with, and attachment to the community, have the right of suffrage, and cannot be taxed, or deprived of their
property for public uses, without their own consent, or that of their representatives so elected, nor bound by any law to which they have not in like
manner assented, for the public good.

VII. That all power of suspending laws, or the execution of laws, by any
authority, without consent of the representatives of the people, is injurious
to their rights, and ought not to be exercised.

VIII. That in all capital or criminal prosecutions a man hath a right
to demand the cause and nature of his accusation, to be confronted with the
accusers and witnesses, to call for evidence in his favour, and to a speedy
trial by an impartial jury of twelve men of his vicinage, without whose unanimous consent he cannot be found guilty; nor can he be compelled to give
evidence against himself; that no man be deprived of his liberty, except by
the law of the land or the judgment of his peers.

IX. That excessive bail ought not to be required, nor excessive fines imposed, nor cruel and unusual punishments inflicted.

X. That general warrants, whereby an officer or messenger may be commanded to search suspected places without evidence of a fact committed, or
to seize any person or persons not named, or whose offence is not particularly described and supported by evidence, are grievous and oppressive,
and ought not to be granted.

XI. That in controversies respecting property, and in suits between man
and man, the ancient trial by jury of twelve men is preferable to any other,
and ought to be held sacred.

XII. That the freedom of the press is one of the great bulwarks of liberty,
and can never be restrained but by despotic governments.

XIII. That a well-regulated militia, composed of the body of the people,
trained to arms, is the proper, natural and safe defence of a free State; that
standing armies in time of peace should be avoided as dangerous to liberty;
and that in all cases the military should be under strict subordination to, and
governed by, the civil power.

XIV. That the people have a right to uniform government; and therefore
that no government separate from or independent of the government of
Virginia ought to be erected or established within the limits thereof.

XV. That no free government, or the blessing of liberty, can be preserved
to any people, but by a firm adherence to justice, moderation, temperance,
frugality and virtue, and by a frequent recurrence to fundamental principles.

XVI. That religion, or the duty which we owe to our Creator, and the manner of discharging it, can be directed only by reason and conviction, not by force or violence; and therefore all men are equally entitled to the free exercise of religion, according to the dictates of conscience; and that it is the duty of all to practice Christian forbearance, love and charity towards each other.[196]

The declarations of rights of 1776 remain America's most notable contribution to universal political thought. Through these eloquent statements of the rights of man political theory became political reality.

CHAPTER FOURTEEN

American Political Thought, 1765-1776: The Pattern of Government

THE political theory of anarchy is concerned almost exclusively with the rights of the individual, the political theory of autocracy with the purposes of the state. The quest of the one is absolute liberty; the passion of the other is absolute order. The political theory of the American Revolution was a notable attempt to strike a balance between these equally dangerous and repulsive extremes. It was a theory of ordered liberty, of the free yet dependent person in the sheltering yet compulsive community. The men who expounded this theory were therefore as concerned with the pattern of government as with the rights of man. Convinced that the concept of man without government was valid only as a useful hypothesis or fact of prehistory, they gave nearly as much attention to political organization as to political liberty. We have heard what they had to say about man—about his nature, his rights, and the higher law that governs and protects him. Now we are to hear them speak about government—about its origin, purpose, nature, structure, and moral basis. Yet even as we divide Revolutionary political thought into the prime categories of man and government, we must remember that these halves made up an indivisible whole. In theory as in fact, man and government could not exist apart from one another.

American speculation about political organization went through three stages in the decade before independence. In the first few years most writers were quite unimaginative, apparently content to parrot the teachings of the great Whigs about the origin and purpose of government and the beauties of the English Constitution. Around 1770, in a few instances even earlier, their writings began to show increased independence of judgment. And finally, in 1775 and 1776, the colonists embarked upon a campaign of constructive thought that was to lead through the first state constitutions to the Convention of 1787 and from there to the triumph of constitutional republicanism in the Federalist and Jeffersonian periods. Rarely have men been privileged to think such influential thoughts about the purpose and form of government. As the most constructive political mind of the era observed to a colleague in greatness:

> You and I, my dear friend, have been sent into life at a time when the greatest lawgivers of antiquity would have wished to live. How few of the human race have ever enjoyed an opportunity of making an election of government, more than of air, soil, or climate, for themselves or their children! When, before the present epocha, had three millions of people full power and a fair opportunity to form and establish the wisest and happiest government that human wisdom can contrive? [1]

And rarely has such a measure of practical success crowned the speculative efforts of a school of political thought.

THE ORIGIN OF GOVERNMENT

Revolutionary thinkers followed a well-worn path to a standard explanation of the origin of government. The concept of the contract or compact is nearly as old as political theory itself, and we have already noted the universality of its appeal to early Americans. The men of the Revolution honored their Christian and colonial past in clinging to a belief that men institute government as an act of will. Their lack of originality in handling this crucial problem of political theory was a tribute to the vigor and utility of a great tradition rather than a sign of mental indolence or incuriosity.

The opening pages of *Common Sense* present one of the most precise renditions of the mechanistic theory in Revolutionary literature. Although many American thinkers disagreed strongly with Paine's unrelenting belief that the "rise of government" results solely from "the inability of moral virtue to govern the world," almost all of them subscribed to some such explanation as this:

> In order to gain a clear and just idea of the design and end of government, let us suppose a small number of persons settled in some sequestered part of the earth, unconnected with the rest; they will then represent the first peopling of any country, or of the world. In this state of natural liberty, society will be their first thought. A thousand motives will excite them thereto; the strength of one man is so unequal to his wants, and his mind so unfitted for perpetual solitude, that he is soon obliged to seek assistance and relief of another, who in his turn requires the same. Four or five united would be able to raise a tolerable dwelling in the midst of a wilderness, but

one man might labor out the common period of life without accomplishing anything; when he had felled his timber he could not remove it, nor erect it after it was removed; hunger in the meantime would urge him to quit his work, and every different want would call him a different way. Disease, nay even misfortune, would be death; for though neither might be mortal, yet either would disable him from living, and reduce him to a state in which he might rather be said to perish than to die.

Thus necessity, like a gravitating power, would soon form our newly arrived emigrants into society, the reciprocal blessings of which would supersede and render the obligations of law and government unnecessary while they remained perfectly just to each other; but as nothing but heaven is impregnable to vice, it will unavoidably happen that in proportion as they surmount the first difficulties of emigration, which bound them together in a common cause, they will begin to relax in their duty and attachment to each other; and this remissness will point out the necessity of establishing some form of government to supply the defect of moral virtue.

Some convenient tree will afford them a statehouse, under the branches of which the whole colony may assemble to deliberate on public matters. It is more than probable that their first laws will have the title only of REGULATIONS and be enforced by no other penalty than public disesteem. In this first parliament every man by natural right will have a seat.

But as the colony increases, the public concerns will increase likewise, and the distance at which the members may be separated will render it too inconvenient for all of them to meet on every occasion as at first, when their number was small, their habitations near, and the public concerns few and trifling. This will point out the convenience of their consenting to leave the legislative part to be managed by a select number chosen from the whole body, who are supposed to have the same concerns at stake which those have who appointed them, and who will act in the same manner as the whole body would act were they present.[2]

Paine's account is especially important for its careful distinction between society and government. Some thinkers confounded these two aspects of the total community, but the best of them agreed with Paine that these were different levels of organization with "different origins." Society was the involuntary, unconscious, natural result of the presence of a group of men "in the midst of a wilderness." Man's need for companionship as well as for "assistance and relief" made society rather than isolation his natural condition. The true state of nature was not an area full of hermits or self-sustaining families, but a true community in which men lived and worked together without government, "without a common superior on earth . . . to judge between them."[3] Government, too, was a natural institution, but with this difference: The vital questions—Who shall govern? For what purposes? Through what methods?—were to be answered by men capable of exercising free choice. If nature forced men to submit to government, it left them free to decide upon its form and personnel, and they might therefore properly insist that it was "the *ordinance of men—an human institution*."[4]

This, then, was the contract in Revolutionary theory: an agreement of free and equal men, not to enter into society, but to institute government on terms mutually satisfactory to them and their prospective rulers. Having agreed among themselves to form a government—a step they had to take whether they liked it or not—they then agreed upon its structure, functions, powers, and limitations. Finally, they bargained with one or more wise men to rule them, at the same time making clear that all future rulers would become parties to this contract upon entering office. The first contract was a promise among free men to respect and sustain one another; the second was a promise of free men to give allegiance and of wise men to extend protection. Actually, the two contracts—of man with man and of men with their governors—were one.[5] When Revolutionary theorists talked of "the social compact," they meant an agreement to form government, not society.

Colonial writers used the words compact, contract, or covenant to refer to several situations of actual bargaining or constitution-making:

(1) The original charters and their many renewals.[6] This assumption made it necessary to argue that the first colonists had exercised the natural right of migration, had settled the wilderness "at their own Expence, & not the Nations,"[7] and had then contracted voluntarily with the sovereign left behind;

(2) the agreement with William and Mary, in which the colonists joined, upon their accession following the Glorious Revolution;[8]

(3) the continuous agreement through which "America has all along consented, still consents, and ever will consent, that parliament, being the most powerful legislature in the dominions, should regulate the trade of the dominions";[9]

(4) a possible new agreement with the King, which would adjust all outstanding differences and contain a renewed promise of popular allegiance and royal protection;[10]

(5) the many associations, leagues, covenants, and other pledges of faith into which various groups of colonists entered in this decade of crisis;[11]

(6) the new state constitutions and, in time, the Articles of Confederation and Constitution of 1787.[12]

The compact argument was especially serviceable in the first of these instances. It brought new dignity and meaning to the charters themselves; it provided philosophical and historical support for the dominion theory implicit in the Declaration of Independence. Arguments of this nature were extremely convincing to colonial minds:

> When the first settlers of this country had transplanted themselves here, they were to be considered, either as in a state of nature, or else as subjects of that kingdom from whence they had migrated: If they were in the state of nature, they were then entitled to all the rights of nature. . . . They had a right to erect a government upon what form they thought best; or to connect themselves, for the sake of their own advantage and security, either with the natives or any other people upon the globe, who were willing to be connected with them: It is a fact, that they chose to erect a government of their own, much under the same form, as that was, which they had formerly

been under in Europe; and chose the King of England for *their* King. . . .
The people here still remain under the most sacred tie, the subjects of the
King of Great Britain; but utterly unaccountable to, & uncontroulable by
the *people* of Great Britain, or any body of them whatever; their compact
being with the King only, to him alone they submitted, to be govern'd by
him, agreeable to the terms of that compact, contained in their charter.[13]

Designation of the charter as an original contract permitted orators to
ask indignantly:

> I would be glad to know, my Lord, what right the King of England has to
> America? it cannot be an hereditary right, that lies in Hanover, it cannot
> be a parliamentary right, that lies in Britain, not a victorious right. . . . Then
> he can have no more right to America, than what the people have by com-
> pact, invested him with, which is only a power to protect them, and defend
> their rights civil and religious; and to sign, seal, and confirm, as their steward,
> such laws as the people of America shall consent to.[14]

The men of the Revolution were convinced that they, like their ancestors,
were happily privileged to form new compacts. The Continental Congress
appealed to the inhabitants of Quebec "to unite with us in one social compact, formed on the generous principles of equal liberty, and cemented
by such an exchange of beneficial and endearing offices as to render it perpetual." [15] The Massachusetts Constitution of 1780 stated:

> The body politic is formed by a voluntary association of individuals. It
> is a social compact, by which the whole people covenant with each citizen,
> and each citizen with the whole people, that all shall be governed by certain
> laws for the common good.[16]

And the men of Massachusetts, in adopting the Constitution of the United
States, acknowledged

> with grateful hearts the goodness of the Supreme Ruler of the Universe, in
> affording the people of the United States, in the course of his providence,
> an opportunity, deliberately and peaceably, without fraud or surprise, of
> entering into an explicit and solemn compact with each other, by assenting
> to and ratifying a new constitution.[17]

These and dozens of other practical applications of the doctrine of contract make clear that Americans were determined to be the one people in
a hundred of whom James Otis had written:

> The form of government is by *nature* and by *right* so far left to the indi-
> viduals of each society, that they may alter it from a simple democracy or
> government of all over all, to any other form they please. Such alteration
> may and ought to be made by express compact: But how seldom this right
> has been asserted, history will abundantly show. For once that it has been
> fairly settled by compact; *fraud force or accident* have determined it an
> hundred times.[18]

The contract was as effective a tool in the construction of the new order of independence as it had been in the destruction of the old order of empire.

But the contract was something more than a clever contrivance with which propagandists could rewrite the past and dignify the present. It was the substance and symbol of the colonists' solution to the problem of obligation, the most perplexing problem in the political theory of freedom, since it poses such questions as: Why do men submit to the compulsions of government? By what authority does government bind men with positive laws? How can men call themselves free if they are subject to a concentration of political power that can restrict their liberty, deprive them of their property, even take away their lives?

To these and other questions of political obligation Revolutionary thinkers advanced a one-word answer as satisfying to them as it was distasteful to their adversaries: *consent*. Men obeyed government because they had consented to obey it. Through the original contract they had exchanged allegiance and obedience for protection and peace. They had agreed to certain well-defined restrictions on their natural freedom as part of a scheme for securing the rest of that freedom against the whims and jealousies of the men with whom they lived. At the same time, they had agreed to representative institutions, notably the legislative assembly and jury of peers, through which they could continue to consent to necessary restrictions on liberty and property. Government, the community organized for political purposes, could restrict men's liberty, deprive them of their property, even take away their lives, because it did all this with their original and continuing consent. The power of government to do these things was not intrinsic but derived, and from the free consent of the very people it governed. In short, the American answer to this troublesome question was simply that the only valid obligation to obey government is self-obligation. "*Resolved,*" voted the freeholders and other inhabitants of Mendon, Massachusetts, "That all just and lawful Government must necessarily originate in the free Consent of the People." [19] The colonists' obsession with the principle of consent is evident in these two representative discussions of the relation of political authority to private property:

> No government can have a RIGHT to obedience from a people, who have not *freely consented* to it; which they can never be supposed to do, till either they are put in a full state of *liberty* to choose their government and governors, or at least till they have such standing laws to which they have by *themselves* or their *representatives given their consent*, and also, till they are allowed their due *property*, which is so to be *proprietors* of what they have, that no body can take away any *part* of it without their *consent*, without which men under any government are not in the *state of freedom*, but are *direct slaves*, under the force of war. The nature of *property* is, that without a man's own consent it cannot be taken from him. [20]

> The supreme power cannot take from any man any part of his property without his own consent; for the preservation of property being the end of

government, and that for which men enter into society; it necessarily requires that the people should have property, without which they must be supposed to lose that by entering into society, which was the end for which they entered into it; too gross an absurdity for any man to own. . . .

It is true, government cannot be supported without great charge, and 'tis fit that every one who enjoys protection should pay out of his estate his proportion for the support of it; but still it must be done with his own consent, or by his representative chosen by him, for if any one shall lay and levy taxes by his own authority, and without such consent of the people, he thereby invades the fundamental law of property, and subverts the end of government, for what property have I in that which another may by right take when he pleases to himself? [21]

To these revealing comments should be added Theophilus Parsons's definition of political liberty:

Let it be thus defined; political liberty is the right every man in the state has, to do whatever is not prohibited by laws, TO WHICH HE HAS GIVEN HIS CONSENT. This definition is in unison with the feelings of a free people.[22]

The notion of consent doubtless had a good deal more appeal to "the feelings of a free people" than to the reasoning powers of their philosophers; yet if sophisticated exponents of the American consensus were troubled by the dangers and ambiguities of this notion, they failed to reveal it in their pamphlets, sermons, and letters. The great framework of Anglo-American constitutionalism—charters, constitutions, bills of rights, elections, assemblies, juries, representation, common law, limited prerogative, majority rule— seemed to them to be rationalized only by the principle of popular consent.[23] This principle, in turn, found rationalization in the compact or contract, the symbol of political obligation derived from free consent. In this sense, the contract was the logical justification rather than historical explanation of the existence and authority of the political community. It answered the great question—What authority should government exercise?—by stating: the authority that free and reasonable men consent to its exercising. If consent was the key to limited and popular government, the compact was the key to consent. Only thus could men secure "mutual harmony, unanimity and concord . . . the great cement and connecting bands of human society." [24]

A corollary of the contractual origin of government was the doctrine of popular sovereignty, a very simple solution to a very complex problem. Colonial thinkers, unlike many of their children and grandchildren, were generally ready to concur in Blackstone's dictum that in all governments "there is and must be . . . a supreme, irresistible, uncontrolled authority, in which the *jura summi imperii*, or the rights of sovereignty, reside," [25] but they were quick to add that in all free governments this authority resided in the people. In a proclamation dated January 23, 1776, the General Court of Massachusetts announced:

It is a maxim that in every government, there must exist, somewhere, a supreme, sovereign, absolute, and uncontrolable power; but this power resides always in the body of the people; and it never was, or can be delegated to one man, or a few; the great Creator having never given to men a right to vest others with authority over them unlimited either in duration or degree.[26]

Blackstone, of course, had been speaking of *legal* sovereignty, of "a supreme, irresistible, uncontrolled authority" residing in government itself. The Americans, on the other hand, were speaking of *political* sovereignty, of the ultimate source from which all legitimate power must be derived. Some of them were quite uninterested in legal sovereignty; others, like James Wilson, were prepared to deny its existence.[27] All of them agreed that even the sovereign people were to be guided and restricted by the laws of nature in exercising their original authority. Political sovereignty was "supreme, irresistible, uncontrolled" only within the sphere assigned to it in the great plan of nature.

In short, the Americans, to the extent that they thought about the problem at all, rejected the concept of supreme legal sovereignty in favor of limited political sovereignty. To the observation that "limited sovereignty" was a contradiction in terms, they would doubtless have replied that they proposed to define their terms to suit themselves. By insisting so vigorously on the necessity and viability of limited government, they actually converted "sovereignty" into a virtually meaningless term. Whatever their conclusions about the scope of political power, all shared the belief expressed by General Washington:

> I cannot conceive [of authority] more honourable, than that which flows from the uncorrupted choice of a brave and free people—the purest source and original fountain of all power.[28]

THE PURPOSE AND NATURE OF GOVERNMENT

In the process of denying parliamentary and asserting provincial or independent authority, colonial theorists had a good deal to say about the purpose of government. Most were in accord with Hamilton, Paine, and Otis that the purpose of society was to extend to each man in it, in return for his talents and exertions, the benefits of the strength, skills, and benevolence of the other men with whom he was associated.[29] The purpose of government, however, evoked a more varied range of comment. Here, in the words of some of the best colonial thinkers, were the reasons why men chose to submit to government:

Samuel Adams, rejecting the doctrine of taxation without representation:

> It destroys the very end for which alone man can be supposed to submit to civil government, which is not for the sake of exalting one man, or a few men above their equals, that they may be maintained in splendour and greatness; but that each individual, under the joint protection of the whole community, may be the Lord of his own possession, and sit securely under his own vine.[30]

"Hampden," in "The Alarm":

> The chief End of all free Government, is the Protection of Property. . . .
> Property is here used in the Large Sense in which Mr. Locke used it, as
> comprehending Life, Liberty, and Estate.[31]

A gentleman writing "From the County of Hampshire" to the *Massachusetts Spy:*

> Personal liberty, personal security, and private property are the three
> only motives, the grand objects for which individuals make a partial sur-
> render of that plenitude of power which they possess in a state of nature,
> and submit to the necessary restrictions, and subordinations of government.[32]

"Spartanus," on "The Interest of America," in the *New-Hampshire
Gazette:*

> Let us now consider what men *relinquish,* and what they *obtain,* by pass-
> ing out of a state of nature, and entering into society, or a state of civil
> government. 1st.—They give up their right to judge between themselves and
> those that offend or injure them, and leave this to the civil magistrate; con-
> sequently they give up the right to vindicate or revenge themselves, any
> other way than by the magistrate or proper officers. 2d.—They give up part
> of their estates, for the support of government. 3d.—They are under obliga-
> tion to expose their lives for the safety of the state when necessary, and
> when called upon to do it. If money will not answer, each man must bear
> his proper part in the defence of the whole. The proper support of gov-
> ernment, supposes that we are ready, with our lives and fortunes, to engage
> in it's defence. Shall it now be asked, what we obtain by entering into civil
> government? I answer we gain *protection,* the protection of our lives and
> properties; that we may without violence enjoy our *own.*[33]

Rev. Samuel Cooke:

> In a civil state, that form is most eligible which is best adapted to promote
> the ends of government—the benefit of the community.[34]

John Adams:

> Government is a frame, a scheme, a system, a combination of powers for
> a certain end, namely,—the good of the whole community. The public good,
> the *Salus populi,* is the professed end of all government.[35]

The Continental Congress:

> A reverence for our great Creator, principles of humanity, and the dic-
> tates of common sense, must convince all those who reflect upon the subject,
> that government was instituted to promote the welfare of mankind, and
> ought to be administered for the attainment of that end.[36]

James Wilson:

> All lawful government is founded on the consent of those who are sub-
> ject to it: such consent was given with a view to ensure and encrease the hap-

piness of the governed. . . . The consequence is, that the happiness of the society is the *first* law of every government.[37]

James Iredell:

The object of all government is, or ought to be, *the happiness of the people governed.*[38]

And finally, the people of Mendon, Massachusetts:

Resolved, That the Good, Safety and Happiness of the People, is the great End of civil Government; and must be considered as the only rational Object, in all original Compacts, and political Institutions.[39]

One major point of agreement and one of disagreement appear in this variety of opinions about the purpose of government. Colonial theorists agreed almost unanimously that government existed only for the benefit of the men who had submitted to it. Even when they used such collective phrases as "the welfare of mankind," "the public good," and "the benefit of the community," they were thinking in terms of the welfare, good, or benefit of each individual. Government had no purpose of its own. The only purpose that counted was that of the men who had instituted it: to seek protection for their "personal liberty, personal security, and private property."

The major point of disagreement, of which few thinkers were fully conscious, was between those who continued to emphasize the protection of life, liberty, and property and those who now began to look upon government as an agency designed "to ensure and encrease the happiness of the governed." Wilson, Iredell, and Jefferson were among those who moved beyond Locke to proclaim, however vaguely, a more positive purpose for the political community. It is doubtful that any one of these men, even the clear-headed Wilson, realized how revolutionary a step it was to salute the pursuit of happiness as a natural right to be protected and even encouraged by government. Nevertheless, it is worth observing that a few imaginative Americans, most of whom seem to have picked up the notion from Burlamaqui, added a new right to man's natural heritage and thus a new purpose to government. And if they spoke occasionally of the happiness of the community as a chief end of government, they meant the happiness of all the persons who had initiated it. Revolutionary thinkers were completely oriented to individualism in their discussions of the purpose of the political community.

Those two supposedly like-minded rabble-rousers, Tom Paine and Sam Adams, were actually some distance apart on several important points. Certainly they had different opinions about the nature of government. Paine based much of his philosophy on the fundamental assumption that "government, even in its best state, is but a necessary evil"; Adams considered it "an ordinance of Heaven, design'd by the all-benevolent Creator, for the general happiness of his rational creature, man." [40] Which one expressed more accurately the prevailing sentiment of the time? Was government a *good* institution for which men could thank wise Providence, or an *evil* one for which they could blame their own moral insufficiencies?

The answer is that Adams spoke for an overwhelming majority of colonial opinion, Paine for few men other than himself. A scattering of preachers like Judah Champion voiced much the same opinion as the opening pages of *Common Sense*,[41] but most thinkers, lay and clerical, rejected the notion that there was something intrinsically evil about government. The assumption that government was "this richest of temporal blessings to mankind"[42] generally proceeded from these other assumptions about its inherent nature: that it was natural, necessary, and derived.

The concept of government as a natural institution was the obvious corollary to the concept of man as a social and political animal. "Certain it is," wrote R. H. Lee, "that there is nothing more becoming to human nature than well-ordered government."[43] "Civil government is founded in the very nature of man, as a social being, and in the nature and constitution of things," stated Rev. John Tucker. "It is manifestly for the good of society."[44] Civil government, echoed John Adams, is "founded in nature and reason."[45] And James Otis, always something of a maverick, went so far as to say, "*Government* is . . . most evidently founded *on the necessities of our nature.* It is by no means an *arbitrary* thing, depending merely on *compact* or *human will* for its existence.*"[46] Even those writers who emphasized the importance of "compact or human will" in the formation of government agreed that men were impelled "to covenant each with the other" by an irresistible, higher force. Civil government, wrote Stephen Johnson, was "the dictate of reason, of nature, and the will of God."[47] Government was artificial only in the sense that men had some control over its structure and complete control over its personnel.

If government was good because it was natural, it was natural because it was necessary. James Otis expressed this sentiment in his *Rights of the British Colonies:*

> The *end* of government being the *good* of mankind, points out its great duties: It is above all things to provide for the security, the quiet, and happy enjoyment of life, liberty, and property. There is no one act which a government can have a *right* to make, that does not tend to the advancement of the security, tranquility and prosperity of the people. If life, liberty and property could be enjoyed in as great perfection in *solitude*, as in *society*, there would be no need of government. But the experience of ages has proved that such is the nature of man, a weak, imperfect being; that the valuable ends of life cannot be obtained without the union and assistance of many. Hence 'tis clear that men cannot live apart or independent of each other: In solitude men would perish; and yet they cannot live together without contests. These contests require some arbitrator to determine them. The necessity of a common, indifferent and impartial judge, makes all men seek one.[48]

Paine found government a necessary evil since "produced by our wickedness." Otis found it a necessary good since produced by our wants. The men of Massachusetts were inclined to agree with Otis. Said the General Court in 1776:

> The frailty of human nature, the wants of individuals, and the numerous dangers which surround them, through the course of life, have, in all ages, and in every country, impelled them to form societies and establish governments.[49]

Good government was something more than a punitive agency. Even if men should become angels, some political organization would be necessary to adjust, of course without compulsion, the complexity of human (or angelic) relations and to do for the people what they could not do as individuals or families. If colonial spokesmen had no vision of the welfare or insurance state, neither did they subscribe to the concept of government as "anarchy plus a street constable."

The men of the Revolution would have been quite unconvinced by the argument that it is a dangerous thing to consider government an inherently good, even divine, institution. Government, they would have answered, can be safely acknowledged a temporal blessing because, in terms of the power it wields, there is nothing inherent about it. Government is not an end in itself but the means to an end. Its authority is the free and revocable grant of the men who have promised conditionally to submit to it. Its organs, however ancient and august, are instruments that free men have built and free men can alter or even abolish. Government can be arbitrary, corrupt, oppressive, wicked—but not if men are conscious of its origin, purpose, proper limits, and source of authority. Indeed, tyranny is not government but an abuse of government. True government is a good, natural, necessary institution ordained by providence to serve man's higher earthly purposes. This was the firm belief of most Revolutionary thinkers:

Q. What is government?
A. Certain powers vested by society in public persons for the security, peace, and happiness of its members.
Q. What ought a society to do to secure a good government?
A. Any thing. The happiness of man, as an inhabitant of this world, depends intirely upon it.[50]

In conclusion to this section, we might note two facts about colonial discussions of society and government: first, that many writers who should have been more careful used these words interchangeably, thereby befogging the vital and acknowledged distinction between the two levels or stages of the community; second, that the colonists had no theory of the state in the modern sense. They occasionally used this word to denote society or government or the total community, but they did not conceive of the state as a third entity that embraced, yet stood apart from, the two natural types of human association. And this, of course, permitted them to argue that sovereignty remained fixed and absolutely unalienable in the people.

THE FORM OF GOVERNMENT: I

"The blessings of society," wrote John Adams to George Wythe, "depend entirely on the constitutions of government." [51] Government might be good and necessary, but like all other gifts of God and nature it was subject to abuse. The pages of history bore grim witness to the fact that government could be so far abused as to defeat rather than gratify the purpose of its institution. Wrote Phillips Payson:

> Much depends upon the mode and administration of civil government to complete the blessings of liberty; for although the best possible plan of government never can give an ignorant and vicious people the true enjoyment of liberty, yet a state may be enslaved though its inhabitants in general may be knowing, virtuous, and heroic. [52]

Government, if not corrupt, was corruptible. The business of "the divine science of politics" was to discover the form least likely to be corrupted and most likely to fulfill the accepted ends of the free political community. "We ought to consider," wrote John Adams,

> what is the end of government, before we determine which is the best form. Upon this point all speculative politicians will agree, that the happiness of society is the end of government, as all divines and moral philosophers will agree that the happiness of the individual is the end of man. From this principle it will follow, that the form of government which communicates ease, comfort, security, or, in one word, happiness, to the greatest number of persons, and in the greatest degree, is the best. [53]

Or as "Spartanus" stated the issue in the *New-Hampshire Gazette:*

> The important day is come, or near at hand, that America is to assume a form of government for herself. We should be very desirous to know what form is best.—And that surely is best which is most natural, easy, cheap, and which best secures the rights of the people. We should always keep in mind that great truth, viz. That the good of the people is the ultimate end of civil Government. [54]

To hit upon and help initiate this ideal form of government was the consuming passion of men like Adams in the years immediately before and after independence. After generations of slavish, uncritical praise of the English system of government, they were now, as if for the first time, forced to consider candidly the problem of political organization. For the most part, they seemed delighted with the opportunity thrust upon them. Said John Witherspoon:

> All the governments we have read of in former ages were settled by caprice or accident, by the influence of prevailing parties or particular persons, or prescribed by a conqueror. Important improvements indeed have been forced upon some constitutions by the spirit of daring men, supported by successful insurrections. But to see government in large and populous

countries settled from its foundation by deliberate counsel, and directed immediately to the public good of the present and future generations . . . is certainly altogether new.[55]

If Americans were not quite the free agents they fancied themselves, still they had more right than most men to boast:

> We have opportunity to form with some deliberation, with free choice, with good advantages for knowledge; we have opportunity to observe what has been right, and what wrong in other states, and to profit by them.[56]

Before we examine the constitutional theory of the Revolutionary period, we should call attention to the emotional context in which the Americans spun out their new plans of government. These two passages are representative of the spirit of the times:

> The affair now in view is the most important that ever was before America. In my opinion it is the most important that has been transacted in any nation for some centuries past. If our civil Government is well constructed, and well managed, America bids fair to be the most glorious state that has ever been on earth. We should now at the beginning lay the foundation right.[57]

> I cannot help cherishing a secret hope that God has destined America to form the last and best plan that can possibly exist, and that he will gradually carry those who have long been under the galling yoke of tyranny in every other quarter of the globe, into the bosom of perfect liberty and freedom in America. Were the great men of the present day, and all those who choose to interfere in public affairs, only to set before them the godlike pleasure of conferring the most lasting and complete state of happiness human nature is capable of, in a state of civil society, on millions yet unborn, and the eternal reward which must attend the doing so much good, I cannot help thinking but contracted views, partial interest, and party factions would sink under, and yield to considerations of so greatly superior a nature.[58]

This sense of a higher destiny, of acting for countless descendants and perhaps for all mankind, gave added dignity to the processes of constitution-making in the Revolutionary era. Generations yet unborn will rise up to honor these men and prove them to have been neither fools, braggarts, nor hypocrites for having exhorted one another:

> It is high time to attend in good earnest to the dictates of common sense, and to be collecting the materials and laying the plan for a more sound Constitution and perfect scheme of Government among ourselves, that will never wax old or decay, nor prove rotten and defective, as all others of human invention have done; but be so wise, permanent, and solid, as to stand in full vigour and glory as long as the sun and moon endureth, and afford to every individual in the present and in all future generations ample security and indemnification of his life, his liberty, and property. Then our peace will be as a river, and our righteousness as the waves of the sea.[59]

Historians have made much of the squabble between radicals and conservatives over legislative-executive relations and the suffrage in the first state constitutions, so much indeed that they have succeeded in concealing the broad agreement among Revolutionary thinkers over constitutional fundamentals. Rare indeed was the American writer who did not concur wholeheartedly with these propositions about the structure and functioning of government:

Whatever the form of government—and there is no one plan good for all men at all times—it should be designed to preserve the maximum liberty and equality of the persons under it.

In the words of "Democraticus," who wrote for a Virginia audience:

Political liberty will always be most perfect where the laws have derogated least from the original rights of men, the *rights to equality*, which is adverse to every species of subordination, besides that which arises from the difference of capacity, disposition, and virtue. It is this sense of equality which gives to every man a right to frame and execute his own laws, which alone can secure the observance of justice, and diffuse equal and substantial liberty to the people. . . . It is this principle of equality, this right, which is inherent in every member of the community, to give his own consent to the laws by which he is to be bound, which alone can inspire and preserve the virtue of its members, by placing them in a relation to the publick, and to their fellow citizens, which has a tendency to engage the heart and affections to both. Men love the community in which they are treated with justice, and in which they meet with considerations proportioned to the proofs they give of ability and good intentions. They love those with whom they live on terms of equality, and under a sense of common interests. It engages them in the exercise of their best talents and happiest dispositions, for the government and defence of their country are the best and noblest occupations of men. They lead to the exercise of the greatest virtues and most respectable talents, which is the greatest blessing that any institution can bestow.[60]

Equality in liberty was both more possible and necessary than equality in property. Government should not engage, said Samuel Adams, in "Utopian schemes of levelling." [61] Rather, wrote an anonymous citizen to the *Boston Gazette*, government must honor an obvious distinction between liberty and property:

Liberty and *Property* are not only join'd in common discourse, but are in their own natures so nearly ally'd, that we cannot be said to possess the one without the enjoyment of the other; and yet there is this distinction to be made between them: All men in their natural and primitive state had an equal right to *possessions*, but when mankind were increased and formed into civil communities, and the whole mass of *property* become unequally divided among them, according to every ones industry and merit, they made laws unanimously for securing each other in their respective acquisitions. Hence it came about, that all men have a right to whatever *property* they can acquire by the laws of a free country; and the principle on which this is founded, is the common good of mankind.

But *liberty*, the source and pillar of all true *property*, cannot be preserved in society while the members possess it unequally. It can no way exist but in its original and native capacity. All men are equally entitled to it. He who assumes more than his just share of *liberty* becomes a tyrant in proportion to what he assumes; and he who loses it becomes so many degrees a slave.[62]

Government should be designed to prevent some men from rising to tyranny and others falling to slavery. "Liberty, charming liberty," which included the right to pursue happiness, was the central object of the well-planned polity. Liberty was the paramount consideration of the individual, for he had submitted to government primarily to secure it. Liberty was the paramount consideration of the community, because it was "the parent of felicity, of every noble virtue, and even of every art and science." [63] "Liberty effects, and naturally produces Population, Riches, Magnanimity, Arts, Science and Learning,—Trade flows from the same Fountain," [64] wrote a gentleman in Connecticut. More than that, added "I. H." in the *Boston News-Letter*, liberty is "the cement of society, and the band of peace, love and unity." [65] In short, echoed a Pennsylvanian:

> I take the essential benefit of civil liberty, wheresoever and in whatever degree it is found, to be, its tendency to put in motion and encourage the exertion of all the human powers. It must therefore evidently improve the human mind, and bring with it, in highest perfection, all the advantages of the social state. It is the parent or the nurse of industry, opulence, knowledge, virtue, and heroism.[66]

The makers of constitutions were to keep this one object in view, if necessary to the exclusion of all others: to preserve as much liberty to each man and as much equality among men as were consistent with the need for a well-ordered society. In practice, of course, this left conservatives and radicals entirely free to haggle over the amount of inequality a well-ordered society demands.

Government should always be "a plain, simple, intelligible thing . . . quite comprehensible by common sense." [67]

Governments in the past had been made unnecessarily complex by elites or tyrants bent on enslaving the mass of the people. "Mysteries of law and government," wrote Samuel Cooke, were "made a cloak of unrighteousness." "Fidelity to the public," to this free and upright people, required that the new laws and constitutions "be as plain and explicit as possible." [68] It required, too, that "every unnecessary power [be] withheld" from government.[69] Although few thinkers except Paine went out of their way to make this point, most would have concurred in a Connecticut author's warning that "No business that can be done by the people themselves should ever be trusted to their Delegates." [70]

The most important step to take toward "plain, simple, intelligible" government was to adopt the only form "consonant to the feelings of the generous and brave Americans . . . a FREE republic." [71] The colonial experience, the events of 1765-1775, and such dramatic assaults on the hereditary system as Paine's *Common Sense* all contributed to the spirit of republicanism in the air in 1776. "Kings and nobles are artificial beings," wrote "Salus Populi" to "the People of NORTH AMERICA,"

> for whose emolument civil society was never intended, and notwithstanding they have had the good fortune to escape general censure from the world, yet I will boldly affirm that nine tenths of all the public calamities which ever befel mankind were brought on by their means. . . .
> Mankind never suffered so much during the existence of a republic, as they have suffered in the short reigns of many kings. A Harry VIII did more mischief to his subjects than any republic ever did to its members, notwithstanding that they were so ill constituted. But the true principles of republicanism are at present so well understood, and the mode of conducting such a government so simple and easy, and America so fit for its reception, that a dozen of wise heads and honest hearts might in one day form a plan for the United Colonies, which would as much excel any one now existing, as the British constitution does that of Caffreria.[72]

Republican government was as good as monarchical or aristocratic government was bad. Said Phillips Payson:

> The voice of reason and the voice of God both teach us that the great object or end of government is the public good. Nor is there less certainty in determining that a free and righteous government originates from the people, and is under their direction and control; and therefore a free, popular model of government—of the republican kind—may be judged the most friendly to the rights and liberties of the people, and the most conducive to the public welfare.[73]

By 1776 most American thinkers were quite ready to agree with John Adams that "there is no good government but what is republican." [74]

Government should be kept as near to the people as possible, chiefly through frequent elections and rotation-in-office.

"All political distinctions ought to be the gift of the free people at large," warned "Salus Populi," "and continually to revert to them at the end of the political year, to be renewed or otherwise, as they shall think proper." [75] Agreed, wrote an anonymous publicist to the *Pennsylvania Packet,* and, what is equally important, "A rotation of offices is one of the lifeguards of liberty." [76] Frequent elections meant, of course, annual elections, and all but one new state constitution made some provision for this method of preserving liberty and equality. Roughly half of them forbade indefinite reeligibility to the most important executive offices.[77] Most leading thinkers of the period had praise for this author's recipe for freedom:

> An annual, or frequent choice of Magistrates, who in a year, or after a few years, are again left upon a level with their neighbours, is most likely to prevent usurpation and tyranny, and most likely to secure the privileges of the people. If rulers know that they shall, in a short term of time be again out of power, and it may be liable to be called to an account for misconduct, it will guard them against maladministration.[78]

The concept of rulers as servants of the people must be central to all planning for constitutional government.

This common assumption found expression in the Virginia and Massachusetts Constitutions:

> All power is vested in, and consequently derived from, the people; magistrates are their trustees and servants, and at all times amenable to them.

> All power residing originally in the people, and being derived from them, the several magistrates and officers of government, vested with authority, whether legislative, executive, or judicial, are their substitutes and agents, and are at all times accountable to them.[79]

"Rulers are no more than attorneys, agents, and trustees, for the people," wrote John Adams, "and if the cause, the interest and trust, is insidiously betrayed, or wantonly trifled away, the people have a right to revoke the authority that they themselves have deputed, and to constitute abler and better agents, attorneys, and trustees." [80] The new state constitutions were full of provisions that expressed or guaranteed this belief.

Government must be constitutional, an empire of laws and not of men: The discretion and whim of all men in power must be reduced to the lowest level consistent with effective operation of the political machinery.

The rule of law demanded the existence of a written constitution, to be acknowledged and administered as law superior to the acts of the legislature, decrees of the judiciary, and ordinances of the executive. Only thus could liberty be secured against defections of weak rulers and designs of strong. Said Stephen Johnson to the Connecticut legislature:

> A good constitution of civil polity, by which, rulers of every rank and order from the highest to the lowest, hold all their powers and prerogatives, emoluments and honors; and the subjects, all their rights and liberties, privileges and immunities; is of very interesting importance to every free state; without which, all the rights and privileges of subjects, rest upon a very weak foundation, and are held by a very slippery and uncertain tenure, the will and caprice of rulers in power.[81]

Charles Turner expressed much the same idea to the Massachusetts legislature:

> All the wisdom, however, religion and publick spirit, which have generally existed, or can be expected soon to take place, among *the great men of the earth*, are by no means a sufficient security to the people, that the end of government will be honorably answered. Rulers are so prone to have, vastly at heart, certain worldly interests, inconsistent with the publick welfare, and the duty they owe to the community, that it is incumbent on the people (whose right it is to do this, on proper consideration, and everything else, respecting government, which they judge will be for the salvation and advantage of the whole) to fix on certain regulations, which if we please we may call a *constitution*, as the standing measure of the proceedings of government; so determining what powers they will invest their rulers with, and what privileges they will retain in their own hands.[82]

The written constitution was a major contribution of Revolutionary thinkers and doers—generally the same men—to the development of modern political thought and practice. In one sense, of course, they had no choice in the matter. The colonial heritage,[83] the recent frustrations of defending an unwritten constitution against parliamentary intrusion,[84] the withdrawal of viceregal power and consequent demand for new organs of government—all these factors made the Revolutionary constitutions an inevitable next step in the progress of political liberty.[85] Yet the men of this period deserve credit for insisting, at the very moment of revolution, upon the constructive principle "that PUBLIC HAPPINESS DEPENDS ON A VIRTUOUS AND UNSHAKEN ATTACHMENT TO A FREE CONSTITUTION." [86] Such popular attachment to a free constitution as higher and controlling law was justified by one, two, or all, of three assumptions: that the constitution was the command of the people, an original compact expressing their unalienable sovereignty; that it was the handiwork of the wisest men in the body politic; [87] that it was an earthly expression of the eternal principles of the law of nature.

Three corollaries of the written constitution are usually traced to or back through this decade of ferment: judicial review, the constitutional convention, and popular ratification. Actually, no one of them secured widespread acceptance until some years after 1776. James Otis's memorable harangue in the writs-of-assistance case (1761),[88] the action of a Virginia county court in declaring the Stamp Act unconstitutional,[89] and the general popularity of an American rather than English concept of unconstitutionality [90] were heralds of a truly original contribution to constitutional government, but no one was yet so bold or irritated as to assert that the judiciary could refuse to enforce the unconstitutional acts of a representative legislature. Most new state constitutions were written by the provincial legislatures, several of which had some sort of special permission to do this. John Adams and others in theory [91] and Massachusetts in fact (1779) acknowledged that a genuine constitution must be the work of a special convention elected by the people. Likewise, the first formal submission of a draft constitution to a vote of the people took place in Massachusetts in 1778. (And it should be added in passing that the people rejected it.) In general, however, popular election of members of the constitutional convention and popular ratification of their handiwork remained a hope of radical thinkers. Rev. Jonas Clarke of Lexington, a superior political mind, wrote this hope into some town resolutions:

> It appears to us that as all government originates from the people; and the great end of government is their peace, safety and happiness; so it is with the people at large, or where that is impracticable, by their Representatives freely and equally elected and empowered for that purpose, to form and agree on a Constitution of government, which being considered and approved by the body of the people, may be enacted, ratified and established.[92]

In May 1776 the townsmen of Pittsfield, for whom Rev. Thomas Allen served as penman, sent a long memorial to the Massachusetts legislature calling for a new and popular constitution. Several passages in this document merit quotation, for they express in earnest fashion the dominant spirit of the time concerning the need of a written constitution, as well as the steadily rising demand for popular participation:

We beg leave, therefore, to represent that we have always been persuaded that the people are the fountain of power; that, since the dissolution of the power of Great Britain over these Colonies, they have fallen into a state of nature.

That the first step to be taken by a people in such a state for the enjoyment or restoration of civil government among them is the formation of a fundamental constitution as the basis and ground-work of legislation. . . .

A representative body may form, but cannot impose said fundamental constitution upon a people, as they, being but servants of the people, cannot be greater than their masters, and must be responsible to them; that, if this fundamental constitution is above the whole legislature, the legislature certainly cannot make it; it must be the approbation of the majority which gives life and being to it; that said fundamental constitution has not been formed for this Province; the corner-stone is not yet laid, and whatever building is reared without a foundation must fall to ruins. . . .

What is the fundamental constitution of this Province? What are the inalienable rights of the people? the power of the rulers? how often to be elected by the people, &c.? Have any of these things been as yet ascertained? Let it not be said by future posterity, that, in this great, this noble, this glorious contest, we made no provision against tyranny among ourselves.

We beg leave to assure your Honors, that . . . *all is to us nothing* while the foundation is unfixed, the corner-stone of government unlaid. We have heard much of government being founded in compact: what compact has been formed as the foundation of government in this Province? We beg leave further to represent, that we have undergone many grievous oppressions in this county, and that now we wish a barrier might be set up against such oppressions, against which we can have no security long till the foundation of government be well established. . . .

Your petitioners, therefore, beg leave to request that this honorable body would form a fundamental constitution for this Province . . . and that said constitution be sent abroad for the approbation of the majority of the people of this Colony; that, in this way, we may emerge from a state of nature, and enjoy again the blessings of civil government.[98]

To this magnificent statement should be added Paine's prophetic burst of eloquence:

But where, say some, is the king of America? I'll tell you, friend, he reigns above, and doth not make havoc of mankind like the Royal Brute of Great Britain. Yet that we may not appear to be defective even in earthly honors, let a day be solemnly set apart for proclaiming the charter; let it be brought forth placed on the divine law, the Word of God; let a crown be placed thereon, by which the world may know, that so far as we approve of monarchy, that in America THE LAW IS KING. For as in absolute governments the king is law, so in free countries the law *ought* to BE king, and there ought to be no other. But lest any ill use should afterwards arise, let the crown at the conclusion of the ceremony be demolished, and scattered among the people whose right it is.[94]

Here, it would seem, in the teachings of a great radical, was the beginning of constitution worship among the North Americans!

THE FORM OF GOVERNMENT: II

No written constitution can be considered complete unless it embodies a specific declaration of rights.

Theophilus Parsons made this point repeatedly in his *Essex Result:*

> A bill of rights, clearly ascertaining and defining the rights of conscience, and that security of person and property, which every member in the State hath a right to expect from the supreme power thereof, ought to be settled and established, previous to the ratification of any constitution for the State.[95]

Rev. Jonas Clarke expressed the same thought for the people of Lexington:

> It appears to us that in emerging from a state of nature into a state of well-regulated society, mankind give up some of their natural rights in order that others of greater importance to their well-being, safety and happiness, both as societies and individuals, might be the better enjoyed, secured and defended. That a civil Constitution or form of government is of the nature of a most sacred covenant or contract entered into by the individuals which form the society, for which such Constitution or form of government is intended, whereby they mutually and solemnly engage to support and defend each other in the enjoyment of those rights which they mean to retain. That the main and great end of establishing any Constitution or form of government among a people or in society, is to maintain, secure and defend those natural rights inviolate. And, consequently, that it is of the highest importance, both to the public peace and utility, and to the safety and security of individuals, that said rights intended to be retained, at least those that are fundamental to the well-being of society and the liberty and safety of individuals, should be in the most explicit terms declared.[96]

The bill of rights was to be something more than a symbol or incantation. The plan and powers of government had to conform to the people's own statement of the rights they were retaining.[97] Maryland, Massachusetts, New Hampshire, North Carolina, Pennsylvania, Vermont, and Virginia all honored this dictate of political liberty in their Revolutionary constitutions. The speed with which a bill of rights emerged from the First Congress is evidence of the strength and persistence of this Revolutionary principle.

A representative legislature is essential to free government.

We have already noted the central place of the right of representation in Revolutionary theory. We need only recall the primary function of the representative assembly—to serve as instrument of consent through which the people tax and restrict themselves—to understand why it was the pivot in any and all schemes of government advanced for consideration in this period.[98] For centuries in England, for generations in the colonies, the legislature had been the popular organ of government. It had served the colonists well in the ceaseless campaign against imperial authority, and they had learned to look to it alone for some show of response to their hopes and convictions. Now, with the departure of the royal governor and his retinue, the provincial legislature was not only the essence but the whole of government. This was a condition distasteful, but not yet alarming, to many keen minds. The antics of some of the state legislatures in the first years of independence were to lead in time to the sentiment expressed in Jefferson's *Notes on Virginia*—that "173 despots would surely be as oppressive as one." [99] But in 1776, in theory as in fact, the legislature occupied a dominant position. It was assumed, of course, that American assemblies would observe the four intrinsic limits that Locke had placed upon all legislatures:

142. These are the bounds which the trust that is put in them by the society and the law of God and Nature have set to the legislative power of every commonwealth, in all forms of government. First: They are to govern by promulgated established laws, not to be varied in particular cases, but to have one rule for rich and poor, for the favourite at Court, and the countryman at plough. Secondly: These laws also ought to be designed for no other end ultimately but the good of the people. Thirdly: They must not raise taxes on the property of the people without the consent of the people given by themselves or their deputies. . . . Fourthly: Legislative neither must nor can transfer the power of making laws to anybody else, or place it anywhere but where the people have.[100]

The framers of several of the first state constitutions inserted provisions in their bills of rights and legislative articles to remind the assembly of these limits so essential to the conduct of government by consent.[101]

A representative legislature is essential to free government, but so, too, are the twin doctrines of the separation of powers and checks and balances. A few colonial writers swung violently in the direction of government by an unrestrained, one-house legislature.[102] A few others clung to a theory of balanced government based on different estates or interests.[103] But most thinkers took a position somewhere between these two extremes, acknowledging both the primacy of the legislature and the necessity for separation and balance. These passages reveal the trend of Revolutionary thinking about the separation of powers and balanced government:

John Adams, in a letter to R. H. Lee:

A legislative, an executive, and a judicial power comprehend the whole of what is meant and understood by government. It is by balancing each of these powers against the other two, that the efforts in human nature towards tyranny can alone be checked and restrained, and any degree of freedom preserved in the constitution.[104]

Article 30 of the Massachusetts Declaration of Rights:

In the government of this commonwealth, the legislative department shall never exercise the executive and judicial powers, or either of them; the executive shall never exercise the legislative and judicial powers, or either of them; the judicial shall never exercise the legislative and executive powers, or either of them, to the end it may be a government of laws and not of men.[105]

Rev. Samuel Cooke to the Massachusetts legislature:

In a civil state, that form is most eligible which is best adapted to promote the ends of government—the benefit of the community. Reason and experience teach that a mixed government is most conducive to this end. In the present imperfect state, the whole power cannot with safety be entrusted with a single person; nor with many, acting jointly in the same public capacity. Various branches of power, concentring in the community from which they originally derive their authority, are a mutual check to each other in their several departments, and jointly secure the common interest. This may indeed, in some instances, retard the operations of government, but will add dignity to its deliberate counsels and weight to its dictates.[106]

"C. X." in *Dunlap's Maryland Gazette:*

What is it that constitutes despotism, but the assemblage and union of the legislative, executive, and judicial functions, in the same person, or persons? [107]

Theophilus Parsons, in the *Essex Result:*

If the legislative and judicial powers are united, the maker of the law will also interpret it; and the law may then speak a language, dictated by the whims, the caprice, or the prejudice of the judge, with impunity to him— And what people are so unhappy as those, whose laws are uncertain. . . .

Should the executive and legislative powers be united, mischiefs the most terrible would follow. The executive would enact those laws it pleased to execute, and no others—The judicial power would be set aside as inconvenient and tardy— The security and protection of the subject would be a shadow— The executive power would make itself absolute, and the government end in a tyranny. . . .

Should the executive and judicial powers be united, the subject would then have no permanent security of his person and property. The executive power would interpret the laws and bend them to his will; and, as he is the judge, he may leap over them by artful construction, and gratify, with impunity, the most rapacious passions. . . . Indeed the dependence of any of these powers upon either of the others, which in all states has always been attempted by one or the other of them, has so often been productive of such calamities, and of the shedding of such oceans of blood, that the page of history seems to be one continued tale of human wretchedness.[108]

Here, in the words of framers and critics of the first constitutions, are the major considerations that impelled them to choose divided and balanced government. Their central object, of course, was human liberty. Whatever ends mixed government had served in the past, such as to represent different estates or interests in the community, its prime purpose now was to divide the totality of governmental power into separate portions, to be exercised by separate organs under a system of restraints held in delicate balance. Only one estate or interest could be recognized in a free constitution—that of all the people voluntarily associated in the commonwealth.[109] It was their power that each branch exercised, their interest that each represented. The separation of powers was something of a retreat from the principle that government should be "a plain, simple, intelligible thing." A unified government would certainly be easier to run and understand. Yet the advantages to be gained from separation and balance far outweighed those to be gained from union.[110] Liberty rather than authority, protection rather than power, delay rather than efficiency were the concern of these constitution-makers. Unrestrained government had led to their distress, and unrestrained government, even by their own representatives, was not to be countenanced again. Once again the conservative Revolutionists drew upon the Anglo-American past in a selective way,[111] and once again the criterion of choice was their passion for liberty. Whatever the difficulties of balanced government, such a system was "essential to Liberty." [112]

Government in a free state is properly the concern of all those who have "a common interest with, and an attachment to the community." [113] The right to vote, as well as to hold office, should be limited to men who have an evident "stake-in-society"—first, because they alone can make competent, responsible, uncorrupted judgments; second, because they alone have a clear right to consent to laws regulating or restricting the use of property.

The appeal of the principle of natural equality was not strong enough at this time to overcome inherited traditions and prejudices. Few voices were raised for universal suffrage, even universal white male suffrage. Only in leveling Vermont, as portent of things to come, was the traditional property qualification abandoned without reserve.[114] The men who wrote the other state constitutions restricted political participation to those who held property or paid taxes. In so doing, they remained true to a fundamental political principle of the colonial period, a principle expressed by Nathaniel Ames in his almanac for 1774: "Law in a free country is or ought to be the determination of those who have property in land." [115] By this time, of course, the growth of trade and cities had brought political recognition to other types of property. Out of a wide variety of qualifications for suffrage in the new constitutions, these may be noted as representative of different shades of emphasis within the area of general agreement: in conservative South Carolina, "a freehold at least of fifty acres of land, or a town lot," or equivalent property; in conservative Maryland, "real or personal property above the value of five hundred pounds current money"; in middle-of-the-road Massachusetts, "a freehold estate" with an "annual income of three pounds, or any estate of the value of sixty pounds"; in liberal Pennsylvania, mere payment of "public taxes." [116] In the more conservative states these provisions were backed up by other provisions limiting office-holding to men of property. The oligarchs of South Carolina pushed this practice to the limit in setting this qualification for governor or councilor: "a settled plantation or free-hold . . . of the value of at least ten thousand pounds currency, clear of debt." [117]

It is surprising how small an output of theory seemed necessary to justify this practice. One of the few men to face this question squarely was Theophilus Parsons, who answered it thus in the *Essex Result:*

> The only objects of legislation . . . are the person and property of the individuals which compose the state. If the law affects only the persons of the members, the consent of a majority of any members is sufficient. If the law affects the property only, the consent of those who hold a majority of the property is enough. If it affects, (as it will very frequently, if not always,) both the person and property, the consent of a majority of the members, and of those members also who hold a majority of the property, is necessary. If the consent of the latter is not obtained, their interest is taken from them against their consent, and their boasted security of property is vanished. Those who make the law, in this case give and grant what is not theirs. . . .
>
> If each member, without regard to his property, has equal influence in legislation with any other, it follows, that some members enjoy greater benefits and powers in legislation than others, when these benefits and powers are compared with the rights parted with to purchase them. For the property-holder parts with the controul over his person, as well as he who hath no property, and the former also parts with the controul over his property, of which the latter is destitute. Therefore to constitute a perfect law in a free state, affecting the persons and property of the members, it is necessary that the law be for the good of the whole, which is to be determined by a majority of the members, and that majority should include those, who possess a major part of the property in the state.[118]

Actually, Parsons was more advanced than most men in his ideas about representation of persons. So, too, was Joseph Hawley, who argued for the town of Northampton that the upper house should represent property and the lower house persons.[119] Most writers simply remained silent on this question, for the stake-in-society principle seemed too essential a part of ordered liberty to require justification or merit indignation. It was left to the next two generations to search this problem exhaustively. The men of the Revolution were sure that this was one of those instances in which natural equality should give way to the need for a well-ordered society. Property qualifications for office-holding were justified on the same general principle: the importance of a citizenry attached by more than accident of birth to the common weal. Fifty acres of land or an income of three pounds were evidence of such attachment. The plea of a New Hampshire radical—"Let it not be said in future generations that money was made by the founders of the American States an essential qualification in the rulers of a free people" [120]—was considered premature and demagogic. Any man worth his salt could get fifty acres or earn three pounds.

Parsons was also one of the few men to consider the problem of women's suffrage, which he disposed of neatly in this solemn passage:

> Women what age soever they are of, are . . . considered as not having a sufficient acquired discretion; not from a deficiency in their mental powers, but from the natural tendency and delicacy of their minds, their retired mode of life, and various domestic duties. These concurring, prevent that promiscuous intercourse with the world, which is necessary to qualify them for electors.[121]

Hawley agreed that Parsons had handled this problem "very sensibly, as well as genteely," [122] all of which proves that words are what each generation makes them.

Within the broad area of patriot consensus we have already noted several sharp differences of opinion. We may conclude this section with an ordered review of the disputes that enlivened the writing of the new state constitutions. For the most part, these disputes were political rather than theoretical in nature and are therefore not properly the concern of this discussion. Conservatives and radicals who struggled for supremacy in states like Pennsylvania and Maryland agreed with few exceptions on such fundamental points as republicanism, a strong legislature, declarations of rights, the separation of powers, and property qualifications. The differences between them, irreconcilable as they must have seemed at the time, were the differences of men who spoke the same political language:

First, conservatives emphasized divided and balanced government, radicals legislative dominance. All insisted on an executive branch separate from the legislature, but fell out over questions of tenure, number, independence, qualifications, powers, and mode of election. Conservatives tended to favor the type of executive outlined in the New York Constitution of 1777 and the Massachusetts Constitution of 1780. Radicals showed what they had in mind in the Pennsylvania, North Carolina, and New Hampshire constitutions. The manner in which selective emphasis on different points in a common and not wholly symmetrical political theory can lead to a bitter clash of opinions was also illustrated in the problem of the judiciary. Few radicals could take pleasure in John Adams's prescription for an independent judiciary: appointment by governor and council, tenure "for life," salaries "ascertained and established by law." [123]

Second, conservatives considered the doctrine of popular sovereignty a useful notion that was not to be applied too literally in concrete situations. Radicals were inclined to accept popular sovereignty at face value. A consistent radical thinker, a man who was of course not easy to find, favored male taxpayer suffrage, popular participation in framing and ratifying constitutions, no property qualifications for office-holding, a popularly elected governor (if to be elected by a source other than the legislature),[124] and annual elections for all offices.[125] A consistent conservative, perhaps a little easier to unearth, pushed for high property qualifications for voting,[126] even higher qualifications for office-holding, appointments to office, and longer terms.

Finally, the whole emphasis of the conservative was on government more complicated, delaying, "high-toned" than that simple scheme fixed in the minds of democrats like Franklin and Paine. The healthy difference of opinion between unicameralists and bicameralists is perhaps the most instructive case in point. To the argument of the former that the scheme of two houses was "a feudal relict," "a source of trouble," and "a step towards arbitrary power," [127] the advocates of a two-chambered legislature replied:

> But the legislative power must not be trusted with one assembly. A single assembly is frequently influenced by the vices, follies, passions, and prejudices of an individual. It is liable to be avaricious, and to exempt itself from the burdens it lays upon it's constituents. It is subject to ambition, and after a series of years, will be prompted to vote itself perpetual. . . .
> The result of a single assembly will be hasty and indigested, and their judgments frequently absurd and inconsistent. There must be a second body to revise with coolness and wisdom, and to controul with firmness, independent upon the first, either for their creation, or existence. Yet the first must retain a right to a similar revision and controul over the second.[128]

Supporters of unicameralism achieved their only constitutional successes in Pennsylvania, Georgia, and Vermont, and many of them lived to regret it.

The struggle for political supremacy in each of the new states was accompanied by violent literary debate over the structure, authority, and basis of government. The distance between conservative and radical in Pennsylvania or South Carolina, or between Carter Braxton's *Address to the Convention . . . of Virginia* and the anonymous New Hampshire tract *The People the Best Governors*,[129] was enormous, yet it was the distance between men who stood at opposite edges of a broad, unbroken plateau. Each could look back over his shoulder at the great mass of patriots, perhaps nine in ten of whom were in accord on fundamentals of constitutional theory. At the center of the plateau and of the people who stood upon it was John Adams of Massachusetts. His little pamphlet *Thoughts on Government*, published in Philadelphia and Boston in 1776, was the most lucid, moderate, representative statement of the theory of ordered liberty out of which the best of the new constitutions arose.[130] And its message about the structure of government was simply this: The great ends of the political community, the liberty and happiness of the men who have created it, will be most successfully answered by government that is limited, divided, balanced, representative, republican, responsible, and constitutional.

We must not overstate the success or originality of the Revolutionary constitutions. Several of them created governments that oscillated violently between anarchy and tyranny; others were little better than a mask for the oligarchy of the "eastern bashaws." The failure of such innovations as Pennsylvania's fantastic Council of Censors leads straight to the judgment that the more faithfully the patriots modeled their new governments on colonial precedents, the more success they achieved as constitution-makers.[131] Yet this period of trial-and-error, which was also, be it remembered, a period of war and desolation, was a necessary prelude to the triumph of republican government under Washington, Adams, and Jefferson. As the second of these men wrote of the state constitutions:

> The United States of America have exhibited, perhaps, the first example of governments erected on the simple principles of nature; and if men are now sufficiently enlightened to disabuse themselves of artifice, imposture, hypocrisy, and superstition, they will consider this event as an era in their history. . . . Thirteen governments . . . founded on the natural authority of the people alone, without a pretence of miracle or mystery, and which are destined to spread over the northern part of that whole quarter of the globe, are a great point gained in favor of the rights of mankind. The experiment is made, and has completely succeeded; it can no longer be called in question, whether authority in magistrates and obedience of citizens can be grounded on reason, morality, and the Christian religion, without the monkery of priests, or the knavery of politicians.[132]

THE MORAL BASIS OF GOVERNMENT

However angrily they might argue over points of constitutional structure, colonial theorists agreed unanimously that it would take more than a perfect plan of government to preserve ordered liberty. Something else was needed, some moral principle diffused among the people to strengthen the urge to peaceful obedience and hold the community on an even keel. The wisest of political philosophers had spoken of three possibilities: fear, honor, virtue. Which were Americans to choose?

The answer, of course, was virtue, for as the author of *The People the Best Governors* observed, "Fear is the principle of a despotic, honour of a kingly, and virtue is the principle of a republican government." [133] "The spirit of a free republican constitution, or the moving power which should give it action," wrote Theophilus Parsons at the end of his great *Essex Result*, "ought to be political virtue, patriotism, and a just regard to the natural rights of mankind." [134] And Samuel Adams spoke for all American thinkers when he reminded James Warren:

> We may look up to Armies for our Defence, but Virtue is our best Security. It is not possible that any State shd long remain free, where Virtue is not supremely honord.[135]

"Liberty cannot be preserved," added another Bostonian, "if the manners of the people are corrupted, nor absolute monarchy introduced, where they are sincere." [136] Free government rested on a definite moral basis: a virtuous people. Conversely, the decay of a people's morals signaled the end of liberty and happiness.[137] On no point in the whole range of political theory were the colonists more thoroughly in accord. Free government, and thus personal liberty, was in large part a problem in practical ethics.

Revolutionary thinkers drew heavily on their colonial heritage in proclaiming virtue the essence of freedom. The decade of crisis brought new popularity to the cult of virtue. All the familiar techniques that earlier colonists had borrowed from England and converted to their purposes were revived for the emergency.[138] The appeal to ancient Rome for republican inspiration was especially favored. The nicest compliment Samuel Adams could pay Joseph Hawley was to say that he had "as much of the stern Virtue and Spirit of a Roman Censor as any Gentleman I ever conversed with." [139] John Dickinson had spoken "with Attick Eloquence and Roman Spirit"; the dead of Concord were "like the Romans of old"; the way to exhort the Americans was to "stir up all that's Roman in them." [140] The Roman example worked both ways: From the decline of the republic Americans could learn the fate of free states that succumb to luxury.[141] The colonists' own ancestors proved equally useful. Thousands of farmers read in Nathaniel Ames's almanac for 1769:

> When our Forefathers firm maintain'd the cause
> Of true Religion, Liberty and Laws,
> Disdaining down the golden Stream to glide,
> But bravely stem'd Corruptions rapid Tide,
> Shall we, by Indolence, supinely doom
> To Sweat and Toil the Nations yet to come? [142]

The praise of virtue and dispraise of corruption served two very practical purposes in the pre-Revolutionary decade: to mobilize public opinion as sanction for various extra-legal associations and governments, and to tear men loose from their traditional deference to all things British. Most of the ceaseless theorizing about "the fatal effects of luxury to a free state" was directed at the mother country. This was especially true in the last months before independence, when radicals began to argue that the "Effeminacy, Luxury, and Corruption, which extend to all Orders of Men" in England would poison the youthful body of America unless it were to cut short its dependence.[143] "Americans!" exclaimed a writer in March 1776,

> Remember the long, habitual, base venality of *British* Parliaments.
> Remember the corrupt, putrefied state of that nation, and the virtuous, sound, healthy, state of your own young constitution.
> Remember the tyranny of *Mezentius,* who bound living men face to face with dead ones, and the effect of it.[144]

"Caractacus" wrote to the *Pennsylvania Packet:*

> We thrived upon her wholesome milk during our infancy. She then enjoyed a sound constitution. I will not say that it is high time we should be taken from her breasts, but I will say, that she has played the harlot in her old age, and that if we continue to press them too closely we shall extract nothing from them but disease and death.[145]

To a British officer's sneer that "the People of America are at least an hundred Years behind the old Countries in Refinement," "An American" replied in the New London *Connecticut Gazette:*

As to Humanity, Temperance, Chastity, Justice, a Veneration for the Rights of Mankind, and every Moral Virtue, they are an hundred years behind us.[146]

This, of course, was why Americans could launch a republic with some hope of success, for it was the one form of government "whose principle and foundation is virtue." [147]

In the process of exhorting one another to be brave, frugal, and honest, and of damning England as "that degen'rate land," [148] American writers worked out a well-rounded theory of the ethical basis of free government. In particular, they identified the essential public virtues, described the contrasting political fates of good men and bad, and recommended techniques for promoting virtue and discouraging vice.

In addition to approving all recognized Christian, Roman, and English virtues, colonial theorists singled out several attitudes or traits of special consequence for a free republic: first, the willingness to act morally without compulsion, to obey the laws of nature as interpreted by reason and the laws of man as established in consent; [149] second, the love of liberty, the desire for the adventure and sacrifices of free government rather than the false security of tyranny; [150] third, public spirit and patriotism, "a disinterested attachment to the publick good, exclusive and independent of all private and selfish interest"; [151] fourth, official incorruptibility, a state of virtue saluted by Jefferson in the *Summary View* when he reminded George III that "the whole art of government consists in the art of being honest"; [152] and fifth, industry and frugality, hard work and plain living, the only path to personal liberty and national independence.[153] Special attention was devoted to the fifth of these qualities, for industry and frugality were essential to the success of America's program of economic resistance. The uproar over industry and frugality, private no less than public virtues, reached such a pitch in New England as to call forth this reminder from "A Freeholder":

Whilst Frugality and Industry are strongly recommended at this Juncture of Time, I think Cleanliness in our public Ways or Streets may not be an Object unworthy of our particular Attention.[154]

Whether cleanliness, too, was essential to liberty was never made clear in Revolutionary literature, but the cultivation of these great public virtues—moral action without compulsion, love of liberty, public spirit, incorruptibility, and industry and frugality—was considered the first duty of a free people. Men who displayed these qualities were the raw materials of liberty. Without such men, in low places as well as high, free government could not possibly exist.

The fruits of virtue, for nations as well as men, were liberty, prosperity, and happiness; the fruits of corruption and luxury were tyranny, poverty, and misery. "The peculiar blessings of heaven," said Rev. Thomas Coombe, "do indeed seem generally to be the reward of DETERMINED VIRTUE in a people." [155] "And as too great authority intoxicates and poisons Kings,"

warned Nathaniel Ames, "so luxury poisons a whole nation." [156] True, echoed
Rev. Phillips Payson, and the upshot is this:

> The baneful effects of exorbitant wealth, the lust of power, and other evil
> passions, are so inimical to a free, righteous government, and find such an
> easy access to the human mind, that it is difficult, if possible, to keep up the
> spirit of good government.[157]

How to encourage virtue and thus "keep up the spirit of good government"? To this key question of political liberty the colonial spokesmen
replied: hortatory religion, sound education, honest government, and a
simple economy.

The deep strain of piety in the philosophy of American liberty is evident
in the appeal of the Declaration of Independence to "Nature's God," the
"Creator," and "the Supreme Judge of the World." Few thinking laymen,
whether believers like Samuel Adams or skeptics like Franklin, ever doubted
the indispensability of organized religion in the preservation of public and
private morality. The former wrote to his friend John Scollay:

> I fully agree in Opinion with a very celebrated Author, that "Freedom or
> Slavery will prevail in a (City or) Country according as the Disposition &
> Manners of the People render them fit for the one or the other"; and I have
> long been convinced that our Enemies have made it an Object, to eradicate
> from the Minds of the People in general a Sense of true Religion & Virtue,
> in hopes thereby the more easily to carry their Point of enslaving them.
> Indeed my Friend, this is a Subject so important in my Mind, that I know
> not how to leave it. Revelation assures us that "Righteousness exalteth a
> Nation"—Communities are dealt with in this World by the wise and just
> Ruler of the Universe. He rewards or punishes them according to their gen-
> eral Character. The diminution of publick Virtue is usually attended with
> that of publick Happiness, and the publick Liberty will not long survive the
> total Extinction of Morals.[158]

Patriot preachers, of course, found this a favorite theme. The practice
of the Christian religion was as essential to virtue as was virtue to freedom.
"Survey the globe," urged Rev. John Joachim Zubly, "and you will find
that liberty has taken its seat only in Christendom, and that the highest
degree of freedom is pleaded for and enjoyed by such as make profession of
the gospel." [159] Rev. Phillips Payson put the case for religion to the Massachusetts legislature in these blunt words:

> The importance of religion to civil society and government is great in-
> deed, as it keeps alive the best sense of moral obligation, a matter of such
> extensive utility, especially in respect to an oath, which is one of the prin-
> cipal instruments of government. The fear and reverence of God, and the
> terrors of eternity, are the most powerful restraints upon the minds of men;
> and hence it is of special importance in a free government, the spirit of
> which being always friendly to the sacred rights of conscience, it will hold
> up the gospel as the great rule of faith and practice. . . . The thoughtful
> and wise among us trust that our civil fathers, from a regard to gospel wor-

ship and the constitution of these churches, will carefully preserve them, and at all times guard against every innovation that might tend to overset the public worship of God, though such innovations may be urged from the most foaming zeal. . . . Let the restraints of religion once be broken down . . . and we might well defy all human wisdom and power to support and preserve order and government in the state. Human conduct and character can never be better formed than upon the principles of our holy religion; they give the justest sense, the most adequate views, of the duties between rulers and people.[160]

In short, religion helped put the order in ordered liberty, especially by emphasizing the dependence of public morality on private virtue.[161] The Massachusetts Convention of 1779 responded to this sort of exhortation by inserting these words in the Declaration of Rights:

As the happiness of a people, and the good order and preservation of a civil government, essentially depend upon piety, religion, and morality; and as these cannot be generally diffused through a community, but by the institution of the public worship of GOD, and of public instruction in piety, religion, and morality—therefore, to promote their happiness, and to secure the good order and preservation of their government, the people of this commonwealth have a right to invest their legislature with power to authorize and require, and the legislature shall, from time to time, authorize and require the several towns, parishes, precincts, and other bodies politic or religious societies, to make suitable provision, at their own expense, for the institution of the public worship of God, and for the support and maintenance of public Protestant teachers of piety, religion, and morality, in all cases where such provision shall not be made voluntarily.[162]

The doctrine of religious necessity had not yet given way to the doctrine of full religious liberty.

The second means of promoting virtue was public and private education. Like their colonial forebears, the men of the Revolution considered the inculcation of morality one of the three or four basic purposes of all instruments of education. Said Rev. Simeon Howard:

Liberty and learning are so friendly to each other, and so naturally thrive and flourish together, that we may justly expect that the guardians of the former will not neglect the latter. The good education of children is a matter of great importance to the commonwealth. Youth is the time to plant the mind with the principles of virtue, truth and honor, the love of liberty and of their country, and to furnish it with all useful knowledge; and though in this business much depends upon parents, guardians, and masters, yet it is incumbent upon the government to make provision for schools and all suitable means of instruction.[163]

Natural law and virtue were closely identified in the Revolutionary mind. Since God and nature told men not only what they had a right to do, but what it was right for them to do, the practice of virtue was simply obedience to natural law. It was the business of educators and ministers to instruct their charges that the fairest right of all was to do what was right, that true liberty was the liberty to follow God's plan for human happiness. John Winthrop had expressed exactly the same idea in defense of theocratic oligarchy, but John Winthrop's God had long since mellowed.

We have already quoted John Adams's hope that colleges would be "instruments of impressing on the tender mind, and of spreading and distributing far and wide, the ideas of right and the sensations of freedom."[164] Fourteen years later he drafted this clause of the Massachusetts Constitution of 1780:

> Wisdom and knowledge, as well as virtue, diffused generally among the body of the people, being necessary for the preservation of their rights and liberties, and as these depend on spreading the opportunities and advantages of education in the various parts of the country, and among the different orders of the people, it shall be the duty of legislators and magistrates, in all future periods of this commonwealth, to cherish the interests of literature and the sciences, and all seminaries of them; especially the university at Cambridge, public schools and grammar schools in the towns; to encourage private societies and public institutions, rewards and immunities for the promotion of agriculture, arts, sciences, commerce, trades, manufactures, and a natural history of the country; to countenance and inculcate the principles of humanity and general benevolence, public and private charity, industry and frugality, honesty and punctuality in their dealings, sincerity, good humor, and all social affections and generous sentiments among the people.[165]

The two passages just quoted from the Massachusetts Constitution indicate something of the importance of government as a promoter of virtue. Not only did it nourish morality indirectly by encouraging and protecting, and perhaps supporting, the instruments of religion and education, but it was expected to make a number of direct contributions: by passing sumptuary laws "to discourage prodigality and extravagance, vain and expensive amusements and fantastic foppery, and to encourage the opposite virtues";[166] by making proclamations from time to time of days "of public humiliation, fasting and prayer";[167] and by itself operating at the highest level of justice, virtue, and incorruptibility. Preachers never tired of exhorting legislators and judges to be men of spotless integrity in both public and private dealings.[168] Orators never tired of reminding the public that it should look for virtue before all other qualities in selecting candidates for public office.[169]

Finally, one influential group of colonial theorists asserted that the virtues necessary to maintain free government were more likely to flourish in an agrarian than in a manufacturing or commercial economy. "Would you extinguish luxury?" asked a South Carolinian. "Give a singular protection to agriculture, which engages men to live in temperance and frugality."[170] A Connecticut gentleman quoted Pitt on the importance to freedom of "the proprietors, and tillers of the ground—men who have a permanent, natural right in the place—and who from being nursed in the bosom of cultivation, form strong and honorable attachments to their country."[171] And Josiah Quincy, jr., saluted "the FREEHOLDERS and YEOMANRY of my country . . . the LANDED INTEREST" as "the virtue, strength, and fortitude" of the state.[172]

The strong agrarian bias of Jeffersonian democracy had roots in the colonial and Revolutionary past.

Colonial writers stressed the interdependence of virtue and each of these forces. Just as religion, education, government, and agriculture could raise the level of public and private morality, so morality could strengthen each of these great human undertakings. This was especially true of morality and government. Virtue fed liberty, liberty fed virtue. More to the point, wrote John Adams, vice brought tyranny, which in turn brought more vice:

> Obsta principiis, nip the shoots of arbitrary power in the bud, is the only maxim which can ever preserve the liberties of any people. When the people give way, their deceivers, betrayers, and destroyers press upon them so fast, that there is no resisting afterwards. The nature of the encroachment upon the American constitution is such, as to grow every day more and more encroaching. Like a cancer, it eats faster and faster every hour. The revenue creates pensioners, and the pensioners urge for more revenue. The people grow less steady, spirited, and virtuous, the seekers more numerous and more corrupt, and every day increases the circles of their dependents and expect- ants, until virtue, integrity, public spirit, simplicity, and frugality, become the objects of ridicule and scorn, and vanity, luxury, foppery, selfishness, meanness, and downright venality swallow up the whole society.[173]

The business of political philosophers is to discover the virtues that lead to free government and the form of government that leads men to virtue.[174] In fact, said Americans, expressing an opinion more than two thousand years old, that form of government is best which produces the greatest number of good, free, happy men.[175] The colonies had enough virtue to be republics,[176] and as republics they could look forward to an increase in virtue. Said David Ramsay on the second anniversary of independence:

> Our present form of government is every way preferable to the royal one we have lately renounced. It is much more favorable to purity of morals, and better calculated to promote all our important interests. Honesty, plain- dealing, and simple manners, were never made the patterns of courtly be- havior. Artificial manners always prevail in kingly governments; and royal courts are reservoirs, from whence insincerity, hypocrisy, dissimulation, pride, luxury, and extravagance, deluge and overwhelm the body of the people. On the other hand, republics are favorable to truth, sincerity, fru- gality, industry, and simplicity of manners. Equality, the life and soul of commonwealth, cuts off all pretensions to preferment, but those which arise from extraordinary merit.[177]

Whether this youthful, virtuous people would lose its virtue with its youth and its freedom with its virtue was a question much debated by colonial writers. Young John Adams could write:

> If ever an infant country deserved to be cherished it is America. If ever any people merited honor and happiness they are her inhabitants. They are a people whom no character can flatter or transmit in any expressions equal

to their merit and virtue; with the high sentiments of Romans, in the most prosperous and virtuous times of that commonwealth, they have the tender feelings of humanity and the noble benevolence of Christians; they have the most habitual, radical sense of liberty, and the highest reverence for virtue; they are descended from a race of heroes, who, placing their confidence in Providence alone, set the seas and skies, monsters and savages, tyrants and devils, at defiance for the sake of religion and liberty.[178]

But young Theophilus Parsons could ask:

The most virtuous states have become vicious. The morals of all people, in all ages, have been shockingly corrupted. . . . Shall we alone boast an exemption from the general fate of mankind? Are our private and political virtues to be transmitted untainted from generation to generation, through a course of ages? [179]

Two things were certain: First, the end of virtue and liberty would come by easy stages rather than in one grand cataclysm. "History does not more clearly point out any fact than this," warned Richard Henry Lee, "that nations which have lapsed from liberty, to a state of slavish subjection, have been brought to this unhappy condition, by gradual paces." [180] Eternal vigilance was the price of virtue as well as liberty. Second, should Americans sink from virtue and liberty to vice and slavery, they would have only themselves to blame. It was clearly in their power to build and preserve a free republic. Rev. Samuel Webster of Salisbury, delivering the Massachusetts election sermon for 1777, laid down eleven commandments for a people determined to be free:

1. Let the people by all means encourage *schools* and *colleges*, and all the means of *learning* and *knowledge*, if they would guard against *slavery*. For a *wise*, a *knowing* and a *learned* people, are the least likely of any in the world to be enslaved.

2. Let them do all in their power to *suppress* vice and *promote religion* and *virtue*. For, besides their *natural* efficacy, I am persuaded no people were ever yet given up by God to *slavery*, till they had first given themselves up to *wickedness*.

3. Let only men of *integrity* be entrusted by you with any *power*. I think power is much safer in their hands than in men of *greater abilities*, but who are wanting in this essential point.

4. Let not *too much power* be trusted in the hands of any. It may hurt them, and then they may hurt the public. Or if it seem necessary in some critical time (like the present) to lodge great power in some *hand* or hands, let it be for a *limited time*, and the power renewed *annually*, if there is occasion.

5. Let elections of the *Legislators* be *frequent;* and let *bribery* and *corruption* be guarded against to the utmost. Methinks, those who are guilty of these should be forever rendered incapable of any place of *power* or *trust;* and this by a fundamental law of the constitution.

6. Let the *militia* be kept under the best regulation, and be made *respectable*. This will be a great security a great many ways.

7. Let *standing armies* be only for *necessity* and for a *limited time.* For, when corrupted, they have been the ruin of many a country's *liberty.*

8. Let these *armies* never be put under the absolute power of any magistrate in time of peace, so as to act in any *cause*, till that *cause* is approved by the *Senate* and *people.*

9. Let *monopolies* and all *kinds* and degrees of *oppression* be carefully guarded against. They are dangerous to the *peace* of a *people*, and they are dangerous to their *liberties!* I am mistaken if the present time does not prove it.

10. Let a *careful watch* be kept, and if any is found *grossly* and *notoriously* exceeding the *limits* of his power, methinks, it should be a standing invariable rule never to trust him with any power more.

Finally, let the *powers* and *prerogatives* of the *rulers* and the *rights* and *priviledges* of the people, be determined with as much precision as possible, that all may know their *limits*. And where there is any dispute, *let nothing be done*, till it is settled by the people, who are the fountain of power.[181]

"A STUMBLING-BLOCK TO . . . TYRANNY AND OPPRESSION"

Were we to judge even the most lucid and subtle of Revolutionary thinkers by standards usually applied to such as Aristotle, Hobbes, or Hegel, we should have to write a rather savage critique of the principles, organization, and mode of expression of their political theory. Not only were they guilty of all the sins against logic, history, and psychology committed by the long line of philosophers dedicated to natural law and the compact, but they were open to reproach on other counts. Certainly it would not be difficult to make a case for each of these criticisms of the Revolutionary school: Mediocrity—it failed to produce, at least during the Revolution itself, a single thinker or book worthy of universal attention. Superficiality—it refused to probe more than a few inches beneath the surface of such problems as obligation and the origin of government. Lack of originality—it accepted almost without reservation the most universal of political theories and added few refinements or doctrines of its own. Confusion—it answered the hard question, Is government natural or mechanistic in origin? by insisting that it was both. Hypocrisy—out of the mouths of slave-holders and slave-traders the world heard the passionate scriptures of natural justice and equality.

Yet how damning are these criticisms? Are all schools of political thought to be judged mediocre and superficial if they cannot produce an Aristotle or *Contrat Social?* The political theory of the Revolution was the faith of a people in hot pursuit of liberty rather than the dialectic of an intellectual elite detached from the stress of affairs, and it should be judged as such by historians of political thought. Moreover, John Adams and George Mason might well ask their critics whether the Massachusetts Constitution and Virginia Declaration of Rights were not among the world's most memorable triumphs in applied political theory. The charge of intellectual confusion is impossible to refute, but at least some of this confusion may be written off to the activist careers of the great spokesmen of the Revolution.

Two points can be made in rebuttal to the alleged lack of originality in Revolutionary thought: First, the colonists were, as we have insisted repeatedly, conscious conservatives. In proclaiming the doctrines of natural law and the contract, they held fast to their colonial and English heritage. Not indifference or poverty of intellect, but pride and a sense of history persuaded the colonists to take their stand at the end of the heroic line of Protagoras, Cicero, Aquinas, Hooker, Locke, and Burlamaqui. Second, we should not forget how rare a thing it is for a man or school to make a genuinely original contribution to political thought. The Revolutionists would appear to have done their share by providing theoretical justification of written constitutions and bills of rights. Through these noble instruments they converted the contract into a working principle of constructive statesmanship.

The mark of hypocrisy must not be stamped too impetuously upon the philosophers of the Revolution, for slavery was an inherited fact of infinite complexity that most of them looked forward confidently to ending in a generation or two. Indeed, the intense popularity of natural law and rights accelerated the movement toward abolition of slavery, or at least suppression of the slave trade, to a noticeable degree. Most petitions, letters, and pamphlets that demanded emancipation labeled slavery "the most shocking violation of the law of nature" [182] and called blunt attention to the moral inconsistency of legislatures that proclaimed natural rights yet failed to repeal their slave codes.[183] The moral case against slavery had more appeal than the practical or economic in this decade of concern for liberty and equality. An anonymous author spoke for tens of thousands of colonists when he wrote in Rind's *Virginia Gazette:*

> As freedom is unquestionably the birthright of all mankind, Africans as well as Europeans, to keep the former in a state of slavery is a constant violation of that right, and therefore of justice.[184]

In conclusion, we may well ask: By what tests is the historian of ideas to measure the excellence of a political philosophy? By its conformity to truth? By its logic, precision, profundity, and symmetry? By its purpose? By the past on which it draws and the future to which it in turn communicates? By its influence on the world of political reality?

The truth of the Revolutionary theory is for philosophers to ponder, and while they ponder they would do well to remember three oft-forgotten facts: The Declaration of Independence was written in 1776, not 1861 or 1932 or 1953; the men who signed it were entirely sincere, never doubting for a moment that the truths announced in the first paragraph were "self-evident"; the men who wrote it—Jefferson, Adams, Franklin—had a unique grasp of the relationship between ideal and reality in successful self-government. As to the second test, no one, least of all the Revolutionists themselves, would deny that this theory could easily have been rendered more logical, precise, profound, and symmetrical. The plea of the defense is that these men were makers of history with a flair for speculative generalization, not philosophers in singleminded search of ultimate truth.

The philosophy of the Revolution was earnest faith rather than ordered theory. Would it not therefore be fitting and honorable to judge it by the last three of the tests we have established? Judged in this manner, it stands forth as one of the most noble and influential of all political philosophies. Its purpose was liberty and happiness for all men everywhere. The past on which it drew was that of Locke rather than Hobbes, of the *Vindiciae contra tyrannos* rather than *The Prince*, of Chrysippus rather than Thrasymachus. The future to which it communicated was that of constitutional democracy rather than the omnipotent state. And as for its influence on the world of political reality, it justified and inspired the makers of the greatest of revolutions, teaching them to build the new temple of ordered liberty even as they tore down the old one of imperial dependence. Lincoln caught the true meaning of the principles of the Revolution when he wrote of the document in which they were recommended "to the opinions of mankind":

> All honor to Jefferson—to the man, who, in the concrete pressure of a struggle for national independence by a single people, had the coolness, forecast, and capacity to introduce into a merely revolutionary document an abstract truth, applicable to all men and all times, and so to embalm it there that today and in all coming days it shall be a rebuke and a stumbling-block to the very harbingers of reappearing tyranny and oppression.[185]

Conclusion

CONSERVATISM, we are told, is the worship of dead revolutionists. If this is true, then Americans are conservatives twice over. Not only do we worship long-dead revolutionists, responding with religious fervor to the cadences of the great Declaration in which they appealed to a candid world, but the Revolution itself was as respectful of the past as a genuine revolution can be. Not only does our political faith stem directly from that of the American Revolution, but the latter reached back through the colonial past almost to the beginning of Western political thought. The Americans of 1776 were among the first men in modern history to defend rather than seek an open society and constitutional liberty; their political faith, like the appeal to arms it supported, was therefore surprisingly sober.

It would seem useful to end this long journey through early American thought by summing up the faith that guided the minds and raised the spirits of the Revolutionists. We must again recall that the Revolution produced neither a universal thinker nor a definitive book. The political theory of this great crisis was a popular creed that hundreds of gifted, hopeful leaders shouted in the midst of combat and tens of thousands of less gifted but no less hopeful followers took to their hearts. But if one able Revolutionist had set himself consciously to express the political consensus of his time, to cast the principles of 1776 in a pattern for later ages to inspect and ponder, this might well have been the outline he would have chosen to follow—this was the political theory of the American Revolution:

I. The political and social world is governed by laws as certain and universal as those which govern the physical world. Whether these laws are direct commands of God, necessities of nature, or simply inescapable lessons of history makes very little practical difference. In any or all of these cases, men are guided and restricted by a moral order that they can defy but not alter. Reason and experience, the means through which men come to understand these laws, point out at least four instances in which they are applicable to the affairs of men. The higher law, or law of nature, is all of these things:

1. A set of moral standards governing private conduct: The law of nature commands men to love, assist, and respect one another and to live godly, righteous, and sober lives.

2. A system of abstract justice to which the laws of men should conform: No human laws are of any validity if contrary to the laws of nature. In practice, this means that positive law which runs directly counter to a community's inherited sense of right and wrong is not only bad law but no law at all.

3. A line of demarcation around the proper sphere of political authority: A government that pushes beyond it into forbidden fields does so at peril of resistance or even revolution. Government must obey the commands of natural law or release men from obedience.

4. The source of natural rights, those rights which belong to man as man: From the law of nature flow man's rights to life, liberty, property, conscience, and happiness. The law of nature wills that men be free and happy.

The law of nature is a call to moral action on the part of men as individuals and the community as their servant. To men and nations who obey this law come prosperity and happiness; to men and nations who defy it come adversity and sadness. History has a way of punishing those who deny the reality of moral restraints on political power.

II. Since men are the raw materials out of which the community is constructed, the nature of man is the key to all major questions of political power and organization. The nature of man is such as to make free government possible but far from inevitable. He is by no means so good and perfectible as one line of philosophers insists; he is by no means so evil or degenerate as another line would have it. He dwells at a moral level considerably lower than that inhabited by angels, yet surely he is something more than a beast walking upright. Man is a composite of good and evil, of ennobling excellencies and degrading imperfections.

The most politically significant of his "good" qualities are sociability, love of liberty, basic human decency, and reasonableness. The first of these—the impulse to associate and co-operate with other men in pursuit of common ends—is unquestionably the most influential. So strong is the urge man feels to live and work with other men that he may properly be considered a political and social animal. The famous "state of nature" is at best a logical hypothesis. Man has no choice, thanks to his own nature, except to be in society and under government.

The most politically significant of his "bad" qualities are selfishness, depravity, passion, moral laziness, and corruptibility. The last of these—the lust for power and the inability to withstand its corrupting effects—is the one vice that constitution-makers must keep constantly in mind. The discretion left to rulers and the duration of their terms of office must each be reduced to the lowest level compatible with the need for effective government.

If man is a composite of good and evil, then one of the chief ends of the community is to separate his vices from his virtues and help him pursue his better nature. True religion, constitutional government, and sound education are the leading types of collective action that can help him to do this. The first of these encourages man to suppress his savage impulses; the second forces him to think before acting; the third teaches him the delights of virtue and liberty and the sorrows of vice and slavery. In short, man's saving grace, at least for earthly purposes, is his capacity for learning. Different men can acquire knowledge in different amounts, but any man can acquire the minimum necessary for survival and citizenship. It is therefore the business of government to encourage the means of general education.

III. If the natural character of man is an alloy of virtue and vice, his natural state is pure freedom and equality. Men may be grossly unequal in appearance, talents, intelligence, virtue, and fortune, but to this extent at least they are absolutely equal: No man has any natural right of dominion over any other; every man is free in the sight of God and plan of nature. This eternal principle of natural equality is not incompatible with political, social, or economic stratification, but the burden of proof rests squarely upon advocates of artificial inequality: It is for them to demonstrate that an unequal arrangement is essential to the stability, prosperity, or independence of the community. Conversely, the goal of political science is to discover a scheme of government that will reduce inequalities without invading individual liberty or menacing the welfare and security of the community.

IV. All men have certain fundamental rights. These rights are natural, traceable directly to the great plan of nature, if not indeed to God; absolute, belonging to men before, outside of, and quite without regard to organized government or society; eternal, never varying in content or identity; essential, since necessary to man's existence as man; and unalienable, impossible to be surrendered either absolutely or permanently. Five rights are clearly of this transcendent character: the right to life, which carries with it the power of self-preservation; the right to liberty, to act as one pleases without external restraint or control of any earthly sort; the right to property, to use and dispose of the fruits of honest industry; the right to happiness, or at least to pursue it on equal terms with other men; and the right to a free conscience, to reach out for God without interference or even assistance.

V. Although the natural rights of man are unalienable and can never be surrendered to any earthly authority, men can surrender their original power to control the exercise of these rights. They do this through a process of free consent in which they give away a certain amount of this power in return for the protection of the community. Just how much of this power they can and should surrender is a key question of political theory. Every man must surrender enough control over his original rights to permit government to maintain an organized, stable, peaceful pattern of human relations. No man should surrender so much that government dictates his every action. Between these two self-evident extremes the balance of liberty and authority must ever be in constant motion. In a free state the balance tips decisively in the direction of liberty. Men in such a state are generally virtuous; they make a conscious effort to use their freedom and property in a way that does not interfere with the freedom and property of the men with whom they must live and do business. Government intervention is the exception rather than the rule. In autocratic states, where men are usually ignorant and immoral, the balance tips just as decisively toward authority. Government is arbitrary because men will not respect one another. The balance between liberty and authority in any particular community is set by the general state of morality, knowledge, and common agreement.

It is, then, possible for government to take a man's life, qualify his liberty, regulate his property, direct his search for happiness—even forbid all anti-social outward manifestations of the inner drives of conscience—if this is done in fulfillment of a contract and in pursuit of known laws. The constitution and laws of every free state must recognize and protect man's natural rights. Whatever restrictions government places upon the free exercise of these rights must result from his freely given consent. The liberty that man retains is then properly styled civil, or, if clearly recognized in fundamental law, constitutional.

VI. In addition to those rights believed to be natural and unalienable, these derivative rights are the possession or aspiration of all men living under free government: the freedoms of speech, press, assembly, and petition; civil supremacy; representation and free elections; jury trial and attendant judicial safeguards. The first four are not only individual rights but social necessities, conditions as essential to the operation of free government as to the happiness of free men. The last two, representation and jury trial, are not only rights but the means of defending all other rights. In order to enjoy and defend their natural liberties a people need not adopt an exact imitation of the English legislative and judicial pattern, but the solid foundation of all free government is some form of equal representation and impartial trial. As to civil supremacy, this means simply that whatever regular armies must be raised for defense are to be subject at all times to civil, legislative control. It means also that the right of a free citizen to be protected against military power and supremacy carries with it a correlative duty: to serve in a well-regulated militia, to combine the characters of citizen and soldier.

VII. Government—that is to say, good government—is a free association of free and equal men for certain well-defined purposes. It is not a necessary evil for which men can blame their moral insufficiencies, but a necessary blessing for which they can thank wise providence. Government is clearly necessary to the happiness of men, for only through the collective techniques that it provides can they order their relations with one another and do for themselves what they cannot do as individuals or in family groups.

Government is both a natural and mechanistic institution. It is natural in the sense that it is founded in the necessities of human nature: Man, a social and political animal, cannot exist without its protection and encouragement. It is mechanistic in the sense that he and his equal fellows have some control over its structure and complete control over its personnel. Though men are forced into government by their wants, they enter it on terms satisfactory to their interests and respectful of human nature. Good government is the result of a voluntary contract, which is another way of saying that good government is based on the consent of the governed.

VIII. The principle of consent, which is made visible in the contract, is the key to the problem of political obligation, the problem that forces men to ask such questions as: Why do we submit to the compulsions of government? By what authority does government bind us with positive laws? How can we call ourselves free if we are subject to a concentration of power that can restrict our liberty, deprive us of our property, even take away our lives? The answer is that men obey government because they have consented to obey it. Through the original contract they have exchanged allegiance and obedience for protection and peace. They have agreed to certain well-defined restrictions on their natural freedom as part of a scheme for securing the rest of that freedom against the whims and jealousies of the men with whom they live. At the same time, they have agreed to representative institutions, notably the legislative assembly and jury of peers, through which they can continue to consent to necessary restrictions on liberty and property. Government, the community organized for political purposes, can restrict men's liberty, deprive them of their property, even take away their lives, because it does all this with their original and continuing consent. The power of government to do these things is not intrinsic but derived, from the free consent of the people it governs. In short, the answer to this troublesome series of questions is simply that the only valid obligation to obey government is self-obligation. The contract is therefore as much a logical justification as an historical explanation of the existence and authority of the political community.

The problem of sovereignty is of little concern to men with a sound grasp of the origin and nature of government. Sovereignty in the sense of supreme, irresistible, uncontrolled authority does not exist in free government and ought not exist in any government. Whatever rights or attributes of sovereignty government may exercise are the free and revocable grant of the people. And even the people, in whom sovereignty rests if it rests anywhere on earth, must be guided and restricted by the laws of nature in exercising their original political authority. They may not commission rulers to do what they may not do themselves: act in defiance of the laws of nature or in derogation from the rights of man.

IX. The purpose of society is to extend to each man in it, in return for his talents and exertions, the benefits of the strength, skills, and benevolence of the other men with whom he is associated. The purpose of government is to protect men in the enjoyment of their natural liberty, secure their persons and property against violence, remove obstructions to their pursuit of happiness, help them to live virtuous, useful lives, and in general preserve the largest degree of natural equality consistent with the welfare of the community and the implications of natural liberty. Neither government nor society, nor any third entity called the state, has any purpose of its own. Although it is proper to say that government exists for the safety, welfare, and happiness of the community, the community itself is nothing more than the individuals who make it up. The purpose of government should never be defined except in terms of the individual.

For this reason, it is not a dangerous thing to consider government an inherently good, even divine institution. Government can be safely acknowledged a temporal blessing because, in terms of the power it wields, there is nothing inherent about it. Government is not an end in itself but the means to an end. Its authority is the free and revocable grant of the men who have promised conditionally to submit to it. Its organs, however ancient and august, are instruments that free men have built and free men can alter or even abolish. Government can be arbitrary, corrupt, oppressive, wicked—but not if men are conscious of its origin, purpose, proper limits, and source of authority. Tyranny is not government but an abuse of government. True government is a good, natural, necessary institution ordained by providence to serve man's higher earthly purposes.

X. Under normal operating conditions of free society and constitutional government, representation and jury trial form the last and firmest line of defence against arbitrary power. When circumstances are abnormal, when this line of defense is irreparably breached, the people may resort to the great right of resistance. Government is divine, an ordinance of God, but governors are human, deriving all power from the consent of the governed. When rulers flout the terms under which they were granted this power, the people are placed in a position where they may, rather must, act to restore ordered liberty.

The right of resistance is the last refuge of a whole people unable to protect their lives, liberties, and properties by normal constitutional methods; it cannot be stretched to justify the *coup d'état* of a militant minority dedicated to the building of a new order. The people have a duty to be peaceful and law-abiding, and history demonstrates that they can be counted on never to resist except under overriding compulsion and to temper their methods to the nature and degree of oppression. The only possible outcome of a full reversion of power to the people is a new contract with new rulers under new terms of reciprocal obedience and protection. God granted men the right of resistance to help them preserve orderly government, not to induce them to fly from the tyranny of arbitrary power to the tyranny of no power at all. In short, resistance, the extreme form of which is revolution, is not so much the right as the solemn, unpleasant duty of a betrayed people.

XI. There is no one form of government good for all men at all times. Different communities may adopt different political systems yet reach the same level of liberty, prosperity, and happiness. A constitution is to be judged not by its logic or symmetry but by its ability to fulfill the great purposes for which all good governments are instituted. Yet if men are entirely free to adopt whatever form they desire, history and reason teach that most successful governments have exhibited the same characteristics and organs. Some structural rules for good government are:

1. Government must be plain, simple, and intelligible. The common sense

of the common man should be able to comprehend its structure and functioning. Too often have governments been made unnecessarily complex by elites or tyrants bent on enslaving the mass of the people.

2. Government must be republican; that is to say, representative and nonhereditary. Not only is simple democracy—government by the people directly—impractical in any community larger than a New England town or Swiss canton, but history demonstrates that representatives of the people, wise men chosen by the community and accountable to it, make more sensible day-to-day decisions than the people themselves. At the same time, there is no reason why these wise men, or one particular wise man as head of state, should occupy positions of decision by accident of birth. A virtuous, alert, liberty-loving people have no need of a king or hereditary aristocracy. They do have need of gifted, accountable leaders.

3. Government must be kept as near to the people as possible, chiefly through frequent elections and rotation-in-office. Frequent elections based on equal representation are the one sure means of keeping rulers responsible, of reminding them that they are servants not masters of the people. Rotation, which is secured by constitutional provisions forbidding indefinite re-eligibility, is an equally sure check against demagoguery or insolence in office. Another method of keeping government near to the people is, of course, to insist that they never delegate any task to government that they can do just as well for themselves.

4. Government must be constitutional, an empire of laws and not of men. The discretion and whim of all those in power must be reduced to the lowest level consistent with effective operation of the political machinery. The rule of law demands the existence of a written constitution, to be acknowledged and administered as law superior to the acts of the legislature, decrees of the judiciary, and ordinances of the executive. It demands, too, the inclusion in this constitution of a specific declaration of natural and civil rights. Only thus can liberty be secured against defections of weak rulers and designs of strong. A true constitution has three sound claims to obedience and even adoration: It is the command of the people, an original compact expressing their unalienable sovereignty; the handiwork of the wisest men in the community; and an earthly expression of the eternal principles of the law of nature. And a true constitution is a constant reminder that the only good government is limited government—limited in purpose, competence, and duration.

5. The one organ essential to free government is a representative legislature. The basic function of this organ—to serve as instrument of consent through which the people tax and restrict themselves—is evidence of its intrinsic character. Free government is difficult without an executive or judiciary; it is impossible without a representative assembly.

6. The fact of legislative primacy does not mean, however, that full, unchecked authority should be lodged in the representative assembly. The most successful and trustworthy governments are those in which the totality of political power is divided among three separate branches: a legislature,

preferably bicameral; an executive, preferably single; and a judiciary, preferably independent. In turn, these branches should be held in position by a system of checks and balances. Divided and balanced government is something of a retreat from the principle that government must be plain, simple, and intelligible. A unified government—a one-chambered, unrestrained assembly—would certainly be easier to run and understand. Yet the advantages to be gained from separation and balance far outweigh those to be gained from union. Liberty rather than authority, protection rather than power, delay rather than efficiency must be the prime concern of constitution-makers. "The nature of man is such as to make free government possible but far from inevitable." Balanced government, which leads to rule by a persistent and undoubted majority, is most likely to strike the proper balance between liberty and authority.

XII. Government in a free state is properly the concern of all those who have an attachment to the community. The right to vote, as well as to hold office, should be limited to men who have an evident stake-in-society—first, because they alone can make competent, responsible, uncorrupted judgments; second, because they alone have the right to consent to laws regulating or restricting the use of property. Participation in public affairs through voting and office-holding is not so much a right as a privilege and duty. This is one instance in which natural equality must give way to the dictates of a well-ordered society. The burden of proof remains, however, on those who would restrict the suffrage: A man who pays taxes or owns a small amount of property would seem to have demonstrated sufficient attachment to the community. The laws should make it possible for any man, however lowly his beginnings, to work his way to first-class citizenship.

XIII. It takes more than a perfect plan of government to preserve ordered liberty. Something else is needed, some moral principle diffused among the people to strengthen the urge to peaceful obedience and hold the community on an even keel. The wisest of political philosophers speak of three possibilities: fear, honor, virtue. There can be little doubt which of these is essential to free government. Such government rests on a definite moral basis: a virtuous people. Men who are virtuous may aspire to liberty, prosperity, and happiness; men who are corrupt may expect slavery, adversity, and sorrow. In addition to such recognized virtues as wisdom, justice, temperance, courage, honesty, and sincerity, these may be singled out as attitudes or traits of special consequence for a free republic: the willingness to act morally without compulsion, love of liberty, public spirit and patriotism, official incorruptibility, and industry and frugality. Men who display these qualities are the raw materials of free government. Without such men, in low places as well as high, free government cannot possibly exist. Hortatory religion, sound education, honest government, and a simple, preferably agrarian economy can all help produce a people sufficiently virtuous to govern themselves. The task of political science is to discover the virtues that lead to free government and the form of government that leads men to virtue. That form of government is best which produces the greatest number of good, free, happy men. The best of all possible governments will be popular, limited, divided, balanced, representative, republican, responsible, constitutional—and virtuous.

The major characteristics of Revolutionary political thought would seem to have been these: individualism, since it placed man rather than the community at the center of political speculation, emphasizing his rights, his happiness, and his power to make and unmake government; optimism, since it chose to stress the good and equal in men rather than the evil and unequal; toughmindedness, since it refused to carry this optimism to extravagant lengths and insisted on calling attention to pitfalls in the way of free government; idealism, since it set out goals for all mankind that few men, even Americans, could hope to attain in their lives on earth; pragmatism, since it tempered this idealism about ends with a refusal to be doctrinaire about means; and morality, since it insisted that free government, and therefore human liberty, is essentially a problem in practical ethics.

Perhaps the most remarkable characteristic of this political theory was its deep-seated conservatism. However radical the principles of the Revolution may have seemed to the rest of the world, in the minds of the colonists they were thoroughly preservative and respectful of the past. Indeed, for generations to come Americans would be conservatives at home and radicals abroad. The explanation of this paradox lies in a decisive fact of history: By 1765 the colonies had achieved a society more open, an economy more fluid, and a government more constitutional than anything Europeans would know for years to come. Americans had secured and were ready to defend a condition of freedom that other liberty-minded men could only hope for in the distant future or plot for in the brutal present. The political theory of the American Revolution, in contrast to that of the French Revolution, was not a theory designed to make the world over. The world—at least the American corner of it—had already been made over as thoroughly as any sensible man could imagine. Americans had never known or had long since begun to abandon feudal tenures, a privilege-ridden economy, centralized and despotic government, religious intolerance, and hereditary stratification. Their goal therefore was simply to consolidate, then expand by cautious stages, the large measure of liberty and prosperity that was part of their established way of life. More than 150 years ago Americans took up their unique role of the world's most conservative radicals, the world's most sober revolutionists. They, like their descendants, spurned the attractive nostrums of both the Enlightenment and Romanticism for a system and philosophy dedicated realistically to individual liberty within a context of communal stability.

Present-day Americans have inherited all characteristics and most principles of Revolutionary political thought. They continue to attack problems of political structure and authority with a thought-process that combines individualism, optimism, toughmindedness, idealism, pragmatism, morality, and conservatism—and thus they continue to horrify philosophers, doctrinaires, and absolutists of right and left. Although they make no fetish of natural law and have wandered far down the road from the agrarian beliefs of Jefferson and the stake-in-society beliefs of John Adams, they talk of fundamental rights, government by consent, the necessity of morality, separation of powers, and checks and balances. They have answered a variety of questions that hardly occurred to the Revolutionists with solutions that do not flout the basic American tradition and are often simply logical extensions of it. Judicial review and federalism, at least in a constitutional sense, are simply two more checks in the system of checks and balances. The secular yet moral state was something to which the men of 1776 were already well on the way. The modern doctrine of empirical collectivism can be traced to the pragmatic strain in Revolutionary thought as well as to the notion that the pursuit of happiness is a natural right to be protected or even encouraged by government. The insistence of one large segment of American thought that political democracy depends absolutely on a free-enterprise economy is not too far removed from Jefferson's insistence that it depended to a large extent on nonfeudal agrarianism. Our modern grasp of the functions of political parties, instruments that the Revolutionists should not be ridiculed for failing to understand, is simply a realistic extension of their belief in free co-operation and majority rule.[1]

What is especially amazing about modern American political thought is not that it continues to employ the idiom and exhibit the mood of the Revolution, but that both idiom and mood seem adequate to deal with many present-day problems. Perhaps this is a huge mistake. Perhaps Americans could achieve a larger measure of liberty and prosperity and build a more successful government if they were to abandon the language and assumptions of men who lived almost two centuries ago. Yet the feeling cannot be downed that rude rejection of the past, rather than levelheaded respect for it, would be the huge mistake. Americans may eventually take the advice of their advanced philosophers and adopt a political theory that pays more attention to groups, classes, public opinion, power-elites, positive law, public administration, and other realities of twentieth-century America. Yet it seems safe to predict that the people, who occasionally prove themselves wiser than their philosophers, will go on thinking about the political community in terms of unalienable rights, popular sovereignty, consent, constitutionalism, separation of powers, morality, and limited government. The political theory of the American Revolution—a theory of ethical, ordered liberty—remains the political tradition of the American people.

NOTES

A Note on the Notes

I MUST apologize in advance to those who dislike footnotes. I have confined my notes rigorously to documentary citations and bibliographical aids, the former as an obligation to those scholars who demand rightfully that an author identify his sources, the latter as a guide for those students who wish to go deeper into some of the subjects discussed in this book. Since the notes contain virtually no explanatory or incidental material, the reader who dislikes them may ignore them with impunity. The notes as finally printed are just about half as numerous and wordy as in the first draft. I was especially ruthless in eliminating bibliographical material. The following abbreviations are used in the interest of economy of space:

COLONIAL NEWSPAPERS

AC (New York) *American Chronicle* (1762)

AG (Salem) *American Gazette* (1776)

AWM (Philadelphia) *American Weekly Mercury* (1719-1746)

AlG *Albany Gazette* (1771-1772)

BCJ (Boston) *Continental Journal* (1776+)

BCh *Boston Chronicle* (1767-1770)

BEP *Boston Evening-Post* (1735-1775)

BG *Boston Gazette* (1719-1776+)

BIA (Boston) *Independent Advertiser* (1748-1749)

BNEC (Boston) *New-England Chronicle* (1776)

BNL *Boston News-Letter* (1704-1776)

BPB *Boston Post-Boy* (1734-1775)

BWR *Boston Weekly Rehearsal* (1731-1735)

CC (Hartford) *Connecticut Courant* (1764-1776+)

CFM (Wilmington) *Cape-Fear Mercury* (1769-1775)

CG (New Haven) *Connecticut Gazette* (1755-1768)

CJ (New Haven) *Connecticut Journal* (1767-1776+)

CNEC (Cambridge) *New-England Chronicle* (1775-1776)

DMG (Baltimore) *Dunlap's Maryland Gazette* (1775-1776+)

EG (Salem) *Essex Gazette* (1768-1775)

EJ (Newburyport) *Essex Journal* (1773-1776+)

ENHG (Exeter) *New Hampshire Gazette* (1776+)

GG (Savannah) *Georgia Gazette* (1763-1776)

MG (Annapolis) *Maryland Gazette* (1727-1734)

MG (2) (Annapolis) *Maryland Gazette* (1745-1776+)

MJ (Baltimore) *Maryland Journal* (1773-1776+)

MS (Boston, Worcester) *Massachusetts Spy* (1770-1776+)

MassG (Boston) *Massachusetts Gazette* (1768-1769)

NCG (New Bern) *North-Carolina Gazette* (1751-1759)

NCG (2) (New Bern) *North-Carolina Gazette* (1768-1776+)

NEC (Boston) *New-England Courant* (1721-1726)

NEWJ (Boston) *New-England Weekly Journal* (1727-1741)

NHG (Portsmouth) *New-Hampshire Gazette* (1756-1776+)

NLG (New London) *Connecticut Gazette* (1763-1776+)

NM *Newport Mercury* (1758-1776+)

NP *Norwich Packet* (1773-1776+)

NVG (Norfolk) *Virginia Gazette* (1774-1775)

NYC *New-York Chronicle* (1769-1770)

NYCG (New York) *Constitutional Gazette* (1775-1776)

NYEP *New-York Evening-Post* (1744-1752)

NYG *New-York Gazette* (1725-1744)

NYG (2) *New-York Gazette* (1747-1773)

NYGWM *New-York Gazette; and the Weekly Mercury* (1768-1776+)

NYJ *New-York Journal* (1766-1776)

NYM *New-York Mercury* (1752-1768)

NYP *New-York Packet* (1776)

NYPa *New-York Pacquet* (1763)

NYWJ *New-York Weekly Journal* (1733-1751)

NYWPB *New-York Weekly Post-Boy* (1743-1747)

PC (Philadelphia) *Pennsylvania Chronicle* (1767-1774)

PEP (Philadelphia) *Pennsylvania Evening Post* (1775-1776+)

PG *Providence Gazette* (1762-1776+)

PJ (Philadelphia) *Pennsylvania Journal* (1742-1776+)

PL (Philadelphia) *Pennsylvania Ledger* (1775-1776+)

PM *Portsmouth Mercury* (1765-1767)

PP (Philadelphia) *Pennsylvania Packet* (1771-1776+)

PPP (Philadelphia) *Penny Post* (1769)

PaG (Philadelphia) *Pennsylvania Gazette* (1728-1776+)

RIG (Newport) *Rhode-Island Gazette* (1732-1733)

RNYG *Rivington's New-York Gazetteer* (1773-1775)

SCAGG (Charleston) *South-Carolina and American General Gazette* (1764-1776+)

SCG (Charleston) *South-Carolina Gazette* (1732-1775)

SCGCJ (Charleston) *South-Carolina Gazette; and Country Journal* (1765-1775)

SG *Salem Gazette* (1774-1775)

SHPM (Philadelphia) *Story and Humphrey's Pennsylvania Mercury* (1775)

VG (Williamsburg) *Virginia Ga-*
zette (1736-1776+). [1736-1766 there
was one *VG*, 1766-1775 two, 1775-
1776 three. All issues before 1766 are
identified as *VG*; all issues after May
16, 1766 are identified as *VG*, with
the name of the publisher (Purdie

and Dixon, Dixon and Hunter, Rind,
Pinkney, or Purdie) in parentheses.]
WNCG (Wilmington) *North-Caro-
lina Gazette* (1764-1766)
*WNYG Weyman's New-York Ga-
zette* (1759-1767)

[This represents a virtually complete list of English-language newspapers published in America up to 1776. To the best of my knowledge, I have seen all issues
printed before 1765 and about ninety-five per cent of those printed in 1765-1776.
I avoided the German press for two reasons: The Pennsylvania Germans were
outside the main stream of colonial culture and politics, and I sampled enough
issues of the (Germantown) *Pensylvanische Berichte* and *Philadelphische Zeitung*
to convince myself that they contained few if any unusual political ideas. Like
all searchers into the colonial mind, I stand in hopeless debt to Clarence S. Brigham for his *History and Bibliography of American Newspapers, 1690-1820,* 2
vols. (Worcester, 1947).]

COLONIAL MAGAZINES

BAM (Boston) *The American Maga-
zine and Historical Chronicle* (1743-
1746)
BC (Boston) *The Censor* (1771-1772)
BWM The Boston Weekly Magazine
(1743)
CH (Boston) *The Christian History*
(1743-1745)
GM (Philadelphia) *The General
Magazine, and Historical Chronicle*
(1741)
IR (New York) *The Independent
Reflector* (1752-1753)
JE (New York) *John Englishman*
(1755)
NAM (Woodbridge, N.J.) *The New
American Magazine* (1758-1760)

NCM (New Bern) *The North-Caro-
lina Magazine* (1764)
NEM (Boston) *The New-England
Magazine* (1758)
OR (New York) *The Occasional Re-
verberator* (1753)
PAM (Philadelphia) *The American
Magazine* (1741)
PAM (2) (Philadelphia) *The Ameri-
can Magazine* (1757-1758)
PAM (3) (Philadelphia) *The Amer-
ican Magazine* (1769)
PaM (Philadelphia) *The Pennsyl-
vania Magazine* (1775-1776)
RAM (Boston) *The Royal American
Magazine* (1774-1775)
TI (New York) *The Instructor*
(1755)

PERIODICALS AND COLLECTIONS OF DOCUMENTS

*AASP American Antiquarian Soci-
ety, Proceedings,* New Series
(1880-   )
*AHAAR American Historical Asso-
ciation, Annual Reports* (1889-   )
AHR American Historical Review
(1895-   )

Amer. Arch. American Archives, 4th
Series (Washington, 1837-1846)
*CCR Public Records of the Colony
of Connecticut* (Hartford, 1850-
1890)
*CSMP Colonial Society of Massachu-
setts, Publications* (1895-   )

CSPC   Calendar of State Papers, Colonial Series (London, 1860-   )

EIHC   Essex Institute, Historical Collections (1859-   )

Hening   W. W. Hening, ed., The Statutes-at-Large; being a Collection of All the Laws of Virginia (New York and Philadelphia, 1823)

JCC   Journals of the Continental Congress (Washington, 1904-1937)

JHB   Journals of the House of Burgesses of Virginia (Richmond, 1905-1924)

MCR   Records of the Governor and Company of the Massachusetts Bay in New England (Boston, 1853-1854)

MHSC   Massachusetts Historical Society, Collections (1792-   )

MHSP   Massachusetts Historical Society, Proceedings (1791-   )

Md. Arch.   Archives of Maryland (Baltimore, 1883-   )

NCCR   Colonial Records of North Carolina (Raleigh, 1886-1890)

NCP   Narragansett Club Publications (Providence, 1866-1874)

NEHGR   New England Historical and Genealogical Register (1842)

NEQ   New England Quarterly (1928-   )

NHCR   Records of the Colony . . . of New Haven (New Haven, 1857-1858)

NYCD   Documents Relative to the Colonial History of the State of New York (Albany, 1856-1887)

NYHSC   New-York Historical Society, Collections (1811-   )

P&A   H. Niles, ed., Principles and Acts of the Revolution (Baltimore, 1822)

PMHB   Pennsylvania Magazine of History and Biography (1877-   )

PSQ   Political Science Quarterly (1886-   )

RICR   Records of the Colony of Rhode Island (Providence, 1856-1865)

RIHSC   Rhode Island Historical Society, Collections (1827-1941)

RIHS Proc.   Rhode Island Historical Society, Proceedings (1872-1892; 1902-1914)

RIHS Pubs.   Rhode Island Historical Society, Publications (1880-1901)

Thorpe   F. N. Thorpe, ed., The Federal and State Constitutions (Washington, 1909)

Va. Mag.   Virginia Magazine of History and Biography (1893-   )

WMQ   William and Mary Quarterly (1892-   )

Notes

PART ONE

INTRODUCTION

1. For examples, see Andrew Burnaby, *Travels through the Middle Settlements in North America* (1759-1760) (3rd ed., London, 1798), 26-27, 67, 97; Lord Adam Gordon (1764-1765), in N. D. Mereness, ed., *Travels in the American Colonies* (New York, 1916), 417, 449-450; *RICR*, III, 385-388, 388-393, 399-400; "John Usher's Report on the Northern Colonies, 1698," *WMQ* (3), VII (1950), 99; *NYHSC* (1869), 75, 118, 119; *NYCD*, VII, 440; *Md. Arch.* (Sharpe Correspondence), I, 96, 97; II, 124, 177, 373, 440.

2. A. H. Smyth, ed., *The Writings of Benjamin Franklin* (New York, 1906), VI, 323. Apparently he forgot to read his friend Joseph Breintnal's contribution to "The Busy-Body," *AWM*, May 1, 1729.

3. C. F. Adams, ed., *The Works of John Adams* (Boston, 1856), X, 282-283, also 172, 359.

4. *The Works of Edmund Burke* (Boston, 1839), II, 32-38.

5. In this discussion I have placed emphasis on the influence of these four major factors in *political* development.

6. *Works*, II, 32-33.

7. Gertrude S. Kimball, ed., *The Correspondence of the Colonial Governors of Rhode Island* (Boston, 1902), I, 10.

8. *Acts and Resolves of Massachusetts Bay*, VIII, 341.

9. D. D. Wallace, *Constitutional History of South Carolina from 1725 to 1775* (Abbeville, S.C., 1899), 50.

10. In a petition of the frontier counties of Pennsylvania—more exactly, of the "Paxton Boys"—printed in *PJ*, March 15, 1764; *NM*, March 19, 1764.

11. Perhaps the finest colonial statement of seventeenth-century English rights was the famed "Remonstrance and Petition" of Robert Child (1646), printed in Thomas Hutchinson, *A Collection of Original Papers* (Boston, 1769), 188-196. Henry Care,

English Liberties, or the Free-born Subject's Inheritance (Boston, 1721), was the most popular statement of English rights during the second half of the colonial period.

12. *A Pillar of Gratitude* (Boston, 1700), 32-33.

13. Jonathan Mayhew, *Two Sermons on Divine Goodness* (Boston, 1761), 72.

14. *Works*, II, 43.

15. The most helpful guides to the intricacies of this conflict are C. M. Andrews, *The Colonial Period of American History* (New Haven, 1934-1938), esp. Vol. IV, and L. H. Gipson, *The British Empire before the American Revolution*, 7 vols. (Caldwell, Idaho, and New York, 1936-1949).

16. For an extraordinarily frank exposition of the orthodox English attitude toward the colonies, see Colonel Martin Bladen's "Short Discourse" in *NCCR*, II, 626-635, or Sir William Keith, *A Collection of Papers* (London, 1740), 169ff.

17. A. H. Buffinton, "The Isolationist Policy of Colonial Massachusetts," *NEQ*, I (1928), 158-179; Viola F. Barnes, *The Dominion of New England* (New Haven, 1923), Chap. 1.

18. *BEP*, March 2, 1747; *NYWJ*, March 23, 1747; *NM*, May 22, 1759.

19. Keith, *Collection of Papers*, 175.

20. Burke, *Works*, II, 37-38.

21. *New Hampshire Provincial Laws*, I, 660-666, 702-705, II, 862-863; *Acts of the Privy Council of England, Colonial Series* (1680-1720), 847.

22. *NCCR*, IV, 756, 792, 797, 844.

23. R. H. Brown, *Historical Geography of the United States* (New York, 1948), Pt. I; Ellen C. Semple, *American History and its Geographic Conditions* (Boston, 1903), Chaps. 1-4; A. M. Schlesinger, *New Viewpoints in American History* (New York, 1923), Chap. 2.

24. *The Frontier in American History* (New York, 1920), 266. For the ob-servations of Turner bearing most directly upon this book, see Chaps. 1, 2, 3, and 9 of the work cited, as well as *The Significance of Sections in American History* (New York, 1932), Chap. 2. For the literature of the frontier, see R. W. G. Vail, *The Voice of the Old Frontier* (Philadelphia, 1949).

25. Andrews, *Colonial Period*, I, 320-343, 400-429; III, 212-226.

26. For an English gentleman's opinion of colonial government at the amateur level, see the Earl of Bellomont's salty comments (1699) on irregularities in Rhode Island, *RICR*, III, 385-388, 388-393, 399-400, as well as other remarks and rejoinders at 543-549. See also *NYCD*, IV, 600.

27. A recent elaboration of the master's teachings is in Avery Craven, *Democracy in American Life* (Chicago, 1941), esp. Chaps. 1-2; a recent questioning in G. W. Pierson, "The Frontier and Frontiersmen of Turner's Essays," *PMHB*, LXIV (1940), 449-478.

28. From a letter of John Pynchon on the defense of the Massachusetts frontier, December 3, 1694, printed in *MHSP*, XLIII, 506. Concerning this frontier, see Lois K. Matthews, *The Expansion of New England* (Boston, 1909), Chaps. 1-5. For the South, see V. W. Crane, *The Southern Frontier, 1607-1732* (Philadelphia, 1929); L. K. Koontz, *The Virginia Frontier, 1754-1763* (Baltimore, 1925); T. P. Abernethy, *Three Virginia Frontiers* (L.S.U., 1940); and that delightful, if not entirely trustworthy, original description, William Byrd, *History of the Dividing Line* (Richmond, 1866).

CHAPTER ONE

1. See the wise words of C. M. Andrews in *Authority and the Individual*, Harvard Tercentenary Publication (Cambridge, 1937), 154-169.

2. The development of political institutions in the colonies is most faithfully described in H. L. Osgood's two great works, *The American Colonies in the Seventeenth Century*, 3 vols. (New York, 1904-1907), and *The American Colonies in the Eighteenth Century*, 4 vols. (New York, 1924). For government in the eighteenth century, there is no better summary than C. P. Nettels, *The Roots of American Civilization* (New York, 1938), Chap. 20. A special study of merit is Louise Kellogg, "The American Colonial Charter," in *AHAAR* (1903), I, 185-341.

3. See especially the fine volume of L. W. Labaree, *Royal Government in America* (New Haven, 1930), and the special studies of W. R. Smith, *South Carolina as a Royal Province* (New York, 1903); W. H. Fry, *New Hampshire as a Royal Province* (New York, 1908); E. J. Fisher, *New Jersey as a Royal Province* (New York, 1911); C. L. Raper, *North Carolina, A Study in English Colonial Government* (New York, 1904); P. S. Flippin, *The Royal Government of Virginia, 1624-1775* (New York, 1919), and "The Royal Government of Georgia," *Georgia Historical Quarterly*, *VIII-XIII* (1921-1929).

4. Andrews, *Colonial Period*, II, 197-240; N. D. Mereness, *Maryland as a Proprietary Province* (New York, 1901); W. R. Shepherd, *History of Proprietary Government in Pennsylvania* (New York, 1896); Edward McCrady, *The History of South Carolina under the Proprietary Government, 1670-1719* (New York, 1897).

5. See the chapters on Connecticut, Rhode Island, and seventeenth-century Massachusetts in Osgood's two works; Jeremiah Dummer, *A Defence of the New-England Charters* (1721) (London, 1765), esp. 43-51.

6. C. M. Andrews, *Connecticut and the British Government* (New Haven, 1933).

7. *Sagittarius's Letters* (Boston, 1775), 20.

8. The influence of the trading corporation on colonial institutions, particularly on those of early Massachusetts, is emphasized by A. C. McLaughlin, *The Foundations of American Constitutionalism* (New York, 1932), 31-52.

9. E. B. Greene, *The Provincial Governor* (New York, 1898).

10. Labaree, *Royal Government*, Chaps. 5-7.

11. Important contemporaneous discussions (from the loyal or royal point of view) of this and other key problems of colonial government are in Thomas Pownall, *The Administration of the British Colonies* (1766) (5th ed., London, 1774); George Chalmers, *An Introduction to the History of the Revolt of the American Colonies* (Boston, 1845), which is excellent on imperial neglect of royal governors; and the same author's *Opinions of Eminent Lawyers*, etc. (London, 1814).

12. A note in R. Frothingham, *The Rise of the Republic* (2nd ed., Boston, 1873), 18-21, presents excellent data concerning the establishment and growth of the assembly in each colony.

13. Alfred de Grazia, *Public and Republic* (New York, 1951), Chap. 3; C. F. Bishop, *History of Elections in the American Colonies* (New York, 1893); McLaughlin, *Foundations of American Constitutionalism*, 52-61; H. Phillips, *The Development of a Residential Qualification for Representatives in Colonial Legislatures* (Cincinnati, 1921).

14. T. F. Moran, *The Rise and Development of the Bicameral System in America* (Baltimore, 1895).

15. See *SCG*, May 6-June 3, 1756, for an orthodox exchange of opinions

between Governor Glen and the South Carolina Assembly on the question whether the latter had the character of a parliament. See also *BWR*, Feb. 5, 1733; *NYWJ*, May 20, 1734; *SCG*, Oct. 1, Dec. 3, 24, 1764.

16. de Grazia, *Public and Republic*, 56.

17. Labaree, *Royal Government*, Chap. 4; Greene, *Provincial Governor*, Chap. 5.

18. For a colonial attack on this technique, see *PAM*, Jan., Feb. 1741.

19. See especially *American Legal Records*, a set of volumes issued at intervals by the American Historical Association in which the original records of representative colonial courts are printed. Volumes dealing with courts in Maryland, New York, Rhode Island, Connecticut, New Jersey, and South Carolina have been published. The introductory essays, particularly that of C. M. Andrews in the Rhode Island volume, are extremely valuable. No less important are two collections of Massachusetts court records: *Records and Files of the Quarterly Courts of Essex County (1636-1683)* (Salem, 1911-1921) and *Records of the Suffolk County Court, 1671-1680*, *CSMP*, XXIX-XXX. See also R. B. Morris, *Studies in the History of American Law* (New York, 1930), and the excellent bibliography at 259-262. I have profited greatly from such special studies as C. J. Hilkey, *Legal Development in Colonial Massachusetts, 1630-1686* (New York, 1910), and O. P. Chitwood, *Justice in Colonial Virginia* (Baltimore, 1905).

20. Thorpe, V, 2781. For some prime examples of attacks on and defenses of lawyers, see *BWR*, Dec. 16, 1734; *VG*, July 18, Oct. 10, 1745; *BEP*, Sept. 23, 1745; *NYEP*, April 15, 1751; *IR*, July 26, 1753; *SCG*, June 12, 1755.

21. See the authoritative treatment in Andrews, *Colonial Period*, Vol. IV.

22. O. M. Dickerson, *American Colonial Government* (Cleveland, 1912); Andrews, *Colonial Period*, IV, Chap. 9; A. H. Basye, *The Lords Commissioners of Trade and Plantations* (New Haven, 1925); M. P. Clarke, "The Board of Trade at Work," *AHR*, XVII (1911), 17-43. For the agency that preceded the Board of Trade, see R. P. Bieber, *The Lords of Trade and Plantations, 1675-1696* (Allentown, Pa., 1919).

23. See the invaluable collection prepared by L. W. Labaree, *Royal Instructions to British Colonial Governors*, 2 vols. (New York, 1935).

24. J. H. Smith, *Appeals to the Privy Council from the American Plantations* (New York, 1950), esp. Appendix A; A. M. Schlesinger, "Colonial Appeals to the Privy Council," *PSQ*, XXVIII (1913), 279-297, 433-450; G. A. Washburne, *Imperial Control of the Administration of Justice in the Thirteen American Colonies, 1684-1776* (New York, 1923); H. D. Hazeltine, "Appeals from Colonial Courts to the King in Council, with Especial Reference to Rhode Island," in *AHAAR* (1894), 299-350. For a discussion of *Winthrop v. Lechmere*, the one clear-cut precedent for the American doctrine of judicial review, see C. M. Andrews, *The Connecticut Intestacy Law* (New Haven, 1933) and Smith, *Appeals to the Privy Council*, 537-560.

25. E. B. Russell, *The Review of American Colonial Legislation by the King in Council* (New York, 1915); Dickerson, *American Colonial Government*, 225-274; C. M. Andrews, "The Royal Disallowance," *AASP*, XXIV, 342-362.

26. Andrews, *Colonial Period*, IV, Chaps. 7-8, and in D. S. Towle, ed., *Records of the Vice-Admiralty Court of Rhode Island, 1716-1752* (Washington, 1936), 1-79.

27. E. P. Tanner, "Colonial Agencies in England during the Eighteenth Century," *PSQ*, XVI (1901), 24-49; B. W. Bond, "The Colonial Agent as a Popular Representative," *PSQ*, XXXV (1920), 372-392; J. J. Burns, *The Colonial Agents of New England* (Washington, 1935); M. Appleton, "Richard Partridge: Colonial Agent," *NEQ*, V (1932), 293-309; M. Wolff, *The Colonial Agency of Pennsylvania, 1712-1757* (Philadelphia, 1933); Ella Lonn, *The Colonial Agents of the Southern Colonies* (Chapel Hill, 1945).

28. A case study of this process is W. T. Root, *The Relations of Pennsylvania with the British Government, 1696-1765* (New York, 1912).

29. A. E. McKinley, *The Suffrage Franchise in the Thirteen English Colonies in America* (Philadelphia, 1905); G. H. Haynes, *Representation and Suffrage in Massachusetts, 1620-1691* (Baltimore, 1894); J. A. C. Chandler, *The History of Suffrage in Virginia* (Baltimore, 1901).

30. A convenient table is in Kirk Porter, *A History of Suffrage in the United States* (Chicago, 1918), 12.

31. Royal instructions to Governor Berkeley of Virginia, November 13, 1676; Hening, II, 425.

32. *PaG*, Dec. 8, 1737.

33. McKinley, *Suffrage Franchise*, 46-47, 217-218, 334-335, 355-357, 471-472; J. F. Jameson, "Did the Fathers Vote?" *New England Magazine* (January 1890), 484-490, and "Virginian Voting in the Colonial Period," *The Nation* (April 27, 1893), 309-310; L. G. Tyler, "Virginians Voting in the Colonial Period," *WMQ*, VI (1897), 7-13; C. S. Sydnor, *Gentlemen Freeholders* (Chapel Hill, 1952), 137-140. R. E. Brown, "Democracy in Colonial Massachusetts," *NEQ*, XXV (1952), 291-313, insists that something very near to white male democracy existed in the New England towns.

34. McKinley, *Suffrage Franchise*, 355-357, and references there cited.

35. Evidence of official concern over nonparticipation in public affairs in the early colonies may be found in *MCR*, II, 208, and Hening, I, 333-334.

36. Lively pictures of colonial elections are in W. B. Reed, *Life and Correspondence of Joseph Reed* (Philadelphia, 1847), I, 36-37, *NYWJ*, Nov. 5, 1733, Oct. 4, 1736; and *The Candidates*, printed in *WMQ* (3), V (1948), 217-257.

37. *AWM*, Sept. 11, 1735; *SCG*, Jan. 6, 1748, March 20, 1749.

38. See the valuable roll of freemen admitted in New York City, 1675-1765, in *NYHSC* (1885), 39-213.

39. Greene, *Provincial Governor*, Chaps. 8-10.

40. *NYWJ*, Dec. 7, 1747, a good recital of the governor's grievances. See also his speech in *NYEP*, May 20, 1745, and Belcher's to the New Jersey Assembly in *PJ*, Feb. 20, 1750.

41. *Writings*, V, 83, also VI, 128-130; *NYGWM*, Dec. 12, 1774. For a typical colonial protest, see *NCCR*, II, 158-160.

42. L. W. Labaree, "The Early Careers of the Royal Governors," in *Essays in Colonial History presented to Charles McLean Andrews* (New Haven, 1931), 168; Louise B. Dunbar, "The Royal Governors, etc.," in R. B. Morris, *The Era of the American Revolution* (New York, 1939), 214-268. See Labaree, *Royal Government*, 466-468, for a bibliography of gubernatorial biographies, as well as J. A. Schutz, *Thomas Pownall* (Glendale, Cal., 1951); L. K. Koontz, *Robert Dinwiddie* (Glendale, 1941); L. Dodson, *Alexander Spotswood* (Philadelphia, 1932).

43. Colonial notions of the qualifications of a good governor are outlined in *AWM*, June 15, 1738.

44. *Journal of the General Assembly of New York*, II, 267.

45. George Bancroft, *History of the United States* (Boston, 1852), IV, 20.

46. *NYEP*, June 8, 1747.

47. Francis Bernard to John Pownall, April 23, 1769; Bernard Papers, VIII (Harvard Library). See also *Md. Arch.* (Sharpe Correspondence), III, 3.

48. *BIA*, Jan. 23, 30, 1749; *NYWJ*, Jan. 21, 1734; *BEP*, July 10, 1738.

49. This point is emphasized by Mary P. Clarke in her competent *Parliamentary Privilege in the American Colonies* (New Haven, 1943).

50. *MG* (2), May 18-June 1, 1758.

51. J. F. Burns, *Controversies between Royal Governors and their Assemblies* (Villanova, Pa., 1923), 57-70, 77-110, 305-313. A good review of the New York situation is in A. C. Flick, ed., *History of the State of New York* (New York, 1933), II, Chap. 5.

52. A splendid case study is D. L. Kemmerer, *Path to Freedom. The Struggle for Self-Government in Colonial New Jersey* (Princeton, 1940).

53. *PaG*, Aug. 26, Sept. 2, 1742; *NYG*, (2), Dec. 23, 1754; *MG* (2), Oct. 1-Nov. 22, 1753, March 7-June 13, 1754; *PAM*, Jan.-March 1741.

54. For evidence of intercolonial interest in the poor relations of governor and assembly, see *NYG*, June 13, 1726, Aug. 5, 26-Oct. 21, Nov. 11, 18, Dec. 2, 31, 1728, Jan. 7-28, April 15, Sept. 15-Oct. 13, 1729, Oct. 26-Nov. 16, 1730, Jan. 26, Feb. 9, March 15, April 26, 1731; *PaG*, Oct. 2, 9, Dec. 9, 30, 1729, Oct. 1-Nov. 5, 1730, Jan. 11-Feb. 22, 1732; *NEWJ*, Dec. 21, 1730-Jan. 11, 1731, Jan. 10, Feb. 7, July 10, 1732; *MG*, Dec. 1-15, 1730; *SCG*, April 7-July 7, 1733; *AWM*, Jan. 22-Feb. 5, 1740, Jan. 21, 28, May 27, June 3, Sept. 2, 1742; *NYWJ*, Oct. 23, 1738, Oct. 12-26, 1741, Jan. 16, 1744; *PJ*, March 5, June 27, 1751, Aug. 21, Oct. 2, Nov.

13, 20, 1755, Jan. 12-26, April 20-May 11, 1758.

55. Andrews, *Colonial Period*, II, 143n.

56. See G. E. Howard, *An Introduction to the Local Constitutional History of the United States* (Baltimore, 1889); E. Channing, *Town and County Government in the English Colonies of North America* (Baltimore, 1884), esp. 55-57; and the many special studies written or directed by H. B. Adams and published in the early volumes of the *John Hopkins University Studies in Historical and Political Science*. The valuable work of Adams and his associates should not be obscured by their devotion to discredited theories of Teutonic origins of local American institutions. For an excellent summary of these and competing theories, see J. F. Sly, *Town Government in Massachusetts* (Cambridge, 1930), Chap. 3.

57. Howard, *Local Constitutional History*, 319-357.

58. Sly, *Town Government*, Chaps. 2, 4; Channing, *Town and County Government*, 26-42; Howard, *Local Constitutional History*, 50-99.

59. Ipswich Town Records, March 8, 1720.

60. These judgments are based on a reading of the published records of the towns of Boston, Salem, Cambridge, Providence, Portsmouth, Warwick, and New Haven, and the unpublished records of Simsbury, Guilford, Greenwich, Stamford, Ipswich, and Little Compton.

61. P. A. Bruce, *Institutional History of Virginia* (New York, 1910), I, 55-93, 478-549, 588-610; Channing, *Town and County Government*, 42-53; Howard, *Local Constitutional History*, 117-134, 388-407; Edward Ingle, *Local Institutions of Virginia* (Baltimore, 1885); L. W. Wilhelm, *Local Institutions of Maryland* (Baltimore, 1885); A. O. Porter, *County*

Government in Virginia (New York, 1947), Chaps. 1-2.

62. For an understanding of local government there is no substitute for the original records. The unpublished county records of the southern colonies which I found most useful (i.e., legible) were: Virginia—Spottsylvania Order Book (1749-1755), Westmoreland Order Book (1731-1739) (1761-1764), Isle of Wight Order Book (1746-1752); North Carolina—Minutes of the County Courts of Chowan (1730-1734) (1740-1748), Hyde (1745-1761), Craven (1712-1715) (1749-1750) (1765), Orange (1752-1762), and Carteret (1723-1747).

63. These judgments are based on a study of the published records of St. Peter's (New Kent and James City), Petsworth, Bristol, Lynnhaven, Stratton Major, Upper (Nansemond), and St. Paul's (Hanover) parishes. Most of these vestry books were printed under the dedicated guidance of G. C. Chamberlayne. A good description of the parish's place in the Virginia scheme of government is in W. L. Hall, ed., *The Vestry Book of the Upper Parish, 1743-1793* (Richmond, 1949), xiii-lxxiv.

64. From "Notes on Virginia," in P. L. Ford, ed., *The Writings of Thomas Jefferson* (New York, 1894), III, 238-239.

65. Howard, *Local Constitutional History*, 100-112, 358-387. For the special problem of New Netherland, see I. Elting, *Dutch Village Communities on the Hudson River* (Baltimore, 1886); A. E. McKinley, "English and Dutch Towns of New Netherland," *AHR*, VI (1900), 1-18; *NYCD*, Vols. I, II, XIII, XIV; E. B. O'Callaghan, *History of New Netherlands* (Philadelphia, 1846-1848); Flick, *History of New York*, I, Chaps. 7-9. It seems clear that Dutch practices had no permanent influence on New York's political institutions.

66. *The Acts of Assembly of the Province of Pennsylvania* (Philadelphia, 1775), 131-138.

67. The records of most of these towns have been published. The most rewarding for the student of local government are those of Brookhaven (Vol. I), Huntington (Vols. I and II), Easthampton (Vol. I), and Jamaica (Vols. I-III).

68. See E. S. Griffith, *History of American City Government. The Colonial Period* (New York, 1938), an admirable study with especially valuable bibliographies in the appendices; J. A. Fairlie, *Essays in Municipal Administration* (New York, 1908), 48-94; and such first-rate local studies as A. E. Peterson and G. W. Edwards, *New York as an Eighteenth Century Municipality* (New York, 1917) and J. T. Scharf and T. Westcott, *History of Philadelphia* (Philadelphia, 1884).

69. Especially valuable are *Minutes of the Common Council of the City of New York, 1675-1776*, 8 vols. (New York, 1905), and *Minutes of the Common Council of the City of Philadelphia, 1704-1776* (Philadelphia, 1847).

70. *NYWJ*, Dec. 2, 1734.

71. For an informative documentary view of primitive government in the early colonies, see *Records of the Town of East-Hampton* (Sag Harbor, L.I., 1887-1905), I, 7ff.

72. The proof of this statement can be read in such unpublished records as the Minutes of the Chowan (N.C.) County Court (1730-1734), and such published records as L. Chalkley, ed., *Chronicles of the Scotch-Irish Settlement in Virginia* (Rosslyn, Va., 1912), I, 13ff.

73. See, for example, the Massachusetts law of 1647 (*MCR*, II, 197), which extended the strictly local suffrage, naturally with some qualifications, to non-freemen over twenty-four. The

city of Philadelphia was one obvious exception to this general rule.

74. See F. L. Mott, *American Journalism* (New York, 1941), 3-110; Sidney Kobre, *The Development of the Colonial Newspaper* (Pittsburgh, 1944); L. C. Wroth, *The Colonial Printer* (Portland, Me., 1938); G. H. Payne, *History of Journalism in the United States* (New York, 1920), 12-99; D. C. McMurtrie, *A History of Printing in the United States* (New York, 1936), Vol. II (only volume ever published); and the fine old work of Isaiah Thomas, *The History of Printing* (1810), reprinted in 1874 with additional material by the American Antiquarian Society.

75. Hening, II, 517.

76. Labaree, *Royal Instructions*, II, 495-496.

77. C. A. Duniway, *The Development of Freedom of the Press in Massachusetts* (New York, 1906); G. E. Littlefield, *The Early Massachusetts Press, 1638-1711* (Boston, 1907).

78. In addition to Brigham's volumes, see the checklist of Boston newspapers (1704-1780) compiled by Mary F. Ayer in *CSMP*, IX.

79. *BG*, March 10, 1752; *NYG* (2), April 13, 1752; *BNL*, March 22, 1753. The palm for the prize horror story in the colonial press goes to *NLG*, April 27, 1764.

80. A. M. Schlesinger, "The Colonial Newspapers and the Stamp Act," *NEQ*, VIII (1935), 63-83.

81. L. N. Richardson, *A History of Early American Magazines, 1741-1789* (New York, 1931), esp. 9-162, 363-367.

82. L. Rutherfurd, *John Peter Zenger* (New York, 1904); L. R. Schuyler, *The Liberty of the Press in the American Colonies Before the Revolutionary War* (New York, 1905), 42-50; and Zenger's own *A Brief Narrative of the Case and Tryal of John Peter Zenger* (New York,

1736), reprinted by Rutherfurd, 173-246.

83. Including the English press: *PaG*, April 6, May 18, 1738.

84. For some representative colonial essays and reprints on freedom of the press, see *NYWJ*, Nov. 12, 19, 1733, Feb. 18-March 4, April 15, 1734, Jan. 24, 1743; *NYG*, April 8, Oct. 14, 28, 1734; *AWM*, March 12, 28, April 4, 25, 1734; *PaG*, Nov. 17-Dec. 8, 1737, April 6, 1738; *BEP*, April 12, May 17, 1742, April 20, 1747; *NYEP*, Nov. 16, 1747; *NYM*, Sept. 2, 1754; *CG*, April 12, 1755; *NHG*, July 13, 1764; *PAM*, Jan. 1741; *IR*, Aug. 30, 1753; *NEM*, Aug. 1758. Cautious views are expressed in *NHG*, Oct. 7, 1756; *CG*, June 7, 1755, Feb. 7, May 22, 1756; *NYG* (2), March 24, 1755, Jan. 26, 1764.

85. *CG*, Feb. 7, 1756.

86. *NYWJ*, Jan. 14, 1734.

87. From *A Fan for Fanning* (Boston, 1771)—generally attributed to Hermon Husband—printed in W. K. Boyd, ed., *Some Eighteenth Century Tracts Concerning North Carolina* (Raleigh, 1927), 353.

88. McLaughlin, *Foundations of American Constitutionalism*, and "A Written Constitution in Some of its Historical Aspects," *Michigan Law Review*, V (1907), 605-626; B. F. Wright, "The Early History of Written Constitutions in America," in *Essays in History and Political Theory in Honor of Charles Howard McIlwain* (Cambridge, 1936), 344-371; S. G. Fisher, *The Evolution of the Constitution of the United States* (Philadelphia, 1897), Chap. 5; C. E. Stevens, *Sources of the Constitution of the United States* (New York, 1894), Chap. 1.

89. From the Virginia charter of 1609; Thorpe, VII, 3801.

90. See the pertinent essays in *Two Centuries' Growth of American Law*, Yale Bicentennial Publications (New York, 1902), and *Select Essays in*

Anglo-American Legal History, Association of American Law Schools (Boston, 1907-1909).

91. The charter of grants and liberties of 1618 supplanted the autocratic "Articles, Lawes, and Orders, Divine, Politique, and Martiall" of 1610, Peter Force, *Tracts and Other Papers* (Washington, 1844), 9-68. No copy of the document of 1618 exists as a whole, but its provisions may be reconstructed by using Andrews, *Colonial Period*, I, 180-184, and references there cited.

92. W. H. Whitmore, ed., *The Colonial Laws of Massachusetts* (Boston, 1887), II, 29-61; F. C. Gray, "Remarks on the Early Laws of Massachusetts Bay," *MHSC*, VIII (3rd ser.), 191-237.

93. *RICR*, I, 157-208; *CCR*, I, 509-563; *NHCR*, II, 561-616. For the famous "Duke's Laws" of New York (1665), see A. E. McKinley, "Transition from Dutch to English Rule in New York," *AHR*, VI (1901), 693-724.

94. J. Goebel, Jr., "King's Law and Local Custom in Seventeenth Century New England," *Columbia Law Review*, XXXI (1931), 416-448, emphasizes the ignorance of the early colonists as a factor in this primitivism. A clear impression of what it meant to go to law in early America may be secured from H. W. K. Fitzroy, "Richard Crosby goes to Court, 1683-1697," *PMHB*, LXII (1938), 12-19.

95. R. B. Morris, "Massachusetts and the Common Law," *AHR*, XXXI (1926), 443-453.

96. St. G. L. Sioussat, *The English Statutes in Maryland* (Baltimore, 1903).

97. *Studies in the History of American Law*. The subjects treated in detail are forms of action, evidence, land laws, women's rights, and torts. Further evidence is supplied by Felix Rackow, *The Right to Counsel*, unpublished doctoral thesis submitted

(1952) to Cornell University, 17-33.

98. *B. C. and M. Railroad v. The State*, 32 N.H. 215, 231 (1855). See Hening, I, 146, for an example of the way in which the colonial assembly aided this simplifying process.

99. Roscoe Pound, *The Spirit of the Common Law* (Boston, 1921), Chaps. 2-5; Flick, *History of New York*, II, Chap. 1.

100. Charles Warren, *A History of the American Bar* (Boston, 1913), Pt. I.

101. E. A. Jones, *American Members of the Inns of Court* (London, 1924).

102. P. S. Reinsch, *English Common Law in the Early American Colonies* (Madison, Wisc., 1899), 8.

103. Reinsch, *Common Law*, 5.

104. *Works*, II, 36.

105. For examples of colonial re-enactment or imitation of the English statute, see *Statutes at Large of South Carolina*, II, 74, 399; *Acts and Resolves of Massachusetts Bay*, I, 95, 99. The latter was disallowed by the Privy Council. See generally A. H. Carpenter, "Habeas Corpus in the Colonies," *AHR*, VIII (1902), 18-27.

CHAPTER TWO

1. J. N. Figgis, *From Gerson to Grotius* (Cambridge, England, 1907), 6, 133. See also his comments at 123-125, 133-135, 138-139, as well as his chapter in Vol. III of *The Cambridge Modern History* (Cambridge, England, 1904).

2. H. Laski, ed., *A Defence of Liberty against Tyrants* (London, 1924), 27; Lord Acton, *The History of Freedom* (London, 1907), 150-155.

3. M. S. Bates, *Religious Liberty* (New York, 1945); J. H. Nichols, *Democracy and the Churches* (Philadelphia, 1951).

4. The most significant treatments of colonial religion are W. W. Sweet, *Religion in Colonial America* (New York, 1942), and S. H. Cobb, *The Rise of Religious Liberty in America*

(New York, 1902). For the history of individual churches, see the thirteen volumes of *The American Church History Series* (New York, 1893-1897), many of which are cited elsewhere in these pages. See also the nine volumes of W. B. Sprague, *Annals of the American Pulpit* (New York, 1859-1869).

5. Studies of the religious situation in particular colonies abound. In addition to those cited elsewhere, see R. C. Strickland, *Religion and the State in Georgia in the Eighteenth Century* (New York, 1939); S. B. Weeks, *The Religious Development in the Province of North Carolina* (Baltimore, 1892), and *Church and State in North Carolina* (Baltimore, 1893); S. M. Reed, *Church and State in Massachusetts, 1691-1740* (Urbana, Ill., 1914). Serious students should not pass over lightly such quaintly disorganized but informative works as J. G. Felt, *The Ecclesiastical History of New England* (Boston, 1855-1862), and Isaac Backus, *A History of New England*, etc. (first published, 1777-1796; reissued at Newton, Mass., 1871).

6. K. S. Latourette, *A History of the Expansion of Christianity* (New York, 1937-1945), III, 186-239; A. L. Drummond, *Story of American Protestantism* (Edinburgh, 1949), Bk. I.

7. *NYM*, Sept. 23, 1754. See Sister M. Augustina (Ray), *American Opinion of Roman Catholicism in the Eighteenth Century* (New York, 1936).

8. *PaG*, July 17, 1755, Dec. 9, 1756; *NAM*, Feb. 1759; *MG* (2), April 29, Oct. 10, 1754, July 1, 1746, Feb. 10, 1747; *BAM*, Jan. 1746. On the related question of church and state in New France and New Spain, see E. B. Greene, *Religion and the State* (New York, 1941), 23-28.

9. T. O'Gorman, *A History of the Roman Catholic Church in the*

United States (New York, 1895), 234-246.

10. Andrews, *Colonial Period*, I, 65-67, 344-354, 369-371; Sweet, *Religion in Colonial America*, Chap. 1; N. M. Crouse, "Causes of the Great Migration," *NEQ*, V (1932), 3-36; Perry Miller, "The Religious Impulse in the Founding of Virginia," *WMQ* (3), V (1948), 492-522, VI (1949), 24-41.

11. L. B. Wright, *Religion and Empire* (Chapel Hill, 1943).

12. E. H. Davidson, *The Establishment of the English Church* (Durham, 1936). For the peculiar case of the establishment in New York, see *Ecclesiastical Records of the State of New York*, II, 1074-1079.

13. A. B. Seidman, "Church and State in the Early Years of the Massachusetts Bay Colony," *NEQ*, XVIII (1945), 211-233.

14. C. O. Paullin, *Atlas of the Historical Geography of the United States* (Washington, 1932), 49-50, Plate 82.

15. Sweet, *Religion in Colonial America*, 163, citing an unpublished thesis, 163n. An excellent contemporaneous report is "The Memorial of Colonel Lewis Morris concerning the State of Religion in the Jerseys" (1700), *New Jersey Historical Society, Proceedings*, IV (1849-1850), 118-121.

16. An informative series of papers on the development of different churches in New England is in J. W. Platner et al., *The Religious History of New England* (Cambridge, 1917).

17. See the brilliant exposition of "American Religion" in H. B. Parkes, *The American Experience* (New York, 1947), Chap. 4.

18. For some of the loudest laments, which eighteenth-century ministers simply echoed, see these memorable election sermons: Thomas Shepard, *Eye-Salve, or a Watch-Word from Our Lord* (Cambridge, 1673); Samuel Torrey, *A Plea for the Life of Dying Religion* (Boston, 1683), esp.

in the colonies is evident in such newspaper debates as that carried on in *NYG* (2), March 14, 1768-Jan. 29, 1770; *NYGWM*, April 4, 1768-July 10, 1769; *NYJ*, Sept. 22, 1768-Feb. 23, 1769; *PJ*, March 24-July 28, 1768, Sept. 8, 1768-Jan. 12, 1769; *PC*, Sept. 19, 1768-Feb. 27, 1769; *PaG*, Sept. 8, 1768-Jan. 5, 1769; *BEP*, April 11-Oct. 24, 1768; *BG*, March 28-June 6, 1768. This journalistic Donnybrook was touched off by Rev. Thomas Chandler's *An Appeal to the Public, in Behalf of the Church of England in America* (New York, 1767).

59. H. J. Eckenrode, *Separation of Church and State in Virginia* (Richmond, Va., 1910), 13. For some remarkable self-portraits of eighteenth-century Virginia ministers, see their answers to certain queries of the Bishop of London (1724) in Perry, *Historical Collections*, I, 261-318.

60. For the early church in Virginia see T. J. Wertenbaker, *The First Americans* (New York, 1938), Chap. 5; P. A. Bruce, *Institutional History of Virginia in the Seventeenth Century* (New York, 1910), I, 3-289; G. M. Brydon, *Virginia's Mother Church* (Richmond, 1947). A defense of the Virginia establishment is E. L. Goodwin, *The Colonial Church in Virginia* (London, 1927). For South Carolina, see F. J. Klingberg, ed., *Carolina Chronicle* (Berkeley, Cal., 1946). For the S.P.G., see H. P. Thompson, *Into All Lands* (New York, 1952).

61. J. D. Anderson, *History of the Church of England in the Colonies* (London, 1845), II, 559, quoting Morgan Godwyn, a Virginia minister.

62. *NCCR*, II, 374.

63. Fulham MSS. (Library of Congress transcripts), No. 230.

64. For the Jews in colonial America, see L. M. Friedman, *Early American Jews* (Cambridge, 1934); Anita Leb-

eson, *Jewish Pioneers in America* (New York, 1931); L. J. Levinger, *A History of the Jews in the United States* (Cincinnati, 1930); David de Sola Pool, *Portraits Etched in Stone* (New York, 1952); A. V. Goodman, *American Overture* (Philadelphia, 1947), esp. the bibliography at 229-251; and the publications of the American Jewish Historical Society. A definitive history of colonial Jewry is badly needed. For the Catholics, see O'Gorman, *History of the Roman Catholic Church*; J. G. Shea, *The Catholic Church in Colonial Days* (New York, 1886), a clear overstatement of the importance of Catholics in English America; W. H. J. Kennedy, "Catholics in Massachusetts before 1750," *Catholic Historical Review*, XVII (1931), 10-28; and Rev. A. J. Riley's remarks in *CSMP*, XXXIV, 389-399.

65. George Petrie, *Church and State in Early Maryland* (Baltimore, 1892).

66. Labaree, *Royal Instructions*, II, 494.

67. Some choice examples are the articles or letters in *NYEP*, Feb. 3, 1746, April 13, 1747, Nov. 21, 1748, Aug. 4, 1755; *BWR*, Nov. 29-Dec. 27, 1731; *VG*, Jan. 16, 23, July 3, 1746, April 11, 18, 1751; *NEWJ*, March 27, April 24, 1727, Nov. 29, 1737; *BNL*, April 15-July 22, 1725; *NM*, Oct. 10, 17, 1763, Sept. 3, 1764; *NHG*, April 15, 29, 1757, June 15, 1759; *PaG*, Sept. 1, 1764; *NLG*, Aug. 31, 1764. This list could be extended to a dozen pages. *The Wiles of Popery* (Boston, 1745); Hugh Jones, *A Protest against Popery* (Annapolis, 1745); and *Popish Cruelty Displayed* (Boston, 1753), were all best-sellers.

68. For most purposes of this discussion "Congregationalism" can be substituted for "Puritanism"; for some purposes, it should be. See generally G. G. Atkins and F. L. Fagley, *History of American Congregationalism* (Boston, 1942), Chaps. 1-9.

69. From the "Replye on the Negative Vote," printed in R. C. Winthrop, *Life and Letters of John Winthrop* (Boston, 1869), II, 430.

70. From the famous "Letter to Lord Say and Seal," printed in Thomas Hutchinson, *The History of the Colony of Massachusetts-Bay* (London, 1760, I, 497.

71. The extreme case for Puritanism as the core of modern democracy is made by C. K. Shipton, "A Plea for Puritanism," *AHR*, XL (1935), 460-467, and "Puritanism and Modern Democracy," *NEHGR*, CI (1947), 181-188. See also H. D. Foster, *Collected Papers* (Hanover, N.H., 1929), 30-76; Ola M. Winslow, *Meetinghouse Hill, 1630-1783* (New York, 1952), a superior book.

72. P. Miller, *The New England Mind* (New York, 1939), Chaps. 13-15, and *Orthodoxy in Massachusetts, 1630-1650* (Cambridge, 1933); P. Miller and T. H. Johnson, eds., *The Puritan Mind* (New York, 1938), 187-193; C. Burrage, *The Church Covenant Idea* (Philadelphia, 1904), which emphasizes Baptist practice; W. S. Carpenter, *The Development of American Political Thought* (Princeton, 1930), Chap. 1.

73. "Common Law," *Encyclopedia of the Social Sciences*, IV, 55. There is no wiser or more urbane discussion of the purposefulness of Puritan individualism than Perry Miller, "Individualism and the New England Tradition," *Journal of Liberal Religion*, IV (1942), 3-21.

74. Colonial attitudes on the right of private judgment are well summed up in *BAM*, Oct. 1744, March 1745; *PaG*, Jan. 19, 1748; *SCG*, July 12, 1760.

75. A provocative essay on Puritanism and American liberty is William Haller, "The Puritan Background of the First Amendment," in Conyers Read, ed., *The Constitution Reconsidered* (New York, 1938), 131-141.

76. W. M. Gewehr, *The Great Awakening in Virginia, 1740-1790* (Durham, 1930); C. H. Maxson, *The Great Awakening in the Middle Colonies* (Chicago, 1920); Joseph Tracy, *The Great Awakening* (Boston, 1842); F. M. Davenport, *Primitive Traits in Religious Revivals* (New York, 1905), Chap. 8; Sweet, *Religion in Colonial America*, Chap. 9.

77. Nettels, *Roots of American Civilization*, 481.

78. Perry Miller, *Jonathan Edwards* (New York, 1949) supplants all other inquiries into this fabulous mind, although the biographies of H. B. Parkes, A. C. McGiffert, and Ola Winslow retain much of their value.

79. L. Tyerman, *The Life of the Rev. George Whitefield* (London, 1876-1877). For a choice example of the effectiveness of Whitefield's preaching, see *Autobiography of Benjamin Franklin*, 130.

80. Not a newspaper in the colonies could ignore his presence. Examples of the space and varied treatment he received are *NYG*, Nov. 26, 1739; *NEWJ*, March 18-Sept. 2, 1740; *BG*, April 20-June 29, 1741, *PaG*, April 7-May 1, 1740; *SCG*, Jan. 5-March 29, 1740, March 11, 18, 1745, May 5, 1746, Oct. 26, Nov. 16, 1747; *CH*, 1743-1745, *passim;* and after his death, *BPB*, Oct. 1, Nov. 12, Dec. 3, 1770, March 18, April 15, May 6, 1771.

81. See his *Seasonable Thoughts on the State of Religion in New England* (Boston, 1743), the most incisive contemporaneous attack on the excesses of the Awakening.

82. Gewehr, *The Great Awakening,* Chaps. 8-11; W. W. Sweet, *Revivalism in America* (New York, 1944), Chap. 2; P. G. Mode, *The Frontier Spirit in American Christianity* (New York, 1923), Chap. 3.

83. Max Savelle, *Seeds of Liberty* (New York, 1948), 69.

84. Some idea of the intensity of the antipathies aroused may be found in the letters to *BPB*, Sept. 28, Oct. 5, 12, 1741; *BG*, July 24, 1744; *BEP*, Jan. 7-May 6, 1745.
85. Husband, *An Impartial Relation*, in Boyd, *Tracts*, 369.

CHAPTER THREE

1. A highly provocative economic interpretation of early American history is L. M. Hacker, *The Triumph of American Capitalism* (New York, 1940), Pts. 1-2. Economic histories of the United States abound. Especially worthy are E. C. Kirkland, *A History of American Economic Life* (New York, 1932), Chaps. 1-3, and the pertinent chapters in Nettels, *Roots of American Civilization*.
2. G. B. Parks, *Richard Hakluyt and the English Voyages* (New York, 1928); W. Cunningham, *The Growth of English Industry and Commerce in Modern Times* (Cambridge, England, 1912), Pt. I, Chap. 9; Nettels, *Roots of American Civilization*, Chaps. 4-6.
3. E. F. Heckscher, *Mercantilism* (London, 1933); G. Schmoller, *The Mercantile System* (New York, 1896), 47-77; E. Lipson, *The Economic History of England* (London, 1931), III, Chap. 4; P. W. Buck, *The Politics of Mercantilism* (New York, 1942).
4. Sir William Ashley, ed., *England's Treasure by Forraign Trade* (New York, 1895), 7. This is the most accessible modern edition of Thomas Mun's celebrated statement of the mercantile position, written about 1630 and first published in 1664.
5. J. F. Rees, "Mercantilism and the Colonies," in *The Cambridge History of the British Empire* (Cambridge, England, 1929), I, Chap. 20.
6. John Campbell, *Political Essays Concerning the Present State of the British Empire* (London, 1772), 327;

Keith, *A Collection of Papers*, 169-172.
7. E. A. J. Johnson, *American Economic Thought in the Seventeenth Century* (London, 1932), and "Some Evidence of Mercantilism in the Massachusetts-Bay," I (1928), 371-395.
8. R. B. Morris, "Labor and Mercantilism in the Revolutionary Era," in Morris, *Era of the Revolution*, 76-139.
9. Americans have always complained of high prices: *NEC*, Dec. 16, 1724, Jan. 11, 18, March 1-15, 1725; *BG*, May 16, 1737; *BEP*, Aug. 21, 1749; *NM*, Dec. 26, 1758; *NYM*, Dec. 31, 1759; *PaG*, Jan. 10, 1760; *SCG*, June 20, 1761.
10. W. Hill, "The First Stages of the Tariff Policy of the United States," *American Economic Association, Publications*, VIII (1893), 453-614.
11. A. A. Giesecke, *American Commercial Legislation Before 1789* (New York, 1910).
12. For the most important regulatory statute, the Virginia inspection act of 1730, see Hening, IV, 247-271. For the corresponding Maryland act of 1747, see *Md. Arch.*, XLIV, 595-630, and V. J. Wyckoff, *Tobacco Regulation in Colonial Maryland* (Baltimore, 1936). The problem of regulation was thoroughly agitated in the Southern press, the general line of argument holding that the tobacco trade was not regulated enough: *VG*, Aug. 5, 12, 1737, April 21, 1738; *MG* (2), April 1-Oct. 28, 1746, April 7-July 28, Dec. 9-30, 1747, April 5-Aug. 16, 1753, March 9, 16, 1758.
13. *NYWJ*, Oct. 12-26, 1741; *SCG*, April 9, 16, 1750; *NYG* (2), March 19, 1753; *WNYG*, Aug. 29, Sept. 12, 19, 1763; *IR*, May 10, 1753.
14. There is a variety of worth-while books on early American agriculture, among which these should be singled out for mention: J. Schafer, *The Social History of American Agricul-*

ture (New York, 1936); L. Carrier, *The Beginnings of Agriculture in America* (New York, 1940); N. S. B. Gras, *A History of Agriculture* (New York, 1940), Chaps. 12-16.

15. *VG*, March 30, 1739; *BG*, Feb. 13, 1753; *BEP*, Oct. 15, 1759.

16. Much of what we know about colonial agricultural methods comes from two important works: Jared Eliot, *Essays upon Field Husbandry* (Boston, 1760), and the anonymously published *American Husbandry* (London, 1775). Both of these have been reprinted under the editorship of H. J. Carman. See also C. R. Woodward's delightful *Ploughs and Politicks* (New Brunswick, N.J., 1941).

17. A stimulating if overreaching treatment of colonial economic theories is J. Dorfman, *The Economic Mind in American Civilization* (New York, 1946), I, Bk. 1.

18. For evidence of this statement in terms of business organization, see J. S. Davis, *Essays in the Earlier History of American Corporations* (Cambridge, 1917), 3-107.

19. D. R. Dewey, *Financial History of the United States* (8th ed., New York, 1922), 9-17. Important studies of colonial taxation and finance are W. Z. Ripley, *The Financial History of Virginia, 1609-1776* (New York, 1893); F. R. Jones, *The History of Taxation in Connecticut, 1636-1776* (Baltimore, 1896); Osgood, *American Colonies in the Seventeenth Century*, I, Chap. 12, and II, Chap. 14.

20. See generally V. S. Clark, *History of Manufactures in the United States, 1607-1860* (Washington, 1916), Chaps. 1-9, and the amorphous but fact-laden compendium of J. L. Bishop, *A History of American Manufactures from 1608 to 1860* (Philadelphia, 1861-1864), Vol. I. The colonial case for manufactures is stated in *NYWJ*, March 28, May 2, 23, 1737.

21. C. B. Kuhlmann, *The Development of the Flour-Milling Industry in the United States* (Boston, 1929), Chap. 1, is a first-rate piece of economic history.

22. See especially C. P. Nettels, *The Money Supply of the American Colonies Before 1720* (Madison, Wisc., 1934), a model for all special investigations of colonial economic themes.

23. R. M. Tryon, *Household Manufactures in the United States, 1640-1860* (Chicago, 1917), Chaps. 2-3.

24. See E. Johnson, *et al.*, *History of Domestic and Foreign Commerce of the United States* (Washington, 1915), I, Pt. 1; C. M. Andrews, "Colonial Commerce," *AHR*, XX (1914), 43-63, a brilliant short review; and such special studies as M. S. Morriss, *Colonial Trade of Maryland, 1689-1715* (Baltimore, 1914), and R. M. Hooker, *The Colonial Trade of Connecticut* (New Haven, 1936).

25. And to a degree not always palatable to contemporary generations. See *BNL*, March 7, 1734; *NEWJ*, March 11, 1734. For a contrary attitude, see *MG* (2) March 11, April 8, 1762.

26. W. T. Baxter, *The House of Hancock* (Cambridge, 1945), and J. B. Hedges, *The Browns of Providence Plantations, Colonial Years* (Cambridge, 1952), are outstanding studies of great merchant families.

27. An excellent summary of colonial production and trade is H. J. Carman, *Social and Economic History of the United States* (Boston, 1930), I, Chap. 3.

28. A confusing but valuable description of the New England economy is W. B. Weeden, *Economic and Social History of New England* (Boston, 1890).

29. *Johnson's Wonder-Working Providence* (1654) (Andover, Mass., 1867), 163.

30. For New England agriculture, see P. W. Bidwell and J. I. Falconer, *History of Agriculture in the Northern United States, 1620-1860* (Washington, 1925), Pts. 1-2; R. R. Walcott, "Husbandry in Colonial New England," *NEQ*, IX (1936), 218-252.

31. W. S. Tower, *A History of the American Whale Fishery* (Philadelphia, 1907), Chap. 3; E. P. Hohman, *The American Whaleman* (New York, 1928), Chap. 3; A. Starbuck, *History of the American Whale Fishery* (Waltham, Mass., 1878).

32. For an informative account of a special problem in lumbering, the supply of masts to the English fleet, see R. G. Albion, *Forests and Sea Power* (Cambridge, 1926), Chap. 6. J. E. Defebaugh, *History of the Lumber Industry in America* (Chicago, 1906-1907), II, is disorganized but full of information. For the story of government regulation of the forests, see Jenks Cameron, *The Development of Governmental Forest Control in the United States* (Baltimore, 1928), Chap. 2.

33. On the New England fur trade, see A. H. Buffinton, "New England and the Western Fur Trade," *CSMP*, XVIII, 160-192. For a survey of this trade in all sections, see the introduction in C. H. McIlwain, ed., *Wraxall's Abridgment of the Indian Affairs* (Cambridge, 1915).

34. R. McFarland, *A History of the New England Fisheries* (New York, 1911), Chaps. 2-6; H. A. Innis, *The Cod Fisheries* (New Haven, 1940), Chaps. 4-7.

35. *Works*, X, 345.

36. See especially the widely reprinted "An Essay on the Trade of the Northern Colonies," *PJ*, March 8, 1764; *NYM*, Feb. 6, 1764; *PG*, Jan. 14, 21, 1764; *NLG*, Feb. 3, 1764; *NYG* (2), Feb. 9, 1764; *NM*, Feb. 6, 13, 1764. Other provocative statements of the position of the Northern colonies are in *NEWJ*, Sept. 6,

13, 1731; *PaG*, July 15, 1731; *BEP*, March 2, 1747.

37. On this great extractive industry, see E. L. Lord, *Industrial Experiments in the British Colonies of North America* (Baltimore, 1898; C. P. Nettels, "The Menace of Colonial Manufacturing," *NEQ*, IV (1931), 230-269, 240ff.; L. C. Gray, *History of Agriculture in the Southern United States to 1860* (Washington, 1933), I, 151-160.

38. On the Southern fur trade, see Crane, *Southern Frontier*, Chap. 5.

39. See especially the magnificent volumes of L. C. Gray, *History of Agriculture in the Southern United States*.

40. L. Sellers, *Charleston Business on the Eve of the Revolution* (Chapel Hill, 1934), is a model study of a colonial center of commerce.

41. K. Bruce, *Virginia Iron Manufacture in the Slave Era* (New York, 1931), 3-23.

42. P. A. Bruce, *Economic History of Virginia in the Seventeenth Century* (New York, 1896), I, Chaps. 4-7.

43. M. Jacobstein, *The Tobacco Industry in the United States* (New York, 1907), Chap. 1; Gray, *History of Agriculture*, Chaps. 10-12; Avery Craven, *Soil Exhaustion as a Factor in the Agricultural History of Virginia and Maryland, 1606-1860* (Urbana, Ill., 1926), Chaps. 1-2; J. C. Robert, *The Story of Tobacco in America* (New York, 1949), Chaps. 1-2.

44. And irritated colonials: *MG* (2), Oct. 28, 1746. See generally J. S. Bassett, "The Virginia Planter and the London Merchant," *AHAAR*, 1901 (I), 551-575.

45. *VG*, March 20, 1752.

46. Gray, *History of Agriculture*, Chap. 13.

47. An interesting special study of this region is Anne Bezanson *et al.*, *Prices in Colonial Pennsylvania* (Philadelphia, 1935). For New York,

see Flick, *History of New York*, II, Chaps. 7-9.

48. A. C. Bining, *Pennsylvania Iron Manufacture in the Eighteenth Century* (Harrisburg, Pa., 1938).

49. Peter Kalm, *Travels into North America* (2nd ed., London, 1772), I, 70.

50. For a difference of opinion on the actual extent of the manorial system in Maryland, see the comments of Gray, *History of Agriculture*, 372-377, on L. W. Wilhelm, *Local Institutions of Maryland* (Baltimore, 1885), Chap. 1, and J. Johnson, *Old Maryland Manors* (Baltimore, 1883).

51. For a discussion of free and common socage and related matters, see V. F. Barnes, "Land Tenure in English Colonial Charters of the Seventeenth Century," in *Essays in Colonial History*, 4-40.

52. B. W. Bond, jr., *The Quit-Rent System in the American Colonies* (New Haven, 1919), 444. This is an extremely valuable work, not least because of C. M. Andrews's introductory musings on historiography, land tenure, and freedom.

53. Important recent studies in the land history of colonial New York are Edith M. Fox, *Land Speculation in the Mohawk Country* (Ithaca, N.Y., 1949), and D. M. Ellis, *Landlords and Farmers in the Hudson-Mohawk Region* (Ithaca, 1946), 7-15. C. W. Spencer, "The Land System of Colonial New York," *Proceedings, N. Y. State Historical Association*, XVI, (1917), 150-164, has some interesting general observations. See also S. G. Nissenson, "The Development of a New York Land Registration System," *New York History*, XX (1939), 16-42, 161-188; R. L. Higgins, *Expansion in New York* (Columbus, Ohio, 1931), Chap. 3; E. W. Spaulding, *New York in the Critical Period* (New York, 1932), Chap. 3.

54. M. Egleston, *The Land System of the New England Colonies* (Balti-more, 1886); R. H. Akagi, *The Town Proprietors of the New England Colonies* (Philadelphia, 1924); Bidwell and Falconer, *History of Agriculture*, Chap. 5; Osgood, *American Colonies in the Seventeenth Century*, I, Chap. 11; A. N. B. Garvan, *Architecture and Town Planning in Colonial Connecticut* (New Haven, 1951), Chap. 3, a brilliant study.

55. *MHSC*, VIII (3rd ser.), 218, 230. See R. B. Morris, "Primogeniture and Entailed Estates in America," *Columbia Law Review*, XXVII (1927), 24-51, and *Studies in American Law*, Chap. 2.

56. William Haller, jr., *The Puritan Frontier* (New York, 1951), is a study of the interaction of Puritan institutions and wilderness environment during the first period of expansion, 1630-1660.

57. *MCR*, V, 214.

58. A. B. MacLear, *Early New England Towns* (New York, 1908), Chap. 4.

59. See particularly the invaluable articles of G. L. Haskins, "The Beginnings of Partible Inheritance in the American Colonies," *Yale Law Journal*, LI (1942), 1280-1315; "The Beginnings of the Recording System in Massachusetts," *Boston Univ. Law Review*, XXI (1941), 281-304; and "Gavelkind and the Charter of Massachusetts Bay," *CSMP*, XXXIV, 483-498.

60. For a famous blast at those whose lust for land made it "one of the Gods of New England," see Roger Williams's words in *NCP*, VI, 342.

61. For land-holding in Connecticut, see C. M. Andrews, *The River Towns of Connecticut* (Baltimore, 1889), Chap. 2, and *Connecticut Intestacy Law*.

62. From his speech at Plymouth, December 22, 1820; *The Writings and Speeches of Daniel Webster* (Boston, 1903), I, 211-212.

63. The best summary of land tenure in the Southern colonies is Gray, *History of Agriculture*, I, Chap. 17; in the middle colonies Bidwell and Falconer, *History of Agriculture*, 60-66. See also Osgood, *American Colonies in the Seventeenth Century*, II, Chap. 2; Shepherd, *Proprietary Government in Pennsylvania*, Pt. I.

64. I. D. Rupp, *History of Berks and Lebanon Counties* (Lancaster, 1844), 115. On this problem, see A. C. Ford, *Colonial Precedents of Our National Land System* (Madison, 1910), Chap. 7.

65. For the influence of Dutch practices on land-holding in New York, see C. W. Rife, "Land Tenure in New Netherland," in *Essays in Colonial History*, 41-73. A severe contemporary indictment of the situation in New York may be found in a letter of "Manius Currius" to *MS*, June 4, 1772.

66. Dr. Alexander Hamilton (1744) in C. Bridenbaugh, ed., *Gentleman's Progress* (Chapel Hill, N.C., 1948), 39.

67. Ingle, *Local Institutions of Virginia*, Chap. 2; C. P. Gould, *The Land System in Maryland, 1720-1765* (Baltimore, 1913); J. S. Bassett, "Landholding in Colonial North Carolina," *Law Quarterly Review*, XI (1895), 154-166; Smith, *South Carolina as a Royal Province*, Sec. 1.

68. J. C. Ballagh, "Introduction to Southern Economic History—The Land System," *AHAAR* (1897), 101-129; M. C. Voorhis, "Crown versus Council in the Virginia Land Policy," *WMQ* (3), III (1946), 499-514.

69. T. P. Abernethy, *Western Lands and the American Revolution* (New York, 1937), Chaps. 1-12; Akagi, *Town Proprietors*, Pt. II; F. T. Volwiler, *George Croghan and the Western Movement* (Cleveland, 1926); Fox, *Land Speculation in the Mohawk Country*.

70. *PMHB*, XI (1887), 277.

71. Turner, *Significance of Sections*, 293.

72. Hector St. John de Crèvecoeur, *Letters from an American Farmer* (1782), (London, 1912), 24-25.

73. *Triumph of American Capitalism*, 5.

74. *Triumph of Capitalism*, 27.

75. Samuel Whitman, *Practical Godliness the Way to Prosperity* (New London, 1714); James Lockwood, *Religion the highest Interest of a civil Community, and the surest Means of its Prosperity* (New London, 1754).

76. See especially "The Watchman," *PJ*, April 27, 1758: "*Trade* much delights in *Freedom* and *Ease*."

77. A highly suggestive treatment of the influence of the forest on colonial history is R. G. Lillard, *The Great Forest* (New York, 1948), Pt. I.

78. An equally suggestive discussion of the role of the soil is A. B. Hulbert, *Soil: Its Influence on the History of the United States* (New Haven, 1930).

79. Buck, *Politics of Mercantilism*, 88. See E. S. Furniss, *The Position of the Laborer in a System of Nationalism* (Boston, 1920).

80. Buck, *Politics of Mercantilism*, 88.

81. Johnson, *American Economic Thought*, 205-213.

82. J. K. Hosmer, ed., *Winthrop's Journal* (New York, 1908), II, 24. See also his complaints at I, 112.

83. For the Massachusetts General Court's reaction to "excessive prizes," see *MCR*, I, 79, 83, 88, 109, 223.

84. R. B. Morris, *Government and Labor in Early America* (New York 1946), Introduction and Chap. 1. This is one of the most valuable studies in the political economy of the colonies. A special study of importance is S. McKee, jr., *Labor in Colonial New York* (New York, 1935).

85. Clark, *History of Manufactures*, 207.
86. *NYCD*, VII, 888-889.
87. *American Husbandry*, I, 73.
88. John Oldmixon, *The British Empire in America* (London, 1741), I, 316.
89. Morris, *Government and Labor*, 45.
90. See *History of Wages in the United States from Colonial Times to 1928*, Bulletin of the U.S. Bureau of Labor Statistics (Washington, 1929), Pt. I; Clark, *History of Manufactures*, 152-158; and T. J. Wertenbaker's engaging pamphlet *Labor Costs and American Democracy* (Princeton, 1938).
91. See the advertisement in *NYWJ*, Oct. 18, 1742.
92. C. T. Eben, transl., *Gottlieb Mittelberger's Journey to Pennsylvania, 1750-1754* (Philadelphia, 1898), 56.
93. Morris, *Government and Labor*, 363-389.
94. Morris, *Government and Labor*, Chap. 3.
95. J. R. Commons *et al.*, *History of Labor in the United States* (New York, 1918), I, 25-26.
96. An important study of the slave artisan is M. W. Jernegan, *Laboring and Dependent Classes in Colonial America* (Chicago, 1931), Chap. 1.
97. Carl Bridenbaugh, *The Colonial Craftsman* (New York, 1950), Chap. 6, a book of charm and distinction. See also the fascinating material in *The Arts and Crafts in New York, 1726-1776*, *NYHSC*, LXIX (1938); G. F. Dow, *The Arts and Crafts in New England, 1704-1775* (Topsfield, Mass., 1927); A. C. Prime, *The Arts and Crafts in Philadelphia*, etc. (Topsfield, 1929).
98. 12 Car. II c. 18; 14 Car. II c. 7; 7 & 8 Gul. III c. 22, respectively. See generally L. A. Harper, *The English Navigation Laws* (New York, 1939), a work of rare scholarship and insight.

99. 10 & 11 Gul. III c. 10; 5 Geo. II c. 22; 23 Geo. II c. 29, respectively.
100. Gipson, *British Empire*, III, Chap. 8.
101. 6 Geo. II, c. 13; A. B. Southwick, "The Molasses Act," *WMQ* (3), VIII (1951), 389-405. For the background of this act, see C. M. Andrews, "Anglo-French Commercial Rivalry, 1700-1750: The Western Phase," *AHR*, XX (1915), 539-556, 761-780.
102. Harper, *English Navigation Laws*, Pts. III-IV.
103. A. H. Cole, *The American Wool Manufacture* (Cambridge, 1926), I, 38-47; A. C. Bining, *British Regulation of the Colonial Iron Industry* (Philadelphia, 1933).
104. W. S. McClellan, *Smuggling in the American Colonies at the Outbreak of the Revolution* (New York, 1912); A. M. Schlesinger, *The Colonial Merchants and the American Revolution, 1763-1776* (New York, 1917), 39-49; W. J. Ashley, *Surveys Historic and Economic* (London, 1900), 336-360; Harper, *English Navigation Laws*, 247-271.
105. A powerful defense of this trade is printed in *WNYG*, May 19, 1760; *PJ*, May 29, 1760.
106. Russell, *Review of American Colonial Legislation*, Chap. 4.
107. "The Effect of the Navigation Acts on the Thirteen Colonies," in Morris, *Era of the Revolution*, 3-39, esp. 37. And see O. M. Dickerson, *The Navigation Acts and the American Revolution* (Philadelphia, 1951), esp. 290ff.
108. See the table on tobacco shipments in David Macpherson, *Annals of Commerce, Manufactures, Fisheries, and Navigation* (London, 1805), III, 583. For other sources of statistics on the trade of the colonies, see Johnson, *History of Domestic and Foreign Commerce*, 112-117. I found Lord Sheffield's *Observations on the Commerce of the American States*

(London, 1784) especially useful and informative. The colonial newspapers offer all manner of information to the student of economic history; e.g., the ship clearings and cargoes listed in *VG*, May 18, Aug. 10, 24, Nov. 2, Dec. 14, 1739; tables of imports and exports in *SCG*, Nov. 8, 1735, Aug. 8, Sept. 8, Dec. 8, 1759; and "prices current" in *BG*, 1719-1720, *SCG*, 1749-1750, *passim*.
109. The great American spokesman for this point of view was G. L. Beer, as he made abundantly clear in *British Colonial Policy, 1754-1765* (New York, 1908), and especially *The Old Colonial System* (New York, 1912).
110. Kalm, *Travels*, I, 206; *NYG*, July 14, 1729.
111. An extremely useful summary of the arguments of Hacker, Andrews, Miller, J. T. Adams, Becker, and others over the importance of economic forces in the coming of the Revolution is J. C. Wahlke, ed., *The Causes of the American Revolution* (Boston, 1950).
112. A work of prime significance for this subject is C. W. Alvord's *The Mississippi Valley in British Politics* (Cleveland, 1917).
113. Campbell, *Political Essays*, 273. Pages 416-433 of this surprisingly judicious work offer an interesting view of the moderate imperial attitude on the subject of American independence.
114. *Works*, II, 30-31.

CHAPTER FOUR

1. The most useful of the many social histories of the colonies are T. J. Wertenbaker, *The First Americans* (New York, 1927); J. T. Adams, *Provincial Society* (New York, 1927); Nettels, *Roots of American Civilization*, Chaps. 12, 13, 17, 19. C. M. Andrews, *Colonial Folkways* (New

Haven, 1920) is a masterpiece of synthesis.
2. Dixon Wecter, *The Saga of American Society* (New York, 1937), Chap. 2.
3. The best single book on the colonial aristocracy is L. W. Labaree, *Conservatism in Early American History* (New York, 1948).
4. Hutchinson, *History of Massachusetts-Bay*, I, 490.
5. *MCR*, III, 243. For a phase of social distinctions in New England, see N. H. Dawes, "Titles as Symbols of Prestige in Seventeenth-Century New England," *WMQ* (3), VI (1949), 69-83.
6. *WMQ*, III (1894), 136-137.
7. *CSMP*, III, 411, XV, cxl, XVIII, 68, XXV, 420-427; *MHSP*, IX, 252; *AASP*, IX, 34-59, XLII, 371-431.
8. *Proceedings of the Convention of Delegates* (March 1775), 5.
9. L. Wright, *The First Gentlemen of Virginia* (San Marino, 1940), Chap. 1; E. H. Cady, *The Gentleman in America* (Syracuse, 1949), Chaps. 1-2.
10. W. D. Miller, "The Narragansett Planters," *AASP*, XLIII, 49-115; E. Channing, *The Narragansett Planters* (Baltimore, 1886).
11. Gipson, *British Empire*, III, 5. On the Boston aristocracy, see Justin Winsor, ed., *The Memorial History of Boston* (Boston, 1880-1881), II, Chaps. 16, 18. N. H. Chamberlain, *Samuel Sewall and the World He Lived In* (Boston, 1897) is a rewarding account of the mores and habitat of an indigenous New England aristocrat of the middle period.
12. Carl Becker, *The History of Political Parties in the Province of New York, 1760-1776* (Madison, 1909), Chap. 1; I. Mark, *Agrarian Conflicts in Colonial New York, 1711-1775* (New York, 1940), Chaps. 1-3; M. Schuyler, *Patroons and Lords of Manor of the Hudson* (New York,

1932); Flick, *History of New York,* II, Chap. 10, III, Chap. 5.

13. D. R. Fox, *Caleb Heathcote* (New York, 1926), is a delightful portrait of a great aristocrat of the middle period. Alice M. Keys, *Cadwallader Colden* (New York, 1906), pictures the aristocrat as public figure. G. W. Schuyler, *Colonial New York. Philip Schuyler and his Family* (New York, 1885), and E. B. Livingston, *The Livingstons of Livingston Manor* (New York, 1910), are remarkably good studies—considering the thickness of New York blood—of two great families.

14. Virginia Harrington, *The New York Merchant on the Eve of the Revolution* (New York, 1935), Chap. 1.

15. Jan. 27, 1765; *Colden Letter Books, NYHSC,* IX, 462.

16. Esther Singleton, *Social New York under the Georges, 1714-1776* (New York, 1902). For a documentary picture of New York in 1738, see E. B. O'Callaghan, *The Documentary History of the State of New York* (Albany, 1849-1851), I, 163-241. See also Colden's report on land-holdings, I, 375-389.

17. F. B. Tolles, *Meeting House and Counting House* (Chapel Hill, 1948), esp. Chap. 6.

18. Few students of colonial history will now disagree with the thesis of T. J. Wertenbaker's authoritative books: the middle-class origins of the Virginia aristocracy, especially as documented in his *Patrician and Plebeian in Virginia* (Charlottesville, 1910), *The Planters of Colonial Virginia* (Princeton, 1922), *The Old South* (New York, 1942), *Virginia under the Stuarts* (Princeton, 1914), and other works cited in these pages. For a judicious appraisal of various aspects of Southern society, see Carl Bridenbaugh, *Myths and Realities: Societies of the Colonial South* (L.S.U., 1952).

19. Two magnificent views of the lives and customs of this great family are to be found in L. Morton, *Robert Carter of Nomini Hall* (Williamsburg, 1941) and H. D. Farish, ed., *Journal and Letters of Philip Vickers Fithian, 1773-1774* (Williamsburg, 1943). See also such originals as Robert Beverley, *The History and Present State of Virginia* (1705, 1722) (Chapel Hill, 1947) and Hugh Jones, *The Present State of Virginia* (1724) (New York, 1865).

20. A. Craven, *Soil Exhaustion,* esp. Chap. 2.

21. C. A. Barker, *The Background of the Revolution in Maryland* (New Haven, 1940), Chaps. 1-3.

22. C. Eaton, *A History of the Old South* (New York, 1949), Chap. 3.

23. H. H. Ravenel, *Eliza Pinckney* (New York, 1896), 5.

24. Burnaby, *Travels,* 61.

25. The most conclusive of the many studies of white servitude in the colonies are A. E. Smith, *Colonists in Bondage* (Chapel Hill, 1947) and Morris, *Government and Labor,* Chaps. 7-9. For servitude and slavery in New York, see McKee, *Labor in Colonial New York,* Chaps. 3-4.

26. E. I. McCormac, *White Servitude in Maryland* (Baltimore, 1904).

27. C. A. Herrick, *White Servitude in Pennsylvania* (Philadelphia, 1926).

28. Bruce, *Economic History of Virginia,* I, Chap. 9; J. C. Ballagh, *White Servitude in the Colony of Virginia* (Baltimore, 1895).

29. K. F. Geiser, *Redemptioners and Indentured Servants in Pennsylvania* (New Haven, 1901), 41.

30. *Travels,* I, 304.

31. *Colonists in Bondage,* 298-303.

32. Geiser, *Redemptioners and Indentured Servants,* 110-112, presents a thoughtful balance-sheet. See also Jernegan, *Laboring and Dependent Classes,* Chap. 3.

33. E. McCrady, "Slavery in . . . South Carolina, 1670-1770," *AHAAR* (1895), 631-673.

34. L. J. Greene, *The Negro in Colonial New England* (New York, 1942); E. R. Turner, *The Negro in Pennsylvania* (Washington, 1911), Chaps. 1-6; H. S. Cooley, *A Study of Slavery in New Jersey* (Baltimore, 1896); E. Olson, "Social Aspects of Slave Life in New York," *Journal of Negro History*, XXVI (1941), 66-77.

35. J. C. Hurd, *The Law of Freedom and Bondage in the United States* (New York, 1858-1862), I, 228-311; Helen T. Catterall, *Judicial Cases concerning American Slavery and the Negro* (Washington, 1926-1937), Vols. I, II, IV; W. E. Moore, "Slave Law and the Social Structure," *Journal of Negro History*, XXVI (1941), 171-202.

36. On the slave trade and attempts to restrict it, see W. E. B. Du Bois, *The Suppression of the African Slave Trade* (New York, 1896), Chaps. 2-4; Elizabeth Donnan, ed., *Documents Illustrative of the History of the Slave Trade to America* (Washington, 1930-1935), Vols. III, IV; Eric Williams, *Capitalism and Slavery* (Chapel Hill, 1944).

37. O. and M. Handlin, "Origins of the Southern Labor System," *WMQ* (3), VII (1950), 199-222.

38. See generally and circumspectly J. H. Franklin, *From Slavery to Freedom* (New York, 1947), Chaps. 6-8, and the bibliography at 596-600; C. G. Woodson, *The Negro in Our History* (7th ed., Washington, 1941), Chaps. 5-8; U. B. Phillips, *American Negro Slavery* (New York, 1918), Chaps. 2-7; Benjamin Brawley, *A Social History of the American Negro* (New York, 1921), Chaps. 1-2.

39. *NYG*, Sept. 4, 11, 1732; *PaG*, Feb. 16, 1744; *BG*, Jan. 10, 1763.

40. Greene, *Negro in New England*, Chap. 11; J. H. Russell, *The Free Negro in Virginia* (Baltimore, 1913).

41. *AWM*, Aug. 10, 1738; *VG*, April 3, 10, 1752; *SCG*, March 28, 1743, Nov. 5, 1744, Oct. 17, 1754, May 1, 1756. are good examples of this constant concern over the Negroes. The South Carolina slave code of 1740, the most severe in America, was the legal expression of this fear; *S. C. Stat.*, VII, 397-417.

42. On slavery in the South, see the pertinent works cited in the notes above as well as Gray, *History of Agriculture*, Chaps. 16, 22; J. C. Ballagh, *A History of Slavery in Virginia* (Baltimore, 1902); J. S. Bassett, *Slavery and Servitude in North Carolina* (Baltimore, 1896); C. G. Woodson, *The Education of the Negro prior to 1861* (New York, 1915), Chaps. 1-4; Jernegan, *Laboring and Dependent Classes*, Chaps. 1-2; R. B. Pinchbeck, *The Virginia Negro Artisan and Tradesman* (Richmond, 1926).

43. Still the basic, but by no means the definitive, study of the colonial family is A. W. Calhoun, *A Social History of the American Family* (Cleveland, 1917), Vol. I. See also W. Goodsell, *A History of Marriage and the Family* (New York, 1935), Chap. 9 and the bibliography at 426-427.

44. E. S. Morgan, *The Puritan Family* (Boston, 1944).

45. *NHCR*, II, 608.

46. *Va. Mag.*, XXXII, 30.

47. See especially the revealing entries in Sewall's diary, *MHSC*, VII (5th ser.), 204-208, 262-275, 302-303.

48. The books of Alice M. Earle have lost none of their charm and little of their value as repositories of original material. See especially *Home Life in Colonial Days* (New York, 1896); *Customs and Fashions in Old New England* (New York, 1893); *Colonial Days in Old New York* (New York, 1897); and *Two Cen-*

turies of Costume in America (New York, 1903). S. G. Fisher, *Men, Women, and Manners in Colonial Times* (Philadelphia, 1898), is equally informative.

49. Tryon, *Household Manufactures,* Chaps. 2-3.

50. An article of distinction is G. T. Trewartha, "Types of Rural Settlement in Colonial America," *Geographical Review,* XXXVI (1946), 568-596.

51. See Dr. Hamilton's testimony (1744) in Bridenbaugh, *Gentleman's Progress,* 39.

52. Burnaby, *Travels,* 109.

53. See again Morton, *Robert Carter,* and Farish, *Journal of P. V. Fithian,* as well as U. B. Phillips, *Life and Labor in the Old South* (Boston, 1929), Chaps. 2-3; Eaton, *History of the South,* Chap. 2; Mary N. Stanard, *Colonial Virginia* (Philadelphia, 1917).

54. On the rise of the plantation system and Southern social order, see the many studies of Wertenbaker and Bruce as well as W. F. Craven, *The Southern Colonies in the Seventeenth Century* (Baton Rouge, 1949), which has a superb critical essay on authorities at 417-433; W. E. Dodd, "The Emergence of the First Social Order in the United States," *AHR,* XL (1935), 217-231, and *The Old South* (New York, 1937); Gray, *History of Agriculture,* I, Chaps. 14-15.

55. See the works cited in notes 58, 60, 67, and 71, Chapter 1, and notes 54, 56, and 58, Chapter 3, as well as C. Bridenbaugh, "The New England Town: A Way of Life," *AASP,* LVI, 19-48. A full understanding of the New England town can be won only through study of local records and the better town-histories. The town records I have examined are listed in notes 60 and 67, Chapter 1, while the town histories I found most illuminating were T. F. Waters, *Ipswich in the Massachusetts Bay*

Colony (Ipswich, 1905); Ellen D. Larned, *History of Windham County, Connecticut* (Worcester, 1874-1880); C. F. Adams, *Three Episodes of Massachusetts History* (Boston, 1893), II, 581-837; G. Lincoln et al., *History of the Town of Hingham* (Hingham, Mass., 1893); J. T. Adams, *History of Southampton, Long Island* (Bridgehampton, L.I., 1918). The rise and fall of the favorite laboratory of Puritanism is chronicled in Isabel M. Calder, *The New Haven Colony* (New Haven, 1934).

56. *Records of the Town of East-Hampton* (Sag Harbor, L.I., 1887-1905), I, 7 (1650); *Records of East-Hampton,* II, 18 (Oct. 7, 1651); *Huntington Town Records, 1653-1775* (Huntington, L.I., 1887-1888), II, 63.

57. May 1, 1673; *Brookhaven Town Records* (New York, 1924), I, 140.

58. John Adams to Abigail, Oct. 29, 1775; C. F. Adams, *Familiar Letters of John Adams and his Wife Abigail Adams* (New York, 1876), 120-121. A rewarding study of early New England is G. F. Dow, *Every Day Life in the Massachusetts Bay Colony* (Boston, 1935).

59. July 21, 1786; *Works,* III, 400; V, 494-496.

60. Bridenbaugh, "New England Town," *AASP,* LVI, 36-40.

61. J. H. Benton, *Warning Out in New England* (Boston, 1911). For an idea of the extent to which this technique was used in one New England town (Newbury, 1734-1776), see *EIHC,* LXIX, 36-48.

62. Carl Bridenbaugh's *Cities in the Wilderness* (New York, 1938) is in a class by itself as a social survey of our first cities. See also such excellent special studies as C. and J. Bridenbaugh, *Rebels and Gentlemen. Philadelphia in the Age of Franklin* (New York, 1942); Winsor, *Memorial History of Boston,* Vols. I and II; Scharf and Westcott, *History of*

Philadelphia; J. G. Wilson, *Memorial History of the City of New York* (New York, 1892-1893), Vols. I and II; I. N. Phelps Stokes, *Iconography of Manhattan Island* (New York, 1915-1928), Vols. I, II, IV, VI; r. J. Wertenbaker, *Norfolk: Historic Southern Port* (Durham, 1931), Chaps. 1-3; F. B. Bowes, *The Culture of Early Charleston* (Chapel Hill, 1942).

63. *Cities in the Wilderness*, 466.

64. Mary S. Benson, *Women in Eighteenth-Century America* (New York, 1935), esp. Chaps. 8-9, and the bibliography at 317-332; Calhoun, *American Family*, I, Chaps. 3, 5, 8, 16; Earle, *Home Life*, and *Colonial Dames and Goodwives* (New York, 1895); *Commonwealth History of Massachusetts*, II, 355-385.

65. Elisabeth A. Dexter, *Colonial Women of Affairs* (Boston, 1924). For a representative opinion of women in politics, see *NYWJ*, Aug. 19, 1734.

66. *NYWJ*, Sept. 8, 22, 1740.

67. T. Woody, *A History of Women's Education in the United States* (New York, 1929), I, Chaps. 4-6. An interesting dissenting opinion from common beliefs is in *NYWJ*, May 19, 1735.

68. G. E. Howard, *A History of Matrimonial Institutions* (Chicago, 1904), II, Chaps. 12-15; Goodsell, *History of Marriage*, 366-397.

69. The portrait of the ideal woman of the better sort may be found in the occasional funeral sermon, of which Charles Chauncy, *A Funeral Discourse on the Death of Mrs. Lucy Waldo* (Boston, 1741) and Thomas Prince, *A Sermon Occasioned by the Decease of Mrs. Deborah Prince* (Boston, 1744) are classic instances.

70. Julia C. Spruill, *Women's Life and Work in the Southern Colonies* (Chapel Hill, 1938), 65-79.

71. From the journal (1764-1765) of Lord Adam Gordon, in Mereness, *Travels*, 406.

72. H. Moller, "Sex Composition and Correlated Culture Patterns of Colonial America," *WMQ* (3), II (1945), 113-153.

73. Morris, *Studies in American Law*, Chap. 3.

74. For an observing colonial's testimony on the more genuine godliness of women, see Cotton Mather's *Ornaments of the Daughters of Zion, or, the Character and Happiness of a Virtuous Woman* (Boston, 1691), 56-57.

75. Calhoun, *American Family*, I, Chaps. 6, 17; Alice M. Earle, *Child Life in Colonial Days* (New York, 1899); Sister M. Kiefer, "Early American Childhood in the Middle Atlantic Area," *PMHB*, LXVIII (1944), 3-37.

76. Bridenbaugh, *Cities in the Wilderness*, 71. The sections on crime (68ff., 220ff., 379ff.) are among the most informative parts of this wonderful book.

77. For the prosecution: C. F. Adams, "Some Phases of Sexual Morality and Church Discipline in Colonial New England," *MHSP*, VI (2nd ser.), 477-516. For the defense: H. B. Parkes, "Morals and Law Enforcement in Colonial New England," *NEQ*, V (1932), 431-452.

78. H. R. Stiles, *Bundling* (Albany, 1869).

79. *Bradford's History* (1912 ed.), II, 309.

80. *NYG*, May 11, 1730; *BEP*, Aug. 10, 1741; *BIA*, May 29, 1749.

81. A rare instance is in *PJ*, Nov. 30, 1758, Jan. 25, 1759, with rejoinders and fresh attacks Feb. 1-March 15, 1759. Newspapers carried advertisements and lists of winners constantly. The classic example is *NYWPB*, Sept. 8-Oct. 6, 1746. For five weeks the *Post-Boy's* subscribers got nothing but numbers. See J. Ezell, "The

Lottery in Colonial America," *WMQ* (3), V (1948), 185-200.
82. P. Klein, *Prison Methods in New York State* (New York, 1920), Chap. 1; H. E. Barnes, *A History of the Penal . . . Institutions of the State of New Jersey* (Trenton, 1917), Pt. I, Chap. 1, and Pt. II, Chap 1.
83. H. W. K. Fitzroy, "The Punishment of Crime in Provincial Pennsylvania," *PMHB*, LX (1936), 242-269; L. H. Gipson, *Crime and its Punishment in Provincial Pennsylvania* (Bethlehem, 1935).
84. See Israel Acrelius, "Description of . . . the Swedish Churches in Pennsylvania," *Memoirs of the Historical Society of Pennsylvania*, XI, 160-164, for a colonial list of 48 common American drinks, all but three or four of them alcoholic.
85. F. R. Dulles, *America Learns to Play* (New York, 1940), Chaps. 1-3.
86. *BG*, July 17, 1750. Dean Albertson, "Puritan Liquor in the Planting of New England," *NEQ*, XXIII (1950), 477-490, gives a bibulous account of the first settlements.
87. *Kalm*, Travels, I, 56-57; Lord Adam Gordon, in Mereness, *Travels*, 451.
88. *The Private Journal of a Journey from Boston to New York, in the Year 1704* (Albany, 1865), 20. No student of colonial life should fail to taste the tartness of Madam Knight's observations.
89. Carman, *Social and Economic History*, 111.
90. Representative newspaper atttacks on excessive drinking are in *NEC*, Dec. 25, 1721, Sept. 10, 1722, Feb. 26, 1726; *AWM*, July 21, 1726; *NYWJ*, Aug. 16, 23, 30, 1736; June 5, 1749; *PaG*, Jan. 13, 1737 (widely copied), Jan. 5, 1748; *VG*, Sept. 15, 1738, Sept. 21, 1739, April 11, 1751; *BEP*, June 26, 1738; *NEWJ*, March 22, 29, April 5, 1737; *NYG* (2), Dec. 19, 1748; *NM*, Sept. 5, 1763; *Tl*, March 27, 1755.

91. J. A. Krout, *The Origins of Prohibition* (New York, 1925), Chaps. 1-3.
92. Respectively: Boston, 1726; Philadelphia, 1740; Boston, 1673.
93. G. Thomann, *Colonial Liquor Laws* (New York, 1887).
94. *Travels*, 118; *CCR*, III, 300.
95. Jernegan, *Laboring and Dependent Classes*, Chaps. 12-13. M. Creech, *Three Centuries of Poor Law Administration . . . in Rhode Island* (Chicago, 1935), Chaps. 2-5, is the best study of its kind. See also A. Deutsch, "The Sick Poor in Colonial Times," *AHR*, XLVI (1941), 560-579.
96. *CCR*, III, 300; E. W. Capen, *The Historical Development of the Poor Law of Connecticut* (New York, 1905), Chaps. 1-2.
97. Benjamin Franklin to Peter Collinson, May 9, 1753; C. Van Doren, ed., *Letters and Papers of Benjamin Franklin and Richard Jackson* (Philadelphia, 1947), 34.
98. A. Deutsch, *The Mentally Ill in America* (New York, 1937), Chap. 3.
99. *Records of Boston Selectmen* (1736-1742), 366.
100. An extraordinary colonial attempt to educate the Negro, the Charleston Negro School, is chronicled in F. J. Klingberg, *An Appraisal of the Negro in Colonial South Carolina* (Washington, 1941), Chap. 5. See also E. L. Pennington, *Thomas Bray's Associates and their Work among the Negroes* (Worcester, 1939), 65-73; F. J. Klingberg, *Anglican Humanitarianism in Colonial New York* (Philadelphia, 1940).
101. For these and other opponents of slavery, see M. S. Locke, *Anti-Slavery in America* (Boston, 1901), Chap. 1. The most memorable antislavery tracts in the colonial era were Woolman's *Some Considerations on the Keeping of Negroes*, Pt. I (Philadelphia, 1754), Pt. II (Philadelphia, 1762); Benezet's *Observations on the inslaving . . . of Negroes* (German-

town, 1759); and Ralph Sandiford, *A Brief Examination* (Philadelphia, 1729).

102. See the varied testimony of Eaton, *Old South*, 63; Gipson, *British Empire*, III, 85, 91-92; Bridenbaugh, *AASP*, LVI, 34-35; Adams, *Three Episodes*, II, 264-265; *VG*, Oct. 27, 1738; *AWM*, May 13, 1731; A. French, *The First Year of the Revolution* (Boston, 1934), 32-36; H. T. Mook, "Training Day in New England," *NEQ*, XI (1938), 675-697.

103. Eben, *Gottlieb Mittelberger's Journey* (1756), 63.

104. Below, Chap. 5.

105. *NYG* (2), Sept. 17, 1759.

106. Mereness, *Travels*, 450.

107. *PJ*, March 25, 1756; *NYG* (2), April 5, 1756; *NYM*, April 5, 1756.

108. A gentleman of New Jersey to Dr. Hamilton, in Bridenbaugh, *Gentleman's Progress*, 31.

109. A case study of the act of self-creation may be found in Wertenbaker, *Patrician and Plebeian*, Pt. I, and from a somewhat different point of view in P. A. Bruce, *Social Life of Virginia in the Seventeenth Century* (Richmond, 1907).

110. *NYCD*, VII, 705. For an example of this process, see A. C. Land, "Genesis of a Colonial Fortune: Daniel Dulany of Maryland," *WMQ* (3), VII (1950), 255-269.

111. Becker, *Political Parties*, Chap. 1; Mark, *Agrarian Conflicts*, Chap. 3.

112. C. H. Levermore, "The Whigs of Colonial New York," *AHR*, I (1896), 238-250, 245.

113. Dorothy R. Dillon, *The New York Triumvirate* (New York, 1949).

114. *Works*, II, 35-36.

115. Burnaby, *Travels*, 26-27.

116. An interesting phase of intercolonial contact at the upper-class level is described in C. Bridenbaugh, "Baths and Watering Places of Colonial America," *WMQ* (3), III (1946), 151-181.

117. J. E. Johnson, ed., "A Quaker Imperialist's View of the British Colonies in America: 1732," *PMHB*, LX (1936), 97-129, 127-128.

118. "Queries to Cato," *PEP*, March 14, 1776.

119. A bold (and Franklinian) attack on titles may be found in *NEC*, Feb. 18, Dec. 2, 30, 1723.

120. For some stimulating general observations, see H. B. Parkes, "New England in the 1730's," *NEQ*, III (1930), 397-419. Four imaginative reconstructions of life in the colonies are in W. E. Woodward, *The Way Our People Lived* (New York, 1944), Chaps. 1-4.

121. Franklin to Galloway, Feb. 6, 1772 (Yale Library).

122. T. J. Wertenbaker, *Torchbearer of the Revolution* (Princeton, 1940); W. F. Craven, *Southern Colonies*, Chap. 10; C. M. Andrews, ed., *Narratives of the Insurrections, 1675-1690* (New York, 1915), 11-141.

123. Mark, *Agrarian Conflicts* is a solid study of land grievances and controversies in New York; D. R. Fox, *Yankees and Yorkers* (New York, 1940), esp. Chap. 5, is a delightful treatment of the protracted struggle over the "disputed section" that is now Vermont.

124. Gipson, *British Empire*, III, 149-154, and references there cited; Kemmerer, *Path to Freedom*, Chaps. 10-12; Fisher, *New Jersey as a Royal Province*, Chap. 6.

125. *NYWPB*, June 9, 1746; *N. J. Archives*, XII (1st. ser.), 308-309; *NYEP*, Aug. 3, Sept. 7, 1747.

126. J. T. Adams, *Revolutionary New England* (Boston, 1923), 154-160, and references there cited; J. C. Miller, "Religion, Finance, and Democracy in Massachusetts," *NEQ*, VI (1933), 29-58. The bitterness and class-consciousness of this incident is plain in *BPB*, Jan. 21, 28, April 7, 21, Aug. 18, Sept. 22, Dec. 8, 1740; Jan. 12, April 13, May 11, 1741; *BG*, June

18, Aug. 6, 27, Sept. 17, Dec. 10, 1739; Jan. 28, Sept. 29, 1740; March 30, Sept. 13, 1741.

127. *Some Cursory Remarks made by James Birket in his Voyage to North America, 1750-1751* (New Haven, 1916), 31.

128. For an example of the impact on a stable community of religious antagonism, especially as sharpened by tensions over land and currency, see O. Zeichner, *Connecticut's Years of Controversy, 1750-1776* (Williamsburg, 1949), Chap. 2.

129. To Experience Mayhew, October 5, 1747 (Boston University Library). Conservative reaction to the Awakening is well summarized by Labaree, *Conservatism*, 76-89.

130. W. A. Schaper, "Sectionalism and Representation in South Carolina," *AHAAR* (1910), I, 237-463, esp. 338-354.

131. From *An Impartial Relation* (1770), printed in Boyd, *Tracts*, 256.

132. On sectional conflict in Virginia, see Wertenbaker, *Old South*, Chap. 5; C. H. Ambler, *Sectionalism in Virginia* (Chicago, 1910), Chap. 1. And see again Turner, *Significance of Sections*, Chap. 2.

133. Still the best treatment of the Regulators is J. S. Bassett, "The Regulators of North Carolina," *AHAAR* (1894), 141-212. See *NCCR*, Vols. VII and VIII, and Boyd, *Tracts*, for the documents and literature of this movement.

134. Burnaby, *Travels*, xiv.

135. Evidence of this fact is best displayed in the evolution of colonial architecture. Most books—there are hundreds—on the houses of colonial America actually describe the mansions. An example of this is T. T. Waterman's elegant *The Dwellings of Colonial America* (Chapel Hill, 1950). The best studies are F. Kimball, *Domestic Architecture of the American Colonies* (New York, 1922); H. D. Eberlein, *The Archi-*

tecture of Colonial America (Boston, 1924); H. R. Shurtleff, *The Log Cabin Myth* (Cambridge, 1939); and H. Morrison, *Early American Architecture* (New York, 1952).

136. Gipson, *British Empire*, II, Chap. 6.

137. R. B. Flanders, *Plantation Slavery in Georgia* (Chapel Hill, 1933), Chaps. 1-3.

CHAPTER FIVE

1. There have been two serious and largely successful attempts to come to grips with the colonial mind: S. E. Morison's lectures on seventeenth-century New England, *The Puritan Pronaos* (New York, 1936), and Max Savelle's survey of the eighteenth century, *Seeds of Liberty*. Although I cannot agree with some of the main assumptions and conclusions in these books, I can acknowledge gratefully their value as guides to my own explorations.

2. March 25, 1763; *Writings*, IV, 193.

3. N. J. Historical Society, *Collections*, IV, 278, from *Ecclesiasticus*, 38:25.

4. *RIG*, Oct. 25, 1732.

5. F. J. Klingberg, "Ideas that did not Migrate from England to America," *PMHB*, LXIII (1939), 380-389.

6. The intellectual spirit of the age in which the colonies came to maturity is caught with delicacy by J. H. Randall, *The Making of the Modern Mind* (rev. ed., Boston, 1940), and Carl Becker, *The Heavenly City of the Eighteenth Century Philosophers* (New Haven, 1932).

7. Thanks principally to local pride, antiquarianism, and the requirement that doctoral candidates in education submit a dissertation, there is an enormous literature, much of it quite misleading, on education in the colonies. Several items cited in these notes must be used with care. Furthermore, there is a crying need for a good standard history of the sub-

ject. E. P. Cubberley, *Public Education in the United States* (Boston, 1934), Chaps. 1-3, E. G. Dexter, *A History of Education in the United States* (New York, 1904), esp. Chaps. 1-6, 15, E. W. Knight, *Education in the United States* (Boston, 1951), Chaps. 4-5, and N. Edwards and H. G. Richey, *The School in the American Social Order* (Boston, 1947), Chaps. 1-5, are the best surveys available, but the inadequacies of these texts can be appreciated by setting them alongside the brilliant few pages of Labaree, *Conservatism in Early American History*, 90-101, and Merle Curti, *The Social Ideas of American Educators* (New York, 1935), 3-13, 21-24.

8. *A General Idea of the College of Mirania* (New York, 1753), 14.

9. C. K. Shipton, "Secondary Education in the Puritan Colonies," *NEQ*, VII (1934), 646-661.

10. Magnificent statements of the Puritan ideal of general education are Thomas Shepard, *Eye-Salve, or a Watch-Word from our Lord*, 44-45, and Benjamin Wadsworth, *Rulers Feeding and Guiding their People* (Boston, 1716), 14-16.

11. For an instance of the noble work of the S. P. G., see W. W. Kemp, *The Support of Schools in Colonial New York by the Society* (New York, 1913).

12. Archibald Kennedy, *A Speech said to have been Delivered Some Time Before the Close of the Late Sessions* (New York, 1755), 13; *NEM*, Aug. 1758.

13. *MCR*, II, 6-9, 203; *NHCR*, II, 583-584, 376; *CCR*, I, 520-521, 554-555. The definitive survey of this legislation is Jernegan, *Laboring and Dependent Classes*, Chaps. 4-8.

14. Jernegan, *Laboring and Dependent Classes*, Chap. 10; G. F. Wells, *Parish Education in Colonial Virginia* (New York, 1923).

15. B. C. Steiner, *The History of Education in Connecticut* (Washington, 1893), Chaps. 1-2; G. H. Martin, *The Evolution of the Massachusetts Public School System* (New York, 1894), Lectures 1-2; H. Updegraff, *The Origin of the Moving School in Massachusetts* (New York, 1907).

16. T. Woody, *Early Quaker Education in Pennsylvania* (New York, 1920), and *Quaker Education in . . . New Jersey* (New York, 1923); D. Murray, *History of Education in New Jersey* (Washington, 1899), Chaps. 1-2, 8; W. H. Kilpatrick, *The Dutch Schools of New Netherlands and Colonial New York* (Washington, 1912).

17. C. J. Heatwole, *A History of Education in Virginia* (New York, 1916), Chaps. 1-4. See also B. C. Steiner, *A History of Education in Maryland* (Washington, 1894), Chap. 1; C. L. Smith, *The History of Education in North Carolina* (Washington, 1894), Chaps. 1-2; and E. W. Knight's useful *A Documentary History of Education in the South* (Chapel Hill, 1949), Vol. I.

18. On education through apprenticeship, see Jernegan, *Laboring and Dependent Classes*, Chaps. 6, 7, 8, 11; R. F. Seybolt, *Apprenticeship and Apprenticeship Education in Colonial New England and New York* (New York, 1917).

19. R. F. Seybolt has written a number of informative studies on education in Boston, among them *The Private Schools of Colonial Boston* (Cambridge, 1935) and *The Public Schools of Colonial Boston* (Cambridge, 1935).

20. E. E. Brown, *The Making of our Middle Schools* (New York, 1903), Chaps. 1-7.

21. Most of these dates are at best approximations, for it is often difficult to state precisely just when a college in name became a college in fact. The Harvard, William and Mary,

and Pennsylvania dates are particularly open to challenge. Out of the varied literature on these colleges, see particularly S. E. Morison, *The Founding of Harvard College* (Cambridge, 1935), *Harvard in the Seventeenth Century* (Cambridge, 1936), and *Three Centuries of Harvard* (Cambridge, 1937), Pts. I and II; E. P. Cheyney, *History of the University of Pennsylvania* (Philadelphia, 1940), Bk. I; T. J. Wertenbaker, *Princeton, 1746-1896* (Princeton, 1946), Chaps. 1-3; E. Oviatt, *The Beginnings of Yale, 1701-1726* (New Haven, 1916); F. L. Broderick, "Pulpit, Physics, and Politics," *WMQ* (3), VI (1949), 42-68. Brown, Columbia, William and Mary, and Yale await the touch of the modern professional historian.

22. E. J. Young, "Subjects for Master's Degree in Harvard College from 1653 to 1791," *MHSP*, XVIII (1st ser.), 119-151, reveals the content of college education in the colonies.

23. For a powerful but, I fear, twisted argument for the primacy of scholasticism in colonial colleges, see J. J. Walsh, *Education of the Founding Fathers of the Republic* (New York, 1935), and with it S. E. Morison's review in *NEQ*, VIII (1935), 455-457.

24. *NYG* (2), June 3, 1754; *NYM*, June 3, 1754; G. H. Moore, *The Origin and Early History of Columbia College* (New York, 1890), App. III. Franklin's proposals, of course, were even further ahead of the times. See his *Writings*, II, 386-396; X, 9-31. Excellent statements of the purposes of higher education in the eighteenth century can be found in various proposals for a college in Charleston, *SCG*, April 1, 22, 1732, Feb. 19, April 23, Aug. 6, 13, 1750, Oct. 8, 1764; *SCAGG*, Nov. 20, 1769.

25. R. A. Guild, *Early History of Brown University* (Providence, 1897), 540-541.

26. R. F. Seybolt, *The Evening School in Colonial America* (Urbana, 1925).

27. *BEP*, Oct. 7, 1751; W. N. Morse, "Lectures on Electricity in Colonial Times," *NEQ*, VII (1934), 364-374.

28. The scandalous state of education in North Carolina is dwelled upon by Governor Johnston in one of his famous deprecatory speeches, *VG*, Oct. 15, 1736. The hardly less scandalous state of education in Rhode Island is a subject of exhortation in *PG*, Oct. 20, 1762, Feb. 26, 1763.

29. *New Englands First Fruits* (London, 1643), 12. The text of this priceless tract is reproduced in Morison, *Founding of Harvard*, App. D.

30. From "A General Account of . . . the College . . . of New Jersey," *PJ*, April 26, 1753.

31. From an oration of Francis Hopkinson at the Philadelphia Academy, Nov. 12, 1754; *PaG*, Nov. 21, 1754. See also *NEWJ*, July 13, 1730; *NYG*, Dec. 18, 1732; *BG*, Oct. 25, 1736; *NYWJ*, Feb. 14, Nov. 7, 14, 1737; *SCG*, Dec. 7-21, 1747; *NYEP*, May 29, 1749; *NHG*, Nov. 18, 1756.

32. *NEWJ*, March 7, 1738.

33. See especially Savelle, *Seeds of Liberty*, Chaps. 7-9; Adams, *Provincial Society*, Chaps. 5, 6, 10, 11. Michael Kraus has written two important books in this area: *Intercolonial Aspects of American Culture on the Eve of the Revolution* (New York, 1928), and *The Atlantic Civilization* (Ithaca, 1949).

34. T. J. Wertenbaker, *The Golden Age of Colonial Culture* (New York, 1949), and Bridenbaugh, *Cities in the Wilderness*, are the best treatments of urban culture. Bridenbaugh, *Rebels and Gentlemen;* Tolles, *Meeting House and Counting House*, Chaps. 7-9; and Bowes, *Culture of Early Charleston*, are special studies that friends of New York, Newport, and Boston might well be moved to imitate.

35. For conclusive evidence, see E. C. Cook, *Literary Influences in Colonial Newspapers, 1704-1750* (New York, 1912); C. K. Shipton, "Literary Leaven in Provincial New England," *NEQ*, IX (1936), 203-217.

36. *An Addition to the Present Melancholy Circumstances of the Province Considered* (Boston, 1719), 7.

37. R. E. Spiller *et al.*, *Literary History of the United States* (New York, 1948), I, 3-112, and bibliography at III, 72-86; W. P. Trent *et al.*, *The Cambridge History of American Literature* (New York, 1917), I, Bk. I, 365-467; M. C. Tyler, *A History of American Literature, 1607-1765* (New York, 1878); Charles Angoff, *A Literary History of the American People, 1607-1815* (New York, 1931), an antidote to Tyler's anthem; and V. F. Calverton, *The Liberation of American Literature* (New York, 1932), Chaps. 1-3, a provocative expression of Marxist criticism.

38. *NEC*, March 12, 1722, probably written by Dr. William Douglass.

39. J. H. Shera, *Foundations of the Public Library* (Chicago, 1949), esp. the table at 55; A. K. Gray, *Benjamin Franklin's Library* (New York, 1937), Chaps. 1-3; A. B. Keep, *The Library in Colonial New York* (New York, 1909); E. V. Lamberton, "Colonial Libraries of Pennsylvania," *PMHB*, XLII (1918), 193-234; C. T. Hollenbeck, "A Colonial Reading List from the Union Library of Hatboro, Pennsylvania," *PMHB*, LVI (1932), 289-340; L. Shores, *Origins of the American College Library* (New York, 1935).

40. For catalogues of private libraries, see L. C. Wroth, *An American Bookshelf, 1755* (Philadelphia, 1934); Farish, *Journal of Philip Fithian*, 285-294; T. G. Wright, *Literary Culture in Early New England* (New Haven, 1920), Chaps. 2, 7, 12; and the articles in the following publica-

tions: *Huntington Library Quarterly*, I, 3-61; *CSMP*, XIII, 288-292, XIV, 63-66, XXI, 190-230, XXVIII, 107-175, 449-461; *NEQ*, VIII, 277-283; *MHSP*, XXV, 37-85; *AASP*, XVII, 135-147, XX, 269-356; *Maryland Historical Magazine*, XXXVI, 184-201, XXXVII, 26-41, 291-310; *American Literature*, X, 24-52.

41. *Writings*, I, 312.

42. The case for classical learning is stated in *SCG*, Dec. 21, 1769.

43. Representative tributes to "the immortal Mr. Addison" are in *SCG*, Feb. 26, 1732; *NYG*, Jan. 28, 1734; *PaG*, April 4, 1734. Franklin's sizable debt to Addison is too well known to need elaboration here. Representative tributes to Pope ("The GREATEST POET and the BEST OF MEN") are in *SCG*, June 8, Dec. 21, 1734, June 17, 1745; *BAM*, Nov. 1744; *MG* (2), Nov. 8, 1745.

44. And some 160 times before 1850! See A. M. Sibley, *Alexander Pope's Prestige in America, 1725-1835* (New York, 1949), App. I.

45. For his unusual popularity, see M. M. Barr, *Voltaire in America, 1744-1800* (New York, 1941), and excerpts in *BAM*, Nov. 1746; *NAM*, June, Nov. 1758, May 1759. See generally H. M. Jones, *America and French Culture, 1750-1848* (Chapel Hill, 1927).

46. For lists of colonial "best-sellers," see F. L. Mott, *Golden Multitudes* (New York, 1947), 303-304; J. D. Hart, *The Popular Book* (New York, 1950), 301-303.

47. See particularly Cyclone Covey's chapter in Savelle, *Seeds of Liberty*, 490-552, and references there cited. The Puritans and (or versus) music is a subject that continues to fascinate. For differing views, see P. A. Scholes, *The Puritans and Music* (London, 1934); C. Covey, "Puritanism and Music in Colonial America," *WMQ* (3), VIII (1951), 378-388; and the Scholes-Covey exchange

in *WMQ* (3), IX (1952), 128-133, 288.

48. O. G. Sonneck, *Early Concert-Life in America* (Leipzig, 1907) and *Early Opera in America* (New York, 1915).

49. Arthur Quinn, *A History of the American Drama* (New York, 1923), Chap. 1; Arthur Hornblow, *A History of the Theatre in America* (Philadelphia, 1919), I, Chaps. 1-5.

50. *AWM*, Aug. 7, 1729; *BG*, Nov. 20, 1732.

51. *BEP*, April 6, 1767; *PJ*, Feb. 19-March 12, 1767; *PP*, Nov. 8, 15, 29, 1773; *PG*, Jan. 22-Feb. 12, 1763.

52. J. T. Flexner, *First Flowers of Our Wilderness* (Boston, 1947), easily the best book on the subject, and *America's Old Masters* (New York, 1939); O. W. Larkin, *Art and Life in America* (New York, 1949), Bk. I; Savelle, *Seeds of Liberty*, 428-460; Alan Burroughs, *Limners and Likenesses* (Cambridge, 1936); and Oskar Hagen, *The Birth of the American Tradition in Art* (New York, 1940), a book to be used with care.

53. See the works listed above, Chap. 4, n. 135, as well as T. B. Hamlin, *The American Spirit in Architecture* (New Haven, 1926), Chaps. 3-8, and Lewis Mumford, *Sticks and Stones* (New York, 1924), Chaps. 1-3.

54. C. Bridenbaugh, *Peter Harrison, First American Architect* (Chapel Hill, 1949), a delightful book.

55. Bridenbaugh, *The Colonial Craftsman*.

56. It was in this strange medium that the Puritan achieved a minor triumph. See Harriette M. Forbes, *Gravestones of Early New England* (Boston, 1927).

57. Samuel Briggs, ed., *The Essays, Humor, and Poems of Nathaniel Ames, Father and Son* (Cleveland, 1891); *AASP*, XXII, 15-134, XXIV, 11-64, 93-215, XXV, 19-54, XXXV, 1-25, 194-209, XXXVIII, 63-163; *NEQ*, VIII (1935), 264-277.

58. Singleton, *Social New York*, 315.

59. A history of colonial science would be a welcome addition to our knowledge of the American past. In addition to other items cited in these notes, see Savelle, *Seeds of Liberty*, Chap. 2; Kraus, *Atlantic Civilization*, Chap. 7, and *Intercolonial Aspects*, Chap. 8; D. J. Struik, *Yankee Science in the Making* (Boston, 1948), Chap. 1; and Merle Curti, *The Growth of American Thought* (New York, 1943), 86-99.

60. F. E. Brasch, "The Newtonian Epoch in the American Colonies (1680-1783)," *AASP*, XLIX, 314-333.

61. *The Declaration of Independence* (New York, 1948), 43.

62. In a communication to the Royal Society, quoted in Kraus, *Atlantic Civilization*, 186.

63. *Philosophic Solitude* (Boston, 1762), 39. For other tributes, see *NYG*, March 24, 31, 1729, Aug. 23, 1731; *NEWJ*, May 26, 1729; *BG*, July 5, 1731; *BAM*, Jan. 1745.

64. F. E. Brasch, "Newton's First Critical Disciple in the American Colonies," in *Sir Isaac Newton, 1727-1927* (Baltimore, 1928), 301-338. Winthrop's most famous writings were his *Relation of a Voyage . . . for the Observation of the Transit of Venus* (Boston, 1761), and *Two Lectures on the Parallax and Distance of the Sun* (Boston, 1769). For evidence of widespread interest in Winthrop's work, see *BPB*, April 6, 1761; *NHG*, April 10, 1761; *CG*, April 25, 1761; *BNL*, April 2, 30, July 30, 1761; *MG* (2), April 20, 1761.

65. On Rittenhouse and other Philadelphians, see Bridenbaugh, *Rebels and Gentlemen*, Chap. 9.

66. *NYG*, July 8, 1734; *BAM*, Jan. 1743; *BEP*, Feb. 27, 1744; *NYWJ*, Feb. 13, 1744; *BNL*, March 29, 1753; *NHG*, July 29, 1757.

67. The definitive edition was published in London in 1751.

68. The biggest battle in the colonies was over inoculation for smallpox, as witness *NEWJ*, Jan. 5, March 2, 1730; *PaG*, March 11, 1731; *NYG*, March 22-April 5, 1731; Oct. 23, Dec. 11-25, 1738; *SCG*, May 25-Sept. 14, 1738; *GG*, June 7-July 12, 1764.

69. Kraus, *Atlantic Civilization*, 192. See generally F. R. Packard, *History of Medicine in the United States* (New York, 1931); M. B. Gordon, *Aesculapius Comes to the Colonies* (Ventnor, N.J., 1949), a work to be used only by those who have read the review of it in *WMQ* (3), VI (1949), 660-664; Bridenbaugh, *Rebels and Gentlemen*, Chap. 8; H. R. Viets, *A Brief History of Medicine in Massachusetts* (Boston, 1930), Chaps. 1-3; Kraus, *Atlantic Civilization*, Chap. 8.

70. The progress and yet continued primitivism of colonial medicine is clearly perceived in such items as those in *NYG*, Jan. 18, 1732, on the "stone and gravel"; *NEWJ*, Aug. 14, 21, Sept. 11, 1739, on fevers, and Sept. 18, 1739, on the gout; *NYWJ*, Sept. 7, 1741, on corns, and Sept. 6, 1742, on the uses of vinegar; *VG*, Dec. 19, 1751, on amputation techniques; *BNL*, Feb. 27, March 5, 1752, on the "ulcerated sore-throat."

71. Franklin, *Writings*, II, 228.

72. T. Hornberger, *Scientific Thought in the American Colleges, 1638-1800* (Austin, Tex., 1945); I. B. Cohen, *Some Early Tools of American Science* (Cambridge, 1950); Louis W. McKeehan, *Yale Science, 1701-1801* (New York, 1947).

73. S. E. Morison, "The Harvard School of Astronomy in the Seventeenth Century," *NEQ*, VII (1934), 3-24.

74. *Writings* (Memorial ed.), XIV, 231.

75. Although it overstates Masonic influence, B. Faÿ, "Learned Societies in Europe and America in the Eight-

eenth Century," *AHR*, XXXVII (1932), 255-266, is a useful guide.

76. For the one purposeful attempt, see Franklin's proposal of 1743, *Writings*, II, 228-232.

77. The contributions of each of these men is reviewed in F. E. Brasch, "The Royal Society of London and its influence upon Scientific Thought in the American Colonies," *Scientific Monthly*, XXXIII (1931), 336-355, 448-469. See also R. P. Stearns, "Colonial Fellows of the Royal Society," *WMQ* (3), III (1946), 208-268.

78. *BAM*, Sept. 1746. *SCG*, April 29, 1732, carries a typical encomium of "the right Use of Reason in our Enquiries after Truth."

79. J. G. Crowther, *Famous American Men of Science* (New York, 1937), 135-154; Woodrow Wilson, *Constitutional Government* (New York, 1908), 54-56.

80. *Relation of a Voyage*, 6.

81. C. E. Jorgenson, "The New Science in the Almanacs of Ames and Franklin," *NEQ*, VIII (1935), 555-561.

82. Science in the newspapers tended to emphasize the sensational; e.g., *VG*, Jan. 27, Feb. 3, 1737; *PaG*, Dec. 15, 22, 1737; *BAM*, Jan. 1744.

83. *VG*, Jan. 14, 1737; *SCG*, March 19, 1737; *BAM*, Oct. 1743.

84. See I. W. Riley, *American Philosophy. The Early Schools* (New York, 1907), easily the most exhaustive book on the subject; H. W. Schneider, *A History of American Philosophy* (New York, 1946), Pts. I-II; H. G. Townsend, *Philosophical Ideas in the United States* (New York, 1934), Chaps. 1-4, a brief review; and Savelle, *Seeds of Liberty*, Chap. 3.

85. (Philadelphia, 1752.) See H. and C. Schneider, eds., *Samuel Johnson, His Career and Writings* (New York, 1929), II. Colonials were far more interested in Berkeley's treatise on tar-water (*NYWPB*, Feb. 18-March 11, 1745; *VG*, May 9-23, 1745) than

in his speculations on the meaning of reality.

86. Riley, *American Philosophy*, 329-372, a brilliant exposition.

87. See Miller, *New England Mind;* Miller and Johnson, *The Puritans;* Morison, *Puritan Pronaos;* and H. W. Schneider, *The Puritan Mind* (New York, 1930).

88. Although Chauncy was a force to be reckoned with as early as 1739, especially for his *Seasonable Thoughts* (1743), his mature theology is to be sought in *The Benevolence of the Deity* (Boston, 1784), written thirty years before publication, and *Salvation for All Men* (Boston, 1782).

89. W. H. Werkmeister, *A History of Philosophical Ideas in America* (New York, 1949), 12. On this whole subject, see Joseph Haroutunian, *Piety versus Moralism* (New York, 1932), which has a notable bibliography at 307-322.

90. *A Careful and Strict Enquiry into . . . Freedom of the Will* (Boston, 1754).

91. *A Brief History and Vindication* (New Haven, 1755); *An Essay on the Nature and Foundation of Moral Virtues and Obligation* (New Haven, 1765).

92. A representative discussion of "Reason and Science" is in *NYG*, July 17, Sept. 4-Oct. 2, 1732. E. A. Burtt, *The Metaphysical Foundations of Modern Physical Science* (New York, 1927), Chap. 7, is excellent on Newton's philosophy.

93. For documentary evidence, see Cotton Mather's *Reasonable Religion* (Boston, 1713).

94. One excellent example is "The Plain Dealer," *MG*, Dec. 17, 1728-Jan. 21, 1729. See also the interesting exchange in *NYG* (2), April 27, May 4, Aug. 23, 1752, and *BEP*, Jan. 4, 1742, July 28, 1755.

95. H. M. Morais, *Deism in Eighteenth Century America* (New York, 1934). The bitterness of the reaction to de-

ism, which few traditionalists could distinguish from rationalism (or vice versa), is apparent in the reprinting of Charles Leslie's *A Short and Easie Method with the Deists* (Williamsburg, 1733) (New York, 1745), as well as in communications in *NYG*, May 21, 1738; *BEP*, June 7, 1742; *BAM*, Aug. 1744, Sept. 1746.

96. See the frank article, "Some Thoughts on Infidelity," in *BAM*, Jan. 1745.

97. *NYG* (2), Oct. 18, 1764; *PaG*, March 4, 1736.

98. *BAM*, Oct. 1744.

99. A great and often reprinted favorite that sang of good manners and other virtues was Robert Dodsley, *The Family Companion; or the Oeconomy of Human Life* (1st American printing, Philadelphia, 1751). The classic statement of American middle-class morality is, of course, to be found in Franklin's *Autobiography*, 101-111.

100. Examples of moral preaching are so profuse as to make "see any convenient colonial newspaper" the most useful reference. A few choice instances will nevertheless be cited: *NEWJ*, May 29, June 26, 1727, June 7, 14, 1731, April 3, Dec. 11, 1732, Sept. 28, 1736; *AWM*, June 18, 1730, Jan. 25, 1732; *PaG*, Oct. 14, 1731, Aug. 22, 1734, Feb. 1, 1739; *SCG*, July 8, Aug. 12, Sept. 2-30, 1732, Aug. 18, 1733, June 1, 1734, May 10, 1740, April 25, Nov. 21, 1743, Aug. 24, 1747, Dec. 31, 1750, Jan. 1ff., 1754; *NYG*, Feb. 15, 1732, Jan. 7, 14, 1735, Jan. 20, 1736, April 17, 1738; *BWR*, March 12, 1733; *VG*, Feb. 24, 1737, Aug. 3, 1739; *BEP*, June 20, 1737, Nov. 15, 1742, July 11, 1753; *MG* (2), Feb. 13, Sept. 14, Oct. 19, Dec. 28, 1752, March 25, May 6, 1756; *PJ*, Dec. 19, 1745, Dec. 27-Jan. 10, 1753, July 11, 1754, Aug. 4, 11, 1757; *BIA*, March 20, July 24, 1749; *NYG* (2), March 13, 1749; *NYEP*, March 26, 1750, May 13, Nov. 18,

1751; *NYM*, Jan. 14, 1754; *CG*, Nov. 27, 1757; *BPB*, June 12, Aug. 14, 1758.

101. For which couplets from Pope's *Essay on Man* were particularly favored as mottoes. A model of the essay on the good man is in *VG*, Sept. 29, 1752.

102. *BWR*, Oct. 18, 1731; *AWM*, May 25, 1738; *BIA*, March 20, 1749; *BG*, May 25, 1755; *CG*, Dec. 18, 1756; *NYM*, March 21, 1757; *IR*, Nov. 30, 1752. At least one correspondent got quite tired of seeing "the venerable names of Antiquity prostituted by every paltry Scribbler," *PaG*, Oct. 11, 1733.

103. *MG* (2) Dec. 12, 1754; Feb. 27, 1755; *BEP*, Nov. 24, 1755; *CG*, May 1, 1756; *PJ*, March 10, 1757; *NYM*, April 25, 1757.

104. *PaG*, June 17, 1756. See also *NYG*, Nov. 3, 1729; *PaG*, Feb. 12, 1741, Jan. 8, 1759; *BEP*, April 18, 1748; *MG* (2), Jan. 25, 1753. This was a favorite theme of royal governors: *MG* (2), Jan. 30, 1755.

105. *NYG*, May 11, 1730.

106. Surveys of colonial political thought, most of them much too concerned with Puritanism, may be found in C. E. Merriam, *A History of American Political Theories* (New York, 1920), Chap. 1; R. G. Gettell, *History of American Political Thought* (New York, 1928), Chap. 3; J. M. Jacobson, *The Development of American Political Thought* (New York, 1932), Chap. 1; F. G. Wilson, *The American Political Mind* (New York, 1949), Chap. 2. V. L. Parrington, *Main Currents in American Thought* (New York, 1930), Vol. I, and R. B. Perry, *Puritanism and Democracy* (New York, 1944), are memorable expositions, to be handled with care.

107. Excellent examples are *PAM*, Jan., Feb. 1741; *MG* (2), Jan. 20-June 29, 1748; *PJ*, Feb. 23-Oct. 5, 1758.

108. *Gentleman's Progress*, 163.

109. L. Swift, *The Massachusetts Election Sermons* (Cambridge, 1897), reprinted from *CSMP*, I, 388-451. Most of the pamphlets cited in the notes of the next few pages are Massachusetts or Connecticut election sermons. On the importance of the colonial clergy in spreading popular political ideas, see A. M. Baldwin, *The New England Clergy and the American Revolution* (Durham, 1928) and "Sowers of Sedition," *WMQ* (3), V (1948), 52-76.

110. The political essays in the *Courant* were chiefly written by the Franklin brothers and William Douglass, in the *Journal* by the Lewis Morrises, in the *Advertiser* by Sam Adams and his circle, and in the *Independent Reflector* by William Livingston, William Smith, jr., and John Morin Scott. The citations of these four journals in the notes that follow are intended as guides to a unique source of early American political thought.

111. His chief works were listed in the inventories of almost every bookseller and private library. The one important American reprint, the work of the senior class at Yale, was *A Letter Concerning Toleration* (Boston, 1743; also Wilmington, Del., 1764).

112. Although none of his works was reprinted in colonial America, they were imported in unusual quantities. His ideas were also made widely available through *Cato's Letters*.

113. *Letters on the Spirit of Patriotism* (Philadelphia, 1749; New York, 1756); *The Freeholder's Political Catechism* (Boston?, 1757).

114. *The Security of Englishmen's Lives* (Boston, 1720).

115. *An Enquiry into the Reasons for the Conduct of Great Britain* (Boston, 1727).

116. *English Liberties, or the Free-born Subject's Inheritance* (Boston, 1721),

an especially popular collection of basic documents with commentaries.

117. *Britain's Remembrancer* (Philadelphia, 1747, 1748; New York, 1748; Boston, 1759); *Thoughts on Education* (Boston, 1749).

118. Examples of the political uses of *The Spectator* and other Addison pieces are in *NYG*, March 4, April 8, 1734, July 18, 1736; *NYWJ*, Jan. 28, 1734, May 26, June 2, 1735, July 26, 1736.

119. On the English and Continental background of American political thought, see G. H. Sabine, *A History of Political Theory* (rev. ed., New York, 1950), Chaps. 18, 19, 21, 22, 25, 26, and references there cited. More's *Utopia* was reprinted in Philadelphia in 1753.

120. The four volumes of *Cato's Letters* (the most popular editions: London, 1733, 1748) were imported in astonishing quantities into the colonies but were never reprinted. Gordon's *The Craftsman* (New York, 1753) and the jointly authored *The Independent Whig* (Philadelphia, 1724, 1740) were also extremely popular. Some examples of the widespread use of *Cato's Letters* in the press are *NEC*, Sept. 11-Oct. 30, 1721; *AWM*, Feb. 20, March 29, April 19, June 7, 21, 1722, Feb. 11-March 3, 1724, March 13, 1729, April 9-June 4, 1730; *NYWJ*, Nov. 12, 1733-Nov. 11, 1734, July 7-21, Aug. 25-Sept. 22, 1735; *PaG*, April 1-May 13, and esp. June 10, 1736. The great favorites were essays No. 38, "The Right and Capacity of the People to judge of Government" (*BG*, May 12-19, 1755; *SCG*, Aug. 8, 1748); No. 15, "Of Freedom of Speech" (*NEC*, July 9, 1722; *NYWJ*, Feb. 18, Nov. 11, 1734); and No. 37, "Character of a good and of an evil Magistrate" (*NYWJ*, July 21, 1735; *SCG*, July 29, 1748). The student who is anxious to explore for himself the true sources of colonial political thought

should also read these numbers of *Cato's Letters*: 18, 26, 27, 108 (corruption and virtue); 25, 66, 72, 73, 115 (arbitrary power); 35 (public spirit); 45 (equality); 59, 62-65, 67, 68, 71 (liberty); 60, 61 (nature of government); 75, 76 (restraints on rulers); 84 (property); 94-95 (standing armies).

121. "A. P." in *NYG* (2), April 16, 1753. For other original and borrowed salutes to liberty, see *NEC*, April 16, 1722; *NEWJ*, May 27, 1728; *BWR*, Jan. 24, 1732, Jan. 1, 1733; *NYWJ*, Nov. 19, 1733; *BIA*, April 10, 1749; *PJ*, Sept. 28, 1758; *AC*, April 19, 1762; *NM*, Aug. 22, 1763; Nathaniel Hunn, *The Welfare of a Government Considered* (New London, 1747), 14-15.

122. *NEWJ*, May 27, 1728; *BEP*, July 4, 1737.

123. At least one correspondent complained that there was too much shouting about liberty by people who didn't know what the word meant, in *BG*, April 30, 1739. See also Charles Chauncy, *Civil Magistrates must be just* (Boston, 1747), 34-35.

124. *IR*, Nov. 30, 1752.

125. A brief survey of natural law in the colonies is B. F. Wright, *American Interpretations of Natural Law* (Cambridge, 1931), Chaps. 1-3. Wright underestimates the popularity of natural-law ideas in the middle and later periods. Some of the best colonial expositions of the natural-law theory (in addition to the works discussed in Part 2) are Jared Eliot, *Give Cesar his Due* (New London, 1738), Samuel Quincy, *Twenty Sermons* (Boston, 1750), and the sermons of Hobart, Barnard, A. Williams, E. Williams, and Chauncy mentioned in the notes to follow.

126. *NEC*, May 14, 1722; *NYWJ*, July 7, 14, 1735; *PAM*, Jan. 1741. The New England clergy, with few exceptions, continued to identify the

law of nature with the law of God. For an excellent example, see Solomon Williams, *A Firm and Immovable Courage to Obey God* (New London, 1741), 18. On higher law among the Puritans, see Wright, *American Interpretations*, Chap. 2. See also the entry in Sewall's Diary, *MHSC*, VII (5th), 65.

127. *CG*, Aug. 7, 1756.

128. *BIA*, April 10, 1749; Elisha Williams, *A Seasonable Plea for the Liberty of Conscience* (Boston, 1744), 4-5.

129. *NYWJ*, Aug. 25, 1735; *BIA*, April 10, 1749; Joseph Moss, *An Election Sermon* (New London, 1715), 6-7; Timothy Cutler, *The Firm Union of a People* (New London, 1717), an especially positive assertion of "compactness" as the basis of society; John Barnard, *The Throne Established by Righteousness* (Boston, 1734), 13-19; Abraham Williams, *A Sermon Preach'd at Boston . . . May 26, 1762* (Boston, 1762), 5-6; William Welsteed, *The Dignity and Duty of the Civil Magistrate* (Boston, 1751), 11-12. For the contract as reality, see *CCR*, I, 20; *RICR*, I, 52, 112; *New Hampshire Provincial Papers*, I, 132; F. J. Turner, "Western State-Making in the Revolutionary Era," *AHR*, I (1895), 70-87.

130. *NEWJ*, May 21, 1733; *MG*, July 15, 1727, May 26, 1730; *NYG* (2), Oct. 18, 1764; Barnard, *The Throne Established*, 23-24.

131. *BG*, May 10, 1756; *BAM*, Sept. 1744. On Sept. 19, 1754 the town meeting of Newbury, Mass., voted that a tax on "the consumption of distilled spirits in private families" was "an infringement on the natural rights of Englishmen." J. Coffin, *History of Newbury* (Boston, 1845), 221.

132. Actually there was surprisingly little discussion of property in colonial political theory. For an example, see *NYWJ*, June 16, 23, 1735.

133. The interest of the colonists in the doctrine of equality may be traced in *AWM*, April 9, 1730; *BWR*, Jan. 1, 1733; *PaG*, April 15, 1736, Dec. 8, 1737; *BIA*, Jan. 11, 1748; *NYG* (2), April 2, 1753; *IR*, Aug. 2, 1753; *BG*, May 12, 19, 1755; E. Williams, *A Seasonable Plea*, 2-3; A. Williams, *Sermon*, 5, 21.

134. *NEC*, Feb. 17, 1724.

135. *NEC*, May 28, 1722; *NYWJ*, May 27, 1734, July 21, Sept. 27, 1735; *AWM*, May 25, 1738; *SCG*, July 29, 1748; *BG*, May 12, 1755, May 31, 1756; *NM*, April 10, 1759; *AC*, March 20, 1762; Ebenezer Pemberton, *The Divine Original and Dignity of Governments Asserted* (Boston, 1710); John Woodward, *Civil Rulers are God's Ministers, for the Peoples Good* (Hartford, 1712); John Hancock, *Rulers should be Benefactors* (Boston, 1722).

136. *NEC*, May 14, 1722, June 24, 1723; *NEWJ*, Jan. 25, 1731; *NYWJ*, Dec. 31, 1733, July 14, 1735; *AWM*, May 25, 1738; *MG* (2), Aug. 26, 1746; *BIA*, Jan. 11, Feb. 8, 1748; *BEP*, April 2, 1750; *NYG* (2), Oct. 18, 1764; *PAM*, Jan. 1741; *IR*, Dec. 21, 1752, July 12, 1753; *PAM* (2), March 1758; Eliot, *Give Cesar his Due*, 13-14; E. Williams, *A Seasonable Plea*, 26-27. For other flirtations with the right of resistance, see the commencement theses listed by Morison, *Three Centuries of Harvard*, 90-91.

137. *NEC*, Sept. 11, 1721.

138. *BIA*, Jan. 11, 1748; *NEC*, May 28, 1722; *NEWJ*, Jan. 20, 1736; *IR*, July 12, 1753; Noah Hobart, *Civil Government the Foundation of Social Happiness* (New London, 1751).

139. *NAM*, Jan. 1759; *BWR*, June 11, 1733; *NYG*, April 11, 1735; *BIA*, April 10, May 29, 1749; *CG*, April 10, 1756; *BEP*, April 27, 1761; *NYG* (2), Oct. 18, 1764; *IR*, Dec. 21, 1752; Thomas Frink, *A King reigning in Righteousness* (Boston, 1758), a typical paean to English government;

James Lockwood, *The Worth and Excellence of Civil Freedom* (New London, 1759), 13; William Smith, *A True and Faithful Narrative* (1740), in Boyd, *Tracts*, 52. The royal governors were only too happy to agree: *SCG*, Nov. 31, 1754.

140. *BIA*, Jan. 11, 1748; *BNL*, Jan. 9, 1755; *BG*, May 10, 1756; *PJ*, Sept. 28, 1758; *BEP*, April 27, 1761; W. H. Whitmore, ed., *The Andros Tracts* (Boston, 1868), I, 11-19, 71-132; Daniel Dulany, *The Right of the Inhabitants of Maryland to the Benefit of the English Laws* (Annapolis, 1728), reprinted in Sioussat, *English Statutes in Maryland*, App. II.

141. *NYG*, March 18, 1734, April 11, 1735; *NYWJ*, June 2, 1735; *PaG*, April 1, 1736; Chauncy, *Civil Magistrates must be just*, 15-16; Samuel Haven, *A Sermon occasioned by the Death of King George* (Portsmouth, 1761), 18. For early defenses of the separation of powers, see *BG*, Jan. 2, 1758 (citing Montesquieu), May 16, 23, June 6, 1763.

142. *NYWJ*, Dec. 3, 1733, July 28, 1735; *BIA*, Feb. 6, April 10, 1749; *MG* (2), Oct. 19, 1752; *NYM*, July 28, 1755. Favorite colonial reprints and originals on this great possession were Sir John Hawles, *The Englishman's Right* (Boston, 1693); Somers, *Security of Englishmen's Lives*; and *The Nature and Importance of Oaths and Juries* (New York, 1747).

143. *NAM*, April 1759. For a loud salute to Magna Charta, see *NEC*, July 30, 1722.

144. *IR*, Dec. 21, 1752; *NYWJ*, Jan. 11, 1734.

145. Eliot, *Give Cesar his Due*, 36; *NYWJ*, Nov. 19, 1733, Jan. 28, March 11, 1734, June 2, 1735; *BPB*, Nov. 6, 1749; *BG*, May 12, 1755; *IR*, Dec. 21, 1752; E. Williams, *A Seasonable Plea*, 6.

146. *AWM*, Sept. 18, 1729, May 4, 1738; *RIG*, Jan. 11, 1733.

147. *AWM*, Aug. 15-Sept. 5, 1734; *NYWJ*, Aug. 26, 1734. A number of interesting broadsides on annual elections issued from Zenger's press in 1732; e.g., *Maxima Libertatis Custodia Est* and *Vincit Amor Patriae*.

148. *NYWJ*, Sept. 22, 1735; Sept. 27, 1736, May 23, 30, 1737.

149. *SCG*, March 30, 1747; *MG* (2), Feb. 27, 1752. Trenchard's *An Argument Shewing, that a Standing Army is inconsistent with a Free Government* (London, 1697) was a great favorite.

150. Above, Chap. 1, n. 84.

151. *NYG*, Sept. 8, 1729; *BEP*, Nov. 26, 1739; *NYEP*, March 7, 1748.

152. *NYWJ*, Dec. 16-30, 1734, Feb. 3, 1735; *NYM*, Dec. 30, 1754.

153. Probably the favorite topic of writers to the colonial press was the curse of "faction" and "cabal," also known as "Party-Heat," "Party-Malice," and "Party-Rage." See *AWM*, Dec. 31, 1723, June 17, 1736, Jan. 31, 1738; *NEWJ*, Aug. 25, 1729; *SCG*, Jan. 8, 1732; *PaG*, Sept. 28, 1733; *BEP*, April 13, 1741, April 5, 1742, July 2, 1750, April 12, 1756; *GM*, June 1741; *IR*, Feb. 22, 1753; *PJ*, March 25, 1756; *NEM*, Aug. 1758; *NM*, April 17, 1759, April 18, 1763, April 23, May 28, 1764; *PG*, Jan. 29, 1763, March 3, 1764. A more realistic view of the functions of parties in free government may be found in *NYG*, March 18, 1734, March 18, 1735; *NYWJ*, March 17, 1735; *NYG* (2), Jan. 9, 1749; *PAM* (2), Oct. 1757.

154. *BEP*, March 15, 1736; Frink, *A King reigning in Righteousness*, 82.

155. *SCG*, Dec. 14, 1734, a great favorite; *NYG*, Dec. 24, 1734.

156. *NEC*, June 24, 1723; *NYWJ*, Dec. 31, 1733; *NYG*, Dec. 24, 1734; *MG* (2), Aug. 26, 1746; *PAM* (2), March 1758; *IR*, Aug. 16, 1753.

157. Some excellent examples of conservative political thought in the colonies are *AWM*, June 17, 1736;

NEWJ, Nov. 8, 1731, Jan. 20, 1735; May 29, 1737; *NYG*, April 11, 1735; *BEP*, Nov. 29, 1742; *BNL*, Oct. 17, 1751; *NM*, April 23, 1764, a brilliant attack on Rhode Island democracy; William Cooper, *The Honours of Christ demanded of the Magistrate* (Boston, 1740), esp. 6, 9; *Colden Papers, NYHSC* (1935), IX, 241-257; Schneider, *Samuel Johnson*, I, 148-150, 349; Keith, *Collection of Papers*, Essay 3. Labaree, *Conservatism*, Chap. 5, is a fine discussion of political conservatism. The political theory of American Puritanism is expounded in Perry, *Puritanism and Democracy*, Chaps. 4-5; Parrington, *Main Currents*, I, Bk. I; H. L. Osgood, "The Political Ideas of the Puritans," *PSQ*, VI (1891), 1-28, 201-231; S. Gray, "The Political Thought of John Winthrop," *NEQ*, III (1930), 681-705; Miller and Johnson, *The Puritans*, Chap. 2.

158. *Writings* (Ford ed.), I, 112.

159. *NYWPB*, March 17, 1746; *NYWJ*, Jan. 7, 14, 1734; *NYM*, Feb. 28, 1763.

160. *BIA*, April 10, 1749; *BEP*, April 27, 1761.

161. *PJ*, Sept. 28, 1758.

162. *CG*, April 10, 1756.

163. *BIA*, April 10, May 29, 1749.

164. *BG*, Sept. 17, 1764; *NYG*, Nov. 3, 1729; *NYWJ*, June 30, 1735, Jan. 11, 1739.

165. Hunn, *Welfare of a Government*, 3-6; Nathanael Eells, *The Wise Ruler a Loyal Subject* (New London, 1748), 5ff.; Benjamin Lord, *Religion and Government subsisting together in Society* (New London, 1752).

166. *CG*, April 12, 1755; *PJ*, June 17, 1756; Franklin, *Writings*, II, 392.

167. *BG*, May 19, 1755; *BPB*, Jan. 8, 1739; *NYEP*, Nov. 16, 1747; *NM*, April 10, 1759; Samuel Willard, *The Character of a Good Ruler* (Boston, 1694).

168. *BIA*, March 20, 1749; *BEP*, Aug. 10, 1741; *NYEP*, Jan. 8, 1750; *PAM* (2), Nov., Dec. 1757, Jan. 1758.

169. *NYM*, March 21, 1757; *BIA*, March 20, 1749; *BPB*, March 20, 1749.

170. Which was carefully distinguished from chauvinism: *NEWJ*, April 6, 1730; *NYWJ*, Jan. 27, 1735; *SCG*, May 10, 1740; *NYM*, Dec. 11, 1752; *BNL*, Dec. 28, 1752; *IR*, May 3, 1753; *NM*, April 17, 1759; Nathanael Walter, *The Character of a True Patriot* (Boston, 1745); Thomas Pollen, *The Principal Marks of True Patriotism* (Newport, 1758); Samuel Davies, *Religion and Public Spirit* (Portsmouth, 1762), a great favorite; Noah Welles, *Patriotism Described and Recommended* (New London, 1764).

171. *NEWJ*, May 29, 1727; Increase Mather, *The Excellency of a Publick Spirit* (Boston, 1702), 3-11, a noble statement.

172. *Industry and Frugality Proposed as the Surest Means to Make us a Rich and Flourishing People* (Boston, 1753); *BNL*, July 5, 19, Aug. 2, 16, 23, 1750; *MG* (2), Dec. 16, 23, 1746.

173. *VG*, Aug. 16, 1751.

174. *BNL*, May 9, 1751; Edward Holyoke, *Integrity and Religion to be principally regarded, by such as design others to Stations of publick Trust* (Boston, 1736).

175. *BAM*, Aug. 1745.

176. *NEWJ*, May 5, 1735; *NYWJ*, July 18, 1737, March 5, 1739; *BIA*, May 8, 1749; *BNL*, May 9, 1751; *BG*, May 31, 1756; *BEP*, May 14, 1759, April 27, May 4, 1761.

177. *SCG*, June 11, 1763; *NCG*, April 15, 1757; *BNL*, March 30, 1758, quoting Smollett; *BPB*, May 29, June 5, 1758; *NYG* (2) Sept. 18, 1758, Nov. 19, 1759; *NAM*, Oct. 1759; *NHG*, Sept. 7, 1759; Oct. 5-Nov. 23, 1759; *NM*, Dec. 20, 1762, Jan. 3, April 4, 1763; *PG*, Jan. 1, June 4, July 30, 1763, Dec. 15, 1764, in which he is equated (like Cato) with liberty itself.

178. *BEP*, Nov. 15, 1742; Jonathan Todd, *Civil Rulers the Ministers of God* (New London, 1749); Benjamin Wadsworth, *Rulers Feeding, and Guiding their People* (Boston, 1716), 22-55, by all odds the finest sermon of this type; Chauncy, *Civil Magistrates must be just*, 13ff.

179. Labaree, *Royal Instructions*, II, 503-505; *BNL*, March 16, 1758; *BG*, Oct. 5, 1730, Dec. 5, 1737; *BNL*, Nov. 6, 1704; Aug. 14, 21, 1755, March 9, 1758; *SCG*, May 26, 1757; *NCG*, April 14, 1757.

180. *NYEP*, Nov. 16, 1747, Oct. 2, 1749.

181. *IR*, Jan. 18, 1753.

182. *BG*, Feb. 11, 1760, July 18; 1763; *NYG*, Feb. 25, 1735; *NEWJ*, Dec. 19, 1738; *VG*, March 30, 1739; *SCG*, April 5, 1739; *NYWJ*, Aug. 21, 1749; *BNL*, Sept. 21, 1752; *NEM*, No. 3 (1758).

183. *NYWJ*, March 28, 1737; *AWM*, April 20, 1738.

184. See also *PAM*, Jan. 1741. The Winthrop quote is on the Tercentenary Monument in Boston Common, the Stoughton boast from his *New-England's True Interest* (Cambridge, 1670). See C. Rossiter, "The American Mission," *The American Scholar*, XX (1950-1951), 19-28.

PART TWO

INTRODUCTION

1. *Letters from an American Farmer*, 58.

2. The horrors of the Atlantic passage are chronicled in dozens of diaries and original narratives. See the protest of five Palatine Germans printed in *PaG*, Feb. 15, 1732, and B. R. James, ed., *Journal of Jasper Danckaerts, 1679-1680* (New York, 1913), 39-42.

3. Smith, *Colonists in Bondage*, Chaps. 5-7, and the table at 311-312; J. D. Butler, "British Convicts shipped to American Colonies," *AHR*, II (1896), 12-33; McCormac, *White Servitude in Maryland*, Chap. 8. For the transportation of military and political prisoners, see Smith, *Colonists in Bondage*, Chaps. 8-9.

4. James Boswell, *The Life of Samuel Johnson* (London, 1904), I, 560.

5. *Writings*, III, 45-48; *PaG*, May 24, 1751; *VG*, May 30, 1751. For other protests, see *AWM*, Oct. 29, 1720, Feb. 7, 14, 1721; *IR*, March 15, 1753;

MG (2), July 30, 1767. The latter also carries a spirited defense of their importation.

6. *BNL*, April 17, 1755.

7. See the examples printed in Edith Abbott, ed., *Historical Aspects of the Immigration Problem* (Chicago, 1926), 542-547. Useful studies of legislation dealing with the immigrant are Cora Start, "Naturalization in the English Colonies of North America," *AHAAR* (1893), 317-328; E. E. Proper, *Colonial Immigration Laws* (New York, 1900); E. A. Hoyt, "Naturalization under the American Colonies," *PSQ*, LXVII (1952), 248-266.

8. The best studies of colonial immigration are M. L. Hansen, *The Atlantic Migration, 1607-1860* (Cambridge, 1940), Chap. 2, and Carl Wittke, *We Who Built America* (New York, 1939), Pt. I.

9. I base these rough percentages on the census of 1790, first interpreted (or misinterpreted) by W. S. Rossiter in his *A Century of Population*

Growth (Washington, 1909), then reinterpreted by a distinguished committee of the American Council of Learned Societies in *Report* . . . *on* . . . *the Population of the United States, AHAAR* (1931), I, 105-441, as well as on a number of other works cited in these pages, all of which helped me project the best 1790 figures [*AHAAR* (1931), I, 124] back to 1765.

10. To Richard Jackson, Dec. 6, 1753; Van Doren, *Letters of Franklin and Jackson,* 41.

11. For these and other population figures I have used (with some figuring of my own) E. B. Greene and Virginia Harrington, *American Population before the Federal Census of 1790* (New York, 1932) and S. H. Sutherland, *Population Distribution in Colonial America* (New York, 1936).

12. Although some Welsh immigrants came to the colonies as conscious nationalists, they were speedily absorbed into the English community. See generally C. H. Browning, *Welsh Settlement of Pennsylvania* (Philadelphia, 1912). For another group of immigrants to Pennsylvania more English than not, see A. C. Myers, *Immigration of the Irish Quakers into Pennsylvania, 1682-1750* (Swarthmore, 1902).

13. See the evidence adduced by Franklin in his *Observations concerning the Increase of Mankind* (1751) and *The Interest of Great Britain Considered* (1760), in *Writings,* III, 63-73, IV, 32-82. See also Kalm, *Travels,* 313-315.

14. W. F. Dunaway, "The English Settlers in Colonial Pennsylvania," *PMHB,* LII (1928), 317-341, swings a little too far in the direction of the English.

15. J. P. MacLean, *An Historical Account . . . of Scotch Highlanders in America* (Cleveland, 1900).

16. The literature on the Scotch-Irish is enormous and checkered. See H. J. Ford, *The Scotch-Irish in America* (Princeton, 1915); C. A. Hanna, *The Scotch-Irish* (New York, 1902), an example of overenthusiasm; W. F. Dunaway, *The Scotch-Irish of Colonial Pennsylvania* (Chapel Hill, 1944), which has a fine bibliography at 233-257; and C. K. Bolton, *Scotch-Irish Pioneers* (Boston, 1910), Chaps. 8-13 of which deal with the great invasion of New England, 1718-1720. The publications of the Scotch-Irish Society of America must be used with care.

17. C. K. Shipton, "Immigration to New England, 1680-1740," *Journal of Political Economy,* XLIV (1936), 225-239.

18. See Governor Shute's observations in *BNL,* Nov. 9, 1719; for a later manifestation of nascent nativism, see *NHG,* Dec. 31, 1762. The typical colonial attitude, which welcomed all hardworking, Protestant aliens, is expressed in *IR,* Dec. 28, 1752.

19. *New Hampshire Provincial Papers,* III, 770-771.

20. Most notably Michael J. O'Brien of the Irish American Historical Society. Mr. O'Brien, who writes books with titles like *Timothy Murphy, Hero of the American Revolution* (New York, 1941) and *The McCarthys in Early American History* (New York, 1921), reached his extravagant peak in *A Hidden Phase of American History* (New York, 1919), Chaps. 14-22. See the review by J. F. Jameson, *AHR,* XXVI (1921), 797-799.

21. The best study of the colonial Germans, despite its tendency to claim too much, is A. B. Faust's exhaustive *The German Element in the United States* (Boston, 1909), I, Chaps. 2-10. See also Lucy F. Bittinger, *The Germans in Colonial Times* (Philadelphia, 1901); Wertenbaker, *Middle Colonies,* Chaps. 8-9; Wittke, *We*

Who Built America, Chap. 6; O. Kuhns, *The German and Swiss Settlements of Colonial Pennsylvania* (New York, 1901).

22. W. A. Knittle, *Early Eighteenth Century Palatine Emigration* (Philadelphia, 1937).

23. D. Cunz, *The Maryland Germans* (Princeton, 1948), Pt. I; H. Schuricht, *History of the German Element in Virginia* (Baltimore, 1899), Vol. I; J. W. Wayland, *The German Element . . . of Virginia* (Charlottesville, 1907).

24. F. R. Diffenderfer, *The German Immigration into Pennsylvania* (Lancaster, Pa., 1900); Ralph Wood, ed., *The Pennsylvania Germans* (Princeton, 1942). See also the many publications of the Pennsylvania German and Lancaster County Historical Societies.

25. *NYG* (2), June 18, 1750; *AWM*, Jan. 21, 1742; *SCG*, Dec. 4, 1749.

26. A. B. Faust, "Swiss Emigration to the American Colonies in the Eighteenth Century," *AHR*, XXII (1916), 21-44, 98-132.

27. L. J. Fosdick, *The French Blood in America* (Boston, 1906), Bk. III, Pts. 1-3; C. W. Baird, *History of the Huguenot Emigration to America* (New York, 1885); C. F. Dunaway, "The French Racial Strain in Colonial Pennsylvania," *PMHB*, LIII (1929), 322-342, a study that emphasizes the process of assimilation.

28. A. H. Hirsch, *The Huguenots of Colonial South Carolina* (Durham, 1928).

29. *Records of the Town of New Rochelle, 1699-1828* (New Rochelle, 1916). See also the records of King William Parish in *Va. Mag.*, XI-XIII.

30. See Flick, *History of New York*, I, Chaps. 7-10, II, Chap. 1; the old but still valuable works of E. B. O'Callaghan, *History of New Netherland* (New York, 1846-1848), and J. R. Brodhead, *History of the State of New York* (New York, 1853),

Vol. I; Wertenbaker, *Middle Colonies*, Chap. 2; J. F. Jameson, ed., *Narratives of New Netherland, 1609-1664* (New York, 1909). A recent scholarly treatment marked by a strong feeling for the Dutch is E. L. Raesly, *Portrait of New Netherland* (New York, 1945).

31. The absurd claims put forward by Douglas Campbell in *The Puritans in England, Holland, and America* (New York, 1892) are exploded by the articles of H. T. Colenbrander and Ruth Putnam in *AHAAR* (1909), 191-218. See also H. I. Priestley, *The Coming of the White Man* (New York, 1930), Chaps. 11-12, and the bibliography at 380-386.

32. Lord Adam Gordon, in Mereness, *Travels*, 416.

33. A. B. Benson and N. Hedin, *Americans from Sweden* (Philadelphia, 1950), Chaps. 1-2. Amandus Johnson, *The Swedish Settlements on the Delaware, 1638-1664* (Philadelphia, 1911), leaves nothing to be said, but C. Ward, *The Dutch and Swedes on the Delaware* (Philadelphia, 1930), says it more economically. Israel Acrelius, *Description of . . . New Sweden* (1759), reprinted in *Memoirs of the Historical Society of Pennsylvania*, XI (1874), is the best colonial account.

34. The best study of intercolonial migration is W. F. Dunaway, "Pennsylvania as an Early Distributing Center of Population," *PMHB*, LV (1931), 134-169.

35. Above, Chap. 2, n. 64.

36. M. A. Gutstein, *The Story of the Jews of Newport* (New York, 1936), Chaps. 1-9; B. M. Bigelow, "Aaron Lopez," *NEQ*, IV (1933), 757-776.

37. Kalm, *Travels*, 191.

38. Clark Wissler, *Indians of the United States* (New York, 1940); D'Arcy McNickle, *They Came Here First* (Philadelphia, 1949), Pt. II, and bibliography at 306-310. An interesting phase of colonial-Indian relations

is chronicled in A. W. Lauber, *Indian Slavery in Colonial Times* (New York, 1913).

39. *Letters from an American Farmer,* 43.

40. H. P. Fairchild, *Immigration* (New York, 1913), Chap. 2. H. E. Bolton and T. M. Marshall, *The Colonization of North America* (New York, 1920), sets migration into the British colonies in a larger perspective.

41. *VG,* March 5, 1752; Kalm, *Travels,* 46-47.

42. See the letter of "Caius Memmius" in *MG* (2), Dec. 1, 1768. The Boston Tories did their best to spread the notion that the Sons of Liberty were an Irish mob, as in the letter of "Honourable Patrick McAdam O'Flagharty" in *BC,* Feb. 29, 1772.

43. Burnaby, *Travels,* 67; William Douglass, *A Summary, Historical and Political, of the British Settlements in North-America* (London, 1755), I, 209-210, II, 326.

44. Serious consideration was accorded Daniel Dulany the elder (1685-1753) for his *The Rights of the Inhabitants of Maryland to the Benefit of the English Laws* (Annapolis, 1728), reprinted in Sioussat, *English Statutes in Maryland,* App.

45. For some classic examples, see Boyd, *Tracts,* 180-192; Ford, *The Scotch-Irish,* 576-582 (also in *PJ,* March 15, 1764; *NM,* March 19, 1764); *NCCR,* VII, 671-672, 699-700, 759-766, 770-771; J. R. Robertson, ed., *Petitions of the Early Inhabitants of Kentucky* (Louisville, 1914), Nos. 2, 3, 8, 9, 15, 24; Fulham MSS., N.C., S.C., Ga. (Library of Congress transcripts), No. 72; *Amer. Arch.,* I, 275-276, VI, 1528-1529.

46. See the pamphlets attributed to Husband in Boyd, *Tracts,* 193-392.

CHAPTER SIX

1. Cotton Mather, *Magnalia Christi Americana* (1702) (Hartford, 1820), I, 311, 313. Mather's account of Hooker was also printed separately in his *Johannes in Eremo* (Boston, 1695).

2. G. P. Gooch, *Political Thought in England from Bacon to Halifax* (London, 1914), 142. For treatments of Hooker as democrat and Connecticut as democracy, see John Fiske, *The Beginnings of New England* (Boston, 1890), 123-128; W. D. Love, *The Colonial History of Hartford* (Hartford, 1914), Chap. 5; Parrington, *Main Currents,* I, 53-62; J. T. Adams, *The Founding of New England* (Boston, 1921), 192-195; Jacobson, *Development of American Political Thought,* 17. And see J. M. Taylor, *Roger Ludlow* (New York, 1900), 82-86, for a crushing array of eulogies of the Fundamental Orders as "the first example in history of a written constitution," including contributions by Bancroft, Palfrey, J. R. Green, Bryce, and Bushnell.

3. Examples enough are Mrs. J. M. Holcombe, "The Birthplace of American Democracy," *Connecticut Magazine,* VIII (1904), 489-504; L. E. Whiton, "Aristocracy versus Democracy," *Conn. Mag.* IX (1905), 33-48.

4. Alexander Johnston, *Connecticut* (Boston, 1893), 73.

5. Miller and Johnson, *The Puritans,* 291. See Miller's briskly argued "Thomas Hooker and the Democracy of Early Connecticut," *NEQ,* IV (1931), 663-712; Osgood, *American Colonies in the Seventeenth Century,* I, 308-309; Andrews, *Colonial Period,* II, 142-143.

6. C. M. Andrews, "On Some Early Aspects of Connecticut History," *NEQ,* XVII (1944), 3.

7. Mather, *Magnalia,* I, 302.

8. J. F. Jameson, ed., *Johnson's Wonder-Working Providence* (1653) (New York, 1910), 87, 90.

9. The standard biography of Hooker is G. L. Walker, *Thomas Hooker.*

Preacher, Founder, Democrat (New York, 1891). See also E. W. Hooker, *The Life of Thomas Hooker* (Boston, 1849); Sprague, *Annals of the American Pulpit*, I, 30-37; W. S. Archibald, *Thomas Hooker* (New Haven, 1933). These works are sketchy and do little more than repeat the facts presented by Mather in the *Magnalia* and Winthrop in his *Journal.*

10. For evidence of the confusion surrounding the facts of Hooker's life, see *NEHGR*, XLVII (1893), 189-192; *New York Genealogical and Biographical Record*, LXIV (1933), 2; J. Savage, ed., *Genealogical Dictionary* (Boston, 1860), II, 459-460.

11. *Magnalia*, I, 303.

12. Mather, *Magnalia*, I, 308.

13. Miller, *New England Mind*, 58, 62, 218, 258, 283, 300-301, 356-358; Tyler, *History of American Literature*, I, 193-204.

14. Walker, *Thomas Hooker*, 45-46; John Waddington, *Congregational History* (London, 1874), II, 292; paraphrased in *Calendar of State Papers (Domestic Series), 1628-1629*, 554. For other tantalizing glimpses of Hooker in England and Holland, see *Calendar of State Papers (Domestic Series), 1628-1629*, 567; *1629-1631*, 87, 92; *1631-1633*, 411; *1633-1634*, 30-31, 324.

15. *Winthrop Papers* (Boston, 1929-1947), I, 178, 336.

16. *Winthrop's Journal*, I, 106.

17. *Winthrop's Journal*, I, 111.

18. *Winthrop's Journal*, I, 110-111. On the purported influence of Plymouth, see the evidence in *Bradford's History* (Boston, 1899), 316-317. For Perry Miller's dissenting view, see his *Orthodoxy in Massachusetts*, 127-147; and on this whole question, see W. Walker, *A History of the Congregational Churches in the United States* (New York, 1894), 100-114.

19. *Winthrop's Journal*, I, 124.

20. *Winthrop's Journal*, I, 132-134.

21. *Winthrop's Journal*, I, 113-114, 142, 162-163.

22. The evidence on these points is reviewed by Walker, *Thomas Hooker*, 86-90; Andrews, *Colonial Period*, II, 84-91; and Miller, *NEQ*, IV, 675-679. William Hubbard's *General History of New England* (c. 1680), printed in *MHSC*, V-VI (1815), is the authority upon which later historians have relied in this matter. At page 173 he makes the oft-quoted statement, "Two such eminent stars, such as were Mr. Cotton and Mr. Hooker, both of the first magnitude, though of differing influence, could not well continue in one and the same orb." See also Benjamin Trumbull, *A Complete History of Connecticut* (New Haven, 1818), I, 216.

23. For the testimony of Roger Williams on this point, see *NCP*, VI, 344. For evidence of religious differences between Hooker and the Bay ministers, see *Winthrop Papers*, III, 199-200, 389-390, and his own account of the famous controversy over the cross in the ensign, *MHSP*, XLII, 272-280.

24. *MCR*, I, 170-171.

25. *Winthrop's Journal*, I, 180-181.

26. *MCR*, I, 159-160.

27. *MCR*, I, 170-171.

28. *CCR*, I, 9.

29. C. E. Cunningham, "John Haynes," *NEQ*, XII (1939), 654-680.

30. Taylor, *Roger Ludlow*; R. V. Coleman, *Roger Ludlow in Chancery* (Westport, Conn., 1934) and *Mr. Ludlow Goes for Old England* (Westport, 1935).

31. The text of the Fundamental Orders is in Thorpe, I, 519-523; *CCR*, I, 20-25; G. M. Dutcher and A. C. Bates, *The Fundamental Orders of Connecticut* (New Haven, 1934).

32. C. M. Andrews, *The Beginnings of Connecticut* (New Haven, 1934), 42-44.

33. Another "first" claimed for Connecticut by some enthusiastic chron-

iclers was thus neatly punctured by Osgood, *American Colonies in the Seventeenth Century*, I, 306: "Connecticut was in no sense formed by a 'consociation' of independent towns, for the simple reason that its towns were never independent. No imposing theory of federal union can be evolved from the early history of the River Towns without drawing very heavily on the imagination."

34. *CCR*, I, 36, 39, 138, 509-563

35. *CCR*, I, 119.

36. *CCR*, I, 293.

37. *CCR*, I, 347.

38. *Magnalia*, I, 302-303.

39. *Founding of New England*, 193, 258; *Main Currents*, I, 54, 57, 60.

40. The antidote for an overdose of Parrington is a "shot" of Perry Miller, especially his *Orthodoxy in Massachusetts* and *New England Mind*. The indices of these two books are a gold mine for diggers into Hooker's religious ideas, and I gratefully acknowledge that I have dug with profit.

41. *Winthrop's Journal*, I, 162-163, 229, 232; II, 139, 257.

42. Hooker's religion is most perfectly represented in *The Poore Doubting Christian* (London, 1629); *The Application of Redemption* (London, 1657); *The Soules Preparation* (London, 1632); *The Soules Humiliation* (London, 1637); *The Soules Implantation* (London, 1637); and *The Soules Exaltation* (London, 1638). See the excerpts from his fire-and-brimstone farewell to England, *The Danger of Desertion* (London, 1641), in *MHSP*, XLVI (1913), 253-274, as well as excerpts from his sermons in G. L. Walker, *History of the First Church in Hartford* (Hartford, 1884), Chap. VI. The appendix of this book and that of Walker's *Thomas Hooker* carry the bibliography of Hooker's writings prepared by J. H. Trumbull.

43. *A Survey of the Summe of Church-Discipline* (London, 1648), Pt. I, 50.

44. Hooker's strictly Congregational views on the purposes and powers of synods are plain in the fragmentary part 4 of *The Summe of Church-Discipline*, esp. 19, 23-24, 45-54.

45. *NEQ*, IV, 689.

46. *Winthrop's Journal*, II, 346; Mather, *Magnalia*, I, 77.

47. The London, 1648, edition of this book was the only one ever printed. The preface is reprinted in full in *Old South Leaflets* (Boston, n.d.), No. 55, in part in W. Walker, *The Creeds and Platforms of Congregationalism* (New York, 1893), 132-148. To some copies of the 1648 edition, including the one I have used, Cotton's *Way of the Congregational Churches Cleared* was appended. Rutherford's answer was *A Survey of the Survey of that Summe of Church-Discipline* (London, 1658).

48. *Winthrop's Journal*, I, 231-232, 287-289.

49. *Winthrop Papers*, IV, 53-54, 75-84, 99-100. Hooker's letter is also in *Connecticut Historical Society Collections*, I, 1-18.

50. *Connecticut Historical Society Collections*, I, 20-21. The bracketed words are those of whose identity Trumbull was not certain.

51. Miller, *New England Mind*, esp. 116-153, 312-330, 493-501.

52. Andrews, *Beginnings of Connecticut*, 21.

53. *Summe of Church-Discipline*, Pt. I, 46-50, 69, 187-188.

54. *Summe of Church-Discipline*, Pt. I, 78-81.

55. *Winthrop Papers*, II, 282-295; *Winthrop's Journal*, II, 237-239. See also *A Replye*, etc., and *Arbitrary Government Described*, in R. C. Winthrop, *Life and Letters of John Winthrop* (Boston, 1869), II, 427-438, 440-460. See Stanley Gray, "The Political Thought of John Winthrop," *NEQ*, III (1930), 681-705.

56. *Winthrop's Journal,* II, 326-327; letter of Samuel Stone to Thomas Shepard, *MHSC,* VIII (4th ser.), 544-546; Mather, *Magnalia,* I, 317.
57. *CCR,* I, 124. The most informative piece of evidence we have of Hooker's life in Connecticut is his will, which may be found in *CCR,* I, 498-502, or Walker, *Thomas Hooker,* 178-183.
58. *A General History of Connecticut* (2nd ed., London, 1787), 59.
59. *The Puritans,* 291.
60. Mather, *Magnalia,* I, 316-317. The quotation is from the preface to *The Summe of Church-Discipline.* See also Hooker's letter of July 15, 1643, "to his much Honoured freind John Wyntropp Esquier," *Winthrop Papers,* IV, 401-402.
61. Mather, *Magnalia,* I, 302.
62. For Hooker's orthodox opinion of the support owed one another by magistrate and minister, see *Summe of Church-Discipline,* Pt. II, 79-80; Pt. IV, 54-59.
63. *Main Currents,* I, 59.

CHAPTER SEVEN

1. *Magnalia,* II, 430.
2. *Magnalia,* II, 433.
3. Williams has had more than his share of biographies, especially poor ones. The list is far too long to be recorded here, but attention should be called to these books: J. D. Knowles, *Memoir of Roger Williams* (Boston, 1834), a surprisingly judicious and brightly written treatment, containing many letters and documents; O. S. Straus, *Roger Williams* (New York, 1894); E. J. Carpenter, *Roger Williams* (New York, 1909); Emily Easton, *Roger Williams* (Boston, 1930); James Ernst, *Roger Williams* (New York, 1932), a learned and valuable work, despite the shameful job of editing bestowed upon it; and S. H. Brockunier, *The Irrepressible Democrat* (New York, 1940), the latest and best.
4. *NEHGR,* XLIII, 290-303, 427, XLVII, 498-499, LXVII, 90-91, LXXV, 234-235, LXXVIII, 272-276, XCVII, 173-181; *Book Notes,* XXIX, 81-93; *Rhode Island History,* III, 23-30, 67-71, 91-102; *RIHSC,* XXVIII, 112-115.
5. *NCP,* VI, 2. The six volumes of this series are the most reliable and accessible printed source of the bulk of Williams's writings. For other letters of Williams, see *NEHGR,* XXXVI, 78, LIII, 314-320; *Providence Records,* XV, 209, 219-220; *RIHSC,* XXVII, 85-92; *RIHS Pubs.,* VIII, 141-161; *RIHS Proc.* (1877-1878), 62-73; *An Answer to a Letter,* etc. (Boston, c. 1678; reprinted, Providence, 1876). See *RIHSC,* XI, 12-17, for a chronological list of his letters, indicating location of originals and the various books and collections in which each is printed. Several of his most important letters have been published in special editions. A. B. Strickland, *Roger Williams* (Boston, 1919), reproduces many interesting items concerning Williams's life and work.
6. *NCP,* VI, 252-253. These lines were an endorsement by Coke's daughter, Anne Sadleir, on a letter from Williams, probably written in 1652. For the facts and letters of the spirited exchange between the rebel preacher and the orthodox lady, see *NCP,* VI, 237-253; Ernst, *Roger Williams,* 324-327.
7. See his fantastic and revealing letters to Lady Joan Barrington, aunt and guardian of Jane Whalley, in *NEHGR,* XLIII, 315-320.
8. *RIHSC,* XXIX, 66-80.
9. *Winthrop's Journal,* I, 57.
10. *NCP,* VI, 356.
11. *Winthrop's Journal,* I, 61-62.
12. *Bradford's History,* 369-370.
13. *Winthrop's Journal,* I, 105-107, 110, 112.

14. *Winthrop's Journal*, I, 112-113, 116-117, 142, 149, 154, 155, 157, 162-163. The order of banishment is in *MCR*, I, 160-161.

15. For the payment of the bribe, see *MCR*, I, 165. Another early Massachusetts controversy in which Williams took an active part is chronicled in H. M. Chapin, *Roger Williams and the King's Colors* (Providence, 1928).

16. For a judicious summary of the Williams incident as one aspect of an unintended three-pronged attack on the oligarchy (the other rebels being Anne Hutchinson and Dr. Robert Child), see Andrews, *Colonial Period*, I, 470-495. The case for Massachusetts was stated once and for all time by H. M. Dexter, *As to Roger Williams* (Boston, 1876). See also G. A. Stead, "Roger Williams and the Massachusetts-Bay," *NEQ*, VII (1934), 235-257; Brockunier, *Roger Williams*, 68-81; Osgood, *American Colonies in the Seventeenth Century*, I, 224-235; and Charles Deane, "Roger Williams and the Massachusetts Charter," *MHSP*, XII, 341-358. The exchange of views of Williams and Cotton is in *NCP*, I, 324-325; II, 14, 40-55, 90; IV, 506.

17. *Winthrop's Journal*, I, 168.

18. *NCP*, VI, 335.

19. *NCP*, VI, 335.

20. *Providence Records*, V, 307.

21. *RICR*, I, 18-27, 45-51, 130-131.

22. From the "Epistle Dedicatory" to *The Hireling Ministry None of Christ's* (London, 1652).

23. *NCP*, VI, 263. The documents of Williams's transfer of his own rights to others are in *RICR*, I, 18-41; *NCP*, VI, 305-306, 316-317, 406-408. On this point, see Brockunier, *The Irrepressible Democrat*, 101-106, 113-117, 163-167, 260-263, 268-272.

24. *NCP*, VI, 318.

25. For glimpses of Williams as peacemaker, see *Winthrop's Journal*, I, 192-194, 221n., 272, II, 96, 350; *Win-throp Papers*, IV, *passim;* and several of his own letters in *NCP*, VI, 231-232, 269-276, 321-324.

26. This book is reprinted in *NCP*, I, 17-222, and was also republished separately in 1936.

27. *NCP*, VI, 338-340.

28. I am particularly indebted for my understanding of Williams's religion to C. S. Roddy, *The Religious Thought of Roger Williams*, an unpublished doctoral thesis submitted (1948) to New York University.

29. See his cantankerous and untypical tract, *George Fox Digg'd out of his Burrowes* (Boston, 1676), reprinted with comments in *NCP*, V, as well as his letter to Fox, July 15, 1672; *NCP*, VI, 357-360.

30. *RICR*, I, 374-380.

31. *The Fourth Paper, Presented by Major Butler* (London, 1652), reprinted by the Club for Colonial Reprints (Providence, 1903), 18-19.

32. R. B. Morris, "The Jewish Interests of Roger Williams," *American Hebrew*, December 9, 1921; C. P. Daly, *The Settlement of the Jews in North America* (New York, 1893), 12-15; *American Jewish Historical Society Publications*, VI, 62-73, XX, 140-142; XXXIV, 1-10; Goodman, *American Overture*, Chap. 3.

33. *CSPC* (1574-1660), 325-326.

34. *CSPC* (1574-1660), 338, 353-354, 377, 390, 414.

35. *NCP*, VI, 258-262; James Ernst, "Roger Williams and the English Revolution," *RIHSC*, XXIV, 1-58, 118-128, an overdrawn but informative account of his influence in the events of the time; David Masson, *The Life of John Milton* (London, 1881-1894), III, 112-129, 153-155, IV, 395-397, 528-533; G. R. Potter, "Roger Williams and John Milton," *RIHSC*, XIII, 113-125.

36. See Andrews, *Colonial Period*, II, 1-66; I. B. Richman, *Rhode Island. Its Making and Meaning* (New York, 1902); H. M. Chapin, *Documentary*

History of Rhode Island (Providence, 1916); and S. G. Arnold, *History of Rhode Island* (New York, 1859-1860), I.

37. *Harris Papers, RIHSC,* X; Andrews, *Colonial Period,* II, 55-66.

38. Three entries in *Winthrop's Journal* (I, 286, 297, 309) for 1638-1639 begin respectively: "At Providence, also, the devil was not idle"; "At Providence things grew still worse"; "At Providence matters went after the old manner."

39. *RICR,* I, 14.

40. *NCP,* VI, 3-7.

41. *RICR,* I, 52-53, 63-65, 69-71, 87.

42. K. W. Porter, "Samuell Gorton," *NEQ,* VII (1934), 405-444.

43. *RICR,* I, 112-113.

44. *RICR,* I, 143-146. The colony was styled "Providence Plantations."

45. *RICR,* I, 147-208.

46. *RICR,* I, 214-216. For light on the background of this federal pattern, see the "Instructions from the Town of Providence" to its delegation, *Providence Records,* XV, 9-10; *RICR,* I, 42-44.

47. *RICR,* I, 148-149. For the rise and fall of popular lawmaking in Rhode Island, see C. S. Lobingier, *The People's Law* (New York, 1909), 78-88.

48. *RICR,* I, 319, 320, 328, 365, 420-421, 442, 468, 496, 505, etc.

49. *RICR,* I, 327.

50. *RICR,* I, 432, 442-447; Andrews, *Colonial Period,* II, 38-49; T. W. Bicknell, *Story of Dr. John Clarke* (Providence, 1915).

51. *RICR,* I, 490-491.

52. The charter is printed in *RICR,* II, 3-21, its receipt recorded in *RICR,* I, 509-511. See also *CSPC* (1661-1668), 4, 110, 148-150, 341-343, 373; *NCP,* VI, 346.

53. W. E. Foster, *Town Government in Rhode Island* (Baltimore, 1886), 7-12.

54. *NCP,* VI, 268.

55. Williams's intellectual loneliness is emphasized by R. E. E. Harkness,

"Roger Williams—Prophet of Tomorrow," *Journal of Religion,* XV (1935), 400-425.

56. James E. Ernst has devoted an entire monograph to *The Political Thought of Roger Williams* (Seattle, 1929). This is a valuable if oversystematized and repetitious work. Its chief defect lies in its presentation of Williams's ideas in much too modern, expansive, and professional terms.

57. *NCP,* VI, 149-151, 262-266, 278-279, 400-403. See also *NCP,* VI, 266-268; *RIHS Pubs.,* VIII, 147-154.

58. The first four and the eighth of these writings are reprinted in *NCP,* I-V. For a modern edition of *The Fourth Paper,* see above, n. 31. *Experiments* was reprinted in Providence, 1863, and Philadelphia, 1951; *The Hireling Ministry* in Utica, N. Y., 1847. See also *Christenings Make No Christians* (London, 1645; reprinted, Providence, 1881).

59. Parrington, *Main Currents,* I, 66-73; Ernst, *Roger Williams,* 207.

60. *NCP,* III, 366.

61. *NCP,* III, 384.

62. *NCP,* IV, 222.

63. *NCP,* III, 355.

64. *NCP,* IV, 187.

65. *NCP,* III, 349-250.

66. *NCP,* III, 338; IV, 80.

67. Ernst, *Political Thought of Roger Williams,* 29, 44, 196-197, is the most obvious example.

68. *RIHS Pubs.,* VIII, 149.

69. See the translation (by J. E. Ernst) of an important chapter of M. Freund, *Der Idee der Toleranz* (Halle, 1927), in *RIHSC,* XXVI, 101-133; Johannes Kühn, *Toleranz und Offenbarung* (Leipzig, 1923); Mecklin, *Story of American Dissent,* 82-115.

70. *NCP,* III, 333.

71. *NCP,* III, 3-4, 202.

72. *NCP,* III, 72-73.

73. *NCP*, III, 252. For evidence of the reality of religious liberty in Rhode Island, see *RICR*, I, 14, 16, 376-378.

74. *NCP*, III, 171.

75. *NCP*, IV, 71.

76. *The Hireling Ministry*, intro.

77. *NCP*, III, 4; IV, 7-8.

78. Miller and Johnson, *The Puritans*, 186. They set up a plausible distinction between Williams and Jefferson as "apostles of religious liberty." Each wanted separation—Williams because he feared state would contaminate church, Jefferson because he feared church would contaminate state. The philosophical differences of Cotton and Williams are emphasized in H. B. Parkes, "John Cotton and Roger Williams Debate Toleration," *NEQ*, IV (1931), 735-756. For a view more friendly to Cotton, see Elizabeth F. Hirsch, "John Cotton and Roger Williams," *Church History*, X (1941), 38-51.

79. *NCP*, IV, 30.

80. *An Answer to a Letter*, 10.

81. *NCP*, V, 13, 59-62, 242.

82. *NCP*, VI, 149-150.

83. *RICR*, I, 28-29.

84. *MCR*, I, 151.

85. February 17, 1655; *NCP*, VI, 287.

86. *NCP*, VI, 278-279; *PG*, Feb. 16, 1765. See also *NCP*, VI, 400-403, and *RICR*, I, 158, in which the "founding fathers" of 1647 stated their unwillingness "that our popularity should prove (as some conjecture it will), an Anarchie, and so a common Tyranny."

87. *RICR*, I, 157-158.

88. *NCP*, VI, 263. See also *RIHS Pubs.*, VIII, 158.

89. *NCP*, IV, 12.

90. John Callender, *An Historical Discourse* (1738-1739) (Providence, 1838), 147-148; Brockunier, *The Irrepressible Democrat*, 281; RIHSC, XXVII, 54.

91. For the revival of Williams's fame, see Brockunier, *The Irrepressible Democrat*, 285-289. Callender's "Cen-

tury Sermon" did much to keep the memory of this "most pious and heavenlyminded soul" alive in the colony, while Stephen Hopkins's excellent "An Historical Account of the Planting and Growth of Providence" (*PG*, Jan. 12, 19, Feb. 2-16, March 16, 30, 1765; *MHSC*, IX (2nd ser.), 166-203; *RIHSC*, VII, 13-65) called the attention of the Revolutionary generation to the greatness of the founder. The letter of "William Freeborn," *RIG*, Jan. 11, 1733, is evidence that Rhode Islanders knew they had something special in their form of government.

92. For an interesting if typically hyperbolic account of the significance of Williams's doctrines, see John Dos Passos, *The Ground We Stand On* (New York, 1941), 23-183. More judicious appraisals are F. B. Wiener, "Roger Williams' Contribution to Modern Thought," *RIHSC*, XXVIII, 1-20, and L. C. Wroth, "Roger Williams," *Brown Univ. Papers*, XIV (1937).

93. G. P. Gooch, *English Democratic Ideas in the Seventeenth Century* (Cambridge, Eng., 1927), 72.

94. *NCP*, VI, 238, 242.

CHAPTER EIGHT

1. Parrington, *Main Currents*, I, vii.

2. Miller and Johnson, *The Puritans*, 193.

3. From "A Character of the Reverend Mr. John Wise," appended to John White's funeral sermon, *The Gospel Treasure in Earthen Vessels* (Boston, 1725).

4. *History of American Literature*, II, 115; *History of the Congregational Churches*, 209; *Main Currents*, I, 119.

5. *NEHGR*, II, 104.

6. Savage, *Genealogical Dictionary*, I, 21; II, 23; IV, 614.

7. Morison, *Harvard in the Seventeenth Century*, I, 75. The first full-

length biography of Wise (by George A. Cook) was published in late 1952, but I was unable to see it until this book was in page-proofs. See also J. L. Sibley, *Biographical Sketches of Graduates of Harvard University* (Cambridge, 1881), II, 428-441; T. F. Waters, *Two Ipswich Patriots* (Ipswich, 1927), 5-23; S. L. Cook, "John Wise," *Proceedings of the Boston Society* (1924), 28-40; P. S. McElroy, "John Wise," *EIHC*, LXXXI, 201-226; H. M. Dexter, "Address on Rev. John Wise," in *Celebration of the Two Hundredth Anniversary . . . of the Congregational Church and Parish in Essex, Mass.* (Salem, 1884), 113-137.

8. *CSMP*, III, 452-454.

9. *CCR*, II, 399, 402.

10. R. Crowell, *History of the Second Parish in Ipswich* (Andover, 1815), 10-15; *MCR*, V, 146, 175, 225.

11. R. Crowell, *History of the Town of Essex* (Boston, 1853), 124-130; *MCR*, V, 285; Ipswich Town Records, March 23, 1686, and Jan. 22, 1695.

12. *Journals of the House of Representatives of Massachusetts*, II, 108; *MHSC*, VII (5th ser.), 214.

13. J. B. Felt, *History of Ipswich, Essex, and Hamilton* (Cambridge, 1834), 262.

14. *History of American Literature*, II, 104.

15. Felt, *History of Ipswich*, 259.

16. From "A Character of the Reverend Mr. John Wise."

17. Barnes, *Dominion of New England*, esp. Chap. 4; Waters, *Ipswich*, I, 225-273.

18. Felt, *History of Ipswich*, 124.

19. Ipswich Town Records, Aug. 23, 1687.

20. *AASP*, XII, 477; *CSPC* (1685-1688), 473-474.

21. *MHSP*, XII, 109.

22. See Wise's account of this affair, drawn up at the request of the Ipswich town meeting (Ipswich Town Records, Dec. 24, 1689), in Whitmore, *Andros Tracts*, I, 83-87; see also "Proceedings Against Wise and Others of Ipswich for Misdemeanors," in R. N. Toppan, ed., *Edward Randolph* (Boston, 1899), IV, 171-182.

23. From "A Character of the Reverend Mr. John Wise."

24. *MHSP*, XV (2nd ser.), 283-296.

25. *Salem Witchcraft* (Boston, 1867), II, 304-305.

26. Waters, *Ipswich*, I, 290-291.

27. *MHSC*, IX (1st ser.), 276.

28. (Boston, 1721), reprinted in A. M. Davis, ed., *Colonial Currency Reprints* (Boston, 1911), II, 159-223. Wise's chief contribution to a lively controversy over *A Word of Comfort* carried on in *BG* (Feb. 20, March 13, 20, 1721) was *A Friendly Check, from a Kind Relation* (Boston, 1721), reprinted in *Colonial Currency Reprints*, II, 245-250.

29. Walker, *History of the Congregational Churches*, 201.

30. From an endorsement to the second edition of *The Churches' Quarrel Espoused* (Boston, 1715).

31. *The Churches' Quarrel Espoused* was republished in 1715, 1745, and 1772, *A Vindication* in 1772. The most accessible printing of Wise's two books is the combined edition of 1860, published in Boston by the Congregational Board of Publication. It is this edition that I shall cite in this chapter. Wise has been cited as an authority on church government by the courts of Massachusetts. See *Baker v. Fales*, 16 *Mass. Rep.* (1819), 488, 498-499.

32. *MHSC*, VIII (7th ser.), 327. In another entry (VIII, 450), he speaks of the "Poison of Wise's cursed Libel."

33. *MHSC*, VII (5th ser.), 51. Sewall, who was a correspondent of Wise's, wished "the extremity of the censure had been forborn—Lest we be devoured of one another."

34. *Vindication*, 29.

35. The most accessible English edition, which includes a valuable introduction, is the translation of C. H. and W. A. Oldfather (Oxford, 1934).

36. *NEHGR*, XXX, 64-67.

37. All these quotations are from *Churches' Quarrel*, 136, 149, 164, 211, 217, 230, respectively.

38. *History of American Literature*, II, 104. Tyler, it must be admitted, was rarely guilty of understatement.

39. *Vindication*, 25.

40. *Vindication*, 30-31.

41. *Vindication*, 31.

42. *De Jure Belli ac Pacis* (English ed., Oxford, 1925), Bk. I, Chap. 1, Sec. x, 5.

43. *Vindication*, 30.

44. *Vindication*, 31.

45. *Vindication*, 33.

46. *Vindication*, 32-33.

47. *Vindication*, 33.

48. *Vindication*, 33-34.

49. *Vindication*, 34-35.

50. *Vindication*, 54.

51. *Churches' Quarrel*, 207, 208, 209.

52. *Vindication*, 37-38.

53. *Vindication*, 39.

54. *Churches' Quarrel*, 208.

55. *Vindication*, 38.

56. *Vindication*, 64.

57. *Vindication*, 29.

58. *Vindication*, 41-42, 44-45.

59. *Vindication*, 45.

60. *Vindication*, 56.

61. *Vindication*, 60.

62. *Vindication*, 42.

63. *Vindication*, 43-44.

64. *Vindication*, 37.

65. *Vindication*, 42.

66. *A Disquisition on Government*, in *The Works of John C. Calhoun* (Charleston, 1851), I, 14.

67. *Vindication*, 63.

68. *Common Sense*, in M. D. Conway, ed., *The Writings of Thomas Paine* (New York, 1894), I, 69.

69. *Churches' Quarrel*, 139-140.

70. *Vindication*, 54-55.

71. *Vindication*, 40.

72. *Vindication*, 57.

73. *Vindication*, 47.

74. The list of subscribers to the 1772 edition may be found in the 1860 edition, 237-245. Proposals for this edition appeared in *EG*, Jan. 7, 14, 1772.

75. From a brief tribute to Wise in White's otherwise wearing funeral sermon, *The Gospel Treasure in Earthen Vessels*, 38.

76. *Churches' Quarrel*, 116.

CHAPTER NINE

1. To Hezekiah Niles, Feb. 3, 1818; *Works*, X, 284.

2. Adams, *Works*, X, 287-288. For equally strong characterizations of Mayhew, see such diverse sources as George Bancroft, *History of the United States* (rev. ed., Boston, 1876), III, 40-41, and IV, 9; Miller and Johnson, *The Puritans*, 193-194, 277.

3. C. E. Banks, *History of Martha's Vineyard* (Boston, 1911-1925), III, 305. The Mayhew genealogy in Savage, *Genealogical Dictionary*, III, 184-185, is not accurate.

4. A. Bradford, *Memoir of the Life and Writings of Rev. Jonathan Mayhew, D.D.* (Boston, 1838), 12. This curious, formless, and eulogistic work is the only full-length biography of Mayhew. Although Bradford reprinted sizable extracts from Mayhew's sermons and letters, he unfortunately insisted on touching them up with insertions and alterations of his own making. The bulk of the memorable correspondence between Mayhew and Thomas Hollis is preserved in the Massachusetts Historical Society (*MHS*). The Boston University Library (*BU*) has a large number of letters to, from, and about Mayhew.

5. A brief account of his life and writings is in *NEHGR*, XIII, 247-248, and *Sibley's Harvard Graduates*, VII, 632-639. General Jonathan M.

Wainwright is fifth in line from Jonathan Mayhew.

6. Mayhew was twice appointed "Scholar of the House," and also received a grant of money from the college; *Harvard College Records, CSMP*, XVI, 713, 740, 721.

7. Harvard College, Faculty Records, I, 157, 188, 198, 214. Other glimpses of Mayhew are at 149, 156, 158-159, 169, 186, 190.

8. *BG*, July 14, 1766; *NHG*, July 18, 1766; *BPB*, July 21, 1766; *NM*, July 21, 1766.

9. *BNL*, July 17, 1766.

10. Bradford, *Mayhew*, 25n.

11. Bradford, *Mayhew*, 385.

12. See, for example, the blast at the Rev. John Cleaveland of Ipswich, *A Letter of Reproof to Mr. John Cleaveland* (Boston, 1764).

13. (Boston, 1749); reprinted in London, 1750. A full and virtually accurate bibliography of Mayhew may be found in Sprague, *Annals of the American Pulpit*, VIII, 26, or in M. C. Tyler, *The Literary History of the American Revolution* (New York, 1897), I, 126-127.

14. Hollis was responsible for most of the London reprints of Mayhew's works. See Francis Blackburne, *Memoirs of Thomas Hollis* (London, 1790). A notable addition to our understanding of Hollis and his friendship with Mayhew is Caroline Robbins, "The Strenuous Whig, Thomas Hollis of Lincoln's Inn," *WMQ* (3), VII (1950), 406-453.

15. Cross, *The Anglican Episcopate and the American Colonies*, Chap. 6; H. W. Foote, *Annals of King's Chapel* (Boston, 1882-1896), II, 243-280; Perry, *History of the American Episcopal Church*, I, 411ff.; *MHSC*, LXXIV, 103-114; Perry, *Collections*, III, 497, 500, 508; *BG*, 1763-1754, *passim*.

16. *BG*, Feb. 21, 1763; *BEP*, Feb. 28, March 7, 14, 1763.

17. Including such delicious (or malicious) newspaper attacks as those printed in *NM*, June 6, 13, 20, Oct. 10, 1763. The first of these was also printed as an anonymous pamphlet, *Verses on Doctor Mayhew's Book of Observations* (Providence, 1763).

18. *A Review of Dr. Mayhew's Remarks* (London, 1764).

19. Mayhew to Hollis, Aug. 8, 1765; Sept. 26, 1765 (*MHS*).

20. *Observations on the Charter and Conduct of the Society* (Boston, 1763), 156. This and most of the other pamphlets in the controversy were reprinted immediately in London. Mayhew's concern is evident in his letters to Hollis of April 6, 1762; April 27, 1763 (*MHS*).

21. *Works*, X, 185, 187, 312, 313.

22. For the details and documents of this controversy, see President Quincy's noble *History of Harvard University* (Boston, 1860), II, 105-112, 464-479; Mayhew to Hollis, April 6, 1762 (*MHS*).

23. Bradford, *Mayhew*, 416-427; Hutchinson, *History of Massachusetts Bay*, III, 123; *NEHGR*, XLVI, 15-20; Mayhew to Hutchinson, Aug. 27, 1765 (*BU*).

24. The quotation is from the unpaged introduction to Vol. I.

25. *Heralds of a Liberal Faith*, I, 2.

26. *Sermons upon the Following Subjects*, etc. (Boston, 1755), 417-418. This note proved offensive to many, and Mayhew tried unsuccessfully to have it removed from the London edition (1756). In the latter volume the note appears at 322-323. See Sprague, *Annals of the American Pulpit*, I, 23; C. A. Bartol, *The West Church and its Ministers* (Boston, 1856), 98, 129-130.

27. Mayhew to Experience Mayhew, Oct. 5, 1747 (*BU*). In earlier letters he had expressed profound sympathy with the first outbursts of the Awakening; Mayhew to Zachariah May-

hew, Dec. 26, 1741, March 26, 1742 (*BU*).

28. *Seven Sermons* (Boston, 1749), 107.
29. *Two Sermons on . . . Divine Goodness* (Boston, 1763), 23-24, 44.
30. *Seven Sermons*, 108.
31. *Seven Sermons*, 5, 22ff.
32. Schneider, *Samuel Johnson*, I, 346.
33. *Seven Sermons*, 155.
34. *Three Centuries of Harvard*, 190-191.
35. Bradford, *Mayhew*, 432.
36. *Seven Sermons*, 86. The core of Mayhew's personal theology is in the two sermons on private judgment printed in *Seven Sermons*, 41-88.
37. Schneider, *Samuel Johnson*, I, 346.
38. (Boston, 1750), reprinted in 1818. It was made available to British readers in Richard Baron's curious *The Pillars of Priestcraft and Orthodoxy Shaken* (London, 1752). The most accessible edition of this sermon is in J. W. Thornton, ed., *The Pulpit of the American Revolution* (Boston, 1860), 39-104, to which I shall refer in this chapter.
39. That Mayhew had poked at a sensitive spot is plain in the severe counter-attack launched upon him in *BNL*, March 1, 22, 1750; *BEP*, Feb. 19-June 18, 1750. He was staunchly defended in *BG*, March 13-April 3, 1750.
40. Thornton, *Pulpit*, 43.
41. *A Sermon Preach'd in the Audience of his Excellency William Shirley* (Boston, 1754), to be cited as *Election Sermon*. Anti-French excerpts from this sermon were reprinted in *BNL*, May 30, 1754; *MG* (2), Dec. 5, 1754; *NYG* (2) Sept. 2, 1754.
42. (Boston, 1766), reprinted in L. A. Osborne, ed., *The Patriot Preachers of the American Revolution* (New York, 1860), 7-48, to which I shall refer. Mayhew's tribute to Pitt was reprinted in *NHG*, July 25, 1766; *VG* (Rind), Aug. 15, 1766; *PJ*, July 24, 1766.

43. *Seven Sermons*, 137.
44. *Election Sermon*, 6.
45. *Unlimited Submission*, 86n.
46. *Election Sermon*, 4-5. See also his *Sermon . . . on the Death of Frederick, Prince of Wales* (Boston, 1751), and *Unlimited Submission*, 56n., 61-62n., 83-84.
47. *Election Sermon*, 6-7, also 8-10, and *Unlimited Submission*, 60-61.
48. *Unlimited Submission*, 81n.
49. *Election Sermon*, 19.
50. *Election Sermon*, 13, 18, 10.
51. *Unlimited Submission*, 59.
52. *Election Sermon*, 42.
53. *Unlimited Submission*, 59n.
54. *Unlimited Submission*, 49.
55. *Unlimited Submission*, 60-61.
56. *The Snare Broken*, 30, 47.
57. *Unlimited Submission*, 69, 72, 73-74.
58. *Unlimited Submission*, 62.
59. *Unlimited Submission*, 86n.
60. *Unlimited Submission*, 79, 94-95n.
61. *Unlimited Submission*, 87n.
62. *Unlimited Submission*, 89-92.
63. *Unlimited Submission*, 87n.
64. *Unlimited Submission*, 88.
65. (Boston, 1763), ix.
66. *The Snare Broken*, 39-41.
67. Bradford, *Mayhew*, 4; Mayhew to Hollis, Dec. 18, 1764 (*MHS*).
68. Mayhew to Hollis, March 19, 1761 (*MHS*).
69. Mayhew to Hollis, Feb. 9, 1765 (*MHS*). Mayhew's Dudleian lecture at Harvard in 1765, entitled *Popish Idolatry* (Boston, 1765), included a measured attack on the threats to political and religious freedom inherent in ecclesiastical absolutism.
70. *Election Sermon*, 28, 10.
71. *The Snare Broken*, 41-42.
72. *The Snare Broken*, 31-32.
73. Mayhew to Otis, June 8, 1766 (*BU*). A copy of this letter is printed in Mercy O. Warren, *History of . . . the American Revolution* (Boston, 1805), I, 415-416. See also *Election Sermon*, 34-35, 40; *The Snare Broken*, 41-42.

74. Mrs. Mayhew to Hollis, July 27, 1766; Harrison Gray to Hollis, July 27, 1766 (*MHS*).

75. Blackburne, *Thomas Hollis*, I, 339.

76. *Works*, IV, 29.

77. From a poem recited by R. T. Paine, jr., at the 1792 Harvard commencement, quoted in Bradford, *Mayhew*, 449. Another choice poetical tribute was Benjamin Church, *Elegy on the Death of the Reverend Jonathan Mayhew, D.D.* (Boston, 1766). The best of the several eulogies occasioned by his death was Charles Chauncy, *A Discourse Occasioned by the Death of the Reverend Jonathan Mayhew, D.D.* (Boston, 1766).

CHAPTER TEN

1. In the notes to this chapter I have used the system of abbreviations established by E. G. Swem in his invaluable *Virginia Historical Index* (Roanoke, Va., 1934-1936): *V* for *Virginia Magazine of History and Biography; T* for *Tyler's Quarterly Historical and Genealogical Magazine; W(1), W(2),* and *W(3)* for *William and Mary Quarterly* (first, second, and third series, respectively); *H* for *Hening's Statutes at Large; C* for *Calendar of Virginia State Papers; R* for *Virginia Historical Register.* I have also used a few abbreviations of my own: *VG* for *Virginia Gazette; JHB* for *Journals of the House of Burgesses of Virginia* (Richmond, 1905-1924); *EJV* for *Executive Journals of the Council of Colonial Virginia* (Richmond, 1925-1945); *PCD* for *The Proceedings of the Convention of Delegates . . . in the Colony of Virginia* (Richmond, 1816); *JCS* for *Journals of the Council of the State of Virginia* (Richmond, 1931-1932).

2. For the English background and connections of Theodorick Bland, see *Familiae Minorum Gentium* (Harleian Society), II, 421-427.

3. Charles Campbell, ed., *The Bland Papers* (Petersburg, Va., 1840-1843), I, 148. For other evidences of Theodorick Bland, see 4 *V* 245; 5 *V* 22, 24, 113; 8 *V* 73, 107; 3 *W(1)* 65; 4 *W(1)* 167; 8 *W(1)* 185; 1 *H* 527, 543; 2 *H* 9.

4. 1 *V* 234, 365; 4 *V* 161, 163, 169, 174; 15 *V* 348; 1 *C* 122, 146; 3 *W(1)* 175, 180.

5. The will, probated April 12, 1720, is recorded in Prince George County Deed Book (1713-1729), 394.

6. *Works*, II, 362.

7. To Jeremy Belknap, June 15, 1798; *Writings of Washington* (Washington, 1931-1944), XXXVI, 290-291.

8. 6 *V* 129-130; *JHB* (1761-1765), xxix-xxxviii; and Bland's letter to R. H. Lee, May 22, 1766, in *Southern Literary Messenger*, XXVII, 116.

9. To Edward Coles, Aug. 25, 1814; *Writings* (Ford ed.), IX, 477; *Amer. Arch.*, I, 494.

10. William Meade, *Old Churches, Ministers and Families of Virginia* (Philadelphia, 1872-1878), I, 437-438; G. C. Mason, *Colonial Churches of Tidewater Virginia* (Richmond, 1945), 73-79; *Fifth Annual Report of the Archivist, University of Virginia Library* (1935), 15.

11. 6 *V* 133-134; *Writings of Jefferson*, XV, 472.

12. On one occasion he offered himself unsuccessfully as candidate for Speaker of the House; *VG* (Purdie and Dixon), June 27, 1766; *Southern Literary Messenger*, XXVII, 116; *JHB* (1766-1769), 11.

13. H. J. Eckenrode, *The Revolution in Virginia* (Boston, 1916), 11. Just how Eckenrode learned that Bland was "somewhat untidy" is beyond me.

14. Minute Book, Prince George County (1737-1740), 87, 108, 129, 280, 282, 300, 303, 323, 371, 382, 389. Bland seemed content to scare his

opponents, for he failed to prosecute on most occasions.

15. 6 *V* 132; 5 *W(1)* 154-155.
16. 1 *T* 59; *Bland Papers*, I, 149.
17. 12 *W(1)* 239.
18. 15 *V* 356.
19. *VG* (Dixon and Hunter), Nov. 1, 1776.
20. *VG* (Rind), Dec. 13, 1770.
21. *EJV*, IV, 299; V, 162, 388, 394. A favorable glimpse of Bland as justice of the peace, in this case dissenting from a court order to sell a white man for debt, is in 4 *V* 278.
22. *JHB* (1742-1749), viii, 155.
23. Minute Book, Prince George County (1737-1740), 239.
24. 2 *W(1)* 37; 20 *W(2)* 544; 27 *W(2)* 239.
25. *EJV*, IV, 324, V, 208, 342, 404; 7 *H* 637, 8 *H* 169.
26. *The Vestry Book and Register of Bristol Parish . . . 1720-1789* (Richmond, 1898), 148, 152-154, 161, 188, 193, 195, 200, 220, 221.
27. H. B. Grigsby, *The Virginia Convention of 1776* (Richmond, 1855), 57-58.
28. 6 *H* 418, 485, 507; 7 *H* 39, 116, 288, 354; 8 *H* 67, 115, 175, 367, 494, 570, 578, 606; *JHB* (1770-1772), 137; *VG* (Purdie and Dixon), July 19, 1770.
29. *JHB* (1742-1749), 123, 132, 190, 191, 193, 202, 204, 315, 361, 377-378, 391; (1752-1758), 483; (1758-1761), 32, 253-255; (1761-1765), 114; (1766-1769), 91. These examples could be multiplied indefinitely.
30. *JHB* (1742-1749), 249, 327, 347, 358; (1752-1758), 91, 312.
31. *JHB* (1758-1761), 57-58, 199-201; (1761-1765), 68-69.
32. *JHB* (1742-1749), 63, 76, 138, 215, 237, 246, 303, 314, 318, 323, 329, 382; (1752-1758), 5, 8, 44, 73, 88, 105, 159, 167, 184, 197, 203, 233, 235, 299, 327, 337, 383, 388, 403, 415, 482, 487; (1758-1761), 5, 36, 102, 117, 135, 208, 238, 240; (1761-1765), 36, 49, 115, 182, 183, 305, 306; (1776-1769), 19, 45, 50, 52, 53, 171.

33. *JHB* (1766-1769), 112, 256.
34. *JHB* (1742-1749), 290; (1766-1769), xxi-xxvi, 119-120, 154-156, 281-282.
35. For Bland's belief in the inseparability of his interests and those of his constituents, see his letter of February 20, 1745; *Bland Papers*, I, 3-4.
36. The best summary of this episode is G. C. Smith, "The Affair of the Pistole Fee," 48 *V* 209-221. The documentary record may be traced in *JHB* (1752-1758), 129, 132, 136, 141, 143-144, 154-156, 168-169, 171; R. A. Brock, ed., *The Official Records of Robert Dinwiddie* (Richmond, 1883), I, 44-48, 71-73, 100-104, 137-141, 153-155, 362-365, 370-376.
37. *JHB* (1752-1758), 143.
38. *JHB* (1752-1758), 154, 155.
39. W. C. Ford, ed., *A Fragment on the Pistole Fee* (Brooklyn, 1891).
40. 6 *H* 437, 524; 7 *H* 13, 116, 120, 354; *JHB* (1752-1758), 462; *JHB* (1758-1761), 12, 16, 23, 26, 31; 5 *R* 202; *VG*, Nov. 30, 1759.
41. *JHB* (1752-1758), 122, 196, 216, 372; *JHB* (1758-1761), 50.
42. *JHB* (1752-1758), 388, 391.
43. *JHB* (1752-1758), 368, 463; *JHB* (1758-1761), 31; 7 *H* 229.
44. *VG*, Sept. 3, 1756; *MG* (2), Nov. 25, 1756; *PJ*, Nov. 4, 1756; *NYM*, Oct. 25, 1756; *CG*, Dec. 4, 1756. See D. S. Freeman, *George Washington* (New York, 1948), II, Chap. 12; *PMHB*, XXII (1898), 436-451.
45. Bland to Washington, June 7, 1755, *PMHB*, XXII, 437-438; *Letters to Washington* (Boston, 1898-1902), II, 87-89.
46. *PMHB*, XXII, 444-451; *Letters to Washington*, I, 386-395; Washington Papers (Library of Congress), V, Cols. 28-29.
47. W. W. Henry, *Patrick Henry* (New York, 1891), I, 46. For the facts of this incident, see H. J. Eckenrode, *Separation of Church and State in Virginia* (Richmond, 1910), Chap. 2; Meade, *Old Churches*, I, 216-225; L. G. Tyler, "The Leader-

ship of Virginia in the War of the Revolution, Part II," 19 *W(1)* 10-42; *JHB* (1761-1765), xxxviii-liii.

48. 7 *H* 240; 6 *H* 568.

49. J. H. Smith, *Appeals to the Privy Council*, 607-626.

50. Eckenrode, *Separation of Church and State*, 20.

51. *JHB* (1758-1761), 5, 6, 7, 11, 15, 17, 45. For a previous act of 1755, also drafted by Bland, see *JHB* (1752-1758), 322.

52. 7 *H* 276. Proceedings and documents of this committee are in 9 *V* 353-360, 364-368; 10 *V* 337-353; 11 *V* 1-25, 131-143, 345-354; 12 *V* 1-14, 157-169; 225-240, 353-364. See E. I. Miller, "The Virginia Committee of Correspondence, 1759-1770," 22 *W(1)* 1-19.

53. The text of this testy letter was printed by Bland in the introduction to his *Letter to the Clergy*. It may also be found in Perry, *Historical Collections*, I, 461-463. For other documents of the Two-Penny affair, see 434-532. The principal tract stating the case for the Virginia clergy was Camm's *A Single and Distinct View of the Act* (Annapolis, 1763). See also the pamphlets of Bland's colleague Landon Carter, *A Letter to the Right Reverend Father in God* (Williamsburg, 1759) and *The Rector Detected* (Williamsburg, 1764), as well as Camm's answer, *A Review of the Rector Detected* (Williamsburg, 1764).

54. Both pamphlets were printed in Williamsburg. There are four extant copies of *A Letter to the Clergy*, two of *The Colonel Dismounted*. There is no extant copy of *VG* for Oct. 28, 1763, but Bland reprints this letter in the appendix of *The Colonel Dismounted*. The constitutional argument of this pamphlet is reprinted in 19 *W(1)* 31-41.

55. Cross, *Anglican Episcopate and the American Colonies*, Chap. 10.

56. Perry, *Collections*, I, 465. For other glimpses of Bland, which show him an able politician and respected gentleman, see 465-468, 484, 511.

57. The controversy may be followed in *VG* (Purdie and Dixon), June 6-Aug. 22, Oct. 10, 1771; *NYJ*, Aug. 22-Sept. 5, 1771.

58. Grigsby, *Virginia Convention*, 59.

59. 6 *V* 127-134; 5 *W(1)* 150-157.

60. *JHB* (1770-1772), 122.

61. 6 *V* 132. See also his letter in *VG* (Purdie and Dixon), March 10, 1774.

62. J. E. Pate, "Richard Bland's Inquiry into the Rights of the British Colonies," 11 *W(2)* 20-28.

63. E. I. Miller, "The Virginia Legislature and the Stamp Act," 21 *W(1)* 233-248; Henry, *Patrick Henry*, I, 49-106; *JHB* (1761-1765), liii-lxxvi; Eckenrode, *The Revolution in Virginia*, 13-27.

64. 12 *V* 5-14.

65. *JHB* (1761-1765), 256-257, 264, 302-304.

66. 18 *W(1)* 159; 20 *W(1)* 185-186; 21 *W(1)* 236n.; 11 *W(2)* 24; 15 *W(1)* 288; Wirt, *Patrick Henry*, App.; Henry, *Patrick Henry*, I, 61; Swem, *Inquiry* (1922 ed.), v.

67. *Writings of Jefferson* (Ford ed.), IX, 340; William Wirt, *Life of Patrick Henry* (4th ed., New York, 1831), 78; Henry, *Patrick Henry*, I, 82. Jefferson wrote "Blood" for Bland (almost a half-century after the event), but there is no doubt whom he meant.

68. *VG* (Purdie and Dixon), March 7, 1766, carries the news that it is coming, *VG* (Purdie and Dixon), March 14, that it has come. *An Inquiry* is now most readily available in a reprint edited by E. G. Swem (Richmond, 1922).

69. *VG* (Purdie and Dixon), July 27, 1769.

70. To William Wirt, Aug. 5, 1815, *Writings of Jefferson*, XIV, 338. Dickinson's *ignis fatuus* was his dis-

tinction between duties laid for revenue and duties laid to regulate trade.
71. For speculation on Bland's possible
influence on Jefferson, see A. M.
Lewis, "Jefferson's *Summary View
as a Chart of Political Union,*" 5
W(3) 34-51, 41-42. Bland several
times retained Jefferson as legal
counsel; see Marie Kimball, *Jefferson: The Road to Glory* (New York,
1943), 90.
72. *VG* (Rind), May 30, 1766; *VG*
(Purdie and Dixon), April 4, May
30, 1766.
73. General Charles Lee's impatience
with Bland's caution is plain in a
letter to Washington dated April 5,
1776; *Amer. Arch.*, V, 792-793. For
a more favorable impression of
Bland, see Mazzei's comments in 9
W(2) 169-170.
74. *JHB* (1766-1769), 145, 146, 148, 158,
161, 165-173; *VG* (Rind), April 21,
1768.
75. *JHB* (1766-1769), xxxix-xliii; *VG*
(Purdie and Dixon), May 25, 1769.
76. *JHB* (1770-1772), xxvi-xxxi; 3 *R*
17-24; *VG* (Purdie and Dixon), June
28, 1770; 20 *W(2)* 84-98.
77. *JHB* (1773-1776), xi-xii, 28, 39; *VG*
(Rind), March 18, 1773; *VG* (Purdie
and Dixon), March 18, 1773. See E.
I. Miller, "The Virginia Committee
of Correspondence of 1773-1775," 22
W(1) 99-113; J. M. Garnett, "Early
Revolutionary History of Virginia,"
*Proceedings, Virginia Historical So-
ciety,* XI (1892), 3-23.
78. *JHB* (1773-1776), 39-43, 135-140,
287; 8 *C* 1, 2, 9, 10.
79. *JHB* (1773-1776), xiii-xiv; *VG*
(Rind), June 30, 1774.
80. 9 *H* 49, 95; *PCD* (July 1775), 18,
(Dec. 1775), 68; *VG* (Purdie), Aug.
25, Sept. 8, 1775; *VG* (Dixon and
Hunter), Aug. 26, 1775.
81. *VG* (Rind), Aug. 4, 11, 1774; *VG*
(Purdie and Dixon), Aug. 4, 11,
1774; *PCD* (March 1775), 7.
82. *Works,* II, 362.

83. *PCD* (July 1775), 14, 15; *VG*
(Purdie), Aug. 18, 1775; *VG* (Pinkney), Aug. 17, 1775.
84. *PCD* (March 1775), 5; Henry, *Patrick Henry,* I, 258.
85. *PCD* (March 1775), 8, (July 1775),
4-25, (Dec. 1775), 60, 62, 71, 77, 87;
JCS, I, 1-29, II, 405-512; 8 *C* 1-239;
7 *H* 288, 568; *VG* (Pinkney), March
30, 1775; 8 *C* 78, 90, 93, 106, 202.
86. Oct. 29, 1775; *Bland Papers,* I, 37-38.
87. *VG* (Dixon and Hunter), June 3,
Oct. 28, 1775; *VG* (Pinkney), Oct.
19, 1775.
88. *VG* (Purdie), July 7, 21, 1775; *VG*
(Dixon and Hunter), July 8, 22,
1775; *Bland Papers,* I, 36-37.
89. *JCD* (July 1775), 5-8.
90. *VG* (Purdie), Aug. 4, 1775; *VG*
(Dixon and Hunter), Aug. 5, 1775.
91. *Revolution in Virginia,* 11; 19 *V*
108.
92. Swem, *Inquiry,* viii; Grigsby, *Virginia Convention,* 59n.; 15 *V* 356. For
evidence that Bland was a recognized
authority on the land system in Virginia, see *PCD* (March 1775), 8;
JHB (1752-1758), 116; *JHB* (1773-
1776), 98, 106, 110, 112, 114; Grigsby,
Virginia Convention, 201.
93. *Inquiry,* 9-10.
94. *Inquiry,* 26.
95. *Inquiry,* 25.
96. *Colonel Dismounted,* 26, 22.
97. *Inquiry,* 14-15.
98. *Inquiry,* 14, 11.
99. *Inquiry,* 7, 29.
100. *Colonel Dismounted,* 22.
101. *Colonel Dismounted,* 22; *Inquiry,*
7.
102. *Letter to the Clergy,* 6.
103. *Colonel Dismounted,* 21.
104. *Fragment,* 37.
105. *Colonel Dismounted,* 22.
106. *Colonel Dismounted,* 20.
107. *JHB* (1752-1758), 192, 197, 203,
338, 416; *JHB* (1766-1769), 165;
Colonel Dismounted, 16.
108. *JHB* (1752-1758), 235.
109. *Fragment,* 31.
110. *Colonel Dismounted,* 23.

111. *Colonel Dismounted*, 26; *Letter to the Clergy*, 18.
112. *Inquiry*, 28; *Colonel Dismounted*, 16.
113. *JHB* (1761-1765), 256.
114. *Inquiry*, 11-12.
115. *JHB* (1752-1758), 404.
116. *JHB* (1766-1769), 165.
117. *Fragment*, 39; *JHB* (1752-1758), 144, 154; *Inquiry*, 18.
118. *Inquiry*, 9.
119. *Inquiry*, 21.
120. *JHB* (1766-1769), 166.
121. *Fragment*, 37-39.
122. *JHB* (1766-1769), 167.
123. *PMHB*, XXII, 445.
124. *Fragment*, 32.
125. *Letter to the Clergy*, 20.
126. *Colonel Dismounted*, 16.
127. *Letter to the Clergy*, 6.
128. *JHB* (1752-1758), 299.
129. 6 *V* 131.
130. *Colonel Dismounted*, 13; *Letter to the Clergy*, 4; *Inquiry*, 4, 11-12; *JHB* (1752-1758), 9.
131. *JHB* (1770-1772), 138; 3 *T* 108; 6 *V* 132-133.
132. *Inquiry*, 5, 24; *Colonel Dismounted*, 22.
133. See, for example, *Letter to the Clergy*, 5-15; *Colonel Dismounted*, 23-25; *Inquiry*, 6-10, 15-25.
134. *PMHB*, XXII, 444-445.
135. *PMHB*, XXII, 448.
136. *Colonel Dismounted*, 18.
137. *Colonel Dismounted*, 38-39; *JHB* (1766-1769), 168.
138. *Letter to the Clergy*, 20, 16.
139. L. G. Tyler, 19 *W*(1) 25; M. C. Tyler, *Literary History of the Revolution*, I, 229.
140. *Colonel Dismounted*, 22; *Inquiry*, 30.
141. *Colonel Dismounted*, 21-22; *Inquiry*, 20.
142. *Colonel Dismounted*, 20-21; *Inquiry*, 13-14, 17, 20; *JHB* (1766-1769), 166, 167, 169.
143. *Inquiry*, 23, 25-26.
144. *Inquiry*, 4-11; *JHB* (1766-1769), 167, 170.

145. *Inquiry*, 20, 21.
146. *Colonel Dismounted*, 22.
147. *Journal of the House of Delegates of Virginia, 1776* (Richmond, 1828), 10, 12, 13.
148. For the facts and paradoxes of this truly great tradition, see C. S. Sydnor, *Gentlemen Freeholders* (Chapel Hill, 1952).

CHAPTER ELEVEN

1. No attempt will be made here to give even a fragmentary bibliography of works by and about Franklin. See the card catalogue of any convenient library, as well as Carl Van Doren, *Benjamin Franklin* (New York, 1938), 785-788; Carl Becker, *Benjamin Franklin* (Ithaca, 1946), 41-42; Spiller *et al.*, *Literary History of the United States*, III, 507-515; P. L. Ford, *Franklin Bibliography* (Brooklyn, 1889); F. L. Mott and C. E. Jorgenson, *Benjamin Franklin, Representative Selections*, (New York, 1936), cli-clxxiii.
2. The best editions now available are Jared Sparks, *The Works of Benjamin Franklin* (Boston, 1840), 10 vols., to be cited below as *Works;* and A. H. Smyth, *The Writings of Benjamin Franklin* (New York, 1905-1907), 10 vols., to be cited below as *Writings.*
3. Carl Van Doren *et al.*, *Meet Dr. Franklin* (Philadelphia, 1943), 223.
4. Van Doren, *Franklin*, 782.
5. *Writings*, X, 493-510.
6. *Autobiography*, 80-81. I have used the edition begun by Max Farrand and published by the University of California Press in 1949.
7. *Autobiography*, 82.
8. *Autobiography*, 147. See Crowther, *Famous American Men of Science*, 19-134.
9. Lois MacLaurin, *Franklin's Vocabulary* (Garden City, 1928), 55-77.
10. I. B. Cohen, ed., *Benjamin Franklin's Experiments* (Cambridge, 1941);

Brother Potamian and J. J. Walsh, *Makers of Modern Electricity* (New York, 1909), Chap. 2.

11. C. Abbe, "Benjamin Franklin as Meteorologist," *Proceedings of the American Philosophical Society*, XLV (1906), 117-12B.

12. T. Diller, *Franklin's Contribution to Medicine* (Brooklyn, 1912).

13. L. J. Carey, *Franklin's Economic Views* (Garden City, 1928), 46-60; A. Aldridge, "Franklin as Demographer," *Journal of Economic History*, LX (1949), 25-44.

14. John Davy, ed., *The Collected Works of Sir Humphry Davy, Bart.* (London, 1840), VIII, 264-265.

15. For representative attempts, see S. P. Sherman in *Cambridge History of American Literature* (1943 ed.), Bk. I, Chap. 6; Van Doren in *Literary History of the United States*, I, Chap. 8; Tyler, *Literary History of the Revolution*, II, 359-381; J. B. McMaster, *Benjamin Franklin as a Man of Letters* (Boston, 1887).

16. *Writings*, IV, 12-14, 121.

17. *Writings*, X, 85.

18. J. F. Sachse, *Benjamin Franklin as a Free Mason* (Philadelphia, 1906).

19. See J. Bennett Nolan's delightful *General Benjamin Franklin* (Philadelphia, 1936). Whatever his general attitude on their philosophy and works, Franklin had no use for Quaker pacifism in the Indian troubles. "The Way to secure Peace is to prepare for War," and "All we want is Order, Discipline and a few Cannon" were his comments in the crisis of 1747; *Writings*, II, 351, 352.

20. Shepherd, *Proprietary Government in Pennsylvania*; C. H. Lincoln, *The Revolutionary Movement in Pennsylvania* (Philadelphia, 1901), Chaps. 1-3; *PMHB*, LXXII (1948), 215, 376.

21. Thomas Penn to Mr. Peters, June 9, 1748; Penn Letter Book (Historical Society of Pennsylvania), II, 231-232. Franklin's statement on the reciprocity of protection and obedience was delivered in his *Plain Truth* (1747); *Writings*, II, 351.

22. Ruth L. Butler, *Doctor Franklin: Postmaster General* (Garden City, 1928); W. E. Rich, *The History of the United States Post Office to the Year 1829* (Cambridge, 1924).

23. For Franklin's importance as a force for intercolonial understanding, see (with the help of the index) Kraus, *Intercolonial Aspects of American Culture*.

24. *Writings*, II, 7.

25. The most characteristic examples are the eleven letters entitled "The Colonist's Advocate" (1770), printed in V. W. Crane, *Benjamin Franklin's Letters to the Press, 1758-1775* (Chapel Hill, 1950), 167-209.

26. To Benjamin Vaughan, Nov. 9, 1779; *Writings*, VII, 412. Even Franklin's rough drafts and memoranda—for example, those preserved in the American Philosophical Society—are wholly practical and unspeculative in character: Franklin Papers (A.P.S.), Vol. 50, Pt. 1, Folios 7-9, 13; Pt. 2, Folios 4, 9-12, 24, 31, 46, 48, 50, 51.

27. *Writings*, VI, 127-137. This essay was first printed in *Gentleman's Magazine*, Sept. 1773.

28. *Writings*, I, 179, 243; II, 387n.; Franklin's Ramsay, 28, 52 (see below, n. 44).

29. Julian Boyd, *The Declaration of Independence* (Princeton, 1945), 16ff., and references there cited.

30. *PEP*, Jan. 11, 1777.

31. Franklin's Ramsay, 8, 9, 10, 14, 15, 51-54; Franklin's Wheelock, 7.

32. For glimpses of the Lockean theory in his published writings, see *Writings*, II, 25-28, 293, VI, 260, 298, IX, 293, X, 59-60, 72; *Works*, II, 323, 556; Crane, *Benjamin Franklin's Letters to the Press*, 55-56, 169. For glimpses in the marginalia, see Franklin's *Good Humour*, 18-20; Franklin's Ramsay, 8-10, 15, 24, 28, 51-52.

33. Franklin's Ramsay, 27.

34. *Writings*, IX, 138.

35. *Writings*, VII, 172. See *Writings*, IX, 161-168, for his low opinion of the Cincinnati and their abortive attempt to "form an Order of *hereditary Knights*, in direct opposition to the solemnly declared Sense of their Country."

36. *Writings*, X, 59-60; also VI, 291.

37. Franklin's Ramsay, 15.

38. See especially his whimsical speech to the Convention of 1787, in M. Farrand, *The Records of the Federal Convention* (New Haven, 1911), II, 120, as well as Franklin's Ramsay, 33-34.

39. *Writings*, V, 133; Franklin Papers (A.P.S.), Vol. 50, Pt. 1, Folios 4B, 8, 11.

40. For examples of Franklin's concern for English rights, see *Writings*, III, 233, V, 80-81; Crane, *Letters to the Press*, 10-11, 44, 56, 112, 174. And see Conyers Read, "The English Elements in Benjamin Franklin," *PMHB*, LXIV (1940), 314-330.

41. To Galloway, June 10, 1758 (Yale Library).

42. *Writings*, X, 130-131. See also *Writings*, VI, 128, 214-215. Franklin's favorite club in London was known as the "Honest Whigs"; Van Doren, *Franklin*, 421-422.

43. Becker, *Franklin*, 35.

44. *Writings*, IV, v. Fragments of the marginalia are in *Works*, IV, 206-232, 281-301; *Writings*, X, 234-240; *PMHB*, XXV (1901), 307-322, 516-526, XXVI (1902), 81-90, 255-264; *AASP*, XXXIV, 217-218. The pamphlets in which the most revealing marginalia are to be found are (1) *The Claim of the Colonies to an Exemption from Internal Taxes* (London, 1765); (2) *Good Humour: or, a Way with the Colonies* (London, 1766); (3) Allen Ramsay, *Thoughts on the Origin and Nature of Government* (London, 1769); (4) Matthew Wheelock, *Reflections Moral and Political on Great Britain and*

her Colonies (London, 1770). Item 1 is in the New York Public Library, item 2 (in photostat) in the Yale Library, items 3 and 4 in the Library of Congress. They are cited here as Franklin's *Claim of the Colonies*, Franklin's *Good Humour*, Franklin's Ramsay, and Franklin's Wheelock.

45. See particularly the excellent chapter, "Benjamin Franklin: Student of Life," contributed by R. E. Spiller to *Meet Dr. Franklin*.

46. William James, *Pragmatism: A New Name for Some Old Ways of Thinking* (New York, 1907), 54-55.

47. *Writings*, II, 393. For other examples of his regard for the usefulness of religion, see J. M. Stifler, *The Religion of Benjamin Franklin* (New York, 1925), 8, 15, 17, 40, 118; *Writings*, IX, 521.

48. *Writings*, II, 386-396; also III, 16-17; X, 9-32. See Thomas Woody, *Educational Views of Benjamin Franklin* (New York, 1931).

49. *Writings*, IV, 228-229.

50. *Writings*, VI, 290-291; Franklin's *Good Humour*, 18.

51. *Writings*, IX, 607-609; Farrand, *Records of the Federal Convention*, II, 641-643. I have used the copy in the Library of Cornell University transcribed by Franklin for Charles Carroll.

52. *Autobiography*, 112-113, also 21-22.

53. *Autobiography*, 73. See *Writings*, II, 393-394, for his thoughts in this vein in connection with the Academy.

54. *Writings*, VI, 260, 262. See also the piece in Crane, *Letters to the Press*, 107-108.

55. *Autobiography*, 25. Actually it was a later issue, that of Jan. 14, 1723 (in which James Franklin's disrespect for the clergy was a bit too carelessly flaunted), that persuaded the General Court to forbid further publication under his name.

56. *Writings*, II, 25-28; *NEC*, July 9, 1722.

57. Crane, *Letters to the Press,* 193.
58. *Writings,* II, 172-179. This piece was reprinted in other journals; e.g., *SCG,* Oct. 14, 1732.
59. *Writings,* IX, 102.
60. Carey, *Franklin's Economic Views;* W. A. Wetzel, *Benjamin Franklin as an Economist* (Baltimore, 1895).
61. *Writings,* III, 409-413.
62. See the famous (and distorted) treatment of Franklin in Max Weber, *The Protestant Ethic and the Spirit of Capitalism* (English ed., London, 1930), 48-51; A. W. Griswold, "Three Puritans on Prosperity," *NEQ,* VII (1934), 475, 483-488. Franklin's tribute to Mather is in *Writings,* IX, 208-209.
63. F. B. Tolles, "Benjamin Franklin's Business Mentors: The Philadelphia Quaker Merchants," *WMQ* (3), IV (1947), 60-69.
64. *Studies in Classic American Literature* (New York, 1923), 13-31.
65. *Writings,* III, 417.
66. On "Franklin and the Physiocrats," see Carey, *Franklin's Economic Views,* Chap. 7. For evidence of Franklin's acceptance of most of their teachings, see *Writings,* V, 155-156, 200-202.
67. *Writings,* II, 313-314, 232-237; *Works,* II, 366; Van Doren, *Letters of Franklin and Jackson,* 34.
68. C. Gide and C. Rist, *A History of Economic Doctrines* (Boston, n.d.), 9.
69. Examples of his wholly practical arguments against mercantilism may be found in Crane, *Letters to the Press,* 94-99, 116-119, 180-181.
70. *Library of Congress Quarterly Journal of Current Acquisitions,* VIII (1950), 78.
71. *Writings,* IV, 469-470. Franklin has been given a little too much credit for the decline of mercantilism, for it is still assumed by many writers that he had significant face-to-face influence on Smith. The case for this thesis rests on extremely unreliable evidence. See T. D. Eliot, "The Relations between Adam Smith and Benjamin Franklin," *PSQ,* XXXIX (1924), 67-96.
72. To Jonathan Shipley, Sept. 13, 1775 (Yale Library); *Writings,* V, 202, IX, 245-246, X, 61, 121-122; Carey, *Franklin's Economic Views,* Chap. 8; C. R. Woodward, "Benjamin Franklin: Adventures in Agriculture," in *Meet Dr. Franklin,* 179-201; E. D. Ross, "Benjamin Franklin as an Eighteenth-Century Agricultural Leader," *Journal of Political Economy,* XXXVII (1929), 52-72.
73. *Writings,* IV, 49; also VI, 13; VIII, 611.
74. *Writings,* X, 59.
75. *Writings,* VIII, 261; IX, 19, 63, 241, 614-615.
76. *Autobiography,* 159-160. See also his three letters of 1754 to Governor Shirley, *Writings,* III, 231-241. These were reprinted in *PC,* Jan. 16, 1769.
77. For the documents of the Albany Plan, see *Writings,* III, 197-227, 231-241. See Mrs. L. K. Mathews, "Benjamin Franklin's Plans for a Colonial Union, 1750-1775," *American Political Science Review,* VIII (1914), 393-412.
78. *Autobiography,* 161.
79. *Writings,* VI, 420-425.
80. Franklin Papers (A.P.S.), Vol. 50, Pt. 1, Folio 35.
81. *Writings,* III, 207. The "rights of Englishmen" would limit this power in the colonies as in England; *Writings,* III, 232-241.
82. *Writings,* III, 238-241; Crane, *Letters to the Press,* 59, 59n., 72, 129n.; Franklin's *Good Humour,* 22.
83. *Writings,* IV, 424; Crane, *Letters to the Press,* 53-54.
84. *Writings,* IV, 421, 428; Crane, *Letters to the Press,* 201-203; Franklin's *Good Humour,* 20; Franklin's *Claim of the Colonies,* 8; Franklin's *Wheelock,* 26, 29, 44, 48-50; Franklin's *Ramsay,* 62.

85. *Writings*, V, 260, also IV, 445-446, V, 114-115, 280, VI, 260-261; Crane, *Letters to the Press*, 46-49, 110-112, 134-138. For Franklin's conversion, see V. W. Crane, "Benjamin Franklin and the Stamp Act," *CSMP*, XXXII, 56-77, and *Benjamin Franklin: Englishman and American* (Baltimore, 1936), 72-139. For an unguarded version of Franklin's mature opinion of the power of Parliament, see his *Claim of the Colonies*, 5-13.

86. *Writings*, V, 134; VIII, 451-452; IX, 330, 638; X, 7; Farrand, *Records of the Federal Convention*, II, 204-205, 249.

87. Evidence of these principles is to be found in *Writings*, III, 197-227, 307-320; VI, 420-425; IX, 169-170, 590-604, 674; X, 54-60, 501-502. See also Farrand, *Records of the Federal Convention*, I, 47, 48, 54, 61, 77-78, 81-85, 98-99, 103, 106, 197-200, 216, 427, 450-452, 488-489, II, 65, 120, 204, 208; M. R. Eiselen, *Franklin's Political Theories* (Garden City, 1928), Chaps. 8-12. The Pennsylvania Constitution of 1776 was more to Franklin's liking. See J. B. Selsam, *The Pennsylvania Constitution of 1776* (Philadelphia, 1936).

88. *Writings*, IX, 596.

89. Farrand, *Records*, I, 47. The last phrase was his own contribution.

90. *Writings*, X, 86-91, also 66-68, 127-

129. See V. W. Crane, "Benjamin Franklin on Slavery and American Liberties," *PMHB*, LXII (1938), 1-11; R. I. Shelling, "Benjamin Franklin and the Dr. Bray Associates," *PMHB*, LXIII (1939), 282-293; A. S. Pitt, "Franklin and the Quaker Movement against Slavery," *Bulletin, Friends' Historical Association*, XXXII (1943), 13-31; Carey, *Franklin's Economic Views*, Chap. 4.

91. Franklin Papers (Library of Congress), X, 2263-2264; *Writings*, X, 120-121. For earlier judgments, see *Writings*, II, 110, 232, 233, 295; III, 319-320.

92. Becker, *Franklin*, 31-37; Van Doren, *Franklin*, 260-262, 781-782, *Meet Dr. Franklin*, 1-10, 221-234, and a review of Becker in *WMQ* (3), IV (1947), 231-234. An old evaluation of Franklin that has stood up well is Theodore Parker, *Historic Americans* (Boston, 1908), 1-40.

93. This great "examination" is in *Writings*, IV, 412-448. It was widely reprinted in the colonial press and in separate editions.

94. To Lord Kames, January 3, 1760; *Works*, VII, 188.

95. To Galloway (Yale Library), Feb. 17, 1758; March 13, 1768; April 20, 1771.

96. To David Hartley, December 4, 1789; *Writings*, X, 72.

PART THREE

INTRODUCTION

1. *BG*, June 3, 1765; J. Adams, *Works*, III, 54; *JCC*, V, 507; *Amer. Arch.*, VI, 1728.

2. *Works*, X, 172.

3. M. D. Conway, ed., *The Writings of Thomas Paine* (New York, 1894),

I, 92; *A Few Political Reflections . . . by a Citizen of Philadelphia* (Philadelphia, 1774), 33-34; *PJ*, Feb. 6, Aug. 14, 1766; *CC*, July 6, 1773; *BG*, Sept. 27, 1773; *MS*, Nov. 11, 26, 1773, March 24, 1774; *PP*, July 4, 1774; *WNYG*, Jan. 20, 1776.

4. *Amer. Arch.*, III, 931.

5. *NYG* (2), Feb. 24, 1763.

6. J. Adams, *Works*, III, 476, II, 154; *BG*, Jan. 20, 1766.

7. The bibliography of sound historical writing on the events of 1765-1776 is overwhelming. Of the dozens of books I have read with profit, I would single out five for special mention: J. C. Miller, *Origins of the American Revolution* (Boston, 1943); A. M. Schlesinger, *The Colonial Merchants and the American Revolution* (New York, 1918); Carl Becker, *The History of Political Parties in the Province of New York, 1760-1776* (Madison, 1909); J. T. Adams, *Revolutionary New England* (Boston, 1923), Chaps. 13-18; and C. H. Van Tyne, *The Causes of the War of Independence* (New York, 1922). C. M. Andrews, *The Colonial Background of the American Revolution* (New Haven, 1931), is a masterpiece of generalization.

8. *The Works of John Witherspoon* (Edinburgh, 1805), IX, 84.

9. *Works* (Sparks ed.), VII, 328-329.

10. (London) *Morning Post*, Jan. 7, Feb. 17, 1775.

11. *JCC*, I, 15, 20, 82, 83, II, 21; James Wilson, *Works* (B. Wilson ed., Philadelphia, 1804), III, 204.

12. *BG*, July 23, 1764; Thacher, *The Sentiments of a British American* (Boston, 1764). See the letter of "Nov-Anglicanus," *BG*, May 14, 1764, for one of the first constitutional arguments.

13. *BG*, Sept. 16, 1765.

14. *P&A*, 457; *RICR*, VI, 465; *PaG*, April 3, 1766.

15. *BEP, BPB*, Nov. 4, 1765; *NM*, Nov. 11, 1765; H. A. Cushing, ed., *The Writings of Samuel Adams* (New York, 1904), I, 23-26. For the other Stamp Act resolves of the colonial assemblies, see *BPB*, Nov. 4, 11, Dec. 23, 30, 1765; *NM*, Nov. 11, Dec. 16, 30, 1765, Jan. 13, 1766; *GG*, Oct. 10, 17, 1765; *MG* (2), Oct. 3, 1765; *PaG*, Sept. 26, Dec. 5, 1765; *CG*,

Nov. 1, 1765; *WNYG*, Dec. 23, 30, 1765.

16. *JHB* (1761-1765), lxvii.

17. *BPB*, Dec. 16, 1765.

18. Charles Chauncy, *A Discourse on "the good News from a far Country"* (Boston, 1766), 23; *NHG*, May 22, 1766; Nathaniel Appleton, *A Thanksgiving Sermon* (Boston, 1766); Mayhew, *The Snare Broken*.

19. S. Adams, *Writings*, I, 187.

20. *RICR*, VI, 541.

21. *Writings*, II, 178.

22. R. W. Gibbes, *Documentary History of the American Revolution* (New York, 1855), I, 14.

23. *Amer. Arch.*, I, 356; *NM*, May 23, 26, June 13, 20, July 4, 25, Aug. 8, 22, 1774.

24. Jonathan Boucher, *A View of the Causes and Consequences of the American Revolution* (London, 1797), xli.

25. *BG*, April 29, 1765. For other expressions of hostility to these permanent restrictions, see *PG*, March 12, 1766; *VG* (Rind), July 6, 1769; *PaG*, Feb. 22, 1775; S. Adams, *Writings*, I, 142; Boyd, *Papers of Jefferson*, I, 123-125; Arthur Lee, *An Appeal to the Justice . . . of Great Britain* (London, 1775), 56ff.

26. Jacob Duché, *The Duty of Standing Fast* (Philadelphia, 1775), 15; *PP*, July 4, 1774.

CHAPTER TWELVE

1. *A Discourse Preached December 15th, 1774*, in J. W. Thornton, *The Pulpit of the American Revolution* (Boston, 1860), 197.

2. *Amer. Arch.*, I, 301. Anglicans were much in the habit of labeling all dissenters "Presbyterians."

3. P. Oliver, *The Origin & Progress of the American Rebellion* (MS. in Massachusetts Historical Society), 73. See Baldwin, *New England Clergy*, Chaps. 7-10; E. F. Humphrey, *Nationalism and Religion in*

America, 1774-1789 (Boston, 1924), Pt. I; W. W. Sweet, *Religion in the Development of American Culture, 1765-1840* (New York, 1952), Chaps. 1-2.

4. Oliver, *Origin of the Rebellion*, 148. For another Tory protest and Whig defense, see J. Adams, *Works*, IV, 55.

5. H. L. Calkin, "Pamphlets . . . during the American Revolution," *PMHB*, LXIV (1940), 22-42.

6. *PC*, Dec. 2, 1767-Feb. 15, 1768.

7. *BG*, Aug. 1765, Jan. 23-April 17, 1775; *VG* (Rind), Feb. 25-April 28, 1768; *BG*, Sept. 5-26, 1768.

8. All these pseudonyms are from *MS*, representing only a fraction of those used in that journal, 1770-1775.

9. *MG* (2), April 17, 1766. On the press in the Revolution, see Mott, *American Journalism*, Chaps. 4-5; S. I. Pomerantz, "The Patriot Newspaper," in Morris, ed., *Era of the Revolution*, 305-331; Philip Davidson, *Propaganda and the American Revolution* (Chapel Hill, 1941), esp. Chap. 13; and articles by A. M. Schlesinger in *NEQ*, VIII (1935), 63-83; *PMHB*, LX (1936), 309-322; and *CSMP*, XXXII, 396-416.

10. *BEP*, May 22, 1769.

11. Oct. 6, 9, 15, 19, 27, 1773, in the New-York Historical Society. "The Alarm" was reprinted widely; e.g., *NYJ*, Oct. 14-Nov. 18, 1773; *NLG*, Oct. 29, Nov. 5, 19, 1773.

12. Briggs, *Nathaniel Ames*, 371ff.

13. S. Adams, *Writings*, III, 104; *P&A*, 1-26.

14. *JCC*, I, 105-113.

15. *P&A*, 72-79; *Amer. Arch.*, V, 1025-1032.

16. This work is now most readily available in *Memoir of Theophilus Parsons* (Boston, 1859), 359-402.

17. I found the resolutions of town meetings and other local bodies an especially helpful indication of the trend in political attitudes and emphases. A highly selective list of local resolutions at four crucial stages in

the decade is: *the Stamp Act*—Providence, R.I., *NM*, Aug. 19, 1765; Little Compton, R.I., *NM*, Sept. 2, 1765; Litchfield County, Conn., *PaG*, March 13, 1766; Anne Arundel County, Md., *MG* (2), Oct. 25, 1765; *the Tea Act*—Westerly, R.I., *NM*, Feb. 7, 1774; Portsmouth, N.H., *NHG*, Dec. 24, 1773; Charleston, S.C., *NM*, April 4, 1774; Harvard, Mass., *MS*, Jan. 6, 1774; *the Coercive Acts*—Baltimore and Queen Anne Counties, Md., *NM*, June 20, 1774; five North Carolina localities, *NCG* (2), Sept. 2, 1774; Newport, R.I., *NM*, May 23, 1774; *independence*—Massachusetts towns and counties, *Amer. Arch.*, VI, 698-706. See also the answers of the Massachusetts towns to Boston's declaration of rights and grievances in *BEP*, Dec. 14ff., 1772; *EG*, Dec. 15, 1772-April 20, 1773.

18. *Works*, III, 462-463.

19. The bibliography of this problem is extremely good. In addition to the original works cited in these notes, see R. G. Adams, *Political Ideas of the American Revolution* (Durham, 1922); Carl Becker, *The Declaration of Independence* (New York, 1922), Chap 3; C. F. Mullett, *Colonial Claims to Home Rule* (Columbia, Mo., 1927); C. F. McIlwain, *The American Revolution* (New York, 1924); J. P. Boyd, *Anglo-American Union* (Philadelphia, 1941).

20. *A Letter from a Virginian to the Members of Congress* (Boston, 1774), 22.

21. 6 Geo. III c. 12.

22. *A Vindication of the British Colonies* (Boston, 1765), 3-4; *The Rights of the British Colonies Asserted and Proved* (Boston, 1764), 39-40; *Brief Remarks on the Defence of the Halifax Libel* (Boston, 1765), 23ff. On Otis's intellectual confusion, see Ellen E. Brennan, "James Otis: Recreant and Patriot," *NEQ*, XII (1939), 691-725.

23. Samuel Johnson, *Taxation No Tyranny*, in *The Works of Samuel Johnson* (London, 1823), 180-181. See also Soame Jenyns, *The Objections to the Taxation of our American Colonies, Briefly Considered* (London, 1765). A concise review of English thinking on the problem of the colonies is in C. F. Mullett, "English Imperial Thinking, 1764-1783," *PSQ*, XLV (1930), 548-579.

24. *VG* (Rind), March 10, 1768.

25. *Considerations on Behalf of the Colonies* (London, 1765), 6, 51; G. J. McRee, ed., *Life and Correspondence of James Iredell* (New York, 1857), I, 211; *PJ*, July 11, 1765; *NLG*, Sept. 29, 1765; *PC*, April 10, 1769; *NYC*, Sept. 14, 1769; *PEP*, April 18, 1775; *P&A*, 11.

26. *Considerations on the Propriety of Imposing Taxes in the British Colonies* (2nd ed., London, 1766), 9-10. For other lengthy essays, see *GG*, Sept. 19, 1765; *NVG*, June 9, 15, 1774; *Considerations upon the Rights of the Colonies* (New York, 1766), 18-21.

27. Bland, *Inquiry*, 4-11; Maurice Moore, *Justice and Policy of Taxing the American Colonies* (Wilmington, N.C., 1765), in Boyd, *Tracts*, 167ff.; Samuel Cooper(?), *The Crisis* (London, 1766), 3-30; Edward Bancroft, *Remarks on the Review* (London, 1769), 95-96; A. Lee, *An Appeal*, 35-36; *The Political Writings of John Dickinson* (Wilmington, Del., 1801), I, 341ff.

28. Otis, *Rights of the British Colonies*, 65. Otis was also in favor, as was Galloway later in the game, of a "subordinate legislative among themselves" in the colonies; *Rights*, 71.

29. *Rights of the British Colonies*, 35-36; Franklin, *Writings* (Smyth ed.), III, 238-241; Crane, *Franklin's Letters to the Press*, 59, 72, 129n.; *BG*, Jan. 28, June 17, July 29, 1765; *PG*, March 12, 1765. For an English argument for the scheme, see *Reflexions on Representation in Parliament* (London, 1766).

30. *Writings*, I, 67-68, also 25, 178, 182, 191; *NYG* (2), Jan. 9, 1766; *PaG*, Jan. 30, 1766; *PJ*, March 13, 1766, an excellent summary; *NYJ*, Nov. 26, 1767; *NM*, Jan. 23, 1775.

31. *Works*, IV, 139, also 101, 119.

32. E. S. Morgan, "Colonial Ideas of Parliamentary Power, 1764-1766," *WMQ* (3), V (1948), 311-341, and comments in *WMQ* (3), VI (1949), 162-170, 351-355.

33. *Rights of the British Colonies*, 42; *Vindication of the Colonies*, 4.

34. For an excellent review of the fifteen formal resolutions of 1764-1765, see Morgan, *WMQ* (3), VI, 315-325.

35. *Considerations*, 30-35; *Inquiry*, 30; *The Grievances of the American Colonies Candidly Examined* (1764) (London, 1766).

36. *Writings*, IV, 24, 421-422, 424, 226.

37. *Parl. Hist.*, XVI, 105.

38. *Writings*, IV, 446.

39. P. L. Ford, ed., *The Writings of John Dickinson* (Philadelphia, 1895), I, 312-317. Dulany, *Considerations*, 34, and others had already made this distinction but had failed to tackle the specific problem of external taxation for purposes of revenue.

40. *Writings*, I, 348.

41. *The Controversy between Great Britain and her Colonies Reviewed* (Boston, 1769), 19.

42. For example, Philip Livingston, *The Other Side of the Question* (New York, 1774), 11.

43. *Discourse, Delivered in Providence* (Providence, 1768), 6-7.

44. *JHB* (1761-1765), 360; *CCR*, XII, 422; *RICR*, VI, 452; *MG* (2), Oct. 3, 1765.

45. S. Adams, *Writings*, I, 134-152.

46. *An Essay on the Constitutional Power of Great Britain over the Colonies* (London, 1774), reprinted in *Political Writings of John Dickinson*, I, 329ff., esp. 400ff.; Mullett, *Colonial Claims to Home Rule*, 22ff.

47. *Speeches of the Governors of Massachusetts*, etc. (Boston, 1818), 340.
48. *Speeches of the Governors*, 363-364. This great exchange can also be found in *BPB*, Feb. 22ff., 1773; *NYGWM*, Feb. 1ff., 1773; *NYJ*, Feb. 11ff., 1773; *PaG*, March 17ff., 1773.
49. *PG*, May 11, 1765; *MG* (2), May 30, 1765; *BG*, Feb. 24, March 3, 17, 1766; *NYG* (2), Jan. 9, 1766; *VG* (Purdie and Dixon), March 14, April 4, 1766; Downer, *Discourse*, 6-7.
50. *Writings*, V, 115.
51. *Writings*, V, 260; Bancroft, *Remarks*, 75, 83; John Allen, *An Oration upon the Beauties of Liberty* (Boston, 1773); *NHG*, July 26, 1771; *BG*, Jan. 27, Feb. 17, 1772.
52. J. Adams, *Works*, IV, 47, 99, 105, 107, 112, 114, 146; Jefferson, *Papers*, I, 123, 129; H. C. Lodge, ed., *The Works of Alexander Hamilton* (New York, 1885), I, 64, 73, 109; Iredell, *Life and Correspondence*, I, 207, 209, 214, 218-219, 248; *PP*, July 18, 1774.
53. *Works*, III, 201, 226, 238-239, 241, 243-244.
54. See Wilson's note, *Works*, III, 244-246.
55. *Papers*, I, 121-135.
56. The documentation of the intellectual drive toward independence is far too enormous to be set down here, but these few references, if followed in order, will give the serious student a line to follow: Iredell, *Correspondence*, 312; J. Adams, *Works*, IV, 131; *Va. Mag.*, XLII, 14; S. Adams, *Writings*, I, 183, III, 100, 276, 279, 281; Otis, *Rights of the British Colonies*, 81; *BEP*, Aug. 26, 1765; *BG*, Sept. 5, 1768, Nov. 2, 1772, Jan. 11, Oct. 11, 1773; *NYJ*, Jan. 21, 1773; *PG*, Oct. 16, 1773, May 14, 1774; *NM*, March 21, 1774; *PG*, May 14, 1774; *EG*, June 7, 1774, April 20, July 13, 1775; *PP*, Jan. 2, 1775; and the great debate aroused by *Common Sense: PaG*, March 13-May 15, 1776; *PL*, March 9-April 27, 1776; *NLG*,

March 22, 1776; *MJ*, March 20, April 10, May 1, 1776; *Amer. Arch.*, IV, 921, 951, 1013, 1141, 1522, 1168, V, 69, 86, 96, 146, 211, 225, 431, 506, 551, 798, 802, 854, 860, 918, 921, 959, 992, 1036, 1094, 1133, 1206, VI, 392, 399, 629, 698-706.
57. *Beauties of Liberty*, 31. See also Dickinson's apology, *Political Writings*, I, 329n.
58. *MS*, Nov. 28, 1771.
59. Otis, *Rights of the British Colonies*, 35; S. Adams, *Writings*, I, 23ff., 64-65; Jefferson, *Papers*, I, 119; *JCC*, I, 33, II, 14.
60. *JCC*, I, 67.
61. See Davidson, *Propaganda and the American Revolution*, a first-rate study.
62. *NLG*, Sept. 6, 1765; *BG*, Oct. 21, 1765; *NHG*, Dec. 27, 1765; *SCG*, June 1, 1769; *PJ*, Nov. 24, 1773; *VG* (Purdie), March 3, 1774; *NYJ*, May 26, 1774.
63. *NLG*, Aug. 24, 1770; Ballagh, *Letters of R. H. Lee*, I, 10.
64. Franklin Papers (Amer. Phil. Society), Vol. 50, Pt. I, Folio 8.
65. Such as Hamilton, *Works*, I, 37, 178ff., esp. 187-188, and, on a slightly more moderate scale, the Continental Congress, *JCC*, I, 88.
66. *Writings*, I, 201-212; *BG*, April 4-18, 1768. See also *BG*, April 25, May 9, 1768; *PAM* (3), Sept. 1769; *NLG*, May 6, 1768; *EG*, Dec. 8, 1772; *NM*, Nov. 18, 1774; *NYJ*, March 30, 1775; *MJ*, April 19, 1775; *SCGCJ*, Feb. 7, 1775; *GG*, Aug. 30, 1775; *NYGWM*, May 22, July 3, 1775; *CFM*, Aug. 7, 1775; *NEC*, Feb. 1, 1776.
67. *NCCR*, X, 127; *GG*, Sept. 28, 1774; *Amer. Arch.*, I, 1230. And see Boucher's testimony in *American Revolution*, 147ff.
68. *PP*, Oct. 31, 1774.
69. *PJ*, Aug. 17, 1774.
70. A select list of this influential type of propaganda is: *JCC*, I, 116-117, V, 511-514; Drayton, in Gibbes, *Documentary History*, I, 15-16, and

in *P&A*, 73; S. Adams, *Writings*, II, 359-369; Jefferson, *Papers*, I, 123-134; Arthur Lee (Junius Americanus), *The Political Detector* (London, 1770), 89ff.; *Amer. Arch.*, I, 658-661; *NYG* (2), Aug. 14, 1769; *PJ*, March 3, 1773, Aug. 3, 1774.

71. Another triumph of propaganda was the publication of the notorious Hutchinson letters. See almost any Boston paper, esp. *MS* and *BG*, June 1773; *PP*, July 12ff., 1773; *PaG*, June 30ff., 1773; *PJ*, June 23ff., 1773; *NYJ*, July 1ff., 1773; *SCGCJ*, Aug. 3ff., 1773.

72. *Works*, II, 36-37.

73. See, too, the epic exchanges in 1773 between Hutchinson and the Massachusetts legislature over the construction of the charter, in *Speeches of the Governors*, 336ff., as well as the answer to Dickinson in *BEP*, Feb. 6-June 5, 1769.

74. *MG* (2), March 7, 1771, Jan. 21-June 10, 1773; *NYG* (2), Feb. 29, March 7, 14, 1768; *PC*, April 23, July 16, Nov. 19, 1770; R. B. Morris, "Legalism versus Revolutionary Doctrine in New England," *NEQ*, IV (1931), 195-215.

75. *Writings*, IV, 415, 428-429; S. Adams, *Writings*, I, 31-32; A. Lee, *An Appeal*, 40ff.; *NHG*, Oct. 4, 1765; *NM*, Dec. 30, 1765, Jan. 6, 1766.

76. (Philadelphia, 1764; London, 1765). See also *Some Thoughts on . . . the Northern Colonies* (London, 1765); Dickinson, *The Late Regulations* (1765), in *Writings*, I, 213ff.; Thacher, *Sentiments*, 13; Iredell, *Correspondence*, I, 283ff.

77. Paine, *Writings*, I, 88, also 101ff.; Hamilton, *Works*, I, 150ff.; *VG* (Dixon and Hunter), April 6, 13, 1776; *VG* (Purdie), March 29, 1776.

78. *PEP*, Feb. 17, 1776; *Amer. Arch.*, IV, 914-917.

79. Witherspoon, *Works*, V, 224, 226; *NHG*, Aug. 31, 1776.

80. A. Lee, *An Appeal*, 50.

81. *NYJ*, Nov. 16, 1775.

82. S. Adams, *Writings*, I, 192.

83. Franklin Papers (Amer. Phil. Soc.), Vol. 50, Pt. 1, Folio 8.

84. S. Adams, *Writings*, I, 27, also 21, 71-73, 153, 163, 392, III, 33, 115, 128, 171; Otis, *Rights of the British Colonies*, 34; Duché, *The Duty of Standing Fast*, in *Patriot Preachers*, 85; Cooke, *Sermon* (1770), in Thornton, *Pulpit*, 173, 185; Gordon, *Discourse* (1774), in Thornton, *Pulpit*, 207-208; Iredell, *Correspondence*, I, 205, 219, 248-249, 302; Dickinson, *Writings*, I, 175, 193-194, 431; Samuel Webster, *The Misery and Duty of an Oppress'd and Enslav'd People* (Boston, 1774), 21-22; *JCC*, IV, 139.

85. *Works*, III, 462, also 452ff.

86. William Smith, *A Sermon on the Present Situation* (Philadelphia, 1775), 23. Perhaps the greatest statement of ancestral piety was Amos Adams, *A Concise, Historical View of the Perils, Hardships, Difficulties and Discouragements*, etc. (Boston, 1769).

87. *BG*, Jan. 22, 1770, Jan. 2, 1775; *EG*, Feb. 8, 1774.

88. *PG*, Jan. 12, 1765; *Grievances*, 14; Downer, *Discourse*, 3-4, 14; Parsons, *Essex Result*, 378.

89. *Writings*, III, 128.

90. *PJ*, Jan. 28, 1768; Hamilton, *Works*, I, 89-109; Bancroft, *Remarks*, 9ff.; B. Church, in *P&A*, 10; Jonas Clarke, in C. Hudson, *History of Lexington* (Boston, 1868), 89, 91, 92, 94, 96-99. Dummer's *Defence of the New-England Charters* was reprinted in London in 1765.

91. *BNL*, Feb. 16, 1772.

92. Otis, *Rights of the British Colonies*, 34; S. Adams, *Writings*, I, 5, 17, 45, 70. For an exhaustive presentation of the two different views of the Massachusetts charter, see again *Speeches of the Governors*, 336ff.

93. *RICR*, VII, 303; Samuel Lockwood, *Civil Rulers an Ordinance of God* (New London, 1774), 8; S. Adams,

Writings, I, 135, 190, III, 15; *Amer. Arch.*, VI, 748-754; *CG*, Feb. 14, 1766; *SCAGG*, Jan. 1, 1768; *EG*, Oct. 18-Nov. 1, 1768; *BPB*, Dec. 2, 1771, Jan. 6, 13, 27, 1772, a Tory view; *VG* (Purdie and Dixon), July 21, 1774; *EJ*, Feb. 2-23, 1776; *JCC*, II, 67, IV, 134, 145.

94. From a Drayton charge to the grand jury, *SCGCJ*, Dec. 20, 1774; *Amer. Arch.*, II, 340-341; *BG*, Sept. 24, 1764; *NCM*, Nov. 9, 1764; *BEP*, March 1, 1773; *Considerations upon the . . . Colonies* (1766), 16ff.

95. *Writings*, I, 72-75.

96. Gad Hitchcock, *A Sermon Preached . . . May 25th, 1774* (Boston, 1774), 19. For representative uses of this general argument, see S. Adams, *Writings*, I, 2, 5, 9, 18, 65, 90; Wilson, *Works*, III, 220; *JCC*, II, 166, 168.

97. J. Adams, *Works*, IV, 117. But see Ballagh, *Letters of R. H. Lee*, I, 19ff.

98. S. Adams, *Writings*, II, 53, 324-326; *NYG* (2), Aug. 4, 1763; *MG* (2), March 20, 1766; *BG*, Feb. 9, 1767; Clarke, in Hudson, *Lexington*, 90, 95, 97; *JCC*, IV, 137; Drayton, in Gibbes, *Documentary History*, I, 23ff.

99. S. Adams, *Writings*, I, 228, 317; Otis, *A Vindication of the Conduct of the House of Representatives* (Boston, 1762), 20n., and *Rights of the British Colonies*, 32; Hopkins, *Grievances*, 6; *BG*, Feb. 9, 1767.

100. *WNYG*, Aug. 4, 1767; *BG*, Aug. 17, 1767; *PC*, Aug. 31, 1767; *MG* (2), Sept. 10, 1767; *NYG* (2), May 29, 1769.

101. *Works*, V, 223, IX, 67; *NYP*, Aug. 8, 1776; *NHG*, Aug. 31, 1776; *NP*, Sept. 30, 1776.

102. *P&A*, 457.

103. *NM*, Nov. 11, 1765, Feb. 3, 1766; *NHG*, June 20, 1766; *SCG*, Aug. 3, 1769; *NYJ*, March 8, 1770; *PP*, Aug. 29, 1774; S. Adams, *Writings*, I, 18, 74, 91, 349, II, 202; Otis, *Rights of the British Colonies*, 39; Hamilton, *Works*, I, 168; *JCC*, I, 35, 118, II,

160; Dickinson, *Writings*, I, 175, 193, 266, 329; R. C. Nicholas, *Considerations on . . . Virginia Examined* (?, 1774), 5. Stella Duff, "The Case against the King," *WMQ* (3), VI 1949), 383-397, is interesting but unconvincing.

104. *P&A*, 206; S. Adams, *Writings*, I, 91; *JCC*, II, 24, 43, 135, 137.

105. Duché, *Standing Fast*, in *Patriot Preachers*, 85; *DMG*, May 23, 1775; *Amer. Arch.*, I, 382n.

106. *NYG* (2), Jan. 9, 1766.

107. *VG* (Purdie and Dixon), Nov. 11, 1773.

108. Smith, *Sermon* (1775), 24; J. Adams, *Works*, III, 475; Dickinson, *Political Writings*, I, 312; *NM*, Dec. 30, 1765.

109. Paine, *Writings*, I, 84-85.

110. *Works*, IX, 66, also V, 222.

111. *Amer. Arch.*, III, 1561, also V, 213.

112. J. D. Richardson, ed., *Messages and Papers of the Presidents* (Washington, 1896), I, 53; J. Adams, *Works*, I, 66, III, 452n., IV, 293; Smith, *Sermon* (1775), 28; Bradbury, *The Ass* (1768 ed.), 14n.; Timothy Hilliard, *The Duty of a People* (Boston, 1774), 30; Champion, *Christian and Civil Liberty*, 16; Ebenezer Baldwin, *The Duty of Rejoicing* (New York, 1776), 38-40; S. Cooper, *Sermon* (1780), 2, 52-54; Jonas Clarke, *The Fate of Blood-thirsty Oppressors* (Boston, 1776), 81; James Duane, in Burnet, *Letters*, I, 98; *P&A*, 26, 63, 70-71; *NVG*, Aug. 11, 1774; *VG* (Pinkney), Dec. 20, 1775; *CC*, Feb. 19, April 22, 1776.

113. Phillips Payson, *A Sermon Preached . . . May 27, 1778*, in Thornton, *Pulpit*, 348-349; *P&A*, 72, 92; Briggs, *Nathaniel Ames*, 402; *Amer. Arch.*, V, 131; *JCC*, I, 33, 36; *BG*, July 8, 1768; *PJ*, Aug. 28, 1768; *NYG* (2), May 22, 1769; *EG*, July 21, 1772; *PP*, July 4, 1774; *RAM*, Jan. 1774. For the greatest of prophecies, see Freneau's "The Rising

Glory of America," in F. L. Pattee, ed., *Poems of Philip Freneau* (Princeton, 1902), I, 49-83. For the beginnings of American patriotism, see Savelle, *Seeds of Liberty*, Chap. 10; M. Curti, *The Roots of American Loyalty* (New York, 1946), Chap. 1.

114. Classic examples of this are in *SCGCJ*, April 29, 1766; *BG*, March 9, 1767; "The Alarm," Oct. 6, 1773; *NLG*, Oct. 29, 1773.

115. *NYJ*, Jan. 12, 1775; Hamilton, *Works*, I, 108; J. Adams, *Works*, II, 374.

116. *Works*, IV, 15.

117. In addition to the hundreds of examples quoted elsewhere in these notes, see the salutes to this basic political theory in *CG*, Feb. 14, 1766; *MG* (2), May 8, 1766; *NYJ*, Sept. 3, 1767; *MS*, Nov. 8, 1770, Jan. 19, 1776; *NM*, Feb. 7, 1774; *PP*, May 30-June 20, 1774; *CJ*, Feb. 22, 1775; *PL*, Feb. 25, March 4, 1775; *EJ*, March 1-April 5, 1775.

118. *MG* (2), Dec. 31, 1772, Feb. 4, 1773. Another good example of Tory use of the "party line" is in *RNYG*, Dec. 2, 1773.

119. July 9, 1775, in *P&A*, 209; *Amer. Arch.*, II, 1610; *PL*, Aug. 5, 1775; *MJ*, Aug. 9, 1775; *DMG*, Aug. 15, 1775; *GG*, Sept. 20, 1775.

120. *Works*, IV, 73.

121. S. Adams, *Writings*, II, 350ff.; *Report of the Boston Record Commissioners*, XVII, 94ff.; *PJ*, Feb. 3, 1773; *VG* (Purdie and Dixon), Feb. 25, 1773; *VG* (Rind), April 29, 1773. Locke, Vattel, Coke, and Blackstone were the authorities cited or quoted in this statement.

122. *JCC*, V, 510-511.

123. Jefferson, *Writings* (Ford ed.), X, 343.

124. C. F. Mullett, "Classical Influence on the American Revolution," *Classical Journal*, XXXV (1939), 92-104.

125. *Beauties of Liberty*, 17.

126. *A Sermon Preached . . . October 25, 1780* (Boston, 1780), 9.

127. *Political Writings*, I, 396.

128. Hamilton, *Works*, I, 59; J. Adams, *Works*, IV, 16, 56; *NYG* (2), July 18, 1765. In this and each of the following notes I have cited only three or four representative uses selected from tens or even hundreds of examples.

129. Dickinson, *Writings*, I, 364, 388; *NVG*, Aug. 25, 1774; *SCG*, Jan. 19, 1765.

130. J. Adams, *Works*, IV, 80, 82; Bancroft, *Remarks*, 85ff.; Hopkins, *Grievances*, 7; *PaG*, April 13, 1774; *SCGCJ*, July 5, 1774; *RAM*, Sept. 1774. See Caroline Robbins, "Algernon Sidney's *Discourse Concerning Government*," *WMQ* (3), IV (1947), 267-296; Zera Fink, *The Classical Republicans* (Evanston, 1945).

131. Wilson, *Works*, III, 219, 227ff.; S. Adams, *Writings*, I, 271, II, 325-326; Hamilton, *Works*, I, 86; Otis, *Rights of the British Colonies*, 88; *Amer. Arch.*, V, 121; Dickinson, *Writings*, I, 329ff.; Gibbes, *Documentary History*, I, 21, 24.

132. *Works*, III, 493. His "Freeholders Political Catechism" was a great favorite: *SCG*, July 21, 1766; *MS*, July 2, 1772; *RAM*, Feb. 1775; *VG* (Dixon and Hunter), Feb. 18, 1775; *BPB*, Feb. 27, 1775.

133. *NYG* (2), June 6, 1765, Feb. 19-March 12, 1770; *NLG*, Dec. 18, 1767; *MS*, March 28ff., 1771; *PEP*, March 28, 30, April 4, 6, May 23, 1775; *PL*, May 27, 1775.

134. Somers's *Judgment of Whole Kingdoms and Nations* was reprinted in four different places in 1774. And see the use of Hutcheson's *Moral Philosophy* in *MS*, Feb. 13, 1772.

135. T. W. Dwight, "Harrington and . . . American Political Institutions," *PSQ*, II (1887), 1-44, esp. 41-44; C. M. Walsh, *The Political Science of John Adams* (New York, 1915); Zoltán Haraszti, *John Adams and the Prophets of Progress* (Cambridge, 1952), 34-35.

136. *PaG*, Sept. 29, 1768.
137. Representative uses of Locke's ideas may be found in Dickinson, *Writings*, I, 356, 358, 411; Otis, *Vindication of the House*, 18-20n., *Rights of the British Colonies*, 22-23, 30; S. Adams, *Writings*, I, 251, II, 22, 210, 224, 257, 259, 298ff., 316, 350ff.; J. Adams, *Works*, IV, 82ff.; A. Lee, *An Appeal*, 7ff., 29ff., 89; Samuel West, *A Sermon Preached . . . May 29th, 1776* (Boston, 1776), 9ff.; Bancroft, *Remarks*, 42ff.; *Amer. Arch.*, II, 86-87; *PaG*, Sept. 29, 1768; *NYC*, Oct. 19, 1769; *MS*, Aug. 22, 1771, July 30, 1772; *BEP*, May 4, 1772; *MG* (2), July 29, Sept. 9, 1773; *PG*, Aug. 20, 1774; *PP*, Sept. 19, 1774; *SHPM*, May 5-19, 1775; *VG* (Dixon and Hunter), May 25, 1776.
138. *Civil Government* was printed in America (by Edes and Gill) for the first time in 1773. On Locke's political theory, see Sabine, *History of Political Theory*, Chap. 26, and the select bibliography at 541, as well as J. W. Gough, *John Locke's Political Philosophy* (Oxford, 1950).
139. W. Livingston, *Philosophic Solitude*, 38.
140. Briggs, *Nathaniel Ames*, 450; *NYCG*, Nov. 29, 1775.
141. See the exchange between Thomas Chandler, *A Friendly Address to all Reasonable Americans* (New York, 1774), 9, and P. Livingston, *The Other Side of the Question*, 12-13. For the typical Tory approach to Locke, respectful yet questioning—see Boucher, *American Revolution*, 508, 516, 552ff.
142. S. Adams, *Writings*, II, 258, 323, 325, 356, III, 266; Otis, *Rights of the British Colonies*, 5; *NCM*, Sept. 14, 21, 1764; *Amer. Arch.*, IV, 922.
143. And also in Otis, *Rights of the British Colonies*, 25-26; J. Adams, *Works*, IV, 82; Boyd, *Tracts*, 166; Hamilton, *Works*, I, 59; Hopkins, *Grievances*, 13; Dickinson, *Political Writings*, I, 310, 339, 341.

144. Wilson, *Works*, III, 206ff.; Hamilton, *Works*, I, 59; "Demophilus," *Genuine Principles*, 39; Dickinson, *Political Writings*, I, 308ff. See R. F. Harvey, *Jean Jacques Burlamaqui* (Chapel Hill, 1937).
145. Wilson, *Works*, III, 208, 216; Ballagh, *Letters of R. H. Lee*, I, 20; Dickinson, *Writings*, I, 331, 402, and *Political Writings*, I, 313, 338ff.; S. Adams, *Writings*, III, 304, 316, 322; G. Chinard, *The Commonplace Book of Thomas Jefferson* (Baltimore, 1926), 257-296; *JCC*, I, 110ff.; *BPB*, Oct. 19, 1772. See P. M. Spurlin, *Montesquieu in America* (L.S.U., 1940).
146. G. Hunt, "The Virginia Declaration of Rights and Cardinal Bellarmine," *Catholic Historical Review*, III (1917), 276-289, is, I fear, quite unconvincing.
147. J. Adams, *Works*, IV, 17, 57; Dickinson, *Writings*, I, 386.
148. J. Adams, *Works*, II, 454, IV, 216; Otis, *Rights of the British Colonies*, 25-26; *The Nature and Extent of Parliamentary Power Considered* (Philadelphia, 1768), 5-6; Parsons, *Essex Result*, 363-364.
149. J. Adams, *Works*, IV, 37; *GG*, Aug. 1, 1765; *BEP*, Jan. 8, 1768; *CC*, May 31, 1774; *NCG* (2), April 7, May 12, 1775; *MG* (2), Sept. 29, Oct. 6, 1774; *DMG*, March 22, Aug. 15-Oct. 31, 1775; *PEP*, July 22-Sept. 26, 1775; *NVG*, April 20, 1775; *VG* (Dixon and Hunter), May 11-June 1, 1776; *P&A*, 189ff.; *Amer. Arch.*, VI, 1ff.; *RAM*, Aug., Sept. 1774.
150. A tiny but representative fraction of the uses to which Pitt was put are in: *MG* (2), May 1, 8, 1766, Nov. 18, 1773; *VG* (Purdie and Dixon), April 25, 1766; *PJ*, May 8, 15, June 5, 1766; *GG*, May 28, 1766, Jan. 7, 1767; *WNYG*, Sept. 30, 1766; *BPB*, Oct. 27, 1766; *SCG*, April 27, 1767; *VG* (Rind), July 19, 1770; *EG*, Nov. 19, 1773; *CC*, Nov. 30, 1773; *EJ*, April 19, 1775; *NCG* (2), May 5, 1775;

DMG, Jan. 20, May 16, 23, 1775; *NVG*, June 15, 1775; *NP*, Oct. 2, 1775; *VG* (Pinkney), Jan. 2, Aug. 28, 1775; *JCC*, I, 83, II, 143.
151. *PM*, May 5, 1766.
152. *NM*, May 19, 1766.
153. Reprinted in 1776 in Philadelphia, Boston, New York, and Charleston. See *NYP*, June 27, July 4, 1776; *BNEC*, July 4, 11, 1776; *NYGWM*, July 22, 1776; *DMG*, Aug. 13, 1776.
154. *Amer. Arch.*, II, 55ff., reprinted in 1775 in eight different towns and almost all Whig newspapers; e.g., *MS*, May 17ff., 1775; *MJ*, June 14-Nov. 22, 1775; *PG*, June 17-Oct. 7, 1775.
155. His works were reprinted in New York in 1768. See also *An Authentic Account* (Philadelphia, New York, Boston, 1763) and *The North Briton, No. 45* (Boston, 1763).
156. *BEP*, Feb. 3, 1772; *EG*, Feb. 4, 1772; *MG* (2), Feb. 21, 1772; *SCGCJ*, March 10, 1772; *NYP*, Jan. 4, 1776.
157. Note the derogatory judgments in Franklin, *Writings*, V, 121-122, 133-134, and Witherspoon, *Works*, IX, 86, the friendly judgments in *VG* (Purdie and Dixon), April 22, 1769; *SCG*, Nov. 4, 1772; *NYPac*, July 11, 1763.
158. The press was full of his trials, tribulations, and speeches, so full indeed that one may go to almost any issue of any newspaper between 1763-1775 and read of John Wilkes.
159. Wilson, *Works*, III, 203ff.; S. Adams, *Writings*, I, 317; Hamilton, *Works*, I, 60-61, 85; Dickinson, *Political Writings*, I, 308ff., 319, 332ff., 388ff., 400, 411; Otis, *Vindication of the Colonies*, 9; *P&A*, 2, 77, 175; *MassG*, July 18, 1768.
160. *Commentaries* (London, 1778), I, 38ff., 123ff.
161. *NCG* (2), June 24, 1768.
162. *NHG*, June 15, 1776; *PG*, Jan. 12-March 30, 1765.
163. Respectively: Boston, 1775; New York, 1774; New York, 1770; Boston, 1765.

CHAPTER THIRTEEN

1. From the preface to a reprint of Thomas Bradbury, *The Ass: or, The Serpent* (1712) (Boston, 1768).
2. James Bryce, *Studies in History and Jurisprudence* (New York, 1901), 599. For the best works on natural law, see *Encyclopedia of the Social Sciences*, XI, 290; C. F. Mullett, *Fundamental Law and The American Revolution* (New York, 1933), 13-14n.
3. For secondary works on the political theory of the Revolution, see the books cited in Chap. 5, n. 106, and M. C. Tyler, *The Literary History of the American Revolution* (New York, 1897). L. Hartz, "American Political Thought and the American Revolution," *American Political Science Review*, XLVI (1952), 321-342, is a brilliant piece. For the ideas of American Tories, which I have regretfully excluded from this book, see Labaree, *Conservatism*, Chap. 6, and references there cited; Tyler, *American Revolution*, I, Chaps. 14-17, II, Chaps. 27-28; Boucher, *American Revolution*; Samuel Seabury, *A View of the Controversy* (New York, 1774); Daniel Leonard, *Massachusettensis* (London, 1776); Thomas Hutchinson, *Strictures upon the Declaration* (London, 1776), and in *Speeches of the Governors*; Joseph Galloway, *Political Reflections* (London, 1783), and *Historical and Political Reflections* (London, 1780); and the files of *BCh, BC*, and *RNYG*.
4. Locke, *Civil Government*, II, Chap. 3, Sec. 19.
5. "The Interest of America," *NHG*, June 15, 1776.
6. *Sermon* (1770), in Thornton, *Pulpit*, 158; Judah Champion, *Christian and Civil Liberty and Freedom Considered and Recommended* (Hartford,

1776), 7; "The Alarm," No. I, Oct. 6, 1773.

7. John Hurt, *The Love of Our Country* (1777), in *Patriot Preachers*, 146.

8. *Civil Government*, II, Chap. 4, Sec. 19.

9. Parsons, *Essex Result*, 362-363.

10. Otis, for one, had little use for this concept: *Rights of the Colonies*, 8-9, 28.

11. *BG*, March 17, 1766; *NM*, March 24, 1766.

12. *Boston Committee Records*, 198; J. Adams, *Works*, II, 366-367 (the famous remark of Henry at the first Continental Congress); *P&A*, 46, 52; Rev. Thomas Allen, in J. E. A. Smith, *History of Pittsfield* (Boston, 1869), 352, 354. Stephen Johnson, *Some Important Observations* (Newport, 1766), 18n., asserted that the Stamp Act had left the colonies "absolutely in a state of nature and independency."

13. *Civil Government*, II, Chap. 2, Sec. 14.

14. Hamilton, *Works*, I, 60-61; Parsons, *Essex Result*, 371; S. Adams, *Writings*, I, 47; "Freeborn American," in *BG*, March 9, 1767.

15. Parsons, *Essex Result*, 363; Wilson, *Works*, III, 206.

16. Thomas Dawes, jr., in *P&A*, 51-52.

17. In addition to other works cited in these notes, see E. S. Corwin's magnificent treatise, "The Higher Law Background of American Constitutional Law," in *Select Essays on Constitutional Law* (Chicago, 1938), I, 1-67, or *Harvard Law Review*, XLII (1928-1929), 149, 365.

18. *A Sermon, Preached May 11th, 1769* (Hartford, 1769), 42.

19. *Rights of the British Colonies*, 8; Dickinson, *Political Writings*, I, 330.

20. S. Cooper, *Sermon* (1780), 14.

21. Cornelia Le Boutillier, *American Democracy and Natural Law* (New York, 1950), esp. Chap. 3. Examples of this sort of thinking are in Dickinson, *Political Writings*, I, 311, 340-

341; Parsons, *Essex Result*, 363-364; J. Adams, *Works*, III, 462.

22. Le Boutillier, *Natural Law*, 135.

23. *Commentaries*, I, 38-41.

24. Hamilton, *Works*, I, 60-61; Champion, *Christian and Civil Liberty*, 8. And note how Wilson, *Works*, III, 205, 206, summons Blackstone to support him on one page and to be refuted on the next.

25. *NHG*, June 15, 1776.

26. Ebenezer Bridge, *A Sermon Preached . . . May 27th, 1767* (Boston, 1767), 19.

27. Wilson, *Works*, III, 206; J. Adams, *Works*, IV, 122.

28. Lord Camden, speaking against the Declaratory Act, *Parl. Hist.*, XVI, 178, a widely reprinted speech.

29. S. Adams, *Writings*, I, 185.

30. Bancroft, *Remarks*, 45.

31. *Papers*, I, 134; S. Adams, *Writings*, I, 23-24; Wilson, *Works*, III, 204.

32. *BNEC*, April 25, 1776.

33. *PP*, Nov. 25, 1771.

34. *The Works of Jeremy Bentham* (Edinburgh, 1843), I, 287.

35. Witherspoon, *Works*, IX, 80.

36. *VG* (Purdie), June 7, 1776.

37. Otis, *Rights of the British Colonies*, 10-11; Dickinson, *Political Writings*, I, 395; *BEP*, Jan. 14, 1771; *MS*, May 21, 1772, a significant reprint.

38. J. Adams, *Works*, IV, 14; Wilson, *Works*, III, 205; Champion, *Christian and Civil Liberty*, 7; *NYG* (2), May 30, 1765; *NP*, May 11, 1775.

39. J. Adams, *Works*, IV, 15.

40. Dickinson, *Political Writings*, I, 396; Zubly, *The Law of Liberty*, in *Patriot Preachers*, 122; Cooke, *Sermon* (1770), in Thornton, *Pulpit*, 162.

41. *Amer. Arch.*, VI, 751.

42. Witherspoon, *Works*, IX, 80; Ballagh, *Letters of R. H. Lee*, I, 167; Hamilton, *Works*, I, 69; Wilson, *Works*, III, 225; *NM*, July 25, 1768; *BG*, June 7, 1773; *NHG*, June 15, 1776.

43. Payson, *Sermon* (1778), in Thornton, *Pulpit*, 342.

44. S. Adams, *Writings*, II, 164; J. Adams, *Works*, III, 489, IV, 17.

45. *NM*, July 25, 1768; Ballagh, *Letters of R. H. Lee*, I, 191; S. Adams, *Writings*, III, 245; Iredell, *Correspondence*, I, 305; J. Adams, *Works*, III, 448; Hamilton, *Works*, I, 114.

46. Joseph Warren, in *P&A*, 4; Dickinson, *Political Writings*, I, 395.

47. Otis, *Rights of the British Colonies*, 11.

48. Hamilton, *Works*, I, 114.

49. *Correspondence*, I, 305.

50. Smith, *History of Pittsfield*, 352.

51. *Writings*, III, 245.

52. *VG* (Purdie), June 7, 1776.

53. Samuel Webster, *A Sermon Preached . . . May 28, 1777* (Boston, 1777), 29.

54. Simeon Howard, *A Sermon Preached . . . May 31, 1780*, in Thornton, *Pulpit*, 392.

55. *Sermon* (1778), in Thornton, *Pulpit*, 334-337; J. Adams, *Works*, III, 455ff.; S. Adams, *Writings*, III, 235-236; *CG*, Aug. 2, 1765; *NM*, July 14, 1766; *BPB*, July 28, 1766.

56. *P&A*, 63; Gad Hitchcock, *A Sermon Preached . . . May 25th, 1774* (Boston, 1774), 32-33.

57. *P&A*, 66.

58. *JCC*, I, 35.

59. *Works*, III, 205; Hamilton, *Works*, I, 6, 58, 72; Cooke, *Sermon* (1770), in Thornton, *Pulpit*, 162, Hitchcock, *Sermon* (1774), 20; Champion, *Christian and Civil Liberty*, 7; Parsons, *Essex Result*, 362-365; M. C. Clune, ed., *Joseph Hawley's Criticism of the Constitution of Massachusetts* (1780) (Northampton, Mass., 1917), 23; *NYP*, March 28, 1776; *NHG*, June 15, 1776.

60. *NLG*, May 29ff., 1767; *MG* (2), Sept. 11, 1772; *NM*, Sept. 26, 1774.

61. *VG* (Purdie), June 7, 1776; *BG*, Feb. 22, 1768.

62. J. Adams, *Works*, III, 480.

63. *Vindication of the House*, 18-19; *Rights of the British Colonies*, 28.

64. Wilson, *Works*, III, 206; Blackstone, *Commentaries*, I, 123.

65. J. Adams, *Works*, III, 449.

66. Blackstone, *Commentaries*, I, 123.

67. Parsons, *Essex Result*, 365; "The Alarm," No. III, Oct. 15, 1773; A. Lee, *Political Detector*, 68.

68. Otis, *Vindication of the Colonies*, 9-10; Hamilton, *Works*, I, 83; Parsons, *Essex Result*, 365-367; Jason Haven, *A Sermon Preached . . . May 31st, 1769* (Boston, 1769), 26, 40.

69. J. Adams, *Works*, III, 449.

70. Hamilton, *Works*, I, 83; Johnson, *Integrity and Piety*, 1.

71. Dickinson, *Writings*, I, 262; J. Adams, *Works*, III, 449; R. H. Lee, in the introduction to the Williamsburg edition of Dickinson's "Farmer's Letters," in Dickinson, *Writings*, I, 290; Clarke, in Hudson, *Lexington*, 94.

72. *Works*, I, 108.

73. J. Adams, *Works*, IV, 193; Jefferson, *Papers*, I, 124; Parsons, *Essex Result*, 362; Clarke, in Hudson, *Lexington*, 88.

74. W. C. Ford, ed., *The Writings of George Washington* (New York, 1889-1893), X, 256.

75. For excellent examples, see *BG*, March 9, 1767; Jefferson, *Papers*, I, 123; Downer, *Discourse*, 10.

76. *Commentaries*, I, 129.

77. S. Adams, *Writings*, I, 319-320.

78. Briggs, *Nathaniel Ames*, 377; *BNL*, Dec. 12, 1765; *CJ*, Dec. 25, 1767; *BG*, Feb. 22, 1768; *PG*, Jan. 16, 1773, June 24, 1775; *NP*, May 18, 1775; *NYP*, Feb. 1, 1776.

79. Iredell, *Correspondence*, I, 217.

80. *Papers*, I, 135.

81. Hamilton, *Works*, I, 61.

82. *NYG* (2), May 30, 1765, also Aug. 11, Oct. 27, 1763; Downer, *Discourse*, 5; Iredell, *Correspondence*, I, 217.

83. Jefferson, *Papers*, I, 121.

84. *Amer. Arch.*, II, 792; *EG*, Feb. 14, 1769; Downer, *Discourse*, 11. See *BC*, Jan. 25, Feb. 1, 1772, for the opposing argument.
85. *Amer. Arch.*, II, 792.
86. Thorpe, VI, 3741.
87. *NVG*, June 15, 1774.
88. *Writings*, I, 190, 174, 185, 288.
89. S. Adams, *Writings*, I, 137, 156-157, 185; Parsons, *Essex Result*, 371; Elisha Fish, *A Discourse Delivered . . . March 28, 1775* (Worcester, 1775), 8. See R. McKeon, "The Development of the Concept of Property," *Ethics*, XLVIII (1938), 297-366.
90. An exceptional use of the Lockean definition is in "The Alarm," No. I, Oct. 6, 1773; *NYJ*, Oct. 14, 1773.
91. *BG*, Feb. 22, 1768; *PP*, Feb. 27, 1775; Otis, *Rights of the British Colonies*, 38.
92. R. H. Lee, in Dickinson, *Writings*, I, 290.
93. *BG*, Oct. 28, 1765.
94. Ballagh, *Letters of R. H. Lee*, I, 128.
95. Iredell, *Correspondence*, I, 217, 245; *RAM*, March 1775.
96. *Writings*, I, 262.
97. On the sources of this phrase and concept, see H. L. Ganter, "Jefferson's 'Pursuit of Happiness' and Some Forgotten Men," *WMQ* (2), XVI (1936), 422-434, 558-585. Locke used this phrase several times in his *Essay on the Human Understanding*. Blackstone and Burlamaqui are other possible sources.
98. For a debate on this question, see C. M. Wiltse, *The Jeffersonian Tradition* (Chapel Hill, 1935), 136-139; Dumas Malone, *Jefferson and his Time* (Boston, 1948-), I, 228, and references there cited.
99. *P&A*, 306; Parsons, *Essex Result*, 361.
100. *Essex Result*, 365-371.
101. *Essex Result*, 371.
102. *RNYG*, Dec. 2, 1773.
103. *NP*, May 11, 1775.

104. *Works*, I, 83; S. Adams, *Writings*, I, 317, citing Blackstone; Parsons, *Essex Result*, 366-367; *RNYG*, Dec. 2, 1773.
105. Hamilton, *Works*, I, 36; Smith, *Sermon* (1775), 20; S. Adams, *Writings*, II, 336; Paine, *Writings*, I, 108; Clune, *Hawley's Criticism*, 41; J. Adams, *Works*, IV, 221n.; Jefferson, *Papers*, I, 525-558; Baldwin, *New England Clergy*, 108ff.; *Amer. Arch.*, V, 1157; *NYJ*, March 14, 1776; *NYP*, Aug. 15, 1776; Izrahiah Wetmore, *A Sermon Preached . . . May 13th, 1773* (New London, 1773), 29, App.
106. Thorpe, VII, 3814.
107. *NYP*, March 28, 1776; *PEP*, March 16, 1776; *Amer. Arch.*, V, 183.
108. *SCGCJ*, Sept. 25, 1769; Sept. 24, 1770; Parsons, *Essex Result*, 369-370; *VG* (Rind), March 31, June 9, 1768.
109. *The People the Best Governors*, reprinted in F. Chase, *History of Dartmouth College* (Brattleboro, Vt., 1928), I, 654; *NYG* (2), July 18, 1765; *MS*, June 4, 1772; *PJ*, Feb. 14, 1776; *SCGCJ*, April 3, 1776; *Amer. Arch.*, IV, 241.
110. *BG*, March 9, 1767.
111. *Sermon* (1770), in Thornton, *Pulpit*, 167.
112. Payson, *Sermon* (1778), in Thornton, *Pulpit*, 341; *MS*, June 21, 1776.
113. *BG*, March 9, 1767.
114. *SCG*, Jan. 19, 1765, quoting Hume; *CG*, Feb. 14, 1766; *MS*, March 28, 1771, still quoting *Cato's Letters*; *PG*, July 10, 1773, quoting Blackstone: *NM*, April 1, 1776, quoting Wilkes.
115. *NYG* (2), Feb. 19, 1770; *PaG*, March 1, 1770; *BEP*, Aug. 20, 1770; *MS*, Nov. 28, 1771.
116. *PM*, Jan. 21, 1765; *NYG* (2), Aug. 15, 1765, July 10, 1769, Feb. 26, 1770; *BEP*, Oct. 14, 1765; *VG* (Purdie and Dixon), June 22, Aug. 22, 1766; *CC*, Feb. 1, 1768; *NHG*, March 18, 1774.
117. *VG* (Purdie and Dixon), Jan. 7, 1768.
118. For discussions of freedom of press touched off by assaults on this free-

dom in the pre-Revolutionary decade, see *Speeches of the Governors*, 118ff.; *EG*, Aug. 27, Sept. 3, 1771; *BPB*, Sept. 2, 1771; *SCG*, Sept. 13, 15, 1773; *GG*, Oct. 26, 1774; *NM*, March 6, 1775; *NYP*, April 11, 1776; *Amer. Arch.*, II, 13, 35-36, 50, 213, 726, 836, V, 438, 1441.
119. *NHG*, July 13, 1764.
120. *WNCG*, Feb. 12, 1766.
121. *VG* (Pinkney), Sept. 29, 1774; *CFM*, Nov. 24, 1769; *JCC*, I, 70; Clarke, in Hudson, *Lexington*, 95.
122. Cooke, *Sermon* (1770), in Thornton, *Pulpit*, 165.
123. Parsons, *Essex Result*, 380.
124. S. Adams, *Writings*, III, 287.
125. Allen, *Beauties of Liberty*, 10; *CC*, March 27, 1775, a tribute to the Cincinnati who took Louisbourg in 1745.
126. *Writings*, I, 264-265, also 145-146, 249-259, 269, 272-274; *BG*, Dec. 5-26, 1768.
127. *Observations on . . . The Boston Port-Bill* (Boston, 1774), 41.
128. *P&A*, 2. See *P&A*, 1-59, for these annual orations, as well as *Amer. Arch.*, II, 38-44, 881-889; *JCC*, I, 70, IV, 140; *NYG* (2), May 30, 1765; *NYJ*, Dec. 11, 1766-Feb. 5, 1767; Dickinson, *Writings*, I, 390-391.
129. *PG*, May 15, 1773.
130. J. Quincy, *Observations*, 42.
131. *Proceedings of the Virginia Convention of Delegates* (March 1775), 5.
132. S. Adams, *Writings*, I, 8-9; *BG*, Sept. 23, 1765.
133. *JCC*, I, 68, 69, 83, II, 133, 146; Dickinson, *Writings*, I, 194; S. Adams, *Writings*, I, 46; *MG* (2), Nov. 17, 1774.
134. S. Adams, *Writings*, I, 18, 23, 47, 64, 135, 180, 185; J. Adams, *Works*, IV, 124.
135. Hamilton, *Works*, I, 84, also 5, 66-67, 85.
136. J. Adams, *Works*, III, 480-482; *BG*, Jan. 27, 1766.

137. S. Adams, *Writings*, II, 1. For Otis's interesting exposition of representation, see *Rights of the British Colonies*, 13ff.
138. *NLG*, Aug. 24, 1770; *BEP*, May 4, 1772; Dickinson, *Writings*, I, 173-174, 184, 202, 400, 416.
139. *NHG*, March 18, 1774; A. Lee, *Political Detector*, 65.
140. Thorpe, III, 1687.
141. *Writings*, II, 1, 31.
142. *VG* (Purdie), June 7, 1776.
143. *Essex Result*, 376; *BNEC*, June 20, 1776; Clarke, in Hudson, *Lexington*, 262.
144. *Works*, IV, 195.
145. *NHG*, March 18, 1774.
146. De Grazia, *Public and Republic*, Chaps. 3-4.
147. *Amer. Arch.*, V, 71; *NYG* (2), Jan. 6, 1770; Clarke, in Hudson, *Lexington*, 96-99.
148. Otis, *Considerations*, 5-6.
149. Parsons, *Essex Result*, 377.
150. *Works*, III, 208; Clarke, in Hudson, *Lexington*, 263.
151. *VG* (Purdie), June 7, 1776.
152. J. Adams, *Works*, IV, 205, 197, 139; Parsons, *Essex Result*, 390, 396; *NYJ*, Nov. 24, 1774; *PG*, Dec. 17, 1774; *CFM*, July 28, 1775; *NYCG*, May 4, 1776. For evidence of the nearly universal acceptance of this doctrine, see the provisions of the first state constitutions in Thorpe, II, 778, III, 1687, 1895, 1898, V, 2596, 2629, 2790, 3084, VI, 3742.
153. *BPB*, June 5, 1769.
154. Thacher, *Sentiments*, 7; Dickinson, *Writings*, I, 174, 185, 243; Clarke, in Hudson, *Lexington*, 90, 263; Iredell, *Correspondence*, I, 305ff.; *MG* (2), May 16, 23, 1765; *NHG*, June 7, 1765; *BG*, July 15, 1765, June 7, 1773; *NM*, Sept. 9, 1765; *NYG* (2), Oct. 31, 1765, March 30, 1770; *NYC*, Oct. 26, 1769; *NYJ*, March 15, 1770, Nov. 10, 1774; *BEP*, Jan. 28, 1771; *PJ*, Jan. 5, 26, 1774.
155. *JCC*, I, 88. On grand juries, see *NYG* (2), April 16, 1770.

156. *Works*, III, 482-483.
157. J. Adams, *Works*, III, 454.
158. Smith, *Sermon* (1775), 21.
159. *Rights of the British Colonies*, 32; Champion, *Christian and Civil Liberty*, 18; John Tucker, *A Sermon Preached . . . May 29th. 1771* (Boston, 1771), 19, 29-30; *NCM*, Nov. 23, 1764.
160. *PaG*, Feb. 22, 1775; *Amer. Arch.*, II, 9.
161. For examples, see Chandler, *Friendly Address*, 5; Boucher, *American Revolution*, 544ff.
162. *CJ*, March 22, 1775.
163. John Lathrop, *Sermon Preached to the Ancient and Honorable Artillery-Company . . . June 6, 1774* (Boston, 1774), 21.
164. A. Lee, *Political Detector*, 132.
165. *Works*, I, 12; S. Adams, *Writings*, I, 317-318; J. Adams, *Works*, IV, 79; West, *Sermon* (1776), 21; *NM*, Nov. 25, 1765; *BG*, June 7, 1773; Clarke, in Hudson, *Lexington*, 95.
166. *Amer. Arch.*, I, 651; *Nature and Extent of Parliamentary Power*, xv.
167. *SCG*, Oct. 18, 1769, probably Christopher Gadsden.
168. *Papers*, I, 123.
169. For examples of the appeal to each of these sanctions, see *Amer. Arch.*, I, 514, II, 149ff., III, 1106; J. Adams, *Works*, IV, 18; Wilson, *Works*, III, 262-263.
170. *P&A*, 142; *Amer. Arch.*, III, 1106.
171. *Amer. Arch.*, V, 1205.
172. April 23, 1776; *P&A*, 73.
173. *P&A*, 75ff.; Hitchcock, *Sermon* (1774), 21-22; *NYJ*, Nov. 16, 1775.
174. *NYJ*, Oct. 19, 1775; *Amer. Arch.*, III, 1207.
175. Hitchcock, *Sermon* (1774), 22.
176. *PaG*, Sept. 14, 1774; *SG*, Aug. 19, 1774; West, *Sermon* (1776), 14.
177. *NYJ*, Nov. 16, 1775; *Amer. Arch.*, IV, 528. For an earlier use of this argument, see Johnson, *Some Important Observations*, 5, 22, 26, 31-32.
178. *VG* (Purdie), Dec. 8, 1775; *MJ*, Dec. 20, 1775.
179. *PaG*, Sept. 14, 1774.
180. Bancroft, *Remarks*, 99.
181. *CJ*, March 1, 1775.
182. *Beauties of Liberty*, 28, also ix-xii.
183. *Amer. Arch.*, I, 335.
184. *P&A*, 176.
185. *SG*, Aug. 19, 1774. And see General John Sullivan's letter in *Amer. Arch.*, IV, 242.
186. *Sermon* (1770), in Thornton, *Pulpit*, 167.
187. *PaG*, Sept. 14, 1774.
188. *A Sermon Preached . . . May 26th, 1773* (Boston, 1773), 28-29.
189. *BG*, Nov. 18, 1765; *NM*, Nov. 25, 1765; Clarke, in Hudson, *Lexington*, 98.
190. *CJ*, Feb. 22, 1775.
191. *Amer. Arch.*, II, 696.
192. West, *Sermon* (1776), 27.
193. For discussions of resistance in addition to the writings cited in preceding notes, see John Lathrop, *Innocent Blood Crying to God from the Streets of Boston* (Boston, 1770), preface; Samuel Chew, *On the Lawfulness of Defence against an Armed Enemy* (Philadelphia, 1775); Hitchcock, *Sermon* (1774), 21-27; *An Essay upon Government, adopted by the Americans* (Philadelphia, 1775); David Jones, *Defensive War in a Just Cause Sinless* (Philadelphia, 1775); Dan Foster, *A Short Essay on Civil Government* (Hartford, 1775), 70-71; A. Lee, *Political Detector*, 68; Dickinson, *Writings*, I, 325; Hamilton, *Works*, I, 108-109; Iredell, *Correspondence*, I, 246; *P&A*, 9-10; *JCC*, II, 153; *BG*, Dec. 2, 1765; *BEP*, April 6, 1767; *VG* (Purdie and Dixon), Oct. 13, 1774; *PG*, March 18, April 8, 1775; *NHG*, Aug. 29, 1775; *NYCG*, Sept. 9, 1775; *NYJ*, Oct. 19, 1775; *NEC*, Oct. 12, 19, 1775.
194. *P&A*, 77.
195. *JCC*, I, 107-108; *PP*, Nov. 14, 1774. This letter was printed in London under the title *A Clear Idea of the General and Uncorrupted British Constitution* (1774).

196. Thorpe, VII, 3812-3814; *P&A*, 123-124; *Amer. Arch.*, VI, 1537-1538, 1561-1562. Maryland, Massachusetts, North Carolina, and Pennsylvania—as well as Vermont—also adopted specific bills of rights in 1776 or 1777. Delaware and Connecticut acted, too, but in a less clear-cut manner. See Thorpe, III, 1686-1691, 1889-1893, V, 2787-2789, 3082-3084, VI, 3739-3742. For the persistence of natural rights in post-Revolutionary constitutions, see Thorpe, III, 1274, V, 2909, VI, 3422 (Kentucky, Ohio, Tennessee).

CHAPTER FOURTEEN

1. John Adams to George Wythe, in *Works*, IV, 200.
2. *Writings*, I, 70-71; Benjamin Church, in *P&A*, 9; Cooke, *Sermon* (1770), in Thornton, *Pulpit*, 158-159.
3. Locke, *Civil Government*, II, Chap. 3, sec. 19; Otis, *Rights of the British Colonies*, 6.
4. Tucker, *Sermon* (1771), 16.
5. Hamilton, *Works*, I, 61; *PL*, March 4, 1775; *PEP*, May 16, 1776; *VG* (Purdie), June 7, 1776.
6. S. Adams, *Writings*, I, 27-28, 44-45, 139, II, 29, 173, 179, 223, 233, 259, 277, 401ff.; Hopkins, *Grievances*, 8, 15; Jefferson, *Papers*, I, 122; Smith, *Sermon* (1775), 11; Iredell, *Correspondence*, I, 302; Cooke, *Sermon* (1770), in Thornton, *Pulpit*, 174-175; Hamilton, *Works*, I, 64; Bancroft, *Remarks*, 9, 25, 35, 75, 83, 98; Dickinson, *Political Writings*, I, 386, 413; *JCC*, I, 32, 33, 68, 82, II, 130, 142; *Amer. Arch.*, IV, 527; *EG*, Feb. 14, 1769, Aug. 2, 1774; *NM*, June 21, 1774; *EJ*, Sept. 28, 1774; *MS*, Feb. 9-March 2, April 6, May 3, 1775.
7. S. Adams, *Writings*, I, 27-28, 153, II, 259; J. Adams, *Works*, IV, 122, 126; Jefferson, *Papers*, I, 277ff.; Wilson, *Works*, III, 222, 235; *EG*, Feb. 26, March 26, April 9, 1771; *NYJ*, Dec. 16, 1773; *NM*, Feb. 7, March 21, 1774; *PG*, Feb. 19, 1774; *EJ*, Aug. 10,

1774; *PaG*, March 6, 1776; *NYCG*, March 9, 1776. And see Crane, *Franklin's Letters to the Press*, 88, reprinted in *PC*, June 8, 1767; *BEP*, June 22, 1767; *WNYG*, July 6, 1767; *SCG*, July 27, 1767.
8. Drayton, in *P&A*, 70ff.; J. Adams, *Works*, III, 461, IV, 114; S. Adams, *Writings*, I, 269. For Magna Charta as contract, see Tucker, *Sermon* (1771), 17.
9. J. Adams, *Works*, IV, 99-100, 112; E. C. Burnett, ed., *Letters of Members of the Continental Congress* (Washington, 1921-1934), I, 38.
10. Bancroft, *Remarks*, 116-124; Turner, *Sermon* (1773), 16; *Amer. Arch.*, IV, 530, V, 785-786; Dickinson, *Political Writings*, I, 318.
11. For example, the Solemn League and Covenant (June 1774), *Amer. Arch.*, I, 397, and the Association of the Freemen of Maryland (July 26, 1775), *Md. Arch.*, XI, 15ff.
12. Thomas Allen, in Smith, *Pittsfield*, 354; Chandler, *Friendly Address*, 19, a Tory use of this concept; Parsons, *Essex Result*, 364; Dawes, in *P&A*, 52; *PEP*, May 16, 1776; *BCJ*, May 30, 1776.
13. *BG*, March 17, 1766; *NM*, March 24, 1766; P. Livingston, *Other Side of the Question*, 16; Webster, *Misery of an Enslav'd People*, 22.
14. J. Allen, *Beauties of Liberty*, 8.
15. *JCC*, I, 112.
16. Thorpe, III, 1889; J. Adams, *Works*, IV, 219.
17. McLaughlin, *Foundations of American Constitutionalism*, 77.
18. *Rights of the British Colonies*, 11-12.
19. *BG*, June 7, 1773; *RAM*, Feb. 1775; Clarke, in Hudson, *Lexington*, 90, 93, 339-340.
20. *BG*, Nov. 18, 1765; *NM*, Nov. 25, 1765.
21. *SG*, Aug. 19, 1774; Hopkins, *Grievances*, 7, 31; Moore, *Justice and Policy*, in Boyd, *Tracts*, 166; S. Adams, *Writings*, II, 299, III, 268. And see

the debate between Charles Carroll and Daniel Dulany in E. S. Riley, ed., *Correspondence of "First Citizen" and "Antilon"* (Baltimore, 1902).

22. *Essex Result*, 366; J. Adams, *Works*, IV, 28; Dickinson, *Political Writings*, I, 403.

23. Hopkins, *Grievances*, 6.

24. CC, July 30, 1770.

25. *Commentaries*, I, 49.

26. *P&A*, 142; *Amer. Arch.*, IV, 833. For other representative allusions to popular sovereignty, see T. Allen, in Smith, *Pittsfield*, 352; Otis, *Rights of the British Colonies*, 9; Wilson, *Works*, III, 213; Parsons, *Essex Result*, 368; *P&A*, 79; JCC, IV, 135, 141; *Amer. Arch.*, V, 451-452; MS, May 21, June 4, 1772; BPB, Dec. 20, 1773; PEP, March 28, 30, 1775, citing *Cato's Letters;* Thorpe, III, 1686, 1890, V, 2787, 3082, VI, 3740, VII, 3813.

27. *Works*, I, 25, 185ff., 417.

28. To General Gage, Aug. 19, 1775; *Amer. Arch.*, III, 247.

29. Hamilton, *Works,* I, 12; Paine, *Writings*, I, 70ff.; Otis, *Rights of the British Colonies*, 8-9.

30. S. Adams, *Writings*, I, 271; BG, Dec. 19, 1768; SG, Aug. 19, 1774.

31. No. I, Oct. 6, 1773; *Amer. Arch.*, V, 121; S. Adams, *Writings*, I, 138; Hamilton, *Works*, I, 61, quoting Blackstone.

32. Reprinted in PL, March 4, 1775.

33. NHG, June 15, 1776.

34. *Sermon* (1770), in Thornton, *Pulpit*, 159.

35. *Works*, III, 479; Otis, *Rights of the British Colonies*, 10; Payson, *Sermon* (1778), in Thornton, *Pulpit*, 330; *Amer. Arch.*, IV, 241; Andrew Eliot, *A Sermon Preached . . . May 29th, 1765* (Boston, 1765), 8, 22.

36. JCC, II, 140.

37. *Works*, III, 206, 213, citing Burlamaqui.

38. *Correspondence*, I, 217, 246; J. Adams, *Works*, IV, 193; Clarke, in

Hudson, *Lexington*, 88; Briggs, *Nathaniel Ames*, 376; Dickinson, *Political Writings*, I, 332; *P&A*, 142; NYG (2), July 18, 1765; NYP, March 28, 1776; JCC, IV, 342.

39. BG, June 7, 1773.

40. Paine, *Writings*, I, 69; S. Adams, *Writings*, I, 269.

41. Champion, *Christian and Civil Liberty*, 7; Church, in *P&A*, 9.

42. Clarke, in Hudson, *Lexington*, 339.

43. In Dickinson, *Writings*, I, 291.

44. *Sermon* (1771), 12-13; Lockwood, *Sermon* (1774), 8.

45. *Works*, III, 454.

46. *Rights of the British Colonies*, 8.

47. *Integrity and Piety*, 6.

48. *Rights of the British Colonies*, 10-11.

49. *P&A*, 142; Iredell, *Correspondence*, I, 246; Parsons, *Essex Result*, 362-363.

50. PEP, May 16, 1776; BCJ, May 30, 1776.

51. *Works*, IV, 193.

52. *Sermon* (1778), in Thornton, *Pulpit*, 330.

53. J. Adams, *Works*, IV, 193.

54. NHG, June 29, 1776.

55. *Works*, V, 226.

56. NHG, June 29, 1776; Parsons, *Essex Result*, 363-364.

57. NHG, June 29, also June 15, 1776; J. Adams, *Works*, IV, 200; Parsons, *Essex Result*, 370.

58. "Salus Populi," in NYP, March 28, 1776; *Amer. Arch.*, V, 182.

59. *Amer. Arch.*, V, 450.

60. VG (Purdie), June 7, 1776.

61. S. Adams, *Writings*, I, 137; MG (2), Sept. 11, 1772.

62. BG, Feb. 22, 1768.

63. NP, May 11, 1775; BG, March 17, 1766; NM, March 24, 1766.

64. CJ, Dec. 25, 1767; *P&A*, 9; SCG, Sept. 21, 1769, a poetic tribute.

65. BNL, Dec. 12, 1765.

66. PaM, April 1776; Turner, *Sermon* (1773), 36.

67. J. Adams, *Works*, III, 454.

68. *Sermon* (1770), in Thornton, *Pulpit*, 163.

69. Ballagh, *Letters of R. H. Lee*, I, 191.

70. *Amer. Arch.*, V, 452.

71. Parsons, *Essex Result*, 365.

72. *NYP*, March 28, 1776; *Amer. Arch.*, V, 181-182.

73. *Sermon* (1778), in Thornton, *Pulpit*, 330.

74. *Works*, IV, 194.

75. *NYP*, March 28, 1776; *CFM*, July 28, 1775.

76. *PP*, Nov. 17, 1774; *NYJ*, Nov. 24, 1774; *PG*, Dec. 17, 1774; Clarke, in Hudson, *Lexington*, 262-263.

77. Thorpe, II, 778; III, 1687, 1689, 1895, 1898; V, 2595, 2596, 2629, 2790, 3084; VI, 3249, 3742; VII, 3816.

78. *NHG*, June 29, 1776; Jefferson, *Papers*, I, 341, 348, 349, 358, 359, 411; Parsons, *Essex Result*, 399; J. Adams, *Works*, IV, 186, 197, 205, 231, 234, 239, 245; "Demophilus," *Genuine Principles*, 24; *Amer. Arch.*, IV, 242, V, 451; *VG* (Purdie), June 7, 1776.

79. Thorpe, III, 1890; VII, 3813; III, 1687, V, 3082, VI, 3740.

80. *Works*, III, 456-457; *P&A*, 9; *Amer. Arch.*, V, 452-453; *NYP*, Feb. 1, 1776.

81. *Integrity and Piety*, 8-9; Clarke, in Hudson, *Lexington*, 95, 98.

82. *Sermon* (1773), 16.

83. Above, 31-34.

84. S. Adams, *Writings*, I, 156, 171, 174, 185, 196.

85. Wright, *American Interpretations of Natural Law*, Chap. 5; A. Nevins, *The American States During and After the Revolution* (New York, 1924), Chaps. 2-5; W. C. Webster, "Comparative Study of the State Constitutions," *Annals*, IX (1897), 380-420.

86. Joseph Warren, in *P&A*, 5.

87. Parsons, *Essex Result*, 369.

88. Memorable, yes, but probably not too accurately remembered! See J. Adams, *Works*, II, 521-525, X, 232-362; Josiah Quincy, *Reports of Cases* (*1761-1772*) (Boston, 1865), 51-57, 469-485.

89. *VG*, March 21, 1766; J. Adams, *Works*, II, 15, 155.

90. For a few scattering examples, see J. Adams, *Works*, III, 465-466; S. Adams, *Writings*, I, 8, 17, 190, 216, 240, 350; Otis, *Rights of the British Colonies*, 47; Dickinson, *Writings*, I, 195, 243, 312, 415, 440; *JCC*, I, 33, 35, 85.

91. J. Adams, *Works*, III, 16. For the facts of the Massachusetts experience, see H. A. Cushing, *History of the Transition . . . in Massachusetts* (New York, 1896). For the theory that rationalized this triumph in constructive constitutionalism, see J. Adams, *Works*, IV, 193-200; Parsons, *Essex Result*; S. Cooper, *Sermon* (1780).

92. Hudson, *Lexington*, 259. See also the address of the New York mechanics, June 14, 1776, in *P&A*, 441-442; resolves of Concord town meeting, Oct. 22, 1776, in S. E. Morison, *Sources and Documents* (Oxford, 1923), 176-177; *PEP*, May 16, 1776; *PP*, Nov. 12, 1776.

93. Smith, *Pittsfield*, 352-354.

94. *Writings*, I, 99; S. Cooper, *Sermon*, (1780), 31.

95. *Essex Result*, 359, 367, 374.

96. Hudson, *Lexington*, 262.

97. Clune, *Hawley's Criticism*, passim.

98. Thomas Fitch, *Reasons Why the British Colonies . . . Should Not be Charged with Internal Taxes* (New Haven, 1764), 4.

99. *Writings*, II, 162-163. For evidence that Jefferson held this belief in 1774, see *Papers*, I, 124.

100. *Civil Government*, II, Chap. 11, Sec. 142.

101. For example, Thorpe, III, 1891-1892.

102. See the articles of "Spartanus," *NHG*, June 15, 29, 1776, and *NYJ*, June 6-20, 1776; Paine, *Writings*, I, 97-99; and the makeshift New Hampshire Constitution of 1776, in Thorpe, IV, 2451-2453. The most powerful assault on government by

an unchecked legislature is in J. Adams, *Works*, IV, 195-196.

103. This seems to be the hope of the "Braxton Plan" in *Amer. Arch.*, VI, 748-754; *VG* (Dixon and Hunter), June 8, 15, 1776.

104. *Works*, IV, 186, also 195-198, 206-207. See *VG* (Purdie), May 10, 1776, for what appears to be Lee's use of Adams's advice, and Jefferson, *Papers*, I, 340, 347, 358, 366, for the Virginia radical's dedication to this principle. For other newspaper discussions, see *VG* (Purdie), June 7, 1776; *BEP*, Feb. 19, 1770; *SCG*, March 15, 1773; *MS*, May 18, 1776; *PEP*, March 16, June 15, 1776; *PL*, Oct. 26, 1776.

105. Thorpe, III, 1893, also II, 778, III, 1687, IV, 2457, V, 2787, VII, 3813.

106. *Sermon* (1770), in Thornton, *Pulpit*, 159, also 165.

107. *DMG*, March 26, 1776.

108. *Essex Result*, 373-374, also 375ff.; Payson, *Sermon* (1778), in Thornton, *Pulpit*, 330-331; S. Cooper, *Sermon* (1780), 28; Haven, *Sermon* (1769), 11; Edward Barnard, *A Sermon Preached . . . May 28th, 1766* (Boston, 1766), 13.

109. *NYP*, March 28, 1776. For a slight qualification to this statement, see Parsons's discussion of persons and property, below, n. 118.

110. *PEP*, March 16, 1776.

111. *BG*, Feb. 9, 1767; S. Adams, *Writings*, I, 168.

112. *AG*, June 18, 1776; *RAM*, March 1775; Clarke, in Hudson, *Lexington*, 263.

113. Maryland Declaration of Rights (1776), in Thorpe, III, 1687.

114. Thorpe, VI, 3768; Chase, *Dartmouth*, 658, 662.

115. Briggs, *Nathaniel Ames*, 449. See C. E. Eisinger, "The Freehold Concept," *WMQ* (3), IV (1947), 42-59.

116. For suffrage qualifications in the first constitutions, see Thorpe, I, 563, II, 779, III, 1687, 1691, 1895-1896,

1898, IV, 2459, V, 2595, 2630, 2790, 3084, VI, 3251-3252, VII, 3816; Porter, *History of Suffrage*, 13, a convenient table.

117. Thorpe, VI, 3249.

118. *Essex Result*, 371-372, also 360, 389-391.

119. Clune, *Hawley's Criticism*, 19ff., 27-29, 50.

120. Chase, *Dartmouth*, 660.

121. *Essex Result*, 376.

122 Clune, *Hawley's Criticism*, 22.

123. *Works*, IV, 206-207; Parsons, *Essex Result*, 382ff.

124. Clune, *Hawley's Criticism*, 28-29.

125. Chase, *Dartmouth*, 656.

126. The best debate in this period over property qualifications was between "Job" and "Elihu" in *NLG*, May 29, June 19, July 10, 31, 1767, after which the argument degenerated into a typical colonial war of words.

127. *NEC*, May 2, 1776; *NHG*, June 29, 1776; Chase, *Dartmouth*, 657.

128. Parsons, *Essex Result*, 379, apparently a plagiarized version of J. Adams, *Works*, IV, 195-196, 206. See also *VG* (Pinkney), Oct. 6, 1774; *VG* (Purdie), June 7, 1776; *BNEC*, Sept. 5, 1776; *PP*, Sept. 24, 1776.

129. *Amer. Arch.*, VI, 748-754; Chase, *Dartmouth*, 654-663.

130. *Works*, IV, 193-200, in a letter to George Wythe.

131. For radically divergent opinions on the advisability of copying the English Constitution, see *Amer. Arch.*, IV, 241 (Gen. John Sullivan); VI, 750-751 (Carter Braxton).

132. *Works*, IV, 292-293, from the preface of his *Defence of the Constitutions* (1787).

133. Chase, *Dartmouth*, 659; J. Adams, *Works*, IV, 193-194. This notion was probably borrowed from Montesquieu. See Chinard, *Commonplace Book of Thomas Jefferson*, 259.

134. *Essex Result*, 402.

135. *Writings*, III, 235, also 285-286, 305.

136. *BNEC*, July 11, 1776, quoting Sidney; *SHPM*, April 14, 1775; Downer, *Discourse* (1768), 15.
137. *PP*, Feb. 27, 1775.
138. Above, 137-139.
139. *Writings*, III, 238.
140. *PaG*, May 12, 1768; *MS*, May 8, 1775; *NP*, Oct. 28, 1776. See also *NM*, Jan. 4, July 25, 1768; *CC*, Feb. 16, 1768; *VG* (Rind), March 3, 1768; *NYG* (2), May 23, 1768; *PPP*, Jan. 20, 1769; *PJ*, Jan. 20, 1773; *PL*, May 27, 1775; Payson, *Sermon* (1778), in Thornton, *Pulpit*, 337; J. Adams, *Works*, III, 454, Briggs, *Nathaniel Ames*, 437.
141. *CJ*, June 2, 1769.
142. Briggs, *Nathaniel Ames*, 400.
143. Bancroft, *Remarks*, 101; Franklin, *Writings*, VI, 311-312; J. Adams, *Works*, IV, 28, 55; W. Livingston, in *P&A*, 271; A. Lee, *Political Detector*, 79; Peter Thacher, in *P&A*, 23-24; *VG* (Dixon and Hunter), July 6, 1776.
144. *Amer. Arch.*, V, 202; *NYCG*, March 20, 1776.
145. *PP*, Aug. 21, 1775; *BG*, Dec. 23, 1771, Oct. 11, 1773; *PJ*, Jan. 20, 1773; *PEP*, Aug. 29, 1775; *NYJ*, Feb. 22, 1776; *Amer. Arch.*, IV, 952-953.
146. *NLG*, Oct. 20, 1775; *NYJ*, Aug. 25, 1774.
147. J. Adams, *Works*, IV, 194.
148. Briggs, *Nathaniel Ames*, 411; *MG* (2), May 4, 1769; Franklin to Shipley, July 7, 1775 (Yale Library).
149. *GG*, March 11, 1767; *Amer. Arch.*, V, 1206.
150. S. Adams, *Writings*, II, 373, 393.
151. *Amer. Arch.*, VI, 751; Samuel Williams, *A Discourse on the Love of Our Country* (Salem, 1775); Clarke, in Hudson, *Lexington*, 161-162; John Hurt, *The Love of Our Country* (1777), in *Patriot Preachers*, 144ff.; Payson, *Sermon* (1778), in Thornton, *Pulpit*, 337; *NM*, Dec. 30, 1765; *SCGCJ*, March 3, 1767, Nov. 15, 1768; *CC*, April 24, 1769; *NYG*

(2), April 2, 1770; *PJ*, Oct. 20, 1773; *SCG*, Nov. 29, 1773; *BCJ*, Jan. 9, 1777. For the identification of Whiggery and patriotism, see *BEP*, April 6, 1767; *CJ*, Feb. 22, 1775; *BCJ*, Jan. 9, 1777; *NP*, Jan. 20, 1777.
152. *Papers*, I, 134.
153. For evidence of the American obsession with industry and frugality, see *PG*, Sept. 8, 1764, Jan. 12, 1765, Dec. 26, 1767; *NM*, Nov. 12, 1764, Dec. 14, 1767; *NHG*, Jan. 25, Feb. 1, 1765; *BEP*, Jan. 4, 1768; *NCG* (2), Nov. 10, 1769; *NLG*, March 18, 1768; *RAM*, March 1775; "Cethegus," in *NYC*, May 8-June 29, 1769, and Timothy Pickering, in *EG*, Nov. 8, 1768, March 21, Nov. 7, 1769, classics in this vein. And see the contributions of Yale and Harvard recorded in *BG*, Dec. 3, 1764; *BNL*, Jan. 7, 1768. Franklin's *Way to Wealth* was several times reprinted.
154. *NHG*, March 21, 1766.
155. From a sermon (1775) reprinted in *DMG*, Aug. 8, 1775; *Amer. Arch.*, V, 451.
156. Briggs, *Nathaniel Ames*, 445, also 385, 400, 401, 443-446; Cooke, *Sermon* (1770), in Thornton, *Pulpit*, 164; Hamilton, *Works*, I, 21; *JCC*, I, 82; W. M. Smith, in *PL*, May 27, 1775; *NLG*, Aug. 7, 1767, May 6-June 10, 1768; *NYJ*, April 9, 1767; *NYC*, May 8, 1769; *PP*, July 13, 1772; *NYP*, March 7, 1776.
157. *Sermon* (1778), in Thornton, *Pulpit*, 333, also 338.
158. S. Adams, *Writings*, III, 286, also II, 336; Franklin, *Writings*, II, 393.
159. *The Law of Liberty*, in *Patriot Preachers*, 129.
160. *Sermon* (1778), in Thornton, *Pulpit*, 339-341; Bridge, *Sermon* (1767), 22ff.; Edward Dorr, *The Duty of Civil Rulers, to be Nursing Fathers to the Church of Christ* (Hartford, 1765), 7-16.
161. Nicholas, *Considerations Examined*, 37.

162. Thorpe, III, 1889; J. Adams, *Works*, IV, 221; S. Cooper, *Sermon* (1780), 37. For a contrary judgment, see Clune, *Hawley's Criticism*, 41.

163. *A Sermon Preached . . . May 31, 1780*, in Thornton, *Pulpit*, 392.

164. *Works*, III, 463.

165. Thorpe, III, 1907-1908; J. Adams, *Works*, IV, 259; S. Adams, *Writings*, III, 235; *CG*, Aug. 2, 1765; *NM*, July 14, 1766.

166. Howard, *Sermon* (1780), in Thornton, *Pulpit*, 393; *PL*, May 27, 1775.

167. *JCC*, II, 87; *P&A*, 142-143.

168. Cooke, *Sermon* (1770), in Thornton, *Pulpit*, 161-172; Richard Salter, *A Sermon* (New London, 1768), 18; Eliphalet Huntington, *The Freeman's Directory* (Hartford, 1768); S. Johnson, *Integrity and Piety*, 14-29; Bridge, *Sermon* (1767), 19ff.; Tucker, *Sermon* (1771), 26ff., Hitchcock, *Sermon* (1774), 28-40.

169. *MG* (2), Dec. 3, 1767; *EG*, Nov. 6, 1770; *BNEC*, July 11, 1776; Chase, *Dartmouth*, 659.

170. *SCGCJ*, Nov. 2, 1773; *PP*, Feb. 12, 1776. But see *PC*, Feb. 5, 1770.

171. *NLG*, April 21, 1775.

172. *Observations*, dedication.

173. *Works*, IV, 43; Samuel Langdon, *Government Corrupted by Vice, and Recovered by Righteousness* (Watertown, 1775).

174. J. Adams, *Works*, IV, 193-194.

175. For descriptions of such men, see Briggs, *Nathaniel Ames*, 392; *CG*, July 5, 1765; *CC*, April 25, 1768; *DMG*, April 16, 1776.

176. *VG* (Pinkney), May 17, 1776.

177. *P&A*, 64; Cooke, *Sermon* (1770), in Thornton, *Pulpit*, 172.

178. *Works*, III, 475-476.

179. *Essex Result*, 378; Turner, *Sermon* (1773), 41.

180. Ballagh, *Letters of R. H. Lee*, I, 26.

181. *Sermon* (1777), 29-31.

182. Otis, *Rights of the British Colonies*, 29; Jefferson, *Papers*, I, 130, 426; Cooke, *Sermon* (1770), in Thornton, *Pulpit*, 182-183; *CJ*, Dec. 18, 1767, Oct. 8-Dec. 31, 1768; *BEP*, May 2, 1768; *PG*, May 14, 1768; *CC*, June 13, 1768; *BG*, March 2, June 13, Sept. 21, 1767, Nov. 16, 1772; *MS*, Nov. 10, 1774. For two hot debates on the "natural" character of slavery, see *NLG*, Sept. 3-Oct. 1, 15, 1773; *BEP*, Sept. 7-Nov. 30, 1772; *BPB*, Jan. 4, 1773.

183. *BG*, Jan. 8, 1768; *BNL*, March 25, 1773; *RAM*, Jan. 1774; *CC*, Sept. 12, Oct. 3, 10, 1774; *NLG*, Oct. 28, 1764; Locke, *Anti-Slavery in America*, Chap. 2. See the town resolutions reported in *NHG*, April 22, 1774, and *PG*, May 21, 1774, Aug. 26, 1775, as well as slave petitions in *EG*, June 8, Aug. 3, 1773; *SG*, Sept. 16, 1774.

184. *VG* (Rind), March 10, 1767; *PC*, May 11, Sept. 7, 1767.

185. To H. L. Pierce and others, April 6, 1859, in P. Stern, *Life and Writings of Abraham Lincoln* (New York, 1940), 540.

CONCLUSION

1. Revolutionary attitudes on political parties are plain in *CG*, Sept. 6, 1766; *CC*, June 1, 1767; *PaG*, March 22, 1775; *PEP*, April 4, 6, 1775.

INDEX

Index

[A number in bold face indicates full citation of a work referred to more than once in the notes.]